C000186251

1 MONTH OF
FREE
READING

at

www.ForgottenBooks.com

By purchasing this book you are eligible for one month membership to ForgottenBooks.com, giving you unlimited access to our entire collection of over 1,000,000 titles via our web site and mobile apps.

To claim your free month visit:
www.forgottenbooks.com/free978855

* Offer is valid for 45 days from date of purchase. Terms and conditions apply.

ISBN 978-0-260-87197-8
PIBN 10978855

This book is a reproduction of an important historical work. Forgotten Books uses
state-of-the-art technology to digitally reconstruct the work, preserving the original format
whilst repairing imperfections present in the aged copy. In rare cases, an imperfection in
the original, such as a blemish or missing page, may be replicated in our edition. We do,
however, repair the vast majority of imperfections successfully; any imperfections that
remain are intentionally left to preserve the state of such historical works.

Forgotten Books is a registered trademark of FB &c Ltd.
Copyright © 2018 FB &c Ltd.
FB &c Ltd, Dalton House, 60 Windsor Avenue, London, SW19 2RR.
Company number 08720141. Registered in England and Wales.

For support please visit www.forgottenbooks.com

F 2302

San Francisco
Law Library

No. _108607_

....

EXTRACT FROM BY-LAWS

Section 9. No book shall, at any time, be taken from the
Library Room to any other place than to some court room of a
Court of Record, State or Federal, in the City of San Francisco,
or to the Chambers of a Judge of such Court of Record, and
then only upon the accountable receipt of some person entitled
to the use of the Library. Every such book so taken from the
Library, shall be returned on the same day, and in default of
such return the party taking the same shall be suspended from
all use and privileges of the Library until the return of the book
or full compensation is made therefor to the satisfaction of the
Trustees.

Sec. 11. No books shall have the leaves folded down. or be
marked, dog-eared, or otherwise soiled, defaced or injured. Any
party violating this provision, shall be liable to pay a sum not
exceeding the value of the book, or to replace the volume by a
new one, at the discretion of the Trustees or Executive Committee, and shall be liable to be suspended from all use of the
Library till any order of the Trustees or Executive Committee
in the premises shall be fully complied with to the satisfaction
of such Trustees or Executive Committee.

WILCOX & CO

San Francisco
Law Library

No.

No. 8860

Vrb

United States
Circuit Court of Appeals

For the Ninth Circuit /

ABBIE W. QUINN,

                                Appellant,

      vs.

CENTRAL COMPANY, a corporation, as agent for the shareholders of the Central National Bank of Oakland, CENTRAL NATIONAL BANK OF OAKLAND, a national banking association in liquidation, and CENTRAL BANK OF OAKLAND,

                                Appellees.

APPELLANT'S OPENING BRIEF.

CHARLES W. SLACK,
EDGAR T. ZOOK,
        1101 Alaska Commercial Building,
        San Francisco, California,

            Attorneys for Appellant.

FILED

PARKER PRINTING COMPANY, 545 SANSOME STREET, SAN FRANCISCO

JAN 3 - 1939

PAUL P. O'BRIEN,

Index

Table of Authorities Cited

Pages

1. CODES, STATUTES, ETC.

2. TEXT BOOKS AND TREATISES.

Pages

3. Cases.

No. 8860

United States
Circuit Court of Appeals

For the Ninth Circuit

ABBIE W. QUINN,

          Appellant,

vs.

CENTRAL COMPANY, a corporation, as agent
for the shareholders of the Central National
Bank of Oakland, CENTRAL NATIONAL
BANK OF OAKLAND, a national banking
association in liquidation, and CENTRAL
BANK OF OAKLAND,

          Appellees.

APPELLANT'S OPENING BRIEF.

I.

STATEMENT OF PLEADINGS AND FACTS SHOWING JURISDICTION.

This action was commenced in the Superior Court of the State of California, in and for the County of Alameda, by plaintiff, Abbie W. Quinn, against Central National Bank of Oakland, a national banking association, (hereinafter called the "National Bank"), having its principal place of business in Oakland, Alameda County, California, against Joseph H. Grut,

as the receiver of the National Bank, and against Central Bank
of Oakland, a California corporation, (hereinafter called the
"Central Bank"), by the filing of a complaint, entitled "Complaint for rescission and other relief", (R. 2-84).*

The relief sought by the complaint, (R. 56-8), is the rescission, on the ground of constructive fraud upon plaintiff by the
National Bank, of an instrument of trust, dated September 24,
1929, (a copy of which is annexed as an exhibit to the complaint, (R. 59-76)), executed by plaintiff, as trustor, with the
National Bank, as trustee, and for the incidental relief, (a), of
the reconveyance to plaintiff by the Central Bank of an unimproved lot of land, situated in Oakland, California, which
plaintiff, at the time of the execution of the instrument of
trust, had conveyed to the National Bank, and of the reassignment to plaintiff by the Central Bank of a promissory note, and
the mortgage securing the same, which plaintiff, likewise at the
time of the execution of the instrument of trust, had assigned
to the National Bank, (b), of the repayment by the Central
Bank to plaintiff of the sum of $80,642.50, being the total
amount of plaintiff's money invested by the National Bank, at
various times prior to the execution of the instrument of trust,
in bonds and notes of several corporations, bonds of two
provinces of South American republics, and bonds of an irrigation district in Oregon, which the National Bank had purchased, through E. D. Bothwell, as the manager of the bond
department of the National Bank, from itself, for plaintiff, with
plaintiff's funds, and (c), of the repayment to plaintiff of the
additional sum of $22,285.75, being the total amount of money
invested by the National Bank, at various times subsequent to
the execution of the instrument of trust, in bonds of several
corporations and bonds of a municipal utility district of Cali-

---

*NOTE: Throughout the briefs of plaintiff and appellant, unless
otherwise noted, the pages of the printed transcript of record, to which
references are made, are indicated by the letter "R", followed by the
appropriate numbers of the pages of the record, all in parentheses.

fornia, some of which the National Bank had purchased through Bothwell, as the manager of the bond department of the National Bank, from itself, with trust funds, for the trusts created by the instrument of trust.

The National Bank, on or about March 2, 1933, closed its doors, and never thereafter opened its doors, for the transaction of business, (R. 3). A. J. Mount, the then president of the National Bank, was appointed by the then acting comptroller of the currency of the United States, pursuant to the provisions of the Bank Conservation Act of the Congress of the United States, as the conservator for the National Bank, (R. 3), and he thereafter continued to be such conservator until May 8, 1933, when Joseph H. Grut was appointed the receiver of the National Bank by the then acting comptroller of the currency, (R. 3, 4).

With the approval of the comptroller of the currency and of the superintendent of banks of the State of California, and with the approval, also, of the United States District Court, Southern Division, Northern District, on the petition of Mount, as the conservator of the National Bank, and with the consent of stockholders holding of record at least two-thirds of the issued capital stock of the National Bank, the whole of the business of the trust department of the National Bank was sold to the Central Bank, (under its former name of "Central Savings Bank of Oakland"), on April 22, 1933, on the terms and conditions of two contracts approved by the comptroller of the currency and by the superintendent of banks, (R. 43-6). One of these contracts provides, (R. 81-82), that the purchase of the trust department includes all court and private trusts, "subject to the rights of trustors and beneficiaries . . . to nominate another and succeeding trustee of the trusts" so transferred, and includes the right of the Central Bank "to succeed to all of the relations, obligations, trusts and liabilities that are in any way connected with or incidental to the business of said trust department", and further provides, (R. 82), that the Central

Bank, (referred to as the "Savings Bank"), assumed "all fiduciary and trust obligations and liabilities of the National Bank", and also that the Central Bank "agrees to perform all of the trusts of the National Bank and to pay and discharge all the debts and liabilities that are incidental to the said trusts or connected therewith, in the same manner as if the Savings Bank had itself incurred the obligation, debt or liability, or assumed the relation of trust", and also provides, (R. 82), that the Central Bank, (again referred to as the "Savings Bank"), "shall have all the rights, and shall be subject to all the liabilities, and hereby assumes all the obligations, that, according to law, result from or are incidental to the purchase and sale of a trust department of a bank".

The complaint prays, (R. 57), that, in the event that it be adjudged that the Central Bank shall not repay to plaintiff the said sum of $80,642.50, then that it be adjudged that the claim of plaintiff therefor be established as a claim of plaintiff therefor against the National Bank, and that the same, as so established, with legal interest, be paid by said Grut, as the receiver of the National Bank, in due course of his administration, or that he certify the same to the comptroller of the currency to be similarly paid.*

---

*NOTE: This prayer for relief, in the alternative, ·as to the repayment to plaintiff of the total sum of $80,642.50, for bonds and notes purchased, at various times prior to the execution of the instrument of trust, for plaintiff, by the National Bank, from itself, through Bothwell, as the manager of the bond department of the National Bank, is based upon plaintiff's contention that, under the provisions, above referred to, of the contract for the purchase by the Central Bank from the National Bank of the whole of the business of the trust department of the National Bank, (R. 82), the Central Bank became the primary obligor and the National Bank became the secondary obligor, (*Miles v. Macon County Bank*, 187 Mo. App. 230, 244, 173 S. W. 713, 719, (1915)), under the somewhat analogous rule which exists in the case of a grantee of mortgaged real property who assumes the mortgage indebtedness, (18 *Cal. Jur.*, p. 57, sec. 375, tit. "Mortgages", 41 *C. J.*, p. 737, sec. 789, tit. "Mortgages"), the obligation and liability remained. imposed upon the National Bank, but that, if it should be adjudged, contrary to plaintiff's contention, that the obligation or lia-

5

Defendants National Bank and its receiver, Grut, and the Central Bank, filed their petition for the removal of the action to the United States District Court, Southern Division, Northern District, (R. 85-90), and their undertaking on removal, (R. 92-5), whereupon, pursuant to notice thereof, (R. 90-1), and an order therefor, (R. 96-8), the cause was removed to the District Court and was there docketed as a suit in equity, and issue was there joined by the answer of the Central Bank, (R. 99-139), and by the answer of the National Bank and its receiver, Grut, to the complaint, (R. 140-177).

Thereafter, and immediately prior to the commencement of the trial of the action on February 4, 1936, the National Bank and its receiver, Grut, filed a so-called "Supplemental answer" to the complaint, (R. 177-84); and thereafter, and prior to the conclusion of the trial of the action, plaintiff filed, and as so designated, her "amendments and supplements to bill of complaint", (R. 184-97).

After the evidence in the action had been introduced, and pursuant to stipulation, (and acting under the provisions of section 197, chapter 2, title 12, of the *Judicial Code* of the United States), the above named Central Company, a corporation, as agent for the shareholders of the National Bank, was substituted as a defendant for the receiver, Grut, of the National Bank, (R. 198-205), and Ira Abraham, Esq., who had been appointed as the attorney for the National Bank, was substituted as the attorney for the National Bank in the place and stead of Frank S. Richards, Esq., who had heretofore appeared in the action as the attorney for the National Bank, (R. 206-8).

The cause having been argued and submitted to the District Court for decision, the Honorable Michael J. Roche, Judge of the District Court, made and filed his findings of fact and con-

---

bility of the National Bank for the repayment of the said sum to plaintiff was not assumed, under the circumstances, by the Central Bank, then the obligation or liability remained imposed upon the National Bank.

6

clusions of law, and ordered judgment to be entered that defendants were entitled to a "judgment and decree" that plaintiff take nothing, that the bill of complaint, together with
plaintiff's amendments and supplements thereto, be dismissed,
and that defendants were entitled to their proper costs and disbursements, (R. 315-53). Later, a "judgment and decree", so
designated, from which this appeal has been taken by plaintiff,
was signed by the District Judge, and the same was filed and
entered, (R. 353-5).

This Court has jurisdiction of the appeal under section 41,
paragraph 16, chapter 2, title 28, of the *Judicial Code* of the
United States, as a case in which district courts of the United
States have original jurisdiction involving the "winding up the
affairs of any" national banking association, and under section 71, chapter 3, title 28, of the *Judicial Code,* under which
any suit of a civil nature, at law or in equity, of which the district courts of the United States "are given original jurisdiction", "may be removed by the defendant or defendants therein
to the district court of the United States for the proper district": *Studebaker Corporation v. First Nat. Bank,* 10 F.(2d)
590, (D. C., S. Car., 1926); *Bell v. Kelly,* 54 F.(2d) 395,
(D. C., Ill. 1931).

II.

STATEMENT OF THE CASE.

This, as to some extent, above noted, is an appeal by plaintiff from a decree in favor of defendants, in a suit brought by
plaintiff against defendants National Bank, Grut, its receiver,
(for whom defendant Central Company was later substituted),
and Central Bank, to rescind, on the ground of constructive
fraud, an instrument of trust, dated September 24, 1929, executed by plaintiff, as trustor, to the National Bank, as trustee,
and for the incidental relief, (a), of the reconveyance to plaintiff by the Central Bank, (to which the business of the trust

department of the National Bank, involving the trust estate created by the instrument of trust, had been sold by the National Bank after its insolvency), of an unimproved lot of land in Oakland, which, at the time of the execution of the instrument of trust, was conveyed to the National Bank, and of the reassignment to plaintiff by the Central Bank of a promissory note, and its securing mortgage, of Sparks Masonic Building Association, which plaintiff, likewise at the time of the execution of the instrument of trust, had assigned to the National Bank, (b), of the repayment by the Central Bank to plaintiff of the sum of $80,642.50, being the total amount of plaintiff's money invested by the National Bank, at various times prior to the execution of the instrument of trust, in bonds and notes of several corporations, bonds of two provinces of South American republics, and bonds of an irrigation district, which the National Bank had purchased, through Bothwell, as the manager of the bond department of the National Bank, from itself, for plaintiff, with plaintiff's funds, and (c), of the repayment by the Central Bank to plaintiff of the additional sum of $22,-285.75, being the total amount of money invested by the National Bank, at various times subsequent to the execution of the instrument of trust, in bonds of several corporations and in bonds of a municipal utility district, some of which the National Bank had purchased, through Bothwell, as the manager of its said bond department, from itself, with trust funds, for the trust estate created by the instrument of trust.

The pleadings involved on the appeal, and on which the case was tried, are the following: (1), the complaint; (2), the answer of the Central Bank to the complaint; (3), the answer of the National Bank and its receiver, Grut, to the complaint; (4), the amendments and supplements to the complaint; and (5), the supplemental answer of the National Bank and its receiver to the complaint.

A complete copy of each of the pleadings is annexed to this brief, as an appendix thereto, and the same are respectively

8

designated as "Appendix A", "Appendix B", "Appendix C", "Appendix D" and "Appendix E".

A complete copy of each the findings of fact and conclusions of law, the decree, and the assignments of error is also annexed to this brief, as an appendix thereto, and the same are respectively designated as "Appendix F", "Appendix G" and "Appendix H".

There is also annexed to this brief, and designated as "Appendix I", a complete copy of Section 31 of the *California Bank Act,* (1 Deering, General Laws of California, 1931, p. 242), pursuant to the provisions of which, (applicable, at least, to the Central Bank), the whole of the business of the trust department of the National Bank was sold to the Central Bank.*

1. THE COMPLAINT.

The allegations of the complaint relate to the following transactions, (or to the following series of transactions), between plaintiff and the National Bank, and to the following additional transaction between the National Bank and the Central Bank, for the sale to the Central Bank of the whole of the business of the trust department of the National Bank, to which said additional transaction plaintiff was not a party, but in which, nevertheless, she was and is interested as a transaction for her benefit, namely:

1. Various purchases of bonds and notes, owned by the National Bank, made for plaintiff, with her funds, by the National Bank, from itself, and always so purchased at a profit to itself, and always so purchased through said Bothwell, as the

*NOTE: Throughout the briefs of plaintiff and appellant, unless otherwise noted, the various appendixes are indicated by the abbreviation "App.", followed by the particular letters of the alphabet, "A", "B", "C", etc., and by the appropriate numbers of the pages of the appendixes, all in parentheses.

manager of its bond department, from time to time, prior to the execution of the instrument of trust, on September 24, 1929, during the period commencing on January 7, 1926, and ending on September 1, 1929; and always so made, with the approval of plaintiff, on Bothwell's recommendation to plaintiff that the same were safe and desirable for the investment of her funds, and with the intention of plaintiff, and pursuant to Bothwell's advice to plaintiff, that a trust would be created by plaintiff, as trustor, with the National Bank, as trustee, of the bonds and notes so purchased, after the sale by plaintiff of a parcel of improved real property owned by her, known as the "Virginia Street" property, situated on Virginia Street, Reno, Nevada, had been made by plaintiff; and during all of which period of time plaintiff reposed in Bothwell and in said bond department, as he well knew, great trust and confidence.

2. The preparation by S. Berven, (or Sylo Berven), the assistant trust officer of the National Bank, of the instrument of trust, with complicated provisions, difficult to understand, (a copy of which, marked "Exhibit A", is annexed to the complaint), and the execution of the instrument, as so prepared, on September 24, 1929, without any independent advice, by plaintiff, as such trustor, with the National Bank, as such trustee, after the sale of the Virginia Street property had been made, and pursuant to which plaintiff transferred to the National Bank, as such trustee, (1), the bonds and notes so purchased, and then in the possession of the National Bank, (2), an unimproved lot of land, owned by plaintiff, situated in Oakland, (3), $15,000, par value, Washoe County, County Roads and Highways Improvement and Construction bonds, purchased by plaintiff in or about the year 1920, and (4), a promissory note and its securing mortgage, dated June 1, 1923, of certain property situated in Sparks, Nevada, executed to plaintiff by Sparks Masonic Building Association, for the principal sum of $20,000, payable in installments, of which the sum of $11,000 then remained unpaid; during all of which period of time plaintiff

reposed in Berven, the assistant trust officer, and in D. Read, (or Daniel Read), the trust officer, of the National Bank, and in the trust department of the National Bank, as Berven and Read each well knew, great trust and confidence.

3. Various purchases of bonds and notes made by the National Bank for the trust estate, with trust funds, by the National Bank, some of them owned by the National Bank, and, therefore, purchased by the National Bank from itself, and always so purchased at a profit to itself, and so purchased through Bothwell, as the manager of its bond department.

4. The transaction of the sale to the Central Bank, on April 22, 1933, under a contract between the Central Bank and the National Bank, (a copy of which, marked "Exhibit C", is annexed to the complaint), of the whole of the business of the trust department of the National Bank, the substitution of the Central Bank as trustee of the trusts created by the instrument of trust, in the place and stead of the National Bank, the transfer of the trust estate by the National Bank, as such trustee, to the Central Bank, as such substituted trustee, (pursuant to an order of the District Court of the United States, for the Northern District of California, approving the same, in proceedings in the said District Court duly had and taken therefor, and also as provided by said Section 31 of the *California Bank Act*, (1 Deering, General Laws of California, 1931, p. 242), with the consent of stockholders of the National Bank holding of record at least two-thirds of the issued capital stock thereof, and with the approval of the comptroller of the currency of the United States and of the superintendent of banks of the State of California) ; and the assumption by the Central Bank, as such substituted trustee, of "all fiduciary and trust obligations and liabilities of the National Bank", and the agreement of the Central Bank, (named in the transaction as the "Savings Bank"), among other things, "to perform all of the trusts of the National Bank, and to pay and discharge all the debts and liabilities that are incidental to said trusts or connected there-

with, in the same manner as if the Savings Bank had itself
incurred the obligation, debt or liability, or assumed the relation of trust"; and thereby, (as plaintiff contends), the Central
Bank assumed, and agreed to pay and discharge, the obligations
and liabilities incurred by the National Bank to plaintiff in the
purchases for plaintiff by the National Bank from itself,
through Bothwell, as the manager of its bond department, of
the bonds and notes prior to the execution of the instrument
of trust, and also assumed, and agreed to pay and discharge,
the obligations and liabilities incurred by the National Bank to
plaintiff in the purchases of certain bonds for the trust estate
subsequent to the execution of the instrument of trust, from
itself, through Bothwell, as the manager of its bond department.

---

2. THE ANSWER OF THE CENTRAL BANK.

The answer of the Central Bank, in what may be termed as
the "First Separate Defense", (1), admits the allegations of
the complaint, either expressly, or impliedly because of its omission to deny the allegations, or (2), the answer affirmatively
alleges, in confession and avoidance of the allegations of the
complaint, either positively, or according to information and
belief, or (3), the answer denies, either positively, or for want
of information and belief, the allegations of the complaint.

The answer, in the "First Separate Defense", contains many
negatives pregnant, many evasive admissions and allegations,
many allegations, not of ultimate facts, but of conclusions of
law, and many denials, which for one or more reasons do not
respond to any allegations of the complaint. The answer has not
been attacked, in any of these particulars, for insufficiency, (by
the only permissible mode of motion to strike), and, therefore,
while insufficiency of the answer in any matter of form may
have been waived, insufficiency in any matter of substance has
not been waived. It will be assumed, for the purposes of this

brief, that the Central Bank, in this "First Separate Defense", has either denied, in proper form, if denials have been made, the allegations of the complaint, essential for recovery by plaintiff, or has pleaded affirmatively, or by confession and avoidance, if affirmative allegations have been made, sufficient in form, but not in substance, to constitute defenses.

The "Second", "Fourth", "Fifth" and "Sixth" "Separate Defenses", (here, with the exception of the respective titles and prayers, reproduced in full, for convenient reference), respectively "allege" as follows, (App. B 36, 37-40):

1.

"That the complaint does not state facts sufficient to constitute a cause of action."

2.

"That the bill of complaint does not contain a short and simple statement of the ultimate facts upon which the plaintiff asks relief."

3.

"That said complaint is multifarious in that it has too large a scope and embraces more than one subject matter uniting several purported causes of action without separately stating them, as follows:

"1. A purported cause of action, or series of causes of action, alleged to arise by reason of alleged false or fraudulent representations of the national bank as to the safety and desirability of certain bonds and notes specifically described in the complaint as investments for plaintiff and her trust;

"2. A purported cause of action, or series of causes of action, alleged to arise by reason of the alleged fact that the national bank purchased said bonds and notes for plaintiff from itself without plaintiff's knowledge and thereby acted in a dual capacity and also made a secret profit thereon;

"3· A purported cause of action by reason of the alleged fact that the execution of the trust instrument was procured by the National bank by fraud or by violation of trust and confidence reposed by plaintiff in said national bank."

4.

"That the causes of action, or the portion of the cause of action, occurring prior to

"1· November 1, 1928, are barred by the provisions of Section 343 of the *Code of Civil Procedure* of the State of California;

"2· November 1, 1929, are barred by the provisions of subdivision 4 of Section 338 of the *Code of Civil Procedure* of the State of California;

"3· November 1, 1930, are barred by the provisions of subdivision 1 of Section 339 of the *Code of Civil Procedure* of the State of California."

With a prayer for judgment, in each instance of such "Separate Defenses", (1), that plaintiff take nothing by her complaint, (2), for costs of suit, and (3), (although the answer contains no counterclaim or cross bill), "For such other and further relief as to this court may seem proper in the premises".

The "Second", "Fourth" and "Fifth" "Separate Defenses" may be passed by as unprecedented, and as entirely lacking in merit both in form and in substance. The District Court did not find upon any of the "Second", "Fourth", "Fifth" or "Sixth Separate Defenses", and expressly, in its conclusions of law, (App. F 37), declined to find upon the "Sixth Separate Defense", that is, the defense of the statutes of limitation.

The "Third Separate Defense" is also here reproduced in full, for convenient reference, as follows, (App. B 37):

"That paragraph VIII of the trust instrument (Exhibit 'A' attached to the complaint) provides that the trustor, plaintiff, reserves the power to revoke the trusts therein created subject to the payment to the trustee of all sums then due to it and that thereupon the trustee shall be fully released and discharged of all the existing liabilities and obligations of every kind and nature affecting the trust property or the trustee in relation thereto; that prior to the commencement of this suit this defendant, being then the successor trustee, offered to permit plaintiff to revoke the trust and the instrument of trust and to deliver all of the trust properties to plaintiff and offered to agree that such revocation should not be a release or discharge of existing liabilities and obligations of this defendant to plaintiff, if any. That plaintiff refused such offer."

The prayer "for judgment" to this "Third Separate Defense" is as follows, (App. 39-40):

"1. That plaintiff take nothing by her complaint. In this respect the defendant offers, as it offered prior to the commencement of the action, to permit plaintiff to revoke the instrument of trust and it will thereupon deliver all of the trust property to plaintiff subject to the payment of this defendant's proper charges."

With a further prayer for costs of suit, and also with the further inapplicable prayer "For such other and further relief as to this court may seem just and proper in the premises".

Before leaving this outline of the answer of the Central Bank, consideration may here be appropriately given of a considerable number of illustrations:—(1), of evasive allegations of the "First Separate Defense", in matters of substance, pleaded in the "Defense", and which have not been waived by plaintiff's omission to attack directly the allegations of the "Defense", for insufficiency, and which, (differing from negatives pregnant in this respect), present no issues arising from the related allegations of the complaint; (2), of allegations, admissions and denials of the "Defense", which are in contradiction of other allegations and admissions of the "Defense"; and to which are added, (3), of references to many denials, as of allegations of the complaint, in which the complaint contains none of the allegations so denied; and (4), of allegations of the "Defense" that the funds of the trust estate created by the instrument of trust were invested by the National Bank, through Bothwell, as the manager of its bond department, in speculative bonds and notes belonging to the National Bank, because, so it is alleged, of plaintiff's "recommendations", "requests", "directions", "insistencies" and "emphatic desires", notwithstanding, so it is also alleged, that plaintiff was repeatedly "advised", "cautioned" and "admonished" by Berven, the assistant trust officer, and, inferentially, also, by Read, the trust officer, of the National Bank, against the investments of the trust funds in bonds and notes of the speculative character in which, through the fault of plaintiff, the most funds were being invested.

1. It is alleged in the complaint, (App. A 9-10), that to an inquiry made by plaintiff at the time, on or about January 1, 1926, when the first of the purchases of bonds and notes was made for plaintiff from the National Bank, through Bothwell, as the manager of its bond department, as to whether or not her funds should be invested in bonds of the United States, Bothwell replied that bonds of the United States paid a low rate of interest, and he assured her that her funds would be invested by the National Bank, through him, as the manager of its bond department, in safe and desirable bonds, just as good as those of the United States, and paying a much larger rate of interest than was paid on bonds of the United States; that Bothwell thereupon recommended to plaintiff, as safe and desirable investments of her funds, the bonds and notes first so purchased by her; and that plaintiff relied upon such recommendation and approved the purchases. The Central Bank, in its answer, (App. B 5-6), denied these allegations, but alleged, "in reference" thereof, (App. B 6), that

> "from time to time the said Bothwell *may* have informed plaintiff that bonds of the United States paid a low rate of interest",

but, nevertheless, (App. B 6), that Bothwell

> "likewise advised plaintiff that in general it was a good rule to follow that the risk involved was in direct proportion to the amount of interest paid on bonds, that is to say,

that the safest bonds usually paid a lower rate of interest than bonds which were not so well secured, or which were more apt to default";

and, therefore, the result of this evasion is that the allegations of the complaint, in this particular, are not denied.

It may be observed, in this connection, that the advice, unquestionably sound, was no sooner given than it was disregarded, and that the advice continued to be disregarded up to the time, on June 27, 1930, when the last investment was made by the National Bank, through Bothwell, as the manager of its bond department, in speculative bonds and notes, insufficiently secured, or not secured at all, bearing interest at the high rate of from 7½% to 6% per annum, with the result that the bonds and notes so purchased, with the exception of those which had matured or were redeemed, defaulted in the payment of the interest thereon, (Defts' Ex. DD, Schedule C-1, R. 755, Pltf's Ex. 47, R. 645), and in which plaintiff's funds, or any trust funds, should never have been invested.

It is to be borne in mind that these very bonds and notes, as in the case of all the other bonds and notes, in which plaintiff's funds were invested by the National Bank, were unqualifiedly recommended to plaintiff, either by Bothwell, or by Read, or by Berven, as safe and desirable investments for the funds of plaintiff, or of the trust estate. This being true, the following qualification, in the answer of the Central Bank, (App. B 26), of such recommendations, (referring to the bonds and notes purchased both prior and subsequent to the execution of the instrument of trust, by the National Bank, through Bothwell, as the manager of its bond department), is an apparent afterthought:

> "denies that any of the bonds or notes referred to in paragraph XIV were not, at the time when sold to plaintiff, or to her trust, safe or desirable *taking into consideration* the yield on said bonds and notes".

2. In a number of instances, the complaint alleged, (App. A 12, 13, 17, 18-9, 30-3, 33-4), the purchase of bonds and notes for plaintiff from the National Bank, through Bothwell, as the manager of its bond department, and also alleged that the purchases were recommended by him to plaintiff as safe and desirable investments for her funds.

In one of such instances, the answer of the Central Bank, after denying that Bothwell had assured plaintiff that certain of the bonds were a safe and desirable investment for her, alleged, (App. B 7), that, in such instance,

> "as well as in the case of *all* other bonds or notes sold by the bond department to plaintiff",

Bothwell

> "*merely* recommended said bonds or notes basing said recommendation upon the best knowledge, information and belief of the national bank and of said Bothwell".

In another of such instances, the answer, after denying, for want of knowledge, that Bothwell had recommended certain other bonds and notes to plaintiff "as safe or desirable investment", (App. B 9-10),

> "*admits* that said Bothwell *recommended* said bonds or notes to plaintiff".

In still another of such instances, the answer, after similarly denying, for want of knowledge, that Bothwell *recommended* certain bonds and notes to plaintiff "as safe and desirable investments", (App. B 12),

> "*Admits* that said bonds were *recommended* as investments for plaintiff".

In still another of such instances, the answer, after denying, for want of knowledge, that Bothwell had "recommended" to plaintiff certain bonds and notes "as safe or desirable investments", (App. B 13), "*admits* that all bonds or notes which plaintiff purchased from the national bank prior to the execution of the trust were *recommended* by Bothwell".

In still another of such instances of the purchase of bonds and notes, (prior to the execution of the instrument of trust), the answer, after denying, for want of knowledge, that Bothwell had *recommended* to plaintiff the bonds or notes so purchased "as safe or desirable investments for plaintiff", (App. B 17),

"*admits* that said bonds or notes were *recommended* by Bothwell".

In still another of such instances of the purchase of certain bonds and notes, (subsequent to the execution of the instrument of trust), the answer, after denying, for want of knowledge, that Bothwell had recommended the bonds or notes, (App. B 23),

"*admits* that Bothwell *recommended* said bonds",

and denies, for want of knowledge, the fact that plaintiff "*relied* upon *said* recommendation".

In still another of such instances of the purchase of certain bonds and notes, (prior to the execution of the instrument of trust), the answer *denies,* positively, (App. B 25),

"that any of said bonds or notes were sold to plaintiff as safe or desirable investments or that any *guaranty* or *assurance* was made as to the safety or desirability thereof",

and denies, also positively, that $1,000, par value, bond of California Cotton Mills Company, purchased after the execution of the instrument of trust, (App. B 25-6), was or

"were *recommended* as a safe or desirable investment, but *admits* that said purchase carried the *recommendation* of the bond department of the national bank".

There is no allegation of the complaint to which the denial, last but one above quoted, responds, namely, that, in the purchase of certain bonds, "that any *guaranty* or *assurance* was made as to the safety or desirability thereof".

The result of all these foregoing denials, allegations and admissions, in variant, indefinite and evasive language, is that Bothwell, in every instance of the purchase of bonds or notes for plaintiff, or for the trust estate, *recommended* to plaintiff the purchase as a safe and desirable investment, and that, since the recommendations could have had no purpose other than that plaintiff should approve and accept them, plaintiff, in every such instance, *relied* upon the recommendation and approved the purchase.

3. The complaint does not contain any allegation, either in terms or to the effect, that in any instance of the purchase of any bonds and notes for plaintiff from the National Bank, through Bothwell, as the manager of its bond department, Bothwell informed plaintiff that the price which she was paying for the bonds and notes was the price paid therefor by the National Bank. Nevertheless, it is repeatedly either denied or alleged that such was the fact, (App. B 8, 9-10, 13, 14, 17).

Nor does the complaint contain any allegation, either in terms or to the effect, that in any of the transactions of the purchase of any of the bonds and notes by plaintiff from the National Bank, and the sale to plaintiff by the National Bank, plaintiff acted in the capacity of the *purchaser* and the National Bank in the capacity of the *seller* thereof. Nevertheless, it is repeatedly alleged in the answer of the Central Bank, either in terms or to the effect, that such was the fact, and that plaintiff "well knew", or that such fact was "well known" to plaintiff, (App. B 10, 11, 13, 14, 17, 18, 34, 35).

Nor does the complaint contain any allegation, either in terms or to the effect, that plaintiff, in the purchases of any of the bonds and notes prior to the execution of the instrument of trust, acted in the capacity of *principal* and the National Bank acted in the capacity of *agent*, or that the relation between the parties was that of *principal* and *agent*. Nevertheless, it is alleged in the answer, (App. B 8), that, in all instances of purchases of bonds and notes prior to the creation of the trust,

> "plaintiff and the national bank were acting in the capacity of *buyer* and *seller,* and *not* in the capacity of *principal* and *agent";*

and, nevertheless, also, the answer of the Central Bank denies, (App. B 19),

> "that at any time the national bank ever *represented* to plaintiff that it was acting in the capacity of *purchasing agent* for plaintiff".

4. The answer of the Central Bank, in many instances, denies that Bothwell ever informed plaintiff that the prices which she was paying for the bonds and notes purchased for her from the National Bank, through Bothwell, as the manager of its bond department, were the same prices for which the National Bank had itself purchased the bonds and notes, (App. B 8, 10-11, 12-3, 14, 17).

There is no allegation, however, in the complaint to which this denial is directed; and it is difficult to understand why the denial was thus repeatedly made, unless it was intended as an indirect and evasive denial that the National Bank was a trustee and plaintiff a cestui que trust, and, consequently, a *profit* made by the National Bank, as such trustee, on any of the transactions of purchase and sale, would be unlawful, unless consented to or acquiesced in by plaintiff, the cestui que trust, with full knowledge of the fact and of her legal rights appertaining thereto, which was not the case.

The law, as will be shown later on in this brief, does not require that the trustee, dealing with itself, should make a profit on the transaction, but should a profit be made, the relation by the trustee of its duty towards the cestui que trust is aggravated, and particularly so if the trustee, as was the case, failed to disclose to, and, therefore, in legal effect, concealed from, the cestui que trust the fact.

Consequently, the complaint alleged, in aggravation of the unlawful act, that in every instance of the purchases of bonds and notes prior to the execution of the instrument of trust, and in every instance of such purchases subsequent to the execution of that instrument, except the last four purchases made in 1930 and 1932, the National Bank had made a profit on the transaction, which it concealed from plaintiff, (App. A 19-21, 33-4).

The answer of the Central Bank, (1), *admits* the fact that the National Bank, in all said transactions of purchase and sale, had made a profit, but alleges, evasively and indefinitely, (App. B 19), that plaintiff, "at all times",

> "had knowledge of the fact that the national bank was selling her bonds and notes which it owned and was making a *profit* thereon";

and as to the said four instances of purchases of bonds and notes in 1930 and 1932, in particular, the answer, (App. B 23),

> "*Denies* that either Bothwell, or Read, or Berven, did not disclose to, or conceal from, plaintiff that through them, or any of them, the national bank had purchased from itself, or sold to itself, said bonds or any of them or that the bank had *profited* in such, or any, of said instances";

and

> "denies that plaintiff had no knowledge of such facts, or any of them, or that plaintiff did not discover them, until the time, or under the circumstances alleged in the complaint";

and alleges, (App. B 23-4),

> "that in each of the four instances of said purchases of bonds in the year 1930, namely, the instances of said purchases from and including the 8th day of April 1930 to and including the 27th day of June, 1930, plaintiff dealt *directly* with Bothwell, as manager of the bond department,

and *directed* the trust department of the national bank to purchase from the bond department said bonds and notes and in each of said instances plaintiff well knew that the trust department of the national bank was making said purchases of bonds from the bond department";

and, referring to Bothwell, Read and Berven, denies, (App. B 24), that

"any of said persons *concealed* from plaintiff the fact that the national bank had *profited* in each, or any, of the said four (4) instances mentioned".

(2), *denies,* in one instance, the *amount* of the profit, as alleged in the complaint, (App. B 18); (3), denies, (App. B 19), that

"Bothwell did not *disclose* to plaintiff, or *concealed* from her the fact that the national bank made a *profit* on each of the purchases of bonds or notes";

alleges, (App. B 19), that

"at all times plaintiff had *knowledge* of the fact that the national bank was selling her bonds and notes which it owned and was making a profit thereon";

and (4), (App. B 24-5), (referring to Bothwell, the manager of the bond department, to Read, the trust officer, and to Berven, the assistant trust officer, of the National Bank, and to the fact, as alleged in paragraphs XXI and XXII of the complaint, that the National Bank, in 1930, had purchased, and purchased at a profit, from itself, either through Read or through Bothwell, bonds and notes for the trust estate),

"Denies that any of said persons *concealed* from plaintiff the fact that the national bank had *profited* in each, or any, of the first four (4) instances mentioned. *Denies* that plaintiff had no *knowledge* of any or all of said alleged facts complained of or did not discover the same until the time and under the circumstances alleged in the complaint and in this respect this defendant *alleges* that at all times plaintiff had *knowledge* of all of the matters complained of in

said paragraphs XXI and XXII immediately upon their occurrence save that this defendant is without knowledge as to whether plaintiff knew of the *amount* of profit made in said four (4) instances mentioned";

and further *denies,* for want of knowledge, (App. B 25),

"as to whether plaintiff knew of the *amount* of *profit* made in said first four (4) instances mentioned".

The answer of the Central Bank, therefore, does not deny the allegations of the complaint, (App. A 19-21, 33-4), that the National Bank in each instance of the purchases, prior to the execution of the instrument of trust, for plaintiff from the National Bank, through Bothwell, as the manager of its bond department, and in each instance of the purchases subsequent to the execution of that instrument, except the last four purchases in the years 1930 and 1932, made a profit on the transactions; but evasively alleges, in one instance, of the purchase and sale of a bond of Medford Irrigation District, (App. B 18),

"that in the case of said bond as in the case of all other bonds sold by the national bank to plaintiff the same were sold at the current market price, if they had an established market price, or a price *commensurate* with the fair and reasonable value thereof, if they had no established market price",—

an allegation wholly unsupported by any evidence.

The sum and substance of all of this sparring in the answer of the Central Bank appears to be, not that there were no *profits* realized by the National Bank on the various purchases of bonds and notes for plaintiff and for the trust estate, created by the instrument of trust, by the National Bank, through Bothwell, as the manager of its bond department, but that the *profits* which the National Bank made in so doing were not *concealed* by it from plaintiff, and, on the contrary, plaintiff had *knowledge* of them, (from some unnamed source), and that in the instances of the four purchases made by the National Bank from itself for the trust estate, through Bothwell, as the manager of its bond department, plaintiff had even *consented* that the purchases be so made, and, inferentially, that she also had *knowledge* of and *consented* to the fact that the National Bank, in so doing, was *profiting* at her expense. In other words, counsel for the Central Bank, in drafting its answer, seems to have overlooked, or, if not, to have intentionally disregarded, the rule that in the wrongdoing of a trustee, in dealing with itself, it is not a matter of vital importance whether or not the trustee profited.

5. There are several allegations in the answer of the Central Bank, in express terms or to the effect, that plaintiff, (1), *consented* that the purchases of the bonds and notes be so made by the National Bank, through Bothwell, as the manager of its bond department, (2), *directed* that the purchases be made from the National Bank, and (3), *insisted* that the purchases be so made.

Thus the answer, (referring to the bonds and notes so purchased for the trust estate created by the instrument of trust), *alleges,* (App. B 24), that

> "plaintiff dealt *directly* with Bothwell, as manager of the bond department, and *directed* the trust department of the national bank to purchase from the bond department said bonds and notes and in each of said instances plaintiff *well knew* that the trust department of the national bank was making said purchases of bonds from the bond department. This defendant further *alleges* that it was at plaintiff's *express instance and direction* that the trust department of the national bank made said purchases and all of them, from the bond department";

with the conclusion of law, by no means correctly drawn,

> "that due to plaintiff's *own wishes,* she *in effect and in reality* acted as the *principal* in these transactions insofar as the trust department of the national bank was concerned and *directed* said trust department as to the investments she *desired* to make".

The frantic efforts which the National Bank, without success, to prevent plaintiff from making unwise, and otherwise prohibitive, investments, by the National Bank, are frequently portrayed in the answer. Thus it is alleged, (although it is not alleged by whom, but probably by Berven, nor exactly when), that, (App. B 28-9):

> "plaintiff was *cautioned and admonished* from time to time that the investments she was making carried with them a *certain element of risk* in that she sought to obtain the highest return possible on her investments".

With equal uncertainty, in other particulars, but with more evasiveness, the answer had previously alleged, (App. B 27),

> "that the trust department of the national bank from time to time *admonished* plaintiff after the creation of the trust that the securities which she then had on hand in said trust or which she thereafter *recommended* be purchased by the trust department from the bond department *were not legal investments* for savings banks or for trust funds and *advised* her that her trust funds should be invested in bonds, which, though paying a lower rate of interest and yielding a lower return, *were deemed more conservative and better secured*".

But, as early as during the preparation by Berven of the instrument of trust, plaintiff, (so it is alleged in the answer of the Central Bank), (App. B 16),

> "*specifically* informed Berven that she did not want the trust so to operate as to *prevent* her from *controlling* the investments and *informed* Berven that she *wanted* to be able to *dictate* the investments the trust department would make",

And that

> "Again, a few days later, plaintiff *interviewed* Berven and was *informed* by him that trust funds, under *ordinary* circumstances can only be invested in certain types of securi-

ties which ordinarily did not bring a greater yield than five per cent (5%)",

but that

"Plaintiff *responded* that she had to have a return of at least six per cent (6%), and *directed* that the trust instrument when drafted should contain a provision authorizing purchases of securities other than those legal for the investment of trust funds",

and that

"plaintiff further informed Berven that she *wished* the trust department to deal with the bond department of the national bank when purchasing securities for the trust".

But it is not explained in this, or in any other connection, or in any manner whatever, why it was that Berven, in the preparation by him of the instrument of trust, did not comply with plaintiff's wishes that she should be able to control and "dictate" the investments for the trust estate and why it was that the instrument of trust not only did not contain any provision to that effect, but, on the contrary, (par. II of the instrument, App. B 23-4, R. 486), gave the power of "dictation" of the character of investments in which funds of the trust estate should be invested solely to the trustee, the National Bank.

And it may be here observed, in passing, that if it be true, (as the answer of the Central Bank alleges that it was), that plaintiff expressed a wish that the trust department, in purchasing securities for the trust estate, should deal with the bond department, why it was not further alleged that Berven did not inform plaintiff that it would be grossly improper for the National Bank to purchase securities for the trust estate from itself, through Bothwell, as the manager of its bond department, and why it was that Berven subsequently, and on January 14, 1932, recommended to her, (R. 477-8), the purchase for the trust estate of $5,000, par value, bonds of East Bay Municipal

Utility District, at a cost of $5,500, and yielding, not 6%, or
even 5%, but 4.80%, (R. 477), and that plaintiff approved the
purchase, (R. 742, Defts' Ex. V), and why it was that Read
had recommended to her, still earlier, and on July 16, 1930,
(R. 561-2, Plf's Ex. 20), the purchase of $3,000, par value 6%
bonds of Pacific Gas and Electric Company, at the price of
110½, and $2,000, par value, 6% bonds of San Joaquin Light
and Power Corporation, at the price of 114½, or at prices, in
either case, yielding much less than 5% per annum, and that,
in a letter to Read, dated July 26, 1930, (R. 561-4, Plf's Exs.
20-3), she approved Read's recommendation, with the statement that "I certainly disire (sic) safe investments at all times",
and the purchases were accordingly made, not by the National
Bank, through Bothwell, as the manager of its bond department,
but from third persons, without any profit to the National Bank,
(R. 547-51, Plf's Exs. 5, 7 and 8, R. 739-40, Defts' Ex. S).

The answer further *denies,* for want of knowledge, (App.
B 28-9):

> "as to whether at the respective times when purchases were
> made, or at any other time, anyone connected with the
> national bank *recommended* any of the bonds and notes
> purchased by plaintiff or by the trust department as safe
> and desirable bonds or notes; *denies* that plaintiff was at
> any time ignorant of the difference between said bonds and
> notes so purchased and the safety or desirability of the
> same for which her funds or the funds of said trust have
> been invested and in this respect *alleges* that plaintiff was
> *cautioned and admonished* from time to time that the in-
> vestments she was making carried with them a certain ele-
> ment of risk in that she sought to obtain the highest re-
> turn possible on her investments".

The answer, (referring to the purchases of the first three of
the seven blocks of bonds and notes listed in the instrument
of trust, and purchased by the National Bank, through its trust
department, from itself, through Bothwell, as the manager of

the bond department, subsequent to the execution of that instrument), *admits,* (App. B 34), that the same

> "were purchased by the trust department of the national bank from the bond department thereof but *alleges* that this fact was well known to plaintiff and was done at her *express instance and request"*.

And, finally, (referring to the same matter), *denies,* (App. B 35), for want of knowledge, that Bothwell, or anyone else connected with the National Bank,

> *"assured* plaintiff of the safety or desirability of any of said bonds or notes",

and *denies* that the same, (App. B 36),

> "when sold by the bond department of the national bank to the trust department, *were not of such type* or so secured as not to justify the *recommendations* given plaintiff",

and *alleges,* "in this respect", (App. B 36),

> "that the said Berven, as assistant trust officer of the national bank, from time to time, *admonished* plaintiff that the bonds or notes which she was *insisting* be purchased by the trust department from the bond department as trust investments, were *not of the type* usually acquired as a trust investment, but that in each and every instance of such *admonition* plaintiff *emphatically* stated that she *desired* such investments to be made".

It will at once be seen that the foregoing allegations that the funds of the trust estate, created by the instrument of trust, were invested by the National Bank, as trustee of the trust estate, through Bothwell, as the manager of its bond department, in bonds and notes owned by the National Bank, and, therefore, that the National Bank was both the seller and the purchaser of the bonds and notes, and that the flagrant, and otherwise unlawful, violations by the National Bank of its obligations as a trustee are attempted to be excused because of plaintiff's "recommendations", "requests", "directions", "insistencies" and "emphatic desires", notwithstanding, so it is alleged, that she was repeatedly "advised", "cautioned" and "admonished" by Berven, the assistant trust officer, and, inferentially, also, by Read, the trust officer, of the National Bank, against the trust funds being invested in bonds and notes of such a character that the investments would not otherwise be approved by any court. Moreover, the allegations are in direct contradiction of the allegations of the complaint, not denied in the answer, that the purchases of the bonds and notes, prior to the execution of the instrument of trust, were recommended by Bothwell, and, after the execution of that instrument, by either Bothwell, or Read, or, inferentially, even by Berven. Neither Read nor Berven, and much less Bothwell, after having recommended the bonds and notes to plaintiff, and after plaintiff had invariably approved the recommendations, is in a position to contend the contrary.

------

3. THE ANSWER OF THE NATIONAL BANK AND ITS RECEIVER.

The answer of the National Bank and its receiver, Grut, in what may be termed as the "First Separate Defense", is entitled as follows, (App. C 1):

> "Answer of defendants Central National Bank of Oakland, a national banking association, and Joseph H. Grut, as receiver thereof";

and the title has the following introduction, (App. C 1):

> "Comes now the defendant, Joseph H. Grut, as Receiver of Central National Bank of Oakland, a National Banking Association, and answers unto plaintiff's complaint both for himself as Receiver and for Central National Bank of Oakland."

The answer, however, is not a joint answer of the National Bank and the receiver, but is an answer of the receiver only, in which he denies, either positively, or according to information and belief, or for want of knowledge, the allegations of the complaint, or admits, or affirmatively alleges, either positively, or on information and belief, as though he were answering for himself alone, and not, in any respect, for the National Bank.

The answer, as a whole, closely follows, and quite conclusively appears to have been copied from, the answer of the Central Bank, except that it omits any references to the sale to the Central Bank of the whole of the business of the trust department of the National Bank, and this, for the obvious reason that if the National Bank became a secondary obligor upon the sale to the Central Bank of the whole of the business of the trust department of the National Bank, it was and is in the interest of the National Bank to support the contention of plaintiff that such was the fact. The answer alleges, as does the answer of the Central Bank, the same so-called "Second", "Third", "Fourth", "Fifth" and "Sixth" "Separate Defenses", (App. C 34, 35-7), except that the so-called "Third Separate Defense" is on information and belief, and except also that, in many instances, the answer of the National Bank and its receiver to the allegations of the complaint are "without knowledge", whereas the allegations should either have been admitted, or have been denied, expressly and positively, since the National Bank was chargeable with the first-hand knowledge of what its officers, such as Bothwell, knew, or did not know, and, consequently, to deny, as "without knowledge", in many instances, is an obvious abuse of that form of denial. But, notwithstanding this particular defect in the answer, and notwithstanding the fact that the answer, in terms, is the answer of the receiver alone, it will be assumed, for the purposes of this brief, that the answer of the receiver is sufficient in form as an answer of the National Bank.

The so-called "Second", "Fourth", "Fifth" and "Sixth" "Separate Defenses", (App. C 34, 35-7), in the answer of the National Bank and its receiver, are in the identical language, quoted above, of the corresponding "Separate Defenses" of the Central Bank.

With a prayer for judgment, in each instance of such "Separate Defenses", (1), that plaintiff take nothing by her complaint, (2), for costs of suit, and (3), "For such other and further relief as to this court may seem meet and proper in the premises".

As in the case of the answer of the Central Bank, these "Second", "Fourth" and "Fifth" "Separate Defenses" may be passed by as unprecedented, and as entirely lacking in merit both in form and in substance. And, as in the case of the answer of the Central Bank, the District Court did not find upon any of the "Second", "Fourth", "Fifth" or "Sixth" "Separate Defenses", and expressly, in its conclusions of law, (App. F 37), declined to find upon the "Sixth Separate Defense", that is, the defense of the statutes of limitation.

The so-called "Third Separate Defense" is pleaded, in identical language, in the answer of the National Bank and its receiver as in the answer of the Central Bank, (App. C 34-5), except that, in the answer of the National Bank and its receiver, the allegations as to the offer are on information and belief.

But it may be here noted that the offer, alleged in the "Third Separate Defense" of the National Bank and its receiver to have been made by the Central Bank, is an offer, if it is an offer at all, by the Central Bank alone, and is not an offer on behalf of either the National Bank or its receiver; and, therefore, the "Third Separate Defense" of the Central Bank is distinctly out of place in the answer of the National Bank and its receiver. The fact that the "Third Separate Defense" of the Central Bank is not a defense of the National Bank and its receiver, even if it be conceded, for the moment, to be a defense of the Central Bank, is singularly recognized by the omission, (App. C 37), in the answer of the National Bank and its receiver of that portion of the prayer of the Central Bank, (App. B 39), after the words "That plaintiff take nothing by her complaint",

"In this respect the defendant offers, as it offered prior to the commencement of the action, to permit plaintiff to revoke the instrument of trust and it will thereupon deliver all of the trust property to plaintiff subject to the payment of this defendant's proper charges."

4. THE AMENDMENTS AND SUPPLEMENTS TO THE COMPLAINT.

The amendments and supplements to the complaint, filed, as above noted, after the trial of the case had commenced on February 4, 1936, and on to-wit, February 6, 1936, before the trial had been concluded, allege, in substance, as follows, (App. D 1-14):

On June 10, 1933, plaintiff addressed and delivered a letter to the Central Bank, and, on June 12, 1933, the proposal, as contained in the letter, was accepted by the Central Bank, by a writing at the foot of the letter. A copy of the letter and of the writing at the foot of the letter are annexed to the pleading as "Exhibit A", (App. D 8-12).

Since the filing of the complaint, on September 16, 1933, (R. 82), bonds and notes, referred to in the complaint, constituting a part of the trust estate created by the instrument of trust, and of the total sum of $32,744.40, (of the respective designations, par values, dates of sales and maturities and redemptions, and amounts realized, as set forth in the pleading), (1), were sold by the Central Bank, as trustee of the trust estate, pursuant to the said letter and to the acceptance of said proposal, with the approval of plaintiff's attorneys, or (2), have matured, or (3), have been redeemed, and the respective amounts for which said bonds and notes have been so sold, and the respective amounts payable on such maturities and redemptions, have respectively been paid to the Central Bank, (App. D 2-3).

Since the filing of the complaint, installments of the principal of the promissory note of Sparks Masonic Building Association, constituting a part of the trust estate, of the total sum of $3,000, have matured, and were paid to the Central Bank, on the respective dates set forth in the pleading, (App. D 3).

Prior to the filing of the complaint, Fageol Motors Company, (of which $10,000, par value, of its so-called "debenture bonds", constituted a part of the trust estate), was adjudged a bankrupt by the District Court of the United States, for the Northern District of California, Southern Division, and a receiver of the estate of the bankrupt was appointed by the said District Court. Prior to the filing of the complaint, but unknown to plaintiff at the time of such filing, and on August 19, 1933, there was paid to the Central Bank a dividend in liquidation on the said debenture bonds of the sum of $2,178.18, and thereafter, on January 13, 1934, and on January 16, 1935, respectively, there was also paid to the Central Bank additional dividends in liquidation of the respective sums of $418.70 and $329.20, or a total sum of $2,926.08; and, as plaintiff is informed and believes, a final dividend in liquidation, not to exceed the sum of $100, may be paid to the Central Bank in the near future, (App. D 3-4).

The said sums so paid to the Central Bank are now held on deposit to the credit of the trust estate by the Central Bank, as trustee of the said trusts, (App. D 4).

Since the filing of the complaint, the Central Bank, pursuant to the said letter and to the acceptance of the said proposal, has collected the interest on bonds and notes and on the promissory note of Sparks Masonic Building Association, held by the Central Bank, as trustee of the said trusts, amounting to the total sum of $7,747.20. The respective dates when the said interest on the said bonds and notes, and the respective amounts of the said interest so collected thereon, and the respective dates when the said interest on the said promissory note and the respective amounts of the said interest so collected on the said note, are shown on "Exhibit B", annexed to the pleading, (App. D 13-4).

Since the filing of the complaint, the Central Bank, pursuant to the said letter and to the acceptance of the said proposal, has paid to plaintiff the said interest so collected, when and as the same was so collected, after deducting therefrom, pursuant to the said letter and to the acceptance of the said proposal, as and for the compensation of the Central Bank, as trustee of the said trusts, 3% of the said interest so collected, or the total sum of $270.01, the said rate of compensation being the usual rate theretofore charged by the National Bank and by the Central Bank for the respective services thereof as respective trustees of the said trusts, on the collection of the interest on the bonds and notes and on the said promissory note, respectively, constituting portions of the trust estate, (App. D 4-5).

The prayer for judgment, (more complete and, in certain particulars, more definite, than the prayer to the complaint, and in addition to the prayer), being, (App. D 6-8), (1), that the instrument of trust be rescinded, (2), that the Central Bank reconvey to plaintiff the unimproved lot situated in Oakland, and reassign to plaintiff the said promissory note and its securing mortgage of Sparks Masonic Building Association, (3), that the Central Bank pay to plaintiff the sum of $80,642.50, and also pay to plaintiff the sum of $22,285.75, or the total sum of $102,926.25, as prayed for in the complaint, (4), that the total sum of $35,670.48, paid to the Central Bank for said bonds and notes respectively so sold, matured or redeemed and as dividends in liquidation, and, in addition thereto, the sum of $3,000, paid to the Central Bank for installments which had matured on the said promissory note, or the grand total sum of

$38,670.48, held by the Central Bank as trustee of the said trusts, be charged with a lien for the repayment to plaintiff of the said total sum of $102,926.25, (4a), that an accounting be had of the respective amounts of the funds of plaintiff invested by the National Bank in bonds or notes for plaintiff, and of the respective dates on which the respective amounts were so invested, aggregating the said sum of $102,926.25, and that interest at the rate of 7% per annum be charged against the Central Bank on the said respective amounts from the respective dates when the said funds were so invested by the National Bank to the date of the filing of the decree herein, less the respective payments of interest made to plaintiff by the National Bank and the Central Bank, respectively, as in the pleading and in the complaint referred to, (5), that in the event it is decreed that the Central Bank should not pay to plaintiff the said sum of $80,642.50, then that it be decreed that a claim of plaintiff therefor, together with interest thereon, determined and computed as aforesaid, be established as a claim of plaintiff against the National Bank, and that the same, as so established, together with interest thereon, at the rate aforesaid, from the date of the filing of the decree herein until the same shall have been paid to plaintiff, be paid by defendant Grut, as receiver of the National Bank, in due course of his administration, or that he certify the same to the comptroller of the currency of the United States to be similarly paid, and (6), that plaintiff have and recover her costs from defendants and have and recover from defendants, or from such thereof, such further, other and different relief as may be equitable and just in the premises.

No answer to this amendatory and supplementary pleading of plaintiff was filed either by the Central Bank or by the National Bank and its receiver, and, therefore, the allegations thereof have been confessed or admitted by defendants, under *Equity Rule 30. Simpkins, Federal Practice,* sec. 68, p. 647, (Rev. Ed.); *Montgomery v. Pacific Electric Ry.,* 293 Fed. 680, 683, (C. C. A., 9th, 1923).

5. THE SUPPLEMENTAL ANSWER OF THE NATIONAL BANK AND ITS RECEIVER TO THE COMPLAINT.

The supplemental answer of the National Bank and of its receiver sets forth, (App. E 1, 2-3), what are respectively designated therein as (1), "a further, seventh and separate defense", (2), "a further, eighth and separate defense", and (3), "a further, ninth and separate defense".

The introduction to these "separate defenses" is substantially similar in form to the introduction to the answer of the National Bank, (App. C 1), and is as follows:

"Comes now the defendant, Joseph H. Grut, as Receiver of the Central National Bank of Oakland, a national banking association, and by leave of court files this supplemental answer to the plaintiff's complaint both for himself as Receiver and for the defendant, Central National Bank of Oakland, and for such supplemental answer admits, denies and alleges as follows."

1.

The "further, seventh and separate defense" alleges, partly in substance and partly verbatim, (App. E 1-3), as follows, with emphasis supplied, and paragraphs, in some instances, divided:

"This defendant", on information and belief, alleges that, since the filing of plaintiff's complaint, plaintiff, on numerous occasions, has accepted payments of interest on the bonds and notes remaining in the trust estate, the exact times and amounts of which are particularly set forth in "Exhibit A" annexed to the pleading, and plaintiff has appropriated all of such interest payments so received to her own use.

"This defendant" did not consent to such payments, or any of them, and had no knowledge, and was not informed, of such payments, or of the fact that plaintiff was accepting the same and was appropriating the same to her own use, until January, 1936.

"This defendant", on information and belief, alleges that plaintiff, from time to time, since the filing of her complaint, has authorized the sale of a substantial number of the bonds and notes remaining in the trust estate at the time of filing her complaint, and the said bonds and notes have been sold, the said bonds and notes so sold and the respective dates being set forth in "Exhibit A" annexed to the pleading.

"This defendant" did not consent to any of said sales, and had no knowledge of the same, and was not informed thereof, until January, 1936.

"If plaintiff ever had any right to rescind the transactions complained of in this (sic) complaint, *which these defendants deny"*,

then plaintiff, by her actions in accepting said payments of interest and by appropriating the same to her own use, and by authorizing the sale of said bonds and notes,

"has waived any such right to rescind said transactions, and by said actions has ratified all of said transactions, and plaintiff has rendered impossible the restoration to *these defendants* of the bonds and notes the sale of which plaintiff seeks to rescind".

2.

The "further, eighth and separate defense" alleges, likewise partly in substance and partly verbatim, (App. E 3-4), as follows, likewise with emphasis supplied and paragraphs in some instances, divided:

"This defendant", on information and belief, alleges that plaintiff

"received notice of the matters complained of in her complaint upon which her claimed right to rescind the transactions referred to in her complaint is based",

on or before April 15, 1932, and plaintiff

"made no complaint regarding the matters complained of in her complaint, gave no notice of her intention to rescind the transactions complained of therein and made no demand for the purchase price of the bonds, the sale of which is complained of in her complaint",

until on or about June 22, 1933.

"During the period aforesaid, during which plaintiff delayed in giving *these answering defendants* notice of her claimed right to rescind the sales of bonds and notes complained of in her complaint, after plaintiff had notice of the facts upon which her said claimed right to rescind is based, said bonds and notes greatly depreciated in market value";

and, by reason of said depreciation,

"*said defendants* would be prejudiced if plaintiff is permitted to rescind said sales after delaying as aforesaid".

"If plaintiff ever had any right to rescind the transactions complained of in the complaint, which *these defendants deny,* as aforesaid, then, by reason of plaintiff's delay, as aforesaid, in giving notice of her intention to rescind and in making a demand for restitution of the purchase price of said bonds and notes, plaintiff has been guilty of such laches as ought to and does bar this action in a court of equity, and has waived any right which she may have had to rescind said transactions."

3.

The "further, ninth and separate defense", (composed, not of a single, but of two defenses), alleges, likewise partly in substance and partly verbatim, and likewise also with emphasis supplied and paragraphs divided, (App. E 4-5):

"During all of the times during which the transactions between plaintiff and defendant Central National Bank of Oakland complained of in plaintiff's complaint took place",

to-wit, from January 1, 1926, to July 1, 1930,

"it was the uniform practice of the defendant Central National Bank of Oakland when selling bonds and similar securities through its bond department to sell to its customers bonds which it owned and not to act as agent for the purchase of bonds by its customers";

and

"in all of the transactions which plaintiff complains of in her complaint the *said defendant* acted in accordance with this practice",

and

"at the time of each of the transactions complained of by plaintiff, plaintiff knew of this practice of *said defendant*".

"During all of the times aforesaid within which the transactions between defendant, Central National Bank of Oakland, and plaintiff, complained of in plaintiff's complaint, took place, it was the uniform custom of banks in the County of Alameda and in the City and County of San Francisco, State of California, which maintained bond departments, to transact their bond business by selling to their customers bonds which were owned by the banks making the respective sales, and that none of the banks in said county and said city and county acted as agents for the purchase of bonds by customers of their respective bond departments",

and

"said custom was known to all persons dealing with such banks during said times",

and

"all of the transactions between *said defendant* and plaintiff complained of in plaintiff's said complaint were conducted by *said defendant* in conformity with said custom",

and

"said custom was known to plaintiff during the period referred to".

The prayer of the pleading, (App. E 6), is as follows:

"Wherefore, *this defendant* prays judgment", (1), that plaintiff take nothing by her complaint, (2), that *"defendant"* recover costs of suit, and (3), "For such other and further relief as to this court may seem meet and proper in the premises", although, as in the case of the respective answers of the Central Bank, (App. B 40), and of the National Bank, (App. C 37), no counterclaim or cross bill was pleaded.

The District Court made no findings concerning the defenses pleaded in this supplemental answer, and, moreover, expressly declined to find on the defenses of waiver by, and of ratification and of laches of, plaintiff.

Without discussing, in this brief, the question whether or not any of these so-called "separate defenses", constitute a defense of either or both the National Bank and its receiver, and assuming that the indefinite and confused allegations are sufficiently definite and certain to show that the National Bank has been injured by the alleged wrongdoings, if such they were, of plaintiff, it may be here noted that, significantly, no reference is made in the "seventh separate defense" to the letter of June 10, 1933, "Exhibit A", to the amendments of, and supplements to, the complaint, (App. D 8-11), and to the fact, as set forth in the amendments and supplements, that besides the sale of the bonds and notes, and the receipt by the Central Bank, as the substituted trustee of the trust estate, in the place and stead of the National Bank, of the purchase prices of the bonds and notes so sold, the Central Bank, since the filing of the complaint, has also received, as such substituted trustee, the following, constituting portions of the trust estate:

(1), a total of $6,000, par value, bonds and notes, which have matured, (App. D 3); (2), a total of $10,000, par value, bonds and notes which had been redeemed at premiums, (App. D 3); (3), a total of $3,000, installments of principal, which had matured, of the promissory note of Sparks Masonic Building Association, (App. D 3); (4), a total of $2,926.08, dividends, in bankruptcy, on $10,000, par value, "debenture bonds" of Fageol Motors Company, (App. D 3-4); and (5), interest, of the total sum of $7,747.20, on bonds and notes, and on the promissory note of Sparks Masonic Building Association, all constituting parts of the trust estate, (App. D 4-5).

The following questions, therefore, suggest themselves:

(1). If the receipt by the Central Bank of the purchase prices of the bonds and notes sold, whether with or without the authorization of plaintiff, resulted in a legal injury to the National Bank and its receiver, were not the National Bank and its receiver, likewise, legally injured by the receipt by the Central Bank of the money payable on the maturities or redemptions of the bonds and notes, on the maturities of the installments of principal of the promissory note of Sparks Masonic Building Association, and on the dividends, in bankruptcy, on the debenture bonds of Fageol Motors Company, and for interest from various sources payable to, and collected by, the Central Bank? (2). If the interest so collected by the Central Bank was not legally collectible by it, as such substituted trustee, who, if anyone, could have collected the interest, and what would have been the result if the National Bank had failed or refused to collect the interest, and if the interest, or some of it, had been lost by such failure or refusal? (3). Was not plaintiff legally entitled to the interest on all trust funds, whether the instrument of trust be set aside or not? (4). If the instrument of trust is set aside, is there anything, either principal of, or interest on, the trust estate, to be restored either to the National Bank or to its receiver, who have contributed nothing to the trust estate? and (5). If the entire situation, as indicated by the foregoing questions, had been disclosed in the "seventh separate defense", as it should have been, would not such disclosure have been completely destructive of the "seventh separate defense", assuming that the "seventh separate defense" ever had any merit, in any respect?

It may also be here noted that each of the three "separate defenses" is a defense of confession and avoidance, and, ac-

cording to elementary rules, should have confessed, or conceded, for the purposes of the defense, an apparent or prima
facie right or cause of action in plaintiff, which is avoided or
destroyed by the defense, since there cannot be, in its very
nature, a defense of confession and avoidance which does not
unqualifiedly confess, as well as avoid, the apparent right or
cause of action which the plaintiff has pleaded. *Majestic Theatre
Co. v. United Artists Corp.,* 43 F.(2d) 991, 995, (D. C., D.
Conn., 1930); *Cohen v. Superior Oil Corp.,* 16 F. Supp. 221,
227, (D. C., D. Del., 1936). Overlooking or disregarding this
elementary rule, it is pleaded in the "seventh separate defense"
that "If plaintiff ever had any right to rescind the transactions
complained of in this (sic) complaint, *which these defendants
deny",* then plaintiff, by her actions, as alleged in the "defense", has waived her right to rescind and has ratified the
transactions of which she complains, (App. E 2-3); and it is
similarly pleaded in the "eighth separate defense" "That if
plaintiff ever had any right to rescind the transactions complained of in her complaint, *which these defendants deny",*
then, by reason of plaintiff's delay, as alleged in the "defense",
in giving notice of her intention to rescind and in making a
restitution of the purchase prices of the bonds and notes purchased, (App. E 4), plaintiff has been guilty of such laches as
ought to and does bar the action in a court of equity, and has
waived any right she may have had to rescind said transactions;
and, therefore, the denial, in each of these two "separate defenses", has destroyed the "defense".

III.

SPECIFICATION OF ASSIGNED ERRORS.

The assignments of error relate entirely to the findings and
the conclusions of law, and specify that the District Judge
erred:—(1), in that there is no evidence to support certain find-

ings; (2), in that certain of the findings are contrary to the evidence; (3), in that certain of the findings are without the issues raised by the pleadings; (4), in that the District Judge, in certain instances, failed to find, and, in certain instances, expressly declined to find, on certain of the issues raised by the pleadings; and (5), in that certain conclusions of law are erroneously drawn by the District Judge, either because there is no evidence to support the facts from which the conclusions are so drawn, or because the facts from which the conclusions are so drawn are without the issues raised by the pleadings, or because the conclusions are so drawn from facts found contrary to the evidence, or because the conclusions do not follow, as a matter of law, from the facts found.

As above noted, a complete copy of the findings of fact and conclusions of law is annexed to this brief, as an appendix thereto, and the same is designated as "Appendix F".

And, as also above noted, a complete copy of the assignments of error is likewise annexed to this brief, as an appendix thereto, and the same is designated as "Appendix H".

1.
SPECIFICATION BY NUMBERS OF ASSIGNED ERRORS.

Plaintiff and appellant has assigned a total of thirty-five errors, numbered as follows:

1.	App. H	1	12.	App. H	14-15	24.	App. H	38-40
2.	"	2- 3	13.	"	15-16	25.	"	40- 1
3.	"	3- 4	14.	"	16-17	26.	"	41- 3
4.	"	4- 5	15.	"	18-19	27.	"	43- 4
5.	"	5	16.	"	19-20	28.	"	44
6.	"	5- 6	17.	"	20- 2	29.	"	44- 6
7.	"	6- 7	18.	"	22- 6	30.	"	46- 7
8.	"	7-10	19.	"	26- 7	31.	"	47- 8
9.	"	10-11	20.	"	27-30	32.	"	48-51
10.	"	11-12	21.	"	30- 3	33.	"	51- 3
11.	"	13	22.	"	33- 5	34.	"	53- 4
11a.	"	13-14	23.	"	35- 8			

The errors so assigned, and, in this brief, relied upon, are segregated, according to periods of time, into the following four groups:

1. Those which concern the relations and the transactions between the National Bank and plaintiff in the purchases of bonds and notes for plaintiff from the National Bank, through Bothwell, as the manager of its bond department, during the period from on or about the date of such purchases on January 7, 1926, to the date of the last of such purchases, of $5,000 par value, bonds of Central West Public Service Company, on August 16, 1929, (R. 645, Plf's Ex. 47), shortly prior to the execution of the instrument of trust on September 24, 1929.

The errors, so assigned, include, in this group, numbered as follows:

3.	App. H	3- 4	9.	App. H	10-11	15.	App. H	18- 9
4.	"	4- 5	11.	"	13	16.	'	19-20
5	"	5	11a.	"	13- 4	17.	'	20- 2
6.	"	5- 6	12.	"	14- 5	19.	'	26- 7
7.	"	6- 7	13.	"	15- 6	20.	"	27-30
8.	"	7-10	14.		16- 7			

2. Those which concern the relations between the National Bank and plaintiff, (1), in the transaction of the preparation of the instrument of trust after the last of such purchases on August 16, 1929, (2), in the transaction of the execution of the instrument of trust on September 24, 1929, (3), in the purchases of bonds and notes for the trust estate created by that instrument, first, in the year 1930, (R. 645, Plf's Ex. 47), from the National Bank, through Bothwell, as the manager of its bond department, and through either Read, the trust officer, or through Berven, the assistant trust officer, of the National Bank, (4), in the purchases thereafter of bonds and notes for the trust estate, in the years 1930 and 1932, (R. 645, Plf's Ex. 47) by the National Bank, either through Read or Berven, and (5), in the transactions in the latter part of October, or in the early part of Novem-

ber, 1932, between plaintiff and Berven and Bothwell, pursuant
to the letter, (R. 409-10, 673, Plf's Ex. 61), dated October 29,
1932, from Berven to plaintiff, requesting her to call at the
trust department

"regarding the bonds of the Alameda Investment Company which we hold in your trust account",

and in which Berven stated that

"We believe that it is advisable that a portion of your
holdings in said company should be sold at this time and
would appreciate it very much if you would call at your
earliest convenience to discuss the matter with us".

The errors, so assigned, include, in this group, numbered as
follows:

21.	App. H 30- 3	25.	App. H 40- 1	29.	App. H 44- 6
22.	" 33- 5	26.	" 41- 3	30.	" 46- 7
23.	" 35- 8	28.	" 44	32.	" 48-51

Besides the foregoing two groups of errors, so assigned, there
will be considered the following two additional errors:

3. The error of the District Judge in failing and declining,
(in Finding Number 33, App. H 51-3), to find on the issue
presented by the complaint and the answer of the Central Bank,
of the assumption and the agreement of the Central Bank to pay
and discharge the obligations and liabilities incurred by the
National Bank on the sale to the Central Bank of the whole of
the business of the trust department of the National Bank.

4. The error of the District Judge in finding, (in Finding
Number 27, App. H 43-4, and in finding, as a fact, in Finding
Number 31, App. H 47-8, misplaced in the conclusions of law),
referring to the Central Bank as the "savings bank", respectively
as follows:

"That prior to the commencement of this suit the savings
bank, being then the successor trustee under the said in-

strument, offered to permit plaintiff to revoke the trust
and the instrument of trust and offered to deliver all of
the trust properties to plaintiff and offered to agree that
such revocation should not be a release or discharge of
existing liabilities or obligations of said savings bank to
plaintiff, if any; that plaintiff refused such offer, in view
of the fact that the savings bank (Central Bank of Oakland), the successor trustee under said instrument of trust,
prior to the commencement of the action, and in its answer, offered to permit plaintiff to revoke said instrument
of trust, plaintiff may, if she so desires, revoke said instrument of trust, or appoint a new, or successor trustee, as
provided for by the provisions of paragraph 1 of the
contract dated April 22nd, 1933, relative to the purchase
of the trust department of the national bank by the savings bank, and in the event of such revocation, or such
appointment of a successor trustee, the savings bank shall
deliver to plaintiff or to such successor trustee, as the case
may be, all trust assets, subject to such deductions as may
be equitable and just for its compensation and expenditures
as set forth in the letter dated June 10, 1933, and shall
execute such instruments as may reasonably be necessary
to effect the foregoing".

IV.

ARGUMENT.

The principal questions involved in the case are five in number
and are as follows:

1. Whether or not an instrument of trust, under which property, real and personal, including bonds and notes and other
securities, were transferred, without consideration, to a national
bank by one who was a widow, and in poor health, and who
had long been a depositor of, and towards whom, the bank,
through the manager of its bond department, and through its
assistant trust officer of its trust department, sustained a relation
of trust and confidence, should be rescinded in a suit brought

for that purpose, for the reason that the bonds and notes were purchased for the depositor by the bank from itself, prior to, but in contemplation of, the creation of the trust estate by the instrument of trust, without disclosing to, and, therefore, concealing from, the depositor the fact that the bonds and notes were owned by the bank, and were sold to the depositor at a profit, and without disclosing to, and, therefore, concealing from, the depositor the further fact that the bank could not lawfully make the purchases of the bonds and notes from itself, whether with or without a profit, and that the depositor had the consequent legal right to disaffirm the purchases and recover from the bank the purchase money, with interest thereon, unless the depositor, (which was not the case), had either previously consented to, or had subsequently ratified, the purchases, after full knowledge, in either such events, of the facts and of the depositor's legal rights relating to those facts.

2. Whether or not the instrument of trust should be rescinded, in a suit brought for that purpose, for the reason that, subsequent to the execution of the instrument of trust, the bank, (the trustee of the trust estate created by the instrument), had purchased bonds and notes from itself, through the manager of its bond department, for and with the funds of the trust estate, at a profit to itself, without disclosing to, and, therefore, concealing that fact from, the trustor, (and the cestui que trust), and without disclosing to, and, therefore, concealing from, the cestui que trust the further fact that the bank could not lawfully make the purchases of the bonds and notes from itself for the trust estate, whether with or without a profit to itself, and that the cestui que trust had the consequent right to disaffirm the purchases and recover from the bank the purchase money, with interest thereon, unless the cestui que trust, (which was not the case), had either previously consented to or had subsequently acquiesced in the purchases, after full knowledge, in either such events, of the facts and of her legal rights relating to those facts.

3. Whether or not the instrument of trust should be rescinded, if both of the preceding questions are answered in the negative, (and equally so if both questions are answered in the affirmative), for the reason that the instrument of trust, by which the trustor had reserved the right to revoke, in whole or in part, the trusts created by the instrument of trust, by an instrument declaring such revocation, in which event the trust property, or the part thereof to which the trusts are revoked, as the case may be, shall be paid and delivered to the trustor, provided, however, that in no event shall any attempted revocation be of any effect unless and until all sums of money then due the trustee under the terms thereof shall be fully paid and the trustee "shall be fully released and discharged of all then existing liabilities and obligations of every kind and nature affecting the said property or in relation thereto, anything to the contrary notwithstanding".

4. Whether or not the Central Bank, on the sale to it by the National Bank, became liable to the appellant, as the primary obligor, for the violation of the duties of the National Bank to the appellant, (assuming that the first two of the three preceding questions are answered in the affirmative), pursuant to the provisions of section 31 of the *California Banking Act*, (1 Deering, General Laws of California, 1931, p. 242), and to the provisions of one of the two contracts, (R. 81-4), entered into between the National Bank, and its conservator, Mount, and the Central Bank.

5. Whether or not it is a fact that, as alleged in the "Third Separate Defense" of the Central Bank, (App. B 37),

"that prior to the commencement of this suit this defendant, being then the successor trustee, offered to permit plaintiff to revoke the trust and the instrument of trust and to deliver all of the trust properties to plaintiff and offered to agree that such revocation should not be a release or discharge of existing liabilities and obligations of this defendant, if any";

but that "plaintiff refused such offer", and if it is a fact, either admitted as such by plaintiff or established as such by the evidence, whether or not the offer constitutes a defense.

1.

The District Judge answered the first two of the foregoing questions in the negative. The questions which are interrelated will be, for that reason and for the reason that they are governed by the same legal rules, discussed together.

The errors which are relied upon are numbered and fully set forth in "Exhibit H", and may be summarized, for the purposes of this brief, as follows: (1), those relating to the extent of plaintiff's acquaintance with Bothwell, No. 3, App. H 3-4; (2), those which relate to plaintiff's mentality and the exercise by her of her independent judgment with respect to the purchases of bonds and notes, No. 4, App. H 4-5, No. 5, App. H 5; (3), those which relate to the nature of the relationship between plaintiff and the National Bank, that is, whether the relationship was that of buyer and seller or of principal and agent, and the intention of plaintiff in that respect, No. 6, App. H 5-6, No. 7, App. H 6-7; (4), those which relate to the time when plaintiff intended to create a trust, No. 8, App. H 7-10; (5), those which relate to the custody by the National Bank of the bonds and notes purchased prior to the execution of the instrument of trust on September 24, 1929, No. 9, App. H 10-11; (6), those which relate to the purchase prices of the bonds and notes purchased, No. 11, App. H 13; (7), those which relate to the concealments from plaintiff by the National Bank that the Bank was making a profit on the sale of the bonds and notes, No. 11a, App. H 13-4; (8), those which relate to the desire of plaintiff to secure a high rate of return on her purchases of bonds and notes, never less than 6%, and to plaintiff's being actuated primarily in the purchase of the bonds and notes with that end in view, No. 12, App. H 14-5; (9), those which relate to the advice given by Bothwell to plaintiff and by Berven to plaintiff that return or interest on bonds and notes was compensation for the risk taken, and that, in general, the higher the rate of interest the greater the risk was involved, No. 13, App. H 15-6; (10), those which relate to bonds and notes when purchased being of the type desired by plaintiff, and being at that time satisfactory, safe and desirable, and being so considered, not only by the National Bank, but also by investment houses which at the same time were selling the same securities to their customers, No. 15, App. H 18-9; (11), those which relate to the alleged fact that the only recommendation made by Bothwell, or by the National Bank, in the sale of bonds and notes to plaintiff was that the same were considered satisfactory by the National Bank, or that the National Bank considered the same as safe and desirable, such recommendations being based upon the best knowledge, information and belief of the Bank and of Bothwell, No. 16, App. H 19-20; (12), those which relate to the reliance by plaintiff, in purchasing the bonds and notes, in part, upon the recommendations of Bothwell and Berven, and, in part, upon the relatively high rate of interest and return on the bonds and notes purchased, No. 17, App. H 21-2; (13), those which relate to the bonds and notes sold to plaintiff as being sufficiently secured, No. 18, App. H 22-6; (14), those which relate to the first conversations between plaintiff and Bothwell and Read, concerning plaintiff's intended creation of a trust, Nos. 19 and 20, App. H 26-7; (15), those which relate to the alleged wish, expressed by plaintiff to Berven, that the purchase of bonds and notes from the bond department of the National Bank should be continued, and of plaintiff's desire to purchase securities bearing a return of not less than 6%, and of Berven's statement to plaintiff that the type of securities regarded as proper for trust investments usually paid not over 5%, and of her insistence that she needed at least 6%, and of Berven's telling plaintiff that a provision could be inserted in the instrument of trust authorizing such type of investments,

No. 20, App. H 27-30; (16), those which relate to the submission by Berven to plaintiff for her consideration of the instrument of trust, and the reading of the same by plaintiff, and to the explanations by Berven to plaintiff, and her statements to Berven that she understood the same, and to Berven's reply to plaintiff's inquiry as to whether she should submit the instrument of trust to an attorney of her own selection for his advice concerning the same, and to Berven's reply that it was proper for her to do so, and to her statement to Berven that she had not time to do so, No. 21, App. H 30-2; (17), those which relate to the purchases of bonds and notes by the National Bank, through Bothwell, as the manager of its bond department, and to Bothwell's submitting the same to plaintiff, without any recommendation, and to the reliance, in part, by plaintiff upon Bothwell's suggestion and submission, and, in part, to the relatively high rate of return, and to plaintiff's direction to the trust department to purchase the same from the bond department, with the knowledge of plaintiff that the bond department was making a profit thereon, No. 22, App. H 33-5; (18), those which relate to the fact that the National Bank did not conceal from plaintiff the fact that the trust department was purchasing the bonds owned by the bond department, and that in so doing the Bank had profited in each instance of such purchases, and to the fact that the bonds and notes were purchased at the fair value thereof, and were legal trust investments for the trust department to make for the trust estate, No. 23, App. H 35-8; (19), those which relate to the notification by the National Bank to plaintiff of the defaults in the payment of the interest on bonds and notes, No. 25, App. H 40-1, No. 26, App. H 41-3; (20), those which relate to the question whether or not any fraud, concealment or misrepresentation was perpetrated by the National Bank on plaintiff, and whether or not plaintiff was entitled to the relief of rescission, No. 29, App. H 44-6, and No. 30, App. H 46-7; and (21), those which relate to the question whether or not plaintiff expressly authorized and directed the

trust department of the National Bank to make purchases of bonds and notes and to plaintiff's knowledge that the National Bank was the owner of the bonds and notes and would make a profit on the purchases, No. 32, App. H 48-51.

The errors, so assigned, include that the findings are, (1), without the issues, (2), without any supporting evidence, and (3), contrary to the evidence.

The District Judge found that, in the purchases of the bonds and notes, both prior and subsequent to the execution of the instrument of trust, from the National Bank, through Bothwell, as the manager of its bond department, the National Bank did not conceal from plaintiff the fact that it was the owner of the bonds and notes so purchased, and had made a profit thereon, and that plaintiff not only had full knowledge that such were the facts, but had consented, and even directed, that the purchases be so made. But the District Judge did not find that, in addition to such findings, it was essential that plaintiff should have been fully informed of her legal rights concerning the transactions.

The rule is well settled that a trustee, who would excuse himself for a breach of trust on the ground of the confirmation by the beneficiary of the breach, has the heavy burden laid upon him of proving not only that he made a full and fair disclosure to the beneficiary of all the material facts relating to the breach, including his own wrongdoing, and his resulting legal obligations therefrom, but, in addition, that he fully apprised the beneficiary of the beneficiary's legal rights concerning the breach, and that the beneficiary, having been so apprised, freely and deliberately, and with the intention so to do, confirmed the breach:

> 1 *Restatement, Trusts,* sec. 170, sub-sec. 2, p. 441;
> 1 *Id.,* sec. 216, sub-sec. 2(b), p. 609;
> 1 *Id.,* sec. 218, sub-sec. 2(b), p. 622;
> *Lewin, Trusts,* p. 980, (13th Eng. ed.);
> *Adair v. Brimmer,* 74 N. Y. 539, 553-4, (1878);

White v. Sherman, 168 Ill. 589, 605, 48 N. E. 128, 132, 61 A. S. R. 132, (1897);

Joliet Trust & Savings Bank v. Ingalls, 276 Ill. App. 445, 450-4, (1935);

McAllister v. McAllister, 120 N. J. Eq. 407, 414-20, 184 At. 723, 728-30, (aff'd. 121 N. J. Eq. 264, 190 At. 52), (1936);

Gates v. Plainfield Trust Co., 121 N. J. Eq. 460, 484-8, 191 At. 304, 317-9, (1937);

In re Bender's Estate, 122 N. J. Eq. 192, 194-201, 192 At. 718, 721-3, (1937);

In re Young's Estate, 244 App. Div. 495, 501, 293 N. Y. S. 97, 107, (1937);

Jackson v. Smith, 254 U. S. 586, 588-9, 65 L. Ed. 418, 424, (1921);

Kershaw v. Julien, 72 F.(2d) 528, 530, (C. C. A. 10th, 1934);

Gates v. Megargel, 266 Fed. 811, 820, (C. C. A., 2d, 1920);

Thompson v. Park Sav. Bank, 96 F.(2d) 544, 549, (C. A., Dist. Columbia, 1938);

Garret v. Reid-Cashion Land & Cattle Co., 34 Ariz. 245, 267-71, 270 Pac. 1044, 1051-3, (1928).

Thus, in the leading case of *Adair v. Brimmer,* 74 N. Y. 539, 553, (1878), it was said:

"The testimony as to a ratification of these transactions is contradicted by the contestants, and the auditor has found against such ratification. We concur in his conclusion. To establish a ratification by a cestui que trust, the fact must not only be clearly proved, but it must be shown that the ratification was made with a full knowledge of all the material particulars and circumstances, and also in a case like the present that the cestui que trust was fully apprised of the effect of the acts ratified, and of his or her legal rights in the matter. Confirmation and ratification imply to legal minds, knowledge of a defect in the act to be confirmed, and of the right to reject or ratify it. The cestui que trust must therefore not only have been acquainted with the facts, but apprised of the law, how these facts would be dealt with by a court of equity. All that is implied in the act of ratification, when set up in equity by a trustee against his cestui que trust, must be proved, and will not be assumed. The maxim 'ignorantia legis excusat neminem', cannot be invoked in such a case. The cestui que trust must be shown to have been apprised of his legal rights."

Again, the Supreme Court of Illinois, in the frequently cited case of *White v. Sherman*, 168 Ill. 589, 48 N. E. 128, in affirming a judgment of an appellate court, holding that the evidence did not support a ratification by the beneficiaries of unlawful transactions of the trustee, said, (168 Ill. 605, 48 N. E. 132), as follows:

"In order to bind a cestui que trust by acquiescence in a breach of trust by the trustee, it must appear that the cestui que trust knew all the facts, and was apprised of his legal rights, and was under no disability to assert them. Such proof must be full and satisfactory. The cestui que trust must be shown, in such case, to have acted freely, deliberately and advisedly, with the intention of confirming a transaction which he knew, or might or ought, with reasonable or proper diligence, to have known to be impeachable. His acquiescence amounts to nothing if his right to impeach is concealed from him, or if a free disclosure is not made to him of every circumstance which it is material for him to know. He cannot be held to have recognized the validity of a particular investment, unless the question as to such validity appears to have come before him. The trustee setting up the acquiescence of the cestui que trust must prove such acquiescence. The trustee must also see to it, that all the cestuis que trust concur, in order to protect him from a breach of trust. If any of the beneficiaries are not sui juris, they will not be bound by acts charged against them as acts of acquiescence. The trustee cannot escape the liability merely by informing the cestuis que trust, that he has committed a breach of trust. *The trustee is bound to know what his own duty is, and cannot throw upon the cestuis que trust the obligation of telling him what such duty is."* (Italics supplied.)

It is not vital, in the application of this rule, whether or not a profit was made by the wrongdoing trustee; the making of a profit has no effect other than to aggravate the offense.

The foregoing cases of *Jackson v. Smith*, 254 U. S. 586, 65 L. Ed. 418, (1921), *Kershaw v. Julien*, 72 F.(2d) 528, (C. C. A., 10th, 1934), *Gates v. Megargel*, 266 Fed. 811, (C. C. A., 2d, 1920), *Thompson v. Parks Savings Bank*, 96 F.(2d) 244, (C. A., Dist. Columbia, 1938), and *Garret v. Reid-Cashion Land & Cattle Co.*, 34 Ariz. 245, 270 Pac. 1044, (1928), do not involve the conventional relation of trustee and cestui que trust, but involve the fiduciary, or, as it is sometimes termed, the "confidential" relation which exists between a receiver of a building and loan association and those interested in the association, between directors and stockholders, and between promoters of and subscribers to an enterprise; but the rule above formulated has the same application to those relations as in the case of conventional trustees and their cestuis que trustent.

The rule applies with equal force to the multitude of cases in which an agent, authorized to purchase property for his principal, purchased the property from himself, frequently secretly, first taking the title to the property in himself. The law treats the relation between the agent and the principal very much the same as though the relation was that of a trustee and cestui que trust. Thus, in 2 *Pomeroy, Equity Jurisprudence*, sec. 959, p. 2055, (4th ed.), tit. "Constructive Fraud", Professor Pomeroy, in discussing the relation between an agent and his principal, says:

> *"Equity regards and treats this relation in the same general manner, and with nearly the same strictness, as that of trustee and beneficiary.* The underlying thought is, that

an agent should not unite his personal and his representative characters in the same transaction; and equity will not permit him to be exposed to the temptation, or brought into a situation where his own personal interests conflict with the interests of his principal, and with the duties which he owes to his principal. In dealings without the intervention of his principal, if an agent for the purpose of selling property of the principal purchases it himself, *or an agent for the purpose of buying property for the principal buys it from himself, either directly or through the instrumentality of a third person, the sale or purchase is voidable; it will always be set aside at the option of the principal; the amount of consideration, the absence of undue advantage, and other similar features are wholly immaterial;* nothing will defeat the principal's right of remedy except his own confirmation after full knowledge of all the facts." (Emphasis supplied.)

See, also, to the same effect:

1 *Cal. Jur.*, secs. 77-80, pp. 788-92, tit. "Agency";

2 *Restatement, Agency*, sec. 389, pp. 873-4;

2 *Id.*, sec. 390, pp. 877-8, 879-80.

And for recent cases involving the rule decided by the California appellate courts, see the following:

Scovill v. Guy, 205 Cal. 386, 388-9, 270 Pac. 934, 935, (1928);

Bank of America v. Sanchez, 3 Cal. App.(2d) 238, 242-4, 38 Pac.(2d) 787, 789-90, (1934);

Alexander v. State Capital Company, 9 Cal.(2d) 304, 311, 70 Pac.(2d) 619, 622, (1937).

There is no good reason why the rule should not be applied to the case of a seller and a buyer, if there is a fiduciary relation, as there may well be, from which a duty to disclose rests upon the seller, (25 *C. J.*, secs. 8-10, pp. 1118-20, tit. "Fiduciary"); but this application of the rule has been overlooked in the an-

swer of the Central Bank to the complaint and in the findings of
the District Judge, in which a difference between a trustee and
a cestui que trust and a seller and a purchaser is sought to be
supported by mere reiteration of the conclusion of law that the
relation between the National Bank and plaintiff, in the purchases of the bonds and notes, was that of seller and purchaser,
and was not that of principal and agent. The complaint does not
allege, in so many words, that the relation between the National
Bank and plaintiff, in their transactions, was that of trustee and
cestui que trust, and had the relation been so alleged the allegation would have been a conclusion of law, which would not have
added to or detracted from the facts, as alleged in the complaint
in detail. The result, therefore, is that the finding has no foundation either in the issues or in the evidence, and, aside from this
fact, is completely nullified by the finding that plaintiff reposed
"trust and confidence" in the National Bank. In other words,
the Central Bank overshot its mark, and scored nothing.

In Conclusion of Law 1, (App. F 34), the District Judge
found as a fact the following:

> "That prior to the execution of the instrument of trust
> on September 24, 1929 the relationship existing between
> plaintiff and the national bank was that of buyer and seller
> and no fraud, concealment, or misrepresentation was prac-
> ticed upon plaintiff by the national bank either with respect
> to said relationship, or with respect to the value or de-
> sirability of the securities purchased or their market value,
> or with respect to the fact that said national bank was
> making a profit on such sales, or with respect to the fact
> that said bank was selling its own securities to plaintiff,
> and therefore plaintiff is not entitled to rescind any of the
> purchases of securities made by her from the bond depart-
> ment of the national bank prior to the execution of the
> instrument of trust."

This finding is a misconception of what constitutes constructive fraud, as plaintiff contends was practiced upon her by the

National Bank. If it be conceded, for present purposes, that the
relation between plaintiff and the National Bank was that of a
buyer and seller, and that plaintiff reposed in the National Bank
great trust and confidence, the violation of the great trust and
confidence by the National Bank was a constructive fraud, or,
as well expressed in the case of *Kershaw v. Julien,* 72 F.(2d)
528, 530, *supra,*

> "When there is a duty to speak, the suppression of the
> truth is as reprehensible and as actionable as the utterance
> of the false".

Two findings of the District Judge, which have not been
assigned as error, require a special consideration, in this connection. They are respectively as follows:

1. (App. F, Finding 7 of paragraph I), "Plaintiff reposed
in Bothwell and in the bond department trust and confidence,
which Bothwell well knew". This finding covers a period of more
than ten years prior to the date of the first purchases of bonds
and notes on January 7, 1926, during all of which time Bothwell occupied the position of an executive officer, of high rank,
of the National Bank, to-wit, that of an assistant cashier and
the manager of the bond department of the National Bank.

Although it is alleged in the complaint that plaintiff, during
the entire time in which the bonds and notes were purchased,
reposed "great" trust and confidence in the National Bank, in
Bothwell, in Berven and in Read, the superlative adjective
"great" adds nothing of substantial importance to the otherwise
"trust and confidence" so reposed. The effect of the finding, as
made, is important in its relation to other findings, in several
particulars, namely, (1), (App. F, Finding I of paragraph II),
"That at all times mentioned in the complaint plaintiff was a
widow and in poor health; it is a fact, however, that at all
times, both before as well as after the execution of the trust
instrument, plaintiff had a highly developed business sense, and
was extremely able and alert mentally, and was well able to

understand, and did in fact understand, the nature of the transactions complained of in the complaint; plaintiff was accustomed to, and did in fact, exercise her independent judgment with respect to the transactions complained of in the complaint". (Assigned, excluding the first sentence, as error No. 4, App. G 45).

The obvious purpose of the finding, which has no support in any of the allegations of the complaint, or in any of the evidence, is to create the impression that plaintiff's mentality was such that she was not imposed upon by either Bothwell, Berven or Read. But the law does not require that the victim of misplaced confidence in her trustee should have any particular degree of mentality, since a person of the highest mentality, who has trust and confidence in his trustee, may, and often is, imposed upon. The indisputable fact is that the bonds and notes purchased were always recommended, in one form or another, to plaintiff, by one of these three named officials, and that plaintiff relied upon the recommendation. The making of the recommendation had no other object than that it should be relied upon.

2. (App. F 37, Conclusion of Law 4), "Had any liabilities been established as arising out of, or relating or incidental to, the purchase of the securities by the trust department, or the conduct of said trust, after the execution of the trust instrument on September 24, 1929, such liabilities would have been assumed by the savings bank". This is an admission that the liabilities of the National Bank, which resulted from the purchases of bonds and notes from itself for the *trust estate,* through Bothwell, as the manager of the bond department, were assumed by the National Bank stand on precisely the same footing as the purchases of bonds and notes for plaintiff by the National Bank, through Bothwell, as the manager of its bond department, and is a trust department liability of the National Bank.

The District Judge also answered in the negative the third of the foregoing principal questions involved in the case, and found, in so doing, that the instrument of trust should not be rescinded, but, in so doing, the District Judge overlooked the fact that Berven, in the preparation of the instrument, and in the submission of the instrument to plaintiff for her consideration and approval, was conclusively presumed to have had knowledge of the fact that plaintiff reposed great trust and confidence in the National Bank and in Bothwell, as the manager of its bond department, in the purchases of the bonds and notes, and that the great trust and confidence so reposed had been violated, and it was Berven's duty to disclose to plaintiff all the material facts relating to the purchases, and also to have informed plaintiff of her legal rights to rescind the purchases, failing which he was guilty of a constructive fraud. Moreover, the provisions of the instrument of trust, relating to the revocation by plaintiff of the instrument, very plainly, have nothing whatever to do with the question of plaintiff's right to rescind the transactions between the National Bank and plaintiff in the instant action brought by her for that purpose, in which the full measure of relief to which she is entitled may be secured by her. She has the legal right to have that measure of relief determined in this action, and should not be relegated to the inadequate relief which may be afforded her in those provisions of the instrument of trust, the jurisdiction of the District Court to enforce which would have been lost, with the grave possibility that if a new action be instituted by her to enforce her legal rights, should she and the Central Bank be unable to agree, she may be met with the plea of res judicata.

2.

The fourth of the five principal questions involved in the case, (*ante,* p. 48), is here produced, for convenience, and in a somewhat different form, as follows:

Whether or not the Central Bank, on the sale to it of the whole of the business of the trust department of the National Bank, became liable to plaintiff, as primary obligor, for the result of the violation by the National Bank of its duties to plaintiff in the purchases of the bonds and notes, both prior and subsequent to the execution of the instrument of trust, from itself, for plaintiff in the one case, and for the trust estate created by that instrument in the other case.

The District Judge, (App. F 37, Conclusion of Law 4), found that

> "Had any liabilities been established as arising out of, or relating or incidental to, the purchase of the securities by the trust department, or the conduct of said trust, after the execution of the trust instrument on September 24, 1929, such liabilities would have been assumed by the savings bank".

That finding, as it has been contended, (*ante,* p. 59), is an irrevocable admission, for the purposes of this case, that the liabilities of the National Bank which resulted from the purchases, subsequent to the execution of the instrument of trust, of bonds and notes from itself for the trust estate created by that instrument, through Bothwell, as the manager of its bond department, were assumed by the Central Bank; and, since the relation between the National Bank and plaintiff, in the purchases of the bonds and notes prior to the execution of that instrument, was likewise the relation of trustee and cestui que trust, the irrevocable admission also extends to the liabilities of the National Bank to plaintiff concerning the purchases prior, as well as subsequent, to the execution of that instrument. In other words, the liability of the National Bank, in either case, was and is a trust department liability. This liability results from the provisions of the *California Bank Act,* sec. 31, (1 Deering, General Laws of California, 1931, p. 242), reproduced in Appendix I 1-3, and the important or relevant provisions of which have been separated, as an assistance in their construction, (App. I 4-7), and from the provisions of the agreement of sale, ("Exhibit C" annexed to the complaint, (App. A 80-2)).

Irrespective of the admission, however, it is abundantly clear from the provisions of the *California Bank Act* and from the provisions of the contract of sale that the Central Bank assumed the liabilities of the National Bank as trust department liabilities for the purchases of the bonds and notes both subsequent and prior to the execution of the instrument of trust.

Section 31 of the *California Bank Act* (1 Deering, General Laws of California, 1931, p. 242, (App. I, 4, 6-7), provides as follows:

"Upon the approval by the superintendent of banks of an agreement of sale and purchase and the transfer of the business of a trust department or of a bank having a trust department the purchasing bank shall, ipso facto and by operation of law and without further transfer, substitution, act or deed, and in all courts and places, be deemed and held *to have succeeded* and shall become subrogated *and shall succeed to all* rights, obligations, properties, assets, investments, deposits, demands, contracts, agreements, court and private trusts and other relations to any person, creditor, depositor, trustor, principal or beneficiary of any court or private trust, *obligations and liabilities of every nature,* and shall execute and perform all such court and private trusts in the same manner *as though it had itself originally assumed the relation of trust or incurred the obligation or liability."* (Emphasis supplied).

The contract of sale between the National Bank and the Central Bank, ("Exhibit C", pars. 2 and 3, to the complaint), (App. A 81), (referring to the Central Bank as the "Savings Bank"), provides as follows:

"2. In consideration of the said sale, assignment and transfer and of the premises herein set forth, the Savings Bank *hereby assumes all fiduciary and trust obligations and*

liabilities of the National Bank, and agrees to perform all
of the trusts of the National Bank and *to pay and discharge
all the debts and liabilities that are incidental to said trusts
or connected therewith, in the same manner as if the Savings Bank had itself incurred the obligation, debt or liability, or assumed the relation of trust.*

"3· The Savings Bank shall have all the rights, and
shall be subject to all the liabilities, and hereby assumes
all of the obligations, *that, according to law, result from
or are incidental to the purchase and sale of a trust department of a bank;* and the foregoing enumeration of specific
rights, liabilities and obligations *is not intended as a limitation* upon the general provisions of this paragraph".
(Emphasis added).

It is thus seen that the contract of sale, in its provisions, goes
beyond the requirements of the statute in relation to the assumption of the liabilities of the selling bank, (that is, the National
Bank); but it cannot be conceived that there is any reason why
this enlarged assumption of the liabilities should not be perfectly valid and enforceable.

The result is that, under the provisions of the act, and, in
particular, as the same are enlarged by the contract of sale,
the Central Bank assumed and agreed to discharge the liabilities
of the National Bank to plaintiff arising from the purchases of
the bonds and notes by the National Bank, both subsequent and
prior to the execution of the instrument of trust.

3,

The fifth, and last, of the five principal questions involved
in the case, (*ante,* pp. 48-9), is here reproduced, for convenience, as follows:

"Whether or not it is a fact that, as alleged in the
'Third Separate Defense' of the Central Bank, (App.
B 37),

'that prior to the commencement of this suit this defendant, being then the successor trustee, offered to permit

plaintiff to revoke the trust and the instrument of trust and to deliver all of the trust properties to plaintiff and offered to agree that such revocation should not be a release or discharge of existing liabilities and obligations of this defendant, if any';

but that 'plaintiff refused such offer', and if it is a fact, either admitted as such by plaintiff or established as such by the evidence, whether or not the offer constitutes a defense".

In the first place, there is no evidence whatever to support the allegations of the defense. In the next place, even if there were evidence to support the allegations, the following analysis of the offer is sufficient to demonstrate its absurdity as a defense, either in whole or in part. The offer was, (1), "to revoke the trust and the instrument of trust and to deliver all of the trust properties" to plaintiff, and (2), "to *agree* that such revocation should not be a release or discharge of the *existing* liabilities and obligations" of the *Central Bank*, "if any", to plaintiff; with a prayer that, because plaintiff "refused such offer", plaintiff be penalized by a decree that she "take nothing by her complaint"; that is, because plaintiff, (so it is alleged), refused the offer to enter into an agreement with the Central Bank, (the terms of which are not defined), to release or discharge "the existing liabilities and obligations" of the *Central Bank only*, and not those of the National Bank, to plaintiff, plaintiff is to "take nothing by her complaint", not even her costs against either the *Central Bank* or the National Bank and its receiver. Even under such provisions as those of sec. 1997 of the *California Code of Civil Procedure*, and under similar statutory provisions in other jurisdictions, (15 *C. J.*, secs. 133-4, 138), the penalty for the refusal by plaintiff of an offer of defendant relates only to certain of plaintiff's costs.

WHEREFORE, it is respectfully submitted that the decree of the District Judge should be reversed, with instructions to

enter a decree in favor of plaintiff against the Central Bank
and the National Bank in accordance with the prayer to the
amendments and supplements to the complaint, (App. D 6-8).

CHARLES W. SLACK, and

EDGAR T. ZOOK,

Attorneys for Plaintiff and Appellant.

Appendix A

COMPLAINT

Appendix A

In the ... District Court of the District of Columbia

No. ...

ARTHUR W. QUINN,

Plaintiff,

vs.

CENTRAL NATIONAL BANK OF OAKLAND,
a National Banking Association, JOSEPH H.
GRUT, as trustee of the ... Central Bank
of Oakland, a National Banking Association,
and CENTRAL BANK OF OAKLAND, a
...,

Defendants.

COMPLAINT FOR RESCISSION AND
OTHER RELIEF

The above named plaintiff complains of the above
named defendants, and alleges:

I.

That during all the times hereinafter mentioned,
since on or about the 9th day of August, 1920, the
above named defendant Central National Bank of
Oakland was, and it now is, [?] a national banking
association, duly organized and existing under and
by virtue of the laws of the Congress of the United
States, with its principal place of business in the
City of Oakland, County of Alameda, State of California, and that at all times, as those hereinafter

Appendix A

In the Superior Court of the State of California, in and for the County of Alameda.

No. 3644-S

ABBIE W. QUINN,

Plaintiff,

vs.

CENTRAL NATIONAL BANK OF OAKLAND, a national banking association, JOSEPH H. GRUT, as Receiver of Central National Bank of Oakland, a National Banking Association, and CENTRAL BANK OF OAKLAND, a corporation,

Defendants.

COMPLAINT FOR RESCISSION AND OTHER RELIEF.

The above named plaintiff complains of the above named defendants, and alleges:

I.

That during all the times hereinafter mentioned, since on or about the 9th day of August, 1909, the above named defendant Central National Bank of Oakland was, and it now is, [1*] a national banking association, duly organized and existing under and by virtue of the laws of the Congress of the United States, with its principal place of business in the City of Oakland, County of Alameda, State of California; and that during all the times hereinafter

*Page numbering appearing at the foot of page of original certified Transcript of Record.

mentioned, since on or about the said 9th day of
August, 1909, until the 2d day of March, 1933, the
said Bank carried on a banking business, and other
businesses, hereinafter more particularly alleged,
in connection therewith.

II.

That on or about the said 2d day of March, 1933,
the defendant Central National Bank of Oakland,
pursuant to the proclamation of the Governor of
the State of California on the 1st day of March,
1933, declaring the said 2d day of March, 1933, and
the two (2) days next following the said 2d day
of March, 1933, public holidays, closed its doors,
and has never since opened its doors, for the transaction of business; that on or about the 14th day
of March, 1933, A. J. Mount was duly appointed
by the then acting Comptroller of the United
States, under and in accordance with the provisions
of the Bank Conservation Act of the Congress of the
United States, the conservator for the said Bank;
that thereupon the said Mount duly qualified as such
conservator, and he thereafter, until the 8th day
of May, 1933, was, and continued to be, the duly
appointed, qualified and acting conservator for and
of the said Bank; and that the plaintiff is informed
and believes, and, according to such information
and belief alleges, that continuously for more than
five (5) months prior to and up to on or about the
22d day of April, 1933, the said Mount was either
the president or the executive vice-president of the
said Bank. [2]

III.

That on the said 8th day of May, 1933, the above named defendant Joseph H. Grut was duly appointed by the then acting Comptroller of the Currency of the United States the receiver of the defendant Central National Bank of Oakland, as an insolvent bank, unable to pay its just debts and liabilities; and that thereupon the defendant Joseph H. Grut duly qualified as such receiver, and he ever since has been, and he now is, the duly appointed, qualified and acting receiver of the said Bank.

IV.

That during all the times hereinafter mentioned, since on or about the 7th day of September, 1891, the above named defendant Central Bank of Oakland was, and it now is, a corporation duly incorporated, organized and existing as a savings bank under and by virtue of the laws of the State of California, with its principal place of business in the said City of Oakland; that during all the times hereinafter mentioned, until on or about the 21st day of April, 1933, the name of the defendant Central Bank of Oakland was "Central Savings Bank of Oakland"; that on or about the said 21st day of April, 1933, the articles of incorporation of the defendant Central Bank of Oakland were duly amended, and by the amendments thereof the name of the defendant Central Bank of Oakland was changed from the said name "Central Savings Bank of Oakland" to that of "Central Bank of Oakland", and, by the said amendments, the defendant Cen-

4

tral Bank of Oakland was authorized and empowered to transact, in addition to its savings bank business, a commercial banking business, and also a trust business; that during all the times hereinafter mentioned, until on or about the said 21st day of April, 1933, the defendant Central Bank of Oakland was associ- [3] ated with and carried on its banking business in the same premises, in the said City of Oakland, as the premises in which the defendant Central National Bank of Oakland carried on its banking business, and its other businesses, hereinafter more particularly alleged, in connection therewith, and the defendant Central Bank of Oakland ever since on or about the said 21st day of April, 1933, has continued to carry on its banking business, and its said other business, in the said premises; and that the plaintiff is informed and believes, and, according to such information and belief alleges, that ever since on or about the said 21st day of April, 1933, the defendant Central Bank of Oakland has so carried on its said banking and other business with the said A. J. Mount as its president, and with the same executive vice-president and with other executive officers, including S. Berven, as its assistant trust officer, as were the executive vice-president and other executive officers of the defendant Central National Bank of Oakland on the said 2d day of March, 1933.

V.

That during all the times hereinafter mentioned, since on or about the 1st day of January, 1926,* un-

*NOTE: This date in the printed transcript of the record (R. 4) is the ''1st day of *July*, 1926''; but this is an obvious error in the date. The date should be the ''1st day of *January*, 1926'', and it so appears in the original complaint incorporated in the transcript of record on appeal.

til the said 2d day of March, 1933, the defendant
Central National Bank of Oakland carried on, in
connection with its banking business, a so-called
bond business, by and through a department established by it and designated by it as its "Bond Department", and by and through its said Bond Department it purchased and sold, and otherwise dealt
in, bonds and other obligations issued by private and
by quasi public corporations incorporated under the
laws of the State of California and of other states of
the United States, and it also purchased and sold,
and otherwise [4] dealt in, bonds issued by the
United States and by foreign countries, and by political divisions, municipalities, entities and agencies
of the United States and of foreign countries; and
that for more than ten (10) years prior to the said
1st day of January, 1926, E. D. Bothwell was an employee of the defendant Central National Bank of
Oakland, either in its said banking business, or in its
other said businesses connected therewith, and since
on or about the said 1st day of January, 1926, until
on or about the said 14th day of March,1933,the said
Bothwell was an assistant cashier of the said Bank,
and was also the manager of the said Bond Department thereof, to which said latter position the said
Bothwell had been promoted prior to the said 1st
day of January, 1926.

VI.

That during all the times hereinafter mentioned,
since on or about the said 1st day of January, 1926,
until the said 2d day of March, 1933, the defendant

Central National Bank of Oakland also carried on, in connection with its banking business, a so-called trust business, by and through a department established by it and designated by it as its "Trust Department", and by and through its said Trust Department it acted as trustee of funds and other property transferred to it by decrees of courts and by deeds and other instruments executed to and with it by individuals and by corporations, for the uses and purposes specified in such decrees, deeds and other instruments; and that during all the times hereinafter mentioned, since on or about the said 1st day of January, 1926, until on or about the 1st day of January, 1933, Daniel Read was an assistant vice-president and the trust officer of the defendant Central National Bank of Oakland, and since on or [5] about the said 1st day of January, 1926, until on or about the said 21st day of April, 1933, the said S. Berven was the assistant trust officer of the said Bank.

VII.

That for more than ten (10) years prior to the said 1st day of January, 1926, the plaintiff resided, and she thereafter has continued to reside, in the said City of Oakland, and for more than ten (10) years prior to the said 1st day of January, 1926, she had, and she thereafter has continued to have, an account with the defendant Central National Bank of Oakland, and she also had, and she thereafter has continued to have, an account with the defendant Central Bank of Oakland, and, from time to time, during such period of time, until on or about the said 2d day of March, 1933, she made deposits of money in, and withdrew money so deposited from, the said respective accounts; and that, as such depositor, the plaintiff became well acquainted with the said E. D. Bothwell, and, at and during all the times hereinafter alleged, until the time and under the circumstances hereinafter alleged, of and concerning her transactions with the said Bothwell, the plaintiff reposed in the said Bothwell, and in the said Bond Department, as the said Bothwell well knew, great trust and confidence.

VIII.

That during all the times hereinafter mentioned, the plaintiff was, and she now is, a widow, and in poor health, and, because thereof, the plaintiff, prior to the said 1st day of January, 1926, intended to place her property in a trust, pursuant to which she believed that she would be relieved of the burden of caring for her property, and would be provided with an income sufficient for her support during her lifetime, and upon and after her death, her daughter, Ruth Quinn Osborne, [6] and her said daughter's minor son, William Leighton Osborne, who are her only living descendants, would be adequately provided for; that with the said intention in mind, and on or about the said 1st day of January, 1926, the plaintiff interviewed the said E. D. Bothwell, who had theretofore, as aforesaid, been promoted to the position of manager of said Bond De-

partment of the defendant Central National Bank of
Oakland, and requested his advice as to whether or
not it was advisable for her to carry out her said intention of placing her property in such a trust, and,
if so, she requested the information from him as to
whether or not the said Bank could and would act
as the trustee of such a trust; that the said Bothwell thereupon advised the plaintiff that to place
her property in such a trust was just the thing for
her to do, and informed her that the said Bank
could and would act as the trustee of such a trust,
and that the said Bank had a Trust Department, a
particular part of the business of which was the
taking care of the property of widows and orphans;
that the plaintiff, at the same time, also informed
the said Bothwell of what her property then consisted, and that included in her said property was a
parcel of improved business real property situated
in the City of Reno, State of Nevada, which she was
desirous of selling; that the said Bothwell thereupon informed the plaintiff that the said Bank
could not accept a conveyance to it of real property situated in the said State of Nevada, and, for
that reason, he advised the plaintiff that, pending
the sale by her of the said parcel of real property
and the placing by her of her funds in such a trust
with the said Bank, as trustee, the thing for her to
do was to invest her funds, available for investment,
through the said Bond Department, in bonds; that
the [7] plaintiff thereupon accepted the advice of
the said Bothwell, and, accordingly, informed him

that she would postpone the placing of her property in such a trust with the said Bank until after the sale by her of her said parcel of real property, and, in the meantime, would invest her funds, available for investment, through the said Bond Department, in bonds, but that she had but little experience with bonds, and, if such investments were so made, she would have to rely upon him to purchase for her, through the said Bond Department, safe and desirable bonds for the investment of her said funds; that the said Bothwell thereupon assured the plaintiff that her funds would be invested by the said Bank, through him, as the manager of the said Bond Department, in nothing but safe and desirable bonds for her; and that the plaintiff thereupon told the said Bothwell that she desired her funds to be invested not only in safe bonds, but in bonds of such desirability that the same could be readily sold, at any time, and so that she could thus get back the money which she had invested in them, and inquired of the said Bothwell whether or not her funds should be invested in bonds of the United States, and he replied that bonds of the United States paid a low rate of interest, and he assured her that her funds would be invested by the said Bank, through him, as the manager of the said Bond Department, in bonds of the safety and desirability aforesaid, desired by her, and in bonds just as good as those of the United States, and paying a much larger rate of interest than was paid on bonds of the United States.

IX.

That the said E. D. Bothwell thereupon recommended to the plaintiff, as safe and desirable investments aforesaid for her, $10,000, par value, of the so-called "se- [8] cured sinking fund gold bonds" of the Province of Buenos Aires, External Loan, of the Argentine Republic, and $5,000, par value, of the so-called "secured gold notes" of Miller & Lux, Incorporated, a corporation, $5,000, par value, gold bonds of Rhodes-Jamison Co., a corporation, and $5,000 par value. of Western States Gas and Electric Company, a corporation; that the plaintiff thereupon informed the said Bothwell that she doubted the safety and desirability aforesaid of the said bonds of the Province of Buenos Aires for the investment of her funds, but the said Bothwell assured her that the said bonds of the said Province were well secured and were a safe and desirable investment aforesaid for her, and the said doubts of the plaintiff were dispelled by the said assurance of the said Bothwell; that the plaintiff, accordingly, relied upon the said recommendation of the said Bothwell, and approved the purchase for her by the said Bank, through the said Bothwell, as the manager of the said Bond Department, of the said bonds and notes, so recommended to her by him, and on or about the said 1st day of January, 1926,* paid the said Bank the respective prices, which the said Bothwell informed her were the respective purchase prices of the said bonds and notes, to-wit, the sum of $9,900 for the said

*Note: This date in the printed transcript of the record (R. 9) is the "1st day of *July*, 1926"; but this again is an obvious error in the date. The date should be the "1st day of *January*, 1926", and it so appears in the original complaint incorporated in the transcript of record on appeal.

bonds of the Province of Buenos Aires, the sum of $5,000 for the said notes of Miller & Lux, Incorporated, the sum of $5,000 for the said bonds of Rhodes-Jamison Co. and the sum of $4,800.00 for the said bonds of the Western States Gas and Electric Company; and that the plaintiff intended, as the said Bothwell well knew, to place in such a trust with the said Bank the bonds and notes so purchased for her, as also the bonds and notes thereafter purchased for her, by the said Bank prior to the execution by her to and with the said Bank, on the 24th day of September, 1929, of the instru- [9] ment of trust, hereinafter more particularly alleged, after the said parcel of real property, situated in the said City of Reno, had been sold by her.

X.

That during the year 1927, the defendant Central National Bank of Oakland, through the said E. D. Bothwell, as the manager of the said Bond Department, made further purchases for the plaintiff, as safe and desirable investments aforesaid for her, namely, $5,000, par value, of the so-called "gold bonds" of California Cotton Mills Company, a corporation, $5,000, par value, of the so-called "sinking fund gold notes" of Jackson Furniture Company, a corporation, and $5,000, par value, of the so-called "guaranteed and sinking fund gold bonds" of the Province of Callao, Republic of Peru; that in each of the instances of such further purchases for the plaintiff the said Bothwell recommended the said respective bonds or notes to her as a safe and de-

sirable investment aforesaid for her; that, as in the
instance of the said purchase of the said bonds of
the Province of Buenos Aires, the plaintiff informed
the said Bothwell that she doubted the safety and
desirability aforesaid of the said bonds of the Province of Callao for the investment of her funds, but
the said Bothwell assured her that the said bonds
of the said Province of Callao were well secured and
were a safe and desirable investment aforesaid for
her, and the said doubts of the plaintiff were dispelled by the said assurance of the said Bothwell,
as her doubts concerning the safety and desirability
aforesaid of the said bonds of the Province of
Buenos Aires for the investment of her funds had
been similarly dispelled, as aforesaid; that the
plaintiff also informed the said Bothwell that she
doubted the safety and desirability aforesaid of the
said bonds of the California Cotton Mills Company,
as a corpor- [10] ation apparently engaged in the
manufacture of cotton products, but the said Bothwell assured her that the said bonds of the said
California Cotton Mills Company were a safe and
desirable investment aforesaid for her, and her said
doubts were, likewise, dispelled by the said assurance of the said Bothwell; and that the plaintiff,
accordingly, relied upon the said recommendation
of the said Bothwell in each of the instances of the
said further purchases, and approved the purchase
for her by the said Bank, through the said Bothwell, as the manager of the said Bond Department,
of the said bonds or notes, so recommended to her

by the said Bothwell, and paid the said Bank the price, which the said Bothwell informed her was the purchase price thereof.

XI.

That the said parcel of real property, situated in the said City of Reno, was sold by the plaintiff on or about the 8th day of February, 1928, and she realized from the said sale thereof, over and above the expense of the said sale, the sum of $20,000, or thereabouts; that, from time to time, thereafter, during the year 1928, and during the year 1929, until the 24th day of September, 1929, the defendant Central National Bank of Oakland, through the said E. D. Bothwell, as the manager of the said Bond Department, made still further purchases for the plaintiff of bonds and notes, as safe and desirable investments aforesaid for her, with the said money so realized and with other moneys of the plaintiff, and included in the said last mentioned further purchases were $5,000, par value, of the so-called "gold bonds" of Medford Irrigation District, an irrigation district of the State of Oregon, $10,000, par value, of the so-called "debenture bonds" of Fageol Motors Company, a corporation, and $5,000, par value, of the so-called "gold notes" of Central West Public Service Company a corporation; that in each of the in- [11] stances of the said last mentioned further purchases the said Bothwell recommended the said bonds or notes to the plaintiff as a safe and desirable investment aforesaid for her; that the plaintiff would have doubted the safety and desirability aforesaid of the said bonds of the Medford Irrigation District for the investment of her funds, had not the said Bothwell informed her, in writing, that the said Bond Department had "handled several hundred thousand dollars" of the bonds of the said District, and believed that the said bonds contained "all of the elements to make them a safe and desirable investment"; and that the plaintiff, accordingly, relied upon the said recommendation of the said Bothwell in each of the instances of the said last mentioned further purchases, and approved the said purchases for her by the said Bank, through the said Bothwell, as the manager of the said Bond Department, of the said bonds or notes, so recommended to her by the said Bothwell, and paid the said Bank the price, which the said Bothwell informed her was the purchase price thereof.

XII.

That prior to the said 24th day of September, 1929, the said $5,000, par value, bonds of Rhodes-Jamison Co. and the said $5,000, par value, bonds of Western States Gas and Electric Company were redeemed, and the money paid on the said respective redemptions was paid to the said Bank; that the money so paid to the said Bank was reinvested by the said Bank in other bonds, by the purchase thereof for the plaintiff by the said Bank, through the said Bothwell, as the manager of the said Bond Department; that in each of the said instances of the said purchases of the said other bonds the said

Bothwell recommended to the plaintiff the said
other bonds so purchased as a safe and desirable
investment afore- [12] said for her; and that the
plaintiff, accordingly, relied upon the said recommendation of the said Bothwell in each of the said
instances of the said purchases of the said other
bonds, and approved the said purchases for her by
the said Bank, through the said Bothwell, as the
manager of the said Bond Department, of the said
other bonds, so recommended to her by the said
Bothwell, and of the payment therefor by the said
Bank from the money so paid to the said Bank,
which the said Bothwell informed her was the purchase price thereof.

XIII.

That none of the said bonds or notes purchased
prior to the said 24th day of September, 1929, as
aforesaid, for the plaintiff by the defendant Central
National Bank of Oakland, through the said E. D.
Bothwell, as the manager of the said Bond Department, were ever delivered to her, but, upon the respective said purchases thereof, the said bonds or
notes were retained and held by the said Bank, on
deposit with the said Bank, for the plaintiff, awaiting such time when the same would be assigned and
transferred by her to the said Bank, as trustee of
the trusts, in which she intended, as aforesaid, to
place her property after the said parcel of real
property, situated in the said City of Reno, had
been sold by her, and pending such time, and prior
to the consummation of her said intention by the
execution by her, on the said 24th day of September,

1929, as hereinafter more particularly alleged, of the instrument of trust to and with the said Bank, the interest coupons on the said bonds and notes were removed therefrom by the said Bank, when and as the said interest coupons matured, and the money payable thereon was collected by the said Bank and de- [13] posited by the said Bank to the credit of the plaintiff in her said account with the said Bank.

XIV.

That a copy of the said instrument of trust, together with a copy of the statement at the foot thereof, and together with a copy of each of the acknowledgments annexed thereto, are hereunto annexed and together are marked "Exhibit A", and the same are hereby referred to and made a part hereof; and that on the date of the said instrument of trust, to-wit, on the said 24th day of September, 1929, the defendant Central National Bank of Oakland held on deposit with it, as aforesaid, for the plaintiff, after the said redemptions of bonds and the said reinvestments of the money paid on the said redemptions, fifteen (15) blocks of bonds and notes first listed in the said instrument of trust, comprising bonds and notes of various corporations, and also comprising the said respective bonds of the Province of Buenos Aires, of the Province of Callao, and of the Medford Irrigation District, respectively purchased, as aforesaid, for the plaintiff by the said Bank, through the said E. D. Bothwell, as the manager of the said Bond Department.

XV.

That the plaintiff did not, immediately after the said sale by her, on or about the said 8th day of February, 1928, of the said parcel of real property, situated in the said City of Reno, nor did the plaintiff, for some time thereafter, proceed to carry out her said intention of placing her property in the trust aforesaid, with the defendant Central National Bank of Oakland, as trustee, for the following reasons: that, due to her continuing poor health, the plaintiff was disinclined to attend to any matter which required any prolonged [14] mental effort on her part, including the preparation of the instrument of trust, whereby her property would be placed in trust with the said Bank, as trustee; that the plaintiff was referred by the said E. D. Bothwell, first, to the said Daniel Read, and, next, to the said S. Berven, for particulars concerning the subject of the preparation of the said instrument of trust; that in the conference which the plaintiff had with the said Read concerning the said subject, the said Read seemed to her to be so indifferent about the said subject that she doubted whether or not the said Read was interested in having the said Bank act as such trustee, and, as a result, her mind was greatly disturbed; that, due to her said greatly disturbed condition of mind, no progress was made by the plaintiff towards the preparation of the said instrument of trust in the first conference which she next had with the said Berven concerning the said subject; that, finally, the plaintiff, believing it to be

necessary for her to obtain, without further delay,
the medical advice of the well-known Mayo Brothers,
physicians and surgeons, of the City of Rochester,
State of Minnesota, by a journey by her to the said
City of Rochester for that purpose, and of consummating, before that journey, her said intention
of placing her property in trust with the said Bank,
as trustee, she again, and on several occasions
shortly prior to the said 24th day of September,
1929, consulted the said Berven concerning the said
subject, with the result that the said instrument of
trust was executed by her to and with the said Bank
on the said 24th day of September, 1929, as hereinafter more particularly alleged; that following the
said sale of the said parcel of real property, and
prior to the execution of the said instrument of
trust, the plaintiff con- [15] tinued to make further
investments of her funds, through the purchase of
bonds and notes for her by the said Bank, through
the said Bothwell, as the manager of the said Bond
Department, with the intent aforesaid of placing
the bonds and notes so purchased in a trust aforesaid with the said Bank, as trustee, and all the funds
which she then possessed were so invested prior to
the execution of the said instrument of trust; that,
in each of the said purchases of the said other bonds
or notes, the said Bothwell recommended to the
plaintiff the said further bonds or notes so purchased as a safe and desirable investment aforesaid
for her; and that the plaintiff, accordingly, relied
upon such recommendation of the said Bothwell in

each of the said instances of the said further purchases, and approved the said further purchases for
her by the said Bank, through the said Bothwell, as
the manager of the said Bond Department, of the
bonds or notes, so recommended to her by the said
Bothwell, and paid the said Bank the price, which
the said Bothwell informed her was the purchase
price thereof.

XVI.

That, in each instance of the purchase aforesaid
of the said bonds or notes for the plaintiff by the
defendant Central National Bank of Oakland,
through the said E. D. Bothwell, as the manager of
the said Bond Department, the said bonds or notes
were so purchased for the plaintiff by the said Bank
from itself, and were sold to the plaintiff by the said
Bank, through the said Bothwell, as the manager of
the said Bond Department, and thereby the said
Bank, acting through the said Bothwell, as the
manager of the said Bond Department, was both the
purchaser of the said bonds or notes from itself, in
one capacity, for the plaintiff, and the seller, in
another [16] capacity, to the plaintiff, of the said
bonds or notes so purchased; that, in each instance
of the purchase and sale aforesaid of the said bonds
or notes, the said Bank, through the said Bothwell,
as the manager of the said Bond Department, sold
the said bonds or notes to the plaintiff at a larger
price than the said Bank had originally paid for
them, and thereby the said Bank made a profit on
each of the transactions of the purchase and sale

of the said bonds or notes, and the said profits aggregate the sum of $2,360.33; that one of the said fifteen (15) blocks of the said bonds and notes first listed in the said instrument of trust, namely, the $10,000, par value, of the said so-called "debenture bonds" of Fageol Motors Company, were so purchased by the said Bank on the 27th day of March, 1928, for the price of $9,500, and were so sold to the plaintiff by the said Bank, on the same day, for the increased price of the sum of $10,000, or at a profit thereby to the said Bank of the sum of $500; that another of the said fifteen (15) blocks of the said bonds, namely, the $10,000, par value, of the bonds of Alameda Investment Company, were so purchased by the said Bank on the 22d day of March, 1928, for the price of $9,429, and were so sold to the plaintiff by the said Bank, three (3) days later, for the increased price of the sum of $9,750, or at a profit thereby to the said Bank of the sum of $321; that of another of the said fifteen (15) blocks, namely, the $5,000, par value, of Medford Irrigation District bonds, $1,500, par value, were so purchased by the said Bank on the 22d day of March 1926, for the sum of $1,500, and $2,500 par value were so purchased on the 6th day of September, 1927, for the price of $2,500, and the remaining $1000, par value, were so purchased on the 2d day of February, 1928, [17] for the price of $777.50, or for the total price of $4,777.50, and were sold to the plaintiff by the said Bank on the 27th day of February 1928, or 25 days after the said last purchase of the said last mentioned bonds, at the increased price of $4,850, or at a profit thereby to the said Bank of the difference between the said sum of $4,777.50 and the said sum of $4,850, or the sum of $72.50, but instead of selling to the plaintiff the said last mentioned bonds at the rate of the said price of $777.50 per bond, to which the price of the said bonds had depreciated, or for the price of $3,887.50, the profit to the said Bank on the deal was, in fact, the sum of $972.50, thereby increasing the aggregate of the said profits to the sum of $3,-260.33; and that, in violation of the great trust and confidence which the plaintiff reposed, as aforesaid, in the said Bothwell, the said Bothwell did not disclose to the plaintiff, but concealed from her, the fact that the said Bank, through the said Bothwell, as the manager of the said Bond Department, purchased from itself all the said bonds and notes which it sold to the plaintiff, as aforesaid, and also, in violation of the great trust and confidence which the plaintiff reposed, as aforesaid, in the said Bothwell, the said Bothwell did not disclose to the plaintiff, but concealed from her, the fact that the said Bank, through the said Bothwell, as the manager of the said Bond Department, profited, as aforesaid, on each of the said purchases and sales of the said bonds and notes, and the plaintiff had no knowledge of any of the said facts so concealed, and did not discover any thereof until the time and under the circumstances hereinafter alleged.

XVII.

That on the occasions aforesaid, shortly prior [18] to the 24th day of September, 1929, when the plaintiff consulted the said S. Berven concerning the preparation of the said instrument of trust, the plaintiff informed the said Berven of her desires in relation to some of the provisions of the said instrument of trust, and of the property which she desired to assign and transfer to the defendant Central National Bank of Oakland, in trust; and that the said property, besides the said fifteen (15) blocks of the said bonds and notes listed, as aforesaid, in the said instrument of trust, and then held, as aforesaid, by the said Bank, on deposit with the said Bank, for the plaintiff, included the following: an unimproved lot of land, described in the said instrument of trust, situated in the said City of Oakland, which the plaintiff had purchased in or about the year 1925, $15,000, par value, of Washoe County, County Roads and Highways Improvement and Construction Bonds, also listed in the said instrument of trust, and which the plaintiff had purchased in or about the year 1920, through, and on the advice of, her then attorney, and the promissory note, also listed in the said instrument of trust, dated the 1st day of June, 1923, for the principal sum of $20,000, executed to the plaintiff by Sparks Masonic Building Association, secured by a mortgage of the same date, referred to in the said instrument of trust, executed to the plaintiff by the said Association, on which said note there had theretofore been paid, on

account of the said principal thereof, the sum of
$6,000, leaving as the balance of the said principal
unpaid the sum of $14,000.

XVIII.

That during the occasion aforesaid, shortly prior
to the said 24th day of September, 1929, when the
plain- [19] tiff consulted the said S. Berven concerning the preparation of the said instrument of
trust, she inquired of the said Berven whether or
not it was safe for her to place her said property
in trust with the defendant Central National Bank
of Oakland, and the said Berven replied that it was
entirely safe for her to do so, since, as he said to
her, that whatever might happen to the said Bank,
her property so entrusted by her with the said Bank
would be absolutely protected and secure; that at
all times during the said occasions, and during all
the times hereinafter alleged, until the time and
under the circumstances hereinafter alleged, the
plaintiff reposed in the said Berven and in the said
Daniel Read, and in the said Trust Department, as
the said Berven and the said Read each well knew,
great trust and confidence; that during the said
occasions the plaintiff delivered to the said Berven,
on his request therefor, data, in her handwriting,
concerning the provisions desired by her to be inserted in the said instrument of trust, in relation
to the payment to her, during her lifetime, of the
income of the property, contemplated to be assigned
and transferred by her to the said Bank, and in re-

lation to the provisions to be made, after her death, for her said daughter and her said grandson; that the plaintiff is informed and believes, and, according to such information and belief, alleges that the said data were used in the preparation of the said instrument of trust, and that the said instrument of trust was prepared for the plaintiff to execute, by one of the members of a firm of attorneys of the said City of Oakland, and the said data was delivered by the said Berven to the said member of the said firm for the use aforesaid; that the plaintiff is also informed and believes, and, according to such information and [20] belief alleges, that during all the times hereinabove mentioned, since on or about the 1st day of January, 1926, until on or about the 20th day of May, 1933, the said firm of attorneys were the attorneys of the said Bank, and, as such, received from the said Bank a regular periodical compensation for the services thereof as the attorneys of the said Bank; that the plaintiff is also informed and believes, and, according to such information and belief alleges, that ever since on or about the said 20th day of May, 1933, the said firm of attorneys have been, and they now are, the attorneys of the defendant Central Bank of Oakland; and the plaintiff further alleges that she never paid anything to the said firm of attorneys, or to any member thereof, nor did she ever otherwise recompense the said firm, or any member thereof, for any of the services thereof in the preparation of the said instrument of trust, but that she was charged by the said Bank, and thereafter paid to the said Bank, a so-called "acceptance fee", or a fee for the "acceptance" by the said Bank, as trustee, of the trusts declared by the said instrument of trust, amounting to the sum of $100.

XIX.

That none of the members of the said firm of attorneys ever consulted the plaintiff about the preparation of the said instrument of trust, or ever submitted the said instrument of trust to her for her consideration; that the said instrument of trust, in the form of which the same had been so prepared for the plaintiff to execute, was submitted by the said S. Berven to her for her consideration and approval, on the day of the date thereof, to-wit, on the said 24th day of September, 1929; that the plaintiff thereupon read over the said instrument of trust, and, after having done so, inquired of the said [21] Berven whether or not she should submit the said instrument of trust to an attorney of her own selection, for his advice concerning the same; that the said Berven thereupon replied to the plaintiff that she could do so, if she wanted to, but that such submission was unnecessary, since the said instrument of trust, so he said, was in the usual form, and that she was as well protected by the said instrument of trust as was the defendant Central National Bank of Oakland; that the plaintiff, in the said great trust and confidence which she reposed in the said Berven, relied upon what the said Ber-

ven told her, as aforesaid, about the said instrument
of trust, and, accordingly, did not seek or obtain
any independent advice relating to the said instrument of trust, and thereupon executed, as the same
had been so prepared for her to execute, the said
instrument of trust, in duplicate, and acknowledged
such execution before the notary public, whom the
said Berven called in for the purpose of such
acknowledgment; that, at the same time, the plaintiff signed, in duplicate, the statement at the foot
of the said instrument of trust, by which she "certified" and "declared" that—

"said declaration of trust fully and correctly
sets out the power under and by which the said
trust property therein mentioned is to be held
and managed by said trustee, and I do hereby
agree, consent to, approve, ratify and confirm
the same in all particulars";

that the plaintiff is informed and believes, and, according to such information and belief, alleges that
the said statement was prepared for her to sign by
the same attorney who prepared the said instrument
of trust; that none of the members of the said firm
of attorneys ever consulted the plaintiff about the
[22] preparation of the said statement, or ever submitted the said statement to her for her consideration; that the said statement was submitted to the
plaintiff by the said Berven, for her signature, and
was signed by her, as aforesaid, in the form in
which the same had been so prepared for her to
sign, without obtaining or seeking any independent

advice relating thereto; that, in so signing the said statement, the plaintiff relied upon the said great trust and confidence which she reposed in the said Berven; that to the said instrument of trust appears the name of the said Bank, as trustee of the trusts declared in and by the said instrument of trust, as subscribed thereto by Claud Gatch, as a vice-president, and by the said Berven, as the assistant trust officer, of the said Bank, and also appears the corporate seal of the said Bank, as affixed thereto by the said officers of the said Bank, and annexed to the said instrument of trust also appears the acknowledgment of the said Gatch and of the said Berven of the execution by the said Bank of the said instrument of trust, although the plaintiff has no recollection of such subscription, or of such affixing of the said corporate seal, or of such acknowledgment; that a copy of each the said statement and of each the said acknowledgments is a part of the said "Exhibit A", hereunto annexed; that at the time of the execution by her to and with the said Bank, as aforesaid, of the said instrument of trust, the plaintiff also executed to the said Bank, and acknowledged, a deed of conveyance of the said unimproved lot of land in the said City of Oakland, described in the said instrument of trust, and an assignment of the said promissory note and of the said mortgage securing the same, executed to the plaintiff by the said Sparks Masonic Building Association, referred to in the said instru- [23] ment of trust, and the plaintiff thereupon delivered to the

said Berven, for the said Bank, the said deed and
the said assignment, so executed and acknowledged
by her, and also delivered to the said Berven, for
the said Bank, the said $15,000, par value, of
Washoe County, County Roads and Highways Improvement and Construction bonds, listed in the said
instrument of trust, as assigned by her to the said
Bank by the said instrument of trust, without any
other assignment thereof, and the plaintiff, by the
said instrument of trust, and without any other assignment thereof, also assigned to the said Bank
the said fifteen (15) blocks of the said bonds and
notes first listed in the said instrument of trust, and
then held by the said Bank on deposit for her, as
aforesaid; that the said instrument of trust, the
said deed of conveyance, the said assignment of the
said note and mortgage, the said assignments of the
said bonds and notes, were, and each thereof was,
executed and made, as aforesaid, without any consideration therefor to the plaintiff, either from the
said Bank or from anyone else; and that at the time
when the same were so executed and made, as aforesaid, the plaintiff was in great haste to depart on
her said journey to the said City of Rochester, for
the said purpose of there obtaining the medical
advice of the said Mayo Brothers, and she was so
informed the said Berven before the execution by
her of the said instrument of trust, and, accordingly,
she departed on her said journey, on the morning
following, namely, on the morning of the 25th day
of September, 1929.

XX.

That the said S. Berven, in violation of the great trust and confidence which the plaintiff reposed in him, as aforesaid, did not inform her, at the time aforesaid of the execution by her of the said instrument of trust, or at any other time, that it [24] was necessary for her to obtain independent advice in relation to the said instrument of trust before she executed the same, and she did not know that it was necessary, and was never informed by anyone that it was necessary, for her to obtain such independent advice, until the time and under the circumstances hereinafter alleged; that the said Berven, in violation of the said great trust and confidence which the plaintiff reposed in him, as aforesaid, did not inform her at the time aforesaid of the execution by her of the said instrument of trust, or at any other time, that the responsibilities and liabilities of the defendant Central National Bank of Oakland, as trustee of the trusts declared in and by the said instrument of trust, otherwise imposed by the law upon the said Bank, as such trustee, were greatly restricted and limited, or were attempted so to be, by the provisions of the respective paragraphs I and VII of the said instrument of trust, nor did the said Berven, at the time aforesaid of the signing by her of the said statement at the foot of the said instrument of trust, or at any other time, inform her that the restrictions and limitations aforesaid were approved, ratified and confirmed, or were attempted so to be, by the said statement; that the said Berven, in violation of the said great trust and confidence which the plaintiff reposed in him as aforesaid, did not inform her, at the time aforesaid of the execution by her of the said instrument of trust, or at any other time, that the powers of the said Bank, as trustee aforesaid, otherwise conferred by the law upon the said Bank, as such trustee, were greatly enlarged and extended, or were attempted so to be, by the provisions of paragraph II of the said instrument of trust, nor did the said Berven, at the time aforesaid of the signing by her of the said statement, or at any other time, inform her that the powers aforesaid were approved, ratified and confirmed, or [25] were attempted so to be, by the said statement; and that the plaintiff did not know, and was never informed by anyone, until the time and under the circumstances hereinafter alleged, that the said responsibilities and liabilities were restricted and limited, or were attempted so to be, as aforesaid, or that the said powers were enlarged and extended, or were attempted so to be, as aforesaid, or· that the same were approved, ratified and confirmed, or were attempted so to be, by the said statement.

XXI.

That of the said bonds listed in the said instrument of trust, there were redeemed, from time to time, subsequent to the execution aforesaid of the said instrument of trust, $1,000, par value, of the said notes of Miller & Lux, Incorporated, $3,000 par value, bonds of Oakland Meat & Packing Com-

pany and $15,000, par value, Washoe County,
County Roads and Highways Improvement and
Construction bonds, and the money paid on the said
respective redemptions was paid to the defendant
Central National Bank of Oakland; that there were
also paid to the said Bank, on or about the 1st day
of June, of each of the years 1930, 1931 and 1932,
the installment of the sum of $1,000, or the total
sum of $3,000, of the principal of the said promis-
sory note executed to the plaintiff by the said
Sparks Masonic Building Association, leaving unpaid of the principal of the said promissory note
the sum of $11,000; that part of the money so paid
to the said Bank on the said redemptions and for
the said installments of the principal of the said
promissory note was invested, from time to time,
thereafter, by the said Trust Department of the said
Bank, through the said E. D. Bothwell, as the manager of the said Bond Department, by the respective
purchases of bonds, to be held by the [26] said
Bank, as trustee of the trusts declared in and by the
said instrument of trust, and for the respective
prices, or cost, therefor charged to or against the
said trusts by the said Bank, through the said Trust
Department, as follows: on the 8th day of April,
1930, $1,000, par value, of the so-called "first and
collateral trust" serial bonds of Hearst Publications, Incorporated, a corporation, for the price of
$985; on the 5th day of June, 1930, $1,000, par value,
bonds of California Cotton Mills Company, a corporation, for the price of $850; on the 27th day of

June, 1930, $5,000, par value, bonds of Federal
Public Service Corporation, a corporation, for the
price of $4,650; and on the said 27th day of June,
1930, $6,000, par value, additional said bonds of the
said Hearst Publications, Incorporated, for the
price of $5,946; that on or about the 26th day of
July, 1930, the said bonds of the said Federal Public Service Corporation were sold by the said Bank,
through the said Trust Department, at or about the
said price for which the same had been so purchased
by the said Bank; and that the remainder of the
said money, so paid to the said Bank, including
therein the said price of the said bonds of the said
Federal Public Service Corporation, was invested,
from time to time, thereafter, by the said Bank,
through the said Trust Department, acting either
by the said Daniel Read, as the trust officer, or by
the said S. Berven, as the assistant trust officer, of
the said Bank, in the respective purchases of bonds
to be held by the said Bank under the said instrument of trust, and for the respective prices paid
therefor and charged to or against the said trusts
by the said Bank, through the said Trust Department, as follows: on the 31st day of July, 1930,
$2,000, par value, bonds of Pacific Gas and Electric
Company, a [27] corporation, for the price of $2,-
205; on the said 31st day of July, 1930, $2,000, par
value, bonds of San Joaquin Light and Power Corporation, a corporation, for the price of $2,290; on
the 20th day of January, 1932, $5,000, par value,
bonds of East Bay Municipal Utility District a so-

called municipal utility district of the State of California, for the price of $5,082.75; and on the 11th day of July, 1932, $5,000, par value, bonds of Los Angeles Gas and Electric Corporation a corporation, for the price of $4,925.

XXII.

That in each of the first four (4) said instances of the said purchases of bonds in the year 1930, namely, the instances of the said purchases from and including the said 8th day of April, 1930, to and including the said 27th day of June, 1930, either the said E. D. Bothwell, or the said Daniel Read, or the said S. Berven, recommended to the plaintiff the said bonds so purchased, as a safe and desirable investment aforesaid for her and for the said trusts declared in and by the said instrument of trust, and the plaintiff, accordingly, relied upon the said recommendations and approved the said purchases; that in each of the instances of the said purchases of the said bonds, the said bonds were so purchased by the said Bank from itself, through the said Bothwell, as the manager of the said Bond Department, and were sold to itself, either through the said Read, as the trust officer, or through the said Berven, as the assistant trust officer, of the said Bank, and thereby the said Bank was both the purchaser of the said bonds from itself, in one capacity, for the plaintiff, and the seller, in another capacity, to the plaintiff, of the said bonds so purchased; that in each of the said instances of the purchase and sale [28] aforesaid of the said bonds, the said bonds were

so sold at a larger price than the said Bank had
originally paid for them, and thereby the said Bank
made a profit on each of the said transactions of
purchase and sale of the said bonds, and the aggregate of the said profits is the sum of $471; that,
in violation of the great trust and confidence which
the plaintiff reposed, as aforesaid, in the said Bothwell and in the said Read and in the said Berven,
none of them disclosed to, but all of them concealed
from, the plaintiff the fact that through them, or
some of them, the said Bank had purchased from
itself and sold to itself, as aforesaid, the said bonds,
and that the said Bank, in so doing, had profited,
as aforesaid, in each of the said instances of the
purchase and sale of the said bonds; and that the
plaintiff had no knowledge of any of the said facts
so concealed, and did not discover any thereof, until
the time and under the circumstances hereinafter
alleged.

XXIII.

That the said bonds purchased by the defendant
Central National Bank of Oakland, as aforesaid,
subsequent to the execution aforesaid, on the said
24th day of September, 1929, of the said instrument
of trust, were held, after the said respective purchases thereof, by the said Bank, in its possession,
as trustee of the trusts declared in and by the said
instrument of trust, until on or about the said 22d
day of April, 1933, save as to those thereof which
were redeemed, or which were sold by the said Bank,
and until the same were so redeemed or so sold, as

hereinabove alleged, prior to the said last mentioned date; and that the interest coupons on the said bonds, so purchased and held, were removed therefrom by the said Bank, when and as the said interest coupons matured, [29] and the money payable thereon was collected by the said Bank and was paid or accounted for to the plaintiff as the beneficiary, during her lifetime, of the net income of the property held by the said Bank, as trustee of the said trusts.

XXIV.

That the defendant Central National Bank of Oakland held in its possession, as trustee of the said trusts declared in and by the said instrument of trust, from and after the execution aforesaid of the said instrument of trust, on the said 24th day of September, 1929, until on or about the said 22d day of April, 1933, the respective fourteen (14), of the sixteen (16), blocks of the said bonds and notes listed in the said instrument of trust, and purchased by the said Bank, as aforesaid, prior to the execution of the said instrument of trust, of the respective par values, and of the respective costs, as charged by the said Bank, to the plaintiff, as follows:

Par value:		Cost:
$10,000,	Alameda Investment Company,	$ 9,750.00
8,000,	Alameda Park Co.,	8,080.00
2,000,	Berkeley Terminal Properties, Inc.,	1,960.00
10,000,	Province of Buenos Aires,	9,900.00
5,000,	California Cotton Mills Company,	4,750.00
5,000,	Province of Callao,	4,950.00
5,000,	Central West Public Service Company,	4,987.50
10,000,	Fageol Motors Company,	10,000.00
3,000,	Fox Realty Corporation,	2,940.00
5,000,	Jackson Furniture Company,	5,000.00

Forward,
$63,000 $ 62,317.50

[30]

Par value:		Cost:
Forward,		
$63,000		$ 62,317.50
5,000,	Medford Irrigation District,	4,850.00
4,000,	Miller & Lux, Incorporated	4,000.00
5,000,	Southern United Gas Company,	4,675.00
5,000,	St. Louis Gas & Coke Corporation,	4,800.00

Totals,
$82,000 $80,642.50;

that the said Bank also held in its possession, as
trustee of the said trusts, until on or about the said
22d day of April, 1933, the respective seven (7)
blocks of bonds, purchased by it, as such trustee,
as aforesaid, subsequent to the execution of the said
instrument of trust, of the respective par values and
of the respective costs, as charged by the said Bank,
to the said trusts, as follows:

Par value:		*Cost:*
$ 1,000,	Hearst Publications, Incorporated,	$ 985.00
1,000,	California Cotton Mills Company,	850.00
6,000,	Hearst Publications, Incorporated,	5,946.00
2,000,	Pacific Gas and Electric Company,	2,205.00
2,000,	San Joaquin Light and Power Corporation,	2,290.00
5,000,	East Bay Municipal Utility District,	5,082.75
5,000,	Los Angeles Gas and Electric Corporation,	4,925.00

Totals,
$22,000 $22,283.75;

and that the total par value of the said bonds is the
sum of $104,000, and the total said cost was the
sum of $102,926.25. [31]

XXV.

That of the said bonds and notes held in the possession of the defendant Central National Bank of Oakland, as trustee of the trusts declared in and by the said instrument of trust, from and after the execution aforesaid of the said instrument of trust, the following, purchased, prior to the execution of the said instrument of trust, by the said Bank, through the said E. D. Bothwell, as the manager of the said Bond Department, and as safe and desirable investments aforesaid for the plaintiff, defaulted ou the respective dates following, and have ever since been in default, for the failure of the said respective corporations, and of the said respective Province of Buenos Aires, Province of Callao, and Medford Irrigation District, respectively issuing the same, in the payment of the interest thereon, namely:

Par value:		*Date of default:*
$ 2,000,	Berkeley Terminal Properties, Inc.,	Nov. 1, 1930
5,000,	Province of Callao,	Jan. 1, 1932
10,000,	Fageol Motors Company,	Feb. 1, 1932
5,000,	Southern United Gas Company	April 1, 1932
5,000,	Medford Irrigation District,	July 1, 1932
8,000,	Alameda Park Company,	Aug. 1, 1932
4,000,	Miller & Lux, Incorporated,	Oct. 1, 1932

5,000,	California Cotton Mills Company,	Jan. 1, 1933
5,000,	Central West Public Service Company,	Feb. 1, 1933
10,000,	Alameda Investment Company,	April 1, 1933
		[32]
10,000,	Province of Buenos Aires,	May 1, 1933
5,000,	St. Louis Gas & Coke Company,	June 1, 1933

Total,
$74,000;

that the total price, or cost, of the said bonds and notes, as charged by the said Bank to the plaintiff, was the sum of $72,702.50; that there remain, as not yet in default, of the said bonds and notes so purchased by the said Bank prior to the execution of the said instrument of trust, and so held in the possession aforesaid of the said Bank, only $8,000, par value, namely, $3,000, par value of the said bonds of the said Fox Realty Corporation, and $5,000 par value of the said "gold notes" of the said Jackson Furniture Company, or less than 10% of the total par value of $82,000 of all the said bonds and notes so purchased by the said Bank prior to the execution of the said instrument of trust, and so held in the possession aforesaid of the said Bank; and that, in addition to the said defaults, $1,000, par value, of the bonds of the said California Cotton Mills Company, purchased, as aforesaid, subsequent to the execution of the said instrument of trust, by the said Bank, through the said Bothwell, as the manager of the said Bond Department, and as a safe and desirable investment aforesaid for the plaintiff and for the said trusts, and so held in the possession of the said Bank, and for which the said Bank had charged the said trusts the sum of $850, or a profit to the said Bank of the sum of $150, likewise defaulted on the said 1st day of January, 1933, and has ever since been in default, for the failure of the said California Cotton Mills Company in [33] the payment of the interest thereon.

XXVI.

That none of the said fourteen (14) blocks of the said bonds and notes first referred to in the foregoing paragraph XXIV of this complaint, and none of the first three (3) of the seven (7) blocks of the said bonds secondly referred to in the said paragraph XXIV, were, at the respective times when the same were respectively purchased, as aforesaid, by the defendant Central National Bank of Oakland, through the said E. D. Bothwell, as the manager of the said Bond Department, of the safety or desirability aforesaid in which the funds of the plaintiff, or the funds of the trust declared in and by the said instrument of trust, respectively, should have been invested, as aforesaid; that the so-called said bonds, in so far as the same are purported to

be secured by real property, were, at the respective
times of the purchases thereof, as aforesaid, and
they ever since have been, grossly insufficiently so
secured, and the so-called said notes, in so far as the
same are purported to be secured by real property
or by personal property, were not, at the respective
times of the purchases thereof, as aforesaid, and
they never since have been, secured by first mortgages of real property, and were not, and they never
since have been, either secured by any personal
property at all, or, if so secured, they were not, and
they never since have been, secured by any personal
property of any value, or of any substantial value
whatever; that, in particular, the so-called bonds
of the said Province of Buenos Aires, and of the
said Province of Callao, were, at the respective
times when the same were respectively purchased,
as aforesaid, and they ever since have been uncollectible, and the so-called bonds of the [34] said
Medford Irrigation District never have been secured by any lien upon any real property, or upon
any other property whatever, but the same have
always depended for the payment of the principal
thereof and for the payment of the interest thereon
upon the payments, which may never be made, of
assessments levied upon real property situated in
the said District; that the so-called notes of the said
Jackson Furniture Company have never been secured by any lien upon any property, of any kind;
and that, at the respective times when the purchases

of the said respective bonds and notes were respectively recommended to the plaintiff, as aforesaid, as safe and desirable bonds and notes in which her funds, or the funds of the said trusts, should be respectively invested, as aforesaid, she was ignorant, and she continued to be ignorant, until the time and under the circumstances hereinafter alleged, of the difference between the so-called bonds and notes, so purchased, and of the safety and desirability aforesaid of the same for which her funds and the funds of the said trusts should have been invested, as aforesaid.

XXVII.

That on the 20th day of April, 1933, the said A. J. Mount, as the conservator for the defendant Central National Bank of Oakland, filed his verified petition in the Southern Division of the District Court of the United States for the Northern District of California, entitled "In the Matter of the Conservatorshp of Central National Bank of Oakland", numbered 19,458-S, records of the said District Court, for an order of the said District Court approving two (2) proposed contracts, referred to in the said petition, and for general relief; that respective copies of the said respective two (2) proposed [35] contracts are annexed to the said petition, and marked, respectively, Exhibit "A" and Exhibit "B"; that in and by the said petition it is alleged, among other things, that the said petitioner desired to join with the board of directors and of-

ficers of the said Bank, acting with the consent of
stockholders holding of record at least two-thirds
of the issued capital stock of the said Bank, in the
sale to the defendant Central Bank of Oakland,
under its then said name of "Central Savings Bank
of Oakland", of the whole of the business of the
said Trust Department of the defendant Central
National Bank of Oakland, upon the terms and conditions set forth in the said proposed contract, a copy
of which is marked said Exhibit "B"; that the said
last mentioned proposed contract had been approved
by the Comptroller of the Currency of the United
States and by the Superintendent of Banks of the
State of California; that the sale of the said business of the said Trust Department under the said
last mentioned proposed contract, as the said petitioner verily believed, was for the best interests of
the creditors of the defendant Central National
Bank of Oakland, in that it would result in the discharge of the defendant Central Bank of Oakland

"of all liabilities of said department and in
securing for the benefit of creditors of the National Bank of the full value of the said business;"

that a copy of the said petition, omitting therefrom
the said Exhibit "A" and the said Exhibit "B",
but including a copy of the verification of the said
Mount thereto, is hereunto annexed, and marked
"Exhibit B", and is hereby referred to and made
a part hereof; and that on the said 20th day of
April, 1933, the said District Court duly gave and

made its order wherein and whereby the said petitioner was authorized to join with the board of directors [36] and officers of the defendant Central National Bank of Oakland in the execution of the said proposed contract for the sale of the whole of the business of the said Trust Department, upon the terms and conditions set forth in the said proposed contract.

XXVIII.

That the plaintiff is informed and believes, and, according to such information and belief alleges, that stockholders holding of record at least two-thirds of the issued capital stock of the defendant Central National Bank of Oakland consented to the sale to the defendant Central Bank of Oakland of the whole of the business of the said Trust Department of the defendant Central National Bank of Oakland, upon the terms and conditions set forth in the said proposed contract, a copy of which, marked Exhibit "B", is attached to the said petition; that thereafter the said proposed contract, dated the 22d day of April, 1933, was executed by the defendant Central National Bank of Oakland, by the said A. J. Mount, as the conservator therefor and thereof, and thereby the defendant Central Bank of Oakland assumed and agreed to discharge all the liabilities to the plaintiff of the defendant Central National Bank of Oakland relating or incidental to the purchases of the said bonds and notes for her, or for her benefit, as aforesaid, by the defendant Central National Bank of Oakland, through

the said E. D. Bothwell, as the manager of the said
Bond Department; that a copy of the said contract,
as so executed, is hereunto annexed, and marked
"Exhibit C", and is hereby referred to and made
a part hereof; that thereafter, and on or about the
said 22d day of April, 1933, the defendant Central
National Bank of Oakland, pursuant to the said
contract, delivered to the defendant Central Bank
of Oakland, as the trustee of the trusts declared
in and by the said instrument of trust, the said
bonds and notes [37] referred to and listed in paragraph XXIV of this complaint, and the said promissory note and the said mortgage securing the same,
executed to the plaintiff by the said Sparks Masonic
Building Association, on the principal of which
said note there then remained unpaid, as aforesaid,
the sum of $11,000, and the defendant Central Na-
tional Bank of Oakland also delivered to the defendant Central Bank of Oakland, as the trustee of
the trusts declared in and by the said instrument
of trust, the possession of the said unimproved lot
situated in the said City of Oakland; and that the
defendant Central Bank of Oakland ever since has
been, and is now, in the possession, or has the control, of the said bonds and notes, of the said promissory note and of the said mortgage, and of the said
unimproved lot, as the trustee of the trusts declared
in and by the said instrument of trust, under and
pursuant to the said contract.

XXIX.

That the defendant Central National Bank of
Oakland, either through the said Daniel Read, as
the trust officer, or through the said S. Berven, as
the assistant trust officer, of the said Bank, notified
the plaintiff of the respective and several defaults
aforesaid, which had occurred prior to the 1st day
of November, 1932, in the payment of the interest
on the respective and several bonds and notes referred to and listed in paragraph XXV of this complaint, about the respective times when the respective and several defaults occurred, and on several
occasions prior to the 29th day of October, 1932,
told the plaintiff not to worry about the said defaults, since, so he said, the said bonds and notes
were well secured and the said interest would eventually be paid; that the plaintiff, because of the said
great trust and confidence which she reposed in the
said Berven, and in the said Trust De- [38] partment, and in the said E. D. Bothwell, and in the said
Bond Department, believed what the said Berven so
told her, namely, that the said bonds and notes were
well secured and the said interest would eventually
be paid; that on the said 29th day of October, 1932,
the said Berven wrote a letter to the plaintiff, in
which he stated, referring to the bonds of the Alameda Investment Company, which were not then
in default, that—

"We believe that it is advisable that a portion
of your holdings in said company should be
sold at this time and would appreciate it very

much if you would call at your very earliest
convenience to discuss the matter with us'';

that the plaintiff, pursuant to the said letter, thereafter called on the said Berven on or about the said
1st day of November, 1932; that, at the said time of
the said call by the plaintiff on the said Berven, the
following said bonds and notes had defaulted, as
aforesaid:

Par value: *Date of default:*

  $ 2,000, Berkeley Terminal Prop-
              erties, Inc.,   Nov. 1, 1930
    5,000, Province of Callao,   Jan. 1, 1932
  10,000, Fageol Motors Company, Feb. 1, 1932
    5,000 Southern United Gas
              Company   Apr. 1, 1932
    5,000, Medford Irrigation Dis-
              trict,   July 1, 1932
    8,000, Alameda Park Company, Aug. 1, 1932
    4,000, Miller & Lux
              Incorporated,   Oct. 1, 1932

Total,
    $39,000;

that, at the said time of the said call by the plaintiff
on the said Berven, the following said bonds and
notes had not defaulted, but have since defaulted,
as aforesaid: [39]

Par value: *Date of default:*

$ 5,000, California Cotton Mills
Company,   Jan. 1, 1933

5,000, Central West Public
Service Company,   Feb. 1, 1933

10,000, Alameda Investment
Company,   Apr. 1, 1933

10,000, Province of Buenos
Aires,   May 1, 1933

5,000, St. Louis Gas and Coke
Company,   June 1, 1933

Total,
$35,000;

that, at the said time of the said call by the Plaintiff on the said Berven, none of the said following bonds, purchased subsequent to the execution of the said instrument of trust, with the exception of the $1,000, par value, of California Cotton Mills Company, had, nor have any thereof since, defaulted:

Par Value:

$1,000, Hearst Publications, Incorporated,
1,000, California Cotton Mills Company,
6,000, Hearst Publications, Incorporated,

Total,
$8,000;

that, at the said time of the said call by the plaintiff on the said Berven, the said Berven recommended to her that the said bonds and notes, here-

inabove in this paragraph XXIX of this complaint
referred to, be sold and the proceeds of the sales
thereof be invested in, what he termed to be, "better" bonds; that the total cost of the said bonds and
notes, which had been recommended to the plaintiff,
as aforesaid, as safe and desirable bonds and notes
aforesaid for the investment of her funds and the
funds of the said trusts, respectively, and as charged
by the said Bank to her and to the said trusts, respectively, [40] is the sum of $88,423.50; that the
total of the prices for which the said bonds and
notes could then have been sold, according to estimates obtained for the plaintiff by the said Berven,
at the time of her said call on the said Berven, and
as computed, at the said time, for her by the said
Bothwell, was the sum of $28,860; that the loss,
which would have been sustained to the funds held
subject to the said trusts, had the said bonds and
notes been then sold for the total of the said prices,
as so estimated and computed, would have exceeded
67%, or more than two-thirds, of the said total cost
of the said bonds and notes, as charged by the said
Bank to the plaintiff and to the said trusts, respectively; and that the plaintiff is informed and believes, and, according to such information and belief
alleges, that the said bonds and notes could not
then, or at any time thereafter, have been sold for
anything like as much as the said sum of $28,860.

XXX.

That the plaintiff was greatly shocked by the said
recommendation of the said S. Berven that the said

bonds and notes hereinabove in the said paragraph XXIX of this complaint referred to be sold and the proceeds of the sales thereof be invested in the said "better" bonds, whereby the funds held subject to the said trusts would have suffered the huge loss aforesaid, and, as a consequence thereof, the great trust and confidence which she had theretofore reposed, as aforesaid, in the said E. D. Bothwell, and in the said Bond Department, and in the said Berven, and in the said Trust Department, of the defendant Central National Bank of Oakland, had completely shattered and ended; that the plaintiff, accordingly, and thereafter, on or about the 15th day of November, 1932, con- [41] sulted with one of the attorneys whose names are signed to this complaint as the attorneys for the plaintiff for his advice as to what she could and should do about the matter; that the said attorney thereupon commenced an examination of the facts relating to the transactions hereinabove alleged of the plaintiff with the said Bank, through the said Bothwell, as the manager of the said Bond Department, and through the said Daniel Read, as the trust officer, and the said Berven, as the assistant trust officer, of the said Trust Department, and of the law relating to the said transactions, and the said examination has continued, with the interruptions hereinafter referred to, up to the present time; that the said examination has involved the inspection by the said attorney of a large number of documents and other records of the said Bank; that the said examination

has not proceeded as rapidly as it might otherwise
have done for the reason that the said attorney is
not an accountant, and the plaintiff has not been
financially able to employ an accountant to assist
the said attorney in his said examination; that the
said examination has been unavoidedly interrupted
by the closing of the doors, as aforesaid, of the said
Bank on the said 2d day of March, 1933, by the said
appointment of the said A. J. Mount, on or about
the said 14th day of March, 1933, as the conservator
for the said Bank, by the said appointment of the
defendant Joseph H. Grut, on the said 8th day of
May, 1933, as the receiver of the said Bank, by the
said proceedings relating to the said sale of the
business of the said Trust Department by the said
Bank to the defendant Central Bank of Oakland,
by the delay in the appointment of an attorney for
the defendant Joseph H. Grut, as the receiver of the
defendant Central National Bank of Oakland, in
the place of [42] the said firm of attorneys, who,
prior to his appointment as receiver aforesaid, had
been the attorneys of the defendant Central National Bank of Oakland, but who later, and on or
about the said 22d day of April, 1933, had become
the attorneys of the defendant Central Bank of
Oakland, [but who later, and on or about the said
22d day of April, 1933, had become the attorneys
of the defendant Central Bank of Oakland,]* and by
negotiations between the said attorney of the plaintiff, the said firm of attorneys of the defendant
Central Bank of Oakland, and the attorney of the

*NOTE: The words and figures included between the brackets were inad-
vertently a repetition, and should be omitted.

defendant Joseph H. Grut, as the receiver of the defendant Central National Bank of Oakland, relating to a settlement of the claims of the plaintiff involved in this complaint against the defendant Central Bank of Oakland and against the defendant Central National Bank of Oakland, represented by the defendant Joseph H. Grut, as the receiver of the defendant Central National Bank of Oakland, respectively; that the said negotiations for a settlement of the said claims of the plaintiff came to an end on or about the 22d day of June, 1933, by the denial of the defendant Central Bank of Oakland of all liability to the plaintiff relating to her said claims against the defendant Central Bank of Oakland, including her claim for the said sum of $80,-642.50, referred to in paragraph XXIV of this complaint, paid by her to the defendant Central National Bank of Oakland as the total purchase price of the fourteen (14) blocks of bonds and notes first listed in the said paragraph XXIV of this complaint, purchased for the plaintiff by the defendant Central National Bank of Oakland, through the said Bothwell, as the manager of the said Bond Department, prior to the execution of the said instrument of trust, and now held by the defendant Central Bank of Oakland in its possession, or under its control, as the trustee of the said trusts declared in and by the said instrument of trust, [43] under and pursuant to the said contract for the sale by the defendant Central National Bank of Oakland to the defendant Central Bank of Oakland of the whole

of the business of the said Trust Department, and
including also her claim against the defendant Central Bank of Oakland for the said sum of $22,285.75
referred to in the said paragraph XXIV of this
complaint, as the total purchase price of the seven
(7) blocks of bonds secondly listed in the said paragraph XXIV of this complaint, purchased by the
defendant Central National Bank of Oakland, as
such trustee, subsequent to the execution of the said
instrument of trust, and now held by the defendant
Central Bank of Oakland in its possession, or under
its control, as trustee of the said trusts, under and
pursuant to the said contract, and, as the plaintiff
is informed and believes, and, according to such information and belief alleges, by the denial also of
the defendant Central National Bank of Oakland,
represented by the said receiver thereof, of all liability to the plaintiff relating to her claim for the
said sum of $80,642.50 against the defendant Central National Bank of Oakland; and that, ever since
the said negotiations came to an end aforesaid, the
said attorney has been actively engaged in the
preparation of this complaint.

XXXI.

That, as a result of the said examination, the said
attorney for the plaintiff, from time to time, discovered that each of the said purchases of the said
bonds and notes for the plaintiff by the defendant
Central National Bank of Oakland, through the
said E. D. Bothwell, as the manager of the said

Bond Department, had been made from the said
Bank itself, and that thereby the said Bank, acting
through the said Bothwell, as the manager of the
said Bond Department, was the pur- [44] chaser of
the said bonds and notes from itself, and the seller
of the said bonds and notes, so purchased from
itself, to the plaintiff, and that in each instance of
the said purchases and sales the said Bank, through
the said Bothwell, as the manager of the said Bond
Department, sold the said bonds and notes to the
plaintiff at a larger price than the said Bank had
originally paid for them, and that thereby the said
Bank had made a profit on each of the transactions
of the said purchases and sales; that the said attorney, from time to time, as the said discoveries
were made by him, informed the plaintiff thereof;
and that, as a result of the said examination, the
said attorney of the plaintiff, from time to time,
also informed the plaintiff as follows: that it was
necessary that the plaintiff should have had independent advice in relation to the said instrument
of trust before she executed the said instrument of
trust; that the responsibilities and liabilities of the
said Bank, as trustee of the trusts declared in and
by the said instrument of trust, otherwise imposed
by the law upon the said Bank, as such trustee,
were greatly restricted and limited, or were attempted so to be, by the provisions of the respective
said paragraphs I and VII of the said instrument
of trust, and that the said restrictions and limitations were approved, ratified and confirmed, or were

attempted so to be, by the said statement, signed by her, at the foot of the said instrument; that the powers of the said Bank, as trustee of the trusts declared in and by the said instrument of trust, otherwise conferred by the law upon the said Bank, as such trustee, were greatly enlarged or extended, or were attempted so to be, by the provisions of the said paragraph II of the said instrument of trust, and that the said powers were approved, ratified and [45] confirmed, or were attempted so to be, by the said statement, so signed by her; and that none of the said fourteen (14) blocks of the said bonds and notes first referred to in the said paragraph XXIV of this complaint, and none of the first three (3) of the seven (7) blocks of the said bonds secondly referred to in the said paragraph XXIV, were, at the respective times when the same were respectively purchased by the said Bank, through the said Bothwell, as the manager of the said Bond Department, or at any other time, of the safety or desirability aforesaid which the said Bothwell assured the plaintiff they were for the investment of the funds of the plaintiff, or of the funds of the trusts declared in and by the said instrument of trust, respectively.

Wherefore, the plaintiff prays judgment as follows: (1), that the said instrument of trust be rescinded and set aside; (2), that the defendant Central Bank of Oakland reconvey to the plaintiff, by a deed thereof, properly executed by it and acknowledged in its behalf, the said unimproved lot situated

in the said City of Oakland, and reassign to the
plaintiff, by an instrument of reassignment thereof,
properly executed by it and acknowledged in its
behalf, the said promissory note and the said mortgage securing the same executed to the plaintiff by
the said Sparks Masonic Building Association; (3),
that the defendant Central Bank of Oakland repay
to the plaintiff the said sum of $80,642.50, and also
the said sum of $22,285.75, or the total sum of $102,-
926.25, together with legal interest on each of the
said sums from the date of filing this complaint
until the said respective sums shall have been so
repaid to the plaintiff, as the purchase price of the
said [46] bonds and notes purchased as aforesaid
by the defendant Central National Bank of Oakland
for, or for the benefit of, the plaintiff; (4), that, in
the event that it be adjudged that the defendant
Central Bank of Oakland should not repay to the
plaintiff the said sum of $80,642.50, then that it be
adjudged that the claim of the plaintiff therefor
be established as a claim of the plaintiff against the
defendant Central National Bank of Oakland, and
that the same, as so established, together with legal
interest thereon from the date of filing this complaint until the said sum shall have been so repaid
to the plaintiff, be paid by the defendant Joseph H.
Grut, as the receiver of the defendant Central National Bank of Oakland, in the due course of his
administration, or that he certify the same to the
Comptroller of the Currency of the United States,

to be similarly paid; (5), that such deduction be
made from the said respective sums so to be repaid
to the plaintiff by the defendant Central Bank of
Oakland or by the defendant Central National Bank
of Oakland, respectively, as may be equitable and
just, under the circumstances, for the compensation
thereof for their respective services, if any, and for
their respective expenditures, if any; (6), and that
the plaintiff have and recover her costs, and have
and recover such further and other relief as may
be equitable and just in the premises.

> CHARLES W. SLACK and
> EDGAR T. ZOOK,
> > 1101 Alaska Commercial
> > Building,
> > San Francisco, California.
> > Attorneys for Plaintiff.
> A. J. WOOLSEY,
> > 1105 Easton Building,
> > Oakland, California.
> Of Counsel for Plaintiff. [47]

State of California,
County of Alameda.—ss.

Abbie W. Quinn, being first duly sworn, deposes
and says:

That she is the plaintiff named in the foregoing
complaint; that she has read the said complaint and
knows the contents thereof; and that the same is
true of her own knowledge, except as to the matters
which are therein stated on her information or be-

lief, and as to those matters that she believes it to be true.

ABBIE W. QUINN.

Subscribed and sworn to before me this 22d day of August, 1933.

[Notarial Seal]   A. J. WOOLSEY,
Notary Public in and for the County of Alameda, State of California.

"EXHIBIT A"

Know All Men by These Presents:

That Central National Bank of Oakland, a national banking association organized and existing under and by virtue of the laws of the United States of America, and having its principal place of business in the City of Oakland, County of Alameda, State of California, hereinafter called the Trustee, does hereby admit, certify and declare that it has received and accepted from Abbie W. Quinn, a widow, of said City of Oakland, County of Alameda, State of California, hereinafter called the Trustor, conveyances, assignments, and transfers to it, absolute in form, of the following described real and personal property, to-wit:

All that certain lot, piece or parcel of land, situate, lying and being in the City of Oakland, County of Alameda, State of California, and bounded and particularly described as follows, to-wit:

Beginning at the point of intersection of the Southwestern line of Glenview, formerly Folkers Avenue, with the line dividing lots Numbers 87 and 88 as said avenue and lots are shown on the map hereinafter referred to; running thence at a right angle to said line of Glenview Avenue, Southwesterly, one hundred (100) feet; thence at a right angle Southeasterly, twenty-five and 29/100 (25.29) feet to the Northwestern line of Rand Avenue, as said avenue is shown on the said map; thence North 66° 05' East, along said line of Rand Avenue, ninety-five and 02/100 (95.02) feet; thence continuing Northeasterly, along said line of Rand Avenue and Northwesterly along the Southwestern line of Glenview Avenue, on the arc of a curve to the left with a radius of ten (10) feet, a distance of twenty and 18/100 (20.18) feet; thence North 49° 32' West, along said Southwestern line of Glenview Avenue, fifty-seven and 36/100 (57.36) feet to the point of beginning.

Being Lot Number 88 as said lot is delineated and so designated upon that certain map entitled, "Map of Piedmont By the Lake, Oakland, California" filed November 14, 1906 in Liber 21 of Maps at page 87 in the office of the County Recorder of said Alameda County. [49]

$10,000. par value Alameda Investment Company Series "G" first mortgage collateral trust 6% gold bonds, issue #2, due Feb. 1, 1949, No. M1501/10 incl. for $1000. each, with coupons #4, due Feb. 1, 1930 et seq. attached.

$8,000. par value Alameda Park Co. first closed mortgage 6½% serial gold bond, due August 1, 1933, No. 159/164 incl. No. 166, 167 for $1,000. each, with coupon #7 due Feb. 1, 1930 et seq. attached.

$2,000. par value Berkeley Terminal Properties Inc. 6½% first mortgage sinking fund gold bonds due Nov. 1, 1940, No. 247, and 348 for $1000. each with coupon #8 due Nov. 1, 1929 et seq. attached.

$10,000. par value Province of Buenos Aires, External 7½% secured sinking fund gold bond, due Nov. 1, 1947 No. 152/161 incl. for $1000. each, with coupon #8 due Nov. 1, 1929 et seq. attached.

$5,000. par value California Cotton Mills Company, first mortgage 6% sinking fund gold bond due July 1, 1940, No. M102, 105, 106, 1323, and 1324 for $1000. each with coupon #9 due Jan. 1, 1930 et seq. attached.

$5,000. par value Province of Callao, Peru, guaranteed and secured sinking fund 7½% gold bond due Jan. 1, 1944, No. 267 and 268 for $1000. each, No. D66/71 incl. for $500. each, with coupons #6, due Jan. 1, 1930 et seq. attached.

$5,000. par value Central West Public Service Company, three year 7% gold notes due August 1, 1932 No. M889/893 incl. for $1000. each, with coupon #1 due Feb. 1, 1930 et seq. attached.

$10,000. par value Fageol Motors Company 6½% sinking fund debenture bonds due Feb. 1, 1936 No. M213/222 incl. for $1,000. each, with coupon #4, due Feb. 1, 1930 et seq. attached.

$3,000. par value Fox Realty Corporation of California 1st mortgage 6% sinking fund gold bonds due March 1, 1942, No. M245 for $1000. and D70/73 incl. for $500. each with coupons #6 due March 1, 1930 et seq. attached.

$5,000. par value Jackson Furniture Company 6½% sinking fund gold notes due July 1, 1940 No. M150, 188, 189, 395, 396 for $1000. each, with coupon #9 due Jan. 1, 1930 et seq. attached.

$5,000. par value Medford Irrigation District 6% gold bonds due Jan. 1, 1956 No. 1301, 1302, 1307, 1309, 1310, 1328, 1329, 1330, 1392, 1394 for $500. each, with coupons due Jan. 1, 1930 et seq. attached.

$5,000. par value Miller & Lux Incorporated, secured 7% gold notes due Oct. 1, 1935, No. M7297, 7303, 7304, 7315, 7574 for $1000. each with coupon #8, due October 1, 1929 et seq. attached.

$3,000. par value Oakland Meat & Packing Company 1st mortgage 7% gold bond due July 1, 1932, No. M40/42 for $1000. each, with coupon due Jan. 1, 1930, et seq. attached.

$5,000. par value Southern United Gas Company
first lien 6% sinking fund gold bond Series
"A" due April 1, 1937 No. M1996 for $1000.,
and D337/44 incl. for $500. each, with coupons
No. 5 due Oct. 1, 1929 et seq. attached. [50]

$5,000. par value St. Louis Gas & Coke Corpora-
tion first mortgage sinking fund gold bonds,
6% Series due 1947 due June 1, 1947 No.
M2855/59 incl. for $1000. each, with coupon
No. 5, due Dec. 1, 1929 et seq. attached.

$15,000. par value Washoe County, County Roads
and Highways Improvements and Construction
Bonds Series of 1920 6% due July 1, 1930, No.
221/235 incl. for $1000. each, with coupon #19
due Jan. 1, 1930 et seq. attached.

Promissory note in amount of $20,000. dated Sparks,
Nevada, June 1, 1923, executed by Sparks Masonic Building Association to order of Abbie
W. Quinn, bearing interest at the rate of 7%
per annum, payable at rate of $1000. on the 1st
day of June each year until 1938, when on 1st
day of June $6000. is payable, with balance due
of $14,000. and showing interest paid to June 1,
1929.

Secured by mortgage of even date, Recorded on
June 1, 1923, in Vol. 37 of Mortgages page 146
Records of Washoe County, Nevada. [51]

That no consideration was given by the trustee
for said conveyances, assignments and transfers to
it, and that it has accepted, received and will hold

such rights, titles and interests as it has acquired thereunder in trust, for the following uses and purposes:

I.

It is an express condition of this trust that the trustee shall not be responsible nor assume any liability for the nature, value or extent of its title to any of the real or personal property hereinbefore described and accepted in trust hereunder, or that may hereafter be added to this trust, as hereinafter provided, nor for any adverse or conflicting claims or interests therein of other persons, nor for the value, validity or collectibility of any securities or notes or other paper received by it; but that its only liability shall be for such right, title and interest as it may have received or hereafter acquire under such conveyances, assignments and transfers and for such sums as it may collect from the property so received by it.

II.

During this trust, and to enable it to properly execute this trust, the trustee shall have full power to hold, maintain, or continue the securities, properties, or investments so received by it or to be received by it, or to grant, bargain, sell, convey, exchange, convert, lease for terms either within or beyond the duration of this trust, mortgage, encumber, pledge, assign, partition, divide, subdivide, distribute, receive rents and profits, invest, reinvest, loan, reloan, and generally in all respects manage, handle and dispose of each and every part of the

trust estate in such securities, properties, or investments of the character permitted by law for investment of trust funds, or otherwise, and in such
manner and upon such terms and conditions as to it
may seem best. [52]

The trustee also may subscribe for and purchase
any corporate stock to which it may be entitled by
reason of its ownership of any such stock as a part
of the trust estate; it may exercise at the expense
of the trust estate any stock rights to which it may
become entitled, and it may generally exercise each
and all the rights of a stockholder in respect to any
corporate stock or shares which may be included in
the trust.

The trustee may loan or advance its own funds to
the trust estate for any trust purpose, each and all
of which loans or advancements to bear interest at
prevailing rates,—be a first lien and charge on the
entire trust estate, both as to principal and income,
and shall be first repaid to trustee prior to any other
payments or distributions herein provided to be
made.

The trustee is vested with sole discretion and
power to determine what shall constitute principal
of the trust estate and what shall constitute gross
income therefrom, or net income available for payment under the terms of this trust.

III.

From the gross income derived from the trust
estate, or from the principal thereof, if the trustee

deem that advisable, the trustee shall first pay and discharge, as and when due, any and all taxes, assessments, advancements and other expenses of every kind and nature expended or incurred in the management and protection of the trust estate and of this trust, and the payment when due of any and all income taxes, inheritance taxes and estate taxes levied or assessed upon the trust estate and/or the beneficiaries hereunder or the income therefrom and also pay to itself a reasonable compensation for all its services rendered under this agreement and declaration of trust.

IV.

The entire net income derived from the trust property and available for distribution hereunder shall be paid monthly to the trustor Abbie W. Quinn, during her lifetime. [53]

Upon the death of trustor Abbie W. Quinn, the trust shall continue, and the trustee shall handle, manage, control, pay, convey and deliver the income and corpus of the trust property as follows:

1. The trustee shall separate and set aside from the corpus of said trust property as a separate portion of said trust fund, the sum of Eighty Thousand ($80,000.) Dollars, or trust property equivalent in value to said sum of Eighty Thousand ($80,000.) Dollars (and the determination of said trustee as to what property shall be equivalent in value to the said sum of Eighty Thousand ($80,000.) Dollars shall be conclusive), and from the net income of said amount shall pay the sum of Two Hundred

Seventy Five ($275.00) monthly to Ruth Quinn
Osborne, daughter of Trustor, during her lifetime,
and also said trustee shall pay on June 1st and December 1st each year, all the additional accrued and
accumulated annual income from said separate trust
fund to said Ruth Quinn Osborne, during her lifetime.

Upon the death of said Ruth Quinn Osborne
(after the death of trustor) if William Leighton
Osborne, son of Ruth Quinn Osborne be then alive,
then the trust as to said separate trust fund shall
continue and the said income from said trust fund
shall be accumulated until William Leighton Osborne, grandson of trustor, arrives at the age of
thirty years, at which time the said trustee shall pay
to said William Leighton Osborne, the net income
from said trust property and from the said accumulations, during the remainder of his life.

Upon his death (either before or after he arrives
at the age of thirty years) the trust, as to said
separate trust property shall cease and determine
and should he leave lawful issue him then surviving, then said trust property shall go to said issue,
and if he leave no lawful issue him surviving, then
said trust property shall go to those persons who
would then be entitled to succeed to said trust property as the heirs at law of trustor, Abbie W. Quinn,
under the laws of succession of the State of California, then in force.

Upon the death of said Ruth Quinn Osborne (after
the death of Trustor) should William Leighton Os-

borne be then deceased, then said trust as to said portion of said trust property shall cease and determine [54] and should William Leighton Osborne have left lawful issue him then surviving, the said trust property shall go to said issue, and if he leave no lawful issue him surviving, then said trust property shall go to those persons who would then be entitled to succeed to said trust property as the heirs at law of trustor Abbie W. Quinn, under the laws of succession of the State of California, then in force.

Upon the death of said trustor Abbie W. Quinn, should Ruth Quinn Osborne be then deceased and should William Leighton Osborne be then alive, the trust shall continue as to said portion of said trust fund and the said net income therefrom shall be accumulated until said William Leighton Osborne arrives at the age of thirty years of age, at which time the said trustee shall pay to said William Leighton Osborne the net income from said trust property and from said accumulations, during the remainder of his life.

Upon his death (either before or after he arrives at the age of thirty years) this trust shall cease and determine and should he then leave lawful issue him surviving, then said trust property shall go to said issue, and if he leave no lawful issue him surviving, then said trust property shall go to those persons who would then be entitled to succeed to said trust property as the heirs at law of trustor

Abbie W. Quinn, under the laws of succession of the State of California, then in force.

Upon the death of Trustor Abbie W. Quinn, should both Ruth Quinn Osborne and William Leighton Osborne be then deceased then this trust, not only as to said portion of said trust fund considered in this subdivision 1, of said paragraph IV, but also the entire trust fund shall cease and determine and should said William Leighton Osborne leave lawful issue him surviving, said trust property shall go to said issue, and if he leave no lawful issue him surviving, then said trust property shall go to those persons who would then be entitled to succeed to said trust property as the heirs at law of trustor Abbie W. Quinn, under the laws of succession of the State of California, then in force. [55]

2. The trustee shall further separate and set aside from the corpus of said trust property as a separate portion of said trust fund, the sum of Thirty Thousand ($30,000.) Dollars, or trust property equivalent in value to said sum of Thirty Thousand ($30,000.) Dollars (and the determination of said trustee as to what property shall be equivalent in value to the said sum of Thirty Thousand ($30,000.) Dollars shall be conclusive) and the net income derived therefrom, if William Leighton Osborne, grandson of trustor Abbie W. Quinn, be then alive and has not reached the age of twenty-one years, shall be accumulated (with the exception of Twenty ($20.00) Dollars per year which is to be paid each year to William Leighton Osborne until

he reaches the age of twenty-one, as follows: Ten ($10.00) Dollars on his birthday which is August 4th, and Ten ($10.00) Dollars on December 24, annually.

Upon the said William Leighton Osborne arriving at the age of twenty-one years the said trustee shall pay to the said William Leighton Osborne the net income from said portion of said trust fund and from the accumulations thereof until said William Leighton Osborne arrives at the age of twenty-five years, at which time the trust shall cease and determine as to the sum of Ten Thousand ($10,000.) Dollars, and the said sum of Ten Thousand ($10,000.) Dollars shall be by said trustee paid, conveyed and delivered from said portion of said trust fund to William Leighton Osborne; the trust shall thereupon continue as to said portion of said trust fund and said trustee shall pay the entire net income therefrom to William Leighton Osborne until he arrives at the age of thirty-five years, at which time the trust shall cease and determine, as to the remaining portion of said Thirty Thousand ($30,000.) Dollar trust fund, and the remaining portion thereof shall be paid, conveyed, and delivered to William Leighton Osborne.

In the event that said William Leighton Osborne should predecease trustor, leaving lawful issue him surviving at the time of the death of trustor, then upon the death of said trustor Abbie W. Quinn, the trust shall cease and determine as to the said sum of Thirty Thousand ($30,000.) Dollars of said trust property and the trustee shall pay, convey and deliver to such issue, share and share alike, said sum of Thirty Thousand [56] ($30,000.) Dollars or its equivalent in value of said trust property. In the event, however, that said William Leighton Osborne predeceases trustor and leaves no lawful issue him then surviving at the time of the death of trustor, the trust as to said portion of Thirty Thousand ($30,000.) Dollars shall cease and determine and all said portion of said Thirty Thousand ($30,000.) Dollars shall go to those persons who would then be entitled to succeed to said trust property as the heirs at law of trustor, Abbie W. Quinn, under the laws of succession of the State of California, then in force.

In the event that said William Leighton Osborne should die after the death of trustor Abbie W. Quinn, and before he arrives at the age of thirty-five years, then upon the death of said William Leighton Osborne, the trust as to said portion of said trust property consisting of Thirty Thousand ($30,000.00) Dollars or its equivalent in value, as aforesaid, shall cease and determine and in the event that said William Leighton Osborne leave lawful issue him then surviving, then said portion of said trust estate shall go to such issue, or if he leave no lawful issue him surviving, then said trust property shall go those persons who would then be entitled to succeed to said trust property as the heirs at law of trustor, Abbie W. Quinn, under the laws of succession of the State of California, then in force.

3. From the remainder of said trust property the trustee shall pay all the just debts and funeral expenses of said trustor, Abbie W. Quinn, and all inheritance taxes and Federal Estate taxes levied against her estate or any interest therein, and the trust shall terminate as to the remainder of said trust property and one-half (½) thereof be by said trustee paid, conveyed and delivered to Ruth Quinn Osborne, if she be then alive and if she be then deceased, said one-half (½) portion of said remainder of said trust property shall go to augment the said trust fund of Thirty Thousand ($30,000.) Dollars next herein provided for in Subdivision 2 of paragraph IV hereof, and be disposed of in the manner and way and to those persons therein provided.

The remaining one-half (½) portion of said remainder of said trust property shall go to augment the said trust fund of Thirty Thousand ($30,000.) Dollars next herein provided for in Subdivision 2, paragraph IV hereof, and be disposed of in the manner and way and to those persons therein provided.

V.

It is an express provision of this trust that said trustor has reserved and she is hereby given the specific right, at any time, or from time to time hereafter, to convey, transfer, assign and deliver to said trustee *orhter* or additional sums of money and/or other real and/or personal property to become subject to the provisions of this trust, providing, however, that such additional real and/or personal property be of a kind acceptable to said trustee.

Upon the acceptance thereof by said trustee, such additional property shall ipso facto become subject to and held in trust under the terms hereof, and shall be managed, controlled, handled and disposed of by said trustee subject to all the terms, conditions and trusts herein mentioned, and upon any termination hereof shall go in the same manner to the same persons and in the same events as herein provided, as though it had constituted a part of the original trust estate.

VI.

Upon the termination of this trust, the trustee shall first pay from the principal and/or income of the trust estate any and all inheritance, estate or other taxes which it may then or thereafter be required to pay from the trust estate, and shall also retain and fully pay itself all sums then due it under the terms hereof.

VII.

It is a further provision of this trust that said trustor has reserved and said trustee does hereby assent to the express right and power reserved unto said trustor to revoke the trust hereby created, in whole or in part, by an instrument declaring such revocation executed and acknowledged in the same manner required for the execution and acknowledgment of deeds of conveyance of real estate. In the event of such revocation by such trustor, either in whole or in part, the whole of said [57] trust property, or the part thereof as to which this trust is revoked as the case may be, shall be paid and delivered to said trustor, provided, however, that in no event shall any attempted revocation be of any effect unless and until all sums then due the trustee under the terms hereof shall be fully paid, and said Trustee shall be fully released and discharged of all then existing liabilities and obligations of every kind and nature affecting the said property or the trustee in relation thereto, anything to the contrary herein contained notwithstanding.

In Witness Whereof said Central National Bank of Oakland, as trustee, has caused its corporate name to be subscribed and its corporate seal to be affixed hereunto by its officers thereunto duly authorized this 24th day of September, 1929, at Oakland, California.

CENTRAL NATIONAL BANK
OF OAKLAND, a national
banking association, as Trustee.

By CLAUD GATCH

Vice President

[Corporate Seal] And By S. BERVEN

Ass't. Trust Officer.

I, the undersigned, hereby certify and declare that I am the person named in the foregoing declaration of trust and therein called the trustor, and that said declaration of trust fully and correctly sets out the power under and by which the said trust property therein mentioned is to be held and managed by said trustee, and I do hereby agree, consent to, approve, ratify and confirm the same in all particulars.

Dated: September 24th, 1929.

ABBIE W. QUINN [58]

State of California
County of Alameda—ss.

On this 24th day of September, in the year One Thousand Nine Hundred and Twenty-nine, before me, L. M. Griesemer, a Notary Public in and for the County of Alameda, State of California, residing therein, duly commissioned and sworn, personally appeared Claud Gatch, known to me to be the Vice President, and S. Berven, known to me to be the Asst. Trust Officer of the Corporation that executed the within instrument and the officers who executed the within instrument on behalf of the Corporation therein named, and acknowledged to me that such Corporation executed the same.

In Witness Whereof, I have hereunto set my hand and affixed my Official Seal, the day and year in this certificate first above written.

[Notarial Seal]   L. M. GRIESEMER
Notary Public in and for said County of Alameda, State of California. [59]

State of California
County of Alameda—ss.

On this 24th day of September, in the year One
Thousand Nine Hundred and Twenty-nine, before
me, L. M. Griesemer, a Notary Public in and for
the County of Alameda, State of California, residing therein, duly commissioned and sworn, personally appeared Abbie W. Quinn, known to me to
be the person described in and whose name is subscribed to the within instrument, and she acknowledged to me that she executed the same.

In Witness Whereof, I have hereunto set my
hand and affixed my Official Seal, the day and year
in this certificate first above written.

[Notarial Seal]   L. M. GRIESEMER,
Notary Public in and for said County of Alameda,
State of California. [60]

"EXHIBIT B"

In the Southern Division of the District Court of the United States, for the Northern District of California.

No. 19458-S

In the Matter of

Conservatorship of Central National Bank of Oakland.

PETITION OF CONSERVATOR FOR APPROVAL OF CONTRACTS OF SALE OF ASSETS.

The petition of A. J. Mount, Conservator of Central National Bank of Oakland, *respectively* represents unto the Court as follows:

1. Central National Bank of Oakland is a National Banking Association, organized under the laws of the United States, and is herein referred to as the National Bank; prior to March 14, 1933, said National Bank was engaged in business as such banking association in Oakland, California; on March 14, 1933, petitioner was duly appointed Conservator of said National Bank, and ever since said date has been and now is the duly appointed, qualified and acting Conservator thereof.

2. Central Savings Bank of Oakland is a corporation organized under the laws of the State of California, and is hereby referred to as the Savings Bank; for many years last past the Savings

Bank has been and now is engaged in the banking business in Oakland, California.

3. Petitioner desires to enter into a contract with the Savings Bank, whereby petitioner agrees to sell to the Savings Bank and whereby the Savings Bank agrees to purchase from the petitioner certain assets upon the terms and conditions in said proposed contract set forth, a copy of which proposed contract is attached hereto, marked Exhibit "A" and made a part thereof; said proposed con- [61] tract has been approved by the Comptroller of the Currency of the United States and by the Superintendent of Banks of the State of California.

4. The price to be paid by the Savings Bank for said assets will be sufficient to enable the petitioner to pay forthwith in full all secured and preferred claims, and to pay forthwith seventy per cent of all unsecured claims, against the National Bank.

5. Petitioner desires to join with the board of directors and officers of the National Bank, acting with the consent of stockholders holding of record at least two-thirds of the issued capital stock of the National Bank, in the sale to the Savings Bank of the whole of the business of the trust department of the National Bank, upon the terms and conditions set forth in a proposed contract, a copy of which is attached hereto, marked Exhibit "B" and made a part hereof; said proposed contract has been approved by said Comptroller of the Currency and by said Superintendent of Banks.

6. Petitioner verily believes that the sale of said assets under said first mentioned contract is for the best interests of the creditors of the National Bank, in that it will enable petitioner to make said payments to creditors, as aforesaid, and without any sacrifice or shrinkage in the value of the assets sold; all bills receivable will be sold at full face value plus interest accrued to the date of sale, and other assets will be sold at their full value, as in said proposed contract set forth.

7. Petitioner verily believes that the sale of said business of said trust department under said proposed contract, a copy of which is marked Exhibit "B", is for the best interests of the creditors of the National Bank, in that it will result in the discharge by the Savings Bank of all liabilities of said department and in the securing for the benefit of creditors of the National Bank of the full value of said business. [62]

Wherefore, the petitioner prays:

(a) That an order be issued by this Court approving said sale of said assets under the terms of said proposed contract, a copy of which is marked Exhibit "A", and authorizing petitioner to execute said proposed contract;

(b) That an order be issued by this Court approving said sale of said business of said trust department under the terms of said proposed contract, a copy of which is marked Exhibit "B", and authorizing petitioner to execute said proposed contract;

(c)   And for such other and further relief as to the Court may seem meet and proper.

A. J. MOUNT,
Conservator of Central
National Bank of Oakland
CARL H. ABBOTT
CHARLES A. BEARDSLEY
M. W. DOBRZENSKY
Attorneys for Petitioner,
1516 Central Bank Bldg.,
Oakland, California.

State of California,
County of Alameda—ss.

A. J. Mount, being first duly sworn, deposes and says: Affiant is the Conservator of Central National Bank of Oakland; affiant has read the foregoing petition by him subscribed and knows the contents thereof and that the same is true of his own knowledge.

A. J. MOUNT

Subscribed and sworn to before me this 20th day of April, 1933.

[Seal]   CONSTANCE E. MULVANY
Notary Public in and for the County of Alameda,
State of California. [63]

"EXHIBIT C"

Agreement for Sale of Trust Department of Central National Bank of Oakland.

Agreement made April 22, 1933, between Central National Bank of Oakland, a National Banking Association, herein referred to as the National Bank, and A. J. Mount as Conservator of said National Bank, herein referred to as the Conservator, as Sellers and Central Savings Bank of Oakland, a corporation organized under the laws of the State of California, herein referred to as the Savings Bank, as Buyer:

1. The Sellers agree to and do hereby sell, assign and transfer to the Buyer, and the Buyer agrees to and does hereby purchase from the Sellers, the whole of the business of the trust department of the National Bank, including all court and private trusts, subject to the right of trustors and beneficiaries, after such transfers, to nominate another and succeeding trustee of the trusts so transferred, and including all records, books, files and documents relating to or connected with the said trust department and to or with all of the business thereof, and to or with each and all of said trusts, and including all of the right, title and interest of the sellers or of either of them in and to all assets, investments, deposits, demands, contracts, agreements, and all real and personal property held, owned or possessed in trust or by virtue of any trust or fiduciary relationship, in connection with

or incidental to the operation of the said trust department, and including the right to succeed to all of the relations, obligations, trusts and liabilities that are in any way connected with or incidental to the business of said trust department, including appointments to all executorships, trusteeships, guardianships and other fiduciary capacities in which the National Bank is now or may hereafter be named, in wills heretofore or hereafter probated, or in any other instruments.

2. In consideration of the said sale, assignment and trans- [64] fer and of the premises herein set forth, the Savings Bank hereby assumes all fiduciary and trust obligations and liabilities of the National Bank, and agrees to perform all of the trusts of the National Bank and to pay and discharge all the debts and liabilities that are incidental to said trusts or connected therewith, in the same manner as if the Savings Bank had itself incurred the obligation, debt or liability, or assumed the relation of trust.

3. The Savings Bank shall have all the rights, and shall be subject to all the liabilities, and hereby assumes all of the obligations, that, according to law, result from or are incidental to the purchase and sale of a trust department of a bank; and the foregoing enumeration of specific rights, liabilities and obligations is not intended as a limitation upon the general provisions of this paragraph.

4. All accrued or earned fees and other compensation that are connected with or incidental to

the operation of said trust department shall be pro-rated between the Conservator and the Savings Bank, as of the date of transfer; and the Savings Bank shall have the right to collect all of said fees and other compensation, and the same are hereby assigned to the Savings Bank, subject to the obligation of the Savings Bank to account therefor to the Conservator and to pay promptly to the Conservator his pro-rata thereof from time to time as the same are received by the Savings Bank.

5. The Conservator and the National Bank agree, and each of them agrees, to execute such satisfactory instruments of transfer as may, in the opinion of the Savings Bank, be necessary or advisable in order to give effect to the terms of this agreement.

6. This agreement is executed in quadruplicate and shall be binding upon and inure to the benefit of the parties hereto and each of their successors and assigns, and any persons succeeding to the legal rights of each of the parties hereto.

7. This agreement is subject to the approval of the Superintendent of Banks of the State of California, of the Comptroller [65] of the Currency and of a court of record of competent jurisdiction.

In Witness Whereof, the Savings Bank and the National Bank have caused this agreement to be signed by their respective authorized officers, and their respective corporate seals to be affixed hereto,

and the Conservator has hereunto signed his name,
the day and year first above written.

CENTRAL SAVINGS BANK
OF OAKLAND,

By T. A. CRELLIN,

Executive Vice-President,

And

H. C. SAGEHORN,

Cashier.

CENTRAL NATIONAL BANK
OF OAKLAND,

By A. J. MOUNT,

President,

And

J. F. HASSLER,

Cashier.

A. J. MOUNT,

as Conservator of Central
National Bank of Oakland.

[Endorsed]: Filed Aug. 22, 1933. Geo. E. Gross,
County Clerk. By Hal P. Angus, Deputy.

Appendix B

ANSWER OF CENTRAL BANK

Appendix B

In the District Court of the United States, in and for the Northern District of California, Southern Division.

No. 3644-K—In Equity.

ABBIE W. QUINN,

Plaintiff,

vs.

CENTRAL NATIONAL BANK OF OAKLAND, a National Banking Association, JOSEPH H. GRUT, as Receiver of Central National Bank of Oakland, a National Banking Association, and CENTRAL BANK OF OAKLAND, a corporation,

Defendants.

ANSWER OF THE DEFENDANT, CENTRAL BANK OF OAKLAND.

Now comes the defendant, Central Bank of Oakland, a corporation, and answers unto plaintiff's complaint as follows:

I.

Answering paragraph IV this defendant denies that at or during any of the times mentioned in the complaint it was associated with or carried on its banking business in the same premises as the defendant, Central National Bank of Oakland (to be hereinafter referred to as the national bank), save that this defendant admits that the bulk of its banking business was carried on in the same building as that in which the banking business of the national bank was carried on, but in separate portions of said building. Denies that since or on April 21st, 1933, this defendant has had the same executive officers as were the executive officers of the national bank on March 2nd, 1933.

II.

Answering paragraph V this defendant admits that Bothwell was assistant cashier of the national bank but alleges that he was not an executive officer thereof, his duties and authority being confined solely to the bond department and that he had no duties pertaining to, or authority over, any other department or business [79] of said national bank.

III.

Answering paragraph VII this defendant alleges that it is without knowledge as to the period of time plaintiff resided in Oakland; denies that as such depositor or in any other manner or capacity plaintiff became well or otherwise acquainted with Bothwell until the year 1926; this defendant is without knowledge as to whether plaintiff reposed in Bothwell or the bond department great, or any, trust or confidence; denies that Bothwell knew that plaintiff reposed in him or in the bond department great, or any, trust or confidence.

IV.

Answering paragraph VIII this defendant alleges that it is without knowledge as to whether plaintiff was in poor health during any of the times mentioned in the complaint until about 1929; this defendant is without knowledge that plaintiff, prior to the 1st day of January, 1926, or at any other time except immediately prior to September 24th, 1929, intended to place her property, or any part thereof, in the type of trust referred to in paragraph VIII or in any other type of trust. This defendant denies that on or about the 1st day of January, 1926, or at any other time, except immediately prior to September 24th, 1929, plaintiff interviewed Bothwell or requested his advice as to whether or not it was advisable for her to carry out her alleged intention of placing her property, or any part thereof, in a trust, or that at said time, or at any other time except immediately prior to September 24th, 1929, plaintiff interviewed Bothwell relative to placing her property, or any part thereof, in trust; denies that plaintiff requested information from said Bothwell as to whether or not said national bank could or would act as trustee of such a trust. Denies that at said, or any, time the said Bothwell advised plaintiff that to place her [80] property in such, or any, trust was just the thing for her to do; in this respect this defendant alleges that immediately prior to September 24th, 1929, plaintiff informed Bothwell that she had talked with Daniel Read about creating a trust and asked Bothwell if he thought it desirable to which Bothwell responded that in view of the fact plaintiff contemplated going to Rochester, Minnesota, for medical or surgical

treatment he thought her idea of creating a trust
was a good one but that he had nothing to do with
the trust department and then introduced plaintiff
to Berven, assistant trust officer; denies that said
Bothwell advised plaintiff at any time that the national bank had a trust department, or advised her
that a particular, or any, part of the business of
said trust department was the taking care of property of widows or orphans; denies that plaintiff at
said, or any, time informed Bothwell of what her
property consisted or that included in her property
was a parcel of real property situated in the City
of Reno, State of Nevada, or that she was desirous
of selling said property; denies that the said Bothwell at any time ever informed plaintiff that said
national bank could not accept a conveyance to it of
real property situated in the State of Nevada;
denies that for that, or any other, reason the said
Bothwell advised plaintiff that, pending the sale by
her of said, or any other, parcel of real property,
or the placing by her of her funds in a trust with
said national bank as trustee, the thing for her to
do was to invest her funds available for investment,
or any of them, through the bond department in
bonds; denies that plaintiff accepted the advice of
the said Bothwell in relation to creating a trust because of the fact that Bothwell never gave her any
such advice pertaining to the formation of a trust;
denies that plaintiff ever informed Bothwell that
she would postpone the placing of her property in
a trust with the national bank until after the sale by

her of said parcel of real property, or ever informed [81] Bothwell that she would postpone the
placing of her property in a trust; denies that plaintiff informed Bothwell that in the meantime, or at
any other time, she would invest her funds, available for investment, or any of them, through the
bond department in bonds; denies that plaintiff informed Bothwell that she had little experience with
bonds; denies that plaintiff informed said Bothwell
that if such, or any, investments were made she
would have to rely upon him to purchase for her,
through the bond department, or otherwise, or at
all, safe or desirable bonds for the investment of
her said funds; denies that Bothwell assured plaintiff that her funds would be invested by the national bank, through him as manager of the bond
department, or otherwise, or at all, in nothing but
safe or desirable bonds for her; denies that plaintiff thereupon, or at any other time, told Bothwell
that she desired her funds to be invested not only in
safe bonds, but in bonds of such desirability that
the same could be readily sold, at any time, so that
she could thus get back the money which she had
invested in them, or that plaintiff, at any time, inquired of Bothwell whether or not her funds should
be invested in bonds of the United States; denies
that the said Bothwell replied that bonds of the
United States paid a low rate of interest or that
Bothwell assured her that her funds would be invested by the national bank, through him as the
manager of the bond department, or otherwise, or

at all, in bonds of the safety or desirability alleged
to have been desired by her, or in bonds just as
good as those of the United States, or paying a
much larger rate of interest than was paid on bonds
of the United States. In reference to the foregoing
denials this defendant alleges that from time to
time the said Bothwell may have informed plaintiff that bonds of the United States paid a low rate
of interest and likewise advised plaintiff that in
general it was a good rule to follow that the risk
involved was in direct proportion to the amount of
interest paid on bonds, that [82] is to say, that the
safest bonds usually paid a lower rate of interest
than bonds which were not so well secured, or which
were more apt to default. This defendant further
alleges that from time to time plaintiff advised the
said Bothwell that she was extremely anxious to get
a high rate of return on her various investments.

V.

Answering paragraph IX this defendant alleges
that it is without knowledge as to whether Bothwell used words of recommendation such as therein
alleged, namely, "safe and desirable investments."
Admits that Bothwell recommended to plaintiff $10,-
000.00 par value of "secured sinking fund gold
bonds" of the Province of Buenos Aires, $5,000.00
par value of "secured gold notes" of Miller & Lux,
Incorporated, $5,000.00 par value gold bonds of
Rhodes-Jamison Co., and $5,000.00 par value of
Western States Gas and Electric Company. Denies

that plaintiff thereupon, or at any other time, informed Bothwell that she doubted the safety or desirability of bonds of the Province of Buenos Aires for the investment of her funds; denies that the said Bothwell assured or told plaintiff that the bonds of said Province were well secured; denies that said Bothwell assured plaintiff that said bonds were a safe or desirable investment for plaintiff, or that the doubts of plaintiff were dispelled by any such assurance of Bothwell and in this respect this defendant alleges that the said Bothwell in the case of the bonds of said Province of Buenos Aires, as well as in the case of all other bonds or notes sold by the bond department to plaintiff, merely recommended said bonds or notes basing said recommendation upon the best knowledge, information and belief of the national bank and of the said Bothwell. This defendant is without knowledge as to whether plaintiff relied upon the said, or any, recommendation of Bothwell. Denies that plaintiff approved the purchase for her by the national [83] bank, through said Bothwell as manager of the bond department, or otherwise, or at all, of said bonds or notes, or any of them, and in this respect alleges that in none of the instances of the purchases of bonds or notes by plaintiff did the national bank, or Bothwell, or the bond department, purchase bonds for plaintiff or act for plaintiff in the purchase thereof (save in the case of the purchases of Pacific Gas and Electric Company bonds, San Joaquin Light & Power bonds, East Bay Municipal Utility bonds and Los Angeles Gas and Electric bonds referred to in paragraph XXI of the complaint in which case the trust department of said bank purchased said bonds for plaintiff's trust), but instead, as plaintiff well knew, sold bonds to plaintiff which the national bank either then owned and possessed, or had contracted to purchase or in the underwriting of which the national bank had participated or which were available to the national bank by reason of its participation in the underwriting thereof and that in all cases prior to the creation of the trust hereinafter referred to plaintiff and the national bank were acting in the capacity of buyer and seller and not in the capacity of principal and agent. Denies that on or about the 1st day of January, 1926, or at any other time, Bothwell informed plaintiff that the purchase prices which she was paying for said bonds or notes, or any of them, were the purchase prices paid therefor by the national bank and in this respect this defendant alleges that in each and every instance of the purchase by plaintiff from said national bank of bonds or notes the prices at which they were sold to plaintiff were the then current market prices thereof, if they had an established market price, or a price commensurate with the fair and reasonable value thereof if they had no established market price. Denies that plaintiff intended, or that Bothwell, or this defendant, or the national bank knew that plaintiff intended, to place such, or any, bonds or notes so purchased in a trust with the national bank or that at any time except immediately prior to the execution of the trust instrument on September 24th, 1929, plaintiff intended, or Bothwell, or this defendant, or the national bank, knew that plaintiff intended, to place the bonds or notes, or any of them, so purchased from the national bank in a trust with the national bank as trustee. Denies that Bothwell, or this defendant, or the national bank, knew that plaintiff intended to create said, or any, trust after she sold the real property situated in Reno, or knew that she intended to create a trust at any time until immediately prior to the time the trust was actually created, to-wit, September 24th, 1929.

VI.

Answering paragraph X this defendant denies that during the year 1927, or at any other time, the national bank, through Bothwell, as manager of the bond department, or through any other instrumentality, or person, made further, or any, purchases for plaintiff of any bonds or notes. In this respect defendant alleges that the bonds referred to in said paragraph X of the complaint were sold by the national bank to plaintiff and that in such transaction plaintiff and the national bank were acting as buyer and seller, which fact was well known to plaintiff. This defendant is without knowledge as to whether in the instances of such, or any, further sales to plaintiff Bothwell recommended the bonds or notes therein referred to as safe or desirable investments but admits that said Bothwell recom-

mended said bonds or notes to plaintiff. Denies that
plaintiff informed Bothwell that she doubted the
safety or desirability of bonds of the Province of
Callao for the investment of her funds. Denies that
Bothwell assured plaintiff that said bonds of the
Province of Callao were well secured or were a safe
or desirable investment for her but admits that the
said Bothwell recommended said bonds to plaintiff.
Denies that the doubts of plaintiff were dispelled by
any such [84] assurance of the said Bothwell as is
alleged in the complaint. Denies that plaintiff informed Bothwell that she doubted the safety or
desirability of bonds of California Cotton Mills;
denies that Bothwell assured her that said bonds of
California Cotton Mills were safe or desirable investments but admits that Bothwell recommended
said bonds to plaintiff. Denies that plaintiff's
doubts were dispelled by any such assurance of the
said Bothwell as is alleged in the complaint. This
defendant is without knowledge as to whether plaintiff relied upon any recommendation of Bothwell
in any instances of her purchases of bonds or notes.
Denies that plaintiff approved the purchase for her
by this national bank through Bothwell, or otherwise, or at all, of said bonds or notes, or any of
them, and in this respect alleges that in each instance referred to plaintiff purchased said bonds or
notes from the national bank in the capacity of a
buyer dealing with a seller. Denies that in any
instance Bothwell ever informed plaintiff that the
prices she was paying to purchase bonds or notes

from the bank were the prices which the bank had
paid for them when it acquired them.

VII.

Answering paragraph XI this defendant alleges
that it is without knowledge as to whether the real
property situated in Reno was sold by plaintiff on
or about the 8th day of February, 1928, and is, likewise, without knowledge as to whether plaintiff realized from said sale, over and above the expenses of
said sale, the sum of $20,000.00, or what sum was
received. Denies that thereafter during the year
1928, or during the year 1929, or until the 24th day
of September, 1929, or at any other time, the national bank through Bothwell, as manager of the
bond department, or through any other instrumentality, or otherwise, or at all, made still further purchases for plaintiff of bonds or notes, as safe or
desirable investments for plaintiff, or otherwise, or
at [85] all, and in this respect alleges that in each
of the instances of the purchases of bonds or notes
the national bank and plaintiff acted in the capacity
of buyer and seller, a fact well known to plaintiff
(save in the case of the purchase of Pacific Gas and
Electric Company bonds, San Joaquin Light and
Power bonds, East Bay Municipal Utility District
bonds and Los Angeles Gas and Electric bonds referred to in paragraph V hereof, in which case the
trust department of the national bank purchased
said bonds for plaintiff's trust). This defendant is
without knoweldge as to what extent the further

purchases referred to in paragraph XI of the complaint were made with money realized by plaintiff on the sale of the Reno property. This defendant is without knowledge as to whether in the instances of the purchases referred to in paragraph XI of the complaint Bothwell recommended the bonds or notes therein referred to to plaintiff as safe or desirable investments. Admits that said bonds were recommended as investments for plaintiff. This defendant is without knowledge as to whether plaintiff would have doubted the safety or desirability of the bonds of Medford Irrigation District for the investment of her funds had not the said Bothwell informed her in writing that said Bond Department had "handled several hundred thousand dollars" of the bonds of said District, and believed that said bonds contained "all of the elements to make them a safe and desirable investment". This defendant is without knowledge that plaintiff relied upon said recommendation, or any recommendation. Denies that plaintiff approved said purchases, or any of said purchases, for her by said national bank acting through Bothwell, as manager of said bond department, or otherwise, or at all, of said bonds or notes, or any of them, and in this respect alleges that in each of the instances of the purchase of bonds or notes referred to in paragraph XI of the complaint plaintiff and the national bank were acting in the capacity of buyer and seller, a fact well [86] known to plaintiff. Denies that Both-·well or anyone else connected with the national bank informed plaintiff that the prices she was paying to purchase said bonds or notes from the national bank were the prices which the national bank had paid for them when it acquired them.

VIII.

Answering paragraph XII this defendant denies that the national bank in any of the instances therein referred to acted in the capacity of purchasing for plaintiff any bonds or notes whatsoever and in this respect alleges that in each instance of the purchase of any bonds or notes therein referred to plaintiff and the national bank acted in the capacity of buyer and seller, a fact well known to plaintiff. This defendant is without knowledge as to whether Bothwell recommended to plaintiff the bonds or notes therein referred to, or any of them, as safe or desirable investments but admits that all bonds or notes which plaintiff purchased from the national bank prior to the execution of the trust were recommended by Bothwell. This defendant is without knowledge as to whether plaintiff relied upon any recommendation of Bothwell or of any other person. Denies that plaintiff approved the purchase for her by the national bank, through Bothwell, as manager of the bond department, or otherwise, or at all, of the bonds or notes referred to in paragraph XII of the complaint, or any of them, and in this respect alleges that in each instance therein referred to plaintiff and the national bank acted in the capacity of buyer and seller, a fact well known to plaintiff. Denies that in any instance Bothwell, or anyone else, informed plaintiff that the prices she paid to the national bank as the purchase price of bonds or notes from the bank were the prices the national bank had paid for them when it acquired them.

IX.

Answering paragraph XIII this defendant admits that the [87] bonds or notes which plaintiff purchased from the national bank were retained in the possession of the bond department thereof. Denies that said bonds or notes, or any of them, were retained on or were on deposit with the national bank awaiting the time when the same would be assigned or transferred by plaintiff to the national bank, as trustee of the trusts in which it is alleged plaintiff intended to place her property after the sale of the parcel of property in Reno or pending the execution of the trust instrument.

X.

Answering paragraph XIV this defendant denies that any of the bonds or notes therein referred to had been purchased for plaintiff by the national bank, through Bothwell or anyone else, but instead alleges that said bonds and notes were sold to plaintiff by the national bank, a fact well known to plaintiff.

XI.

Answering paragraph XV this defendant alleges that it is without knowledge as to when the parcel

of real property situated in Reno was sold or as to
whether on or about the 8th day of February, 1928,
or at any other time until immediately prior to September 24th, 1929, plaintiff intended to place her
property in trust with the national bank, as trustee,
or whether plaintiff, due to her alleged continuing
poor health, or for any other reason, was disinclined
to attend to any matter which required any prolonged mental effort on her part, or was disinclined
to attend to the preparation of the instrument of
trust referred to. Denies that plaintiff was referred
by Bothwell to Read; denies that Bothwell referred
plaintiff to Berven for particulars concerning the
subject of the preparation of the trust instrument
or that plaintiff was referred to Berven by Bothwell for any purpose or under any circumstances
other than as stated in paragraph IV hereof. This
defendant is without knowledge as to whether Read
seemed to plain- [88] tiff to be indifferent about the
preparation of the trust instrument or about any
other matter or whether plaintiff doubted whether
or not Read was interested in having the national
bank act as trustee or whether plaintiff's mind was
greatly or at all disturbed. Admits that no progress
was made by plaintiff toward the preparation of
the trust instrument in the first conference plaintiff
had with Berven and in this respect this defendant
alleges that at the time of her first conference with
Berven plaintiff was not definitely committed to the
idea of creating a trust and was merely seeking gen-

eral information as to the workings of a trust; that
some time later plaintiff again interviewed Berven
about creating a trust and at this time specifically
informed Berven that she did not want the trust
so to operate as to prevent her from controlling the
investments and informed Berven that she wanted
to be able to dictate the investments the trust department would make. Again, a few days later,
plaintiff interviewed Berven and was informed by
him that trust funds, under ordinary circumstances,
can only be invested in certain types of securities
which ordinarily did not bring a greater yield than
five per cent (5%). Plaintiff responded that she had
to have a return of at least six per cent (6%) and
directed that the trust instrument when drafted
should contain a provision authorizing purchases of
securities other than those legal for the investment
of trust funds; plaintiff further informed Berven
that she wished the trust department to deal with
the bond department of the national bank when purchasing securities for the trust. Denies that the
national bank or Bothwell made any purchases of
bonds or notes for plaintiff as alleged in paragraph
XV of the complaint and in this respect this defendant alleges that all further investments made by
plaintiff at the times specified were made by plaintiff purchasing from the national bank bonds and
notes, plaintiff and the national bank acting in the
capacity of buyer and seller, the national bank [89]
selling to plaintiff bonds and notes which it either
then owned and possessed or had contracted to pur-

chase or in the underwriting of which the national
bank had participated or which were available to
the national bank by reason of its participation in
the underwriting thereof. This defendant is without knowledge as to whether or not plaintiff had
the intent of placing bonds or notes, or any of them,
purchased by her from the national bank in a trust
with said bank as trustee, or whether all of the
funds which plaintiff then possessed were invested
in the purchase of bonds or notes from the national
bank prior to the execution of the trust. This defendant is without knowledge as to whether in the
instances of the purchases of bonds or notes referred to in paragraph XV of the complaint Bothwell recommended to plaintiff the bonds or notes,
or any of them, as safe or desirable investments for
plaintiff; this defendant admits that said bonds or
notes were recommended by Bothwell. This defendant is without knowledge as to whether plaintiff relied upon the recommendation of Bothwell in each
or any of the instances referred to in paragraph
XV of the complaint. Denies that plaintiff approved further or any purchases for her by the
national bank and in this respect alleges that in
each of said instances plaintiff and the national
bank were acting in the capacity of buyer and seller,
a fact well known to plaintiff. Denies that Bothwell, or anyone else, informed plaintiff that the
prices she paid for said bonds or notes were the
prices which the national bank had paid for them
when it originally purchased them.

XII.

Answering paragraph XVI this defendant denies
that in each or any of the instances of the purchases
of bonds or notes the national bank purchased said
bonds or notes, or any of them, for plaintiff from
itself and in this respect alleges that in each and
every instance plaintiff and the national bank were
act- [90] ing in the capacity of buyer and seller.
Denies that the national bank was acting as, or was,
the purchaser of said bonds or notes, or any of
them, from itself in the one capacity, for the plaintiff, and the seller, in another capacity, to the plaintiff. In regard to the Fageol Motors Company and
Alameda Investment Company bonds the national
bank participated in the underwriting thereof. Denies that the Medford Irrigation District bonds had
depreciated to a price of $777.50 per bond at the
time the national bank sold them to plaintiff and in
this respect alleges that in the case of said bonds
as in the case of all other bonds sold by the national
bank to plaintiff the same were sold at the current
market price, if they had an established market
price, or at a price commensurate with the fair and
reasonable value thereof, if they had no established
market price. Denies that the profit to the Bank
on said Medford transaction was the sum of $972.50,
or any other sum whatsoever in excess of $72.50.
Denies that thereby or in any other manner was
the aggregate profit to the national bank increased
to $3,260.33 or to any other sum in excess of
$2,360.33. This defendant is without knowledge as

to whether plaintiff reposed any trust or confidence
whatsoever in the said Bothwell; denies that in violation of any trust or confidence which plaintiff reposed in said Bothwell, or in violation of any other
obligation owing by the national bank, or by Bothwell, to plaintiff, Bothwell did not discolse to plaintiff, or concealed from her, that the national bank
was selling to plaintiff bonds or notes of which it
was the owner; denies that at any time the national
bank ever represented to plaintiff that it was acting in the capacity of purchasing agent for plaintiff; denies that in violation of any trust or confidence which plaintiff might have reposed in this
defendant, the national bank, or in Bothwell, or in
violation of any other obligation whatsoever, Bothwell did not disclose to plaintiff, or concealed from
her, the fact that the national bank made [91] a
profit on each of the purchases and sales of bonds
or notes. Denies that plaintiff had no knowledge
that the national bank was selling to plaintiff bonds
and notes of which it was the owner; denies that
plaintiff did not discover such matters until the
time or under the circumstances thereinafter alleged
in the complaint and in this respect this defendant
alleges that at all times plaintiff had knowledge of
the fact that the national bank was selling her bonds
and notes which it owned and was making a profit
thereon.

XIII.

Answering paragraph XVII this defendant alleges
that in addition to the property therein referred to

which plaintiff alleges she desired to place in trust was a parcel of real property in or near Sparks, Nevada.

XIV.

Answering paragraph XVIII this defendant denies that Berven told plaintiff her property would be absolutely protected or secure and in this respect alleges that plaintiff inquired as to what would happen to the property in the trust in the event the national bank should fail and that Berven informed her that trust assets were not a part of the general assets of the bank, were segregated therefrom and would not be affected by any failure of the bank. This defendant is without knowledge as to whether plaintiff at any time reposed in Berven, or in Read, or in the trust department great, or any, trust or confidence; denies that Berven or Read knew that plaintiff reposed in them, or in either of them, or in the trust department, great, or any, trust or confidence. This defendant is without knowledge as to whether plaintiff delivered to Berven written data concerning the provisions desired by her to be inserted in the instrument of trust in relation to the matters therein referred to or that said alleged data was used in the preparation of the instrument of trust. Denies [92] that said instrument of trust was prepared for plaintiff to execute or was prepared by any member of or person associated with the firm of attorneys mentioned; denies that said data was delivered to said firm of attorneys; denies that said firm of attorneys performed any services in the preparation of said instrument of trust except to approve the form thereof.

XV.

Answering paragraph XIX this defendant alleges that not only did plaintiff read over the instrument of trust but also that the same was read to her paragraph by paragraph by Berven and each paragraph was fully explained to her and that plaintiff stated that she understood not only the instrument of trust as a whole but also each of the paragraphs thereof. This defendant alleges that plaintiff inquired of Berven if she should submit the trust instrument to her own attorney to which Berven replied that it was eminently proper that she should do so. Denies that Berven told plaintiff it was unnecessary for her to do so or that she was as well protected as the national bank. This defendant is without knowledge as to whether, in so signing said statement, or in not seeking independent advice, or in executing said trust instrument, plaintiff relied upon the great, or any, trust or confidence which she is alleged to have reposed in Berven or whether she reposed any trust or confidence in him. Denies that said statement was prepared for her to sign or was prepared by the attorneys for the national bank, or by anyone associated with said attorneys.

XVI.

Answering paragraph XX this defendant denies that Berven acted in violation of the great, or any, trust or confidence which it is alleged plaintiff reposed in him in regard to any of the matters referred to in said paragraph XX. This defendant alleges that it is without knowledge as to whether plaintiff reposed [93] great, or any, trust or confidence in Berven. Denies that Berven did not inform plaintiff that the responsibilities or liabilities of the national bank, as trustee, otherwise imposed by law were restricted or limited, or were greatly restricted or limited, or were attempted so to be, either by the trust instrument or by paragraphs I and VII of the trust instrument, or either of said paragraphs; denies that Berven did not inform plaintiff at the time she signed the statement at the foot of the instrument of trust that the restrictions and limitations were approved, ratified and confirmed, or were attempted so to be, by the said statement. Denies that Berven did not inform her at that time that the powers of the national bank, as trustee, otherwise conferred by law, were greatly enlarged and extended by the provisions of paragraph II of the instrument of trust; denies that Berven did not inform plaintiff at said time that said powers were approved, ratified and confirmed by said statement. Denies that plaintiff did not know, or was never informed by anyone, until the time and under the circumstances alleged in the complaint that the responsibilities and liabilities were restricted and limited or that said powers were enlarged and extended or that the same were approved, ratified and confirmed by said statement. In this respect this

defendant alleges that at the time of the execution
of the trust instrument and the statement at the
foot thereof Berven informed plainiff as to the
matters complained of in said paragraph XX.

XVII.

Answering paragraphs XXI and XXII this
defendant denies that in each or any of the
first four instances mentioned in paragraph XXI
either Read or Berven recommended the bonds
or notes, or any of them, so purchased as safe or
desirable or made any recommendation concerning
said bonds or notes, or any of them. This defendant is without knowledge as to whether Bothwell
[94] recommended said bonds or notes, or any of
them, as safe or desirable, but admits that Bothwell recommended said bonds; this defendant alleges that it is without knowledge as to whether
plaintiff relied upon said recommendation. This
defendant is without knowledge as to whether
plaintiff reposed in Bothwell, or in Read, or in
Berven, great, or any, trust or confidence. Denies
that either Bothwell, or Read, or Berven, did not
disclose to, or concealed from, plaintiff that
through them, or any of them, the national bank
had purchased from itself, or sold to itself, said
bonds or any of them or that the bank had profited
in such, or any, of said instances; denies that plaintiff had no knowledge of such facts, or any of
them, or that plaintiff did not discover them, until
the time, or under the circumstances, alleged in the
complaint. This defendant alleges that in each

of the four instances of said purchases of bonds in
the year 1930, namely, the instances of said purchases from and including the 8th day of April,
1930, to and including the 27th day of June, 1930,
plaintiff dealt directly with Bothwell, as manager
of the bond department, and directed the trust department of the national bank to purchase from
the bond department said bonds and notes and in
each of said instances plaintiff well knew that the
trust department of the national bank was making
said purchases of bonds from the bond department.
This defendant further alleges that it was at plaintiff's express instance and direction that the trust
department of the national bank made said purchases, and all of them, from the bond department;
that due to plaintiff's own wishes she in effect and
in reality acted as the principal in these transactions insofar as the trust department of the national bank was concerned and directed said trust
department as to the investments she desired it to
make. Denies that either Bothwell, or Read, or
Berven, failed to disclose to, or concealed from,
plaintiff the fact that the national bank had purchased from it- [95] self the bonds mentioned in
the first four (4) instances referred to in said paragraphs XXI and XXII. Denies that any of said
persons concealed from plaintiff the fact that the
national bank had profited in each, or any, of the
first four (4) instances mentioned. Denies that
plaintiff had no knowledge of any or all of said
alleged facts complained of or did not discover the

same until the time and under the circumstances
alleged in the complaint and in this respect this
defendant alleges that at all times plaintiff had
knowledge of all of the matters complained of in
said paragraphs XXI and XXII immediately upon
their occurrence save that this defendant is without knowledge as to whether plaintiff knew of the
amount of profit made in said first four (4) instances mentioned.

XVIII.

Answering paragraph XXIV of the complaint
this defendant denies that any of the bonds or
notes therein listed which were acquired by plaintiff prior to the execution of the instrument of
trust were purchased by the national bank from
itself and in this respect alleges that in all instances such bonds or notes were sold by the national bank to plaintiff, a fact well known to her.

XIX.

Answering paragraph XXV this defendant denies that in any instance prior to the execution of
the trust the national bank purchased through
Bothwell, as manager of the bond department, or
otherwise, or at all, or through anyone else, any
bonds or notes for plaintiff but instead alleges that
the national bank sold them to her; denies that any
of said bonds or notes were sold to plaintiff as safe
or desirable investments or that any guaranty or
assurance was made as to the safety or desirability
thereof. Denies that said $1,000.00 par value of

bonds of California Cotton Mills were purchased
or were recommended as a safe [96] or desirable
investment but admits that said purchase carried
the recommendation of the bond department of the
national bank; denies that said bond was recommended by the trust department or by said national bank as a safe or desirable investment for
plaintiff or for said trusts and in this respect this
defendant alleges that from time to time Berven
pointed out to plaintiff that the purchases she was
directing be made from the bond department were
not of the kind usually acquired for trusts.

XX.

Answering paragraph XXVI this defendant denies that any of the fourteen (14) blocks of bonds
or notes first referred to in paragraph XXIV of
the complaint were purchased by the national bank
for plaintiff or for her trusts; denies that any of
the bonds or notes referred to in paragraph XXIV
were not, at the time when sold to plaintiff, or to
her trust, safe or desirable taking into consideration the yield on said bonds and notes; admits that
said bonds and notes were not of the type in which
trust funds were or are usually invested and in
this respect this defendant alleges that this was
called to plaintiff's attention before, at the time
of, and after, the execution of the trust instrument
but that plaintiff insisted on retaining such investments and also, after the execution of the trust
instrument, plaintiff insisted on purchasing the

first three (3) of the seven (7) blocks of bonds
secondly referred to in paragraph XXIV. This
defendant alleges that the trust department of the
national bank from time time admonished plaintiff
after the creation of the trust that the securities
which she then had on hand in said trust or which
she thereafter recommended be purchased by the
trust department from the bond department were
not legal investmnts for savings banks or for trust
funds and advised her that her trust funds should
be invested in bonds, which, though paying a lower
rate of interest and yielding a lower return, were
deemed more conservative and better [97] secured.
Denies that any of said bonds or notes save the
first three (3) of the seven (7) blocks of said bonds
secondly referred to in paragraph XXIV were
purchased by the national bank from itself. Denies that said bonds, or any of them, insofar as the
same are purported to be secured by real property,
were, at the respective times of the purchases
thereof, or at any other time, grossly insufficiently
secured, or were or are insufficiently secured. Denies that said notes, or any of them, insofar as the
same are purported to be secured by real property
or by personal property were not, at the respective
times of the purchases thereof, or at any other
time, secured by first mortgages of real property,
if they purported to be so secured, or that they
were not, when purchased or that they never since
have been, either secured by personal property, if
they purported to be so secured, or that, if so se-

cured, they have been or ever were secured by personal property of no value or without substantial value; denies that the bonds of the Province of Buenos Aires or of the Province of Callao were, when purchased, uncollectible. This defendant is without knowledge as to whether said bonds, or any of them, since the purchase thereof by plaintiff have been, or now are, uncollectible; denies that the bonds of Medford Irrigation District never have been secured by any lien upon any real property, or upon any other property, and in this respect alleges that said bonds were fully secured and were a lien upon the entire real property in the Medford Irrigation District by virtue of the fact that they were payable out of assessments levied upon and which were a lien upon all real property situated in said District; denies that the notes of Jackson Furniture Company have never been secured by any lien upon any property of any kind. This defendant is without knowledge as to whether at the respective times when purchases of bonds or notes were made, or at any other time, anyone connected with the national bank recommended any of the bonds [98] or notes purchased by plaintiff or by the trust department as safe or desirable bonds or notes; denies that plaintiff was at any time ignorant of the difference between said notes and bonds so purchased and the safety or desirability of the same for which her funds or the funds of said trust should have been invested and in this respect this defendant alleges that plaintiff was

cautioned and admonished from time to time that
the investments she was making carried with them
a certain element of risk in that she sought to obtain the highest return possible on her investments.

XXI.

Answering paragraph XXVIII this defendant
denies that by the contract relative to the purchase
by this defendant of the trust department of the
national bank (Exhibit "C" attached to the complaint), or in any other manner or way, did this
defendant ever assume or agree to discharge all,
or any, of the liabilities to the plaintiff of the national bank relating or incidental to the purchases
of bonds or notes, or any of them, for plaintiff or
for her benefit, or arising out of the sale to plaintiff or to the trust department by the national bank
of bonds or notes, or any of them, either through
Bothwell, as manager of the bond department, or
otherwise, or at all, or through anyone else.

XXII.

Answering paragraph XXIX this defendant denies that the national bank either through Read, or
Berven, or through anyone else, on any occasion,
save as hereinafter alleged, told plaintiff not to
worry about the defaults or any of them or told
plaintiff that said bonds or notes, or any of them,
were well secured or that interest would eventually
be paid. In this respect this defendant alleges
that prior to November 1, 1932, in speaking of Alameda Park Bonds, Berven told plaintiff that these

bonds appeared to be protected by sufficient property but that plaintiff could look at the property herself and satisfy herself as to the [99] adequacy of the security. This defendant is without knowledge as to whether plaintiff reposed great, or any, trust or confidence in Berven, or in the trust department, or in Bothwell, or in the bond department; denies that Berven told plaintiff that the bonds or notes, or any of them, were well secured or that interest would be paid. Denies that at the time of said call Berven recommended to plaintiff that the bonds and notes, or any of them, referred to in paragraph XXIX of the complaint, save Alameda Investment Company bonds, be sold, or that the proceeds of the sales, or any part thereof, be invested in better bonds. In this respect this defendant alleges that before, at the time of, and subsequent to, the execution of the trust instrument Berven from time to time recommended to plaintiff that she sell a portion of her bonds and notes and invest the proceeds in bonds paying a lower interest rate but plaintiff refused to do so or to permit the same to be done. This defendant is without knowledge as to whether any bonds or notes were recommended to plaintiff as safe or desirable. Denies that the total prices for which said bonds and notes could have been sold at that time was only $28,860.00. Denies that the loss had said bonds and notes then been sold would have exceeded or been anywhere near as great as sixty-seven per cent (67%) of the total cost of said bonds and notes; denies that any prices were then computed or estimated as alleged in the complaint. In this respect this defendant alleges that said bonds and notes could have been sold for a price greatly in excess of $28,860.00, the exact price being unknown to this defendant because of the fact that many of said bonds and notes were unlisted and had no established market prices at that time; this defendant alleges further that the majority of said bonds and notes were then of a value greatly in excess of the price that could then have been realized on a sale thereof and, further, that the majority of said bonds and notes have greatly increased in price and value [100] since November 1, 1932.

XXIII.

Answering paragraph XXX this defendant alleges that it is without knowledge as to whether upon the said conversation with Berven the great, or any, trust or confidence, if any, which plaintiff is alleged theretofore to have reposed in Bothwell, or in the bond department, or in Berven, or in the trust department of the national bank was completely, or at all, shattered or ended. In this respect this defendant alleges that it is without knowledge as to whether plaintiff reposed any trust or confidence at any time in Bothwell, or in the bond department, or in Berven, or in the trust department. Denies that the examination by plaintiff's attorney continued, only with the interruptions mentioned in said complaint, up to the time of filing of the action; denies that said examination involved the inspection by said attorney of a large number of documents or other records of the national bank; denies that plaintiff was financially unable to employ an accountant to assist said attorney in his examination and in this respect this defendant alleges that at all times, it, and the national bank and the Conservator and Receiver thereof, furnished said attorney with detailed information in writing as required by him and in such form that the services of an accountant were not needed. This defendant alleges that all information sought by plaintiff's attorney was immediately laid before him in both detailed and summarized form as requested and that it was only necessary for said attorney to verify said information which he and his assistants did in approximately two (2) visits to the national bank which, at the outside limit, took in all one day to complete. Denies that said examination was interrupted by the closing of the national bank, or by the appointment of A. J. Mount, as Conservator of the national bank, or by the appointment of the defendant, Joseph H. Grut, as Receiver of the national [101] bank, or by the proceedings relating to the sale of the business of the trust department of the national bank to this defendant, or by the delay in the appointment of an attorney for the defendant, Joseph H. Grut, as Receiver of the national bank, or by negotiations between plaintiff's attorney and the attorneys for this defendant, or

by negotiations between plaintiff's attorney and
the attorney for the defendant, Joseph H. Grut, as
Receiver of the national bank, relating to a settlement of the claims of plaintiff involved in the complaint or relating to a settlement of any other
claims; denies that the fourteen (14) blocks of
bonds or notes first listed in paragraph XXIV of
the complaint were purchased for plaintiff by the
national bank, or through Bothwell, or through
anyone else, and in this respect alleges that said
fourteen (14) blocks of bonds and notes were sold
by the bond department of the national bank to
plaintiff, a fact well known by her. This defendant
is without knowledge as to whether after said negotiations came to an end plaintiff's attorney has
been actively or at all engaged in the preparation
of the complaint.

XXIV.

Answering paragraph XXXI this defendant denies that the attorney for plaintiff ever discovered
that there were, and also denies that there were,
any purchases of the fourteen (14) blocks of bonds
or notes, or any of them, first described in paragraph XXIV of the complaint for plaintiff by the
national bank through Bothwell, as manager of the
bond department, or otherwise, or at all, or that
said purchases, or any of them, had been made from
the national bank by the national bank for plaintiff, or that the national bank was the purchaser
as well as the seller of said fourteen (14) blocks of
bonds or notes, or any of them, and in this respect

this defendant alleges that in each and every instance the national bank sold said fourteen (14) blocks of bonds or notes to plaintiff, the parties acting in the capacity of buy- [102] er and seller, a fact well known to plaintiff. Admits that after the creation of the trust the first three (3) of the seven (7) blocks of bonds or notes secondly set forth in paragraph XXIV of the complaint were purchased by the trust department of the national bank from the bond department thereof but alleges that this fact was well known to plaintiff and was done at her express instance and request. This defendant alleges that it is without knowledge as to whether plaintiff's attorney, from time to time, or at any time, informed plaintiff of any alleged discoveries; denies that any of said alleged discoveries were made by him. This defendant is without knowledge as to whether plaintiff's attorney advised plaintiff, from time to time, or at any time, that it was necessary that she should have had independent advice in relation to the instrument of trust before she executed the same, or that the responsibilities or liabilities of the national bank, as trustee of the trusts declared in and by the instrument of trust, otherwise imposed by law upon said national bank, as trustee, were greatly, or at all, restricted or limited, or were attempted so to be, by the provisions of paragraphs I or VII, or by any other provisions, of said instrument of trust, or that said attorney informed plaintiff that the restrictions or limitations, or any of them, were approved, or ratified, or confirmed, or were attempted so to be, by the statement signed by her at the foot of said instrument, or otherwise, or at all, or that the powers of the national bank, as trustee of the trusts declared in and by the instrument of trust, otherwise conferred by the law upon the national bank, as such trustee, were greatly, or at all, enlarged or extended, or were attempted so to be by the provisions in paragraph II of said instrument of trust, or by any other provisions of said trust instrument, or that said powers were approved, or ratified, or confirmed, or were attempted so to be, by said statement signed by plaintiff, or that said attorney informed [103] plaintiff that none of the fourteen (14) blocks of bonds and notes first referred to in paragraph XXIV of the complaint, or of the first three (3) of the seven (7) blocks of said bonds or notes secondly referred to in said paragraph XXIV were when purchased of the alleged safety or desirability alleged. Denies that any of the fourteen (14) blocks of said bonds or notes first referred to were purchased for plaintiff and in this respect alleges that all of said fourteen (14) blocks were sold by the national bank to plaintiff, a fact well known to plaintiff; this defendant is without knowledge as to whether Bothwell, or anyone else connected with the national bank, assured plaintiff of the safety or desirability of any of said bonds or notes; denies that any of said bonds or notes when sold by the national bank to plaintiff, or, in the case of the first three (3) of the seven (7) blocks of said bonds or notes secondly referred to in paragraph XXIV of the complaint, when sold by the bond department of the national bank to the trust department, were not of such type or so secured as not to justify the recommendations given plaintiff. In this respect this defendant alleges that the said Berven, as assistant trust officer of the national bank, from time to time admonished plaintiff that the bonds or notes which she was insisting be purchased by the trust department from the bond department as trust investments, were not of the type usually acquired as a trust investment, but that in each and every instance of such admonition plaintiff emphatically stated that she desired such investments to be made.

Wherefore, this defendant prays judgment as hereinafter set forth.

Second Separate Defense.

As a further, second and separate defense this defendant alleges [104]

I.

That the complaint does not state facts sufficient to constitute a cause of action.

Wherefore, this defendant prays judgment as hereinafter set forth.

Third Separate Defense.

As a further, third and separate defense this defendant alleges:

I.

That paragraph VII of the trust instrument (Exhibit "A" attached to the complaint) provides that the trustor, plaintiff, reserves the power to revoke the trusts therein created subject to the payment to the trustee of all sums then due to it and that thereupon the trustee shall be fully released and discharged of all the existing liabilities and obligations of every kind and nature affecting the trust property or the trustee in relation thereto; that prior to the commencement of this suit this defendant, being then the successor trustee, offered to permit plaintiff to revoke the trust and the instrument of trust and to deliver all of the trust properties to plaintiff and offered to agree that such revocation should not be a release or discharge of existing liabilities and obligations of this defendant to plaintiff, if any. That plaintiff refused such offer.

Wherefore, this defendant prays judgment as hereinafter set forth.

Fourth Separate Defense.

As a further, fourth and separate defense this defendant alleges:

I.

That the bill of complaint does not contain a short or simple statement of the ultimate facts upon which the plaintiff asks relief. [105]

Wherefore, this defendant prays judgment as hereinafter set forth.

Fifth Separate Defense.

As a further, fifth and separate defense this defendant alleges:

I.

That said complaint is multifarious in that it has too large a scope and embraces more than one subject matter uniting several purported causes of action without separately stating them, as follows:

1. A purported cause of action, or series of causes of action, alleged to arise by reason of alleged false or fraudulent representations of the national bank as to the safety and desirability of certain bonds and notes specifically described in the complaint as investments for plaintiff and her trust.

2. A purported cause of action, or series of causes of action, alleged to arise by reason of the alleged fact that the national bank purchased said bonds and notes for plaintiff from itself without plaintiff's knowledge and thereby acted in a dual capacity and also made a secret profit thereon.

3. A purported cause of action by reason of the alleged fact that the execution of the trust instrument was procured through the national bank by fraud or by violation of trust and confidence reposed by plaintiff in said national bank.

Wherefore, the defendant prays judgment as hereinafter set forth.

Sixth Separate Defense.

As a further, sixth and separate defense this defendant alleges:

I.

That the causes of action, or the portion of the cause of action, occurring prior to [106]

1. November 1, 1928, are barred by the provisions of Section 343 of the Code of Civil Procedure of the State of California;

2. November 1, 1929, are barred by the provisions of subdivision 4 of Section 338 of the Code of Civil Procedure of the State of California;

3. November 1, 1930, are barred by the provisions of subdivision 1 of Section 339 of the Code of Civil Procedure of the State of California.

Wherefore, this defendant prays judgment as hereinafter set forth.

Wherefore, this defendant prays judgment as follows:

1. That plaintiff take nothing by her complaint. In this respect the defendant offers, as it offered prior to the commencement of the action, to permit plaintiff to revoke the instrument of trust and it will thereupon deliver all of the trust property to plaintiff subject to the payment of this defendant's proper charges.

2. For costs of suit herein; and

3. For such other and further relief as to this
court may seem meet and proper in the premises.

CHARLES A. BEARDSLEY
N. W. DOBRZENSKY
CRELLIN FITZGERALD
JAMES H. ANGLIM
EDWARD B. KELLY,
Attorneys for the Defendant
Central Bank of Oakland.
[107]

State of California

County of Alameda—ss.

A. J. MOUNT, being first duly sworn, deposes
and says: That he is an officer, to-wit: President
of Central Bank of Oakland, a corporation, and
makes this verification for and on behalf of said
corporation; that he has read the foregoing answer
and knows the contents thereof; that the same is
true of his own knowledge except those matters
which are therein stated upon information or belief and as to those things so stated that he believes it to be true.

A. J. MOUNT.

Subscribed and sworn to before me this 30th day
of August, 1935.

[Seal]   CONSTANCE E. MULVANY,
Notary Public in and for the County of Alameda,
State of California.

Appendix C

ANSWER OF
CENTRAL NATIONAL BANK AND ITS RECEIVER

Appendix C

[Title of District Court and Cause.]

ANSWER OF DEFENDANTS CENTRAL NA-
TIONAL BANK OF OAKLAND, A NA-
TIONAL BANKING ASSOCIATION, AND
JOSEPH H. GRUT, AS RECEIVER
THEREOF.

Comes now the defendant, Joseph H. Grut, as Receiver of Central National Bank of Oakland, a
National Banking Association, and answers unto
plaintiff's complaint both for himself as Receiver
and for Central National Bank of Oakland, as
follows:

I.

Answering paragraph VII this defendant alleges
that it is without knowledge as to the period of
time plaintiff resided in Oakland, or as to whether
as such depositor or in any other manner or capacity plaintiff became well or otherwise acquainted
with Bothwell until the year 1926; this defendant
is without knowledge as to whether plaintiff reposed
in Bothwell or the bond department great, or any,
trust or confidence; denies that Bothwell knew that
plaintiff reposed in him or in the bond department
great or any, trust or confidence.

II.

Answering paragraph VIII this defendant alleges
that it is without knowledge as to whether plaintiff
was in poor health [110] during any of the times
mentioned in the complaint; this defendant is without knowledge as to whether plaintiff, prior to the

2

1st day of January, 1926, or at any other time except immediately prior to September 24th, 1929, intended to place her property, or any part thereof, in the type of trust referred to in paragraph VIII or in any other type of trust. This defendant is without knowledge as to whether or not on or about the 1st day of January, 1926,* or at any other time, except immediately prior to September 24th, 1929, plaintiff interviewed Bothwell or requested his advice as to whether or not it was advisable for her to carry out her alleged intention of placing her property, or any part thereof, in a trust, or that at said time, or at any time except immediately prior to September 24th, 1929, plaintiff interviewed Bothwell relative to placing her property, or any part thereof, in trust; is without knowledge as to whether plaintiff requested information from said Bothwell as to whether or not said national bank could or would act as trustee of such a trust; is without knowledge as to whether at said, or any time the said Bothwell advised plaintiff that to place her property in such, or any, trust was just the thing for her to do; this defendant is without knowledge as to whether said Bothwell advised plaintiff at any time that the national bank had a trust department, or advised her that a particular, or any, part of the business of said trust department was the taking care of property of widows or orphans; is without knowledge as to whether plaintiff at said, or any, time informed Bothwell of what her property consisted or that included in her property was a parcel

*Note: This date in the printed transcript of the record (R. 111) is the "1st day of *July*, 1926"; but this again is an obvious error in the date. The date should be the "1st day of *January*, 1926", and it so appears in the original complaint incorporated in the transcript of record on appeal.

of real property situated in the City of Reno, State of Nevada, or that she was desirous of selling said property; is without knowledge as to whether the said Bothwell at any time ever informed plaintiff that said national bank could not accept a conveyance to it [111] of real property situated in the State of Nevada; or that for that, or any other, reason the said Bothwell advised plaintiff that, pending the sale by her of said, or any other, parcel of real property, or the placing by her of her funds in a trust with said national bank as trustee, the thing for her to do was to invest her funds available for investment, or any of them, through the bond department in bonds; is without knowledge as to whether plaintiff accepted the advice of the said Bothwell in relation to creating a trust, or that plaintiff ever informed Bothwell that she would postpone the placing of her property in a trust with the national bank until after the sale by her of said parcel of real property, or ever informed Bothwell that she would postpone the placing of her property in a trust; is without knowledge as to whether plaintiff informed Bothwell that in the meantime, or at any other time, she would invest her funds, available for investment, or any of them, through the bond department in bonds; or as to whether plaintiff informed Bothwell that she had little experience with bonds; or as to whether plaintiff informed said Bothwell that if such, or any, investments were made she would have to rely upon him to purchase for her, through the bond department, or otherwise, or at all, safe or desirable bonds for the investment of her said funds; this defendant is without knowledge as to whether Bothwell assured plaintiff that her funds would be invested by the national bank, through him as manager of the bond department, or otherwise, or at all, in nothing but safe or desirable bonds for her; denies that plaintiff thereupon, or at any other time, told Bothwell that she desired her funds to be invested not only in safe bonds, but in bonds of such desirability that the same could be readily sold, at any time, so that she could thus get back the money which she [112] had invested in them, or that plaintiff, at any time, inquired of Bothwell whether or not her funds should be invested in bonds of the United States; denies that the said Bothwell replied that bonds of the United States paid a low rate of interest or that Bothwell assured her that her funds would be invested by the national bank, through him as the manager of the bond department, or otherwise, or at all, in bonds of the safety or desirability alleged to have been desired by her, or in bonds just as good as those of the United States, or paying a much larger rate of interest than was paid on bonds of the United States. In reference to the foregoing denials this defendant is informed, and believes, and therefore alleges that from time to time the said Bothwell may have informed plaintiff that bonds of the United States paid a low rate of interest and likewise advised plaintiff that in general it was a good rule to follow that the risk involved was in direct proportion to the amount of interest paid on bonds, that is to say, that the safest bonds usually paid a lower rate of interest than bonds which were not so well secured, or which were more apt to default. This defendant further alleges that from time to time plaintiff advised the said Bothwell that she was extremely anxious to get a high rate of return on her various investments.

III.

Answering paragraph IX this defendant alleges that it is without knowledge as to whether Bothwell used words of recommendation such as therein alleged, namely, "safe and desirable investments". This defendant is without knowledge as to whether plaintiff thereupon, or at any other time, informed Bothwell that she doubted the safety or desirability of bonds of the Province of Buenos Aires for the investment of her funds; or whether the said Bothwell assured or told plaintiff that the bonds of [113] said Province were well secured, or whether said Bothwell assured plaintiff that said bonds were a safe or desirable investment for plaintiff, or whether the doubts of plaintiff were dispelled by any such assurance of Bothwell and in this respect this defendant is informed, and believes, and therefore alleges that the said Bothwell in the case of the bonds of said Province of Buenos Aires, as well as in the case of all other bonds or notes sold by the bond department to plaintiff, merely recommended said bonds or notes basing said recommendation upon the best knowledge, information and belief of the national bank and of the said Bothwell. This defendant is without knowledge as to whether plaintiff relied upon the said, or any, recommendation of Bothwell. Denies that plaintiff approved the purchase for her by the national bank, through said Bothwell as manager of the bond department, or otherwise, or at all, of said bonds or notes, or any of them, and in this respect alleges that in none of the instances of the purchases of bonds or notes by plaintiff did the national bank, or Bothwell, or the bond department, purchase bonds for plaintiff or act for plaintiff in the purchase thereof (save that this defendant is informed and believes, and therefore alleges that in the case of the purchases of Pacific Gas and Electric Company bonds, San Joaquin Light & Power bonds, East Bay Municipal Utility bonds and Los Angeles Gas and Electric bonds referred to in paragraph XXI of the complaint, the trust department of said bank purchased said bonds for plaintiff's trust), but instead, as plaintiff well knew, sold bonds to plaintiff which the national bank either then owned and possessed, or had contracted to purchase or in the underwriting of which the national bank had participated or which were available to the national bank by reason of its participation in the underwriting thereof and that in all cases prior to the creation [114] of the trust hereinafter referred to plaintiff and the national bank were acting in the capacity of buyer and seller and not in the capacity of principal and agent. Denies that on or about the 1st day of January, 1926, or at any other time, Bothwell informed plaintiff that the purchase prices which she was paying for said bonds or notes, or any of them, were the purchase prices paid therefor by the national bank and in this respect this defendant alleges that in each and every instance of the purchase by plaintiff from said national bank of bonds or notes the prices at which they were sold to plaintiff were the then current market prices thereof, if they had an established market price, or a price commensurate with the fair and reasonable value thereof if they had no established market price. This defendant has no knowledge as to whether plaintiff intended, or that Bothwell, or this defendant, or the national bank knew that plaintiff intended, to place such, or any, bonds or notes so purchased in a trust with the national bank or that at any time except immediately prior to the execution of the trust instrument on September 24th, 1929, plaintiff intended, or Bothwell, or this defendant, or the national bank, knew that plaintiff intended, to place the bonds or notes, or any of them, so purchased from the national bank in a trust with the national bank as trustee, or as to whether Bothwell, or this defendant, or the national bank, knew that plaintiff intended to create said, or any, trust after she sold the real property situated in Reno, or knew that she intended to create a trust at any time until immediately prior to the time the trust was actually created, to-wit, September 24, 1929.

IV.

Answering paragraph X this defendant denies that during the year 1927, or at any other time, the national bank, through [115] Bothwell, as manager of the bond department, or through any other instrumentality, or person, made further, or any purchases for plaintiff of any bonds or notes. In this respect defendant alleges that the bonds referred to in said paragraph X of the complaint were sold by the national bank to plaintiff and that in such transaction plaintiff and the national bank were acting as buyer and seller, which fact was well known to plaintiff. This defendant is without knowledge as to whether in the instances of such, or any, further sales to plaintiff Bothwell recommended the bonds or notes therein referred to as safe or desirable investments. Denies that plaintiff informed Bothwell that she doubted the safety or desirability of bonds of the Province of Callao for the investment of her funds. Denies that Bothwell assured plaintiff that said bonds of the province of Callao were well secured or were a safe or desirable investment for her. Denies that the doubts of plaintiff were dispelled by any such assurances of the said Bothwell as is alleged in the complaint. Denies that plaintiff informed Bothwell that she doubted the safety or desirability of bonds of California Cotton Mills; denies that Bothwell assured her that said bonds of California Cotton Mills were safe or desirable investments. Denies that plaintiff's doubts were dispelled by any such assurance of the said

Bothwell as is alleged in the complaint. This defendant is without knowledge as to whether plaintiff relied upon any alleged recommendation of Bothwell in any instances of her purchases of bonds or notes. Denies that plaintiff approved the purchase for her by the said nation- [116] al bank through Bothwell, or otherwise, or at all, of said bonds or notes, or any of them, and in this respect alleges that in each instance referred to plaintiff purchased said bonds or notes from the national bank in the capacity of a buyer dealing with a seller. Denies that in any instance Bothwell ever informed plaintiff that the prices she was paying to purchase bonds or notes from the bank were the prices which the bank had paid for them when it acquired them.

V.

Answering paragraph XI this defendant alleges that it is without knowledge as to whether the real property situated in Reno was sold by plaintiff on or about the 8th day of February, 1928, and is, likewise, without knowledge as to whether plaintiff realized from said sale, over and above the expenses of said sale, the sum of $20,000.00 or whatever sum was received. Denies that thereafter during the year 1928, or during the year 1929, or until the 24th day of September, 1929, or at any other time, the national bank through Bothwell, as manager of the bond department, or through any other instrumentality, or otherwise, or at all, made still further purchases for plaintiff of bonds or notes, as safe or

desirable investments for plaintiff, or otherwise, or
at all, and in this respect alleges that in each of the
instances of the purchases of bonds or notes the national bank and plaintiff acted in the capacity of
buyer and seller, a fact well known to plaintiff
(save in the case of the purchase of Pacific Gas and
Electric Company bonds, San Joaquin Light and
Power bonds, East Bay Municipal Utility District
bonds and Los Angeles Gas and Electric bonds referred to in paragraph III hereof, in which case
the trust department of the national bank purchased
said bonds for plaintiff's trust). This defendant is
without knowledge as to what extent the further
[117] purchases referred to in paragraph XI of
the complaint were made with money realized by
plaintiff on the sale of the Reno property. This defendant is without knowledge as to whether in the
instances of the purchases referred to in paragraph XI of the complaint Bothwell recommended
the bonds or notes therein referred to to plaintiff
as safe or desirable investments. This defendant is
without knowledge as to whether plaintiff would
have doubted the safety or desirability of the bonds
of Medford Irrigation District for the investment
of her funds had not the said Bothwell informed
her in writing that said Bond Department had
"handled several hundred thousand dollars" of the
bonds of said District, and believed that said bonds
contained "all of the elements to make them a safe
and desirable investment"; or as to whether Bothwell so informed her, in writing or otherwise. This

defendant is without knowledge that plaintiff relied upon said alleged recommendation, or any recommendation. Denies that plaintiff approved said purchases, or any of said purchases, for her by said national bank acting through Bothwell, as manager of said bond department or otherwise, or at all, of said bonds or notes, or any of them, and in this respect alleges that in each of the instances of the purchase of bonds or notes referred to in paragraph XI of the complaint plaintiff and the national bank were acting in the capacity of buyer and seller, a fact well known to plaintiff. Denies that Bothwell or anyone else connected with the national bank informed plaintiff that the prices she was paying to purchase said bonds or notes from the national bank were the prices which the national bank had paid for them when it acquired them. [118]

VI.

Answering paragraph XII this defendant denies that the national bank in any of the instances therein referred to acted in the capacity of purchasing for plaintiff any bonds or notes whatsoever and in this respect alleges that in each instance of the purchase of any bonds or notes therein referred to plaintiff and the national bank acted in the capacity of buyer and seller, a fact well known to plaintiff. This defendant is without knowledge as to whether Bothwell recommended to plaintiff the bonds or notes therein referred to, or any of them as safe or desirable investments. This defendant is

without knowledge as to whether plaintiff relied
upon any alleged recommendation of Bothwell or
of any other person. Denies that plaintiff approved
the purchase for her by the national bank, through
Bothwell, as manager of the bond department or
otherwise, or at all, of the bonds or notes referred
to in paragraph XII of the complaint or any of
them, and in this respect alleges that in each instance therein referred to plaintiff and the national
bank acted in the capacity of buyer and seller, a
fact well known to plaintiff. Denies that in any
instance Bothwell, or anyone else, informed plaintiff that the prices she paid to the national bank
as the purchase price of bonds or notes from the
bank were the prices the national bank had paid
for them when it acquired them.

VII.

Answering paragraph XIII this defendant is
without knowledge as to whether said bonds or notes
or any of them mentioned in said paragraph were
retained on or were on deposit with the national
bank awaiting the time when the same would be assigned or transferred by plaintiff to the national
bank as trustee of the trusts in which it is alleged
plaintiff intended to place her property after the
sale of the parcel of property in Reno by [119]
pending execution of the trust instrument.

VIII.

Answering paragraph XIV this defendant denies
that any of the bonds or notes therein referred to

had been purchased for plaintiff by the national
bank, through Bothwell or anyone else, but instead
alleges that said bonds and notes were sold to plaintiff by the national bank, a fact well known to
plaintiff.

IX.

Answering paragraph XV this defendant alleges
that it is without knowledge to to when the parcel
of real property situated in Reno was sold or as
to whether on or about the 8th day of February,
1928, or at any other time until immediately prior
to September 24, 1929, plaintiff intended to place
her property in trust with the national bank, as
trustee, or whether plaintiff, due to her alleged continuing poor health, or for any other reason, was
disinclined to attend to any matter which required
any prolonged mental effort on her part, or was
disinclined to attend to the preparation of the instrument of trust referred to, or whether plaintiff
was referred by Bothwell to Read; or whether Bothwell referred plaintiff to Berven for particulars concerning the subject of the preparation of the trust
instrument or whether plaintiff was referred to
Berven by Bothwell for any purpose or under any
circumstances other than as stated in paragraph II
hereof. This defendant is without knowledge as to
whether Read seemed to plaintiff to be indifferent
about the preparation of the trust instrument or
about any other matter or whether plaintiff doubted
whether or not Read was interested in having the
national bank act as trustee or whether plaintiff's

mind was greatly or at all disturbed, or whether any progress was made by plaintiff toward the preparation of the trust instrument in the first [120] conference plaintiff had with Berven. In this respect, however, this defendant is informed and believes, and therefore, alleges, that some time later plaintiff interviewed Berven about creating a trust and at this time specifically informed Berven that she did not want the trust so to operate as to prevent her from controlling the investments and informed Berven that she wanted to be able to dictate the investments the trust department would make; that again, a few days later, plaintiff interviewed Berven and was informed by him that trust funds, under ordinary circumstances, can only be invested in certain types of securities which ordinarily did not bring a greater yield than five per cent (5%) and that plaintiff responded that she had to have a return of at least six per cent (6%) and directed that the trust instrument when drafted should contain a provision authorizing purchases of securities other than those legal for the investment of trust funds; plaintiff further informed Berven that she wished the trust department to deal with the bond department of the national bank when purchasing securities for the trust. Denies that the national bank or Bothwell made any purchases of bonds or notes for plaintiff as alleged in paragraph XV of the complaint and in this respect this defendant alleges that all further investments made by plaintiff at the time specified were made by plaintiff purchasing

from the national bank bonds and notes, plaintiff
and the national bank acting in the capacity of
buyer and seller, the national bank selling to plaintiff bonds and notes which it either then owned and
possessed or had contracted to purchase or in the
underwriting of which the national bank had participated or which were available to the national
bank by reason of its participation in the underwriting thereof. This defendant is without knowledge as to whether all of the funds which plaintiff
then possessed were invested in the purchase [121]
of bonds or notes from the national bank prior to
the execution of the trust. This defendant is without knowledge as to whether in the instances of the
purchases of bonds or notes referred to in paragraph XV of the complaint Bothwell recommended
to plaintiff the bonds or notes, or any of them, as
safe or desirable investments for plaintiff; or
whether said bonds or notes were recommended by
Bothwell. This defendant is without knowledge as
to whether plaintiff relied upon the recommendation of Bothwell in each or any of the instances
referred to in paragraph XV of the complaint. Denies that plaintiff approved further or any purchases for her by the national bank and in this
respect alleges that in each of said instances plaintiff and the national bank were acting in the
capacity of buyer and seller, a fact well known to
plaintiff. Denies that Bothwell, or anyone else, informed plaintiff that the prices she paid for said
bonds or notes were the prices which the national

bank had paid for them when it originally purchased them.

X.

Answering paragraph XVI this defendant denies that in each or any of the instances of the purchases of bonds or notes the national bank purchased said bonds or notes, or any of them, for plaintiff from itself and in this respect alleges that in each and every instance plaintiff and the national bank were acting in the capacity of buyer and seller. Denies that the national bank was acting as, or was, the purchaser of said bonds or notes, or any of them, from itself in the one capacity, for the plaintiff, and seller, in another capacity, to the plaintiff. In regard to the Fageol Motors Company and Alameda Investment Company bonds the national bank participated in the underwriting thereof. Denies that the Medford Irrigation District [122] bonds had depreciated to a price of $777.50 per bond at the time the national bank sold them to plaintiff and in this respect alleges that in the case of said bonds as in the case of all other bonds sold by the national bank to plaintiff the same were sold at the current market price, if they had an established market price, or at a price commensurate with the fair and reasonable value thereof, if they had no established market price. Denies that the profit to the Bank on said Medford transaction was the sum of $972.50, or any other sum whatsoever in excess of $72.50. Denies that thereby or in any other manner was the aggregate profit to the national bank in-

creased to $3,260.33 or to any other sum in excess
of $2,360.33. This defendant is without knowledge
as to whether plaintiff reposed any trust or confidence whatsoever in the said Bothwell; denies that
in violation of any trust or confidence which plaintiff reposed in said Bothwell, or in violation of any
other obligation owing by the national bank, or by
Bothwell to plaintiff, Bothwell did not disclose to
plaintiff, or concealed from her, that the national
bank was selling to plaintiff bonds or notes of which
it was the owner; denies that at any time the
national bank ever represented to plaintiff that it
was acting in the capacity of purchasing agent for
plaintiff; denies that in violation of any trust or
confidence which plaintiff might have reposed in
this defendant, the national bank, or in Bothwell,
or in violation of any other obligation whatsoever,
Bothwell did not disclose to plaintiff, or concealed
from her, the fact that the national bank made a
profit on each of the purchases and sales of bonds
or notes. Denies that plaintiff had no knowledge
that the national bank was selling to plaintiff bonds
and notes to which it was the owner; denies that
plaintiff did not discover such matters until the
time or under the circumstances [123] thereinafter
alleged in the complaint and in this respect this
defendant alleges that at all times plaintiff had
knowledge of the fact that the national bank was
selling her bonds and notes which it owned and was
making a profit thereon.

XI.

Answering paragraph XVIII this defendant denies that Berven told plaintiff her property would be absolutely protected or secure and in this respect said defendant is informed and believes and therefore alleges the facts to be that plaintiff inquired as to what would happen to the property in the trust in the event the national bank should fail and that Berven informed her that trust assets were not a part of the general assets of the bank, were segregated therefrom and would not be affected by any failure of the bank. This defendant is without knowledge as to whether plaintiff at any time reposed in Berven, or in Read, or in the trust department great, or any, trust or confidence; denies that Berven or Read knew that plaintiff reposed in them, or in the trust department, great, or any, trust or confidence. This defendant is without knowledge as to whether plaintiff delivered to Berven written data concerning the provisions desired by her to be inserted in the instrument of trust in relation to the matters therein referred to or that said alleged data was used in the preparation of the instrument of trust, or whether said instrument of trust was prepared for plaintiff to execute or was prepared by any member of or person associated with the firm of attorneys mentioned; or whether said data was delivered to said firm of attorneys; or whether said firm of attorneys performed any services in the preparation of said instrument of trust.

XII.

Answering paragraph XIX this defendant is informed and [124] believes and therefore alleges that not only did plaintiff read over the instrument of trust but also that the same was read to her paragraph by paragraph by Berven and each paragraph was fully explained to her and that palintiff stated that she understood not only the instrument of trust as a whole but also each of the paragraphs thereof. This defendant is further informed and believes and therefore alleges that plaintiff inquired of Berven if she should submit the trust instrument to her own attorneys to which Berven replied that it was eminently proper that she should do so; denies that Berven told plaintiff it was unnecessary for her to do so or that she was as well protected as the national bank. This defendenat is without knowledge as to whether, in so signing said statement, or in not seeking independent advice, or in executing said trust instrument, plaintiff relied upon the great, or any, trust or confidence which she is alleged to have reposed in Berven or whether she reposed any trust or confidence in him. This defendant has no knowledge as to whether said statement was prepared for her to sign or was prepared by the attorneys for the national bank, or by anyone associated with said attorneys.

XIII.

Answering paragraph XX this defendant denies that Berven acted in violation of the great, or any, trust or confidence which it is alleged plaintiff reposed in him in regard to any of the matters referred to in said paragraph XX. This defendant alleges that it is without knowledge as to whether plaintiff reposed great, or any, trust or confidence in Berven, or whether Berven did not inform plaintiff that the responsibilities or liabilities of the national bank, as trustee, otherwise imposed by law were restricted or limited, or were greatly restricted or limited, or [125] were attempted so to be, either by the trust instrument or by paragraphs I and VII of the trust instrument, or either of said paragraphs; or whether Berven did not inform plaintiff at the time she signed the statement at the foot of the instrument of trust that the restrictions and limitations were approved, ratified and confirmed, or were attempted so to be, by the said statement. This defendant is without knowledge as to whether or not Berven did inform her at that time that the powers of the national bank, as trustee, otherwise conferred by law, were greatly enlarged and extended by the provisions of paragraph II of the instrument of trust; or whether or not Berven informed plaintiff at said time that said powers were approved, ratified and confirmed by said statement; or whether or not plaintiff did not know or was never informed by anyone, until the time and under the circumstances alleged in the complaint that the responsibilities and liabilities were restricted and limited or that said powers were enlarged and extended or that the same were approved, ratified and confirmed by said statement. In this respect this defendant is informed, and believes, and therefore alleges, that at the time of the execution of the trust instrument and the statement at the foot thereof Berven informed plaintiff as to the matters complained of in said paragraph XX.

XIV.

Answering paragraphs XXI and XXII this defendant denies that in each or any of the first four instances mentioned in paragraph XXI either Read or Berven recommended the bonds or notes, or any of them, so purchased as safe or desirable, or made any recommendation concerning said bonds or notes, or any of the them. This defendant is without knowledge as to whether Bothwell re- [126] commended said bonds or notes, or any of them, as safe or desirable, or whether Bothwell recommended said bonds; this defendant alleges that it is without knowledge as to whether plaintiff relief upon said recommendation. This defendant is without knowledge as to whether plaintiff reposed in Bothwell, or in Read, or in Berven, great, or any, trust or confidence. Denies that either Bothwell, or Read, or Berven, did not disclose to, or concealed from, plaintiff that through them, or any of them, the national bank had purchased from itself, or sold to itself, said bonds or any of them or that the bank had profited in such, or any, of said instances; denies that plaintiff had no knowledge of such facts, or any of them, or that plaintiff did not discover them, until the time, or under the circumstances, alleged in the complaint. This defendant is informed, and believes, and therefore alleges, that in each of the four instances of said purchases of bonds in the year 1930, namely, the instances of said purchases from and including the 8th day of April, 1930, to and including the 27th day of June, 1930, plaintiff dealt directly with Bothwell, as manager of the bond department, and directed the trust department of the national bank to purchase from the bond department said bonds and notes and in each of said instances plaintiff well knew that the trust department of the national bank was making said purchases of bonds from the bond department. This defendant further alleges that it was at plaintiff's express instance and direction that the trust department of the national bank made said purchases, and all of them, from the bond department; that due to plaintiff's own wishes she in effect and in reality acted as the principal in these transactions insofar as the trust department of the national bank was concerned and directed [127] said trust department as to the investments she desired it to make. Denies that either Bothwell, or Read, or Berven, failed to disclose to, or concealed from, plaintiff the fact that the national bank had purchased from itself the bonds mentioned in the first four (4) instances referred to in said paragraphs XXI and XXII. Denies that any of said persons concealed from plaintiff the fact that the national bank had profited in each, or any, of the first four (4) instances mentioned. Denies that plaintiff had no knowledge of any or all of said alleged facts complained of or did not discover the same until the time and under the circumstances alleged in the complaint and in this respect this defendant alleges that at all times plaintiff had knowledge of all of the matters complained of in said paragraphs XXI and XXII immediately upon their occurrence save that this defendant is without knowledge as to whether plaintiff knew of the amount of profit made in said first four (4) instances mentioned.

XV.

Answering paragraph XXIV of the complaint this defendant denies that any of the bonds or notes therein listed which were acquired by plaintiff prior to the execution of the instrument of trust were purchased by the national bank from itself and in this respect alleges that in all instances such bonds or notes were sold by the national bank to plaintiff, a fact well known to her.

XVI.

Answering paragraph XXV this defendant denies that in any instance prior to the execution of the trust the national bank purchased through Bothwell, as manager of the bond department, or otherwise, or at all, or through anyone else, any bonds or notes for plaintiff but instead alleges that the national bank sold [128] them to her; denies that

any of said bonds or notes were sold to plaintiff as
safe or desirable investments or that any guaranty
or assurance was made as to the safety or desirability thereof. Denies that said $1,000.00 par value
of bonds of California Cotton Mills were purchased
or were recommended as a safe or desirable investment; denies that said bond was recommended by
the trust department or by said national bank as a
safe or desirable investment for plaintiff or for
said trusts and in this respect this defendant is informed and believes and therefore alleges that from
time to time Berven pointed out to plaintiff that
the purchases she made were not of the kind usually
acquired for trusts.

XVII.

Answering paragraph XXVI this defendant denies that any of the fourteen (14) blocks of bonds
or notes first referred to in paragraph XXIV of
the complaint were purchased by the national bank
for plaintiff or for her trusts; denies that any of
the bonds or notes referred to in paragraph XXIV
were not, at the time when sold to plaintiff, or to
her trust, safe or desirable taking into consideration
the yield on said bonds and notes; admits that said
bonds and notes were not of the type in which trust
funds were or are usually invested and in this
respect this defendant is informed and believes and
therefore alleges, that this was called to plaintiff's
attention before, at the time of, and after, the execution of the trust instrument but that plaintiff insisted on retaining such investments and also, after
the execution of the trust instrument, plaintiff

insisted on purchasing the first three (3) of the
seven (7) blocks of bonds secondly referred to in
paragraph XXIV. This defendant is informed and
believes, and therefore alleges, that the trust department [129] of the national bank from time to
time admonished plaintiff after the creation of the
trust that the securities which she then had on hand
in said trust or which she thereafter recommended
be purchased by the trust department from the bond
department were not legal investments for savings
banks or for trust funds and advised her that her
trust funds should be invested in bonds, which,
though paying a lower rate of interest and yielding
a lower return, were deemed more conservative and
better secured. Denies that any of said bonds or
notes save the first three (3) of the seven (7) blocks
of said bonds secondly referred to in paragraph
XXIV were purchased by the national bank from
itself. Denies that said bonds, or any of them, insofar as the same are purported to be secured by
real property, were, at the respective times of the
purchases thereof, or at any other time, grossly
insufficiently secured, or were or are insufficiently
secured. Denies that said notes, or any of them,
insofar as the same are purported to be secured by
real property or by personal property were not, at
the respective times of the purchases thereof, or at
any other time, secured by first mortgages of real
property, if they purported to be so secured, or that
they were not, when purchased or that they never
since have been, either secured by personal prop-

erty, if they purported to be so secured, or that, if so secured, they have been or ever were secured by personal property of no value or without substantial value; denies that the bonds of the Province of Buenos Aires or of the Province of Callao were, when purchased, uncollectible. This defendant is without knowledge as to whether said bonds, or any of them, since the purchase thereof by plaintiff have been, or now are, uncollectible; denies that the bonds of Medford Irrigation District never have been secured by any [130] lien upon any real property, or upon any other property, and in this respect alleges that said bonds were fully secured and were a lien upon the entire real property in the Medford Irrigation District by virtue of the fact that they were payable out of assessments levied upon and which were a lien upon all real property situated in said District; denies that the notes of Jackson Furniture Company have never been secured by any lien upon any property of any kind. This defendant has no knowledge as to whether at the respective times when purchases of bonds or notes were made anyone connected with the national bank recommended any of the bonds or notes purchased by plaintiff or by the trust department as safe or desirable bonds or notes; denies that plaintiff was at any time ignorant of the difference between said notes and bonds so purchased and the safety and desirability of the same for which her funds or the funds of said trust should have been invested and in this respect this defendant is informed and believes, and therefore alleges that plaintiff was cautioned and admonished from time to time that the investments she was making carried with them a certain element of risk in that she sought to obtain the highest return possible on her investments.

XVIII.

Answering paragraph XXIX this defendant has no knowledge as to whether the national bank either through Read, or Berven, or through anyone else, on any occasion, save as hereinafter alleged, told plaintiff not to worry about the defaults or any of them or told plaintiff that said bonds or notes, or any of them, were well secured or that interest would eventually be paid. In this respect this defendant is informed and believes, and therefore alleges that prior to November 1, 1932, in speaking of [131] Alameda Park Bonds, Berven told plaintiff that these bonds appeared to be protected by sufficient property but that plaintiff could look at the property herself and satisfy herself as to the adequacy of the security. This defendant is without knowledge as to whether plaintiff reposed great, or any, trust or confidence in Berven, or in the trust department, or in Bothwell, or in the bond department; denies that Berven told plaintiff that the bonds or notes, or any of them, were well secured or that interest would be paid. Denies that at the time of said call Berven recommended to plaintiff that the bonds and notes, or any of them, referred to in paragraph XXIX of the complaint, save Alameda Investment Company bonds, be sold, or that the proceeds of the sales, or any part thereof, be invested in better bonds. In this respect this defendant is informed and believes, therefore alleges that before, at the time of, and subsequent to, the execution of the trust instrument Berven from time to time recommended to plaintiff that she sell a portion of her bonds and notes and invest the proceeds in bonds paying a lower interest rate but plaintiff refused to do so or to permit the same to be done. This defendant is without knowledge as to whether any bonds or notes were recommended to plaintiff as safe or desirable. Denies that the total prices for which said bonds and notes could have been sold at that time was only $28,860.00. Denies that the loss had said bonds and notes then been sold would have exceeded or been anywhere near as great as sixty-seven per cent (67%) of the total cost of said bonds and notes; denies that any prices were then computed or estimated as alleged in the complaint. In this respect this defendant is informed, and believes, and therefore alleges that said bonds and notes could have been sold for a price greatly in excess of $28,860.00, the exact price being unknown to [132] this defendant because of the fact that many of said bonds and notes were unlisted and had no established market prices at that time; this defendant is informed and believes, and therefore alleges, further that the majority of said bonds and notes were then of a value greatly in excess of the price that could then have been realized on a sale thereof and, further, that the majority of said bonds and notes have greatly increased in price and value since November 1, 1932.

XIX.

Answering paragraph XXX this defendant alleges that it is without knowledge as to whether upon the said conversation with Berven, the great, or any, trust or confidence, if any, which plaintiff is alleged theretofore to have reposed in Bothwell, or in the bond department, or in Berven, or in the trust department of the national bank was completely, or at all, shattered or ended. In this respect this defendant alleges that it is without knowledge as to whether plaintiff reposed any trust or confidence at any time in Bothwell, or in the bond department, or in Berven, or in the trust department. This defendant is without knowledge as to whether the examination by plaintiff's attorney continued, only with the interruptions mentioned in said complaint, up to the time of filing of the action, or whether said examination involved the inspection by said attorney of a large number of documents or other records of the national bank; or whether plaintiff was financially unable to employ an accountant to assist said attorney in his examination and in this respect this defendant alleges that at all times the Central Bank of Oakland and the national bank and the Conservator and Receiver thereof, furnished said attorney with detailed information in writing as required by him and in such form that the services of an account- [133] ant were not needed. This

defendant alleges that all information sought by
plaintiff's attorney was immediately laid before him
in both detailed and summarized form as requested
and that it was only necessary for said attorney to
verify said information which he and his assistants
did in approximately two (2) visits to the national
bank which, at the outside limit, took in all one day
to complete. This defendant is without knowledge
as to whether said examination was interrupted by
the closing of the national bank, or by the appointment of A. J. Mount, as Conservator of the national
bank, or by the appointment of this answering defendant, Joseph H. Grut, as Receiver of the national
bank, or by the proceedings relating to the sale of
the business of the trust department of the national
bank to Central Bank of Oakland, or by the delay
in the appointment of an attorney for this answering defendant, as Receiver of the national bank, or
by negotiations between plaintiff's attorney and the
attorneys for this answering defendant, or by negotiations between plaintiff's attorney and the attorney for the defendant, Central Bank of Oakland,
relating to a settlement of the claims of plaintiff
involved in the complaint or relating to a settlement
of any other claims; denies that the fourteen (14)
blocks of bonds or notes first listed in paragraph
XXIV of the complaint were purchased for plaintiff by the national bank, or through Bothwell, or
through anyone else, and in this respect alleges that
said fourteen (14) blocks of bonds and notes were
sold by the bond department of the national bank to

plaintiff, a fact well known by her. This defendant is without knowledge as to whether after said negotiations came to an end plaintiff's attorney has been actively or at [134] all engaged in the preparation of the complaint.

XX.

Answering paragraph XXXI this defendant denies that the attorney for plaintiff ever discovered that there were, and also denies that there were, any purchases of the fourteen (14) blocks of bonds or notes, or any of them, first described in paragraph XXIV of the complaint for plaintiff by the national bank through Bothwell, as manager of the bond department, or otherwise, or at all, or that said purchases, or any of them, had been made from the national bank by the national bank for plaintiff, or that the national bank was the purchaser as well as the seller of said fourteen (14) blocks of bonds or notes, or any of them, and in this respect this defendant alleges that in each and every instance the national bank sold said fourteen (14) blocks of bonds or notes to plaintiff, the parties acting in the capacity of buyer and seller, a fact well known to plaintiff. Admits that after the erection of the trust the first three (3) of the seven (7) blocks of bonds or notes secondly set forth in paragraph XXIV of the complaint were purchased by the trust department of the national bank from the bond department thereof but alleges that this fact was well known to plaintiff and was done at her express instance and request. This defendant alleges

that it is without knowledge as to whether plaintiff's
attorney, from time to time, or at any time, informed plaintiff of any alleged discoveries; denies
that any of said alleged discoveries were made by
him; denies the existence of said facts alleged to
have been discovered. This defendant is without
knowledge as to whether plaintiff's attorney advised
plaintiff, from time to time, or at any time, that it
was necessary that she should have had independent
advice in relation to the instrument of trust before
[135] she executed the same, or that the responsibilities or liabilities of the national bank as trustee
of the trusts declared in and by the instrument of
trust, otherwise imposed by law upon said national
bank, as trustee, were greatly, or at all, restricted
or limited, or were attempted so to be, by the provisions of paragraphs I or VII, or by any other
provisions, of said instrument of trust, or that said
attorney informed plaintiff that the restrictions or
limitations, or any of them, were approved, or ratified, or confirmed, or were attempted so to be, by
the statement signed by her at the foot of said instrument, or otherwise, or at all, or that the powers
of the national bank, as trustee of the trusts declared in and by the instrument of trust, otherwise
conferred by the law upon the national bank, as
such trustee, were greatly, or at all, enlarged or
extended, or were attempted so to be by the provisions in paragraph II of said instrument of trust,
or by any other provisions of said trust instrument,
or that said powers were approved, or ratified, or

confirmed, or were attempted so to be, by said statement signed by plaintiff, or that said attorney informed plaintiff that none of the fourteen (14) blocks of bonds and notes first referred to in paragraph XXIV of the complaint, or of the first three (3) of the seven (7) blocks of said bonds or notes secondly referred to in said paragraph XXIV were when purchased of the alleged safety or desirability alleged. Denies that any of the fourteen (14) blocks of said bonds or notes first referred to were purchased for plaintiff and in this respect alleges that all of said fourteen (14) blocks were sold by the national bank to plaintiff, a fact well known to plaintiff; this defendant is without knowledge as to whether Bothwell, or anyone else connected with the national bank, assured plaintiff of the safety [136] or desirability of any of said bonds or notes; denies that any of said bonds or notes when sold by the national bank to plaintiff, or, in the case of the first three (3) of the seven (7) blocks of said bonds or notes secondly referred to in paragraph XXIV of the complaint, when sold by the bond department of the national bank to the trust department, were not of such type or so secured as not to justify the recommendations given plaintiff. In this respect this defendant is informed and believes, and therefore alleges that the said Berven, as assistant trust officer of the national bank, from time to time admonished plaintiff that the bonds or notes which she was insisting be purchased by the trust department from the bond department as trust investments, were not of the type usually acquired as a trust investment, but that in each and every instance of such admonition plaintiff emphatically stated that she desired such investments to be made.

Second Separate Defense.

As a further, second and separate defense this defendant alleges:

I.

That the complaint does not state facts sufficient to constitute a cause of action.

Wherefore, this defendant prays judgment as hereinafter set forth.

Third Separate Defense.

As a further, third and separate defense this defendant alleges:

I.

That paragraph VII of the trust instrument (Exhibit "A" attached to the complaint) provides that the trustor, plaintiff, [137] reserves the power to revoke the trusts therein created subject to the payment to the trustee of all sums then due to it and that thereupon the trustee shall be fully released and discharged of all then existing liabilities and obligations of every kind and nature affecting the trust property or the trustee in relation thereto; that this defendant is informed and believes, and therefore alleges that prior to the commencement of this suit the defendant, Central Bank of Oakland, being then the successor trustee, offered to permit plaintiff to revoke the trust and the instrument of trust and to deliver all of the trust properties to plaintiff and offered to agree that such revocation should not be a release or discharge of existing liabilities and obligations of this defendant to plaintiff, if any. That plaintiff refused such offer.

Wherefore, this defendant prays judgment as hereinafter set forth.

Fourth Separate Defense.

As a further, fourth and separate defense this defendant alleges:

I.

That the bill of complaint does not contain a short or simple statement of the ultimate facts upon which the plaintiff asks relief.

Wherefore, this defendant prays judgment as hereinafter set forth.

Fifth Separate Defense.

As a further, fifth and separate defense this defendant alleges:

I.

That said complaint is multifarious in that it has too [138] large a scope and embraces more than one subject matter uniting several purported causes of action without separately stating them, as follows:

1. A purported cause of action, or series of causes of action, alleged to arise by reason of alleged false or fraudulent representations of the national bank as to the safety and desirability of certain

bonds and notes specifically described in the complaint as investments for plaintiff and her trust.

2. A purported cause of action, or series of causes of action, alleged to arise by reason of the alleged fact that the national bank purchased said bonds and notes for plaintiff from itself without plaintiff's knowledge and thereby acted in a dual capacity and also made a secret profit thereon.

3. A purported cause of action by reason of the alleged fact that the execution of the trust instrument was procured through the national bank by fraud or by violation of trust and confidence reposed by plaintiff in said national bank.

Wherefore, the defendant prays judgment as hereinafter set forth.

Sixth Separate Defense.

As a further, sixth and separate defense this defendant alleges:

I.

That the causes of action, or the portion of the cause of action, occurring prior to

1. November 1, 1928, are barred by the provisions of Section 343 of the Code of Civil Procedure of the State of California;

2. November 1, 1929, are barred by the provisions of subdivision 4 of Section 338 of the Code of Civil Procedure of [139] the State of California;

3. November 1, 1930, are barred by the provisions of subdivision 1 of Section 339 of the Code of Civil Procedure of the State of California.

Wherefore, this defendant prays judgment as hereinafter set forth.

Wherefore, this defendant prays judgment as follows:

1. That plaintiff take nothing by her complaint.

2. For costs of suit herein; and

3. For such other and further relief as to this court may seem meet and proper in the premises.

FRANK S. RICHARDS

Solicitor for Defendant, Joseph H. Grut, as Receiver of Central National Bank of Oakland, a national banking association in liquidation. [140]

State of California,
County of Alameda—ss.

Joseph H. Grut, being first duly sworn, deposes and says:

That he is one of the defendants in the above entitled action; that he has read the foregoing Answer and knows the contents thereof, and that the same is true of his own knowledge, except as to those matters which are therein stated on information or belief, and as to those matters, that he believes it to be true.

JOSEPH H. GRUT

Subscribed and sworn to before me this 30th day of August, 1935.

[Seal]   LOUISE M. SPERRY
Notary Public in and for the County of Alameda, State of California.

Appendix D

**AMENDMENTS
AND SUPPLEMENTS TO COMPLAINT**

Appendix D

[Title of District Court and Cause.]
AMENDMENTS AND SUPPLEMENTS TO BILL OF COMPLAINT

The plaintiff, by leave of Court first had and obtained, files these her amendments and supplements to her bill of complaint, and alleges as follows:

I.

That on the 10th day of June, 1933, the plaintiff addressed and delivered a letter to the defendant Central Bank of Oakland, and on the 12th day of June, 1933, the proposal, as contained in the said letter, was accepted by the defendant Central Bank of Oakland, by a writing at the foot of the said letter; and that a copy of the said letter, and of the said writing at the foot thereof, is hereunto, annexed, and marked "Exhibit A", and the same is hereby referred to and made a part hereof.

II.

That, since the filing of the said bill of com- [150] plaint on, to wit, the 22d day of August, 1933, bonds and notes, referred to in the said bill of complaint, constituting a part of the estate then held by the defendant Central Bank of Oakland, as trustee of the trusts declared in the indenture of trust, dated the 24th day of September, 1929, referred to in the said bill of complaint, of the respective designations and par values hereinafter alleged, have been sold by the defendant Central Bank of Oakland, pursuant to the said letter and to the said acceptance of the said proposal, and with the approval of the attorneys for the plaintiff, or have matured, or have been redeemed, as the case may be; and that the respective amounts for which the said bonds and notes have been so sold, and the respective amounts payable on such maturities and redemptions, as the case may be, have respectively been paid to the defendant Central Bank of Oakland, on the respective dates, and in the respective amounts, and of the total sum of $32,744.40, as follows:

Par Value	Bonds		Dates	Amounts
$10,000	Alameda Investment Co.	sold	Aug. 17, 1933	$ 3,996.
3,000	Hearst Publications, Inc.	matured	Nov. 1, 1933	3,000.
3,000	Hearst Publications, Inc.	matured	Nov. 1, 1934	3,000.
4,000	Miller & Lux, Inc.	sold	Apr. 2, 1935	3,038.40
1,000	Hearst Publications, Inc.	sold	Apr. 6, 1935	970.
5,000	Medford Irrigation District	sold	Apr. 10, 1935	2,000.
6,000	California Cotton Mills Co.	sold	Nov. 6, 1935	6,390.
5,000	Jackson Furniture Co.	redeemed	Feb. 1, 1936	5,050.
5,000	Los Angeles Gas & Electric Co.	redeemed	Mar. 1, 1935	5,300.
$42,000				$32,744.40

III.

That, since the filing of the said bill of com- [151] plaint, installments of the principal of the promissory note of Sparks Masonic Building Association, referred to in the said bill of complaint, and constituting a part of the said trust estate, of the total sum of $3,000, have matured, and have been paid to the defendant Central Bank of Oakland, on the respective dates, and in the respective amounts, as follows: On May 28, 1934, the sum of $2,000, for the said installments maturing on the 1st day of June, 1933, and on the 1st day of June, 1934, respectively; and on June 1, 1935, the sum of $1,000.

IV.

That, prior to the filing of the said bill of complaint, Fageol Motors Company, referred to in the said bill of complaint, so-called "debenture bonds", of which, of the par value of $10,000, constituted a part of the said trust estate, was duly adjudged a bankrupt by the above entitled District Court of the United States, and a receiver of the estate of the said bankrupt was duly appointed by the said Court; that, prior to the filing of the said bill of complaint, but unknown to the plaintiff at the time of the filing of the said bill of complaint, and on August 19, 1933, there was paid to the defendant Central Bank of Oakland a dividend in liquidation on the said debenture bonds, of the sum of $2,178.18, and that thereafter, on January 13, 1934, and on January 16, 1935, respectively, there were also paid to the defendant Central Bank of Oakland respective additional dividends in liquidation, of the respective sums of $418.70 and $329.20, or a total sum of $2,926.08, and the plaintiff is informed and believes, and according to such information and belief alleges, that a final dividend in liquidation, not to exceed the sum of $100, may be paid to the defendant Central Bank of Oakland in the near future. [152]

V.

That the said sums so paid to the defendant Central Bank of Oakland are now held on deposit to the credit of the said trust estate by the defendant Central Bank of Oakland, as trustee of the said trusts.

VI.

That, since the filing of the said bill of complaint, the defendant Central Bank of Oakland, and pursuant to the said letter and to the said acceptance of the said proposal, has collected the interest on bonds and notes and on the said promissory note of the said Sparks Masonic Building Association, held by the defendant Central Bank of Oakland, as trustee of the said trusts, amounting to the total sum of $7,747.20; and that the respective dates when the said interest on the said bonds and notes, and the respective amounts of the said interest so collected on the said bonds and notes, and the respective dates when the said interest on the said promissory note of the said Sparks Masonic Building Association, and the respective amounts of the said interest so collected on the said promissory note, are shown on an exhibit hereunto annexed, and marked "Exhibit B", and the same is hereby referred to and made a part hereof.

VII.

That, since the filing of the said bill of complaint, the defendant Central Bank of Oakland, and pursuant to the said letter and to the said acceptance of the said proposal, has paid to the plaintiff the said interest so collected, when and as the same was so collected, after deducting therefrom, pursuant to the said letter and to the said acceptance of the said proposal, as and for the compensation of the defendant Central Bank of Oakland, as trustee of the said trusts, 3% of the said interest so collected, [153] or the total sum of $270.01, and that the said rate of compensation was the usual rate theretofore charged by the defendant Central National Bank of

Oakland and by the defendant Central Bank of Oakland for the respective services thereof, as respective trustees of the said trusts, on the collection of the interest on bonds and notes and on the said note of the said Sparks Masonic Building Association, respectively, constituting respective portions of the said trust estate.

Wherefore, the plaintiff prays judgment as follows: (1), that the said instrument of trust be rescinded and set aside; (2), that the defendant Central Bank of Oakland reconvey to the plaintiff, by a deed thereof, properly executed by it and acknowledged in its behalf, the unimproved lot, referred to in the said bill of complaint, situated in the City of Oakland, County of Alameda, State of California, and reassign to the plaintiff, by an instrument of reassignment thereof, properly executed by it and acknowledged in its behalf, the said promissory note and the said mortgage securing the same executed to the plaintiff by the said Sparks Masonic Building Association; (3), that the defendant Central Bank of Oakland pay to the plaintiff the sum of $80,642.50, and also pay to the plaintiff the sum of $22,285.75, or the total sum of $102,926.25, all referred to in the said bill of complaint; (4), that the total sum of $35,670.48, paid as aforesaid to the defendant Central Bank of Oakland for the said bonds and notes which have been respectively sold, matured or redeemed, and as dividends in liquidation, as aforesaid, and, in addition thereto, the said sum of $3,000, paid as aforesaid to the defendant Central Bank of Oakland for installments which had matured on the said promissory note of the said Sparks Masonic Building Association, or the grand total sum of $38,-670.48, now held, as aforesaid, by the defendant Central [154] Bank of Oakland, as trustee of the said trusts, on deposit to the credit of the said trust estate, be charged with a lien for the repayment to the plaintiff of the said total sum of $102,926.25; (4), that an accounting be had of the respective amounts of the funds of the plaintiff invested by the defendant Central National Bank of Oakland in bonds or notes for the plaintiff, and of the respective dates on which the said respective amounts were so invested, aggregating the said sum of $102,926.25, and that interest, at the rate of seven (7) per cent. per annum, be charged against the defendant Central Bank of Oakland on the said respective amounts, from the respective dates when the said funds were so invested by the defendant Central National Bank of Oakland to the date of the filing of the decree herein, less the respective payments of interest made to the plaintiff by the defendant Central National Bank of Oakland and the defendant Central Bank of Oakland, respectively, hereinabove and in the said bill of complaint referred to; (5), that, in the event it be adjudged and decreed that the defendant Central Bank of Oakland should not pay to the plaintiff the said sum of $80,642.50, then that it be adjudged and decreed that a claim of the plaintiff therefor, together with interest thereon, determined and computed as aforesaid, be established as a claim of the plaintiff against the defendant Central National Bank of Oakland, and that the same, as so established, together with interest thereon, at the rate aforesaid, from the date of the filing of the decree herein until the same shall have been paid to the plaintiff, be paid by the defendant Joseph H. Grut, as the receiver of the defendant Central National Bank of Oakland, in due course of his administration, or that he certify the same to the Comptroller of the Currency of the United States to be similarly paid; and (6), that the plaintiff have and recover her costs from the defendants, and have and recover [155] from the defendants, or from such thereof, such further, other and different relief as may be equitable and just in the premises.

CHARLES W. SLACK and
EDGAR T. ZOOK,
Attorneys for the Plaintiff. [156]

"EXHIBIT A"

San Francisco, California,
June 10, 1933.

To Central Bank of Oakland,
 formerly Central Savings Bank of Oakland,
 Oakland, California.

Dear Sirs:

Since the employment by me about December 1, 1932, of Messrs. Charles W. Slack and Edgar T. Zook, as my attorneys, for the purpose of making an examination of and advising me in relation to the instrument of trust, dated September 24, 1929, entered into between myself, as trustor, and Central National Bank of Oakland, as trustee, and in relation to various purchases of bonds made by the said National Bank for me prior to the said instrument and specifically included therein, and in relation to various purchases of bonds made by the said National Bank for me subsequent to the said instrument and as trustee under the said instrument, a considerable amount of time has been expended by my said attorneys in making the said examination, and my said attorneys have informed me that the said examination has not yet been completed by them. Much of the delay in completing the said examination, so my said attorneys have informed me, has been due to the holidays declared by proclamation of the Governor of the State, to the bank holidays declared by proclamation of the President of the United States, to the appointment by the Comptroller of the Currency, first, of a conservator, and, later, of a receiver for the said National Bank, and to the sale by the said National Bank and by its said conservator to, and the purchase by yourselves from, the said National Bank and its said conservator, pursuant to an agreement, dated April 22, 1933, between the said National Bank and its said conservator and yourselves, of the business of the Trust Department of the said National Bank, including all court and private trusts.

Commencing on about December 1, 1932, and continuing until on or about the date of the said sale and purchase of the said business, the said National Bank, and, since on or about the date of the said sale and purchase of the said business, you have made collections of interest on securities held by the said National Bank and by yourselves, respectively, as respective trustees under the said instrument, and have made expenditures, as such respective trustees, from the said collections, and you have furnished my said attorneys, under date of June 5, 1933, with a statement of collections and expenditures so respectively made. Included in the said expenditures are moneys either deposited to my credit in my commercial account in the said National Bank, or for which the said National Bank and yourselves have issued respective checks to me. Most of the moneys so deposited I have withdrawn and at least one of the checks I have cashed. I have done this for the reason that I was and am in urgent need of funds and have no source of income other than from the securities held under the said instrument.

Since on or about December 1, 1932, there have been [157] defaults in the payment of the interest on several of the securities held under the said instrument, and I have been requested by the said National Bank and by yourselves, respectively, to consent to the taking of such action by the said National Bank and by yourselves, respectively, in relation to some of such defaults, as was deemed by the said National Bank and by yourselves, respectively, to be advisable, but thus far, acting under the advice of my said attorneys, I have not complied with any such request.

I have instructed my said attorneys that, after they have obtained the further information desired by them in relation to the said purchases of securities prior and subsequent to the said instrument, to effect, if possible, a settlement satisfactory to me, without litigation, of my claims in relation to and involving the said purchases and the said instrument, but that if such a settlement is not effected, to commence and prosecute such legal proceedings as my said attorneys shall deem to be appropriate and necessary to enforce and protect what they and I believe to be my rights in the premises.

Pending such settlement and the determination, (if such settlement is not effected), of such legal proceedings, and because I do not wish to run the risk of being charged with any laches, in the past or in the future, in making the said examination and in acting promptly upon the information obtained by me, through my said attorneys, therefrom, or to run the risk of being charged with any estoppel in the receipt and use by me, in the past or in the future, of income from the securities held under the said instrument, and in order to avoid possible loss through inaction on my part in relation to the said defaults, which have already occurred, and to similar defaults which may hereafter occur, I hereby propose to you that, pending such further examination and pending efforts to effect such settlement without legal proceedings, and pending the determination of such legal proceedings, (if such settlement is not effected), you shall continue to collect the said interest and other moneys which may now be due, or which may hereafter become due, on the said securities and to make therefrom such usual expenditures and deductions as are indicated in the said statement above referred to, and to pay me the balance of the income so collected, monthly, so far as possible, in order that I may make use thereof for my needs, which are urgent, and you shall take such steps and do such things as you shall deem to be necessary or proper, with the approval, so far as possible, of my said attorneys, in relation to the said defaults which have already occurred and in relation to similar defaults which may hereafter occur, including the deposit of the said securities under reorganization agreements and plans, in order that the loss by reason of such defaults may be minimized, so far as possible, it being understood that, in the efforts to effect the said settlement and in the said legal proceedings, (if such settlement is not effected), I shall not be charged with any laches or with any estoppel and that such rights as you and I, respectively, may have in the premises shall not be prejudiced by the course of conduct on our respective parts as above outlined.

If you agree to the foregoing proposal, please sign your acceptance thereof on a duplicate of this letter and deliver such duplicate, so signed, to my said attorneys.

Yours, etc.,

ABBIE W. QUINN [158]
Oakland, California,
June 12, 1933.

The foregoing proposal is hereby accepted.
CENTRAL BANK OF OAKLAND,
By EDW. GEARY
Vice Pres. & Trust Officer [159]

"EXHIBIT B"

Interest collected on bonds and notes.

Dates			Amounts
September	1,	1933,	$ 300.00
November	1,	"	218.75
December	1,	"	60.
January	2,	1934,	287.50
March	1,	"	300.00
April	3,	'	20.00
May	1,	'	125.00
June	1,	'	60.00
July	2,	'	287.50
September	1,	"	300.00
October	8,	"	20.00
October	19,	"	856.70
November	1,	"	125.00
November	16,	"	290.70
December	1,	"	60.00
December	11,	"	161.48
January	2,	1935,	287.50
March	1,	"	300.00
April	6,		26.39
April	24,		20.00
June	1,		60.00
July	1,	'	287.50
September	3,	"	300.00
October	28,	"	20.00
November	29,	"	150.00
December	2,	"	60.00
December	18,	"	227.28

January	2, 1936,	162.50
January	3, "	125.00
January	10, "	568.40

$6,067.20

Interest collected on promissory note of
Sparks Masonic Building Association

Dates		Amounts
December	4, 1933,	$ 385.00
May	28, 1934,	385.00
November	26, "	315.00
June	1, 1935,	315.00
November	12, "	280.00

$1,680.00

Due service of the within is hereby admitted this
6th day of February, 1936.

> FITZGERALD, ABBOTT &
> BEARDSLEY
> By EDMUND B. KELLY
> Atty. for Defendant Central Bank
> of Oakland
> FRANK S. RICHARDS
> Attorney for Central National Bank
> and Jos. H. Grut, Receiver

[Endorsed]: Filed Feb. 6, 1936. [160]

Appendix E

SUPPLEMENTS TO ANSWER
OF NATIONAL BANK AND ITS RECEIVER

Appendix E

[Title of District Court and Cause.]
SUPPLEMENTAL ANSWER OF DEFEND-
ANTS CENTRAL NATIONAL BANK OF
OAKLAND AND JOSEPH H. GRUT

Comes now the defendant, Joseph H. Grut, as Receiver of the Central National Bank of Oakland, a
national banking association, and by leave of court
files this supplemental answer to the plaintiff's
complaint both for himself as Receiver and for the
defendant, Central National Bank of Oakland, and
for such supplemental answer admits, denies and
alleges as follows:

For a further, seventh and separate defense, this
defendant alleges:

I.

That this defendant is informed and believes and
therefore alleges that since the filing of plaintiff's
complaint herein, plaintiff above named has upon
numerous occasions accepted payments of interest
upon the bonds and notes remaining in the trust referred to in her complaint; that the exact times and
amounts of such payments are more particularly

set forth in the schedule attached hereto and marked
"Exhibit A" and by this reference made [142] a
part hereof; that plaintiff has appropriated all of
said interest payments so received to her own use.

That this defendant did not consent to said payments, or any of them, and had no knowledge of
and was not informed of such payments or of the
fact that plaintiff was accepting the same and was
appropriating the same to her use until January,
1936.

II.

That this defendant is informed and believes and
therefore alleges that plaintiff from time to time
since the filing of her complaint herein has authorized the sale of a substantial number of the bonds
and notes remaining in the trust at the time of
filing her complaint and referred to therein, and
that said bonds and notes have been sold; that the
bonds and notes so sold and the respective dates of
sale are more particularly set forth in the schedule
attached hereto, marked "Exhibit B," and by this
reference made a part hereof; that this defendant
did not consent to any of said sales and had no
knowledge of said sales, or any of them, and was
not informed of said sales until January, 1936.

III.

If plaintiff ever had any right to rescind the
transactions complained of in this complaint, which
these defendants deny, then plaintiff, by her actions
in accepting the payments of interest upon the
bonds and notes as alleged above, by appropriating

such payments to her own use and by authorizing the sale of said bonds and notes, as aforesaid, has waived any such right to rescind said transactions, and by said actions has ratified all of said transactions, and plaintiff by said actions has rendered impossible the restoration to these defendants of the bonds and notes the sale of which plaintiff seeks to rescind.

Wherefore, this defendant prays judgment as hereinafter set forth. [143]

For a further, eighth and separate defense, this defendant alleges:

I.

That this defendant is informed and believes and therefore alleges that the plaintiff above named received notice of the matters complained of in her complaint upon which her claimed right to rescind the transactions referred to in her complaint is based, on or before the 15th day of April, 1932. That plaintiff made no complaint regarding the matters complained of in her said complaint, gave no notice of her intention to rescind the transactions complained of therein and made no demand for the purchase price of the bonds, the sale of which is complained of in her said complaint, until on or about the 22nd day of June, 1933.

II.

That during the period aforesaid, during which plaintiff delayed in giving these answering defendants notice of her claimed right to rescind the sales

of bonds and notes complained of in her complaint,
after plaintiff had notice of the facts upon which
her said claimed right to rescind is based, said
bonds and notes greatly depreciated in market
value; that by reason of said depreciation in market value of said bonds and notes, said defendants
would be prejudiced if plaintiff is permitted to rescind said sales after delaying as aforesaid.

III.

That if plaintiff ever had any right to rescind the
transactions complained of in her complaint, which
these defendants deny, as aforesaid, then by reason
of plaintiff's delay, as aforesaid, in giving notice of
her intention to rescind and in making a demand
for restitution of the purchase price of said bonds
and notes, plaintiff has been guilty of such laches
as ought to and does bar this action in a court of
equity, and has waived any right she may [144] have
had to rescind said transactions.

Wherefore, defendant prays judgment as hereinafter set forth.

As a further, ninth and separate defense, this defendant alleges:

I.

That during all of the times during which the
transactions between plaintiff and defendant Central National Bank of Oakland complained of in
plaintiff's complaint took place, to wit, from the
1st day of January, 1926, to the 1st day of July,
1930, it was the uniform practice of the defendant

Central National Bank of Oakland when selling bonds and similar securities through its bond department to sell to its customers bonds which it owned and not to act as agent for the purchase of bonds by its customers; that in all of the transactions which plaintiff complains of in her complaint the said defendant acted in accordance with this practice; that at the time of each of the transactions complained of by plaintiff, plaintiff knew of this practice of said defendant.

II.

That during all of the times aforesaid within which the transactions between defendant, Central National Bank of Oakland, and plaintiff, complained of in plaintiff's complaint, took place, it was the uniform custom of banks in the County of Alameda and in the City and County of San Francisco, State of California, which maintained bond departments, to transact their bond business by selling to their customers bonds which were owned by the banks making the respective sales, and that none of the banks in said county and said city and county acted as agents for the purchase of bonds for customers of their respective bond departments; that said custom was known to all persons dealing with such banks during said times; that all of the transactions between said defendant and plaintiff [145] complained of in plaintiff's said complaint were conducted by said defendant in conformity with said custom; that said custom was known to the plaintiff during the period referred to.

6

Wherefore, this defendant prays judgment as follows:

1. That plaintiff take nothing by her complaint;
2. That defendant recover costs of suit herein;
3. For such other and further relief as to this court may seem meet and proper in the premises.

FRANK S. RICHARDS
Solicitor for defendants Joseph H. Grut
and Central National Bank of Oakland
[146]

State of California,
County of Alameda—ss.

Joseph H. Grut, being first duly sworn, deposes and says:

That he is one of the defendants in the above entitled action; that he has read the foregoing supplemental answer and knows the contents thereof, and that the same is true of his own knowledge, except as to those matters which are therein stated on information or belief, and as to those matters, that he believes it to be true.

JOSEPH H. GRUT.

Subscribed and sworn to before me this 22nd day of January, 1936.

[Seal]   FRANCIS TUTTLE,
Notary Public in and for the County of Alameda,
State of California. [147]

"EXHIBIT A"

Payments of interest to Mrs. Abbie W. Quinn:

Date of Payment	Amount
1933	
September 29,	$280.96
November 29,	178.30
December 30,	431.61
1934	
January 31,	322.58
March 31,	254.13
April 30,	19.38
May 31,	491.66
June 30,	58.16
July 31,	379.33
September 29,	287.51
October 31,	843.86
November 30,	672.58
December 31,	214.80
1935	
January 31,	451.36
March 30,	254.83
April 30,	45.00
June 29,	316.95
July 31,	465.18
September 30,	264.00
October 31,	19.40
November 30,	382.38

[148]

8

"EXHIBIT B"

Bond	Par Value	Date Sold
Alameda Investment Company Series "G" 1st mortgage collateral trust bonds	$10,000	August 17, 193
Miller & Lux, Inc. Secured 7% Notes	4,000	April 2, 193
Hearst Publications, Inc. 1st mortgage collateral trust 6¼% bonds	1,000	April 6, 193
Medford Irrigation District 6% bonds	5,000	April 10, 193
Calif. Cotton Mills Co. 1st mortgage sinking fund 6% bonds	6,000	November 6, 193
	$26,000	

[Endorsed]: Filed February 4, 1936. [149]

Appendix F

FINDINGS AND CONCLUSIONS OF LAW

Appendix F

[Title of District Court and Cause.]

FINDINGS OF FACT AND CONCLUSIONS OF LAW.

The above cause, under the title "Abbie W. Quinn, Plaintiff, vs. Central National Bank of Oakland, a national banking association, Joseph H. Grut, as Receiver of Central National Bank of Oakland, a national banking association, and Central Bank of Oakland, a corporation, Defendants'' (commenced in the Superior Court of the State of California, in and for the County of Alameda by the filing therein of the complaint on the 22nd day of August, 1933, and thereafter removed to the above entitled court), came on regularly for trial on the 4th day of February, 1936, before the above entitled court, Honorable Michael J. Roche, Judge, presiding [268] upon the bill of complaint of plaintiff and upon the answer thereto of the defendants, Central National Bank of Oakland, a national banking association, and Joseph H. Grut, as Receiver of said Central National Bank of Oakland, and upon the answer of the defendant, Central Bank of Oakland, a corporation, Charles W. Slack, Esq. and Edgar T. Zook, Esq. by Charles W. Slack, Esq. appearing as counsel for plaintiff, Frank S. Richards, Esq. appearing as counsel for the defendants, Central National Bank of Oakland, and Joseph H. Grut as Receiver thereof, and Messrs. Fitzgerald, Abbott & Beardsley by Charles A. Beardsley, Esq. and Edward B. Kelly, Esq. appearing as counsel for the defendant, Central Bank of Oakland, and evidence both oral and documentary having been introduced on said day and the trial of the cause having been duly and regularly continued from day to day thereafter to and including the 17th day of February, 1936, with like introduction of evidence, and plaintiff, pursuant to leave of court, having filed certain amendments and supplements to her bill of complaint, and the defendants, Central National Bank

of Oakland and Joseph H. Grut, pursuant to leave
of court, having filed a supplemental answer, and
the cause having been duly and regularly continued
thereafter to the 24th and 25th days of May, 1937,
for the purpose of certain motions and for argument, and the defendant, Central Bank of Oakland,
having, on the 24th day of May, 1937, made its motion to strike portions of the evidence, which said
motion was denied, and the defendant, Central Company, a corporation, as agent for the shareholders
of Central National Bank of Oakland, having been
substituted as a defendant in the place and stead of
the defendant, Joseph H. Grut as Receiver of Central National Bank of Oakland, and Ira Abraham,
Esq. having been duly substituted as attorney for
Central National Bank of Oakland in the place and
stead of the said Frank S. Richards, Esq. and the
said Ira Abraham, Esq. being likewise the attorney
for the [269] defendant, Central Company, a corporation, as agent for the shareholders of Central
National Bank of Oakland, and the cause having
been submitted to the court for decision on May
25th, 1937, and the court being duly and fully advised in the premises, and good cause appearing
therefor, now makes and files the following

Findings of Fact.
I.

With respect to the allegations of paragraphs I,
II, III, IV, V, VI and VII of the complaint, the
court finds:

1. At all times mentioned in the complaint since August 9th, 1909 the defendant Central National Bank of Oakland (to be hereinafter referred to as the national bank) was a national banking association with its principal place of business in Oakland, California and until March 2nd, 1933 carried on a banking business and other businesses in connection therewith.

2. On March 2nd, 1933 the national bank, pursuant to proclamation of the Governor of California on March 1st, 1933 declaring March 2nd and the next two days following public holidays, closed its doors, and has never since opened its doors, for the transaction of business. On or about March 14th, 1933 A. J. Mount was duly appointed the conservator for said national bank and immediately qualified as such and continued to be the conservator for and of said national bank until on or about May 8th, 1933. Said Mount was either the President or the Executive Vice-President of the national bank for more than five months prior to the 22nd day of April, 1933.

3. On May 8th, 1933 Joseph H. Grut (formerly a defendant herein) was duly appointed the receiver of the national bank, as an insolvent bank, unable to pay its just debts and liabilities. Immediately thereafter said Joseph H. Grut duly qualified as such receiver and continued to be the duly appointed, qualified and acting receiver of the national bank. [270]

4. At all times since September 7th, 1891 the defendant Central Bank of Oakland (to be hereinafter referred to as the savings bank) was and is a California banking corporation with its principal place of business in Oakland, California; that until April 21st, 1933 the name of said savings bank was "Central Savings Bank of Oakland"; on April 21st, 1933 its corporate name was changed from "Central Savings Bank of Oakland" to "Central Bank of Oakland" and it was likewise on or about said day authorized to transact a commercial banking business and also a trust business in addition to its former savings bank business. It is not a fact that the savings bank at any time was associated with the national bank. It is a fact that the savings bank carried on its business in the same premises as the premises in which the national bank carried on its banking business, and its other businesses. Since April 21st, 1933 the savings bank has carried on its banking and other business with A. J. Mount as its President, and with the same Executive Vice-President and other executive officers, including S. Berven as its Assistant Trust Officer, as were the Executive Vice-President and the other executive officers of the national bank on March 2nd, 1933.

5. At all times mentioned in the complaint since prior to January 1st, 1926 and until March 2nd, 1933 the national bank carried on, in connection with its banking business, a bond business by and through a department designated "Bond Depart-

ment''. Said national bank by and through its bond department purchased and sold, and otherwise dealt in, bonds and other obligations. For more than ten years prior to January 1st, 1926 E. D. Bothwell was an employee of the national bank either in its banking business or in its other businesses connected therewith, and since prior to January 1st, 1926 and until March 14th, 1933 Bothwell was Assistant Cashier and Manager of the bond department of the national bank. Said Bothwell was not an executive officer of the [271] national bank but his duties were confined solely to the bond department thereof at all times from and after his appointment as Manager thereof prior to January 1st, 1926; said Bothwell had no duties pertaining to, or authority over, any other department or business of the national bank after his appointment as Manager of the Bond Department thereof.

6. At all times mentioned in the complaint since prior to January 1st, 1926 and until March 2nd, 1933 the national bank carried on a trust business by and through a department established by it and designated as its "Trust Department" and by and through said trust department acted as trustee of funds and other property transferred to it by decrees of courts and by deeds and other instruments executed to and with it by individuals and by corporations. During all of the times mentioned in the complaint since prior to January 1st, 1926 and until January 1st, 1933 Daniel Read was an assistant Vice-President and the Trust Officer of the national bank

and since prior to January 1st, 1926 until on or about April 21st, 1933 S. Berven was the Assistant Trust Officer of said national bank.

7. For more than ten years prior to January 1st, 1926 plaintiff resided and thereafter continued to reside in Oakland and during said period of time she had, and thereafter continued to have, an account with the national bank and with the savings bank and from time to time during such period of time until March 2nd, 1933 plaintiff made deposits of money in, and withdrew money so deposited from, said respective accounts. As such depositor plaintiff became well acquainted with said Bothwell; the acquaintanceship of plaintiff with Bothwell prior to the time of the first of her bond purchases on January 7, 1926 was merely that of a depositor with a bank teller; plaintiff reposed in Bothwell and in the bond department trust and confidence which Bothwell knew. [272]

II.

With respect to the allegations of paragraphs VIII, IX, X, XI, XII, XIII, XIV, XV, XVI, XVII, XXIV, XXV, XXVI, XXVIII, XXX and XXXI of the complaint, insofar as said allegations deal with transactions occurring and conditions existing prior to the execution of the trust instrument on September 24, 1929, the court finds:

8

1. With respect to plaintiff's mental capacity the court finds: That at all times mentioned in the complaint plaintiff was a widow and in poor health; it is a fact however that at all times, both before as well as after the execution of the trust intsrument, plaintiff had a highly developed business sense and was extremely able and alert mentally and was well able to understand, and did in fact understand, the nature of the transactions complained of in the complaint; plaintiff was accustomed to, and did in fact, exercise her independent judgment with respect to the transactions complained of in the complaint.

2. With respect to the nature of the relationship existing between plaintiff and the national bank prior to the execution of the trust instrument on September 24, 1929, the court finds: Prior to the execution of the instrument of trust on September 24th, 1929 the following described securities were purchased by plaintiff from the national bank on the following dates and for the following prices, to-wit:

Date of Purchase	Par Value	Description	Price
January 7, 1926	$10,000	Province of Buenos Aires	$ 9,900
January 7, 1926	5,000	Miller & Lux	5,000
January 7, 1926	5,000	Rhodes-Jamison Co.	5,000
January 7, 1926	5,000	Western States Gas and Electric Co.	4,800
July 25, 1927	5,000	California Cotton Mills	4,750
July 25, 1927	5,000	Jackson Furniture Co.	5,000

[273]

Date of Purchase	Par Value	Description	Price
July 25, 1927	$ 5,000	Province of Callao	$ 4,950
Feb. 27, 28 as of			
March 1, 1928	5,000	Medford Irrigation District	4,850
March 27, 1928	8,000	Alameda Park Co.	8,080
March 27, 1928	2,000	Berkeley Terminal Properties	1,960
March 27, 1928	10,000	Fageol Motors Co.	10,000
March 27, 1928	10,000	Alameda Investment Co.	9,750
March 30, 1928	3,000	Oakland Meat & Packing Co.	3,030
March 30, 1928	5,000	St. Louis Gas & Coke Co.	4,800
March 30, 1928	3,000	Fox West Coast Properties	2,940
July 9, 1929		(Fox Realty Corporation)	
August 16, 1929 as of	5,000	Southern United Gas Co.	4,675
September 1, 1929	5,000	Central West Public Service Co.	4,987.50
		Total	$94,472.50

Prior to September 24, 1929, the relationship existing between plaintiff and the national bank with respect to plaintiff's acquisition of said securities was that of buyer and seller and not that of a principal (on plaintiff's part) and an agent or broker to purchase securities (on the national bank's part). It was intended by plaintiff that she should buy securities from the national bank which said bank owned or had contracted to purchase and that said bank should sell its own securities to her. It was not intended by plaintiff that the bank should purchase securities for plaintiff nor did she ever tell the national bank to do so for her.

3. With respect to plaintiff's trust intent the court finds: Plaintiff did not intend to create a trust

until approximately four (4) or five (5) months
prior to September 24, 1929. Plaintiff did not tell
Bothwell that she intended to create a trust until
approximately four (4) or five (5) months prior to
September 24, 1929; plaintiff at no time asked Bothwell whether [274] the national bank could or would
act as trustee; Bothwell did not inform plaintiff that
the national bank had a trust department, or that a
particular part of the business of said trust department was the taking care of property of widows, or
orphans, or of anyone else; plaintiff did not at any
time inform Bothwell as to what her property consisted of save that from time to time she advised
him of the funds which she had available for the
purchase of securities, nor did plaintiff at any time
inform Bothwell that she had a parcel of real property in Reno, Nevada, or elsewhere. Bothwell did
not inform plaintiff that the bank could not accept
a conveyance of real property in Nevada nor did he
inform her in any way with respect to whether or
not the national bank could or could not accept a
conveyance of real property. Bothwell did not advise plaintiff that pending the sale of said, or any,
real property, or pending the placing of her funds
in, or the creating of, such, or any, trust, or pending
any other contingency, the thing to do was to invest
her funds in, or buy, securities. Of the bonds described in subparagraph 2 of this paragraph II the
Western States Gas and Electric Company bonds
for which plaintiff had paid the price of $4,800.00
were called on March 1st, 1928 at a price of $5,125.00

and the Rhodes-Jamison Company bonds for which plaintiff had paid $5,000.00 were called on September 1st, 1929 at a price of $5,125.00. The proceeds of such redemptions were paid into plaintiff's commercial bank account in the national bank. None of the securities purchased by plaintiff from the national bank prior to September 24, 1929, were delivered to plaintiff, but at plaintiff's request, were held in safe-keeping by the national bank subject to plaintiff's order as a matter of accommodation to plaintiff; said securities were not held by said bank awaiting the time when the same would be assigned or transferred by her to said bank as trustee or until such time as she should create a trust. At plaintiff's request the interest [275] coupons on the securities purchased by plaintiff from the national bank were removed and cashed by said bank and the proceeds deposited in plaintiff's commercial bank account with said bank.

4. With respect to the selling prices of the securities and the profit made by the national bank thereon, the court finds: In each instance of the sale of securities by the national bank to plaintiff said bank sold said securities to plaintiff at a larger price than said bank had itself paid for the aggregate of any block of said securities and consequently made a profit thereon. The aggregate amount of such profit was $2,360.33. The Fageol bonds were purchased by the national bank on March 27th, 1928 for $9,-500.00 and were sold by it to plaintiff on the same day for a price of $10,000.00, a profit to the national

bank of $500.00; the Alameda Investment Company bonds were purchased by the national bank on March 22nd, 1928 for $9,429.00 and were sold by it to plaintiff on March 27th, 1928 for the price of $9,750.00, a profit to the national bank of $321.00; the Medford Irrigation District bonds purchased by the national bank as follows: $1500.00 par value on March 22nd, 1926 for the sum of $1500.00; $2500.00 par value on September 6th, 1927 for the sum of $2500.00; and $1,000.00 par value on February 2nd, 1928 for the sum of $777.50, or a total price to the national bank of $4,777.50, were sold by it to plaintiff on February 27th, 1928 as of March 1st, 1928 at a price of $4,850.00, or a profit to the national bank of $72.50. It is not a fact that at the time of the sale of the Medford bonds to plaintiff the same had dropped to a market price or value of $777.50 per bond. That at all times the securities sold by the national bank to plaintiff were sold at the fair value and market price thereof. Plaintiff was not told that the prices which she was paying to the national bank in purchasing said securities were the prices at which said bank [276] had itself acquired them. Bothwell did not conceal from plaintiff that the national bank was making a profit in the sales of securities to her, a fact well known to plaintiff at all times.

5. With respect to the type of securities sold to plaintiff and recommendations made by the national bank concerning the same, the court finds: At all times plaintiff desired to secure a high rate of re-

turn on her purchases of securities, never less than
six per cent (6%) per annum and in her purchases
of securities plaintiff was actuated primarily with
that end in view. At the time of the first of her
purchases on January 7, 1926, and at various times
thereafter plaintiff was advised by Bothwell that
return or interest was compensation for the risk
taken and that, in general the higher the rate of
interest the greater the risk involved. That shortly
prior to, at the time of, and subsequent to the
creation of the trust instrument on September 24,
1929, plaintiff was similarly so advised by Berven.
Plaintiff did not tell Bothwell she desired her
funds invested in, or to purchase, bonds of such
safety or desirability that the same could be readily
sold at any time at the price at which she purchased
them nor did she ask him whether or not her funds
should be invested in United States Government
bonds nor did Bothwell tell her that her funds
would be invested in, nor that there would be sold
to her, bonds just as good as United States Government bonds. All of the securities purchased by
plaintiff from the national bank prior to the execution of the trust instrument on September 24,
1929, were at the times when purchased by plaintiff of the type desired by her and were at that
time satisfactory, safe and desirable, and were so
considered, not only by the national bank, but also
by investment houses which, at the same time, were
selling the same securities to their customers. In
general the only recommendation made by Both-

well or by the national bank in the [277] sale of the securities to plaintiff was that the securities were considered satisfactory by the national bank or that said bank considered said securities as safe and desirable. Such recommendations were based upon the best knowledge, information and belief of the national bank and Bothwell. In purchasing said securities plaintiff relied in part upon the aforementioned recommendations and also in part upon the relatively high rate of interest and return such securities had. The bonds sold to plaintiff were sufficiently secured by real property insofar as they purported or were represented to be so secured; that the notes sold to plaintiff were sufficiently secured by real and personal property, or by real or personal property insofar as they purported or were represented to be so secured; neither the bonds of the Province of Buenos Aires nor of the Province of Callao were, when purchased, uncollectible, nor have they ever been uncollectible, except in the sense that no obligations of a sovereign power or state are collectible in the event of the failure or refusal of such sovereign power or state to pay the same; the Medford Irrigation District bonds were not, strictly speaking, secured by any direct lien upon real or other property, but said bonds were nevertheless secured by assessments which were liens upon real property situated in said district; the notes of Jackson Furniture Company were never secured by any lien upon property of any kind, nor did they purport nor were they rep-

resented to be so secured; plaintiff did not tell
Bothwell that she doubted the safety or desirability
of the Buenos Aires, or Callao or California Cotton
Mills bonds. Of the securities purchased by plaintiff from the bond department of the national bank
prior to the execution of the instrument of trust,
the following defaults occurred in the payment of
interest, to-wit: [278]

Par Value		Date of Default
$ 2,000	Berkeley Terminal Properties, Inc.,	Nov. 1, 1930
5,000	Province of Callao,	Jan. 1, 1932
10,000	Fageol Motors Company,	Feb. 1, 1932
5,000	Southern United Gas Company,	April 1, 1932
5,000	Medford Irrigation District,	July 1, 1932
8,000	Alameda Park Company,	Aug. 1, 1932
4,000	Miller & Lux, Incorporated,	Oct. 1, 1932
5,000	California Cotton Mills Company,	Jan. 1, 1933
5,000	Central West Public Service Company,	Feb. 1, 1933
10,000	Alameda Investment Company,	April 1, 1933
10,000	Province of Buenos Aires,	May 1, 1933
5,000	St. Louis Gas & Coke Company	June 1, 1933

Total $74,000.

The total price paid by plaintiff to the national bank
for the foregoing securities was $72,702.50.

III.

With respect to the allegations of paragraphs
XIV, XV, XVII, XVIII, XIX, XX and XXXI
of the complaint insofar. as said allegations deal
with the execution of the trust instrument, the
court finds:

1. A copy of the instrument of trust, together with accompanying statement and acknowledgments. is annexed to the complaint and marked Exhibit "A".

2. Bothwell did not refer plaintiff to Daniel Read concerning the subject of the instrument of trust but at the time when plaintiff first spoke to Bothwell concerning her intended creation of the trust she informed Bothwell she had already spoken to Daniel Read but that he had seemed so indifferent about the subject that she did not believe that he was interested in her [279] creating a trust. About four (4) or five (5) months prior to September 24, 1929 plaintiff first told Bothwell that she was about to go to the Mayo Brothers' in Rochester, Minnesota, for treatment and asked him whether he believed it advisable for her to execute a trust and Bothwell stated that in view of the circumstances of her intended trip to Rochester he thought it was the thing to do. Bothwell thereupon introduced plaintiff to Berven and on several occasions shortly prior to September 24, 1929 plaintiff consulted with Berven concerning the creation of a trust and during such consultations told Berven that she wished to continue purchasing securities from the bond department of the national bank and desired to purchase securities bearing a return of not less than six per cent (6%). Berven told her that the type of securities regarded as proper for trust investments usually paid not over five per cent (5%). Upon plaintiff's insistence that she

needed at least six per cent (6%) interest, Berven told plaintiff that a provision could be inserted in the trust instrument authorizing such type of investments. As a result thereof the instrument of trust (Exhibit "A" annexed to the complaint) was executed by plaintiff to and with the national bank as trustee on September 24, 1929. Plaintiff did not at any of the times mentioned in the complaint prior to September 24th, 1929 deliver to Berven data in her handwriting, or other written data, concerning the provisions desired by her to be inserted in the instrument of trust, but did inform Berven of the provisions which she desired to have inserted therein. That the data which was given by plaintiff to Berven at said times was used in the preparation of said instrument of trust. That said instrument of trust was prepared, insofar as the provisions relating to the disposition of income and principal were concerned, by one of the members of the firm of attorneys representing the said national bank at that time, [280] which said firm of attorneys at all times thereafter and until about the 20th day of May, 1933, continued to represent the said national bank as its attorneys and received therefrom regular periodical compensation for their services as such; the remainder of said trust instrument was prepared by Berven; plaintiff never paid anything to said firm of attorneys, or to any member thereof, nor did she otherwise recompense said firm, or any member thereof, for any services in connection with the preparation of said instrument of trust. That said firm of attorneys did not purport to represent plaintiff in connection with the preparation or execution of said instrument of trust but instead were acting for the national bank. Plaintiff was charged by the national bank, and thereafter paid to said bank, an acceptance fee in the sum of $100.00 for the acceptance by said national bank of the trusteeship under said instrument of trust. The instrument of trust was submitted by Berven to plaintiff for her consideration and approval on the 24th day of September, 1929 and was read to plaintiff by Berven, as well as being read by plaintiff, and the provisions thereof, paragraph by paragraph, were explained by Berven to plaintiff and plaintiff stated she understood the same. Plaintiff inquired of Berven whether she should submit the instrument of trust to an attorney of her selection for his advice concerning the same to which Berven replied that it was proper she should do so, whereupon plaintiff stated that her attorney was in Nevada and that as she was about to leave for Rochester, Minnesota, she did not have time to do so. That Berven did not state to plaintiff that the instrument of trust was in the so-called "usual form" but instead stated to her that owing to her own wishes provision was made therein for the investment of the trust funds in securities which, without such provision, would be improper for the investment of trust funds. That plaintiff, in reliance upon her reading of [281] the provisions of the trust and in reliance upon what the said Berven had told her concerning the same, executed said instrument of

trust as the same had been prepared and signed the
statement at the foot thereof. That in so signing
said instrument of trust plaintiff did not seek or
obtain independent legal advice relating thereto
because of the fact that she was in a hurry to leave
for Rochester, Minnesota. That at the time of the
execution of said instrument of trust plaintiff also
executed to the national bank a deed of conveyance
of the unimproved lot of land in Oakland, California, described in the instrument of trust, and
an assignment of a promissory note and mortgage
securing the same, executed to plaintiff by Sparks
Masonic Building Association, referred to in said
instrument of trust, and also delivered to the
national bank $15,000.00 par value Washoe County,
Nevada, County Roads and Highways Improvement
and Construction bonds, likewise referred to in the
instrument of trust, and in addition thereto executed a deed of gift to her daughter covering
property which plaintiff had in Sparks, Nevada,
and over which Berven had previously informed
her the national bank could not act as trustee. The
securities which had previously been purchased by
plaintiff from the bond department of the national
bank which are set forth in paragraph II, subp. 2
hereof less the Western States Gas and Electric
Company bonds and the Rhodes-Jamison bonds
which, as set forth in paragraph II, subp. 3 hereof,
had previously been called, were delivered by plaintiff to the trust department of the national bank
without any assignment other than the execution

of the instrument of trust, but nevertheless plaintiff was required to and did sign a receipt showing the delievery of said securities from the safe-keeping or depositary account under which said securities had previously been retained by the bond department of said national bank. [282]

IV.

With respect to the allegations of paragraphs XXI, XXII, XXIII, XXIV, XXV, XXVI, XXIX, XXX and XXXI of the complaint, insofar as said allegations deal with purchases of securities occurring after the execution of the trust instrument on September 24, 1929 the court finds:

1. That of the bonds listed in the instrument of trust the following were redeemed subsequent to the execution of the instrument of trust, to-wit: $1,000.00 par value of the Miller & Lux Incorporated notes; $3,000.00 par value Ookland Meat & Packing Company bonds; $15,000.00 par value Washoe County, Nevada, County Roads and Highways Improvement and Construction bonds. The moneys paid on the respective redemptions were paid to the national bank in addition thereto on or about the 1st day of June, of each of the years 1930, 1931 and 1932 there were also paid to the national bank the installment of $1,000.00 for each of said years, or a total sum of $3,000.00 on account of the principal of the promissory note executed to plaintiff by Sparks Masonic Building Association, leaving unpaid at that time the principal of said promis-

sory note in the sum of $11,000.00. That part of
the money so paid to the national bank was from
time to time thereafter invested by the trust department of said bank in the purchase of the securities at the times and for the prices hereinafter set
forth:

Date of Purchase	Par Value	Description	Price
April 8, 1930 as of April 15, 1930	$1,000	Hearst Publications, Inc.	$ 985
June 5, 1930	1,000	California Cotton Mills Co.	850
June 27, 1930 as of July 1, 1930	5,000	Federal Public Service Corporation	4,650
June 27, 1930 as of July 1, 1930	6,000	Hearst Publications, Inc.	5,946
			12,431
			[283]
July 31, 1930	$2,000	Pacific Gas & Electric Co.	$2,205
July 31, 1930	2,000	San Joaquin Light & Power Co.	2,290
January 20, 1932	5,000	East Bay Municipal Utility District	5,082.75
July 11, 1932	5,000	Los Angeles Gas & Electric Corporation	4,925
		Total	$26,933.75

Of the purchases so made, the first four blocks of
securities only were purchased by the trust department of the national bank from the bond department thereof (the remainder, or the last four blocks
of said securities, being purchased by the trust
department of the national bank from outside

sources). On or about July 16th, 1930 the Federal
Public Service Corporation bonds were sold by the
national bank at the same principal price as had
previously been paid therefor plus $49.17 interest
accrued thereon in the meantime. The said California Cotton Mills bonds and the said Hearst Publication bonds were thereafter sold at the following
times and at the following prices and had in the
meantime paid the following interest:

$1000.00 par value Hearst Publication bond
purchased on April 8th, 1930, at a price of
$985.00, was sold on April 6th, 1935, at a price
of $970.00, a principal loss of $15.00, and in
the meantime $338.89 interest was received
thereon;

$1000.00 par value California Cotton Mills
bond purchased on June 5th, 1930, at a price
of $850.00, was sold on November 6th, 1935,
at a price of $1065.00, a principal gain of
$215.00, and in the meantime $150.00 interest
was received thereon;

$6000.00 par value Hearst Publications bonds
purchased on June 27th, 1930, at a price of
$5946.00 matured in $3,000.00 lots respectively
on November 1st, 1933 and November 1st, 1934,
at a total price of $6000.00, a principal gain of
$54.00, and in the meantime $1500.00 interest
was received thereon.

2. In the instance of the purchases of the said
Hearst bonds, said California Cotton Mills bond and
said Federal Public [284] Service bonds, Bothwell

suggested and submitted the same to plaintiff without any other recommendation and plaintiff, relying in part upon the said suggestion and submission and in part upon the relatively high rate of return, directed the trust department to purchase the same from the bond department; that no recommendation was made by any officer of the trust department of said bank in connection with said purchases; in the instance of each of said purchases, plaintiff knew that the bond department of the national bank was the owner of the securities so suggested and submitted and, with knowledge of that fact and that the said bond department was making a profit thereon, nevertheless directed the trust department to make such purchases from the bond department. In the instances of said purchases plaintiff dealt directly with the bond department and directed the trust department to follow out her wishes in making such purchases. The aggregate profit made by the national bank on such purchases was the sum of $471.00. The national bank did not conceal from plaintiff the fact that the trust department was purchasing bonds owned by the bond department, nor did it conceal from plaintiff that in so doing the bank had profited in each of the instances of the purchase and sale of said bonds; that said bonds were in each case sold by the bond department to the trust department at the fair value thereof and were legal trust investments for said trust department to make for plaintiff's trust because of the fact that the instrument of trust authorized the national bank, as trustee, to invest the trust funds in securities or investments of the character permitted by law for the investment of trust funds, "or otherwise". That the said words "or otherwise" were inserted in Article II of the instrument of trust (Exhibit "A" annexed to the complaint) in order to comply with plaintiff's desire that the trust funds be invested in securities having a return of not less than six [285] per cent (6%) and it was at the time of the execution of the instrument of trust explained to her that such words had that effect, which was as plaintiff intended.

V.

With respect to the allegations of paragraphs XXVII and XXVIII of the complaint, insofar as said allegations deal with the purchase of the trust department of the national bank by the savings bank on April 22nd, 1933, the court finds: On April 20th, 1933, A. J. Mount, as Conservator of the national bank, filed his verified petition in the Southern Division of the United States District Court for the Northern District of California entitled "In the Matter of the Conservatorship of Central National Bank of Oakland", numbered 19458-S, in the records of said District Court, for an order approving two proposed contracts referred to in said petition, and for general relief. That copies of said two proposed contracts are annexed to said petition and marked respectively Exhibit "A" and "B". In said petition it is alleged, among other things, that

the petitioner desired to join with the board of
directors and officers of the national bank, acting
with the consent of stockholders holding of record
at least two-thirds of the issued capital stock of
said national bank, in the sale to the savings bank
of the whole of the business of the trust department
of the national bank upon the terms and conditions
set forth in said proposed contract, a copy of which
is annexed to the complaint herein and designated
Exhibit "C"; that said last mentioned contract had
been approved by the Comptroller of the Currency
of the United States and by the Superintendent of
Banks of the State of California; that it was re-
cited in said petition that the sale of the business of
the trust department was for the best interests of
the creditors of the national bank in that it would
result in the discharge of the national bank "of all
liabilities of said department and in securing for
the benefit of creditors of the Na- [286] tional Bank
of the full value of the said business"; that a copy
of said petition omitting therefrom Exhibits "A"
and "B", but including a copy of the verification
of the said Mount thereto, is annexed to the complaint and marked "Exhibit B"; on April 20th,
1933 said District Court made its order authorizing
the said petitioner to join with the board of directors and officers of the national bank in the execution of the proposed contract for the sale of the
whole of the business of the trust department, upon
the terms and conditions set forth in said proposed
contract. The stockholders holding of record at least

two-thirds of the issued capital stock of the national
bank consented to the sale to the savings bank of
the whole of the business of the trust department of
the national bank upon the terms and conditions set
forth in said proposed contract; thereafter said
proposed contract, dated April 22nd, 1933, was executed by the national bank, by A. J. Mount, as
Conservator thereof; a copy of said contract is annexed to the complaint and designated "Exhibit
C"; thereafter and on or about April 22nd, 1933
the national bank, pursuant to said contract, delivered to the savings bank, as the successor trustee of
the trusts declared in and by the instrument of trust,
the securities described in subparagraph 2 of paragraph II hereof and in subparagraph 1 of paragraph IV hereof, less such thereof as had been
called, sold or redeemed prior thereto, and also delivered to the savings bank the Sparks Masonic
Building Association promissory note and mortgage,
on the principal of which there then remained unpaid the sum of $11,000.00, together with the pos-
session of the unimproved lot situated in Oakland,
California. The Court makes no finding as to
whether or not, had plaintiff succeeded in establishing the liabilities, matters and things complained
of and alleged in her complaint, the savings bank,
by the contract for the purchase of the trust department, or otherwise, or at all, would [287] have assumed or agreed to pay or discharge any of said
alleged liabilities to plaintiff of the national bank
relating or incidental to, or arising out of, the
purchase of any bonds or notes, or any other matter
or thing occurring, prior to the execution of the

instrument of trust on September 24, 1929 for the
reason that, by virtue of the other findings herein
to the effect that no such liabilities, matters or
things, were established in the first instance, such
finding as to the effect of the contract for the purchase of the trust department by the savings bank
from the national bank, or as to such alleged assumption by the savings bank of the alleged liabilities of the national bank, is rendered immaterial
and unnecessary to the decision of this case. It
was conceded by the savings bank during the trial,
and the court finds, that had any liabilities been
established as arising out of, or relating or incidental to, the purchase of securities by the trust
department, or the conduct of said trust, after
September 24, 1929, such liabilities would have
been assumed by the savings bank under the contract for the purchase of the trust department
dated April 22nd, 1933.

VI.

With respect to the allegations of paragraphs
XXIX, XXX and XXXI of the complaint, insofar
as said allegations deal with the alleged discovery
by plaintiff of certain defaults and matters related
thereto, the court finds:

1. The national bank notified plaintiff of the
respective defaults at or about the respective times
when said defaults occurred. The national bank
neither through Read, nor Berven, nor Bothwell,
nor anyone else, except as hereinafter found, told

plaintiff not to worry about said defaults, or any
of said defaults, nor did it tell plaintiff after said
defaults that said securities were well secured, or
that interest would eventually be paid; in [288] this
respect prior to November 1st, 1932, Berven told
plaintiff that the Alameda Park bonds appeared to
be protected by sufficient property.

2. On October 29th, 1932 Berven wrote a letter
to plaintiff in which, in referring to the bonds of
Alameda Investment Company, which were not then
in default, he said as follows:

> "We believe that it is advisable that a por-
> tion of your holdings in said Company should
> be sold at this time and would appreciate it
> very much if you would call at your earliest
> convenience to discuss the matter with us;"

and thereafter and on or about November 1st, 1932
plaintiff called upon Berven. Berven did not at that
time recommend to plaintiff that the bonds be sold
save as hereinafter found, or that the proceeds of
the sales be invested in so-called "better bonds". In
respect to this finding, not only prior to the execution of the trust instrument, but also subsequent
thereto, Berven from time to time recommended to
plaintiff that she sell a portion of her bonds and
notes and invest the proceeds in bonds paying a
lower rate of interest but having more stability as to
principal, but plaintiff refused to do so or to permit
the same to be done. Berven, on or about the aforesaid 1st day of November, 1932 recommended that

the Alameda Investment Company bonds, or a portion thereof, be sold which plaintiff likewise refused to permit. It is not a fact that at said time, to-wit, on or about the 1st day of November, 1932 the then value of said bonds was computed for plaintiff either by Berven or by Bothwell, but that it is a fact that at or about said time the value of certain, but not all, of said bonds was computed for plaintiff by Wm. Cavalier & Co. at the approximate sum of $28,860.00; that since that time the majority of said bonds have increased substantially in value.

[289]

3. Plaintiff on or about November 15th, 1932 consulted with one of the attorneys who is her counsel in this case; that said attorney thereupon commenced an examination of the facts relating to the transactions alleged in the complaint and of the law relating to said transactions; said examination was interrupted by the closing of the national bank on March 2nd, 1933, by the appointment of Mount as Conservator and Grut as Receiver, and by negotiations between plaintiff's attorneys and the attorneys for the savings bank and the attorneys for Joseph H. Grut, as Receiver of the national bank, relating to a settlement of plaintiff's alleged claims involved in the complaint; said negotiations for a settlement came to an end about June 22nd, 1933.

VII.

With respect to the matters set forth in the third separate defense in both of the answers on file herein, the court finds: That prior to the commencement of this suit the savings bank, being then the successor trustee under said trust instrument, offered to permit plaintiff to revoke the trust and the instrument of trust and offered to deliver all of the trust properties to plaintiff and offered to agree that such revocation should not be a release or discharge of existing liabilities or obligations of said savings bank to plaintiff, if any; that plaintiff refused such offer.

VIII.

With respect to the allegations of the amendments and supplements to the bill of complaint filed herein during the course of the trial, the court finds:

1. On June 10th, 1933 plaintiff delivered a letter to the savings bank which was accepted by the savings bank on June 12th, 1933; a copy of said letter and of said acceptance is annexed to said amendments and supplements to said bill of complaint as Exhibit "A" thereto. [290]

2. Since the filing of the complaint on August 22nd, 1933 and down to the time of the trial, certain of the securities held in trust by the savings bank, as successor trustee, pursuant to said letter and the acceptance thereof, and with plaintiff's approval have been sold by the savings bank pursuant to said letter, or have matured, or been redeemed as the case may be; that the following are the amounts for which said securities have been sold and of the respective amounts payable on such maturities and redemptions, to-wit:

31

Par Value	Bonds		Dates	Amounts
$10,000	Alameda Investment Co.,	sold	Aug. 17, 1933	$ 3,996.
3,000	Hearst Publications, Inc.,	matured	Nov. 1, 1933	3,000.
3,000	Hearst Publications, Inc.,	matured	Nov. 1, 1934	3,000.
4,000	Miller & Lux, Inc.,	sold	Apr. 2, 1935	3,038.40
1,000	Hearst Publications, Inc.,	sold	Apr. 6, 1935	970.
5,000	Medford Irrigation District,	sold	Apr. 10, 1935	2,000.
6,000	California Cotton Mills Co.,	sold	Nov. 6, 1935	6,390.
5,000	Jackson Furniture Co.,	redeemed	Feb. 1, 1936	5,050.
5,000	Los Angeles Gas & Electric Co.,	redeemed	Mar. 1, 1935	5,300.

$42,000 $32,744.40

3. That since the filing of the complaint and down to the time of trial, installments of the principal of the Sparks Masonic Building Association promissory note in the total amount of $3.000.00 have matured and have been paid to the savings bank at the following times and in the following amounts: May 28th, 1934 the sum of $2,000.00 for the installments maturing June 1st, 1933 and June 1st, 1934; June 1st, 1935, the sum of $1,000.00. [291]

4. Prior to the filing of the complaint, the Fageol Motors Company was adjudicated a bankrupt by the above entitled District Court; prior to the filing of the complaint and on August 19th, 1933 the savings bank received a dividend in liquidation on the Fageol Motors Company debenture bonds in the sum of $2,178.18 and thereafter on January 16th, 1935

there were respectively paid to the savings bank additional dividends in liquidation of the respective sums of $418.70 and $329.20. A further dividend is expected, not, however, to exceed the sum of approximately $100.00.

5. The sums so paid to the savings bank are now held on deposit to the credit of the trust estate by the savings bank, as successor trustee.

6. Since the filing of the complaint and down to the time of the trial of the action, pursuant to said letter and the acceptance thereof, the savings bank has collected the interest on bonds and notes and on the promissory note of the Sparks Masonic Building Association amounting to the total sum of $7,747.20; the respective dates when said interest was so collected and the respective amounts thereof are set forth on Exhibit "B" annexed to said amendments and supplements to the bill of complaint.

7. Since the filing of the complaint and down to the time of the trial of the action, the savings bank, pursuant to said letter and the acceptance thereof, has paid to plaintiff the interest so collected after deducting therefrom, pursuant to said letter, three per cent (3%) of the interest so collected as compensation for the savings bank, as successor trustee, making a total of $270.01; said rate of compensation was the usual rate theretofore charged by the national bank while it was trustee and by the savings bank since April 22nd, 1933 when it became successor trustee, for the respective services. [292]

IX.

With respect to the allegations contained in the
supplemental answer of the defendants, Central
National Bank of Oakland and Joseph H. Grut, as
Receiver thereof, the court finds: Since the filing
of the complaint, plaintiff has, upon numerous occasions, accepted payments of interest upon the bonds
and notes remaining in the trust referred to in the
complaint; the exact times and amounts of such
payments are more particularly set forth in Exhibit
"A" annexed to said supplemental answer; plaintiff has appropriated all of said interest payments
so received by her to her own use. Neither the
national bank, nor Joseph H. Grut, as Receiver
thereof, consented to said payments, or to any of
them, nor had they, or either of them, any knowledge of such payments, nor were they, or either of
them, informed thereof or of the fact that plaintiff
was accepting the same and appropriating the same
to her use until January, 1936. From time to time
since the filing of the complaint, plaintiff authorized
the sale, by the savings bank, as successor trustee,
of a substantial number of bonds and notes remaining in the trust at the time of the filing of the
complaint, and that pursuant to such authorization
certain bonds and notes were sold, said bonds so
sold and the dates of sale being more particularly
set forth in Exhibit "B" annexed to said supplemental answer; neither the national bank, nor
Joseph H. Grut, as Receiver thereof, consented to
any of said sales, nor had they, or either of them,

any knowledge of such sales, or any thereof, and were not informed thereof until January, 1936.

Wherefore, and as

Conclusions of Law

this court does determine:

1. That prior to the execution of the instrument of trust on September 24, 1929 the relationship existing between [293] plaintiff and the national bank was that of buyer and seller and no fraud, concealment, or misrepresentation was practiced upon plaintiff by the national bank either with respect to said relationship, or with respect to the value or desirability of the securities purchased or their market value, or with respect to the fact that said national bank was making a profit on such sales, or with respect to the fact that said bank was selling its own securities to plaintiff, and therefore plaintiff is not entitled to rescind any of the purchases of securities made by her from the bond department of the national bank prior to the execution of the instrument of trust.

2. That the national bank was not guilty of any fraud, concealment, or misrepresentation in connection with the execution of the instrument of trust dated September 24, 1929, and therefore plaintiff is not entitled to rescind the same. However, in view of the fact that the savings bank (Central Bank of Oakland), the successor trustee under said instrument of trust, prior to the commencement of the action, and in its answer, offered to permit plaintiff

to revoke said instrument of trust, plaintiff may, if
she so desires, revoke said instrument of trust, or
appoint a new, or successor trustee, as provided for
by the provisions of paragraph 1 of the contract
dated April 22nd, 1933, relative to the purchase of
the trust department of the national bank by the
savings bank, and in the event of such revocation,
or such appointment of a successor trustee, the savings bank shall deliver to plaintiff or to such successor trustee, as the case may be, all trust assets,
subject to such deductions as may be equitable and
just for its compensation and expenditures as set
forth in the letter dated June 10, 1933, and shall
execute such instruments as may reasonably be
necessary to effect the foregoing. Among such trust
assets, to be so delivered, and among such instruments, to be so executed, are the following: A deed
properly executed [294] and acknowledged covering the unimproved lot of land in Oakland, California, which is described in the instrument of
trust; an assignment, properly executed and acknowledged, covering the Sparks Masonic Building
Association note and mortgage; all installments of
principal of the Sparks Masonic Building Association note, and also all interest payments on said
note not heretofore paid to plaintiff, collected by
the savings bank since the filing of the complaint;
all other moneys not heretofore paid to plaintiff,
including all moneys received by the savings bank,
as successor trustee, on redemptions, maturities and
sales of any securities constituting a part of the

trust estate, and also all other interest collected by
the savings bank since the filing of the complaint,
less the aforementioned deductions; all securities
and evidences of indebtedness that came into the
possession of the savings bank, as successor trustee,
less such thereof as may have been called, sold or
redeemed, or, in the case of any of such securities
as may have been deposited with any bondholders'
protective committee, or deposited for any similar
purpose, then the certificate of deposit evidencing
the securities so deposited.

3. That after the execution of the instrument of
trust on September 24, 1929 the national bank, as
trustee of plaintiff's trust, was entitled to, and did
lawfully, purchase the securities which it did in
fact purchase from the bond department by reason
of the fact (a) that plaintiff expressly authorized
and directed the trust department to make such
purchases knowing that the bond department was
then the owner of, and intended to sell to the trust
department, said securities, and that the bond department would make a profit on such sales to the
trust department, and (b) the provisions of Section
25 of the California Bank Act expressly permitted
such purchases by the trust department from the
bond department. Therefore, plaintiff is not entitled to rescind any [295] of the purchases of securities made after the execution of the instrument of
trust.

4. That by reason of the fact that it is hereinabove found and herein determined that plaintiff

has not established any of the liabilities, matters or
things complained of and alleged in her complaint,
on the part of the national bank, the determination
of whether or not the savings bank, by the contract
for the purchase of the trust department, or otherwise, or at all, would have assumed or agreed to
pay or discharge any of said alleged liabilities to
plaintiff of the national bank relating or incidental
to, or arising out of, the purchase of any bonds or
notes, or any other matter or thing occurring, prior
to the execution of the instrument of trust on September 24, 1929 had plaintiff succeeded in establishing the same, is rendered immaterial and unnecessary to the decision of this case. Had any liabilities
been established as arising out of, or relating or
incidental to, the purchase of the securities by the
trust department, or the conduct of said trust, after
the execution of the trust instrument on September
24, 1929, such liabilities would have been assumed
by the savings bank.

5. That by reason of the fact that plaintiff has
not succeeded in establishing any cause or causes
of action against, or liabilities on the part of, any
of the defendants it is unnecessary to determine
whether or not, had such cause or causes of action,
or such liabilities, been established, they would have
been barred by any laches or limitations, or whether
or not plaintiff waived her alleged right to rescind,
or ratified, the alleged transactions complained of.

6. That by reason of the premises the defendants
are entitled to judgment and decree to the effect

that plaintiff take nothing and that the bill of complaint, together with the amendments and supplements thereto, on file herein, be dismissed. [296]

7. That the defendants are entitled to their proper costs and disbursements herein.

Let judgment be entered accordingly.

Dated: September 4, 1937.

MICHAEL J. ROCHE

District Judge.

Proposed by:

IRA ABRAHAM

    Attorney for Central Company as stockholders' agent, etc. and Central National Bank of Oakland.

FITZGERALD, ABBOTT & BEARDSLEY

    Attorneys for Central Bank of Oakland.

Receipt of a copy of the within Findings of Fact and Conclusions of Law is hereby admitted this 23d day of August, 1937.

CHARLES W. SLACK and

EDGAR T. ZOOK

Attorneys for Plaintiff.

Approved as to form, as provided by Rule 22:

....

....

Attorneys for Plaintiff.

[Endorsed]: Filed Sep. 4, 1937. [297]

Appendix G
DECREE

Appendix C

In the District Court of the United States,
Northern District of California, Division ...

No. 2841-K In Equity.

ANNIE W. QUINN,

Plaintiff

vs.

CENTRAL COMPANY, a corporation, as agent
for the shareholders of Central National Bank
of Oakland, CENTRAL NATIONAL BANK
OF OAKLAND, a national banking association,
and CENTRAL BANK OF OAKLAND, a
corporation,

Defendants

JUDGMENT AND DECREE FOR
DEFENDANTS

This cause coming on to be further heard at this
term, and was argued by counsel; and thereupon,
upon consideration thereof, it was ordered, adjudged and decreed as follows, viz.:

1. That the defendants and each of them have
and are hereby granted judgment and decree in their
favor to the effect that plaintiff take nothing and
that the bill of complaint, together with the amendments and supplements thereto on file herein, be and
the same are hereby dismissed with prejudice and
that the defendants, and each of them, have and do
recover their proper costs and disbursements in the
action herein. [317]

Appendix G

In the District Court of the United States, for the Northern District of California, Southern Division.

No. 3644-R. In Equity.

ABBIE W. QUINN,

Plaintiff,

vs.

CENTRAL COMPANY, a corporation, as agent for the shareholders of Central National Bank of Oakland, CENTRAL NATIONAL BANK OF OAKLAND, a national banking association, and CENTRAL BANK OF OAKLAND, a corporation,

Defendants.

JUDGMENT AND DECREE FOR DEFENDANTS.

This cause came on to be further heard at this term, and was argued by counsel; and thereupon, upon consideration thereof, it was ordered, adjudged and decreed as follows, viz.:

1. That the defendants, and each of them, have and are hereby granted judgment and decree in their favor to the effect that plaintiff take nothing and that the bill of complaint, together with the amendments and supplements thereto on file herein, be and the same are hereby dismissed with prejudice and that the defendants, and each of them, have and recover their proper costs and disbursements in the sum of $220.45. [298]

2. Insofar as the present trust relationship existing between plaintiff and the defendant, Central
Bank of Oakland, is concerned, nothing herein contained is intended to preclude plaintiff from revok-
ing the instrument of trust dated September 24th,
1929, or appointing a new or successor trustee thereunder and therefore plaintiff may, if she so desires,
revoke the instrument of trust dated September
24th, 1929, or appoint a new or successor trustee
thereunder, and in the event of such revocation, or
such appointment of a new or successor trustee, the
defendant, Central Bank of Oakland, shall deliver
to plaintiff or to such new or successor trustee, as
the case may be, all trust assets, subject to such deductions as may be equitable and just for its compensation and expenditures as set forth in the letter
dated June 10, 1933, annexed to the amendments and
supplements to the complaint on file herein, and shall
execute such instruments as may reasonably be
necessary to effect the foregoing. Among such trust
assets, to be so delivered by the defendant, Central
Bank of Oakland, and among such instruments, to
be so executed, are the following: A deed properly
executed and acknowledged covering the unimproved
lot of land in Oakland, California, which is described in the instrument of trust; an assignment,
properly executed and acknowledged, covering the
Sparks Masonic Building Association note and
mortgage; all installments of principal of the
Sparks Masonic Building Association note and also
all interest payments on said note, not heretofore

paid to plaintiff, collected by the defendant, Central Bank of Oakland, since the filing of the complaint; all other moneys not heretofore paid to plaintiff, including all moneys received by the defendant, Central Bank of Oakland, as successor trustee, on redemptions, maturities and sales of any securities constituting a part of the trust estate, and also all other interest collected by the defendant, Central Bank of Oakland, since the filing of the complaint, less the [299] aforementioned deductions; all securities and evidences of indebtedness that came into the possession of the defendant, Central Bank of Oakland, as successor trustee, less such thereof as may have been called, sold or redeemed, or, in the case of any of such securities as may have been deposited with any bondholders protective committee, or deposited for any similar purpose, then the certificate of deposit evidencing the securities so deposited.

Dated: October 7th, 1937.

MICHAEL J. ROCHE,

District Judge.

Approved as to form as provided by Rule 22. Counsel refused to approve as to form and did not specify reasons.

EDW. B. KELLY.

Receipt of a copy admitted Oct. 4, '37·

CHARLES W. SLACK and
EDGAR T. ZOOK,

Attorneys for Plaintiff.

[Endorsed]: Filed and Entered October 11, 1937.

[300]

Appendix H

Appendix H

ASSIGNMENTS OF ERROR

Appendix H

[Title of District Court and Cause.]

ASSIGNMENT OF ERRORS.

The above named plaintiff, by and through her attorneys, and in connection with her petition for the allowance of her appeal to the United States Circuit Court of Appeals for the Ninth Circuit, hereby files and presents the following assignment of errors upon which she will rely upon her said appeal:

1. The above named Court erred in finding, in Finding 4, of paragraph I, of its Findings of Fact, made and filed in the above entitled action, (referring to the above named defendant Central Bank of Oakland as the "Savings Bank", and to the above named defendant Central National Bank of Oakland as the "National Bank"), that

"It is not a fact that the savings bank at any time was associated with the national bank."

The said Court so erred for the reason that there [620] is no evidence to support the said Finding 4, but, on the contrary, the evidence shows the facts to be that the said Savings Bank, during all the times alleged in the plaintiff's bill of complaint, since on or about January 1, 1926, until March 2, 1933, was associated with the said National Bank, and carried on its banking business in the said premises, in the City of Oakland, County of Alameda, State of California, as the said National Bank carried on its banking business.

2. The said Court erred in finding, in Finding 5, of paragraph I, of the said Findings of Fact, (re-

ferring to E. D. Bothwell, as the Manager of the
Bond Department of the said National Bank,
through which said Bond Department the said National Bank sold and otherwise dealt in bonds and
other obligations issued by private and by quasi-
public corporations, by the United States and foreign countries, and by political divisions, municipalities, entities and agencies of the United States
and foreign countries), that

> "Said Bothwell was not an executive officer of
> the national bank but his duties were confined
> solely to the bond department thereof at all
> times from and after his appointment as Man-
> ager thereof prior to January 1st, 1926; said
> Bothwell had no duties pertaining to, or au-
> thority over, any other department or business
> of the national bank after his appointment as
> manager of the Bond Department thereof."

The said Court so erred for the reason that there
is no evidence to support the said Finding 5, but,
on the contrary, the evidence shows the facts to be
that the said Bothwell, ever since sometime in the
year 1920, and up to sometime in the month of
February, 1933, when he left his employment with
the said National Bank, was an executive officer of
the said National Bank, to wit, was an Assistant
Cashier and the Manager of the said Bond Department of the said National Bank, and that he had
the authority as such, to bind the said National
Bank, by his [621] representations, statements and
advice to the plaintiff in relation to the purchases of

the bonds and other obligations, (hereinafter sometimes referred to as "securities"), prior to the execution of the instrument of trust, dated September 24, 1929, for the plaintiff from the said National
Bank, through the said Bothwell, as the Manager
of the said Bond Department.

3.   The said Court erred in finding, in Finding 7,
of paragraph I, of the said Findings of Fact, that
     "the acquaintance of plaintiff with Bothwell
     prior to the time of the first of her bond pur-
     chases on January 7, 1926, was merely that of a
     depositor with a bank teller."

The said Court so erred for the reason that the
said Finding 7 is without the issues raised by the
bill of complaint and the answers thereto, and is a
conclusion having no support in any evidence, and
for the further reason that the evidence shows the
facts to be that at the time, to wit, January 7, 1926,
of the first purchases of the said securities for the
plaintiff from the said National Bank, the said
Bothwell was then, and ever since sometime in the
year 1920, and up to sometime in the month of
February, 1933, when he left his employment with
the said National Bank, had been, an Assistant
Cashier and the Manager of the said Bond Department, and that the plaintiff, at the time of the said
first purchases, was well acquainted with the said
Bothwell, and, at the said time of the said first purchases, as well as at all times thereafter until on or
about November 1, 1932, reposed in the said Bothwell, and in the said Bond Department, and in the

said National Bank, as the said Bothwell well knew, great trust and confidence.

4. The said Court erred in finding, in that portion of Finding 1, of paragraph II, of the said Findings of Fact, that, (referring to the poor health of the plaintiff), [622]

"it is a fact however that at all times, both before as well as after the execution of the trust instrument, plaintiff had a highly developed business sense and was extremely able and alert mentally and was well able to understand, and did in fact understand, the nature of the transactions complained of in the complaint."

The said Court so erred for the reasons that the said last quoted portion of the said Finding 1, of paragraph II, is without the issues raised by the said bill of complaint and the answers thereto, and is composed of conclusions having no support, directly or inferentially, in any evidence, and for the further reason that the said portion of the said Finding 1 is contrary to the evidence in that the evidence shows the facts to be: (1), that the plaintiff had no experience in purchasing the kind of securities sold to or for her benefit by the said National Bank, through the said Bothwell, as the Manager of the said Bond Department, and relied upon the recommendations of the said Bothwell that such securities were safe and desirable, or safe and conservative, securities for the investment of her funds; and, (2), that the nature of the transactions of pur-

chase was not explained to her by the said Bothwell
or by any other official of the said National Bank,
and she did not, in fact, understand, or, until subsequent to November 1, 1932, have any knowledge of,
the nature of the said transactions.

5. The said Court erred in finding, in that portion of the said Finding 1, of paragraph II, of the
said Findings of Fact, that

> "plaintiff was accustomed to, and did in fact,
> exercise her independent judgment with respect
> to the transactions complained of in the com-
> plaint."

The said Court so erred for the reason that the
said portion of the said Finding 1, of paragraph II,
is without the issues raised by the said bill of complaint and the answers [623] thereto, and for the
further reason that the evidence shows the facts to
be that the plaintiff was not either accustomed to, or
that she did, in fact, exercise her independent judgment with respect to any of the transactions complained of in the bill of complaint.

6. The said Court erred in finding, in that portion of Finding 2, of paragraph II, of the said
Findings of Fact, that

> "Prior to September 24, 1929, the relationship
> existing between plaintiff and the national bank
> with respect to plaintiff's acquisition of said se-
> curities was that of buyer and seller and not
> that of a principal (on plaintiff's part) and an
> agent or broker to purchase securities (on the
> national bank's part)."

The said Court so erred for the reasons that the said last quoted portion of the said Finding 2, of paragraph II, are contrary to the evidence in that the evidence shows the facts to be that the relation existing between the plaintiff and the said National Bank in the purchase of the securities with the funds of the plaintiff, prior as well as subsequent to the execution of the instrument of trust, was not that of buyer and seller, but was that of trustee and cestui que trust.

7. The said Court erred in finding, in that portion of the said Finding 2, of paragraph II, of the said Findings of Fact, that

"It was intended by plaintiff that she should buy securities from the national bank which said bank owned or had contracted to purchase and that said bank should sell its own securities to her. It was not intended by plaintiff that the bank should purchase securities for plaintiff, nor did she ever tell the national bank to do so for her."

The said Court so erred for the reason that the said last quoted portion of the said Finding 2, of paragraph II, is without the issues raised by the said bill of complaint and the answers thereto, and for the further reason that the said por- [624] tion of the said Finding 2 is contrary to the evidence in that the evidence does not show, either directly or inferentially, the facts to be that it was intended by the plaintiff that she should buy any of the securi-

7

ties from the said National Bank, which the said
National Bank owned or had contracted to purchase, or that the said National Bank should sell to
her its own securities.

8. The said Court erred in finding, in that portion of Finding 3, of paragraph II, of the said
Findings of Fact, as follows:

"Plaintiff did not intend to create a trust until
approximately four (4) or five (5) months prior
to September 24, 1929. Plaintiff did not tell
Bothwell that she intended to create a trust until approximately four (4) or five (5) months
prior to September 24, 1929; plaintiff at no time
asked Bothwell whether the national bank could
or would act as trustee; Bothwell did not inform plaintiff that the national bank had a trust
department or that a particular part of the business of said trust department was the taking
care of property of widows, or orphans, or of
anyone else; plaintiff did not at any time inform Bothwell as to what her property consisted
of, save that from time to time she advised him
of the funds which she had available for the
purchase of securities, nor did plaintiff at any
time inform Bothwell that she had a parcel of
real property in Reno, Nevada, or elsewhere.
Bothwell did not inform plaintiff that the bank
could not accept a conveyance of real property
in Nevada, nor did he inform her in any way
with respect to whether or not the national bank
could or could not accept a conveyance of real

property. Bothwell did not advise plaintiff that
pending the sale of said, or any, real property,
or pending the placing of her funds in, or the
creating of, such, or any, trust, or pending any
other contingency, the thing to do was to invest
her funds in, or buy securities."

The said Court so erred for the reason that the
said last quoted portions of the said Finding 3, of
paragraph II, are contrary to the evidence in that
the evidence shows the facts to be as follows: that
the plaintiff, prior to January 1, 1926, and, because
of her poor health, contemplated placing her property in a trust, so that she would be cared for therefrom, during her lifetime, and so that, after her
death, her daughter, Ruth Quinn Osborne, and her
daughter's minor son, William Leighton Osborne,
who were her only living descendants, would likewise be cared for; [625] that the plaintiff, on more
than one occasion prior to the date of the first purchases of securities, on January 7, 1926, by her from
the said National Bank, through the said Bothwell,
as the Manager of the said Bond Department, informed the said Bothwell of her desire to place her
property in such a trust, for herself, and for her
said daughter and her said grandson, and informed
the said Bothwell of what her said property consisted, and that included in her said property was
real property on Virginia Street, Reno, Nevada,
commonly called the "Virginia Street property",
lots in Sparks, Nevada, and a lot in Oakland, Cali-

fornia, and had inquired of the said Bothwell whether or not the said National Bank had a department which took care of estates; that the said Bothwell informed the plaintiff that the said National Bank had just the department of that kind to take care of estates for widows and orphans, but that the said Bothwell also informed her that the said National Bank could not handle her said Nevada real property, and that the thing for her to do was to dispose of her said Nevada real property and put the money obtained from such disposition in bonds, which could be placed in such a trust later on, and, in the meantime, bonds would be purchased by the said Bothwell, through the said Bond Department, from time to time, for her, as she acquired the money therefor, and the said National Bank would hold the bonds so purchased for her until she had disposed of her said Nevada real property, when the said trust would be created; that the plaintiff thereupon accepted the said advice of the said Bothwell, and, in accepting such advice, it was her intention, as the said Bothwell then knew, to create the said trust of her property, after she had disposed of her said Nevada real property; that the plaintiff further informed the said Bothwell that she had no experience with investments in [626] the bonds proposed to be so purchased by him, and would have to depend on what information about the bonds so purchased she obtained from the said Bond Department; that the said Bothwell thereupon told the plaintiff that the bonds so purchased

would be safe and desirable for the investment of,
and that she would never lose, her money; that to an
inquiry by the plaintiff of the said Bothwell as to
what he thought about investing her money in
United States bonds, he replied that unlimited
means were required for such an investment, since
United States bonds paid but little, and he could
purchase bonds for her that would be just as secure and would pay much more interest; that the
plaintiff did not know the difference, and the said
Bothwell never explained to her the difference, between bonds and notes, or between bonds and debenture bonds or between bonds otherwise secured and
collateral bonds, and she did not know whether or
not the securities, consisting of bonds and notes,
thereafter purchased by her from the said National
Bank, through the said Bothwell, as the Manager
of the said Bond Department, were adequately secured, but was assured by him that they were well
secured.

9. The said Court erred in finding, in that portion of the said Finding 3, of paragraph II, of the
said Findings of Fact, as follows:

"None of the securities purchased by plaintiff
from the national bank prior to September 24,
1929, were delivered to plaintiff, but at plaintiff's request, were held in safe-keeping by the
national bank subject to plaintiff's order as a
matter of accommodation to plaintiff; said securities were not held by said bank awaiting the
time when the same would be assigned or trans-

ferred by her to said bank as trustee or until
such time as she should create a trust.''

The said Court so erred for the reason that the
said last quoted portions of the said Finding 3, of
paragraph II, are contrary to the evidence in that
the evidence shows the facts to [627] be as follows:
that the securities, consisting of bonds and notes,
purchased for the plaintiff by the said National
Bank, through the said Bothwell, as the Manager
of the said Bond Department, were held by the said
National Bank for the plaintiff, pursuant to the advice of the said Bothwell to the plaintiff, awaiting
the time when the said trust was created after the
said Virginia Street property was sold; and that
none of the said securities so purchased prior to the
date, September 24, 1929, of the said instrument of
trust, were held in safe keeping by the said National
Bank, at the request, or for the accommodation of,
the plaintiff.

10.   The said Court erred in finding, in that portion of Finding 4, of paragraph II, of the said
Findings of Fact, (referring to the bonds of Medford Irrigation District), that

"It is not a fact that at the time of the sale of
the Medford bonds to plaintiff the same had
dropped to a market price or value of $777.50
per bond.''

The said Court so erred for the reason that the
said last quoted portion of the said Finding 4, of
paragraph II, is without the issues raised by the

said bill of complaint and the answers thereto, and
for the further reasons that the said portion of the
said Finding 4 is contrary to the evidence in that
the evidence shows the facts to be, (1), that $1,500
par value, of the bonds of the said Medford Irrigation District were purchased by the said National
Bank on March 22, 1926, for the price of $1,500, or
par, (2), that $2,500, par value, of the bonds of the
said District were purchased by the said National
Bank on September 6, 1927, for the price of $2,500,
or par, and (3), that the remaining $1,000, par
value, of the bonds of the said District were purchased by the said National Bank on February 2,
1928, for $777.50, or for the total price of $4,777.50,
and that [628] the entire $5,000, par value, of the
said bonds so purchased were sold to the plaintiff
by the said National Bank, through the said Bothwell, as the Manager of the said Bond Department,
on February 25, 1928, or 25 days after the said last
purchase of the said bonds by the said National
Bank, at the increased price of $4,850, or at a profit
thereby to the said National Bank of the difference
between the said sum of $4,777.50 and the said sum
of $4,850, or the sum of $72.50, but that, instead of
selling to the plaintiff the said bonds at the rate of
$777.50 per $1,000 of the said bonds, to which price
the said bonds had depreciated, or for the price of
$3,887.50, the profit to the said National Bank on
the said purchases by the said National Bank and
the said sale by the said National Bank to the plaintiff was, in fact, the sum of $972.50.

11. The said Court erred in finding, in that portion of the said Finding 4, of paragraph II, of the said Findings of Fact, that

"Plaintiff was not told that the prices which she was paying to the national bank in purchasing the said securities were the prices at which said bank had itself acquired them."

The said Court so erred for the reason that the said last quoted portion of the said Finding 4, of paragraph II, is without the issues raised by the said bill of complaint and the answers thereto, even if it be assumed, to the contrary of the said portion of the said Finding 4, that the plaintiff was told by the said Bothwell, or by some other official of the said National Bank, "that the prices which she was paying to the national bank in purchasing the said securities were the prices at which said bank had itself acquired them", and even if it be also assumed that what was told to the plaintiff was so told at the respective times when the said bonds were sold to the plain- [629] tiff by the said National Bank, through the said Bothwell, as the Manager of the said Bond Department.

11a. The said Court erred in finding, in those portions of the said Finding 4, of paragraph II, of the said Findings of Fact, that

"Bothwell did not conceal from the plaintiff that the national bank was making a profit in the sales of securities, a fact well known to the plaintiff at all times."

The said Court so erred for the reason that the
said last quoted portion of the said Finding 4, of
paragraph II, to wit, that the "fact" referred to as
being a fact "well known to the plaintiff at all
times", is contrary to the evidence, in that the plaintiff was never informed by the said Bothwell, or by
any other official of the said National Bank, of the
fact that the said National Bank was making a
profit on all or any of the sales of securities made by
the said National Bank, through the said Bothwell,
as the Manager of the said Bond Department, and
the plaintiff had no knowledge of the fact that the
said National Bank was making a profit on any of
the sales of securities made by the said National
Bank, until counsel for the plaintiff so informed
her after his examination, commenced on or about
November 15, 1932, of the transactions between the
said National Bank and the plaintiff in the purchases of securities for, or for the benefit of, the
plaintiff, from the said National Bank, through the
said Bothwell, as the Manager of the said Bond
Department.

12. The said Court erred in finding, in that portion of Finding 5, of paragraph II, of the said
Findings of Fact, that [630]

"At all times plaintiff desired to secure a high
rate of return on her purchases of securities,
never less than six per cent (6%) per annum
and in her purchases of securities plaintiff was
actuated primarily with that end in view."

The said Court so erred for the reason that the said last quoted portions of the said Finding 5, of paragraph II, are contrary to the evidence, in that the evidence shows the facts to be that the plaintiff, at no time, desired to secure a high rate of return on her purchases of securities, or that the plaintiff desired never less than 6% per annum, but, on the contrary, did desire a high rate of return on her purchases of securities, but only consistent with safety in such purchases, and that the plaintiff was never actuated, primarily or otherwise, with the end in view that she desired a high rate of interest on her purchases of securities, never less than 6% per annum, if such purchases were not consistent with safety.

13. The said Court erred in finding, in that portion of the said Finding 5, of paragraph II, of the said Findings of Fact, that

"At the time of the first of her purchases on January 7, 1926, and at various times thereafter plaintiff was advised by Bothwell that return or interest was compensation for the risk taken and that, in general, the higher rate of interest the greater the risk involved. That shortly prior to, at the time of, and subsequent to the creation of the trust instrument on September 24, 1929, plaintiff was similarly so advised by Berven."

The said Court so erred for the reason that the said last quoted portions of the said Finding 5, of

paragraph II, are contrary to the evidence, in that
the evidence shows the facts to be that the said
Bothwell did not advise the plaintiff, at the time of
the first of her purchases, on January 7, 1926, or
[631] at any time thereafter, that return or interest
was compensation for the risk taken, and that, in
general, or in particular, the higher rate of interest
the greater the risk involved, and that the evidence
does not show the fact to be that shortly, or at any
time, prior to, or at the time of, or at any time subsequent to the creation of the said trust instrument,
on September 24, 1929, the plaintiff was similarly so
advised by Berven, and that no inference could or
can be drawn from any evidence that the said Bothwell so advised the plaintiff, or that the said Berven similarly so advised the plaintiff.

14. The said Court erred in finding, in those
portions of the said Finding 5, of paragraph II, of
the said Findings of Fact, that

"Plaintiff did not tell Bothwell she desired
her funds invested in, or to purchase, bonds of
such safety or desirability that the same could
be readily sold at any time at the price at which
she purchased them nor did she ask him whether
or not her funds should be invested in United
States Government bonds, nor did Bothwell tell
her that her funds would be invested in, nor
that there would be sold to her, bonds just as
good as United States Government bonds."

The said Court so erred for the reason that the
said last quoted portions of the said Finding 5, of

paragraph II, are contrary to the evidence, in that the evidence shows the facts to be as follows: (1), that the said Bothwell told the plaintiff that the bonds which were to be purchased from the said National Bank, through the said Bothwell, as the Manager of the said Bond Department, pending the creation of the said trust, were to be good, substantial, reliable and safe bonds, and the plaintiff would never lose her money invested in them; (2), that the said Bothwell told the plaintiff, both before and after [632] the execution of the said instrument of trust, that her money would be placed by the said National Bank, through the said Bothwell, as the Manager of the said Bond Department, in bonds that were safe and desirable; and (3), that the plaintiff inquired of the said Bothwell, at the time of the first purchases of the said securities by the plaintiff from the said National Bank, through the said Bothwell, as the Manager of the said Bond Department, what he thought of investing her money in United States Government bonds, and that the said Bothwell replied that the plaintiff should have unlimited means to make such investments, since United States Government bonds paid so little interest, and the said Bothwell told the plaintiff that the bonds purchased for her from the said National Bank, through the said Bothwell, as the Manager of the said Bond Department, would be just as secure as United States Government bonds, and would pay much more interest, and the plaintiff would not lose any of her principal so invested.

15. The said Court erred in finding, in those portions of the said Finding 5, of paragraph II, of the said Findings of Fact, that

"All of the securities purchased by plaintiff from the national bank prior to the execution of the trust instrument on September 24, 1929, were at the times when purchased by plaintiff of the type desired by her and were at that time satisfactory, safe and desirable, and were so considered, not only by the national bank, but also by investment houses which, at the same time were selling the same securities to their customers."

The said Court so erred for the reason that the said last quoted portions of the said Finding 5, of paragraph II, are without the issues raised by the said bill of complaint and the answers thereto, and for the further reasons that the said portions of the said Finding 5 are contrary to the evidence, in that the evidence shows the facts to be as follows: (1), that [633] none of the said securities was, at the time when the same was sold to the plaintiff by the said National Bank, through the said Bothwell, as the Manager of the said Bond Department, of the type desired by the plaintiff, or of the desirable type which the said Bothwell, as the Manager of the said Bond Department, led the plaintiff to believe the said securities so sold were for the investment of her funds; and, (2), that there is no evidence that any of the said securities were so considered by any investment houses, which, at any of the times of any

of the said purchases for the plaintiff of the said
securities, were selling the "same" securities, or
securities of the same issue, to any of their customers, who desired safe and desirable securities for
the investment of their funds.

16. The said Court erred in finding, in those
portions of the said Finding 5, of paragraph II, of
the said Findings of Fact, that

"In general the only recommendation made
by Bothwell or by the national bank in the sale
of the securities to plaintiff was that the securities were considered satisfactory by the national bank or that said bank considered said
securities as safe and desirable. Such recommendations were based upon the best knowledge,
information and belief of the national bank and
Bothwell."

The said Court so erred for the reason that the
said last quoted portions of the said Finding 5, of
paragraph II, are without the issues raised by the
said bill of complaint and the answers thereto, and
for the further reasons as follows: (1), that there is
no evidence that "in general", or in any particular,
the only recommendation made by the said Bothwell,
or by the said National Bank, in the sale, either
prior or subsequent to the date of the execution of
the instrument of trust, on September 24, 1929, of
the securities, or of any of the securities, to the
plaintiff, by the said National Bank, was that the
said [634] securities were considered to be satisfactory by the said National Bank for the investment

of its own funds, rather than for the investment of
the funds of the plaintiff, and that the said National
Bank considered the said securities to be satisfactory
for its purposes, other than for the purpose of selling the said securities, or securities of the same issue, at a profit to itself, to persons who purchased
such securities from it, in the belief that it was a
well managed, reliable and trustworthy bank; and
(2), that there is no evidence that such recommendations were based upon the best knowledge and information, which could, or might, have been reasonably obtainable by the said National Bank, and
upon the justifiable belief of the said National Bank
and of the said Bothwell that such securities were
safe and desirable for the investment of the funds
of persons who purchased such securities for the
purpose of investment.

17. The said Court erred in finding, in that portion of the said Finding 5, of paragraph II, of the
said Findings of Fact, that

"In purchasing said securities plaintiff relied
in part upon the aforementioned recommendations and in part upon the relatively high rate
of interest and return such securities had."

The said Court so erred for the reason that the
said last quoted portion of the said Finding 5, of
paragraph II, is without the issues raised by the
said bill of complaint and the answers thereto, and
for the further reason that the said portion of the
said Finding 5 is contrary to the evidence, in that
the evidence shows the facts to be as follows: (1),

that the plaintiff, in purchasing the said securities
from the said National Bank, through the said
Bothwell, as the Manager of the said Bond Department, did not rely in part, or at all, upon the "relatively", or otherwise, high rate of interest which
such securi- [635] ties bore, or the "return" which
such "securities had", but relied entirely upon the
said National Bank, and the said Bothwell, as the
Manager of the said Bond Department, to select
such securities as were safe and desirable for the
investment of her funds; (2), that the plaintiff
never, either prior or subsequent to the execution
of the said instrument of trust, on September 24,
1929, selected any of the securities in which her
funds, or the funds of the trust estate created by
the said instrument of trust, were invested by the
said National Bank; (3), that, prior to the execution of the said instrument of trust, the said securities were selected by the said Bothwell, and were
recommended to the plaintiff by him as safe and desirable, or as safe and conservative, securities for
the investment of her funds, and, although, in several instances of such recommendations, the plaintiff questioned the securities so selected and recommended by the said Bothwell, as safe and desirable,
or as safe and conservative, she nevertheless approved such recommendations after the said Bothwell had assured her that the securities so questioned by her were safe and desirable, or safe and
conservative, securities for the investment of her
funds, and the securities so selected and recom-

mended by the said Bothwell were accordingly purchased for the plaintiff by the said National Bank, through the said Bothwell, as the Manager of the said Bond Department; and (4), that, subsequent to the execution of the said instrument of trust, the securities for the investment of the trust funds were selected, first, by the said Bothwell, as the Manager of the said Bond Department, and next by the said Read, as the Trust Officer of the Trust Department, of the said National Bank, and lastly by the said Berven, as the Assistant Trust Officer of the said Trust Department, and were recommended to the plaintiff by the said Bothwell, or by the said [636] Read, or by the said Berven, as the case might be, as safe and desirable, or as safe and conservative, securities for the investment of the said trust funds, and that the said recommendations so made were approved by the plaintiff, and the securities so selected and recommended by the said Bothwell, or by the said Read, or by the said Berven, as the case might be, were accordingly purchased for the said trust estate by the said Bothwell, as the Manager of the said Bond Department, or by the said Read, as the Trust Officer of the said Trust Department, or by the said Berven, as the Assistant Trust Officer of the said Trust Department, as the case might be.

18. The said Court erred in finding, in those portions of the said Finding 5, of paragraph II, of the said Findings of Fact, as follows:

"The bonds sold to plaintiff were sufficiently
secured by real property insofar as they purported or were represented to be so secured;
that the notes sold to plaintiff were sufficiently
secured by real and personal property, or by
real or personal property, insofar as they purported or were represented to be so secured;
neither the bonds of the Province of Buenos
Aires nor of the Province of Callao were, when
purchased, uncollectible, nor have they ever
been uncollectible, except in the sense that no
obligations of a sovereign power or state are
collectible in the event of the failure or refusal
of such sovereign power or state to pay the
same; the Medford Irrigation District bonds
were not, strictly speaking, secured by any direct lien upon real or other property, but said
bonds were nevertheless secured by assessments
which were liens upon real property situated in
said district; the notes of Jackson Furniture
Company were never secured by any lien upon
property of any kind, nor did they purport to
be so secured; plaintiff did not tell Bothwell
that she doubted the safety or desirability of
the Buenos Aires, or Callao, or California Cotton Mills bonds."

The said Court erred for the reason that the said
last quoted portions of the said Finding 5, of Paragraph II, are contrary to the evidence, which shows
the facts to be as follows: (1), that such of the said
securities as were purported, or represented, to be

secured by real property, were not sufficiently so
secured to render them safe and desirable for the
investment [637] of the funds of the plaintiff by
the said National Bank, through the said Bothwell,
as the Manager of the said Bond Department; (2),
that such of the said securities as were purported,
or represented, to be secured by real and personal
property, or by personal property, were likewise not
sufficiently so secured as to render them safe and
desirable investments of the funds of the plaintiff
by the said National Bank, through the said Bothwell, as the Manager of the said Bond Department;
(3), that neither the said bonds of the Province of
Buenos Aires, nor the said bonds of the Province of
Callao, were, similarly, at the respective times of
the investment, or at any subsequent time, of the
safety and desirability required for the investment
of the funds of the plaintiff by the said National
Bank, through the said Bothwell, as the Manager
of the said Bond Department, since the government
of the Argentine Republic, of which the Province
of Buenos Aires is a part, was, at the time of such
investment of the funds of the plaintiff in the bonds
of that Province, and it ever since has been, a notoriously politically unstable and financially unreliable government, and since the government of the
Republic of Peru, of which the Province of Callao
is a part, likewise was, at the time of such investment of the funds of the plaintiff in the bonds of
the latter Province, and it ever since likewise has
been, a notoriously politically unstable and finan-

cially unreliable government, with the consequent
result, in each case, that the principal of and the
interest on the said bonds of each of the said respective Provinces are uncollectible by the holders of
the bonds, and the same have not been, and will not
be, paid, unless the said respective Provinces choose
to make such payments; and (4), that the said bonds
of the said Medford Irrigation District, and the
payment of the principal of, or the [638] interest
on, the said bonds, have never been "strictly", or
otherwise, secured by any lien, "direct", or otherwise, upon either any land or any other property,
nor have the said bonds, or the payment of the principal of, or the interest on, the said bonds, ever been
secured by any assessment constituting a lien upon
any real property situated in the said District, with
the qualification that assessments for the payment
of the principal of, and the interest on, the said
bonds constitute liens upon the real property situated in the said District, severally levied against
tracts of land situated in the said District, and
severally payable by the respective owners of such
tracts, with no means for the collection of the respective assessments if the same be not paid, other
than by the sale, almost invariably, of the respective
tracts to the District itself, with the consequent result that the tracts so sold are no longer subject to
any assessment for the payment of the principal of,
or the interest on, any of the said bonds, or for any
other purpose, consequences which should have been
foreseen by the said National Bank, through the

said Bothwell, as the Manager of the said Bond
Department, at the time when the said Bothwell, as
such Manager, recommended to the plaintiff the purchase of $5,000, par value, of the bonds of the said
District, then owned by the said National Bank, as
containing, as he wrote to the plaintiff, on February
28, 1928, "all the elements to make them a safe and
desirable investment" of the funds of the plaintiff,
in contemplation, later fulfilled, of their becoming a
part of the trust estate subsequently created for the
support of the plaintiff and her dependents.

19. The said Court erred in finding, in that portion of Finding 2, of paragraph III, of the said
Findings of [639] Fact, that

> "Bothwell did not refer plaintiff to Daniel
> Read concerning the subject of the instrument
> of trust but at the time when plaintiff first spoke
> to Bothwell concerning her intended creation of
> the trust she informed Bothwell she had already
> spoken to Daniel Read but that he had seemed
> so indifferent about the subject that she did not
> believe that he was interested in her creating a
> trust."

The said Court so erred for the reason that the
said last quoted portion of the said Finding 2, of
paragraph III, is contrary to the evidence, in that
the evidence shows the facts to be as follows: (1),
that the plaintiff did not, at the time when she first
spoke to the said Bothwell concerning her intended
creation of the trust, inform the said Bothwell that
she had already spoken to the said Read; and (2),

that the first conversation which the plaintiff had
with the said Bothwell concerning the creation of a
trust by her, and in which she sought the advice of
the said Bothwell in relation thereto, occurred prior
to the time when she became acquainted with the
said Read, and talked to the said Read about the
creation of a trust.

20. The said Court erred in finding, in those
portions of the said Finding 2, of paragraph III, of
the said Findings of Fact, that

"About four (4) or five (5) months prior to
September 24, 1929 plaintiff first told Bothwell
that she was about to go to Mayo Brothers, in
Rochester, Minnesota, for treatment and asked
him whether he believed it advisable for her to
execute a trust and Bothwell stated that in view
of the circumstances of her intended trip to
Rochester he thought it was the thing to do.
Bothwell thereupon introduced plaintiff to Berven and on several occasions shortly prior to
September 24, 1929 plaintiff consulted with Berven concerning the creation of a trust and during such consultations told Berven that she
wished to continue purchasing securities from
the bond department of the national bank and
desired to purchase securities bearing a return
of not less than six per cent (6%). Berven told
her that the type of securities regarded as
proper for trust investments usually paid not
over five per cent (5%). Upon plaintiff's insistence that she needed at least six per cent

(6%) interest, Berven told plaintiff that a provision could be inserted in the trust instrument authorizing such type of investments. As a result thereof, the instrument [640] of trust (Exhibit 'A' annexed to the complaint) was executed by plaintiff to and with the national bank as trustee on September 24, 1929."

The said Court so erred for the reason that the said last quoted portions of the said Finding 2, of paragraph III, are contrary to the evidence, in that the evidence shows the facts to be as follows: (1), that the first conversation which the plaintiff had with the said Bothwell, concerning the creation of a trust, and in which the plaintiff asked the said Bothwell whether he believed it to be advisable for her to execute a trust, occurred prior to the first purchases of securities, on January 7, 1926, for the plaintiff by the said National Bank, through the said Bothwell, as the Manager of the said Bond Department, and the evidence does not show the fact to be that the plaintiff ever told the said Bothwell that she intended to take a trip to Rochester, Minnesota, for the purpose of treatment by Mayo Brothers; (3), that the said Bothwell, prior to the sale by the plaintiff of the said Virginia Street property, on February 8, 1928, and, therefore, more than a year prior to the execution of the instrument of trust, on September 24, 1929, requested the plaintiff to talk over the matter of the creation of a trust with Read, the Trust Officer of the said National Bank, and gave her a note of introduction to the said Read, and the plaintiff accordingly called on the said Read, in his office in the Central National Bank Building, on two occasions, and told him of her wishes concerning the creation of a trust, but that the said Read seemed to her to be indifferent and not much interested in the matter; (4), that the plaintiff thereafter called on the said Bothwell, and informed him of the result of her interviews with the said Read, and the said Bothwell thereupon told her that he would introduce her to the said Berven, the Assistant Trust [641] Officer of the said National Bank, and thereupon the said Bothwell took the plaintiff to the office of the said Berven, in the said Central National Bank Building, and there introduced her to the said Berven, and explained to the said Berven her desire to create a trust for her benefit during her lifetime, and for the benefit of her daughter and her grandson after her death, and stated to the said Berven that the said National Bank, through him, as the Manager of the said Bond Department, had purchased bonds for her, which the said National Bank was holding for her until such time as the said trust was created, and the said Berven was also informed, during the said interview between the plaintiff, the said Bothwell, and the said Berven, of what her other property, including the said Virginia Street property, consisted, and the said Berven told her that she should sell her said Virginia Street property; (5), that the said Bothwell was present during the entire said interview; (6), that the plaintiff never told the said Berven

that she wished to continue purchasing securities
from the said Bond Department, or that she desired
to purchase securities bearing a return of not less
than 6%, or bearing any other rate of interest; (7),
that the said Berven never told the plaintiff that the
type of securities regarded as proper for trust investments usually paid not over 5% ; (8), that the plaintiff never insisted that she needed at least 6% interest, nor did the said Berven tell the plaintiff that
a provision could be inserted in the trust instrument authorizing such type of investment, nor was
such provision inserted in the said instrument of
trust as a result of anything which the said Berven
had told the plaintiff; (9), and that the said Berven
did not mention to the plaintiff, at any time prior
to the execution of the said instrument of trust,
anything about the type of [642] securities purchased by or for the benefit of the plaintiff, until
subsequent to the execution of the said instrument
of trust, and on or about November 1, 1932.

21. The said Court erred in finding, in those portions of the said Finding 2, of paragraph III, of the
said Findings of Fact, that

"The instrument of trust was submitted by
Berven to plaintiff for her consideration and
approval on the 24th day of September, 1929
and was read to plaintiff by Berven, as well as
being read by plaintiff, and the provisions
thereof, paragraph by paragraph, were explained by Berven to plaintiff and plaintiff
stated she understood the same. Plaintiff inquired of Berven whether she should submit

the instrument of trust to an attorney of her selection for his advice concerning the same, to which Berven replied that it was proper she should do so, whereupon plaintiff stated that her attorney was in Nevada and that as she was about to leave for Rochester, Minnesota, she did not have time to do so. That Berven did not state to plaintiff that the instrument of trust was in the so-called 'usual form' but instead stated to her that owing to her own wishes provision was made therein for the investment of the trust funds in securities which, without such provision, would be improper for the investment of trust funds. That plaintiff, in reliance upon her reading of the provisions of the trust and in reliance upon what the said Berven had told her concerning the same, executed said instrument of trust as the same had been prepared and signed the statement at the foot thereof. That in so signing said instrument of trust plaintiff did not seek or obtain independent legal advice relating thereto because of the fact that she was in a hurry to leave for Rochester, Minnesota.''

The said Court so erred for the reason that the said last quoted portions of the said Finding 2, of paragraph III, are contrary to the evidence in that the evidence shows the facts to be as follows: (1), that the said Berven read to the plaintiff the said instrument of trust from one of the duplicate originals of the said instrument, and the plaintiff followed his reading with the other duplicate original of the said instrument; (2), that the said Berven did not explain to the plaintiff the provisions of the said instrument as he read them, or in any other manner, nor did the plaintiff state to the said Berven at that, or any other, time that she understood them; (3), that the [643] plaintiff asked the said Berven, before she signed the said instrument, if it was necessary for her to have an attorney look over the said instrument for her, and the said Berven replied that it was not necessary for her to do so, since her interests were fully protected by the said instrument; (4), that the plaintiff did not state to the said Berven that her attorney was in Nevada, and that, as she was about to leave for Rochester, Minnesota, she did not have the time for an attorney to look over the said instrument for her; (5), that the plaintiff signed the said instrument, without submitting the same to an attorney of her own selection, because the said Berven told her that such submission was not necessary; (6), that the said Berven did not tell the plaintiff that owing to her own wishes provision was made in the said instrument for the investment of the trust funds in securities which, without such provision, would be improper for the investment of trust funds, nor did the plaintiff ever express the wish to the said Berven that such provision be made in the said instrument; and (7), that the plaintiff did not sign the said instrument without seeking or obtaining legal, or other, advice because she was in a hurry to leave for

Rochester, Minnesota, but she signed the same because, having great trust and confidence in the said National Bank, and in the said Berven, as one of its important officers, she believed it was not necessary for her to have independent advice before she did so.

22. The said Court erred in finding, in those portions of the said Findings of Fact, in paragraph IV, pages 17-8, thereof, (erroneously numbered "2" instead of "3"), that

"In the instance of the purchases of the said Hearst bonds, said California Cotton Mills bond and said Federal Public Service bonds, Bothwell suggested and submitted the same to plaintiff without any other recommendation and plaintiff, relying in part [644] upon the said suggestion and submission and in part upon the relatively high rate of return, directed the trust department to purchase the same from the bond department; that no recommendation was made by any officer of the trust department of said bank in connection with said purchases; in the instance of each of said purchases, plaintiff knew that the bond department of the national bank was the owner of the securities so suggested and submitted and, with knowledge of that fact and that the said bond department was making a profit thereon, nevertheless directed the trust department to make such purchases from the bond department. In the instances of said purchases plaintiff dealt directly with the bond department and directed the trust department to follow out her wishes in making such purchases. The aggregate profit made by the national bank on such purchases was the sum of $471.00.''

The said Court so erred for the reason that the said last quoted portions of the said Findings, pages 17-8, of the said paragraph IV, are contrary to the evidence, which shows the facts to be as follows: (1), that the purchase of $1,000, par value, bond of Hearst Publications, Inc., was made on April 8, 1930, (as of April 15, 1930), the purchase of $1,000, par value, bond of California Cotton Mills Company, was made on June 5, 1930, the purchase of $5,000, par value, bonds of Federal Public Service Corporation, was made on June 27, 1930, (as of July 1, 1930), and the purchase of $6000, par value, bonds of Hearst Publications, Inc., was made on June 27, 1930, (as of July 1, 1930), and, therefore, that the said purchases were made subsequent to the execution of the said instrument of trust on September 24, 1929; (2), that the said purchases were so made for the said trust estate by the said National Bank, through the said Bothwell, as the Manager of the said Bond Department, and the said National Bank was both the seller and the purchaser of the said bonds; (3), that each of the said purchases was made on the recommendation thereof to the plaintiff by the said Bothwell, as the Manager of the said Bond Department, and the plaintiff approved each of the said purchases so recommended by the said Bothwell; (4), that, in approving the said purchases so recommended by the said

35

Both- [645] well, the plaintiff did not rely, in part,
upon the said recommendations of the said Bothwell and, in part, upon the relatively, or otherwise,
high return of interest on the said bonds, but relied
wholly upon the said recommendations of the said
Bothwell, as the Manager of the said Bond Department; and the said Court further so erred for the
reason that the said findings of the said Court, in
this respect, are without the issues raised by the said
bill of complaint and the answers thereto; (5), that
the plaintiff did not direct the said Trust Department, or the said Bothwell, or any other official of
the said National Bank, to make any of the said
purchases, nor did the plaintiff, in any of the
instances of the said purchases, deal directly, or
at all, with the said Bond Department, or direct
the said Trust Department to follow out any
wishes of the plaintiff in making any such purchases; and the said Court further so erred for
the reason that the said findings of the said
Court, in this respect, are likewise without the issues raised by the said bill of complaint and the
answers thereto; and (6), that the plaintiff had no
knowledge of the fact that the said Bond Department, or, more accurately, the said National Bank,
was the owner of the bonds so purchased, and she
did not know that the said National Bank had made
a profit on each of the said transactions of purchase,
aggregating a total of $471, or any other sum, until
she was so informed by her counsel subsequent to
November 15, 1932.

23. The said Court erred in finding, in those por-

tions of the said paragraph IV, pages 18-9, of the
said Findings of Fact, that

"The national bank did not conceal from
plaintiff the fact that the trust department was
purchasing bonds owned by the bond department, nor did it conceal from plaintiff that in so
doing the bank had profited in each of the instances of the purchase and [646] sale of the
said bonds; that said bonds were in each case
sold by the bond department to the trust department at the fair value thereof and were legal
trust investments for said trust department to
make for plaintiff's trust because of the fact
that the instrument of trust authorized the national bank, as trustee, to invest the trust funds
in securities or investments of the character permitted by law for the investment of trust funds,
'or otherwise'. That the said words 'or otherwise' were inserted in article 2 of the instrument of trust ('Exhibit A' annexed to the complaint) in order to comply with plaintiff's desire that the trust funds be invested in securities having a return of not less than six per cent
(6%) and it was at the time of the execution of
the instrument of trust explained to her that
such words had that effect, which was as plaintiff intended."

The said Court so erred for the reason that the
said last quoted portions of the said Finding, pages
18-9, of paragraph IV, are contrary to the evidence,
in that the evidence shows the facts to be as follows:
(1), that neither the National Bank, nor any official

thereof, at any time, informed the plaintiff of the fact that the said National Bank, through its said Trust Department, was purchasing, or had purchased, through its said Bond Department, bonds owned by the said National Bank, and the plaintiff was not informed by the said National Bank that in so doing the said National Bank had profited in each of the instances of the purchase and sale of the said bonds, and, therefore, that the said National Bank had violated its obligation, as a trustee, not to deal with itself in any manner relating to the trust estate, and, whether or not it profited by such dealing, or whether or not it had sold the said bonds to itself at the fair value thereof, the said National Bank, consequently, was guilty of having concealed the facts, in these respects, from the plaintiff, and that the said purchases, for that reason, were unlawful, and could have been disaffirmed the the plaintiff after she had obtained knowledge thereof, unless the plaintiff had ratified the said transactions after she had been informed by the said National Bank, (which was not the case), that the said National Bank [647] was the owner of the said bonds, and had profited in the purchase of them and the resale of them to the plaintiff, and unless, also, the said National Bank had informed the plaintiff of her legal rights in the matter, including her right to disaffirm the said purchases; (2), that the plaintiff never desired that the funds of the said trust estate should be invested in securities having a return of not less than 6%, or a return at any other rate of interest, and that it was not because of the fact that the said instrument of trust authorized the said National Bank, as trustee, to invest the trust funds in securities or investments of the character permitted by law for the investment of trust funds that the words "or otherwise" were inserted in the said article 2 of the said instrument of trust, in order to comply with any desire, or for any other reason, of the plaintiff, that the trust funds be invested in securities having a return of not less than 6%, nor did the plaintiff ever intend that the said trust funds should be so invested, and it was not explained to the plaintiff, at the time of the execution of the said instrument of trust, or at any other time, by any person, whether an official of the said National Bank or not, that such words had such effect.

24. The said Court erred in failing and declining to find, in paragraph V of the said Findings of Fact, as follows (referring to the petition of A. J. Mount, as the Conservator of the said National Bank, filed in this Court, for the approval by this Court, among other things, of the sale by the said National Bank to the said Savings Bank of the business of the said Trust Department of the said National Bank):

"The Court makes no finding as to whether or not, had plaintiff succeeded in establishing the liabilities, matters and things com- [648] plained of and alleged in her complaint, the savings bank, by the contract for the purchase of the trust department, or otherwise, or at all, would have assumed or agreed to pay or discharge any

of the said alleged liabilities to plaintiff of the
national bank relating or incidental to, or arising out of, the purchase of any bonds or notes,
or any other matter or thing occurring, prior to
the execution of the instrument of trust on
September 24, 1929 for the reason that, by virtue of other findings herein to the effect that no
such liabilities, matters or things, were established in the first instance, such finding as to the
effect of the contract for the purchase of the
trust department by the savings bank from the
national bank, or as to such alleged assumption
of the savings bank of the alleged liabilities of
the national bank, is rendered immaterial and
unnecessary to the decision of this case.''

The said Court so erred for the reason that the
responsibility for the obligations and liabilities of
the said National Bank, as well as those of the said
Savings Bank, to the plaintiff, to pay and discharge
all the debts and liabilities that are incidental to, or
connected with, the purchases of the securities for
the plaintiff by the said National Bank, as provided
in and by the contract between the said National
Bank and the said Savings Bank, for the sale by the
said National Bank to the said Savings Bank, is an
issue raised by the said bill of complaint and the
answers thereto, and since, if such obligations and
liabilities of the said National Bank to the plaintiff
were not assumed by the said Savings Bank by the
said contract, the said Savings Bank* would be and
is primarily responsible to the plaintiff as a prin-

*NOTE: This name in the printed Transcript of Record (R. 811) is
an error, and should be ''National Bank''.

cipal, instead of secondarily liable to the plaintiff as a surety, for the said obligations and liabilities.

25. The said Court erred in finding, in that portion of Finding 1, of paragraph VI, of the said Findings of Fact, that

"The national bank notified plaintiff of the respective defaults at or about the respective times when said defaults occurred. The national bank neither through Read, nor Berven, nor Bothwell, nor anyone else, except as hereinafter found, told plaintiff not to worry about said defaults, or any of said defaults, nor did it tell plaintiff after said defaults that said securities were well [649] secured, or that interest would eventually be paid; in this respect prior to November 1st, 1932, Berven told plaintiff that the Alameda Park bonds appeared to be protected by sufficient property."

The said Court so erred for the reason that the said last quoted portion of the said Finding 1, of paragraph VI, is contrary to the evidence, in that the evidence shows the facts to be as follows: (1), that the said Bothwell told the plaintiff that the securities which had defaulted would eventually come back again and would be good securities, and also told the plaintiff not to worry about the matter and that she should not lose her principal; and (2), that the said Berven never told the plaintiff, either prior to November 1, 1932, or at any other time, that the bonds of the said Alameda Park Co., in which $8,000, par value, of the plaintiff's funds had been invested by the said National Bank, through the said Bothwell, as the Manager of the said Bond Department, appeared to be protected by sufficient property, but the said Berven did tell the plaintiff, on or about November 1, 1932, when the plaintiff called upon the said Berven, at his request, that the bonds of the said Alameda Park Co. were secured by the Neptune Beach property in Alameda, and that it was a short way over there and she could take a ride over and look for herself at the property which secured the said bonds, a futile invitation which the plaintiff did not accept.

26. The said Court erred in finding, in those portions of Finding 2, of paragraph VI, of the said Findings of Fact, (referring to the call of the plaintiff upon the said Berven, on or about November 1, 1932, pursuant to a letter which the said Berven wrote to the plaintiff, in which he stated, referring to the bonds of Alameda Investment Company, in which $10,000, par value, of the plaintiff's funds had been invested by the said [650] National Bank for the plaintiff, "We believe that it is advisable that a portion of your holdings in said company should be sold at this time"), that

"Berven did not at that time recommend to plaintiff that the bonds be sold save as hereinafter found, or that the proceeds of the sales be invested in so-called 'better bonds'. In respect to this finding, not only prior to the execution of the trust instrument, but also subsequent thereto, Berven from time to time recommended to plaintiff that she sell a portion of her bonds and notes and invest the proceeds in bonds paying a lower rate of interest, but having more stability as to principal, but plaintiff refused to do so or to permit the same to be done. Berven on or about the aforesaid 1st day of November, 1932, recommended that the Alameda Investment Company bonds, or a portion thereof, be sold which plaintiff likewise refused to permit.''

The said Court so erred for the reason that the said last quoted portions of the said Finding 2, of paragraph VI, are contrary to the evidence in that the evidence shows the facts to be as follows: (1), that the said Berven did recommend to the plaintiff, on the said occasion of her call upon him, that a portion of the said bonds of the said Alameda Investment Company be sold and the proceeds of the sale be invested in better bonds; and (2), that the said Berven did not, from time to time, or at any time, either prior or subsequent to the execution of the said instrument of trust, recommend to the plaintiff that she sell a portion of her bonds and notes and invest the proceeds in bonds paying a lower rate of interest, but having more stability as to principal, with the qualification, however, that the said Berven, on or about November 1, 1932, recommended that a portion of the said bonds of the said Alameda Investment Company be sold, and that the plaintiff declined to approve the sale by the said Central Bank at the heavy loss, for the approximate price, namely, 40 cents per dollar, at which the said bonds could have then been sold.

27. The said Court erred in finding, in paragraph [651] VII of the said Findings of Fact, ("With respect to the matters set forth in the third separate defense in both of the answers on file herein"),

"That prior to the commencement of this suit the savings bank, being then the successor trustee under the said trust instrument, offered to permit plaintiff to revoke the trust and the instrument of trust and offered to deliver all of the trust properties to plaintiff and offered to agree that such revocation should not be a release or discharge of existing liabilities or obligations of said savings bank to plaintiff, if any; that plaintiff refused such offer."

The said Court so erred for the reason that the finding, in the said paragraph VII, of the said Findings of Fact, is not supported by any evidence in that the evidence does not show the fact to be that the offer so found was ever made by the said Savings Bank, but, on the contrary, the evidence shows the fact to be that no such offer, as so found, was ever made by the said Savings Bank, either in its own behalf, or in behalf of the then other defendants to this action, namely, the said National Bank and J. H. Grut, as the receiver of the said National Bank, and for the further reason that, even if had such offer, as so found, been made, such offer would not have constituted a defense to this action of either the said Savings Bank, or of the said National Bank, or its receiver, the said J. H. Grut.

28. The said Court erred in failing to find the facts pleaded in and raised by, (1), the seventh and separate defense of the said National Bank and of its then receiver, the said J. H. Grut, set forth in the supplemental answer of the said National Bank and its then receiver, the said J. H. Grut, filed in this action; or (2), in the eighth and separate defense of the said National Bank and its then receiver, the said J. H. Grut, set forth in the said supplemental answer; or (3), in the ninth and separate defense of the said National Bank and its then [652] receiver, the said J. H. Grut, and in failing to find the respective conclusions of law from the facts found in the respective said answers; for the reason that the plaintiff is entitled to have the facts and the said conclusions of law, raised by the said respective answers, found in favor of, or against, the plaintiff.

29. The said Court erred in finding as a fact, intermingled with, and misplaced in, the Conclusions of the Law found by the said Court

"That prior to the execution of the instrument of trust on September 24, 1929 the relationship existing between the plaintiff and the national bank was that of buyer and seller, and no fraud, concealment, or misrepresentation was practiced upon plaintiff by the national bank either with respect to said relationship, or with

respect to the value or desirability of the securities purchased or their market value, or
with respect to the fact that said national bank
was making a profit on such sales, or with respect to the fact that said bank was selling its
own securities to plaintiff;''

from which the erroneous conclusion of law is found
by the said Court, to-wit,

"and therefore plaintiff is not entitled to rescind any of the purchases of securities made
by her from the bond department of the national bank prior to the execution of the instrument of trust;''

for the reason that the evidence shows the facts to
be that the relation existing between the plaintiff
and the said National Bank, prior to the execution
of the said instrument of trust, was not that of
buyer and seller, but was that of cestui que trust
and trustee; and for the further reason that the
said National Bank, through the said Bothwell, as
the Manager of the said Bond Department, failed
to disclose to, and concealed from, the plaintiff the
facts that the securities sold, prior to the execution
of the said instrument, to the plaintiff by the said
National Bank were owned, in each instance of such
sales, by the said National Bank, and that, in each
instance of such sales, the said [653] National Bank
made a profit thereon, and further failed to disclose
to, and concealed from, the plaintiff that, because of
such facts, the plaintiff had the legal right to dis-

affirm such sales, and, further, that, because of such concealment, the said National Bank had perpetrated, and was guilty of, a fraud, upon the plaintiff.

30. The said Court erred in finding as a fact, likewise, as aforesaid, intermingled with, and misplaced in, the Conclusions of the Law found by the said Court,

> "That the national bank was not guilty of any fraud, concealment, or misrepresentation in connection with the execution of the instrument of trust dated September 24, 1929",

from which the erroneous conclusion of law is found by the said Court

> "and therefore plaintiff is not entitled to rescind the same;"

for the reason that the evidence shows the fact to be that the said National Bank, through the said Berven, the Assistant Trust Officer of the said Trust Department, failed to disclose to, and concealed from, the plaintiff the facts that, in each instance of the sale of the said securities to the plaintiff, by the said National Bank, through the said Bothwell, as the Manager of the said Bond Department, the said securities were owned by the said National Bank, and that, in each instance of such sales, the said National Bank made a profit thereon, and further failed to disclose to, and concealed from, the plaintiff that, because of such facts, the plaintiff had the legal right to disaffirm such sales, and to rescind and set aside the said instrument of trust, and, further, that, because of such concealment, the said Na-

tional Bank had perpetrated, and was guilty of, a
fraud upon the plaintiff; and, further, also, that, irrespective of her said right of rescission, the plaintiff was and is entitled to a decree in [654] this
action rescinding and setting aside the said instrument of trust, in order that her rights, consequent
upon such rescission and setting aside of the said
instrument of trust, might, and should be, judicially
determined, as set forth in the prayer of the said
bill of complaint, and in the prayer of the amendments and supplements to the said bill of complaint, filed in this action.

31. The said Court erred in finding as a fact,
also, likewise, as above, intermingled with, and misplaced in, the Conclusions of the Law found by the
said Court, that,

"in view of the fact that the savings bank
(Central Bank of Oakland), the successor trustee under said instrument of trust, prior to the
commencement of the action, and in its answer,
offered to permit plaintiff to revoke said instrument of trust, plaintiff may, if she so desires, revoke said instrument of trust, or appoint a new, or successor trustee, as provided
for by the provisions of paragraph 1 of the contract dated April 22nd, 1933, relative to the
purchase of the trust department of the national bank by the savings bank, and in the
event of such revocation, or such appointment
of a successor trustee, the savings bank shall
deliver to plaintiff or to such successor trustee,

as the case may be, all trust assets, subject to such deductions as may be equitable and just for its compensation and expenditures as set forth in the letter dated June 10, 1933, and shall execute such instruments as may reasonably be necessary to effect the foregoing."

The said Court so erred for the following reasons: (1), that it is not the fact that the said Savings Bank, either prior to, or since, the commencement of this action, offered to permit the plaintiff to revoke the said instrument of trust; and (2), it is respectfully submitted that the said Court, as a court of equity, should have determined, by its findings and its decree in this action, (as it was incumbent upon the said Court so to do, by a well settled rule of equity practice and procedure), all the rights and duties of the respective parties to the action, and should not leave open and undetermined, as has been done, by the above quoted finding, for the determination hereafter, without [655] the intervention of the said Court, questions of the future conduct, (which may be disputed), of the parties to the action, as set forth in the prayer of the bill of complaint, and in the prayer of the amendments and supplements to the bill of complaint filed in this action.

32. The said Court erred in finding as a fact, also, likewise, as above, intermingled with, and misplaced in, the Conclusions of the Law found by the said Court,

"That after the execution of the instrument
of trust on September 24, 1929 the national
bank, as trustee of plaintiff's trust, was entitled
to, and did lawfully, purchase the securities
which it did in fact purchase from the bond department by reason of the fact (a) that plaintiff expressly authorized and directed the trust
department to make such purchases knowing
that the bond department was then the owner
of, and intended to sell to the trust department,
said securities, and that the bond department
would make a profit on such sales to the trust
department, and (b) the provisions of section
25 of the California Bank Act expressly permitted such purchases by the trust department
from the bond department",

from which the conclusion of law is found by the
said Court to-wit,

"Therefore, plaintiff is not entitled to rescind
any of the purchases of securities made after
the execution of the instrument of trust."

The said Court so erred for the following reasons:
(1), that the following purchases were made by the
said National Bank, through the said Bothwell, as
the Manager of the said Bond Department, subsequent to the execution of the said instrument of
trust, to-wit, $1,000, par value, bond of Hearst Pub-
lications, Inc., on April 8, 1930, (as of April 15,
1930), $1000 par value, bond of California Cotton
Mills Company, on June 5, 1930, $5,000, par value,

bonds of Federal Public Service Corporation, on June 27, 1930, (as of July 1, 1930), and $6,000, par value, bonds of Hearst Publications, Inc., on June 27, 1930, (as of July 1, 1930); (2), that the said purchases were so made by the said National [656] Bank, through the said Bothwell, as the Manager of the said Bond Department, for, and with the funds of, the trust estate created by the said instrument of trust, and, therefore, the said National Bank purchased the said bonds, in one capacity, from itself, and sold the said bonds to itself, in the other capacity, as trustee of the trusts created by the said instrument of trust, and, consequently, was both the purchaser and the seller of the said bonds; (3), that the evidence does not show the fact to be that the plaintiff, expressly or otherwise, authorized or directed the said Trust Department to make any such purchases, and the evidence does not show the fact to be that the plaintiff knew that the said Bond Department was then the owner of, or intended to sell to the said Trust Department, any of the said bonds, or that the said Bond Department would make a profit on any of the said sales to the said Trust Department, and, on the contrary, the evidence shows the facts to be that the plaintiff did not, expressly or otherwise, authorize or direct the said Trust Department to make any such purchases, and that the plaintiff had no knowledge that the said Bond Department, (or, more accurately, the said National Bank), was the owner of, or intended to sell, or did sell, to the said Trust Department, (or,

more accurately, the said National Bank), any of
the said bonds, until she was so informed by her
counsel subsequent to November 15, 1932; (4), that
the provisions of Section 25 of the California Bank
Act did not, and do not, expressly, or inferentially,
permit any such purchases to be made by the said
Trust Department, (or, more accurately, the said
National Bank), from the said Bond Department,
(or, more accurately, the said National Bank), and,
moreover, the provisions of Section 25 of the said
California Bank Act were not pleaded either by the
said Central Bank, or by the said National Bank,
or [657] its receiver, the said J. H. Grut, as a defense to the said transactions of purchase and sale;
(5), that, consequently, the conclusion of law contained in the said above quotation, (referring to the
purchases of the said bonds), that the said National
Bank "was entitled to, and did lawfully, purchase
the securities which it did in fact purchase from the
bond department", is erroneous, and, on the contrary, the fact is that the said National Bank unlawfully purchased the said bonds, and, for that
reason, the plaintiff was and is entitled to findings
accordingly, and was and is entitled to a decree rescinding and setting aside the said purchases and
rescinding and setting aside the said instrument of
trust, as prayed for in the bill of complaint and in
the amendments and supplements to the bill of complaint, filed in this action.

33. The said Court erred in finding as a fact,
also, likewise, as above, intermingled with, and mis-

placed in, the Conclusions of the Law found by the said Court.

"That by reason of the fact that it is hereinabove found and herein determined that plaintiff has not established any of the liabilities, matters or things complained of and alleged in her complaint, on the part of the national bank, the determination of whether or not the savings bank, by the contract for the purchase of the trust department, or otherwise, or at all, would have assumed or agreed to pay or discharge any of the said alleged liabilities to plaintiff of the national bank relating or incidental to, or arising out of, the purchase of any bonds or notes, or any other matter or thing occurring, prior to the execution of the instrument of trust on September 24, 1929 had plaintiff succeeded in establishing the same, is rendered immaterial and unnecessary to the decision of this case. Had any liabilities been established as arising out of, or relating or incidental to, the purchase of the securities by the trust department, or the conduct of the said trust, after the execution of the trust instrument on September 24, 1929, such liabilities would have been assumed by the savings bank."

The said Court so erred for the reason, again respectfully submitted, that the said Court, as a court of equity, should have determined, by its findings and decree in this action, [658] all the rights and duties of the respective parties to the action, and

not leave open and undetermined, as has been done
by the above quoted finding, for the determination
hereafter, without the intervention of the said
Court, questions of the future conduct, (which may
be disputed), of the parties of the action as set forth
in the prayer of the bill of complaint, and in the
prayer of the amendments and supplements to the
bill of complaint, filed in this action.

34. The said Court erred in finding as a fact,
also, likewise, as above, intermingled with, and misplaced in, the Conclusions of the Law found by the
said Court,

> "That by reason of the fact that plaintiff has
> not succeeded in establishing any cause or
> causes of action against, or liabilities on the
> part of, any of the defendants it is unnecessary
> to determine whether or not, had such cause or
> causes of action, or such liabilities, been estab-
> lished, they would have been barred by any
> laches or limitations, or whether or not plaintiff
> waived her alleged right to rescind, or ratified,
> the alleged transactions complained of",

for the reason that the plaintiff is entitled to have
the defense of the statute of limitations, raised by
the sixth separate defense of the respective answers
of the said Central Bank and of the said National
Bank and of its then receiver, the said J. H. Grut,
and also the question of the waiver by the plaintiff
of her right to rescind, or her ratification of, the
transactions complained of by the plaintiff, raised

respectively by the seventh and eighth separate supplemental defenses of the said National Bank and its then receiver, the said J. H. Grut, determined either in favor of, or against, the plaintiff.

Respectfully submitted,

CHARLES W. SLACK and
EDGAR T. ZOOK

Attorneys for Plaintiff.

[Endorsed]: Filed Jan. 10, 1938. [659]

Appendix I

SECTION 31, CALIFORNIA BANK ACT

Appendix I

SECTION 31 OF THE CALIFORNIA BANK ACT.

(1 Deering, General Laws of California, 1931, p. 242.)

§31. Sale of business. Conditions of sale. Rights of creditors. Any bank may sell the whole of its business or the whole of the business of any of its departments or the whole of the business of any of its branches to any other bank which may purchase such business after obtaining the consent of the stockholders of the selling and of the purchasing banks holding of record at least two-thirds of the issued capital stock of each of such corporations; such consent to be expressed either in writing executed and acknowledged by such stockholders and attached to the instrument of sale, or to a copy thereof, or by vote at a stockholders' meeting of each of such banks called for that purpose. The selling and purchasing banks must for such purposes enter into an agreement of sale and purchase, which agreement shall contain all the terms and conditions connected with such sale and purchase. Such agreement shall contain proper provision for the payment of liabilities of the selling bank or of the department sold and the assumption by the purchasing bank of all fiduciary and trust obligations of the selling bank or department sold, and in these particulars shall be subject to the approval of the superintendent of banks; and shall not be valid until such approval is obtained. Such agreement

may contain provisions for the transfer of all deposits to the purchasing bank, subject, however, to
the right of every depositor of the selling bank to
withdraw his deposit in full on demand after such
transfer, irrespective of the terms under which it
was deposited with the selling bank; and such
agreement may also contain provisions for the
transfer of all court and private trusts to the purchasing bank, subject, however, to the right of
trustors and beneficiaries, after such transfer, to
nominate another and succeeding trustee of the
trusts so transferred. The rights of creditors of the
selling bank shall not in any manner be impaired
by any such sale, nor shall any liability or obligation
for the payment of any money due or to become
due, or any claim or demand, in any manner, or for
any cause existing against such selling bank or
against any stockholder thereof, be in any manner
released or impaired, and all the rights, obligations
and relations of all the parties, creditors, depositors,
trustors and beneficiaries of trusts shall remain unimpaired by the sale, but such bank to which the
other shall sell all its business or all the business
of any of its departments, shall succeed to all such
relations, obligations, trusts and liabilities and be
held liable to pay and discharge all such debts and
liabilities and to perform all such trusts of the
selling bank in the same manner as if such bank
to which the other had sold had itself incurred the
obligation or liability or assumed the relation of
trust, and the stockholders of the respective cor-

porations so entering into such agreement shall continue subject to all the liabilities, claims and demands existing against them as such at or before such sale.

Publication of notice. Immediately after the execution of such agreement of sale and purchase and its approval by the superintendent of banks, the original or a duplicate original thereof shall be filed in the office of the superintendent of banks and notice of such agreement shall be published for at least four successive weeks in a newspaper in each of the counties of the state in which either of such banks shall have its principal place of business; provided, however, that no action can be brought against such selling bank or any of its stockholders on account of any deposits, obligations, trusts or liabilities so transferred after the expiration of one year from the last day of publication herein required; and provided, further, that such selling bank shall maintain for a period of one year after the last day of publication herein required such an amount, if any, of capital or capital and surplus as the superintendent of banks, in the exercise of his discretion, may deem necessary.

Affidavit showing publication. An affidavit showing such publication shall be filed in the office of the superintendent of banks within ten days after the last publication thereof. The affairs of such selling bank, or selling department of a bank, shall remain subject to the provisions of this act.

4

Purchasing bank succeeds to rights, when. Upon the approval by the superintendent of banks of an agreement of sale and purchase and the transfer of the business of a trust department or of a bank having a trust department the purchasing bank shall, ipso facto and by operation of law and without further transfer, substitution, act or deed, and in all courts and places, be deemed and held to have succeeded and shall become subrogated and shall succeed to all rights, obligations, properties, assets, investments, deposits, demands, contracts, agreements, court and private trusts and other relations to any person, creditor, depositor, trustor, principal or beneficiary of any court or private trust, obligations and liabilities of every nature, and shall execute and perform all such court and private trusts in the same manner as though it had itself originally assumed the relation of trust or incurred the obligation or liability.

———

The following separation of the important provisions of the Section 31 may be of assistance in their construction (underscoring emphasis being added):

The Section, after providing (p. 242), that,

"Any bank may sell the whole of its business or the whole of the business of any of its departments or the whole of the business of any of its branches to any other bank which may purchase such business after obtaining the consent of the stockholders

of the selling and of the purchasing banks holding
of record at least two-thirds of the issued capital
stock of each of such corporations'',
expressed in a specified manner,—provides (p. 242),
that
"The selling and purchasing banks must for such
purposes enter into an agreement of sale and purchase, which agreement shall contain all the terms
and conditions connected with such sale and purchase'';

and further provides (pp. 242-3), that
"Such agreement shall contain proper provision for
the payment of the selling bank or of the department sold—

"and the assumption by the purchasing bank of all
fiduciary and trust obligations of the selling bank
or department sold, and in these particulars shall
be subject to the approval of the superintendent of
banks; and shall not be valid until such approval
is obtained'';

and, after providing (p. 243), that
"Such agreement may contain provisions for the
transfer of all deposits to the purchasing bank'',

"and such agreement may also contain provisions
for the transfer of all court and private trusts to
the purchasing bank'',

subject, in these respective two instances, to what
amounts to the approval thereof by the depositors
or by the trustors and beneficiaries, respectively,
continues (p. 243):

"The rights of creditors of the selling bank shall not in any manner be impaired by any such sale, nor shall any liability or obligation for the payment of any money due or to become due, or any claim or demand, in any manner, or for any cause existing against such selling bank or against any stockholder thereof, be in any manner released or impaired, and all the rights, obligations and relations of all the parties, creditors, depositors, trustors and beneficiaries of trusts shall remain unimpaired by the sale, but such bank to which the other shall sell all its business or all the business of any of its departments, shall succeed to all such relations, obligations, trusts and liabilities—

"and be held liable to pay and discharge all such debts and liabilities and to perform all such trusts of the selling bank in the same manner as if such bank to which the other had sold had itself incurred the obligation or liability or assumed the relation of trust, and the stockholders of the respective corporations so entering into such agreement shall continue subject to all the liabilities, claims and demands existing against them as such at or before such sale".

Concluding with the following particular provisions relating to the sale of the business of a trust department of a bank (pp. 243-4):

"Upon the approval by the superintendent of banks of an agreement of sale and purchase and the transfer of the business of a trust department or of a bank having a trust department the purchasing bank shall, ipso facto and by operation of law and without further transfer, substitution, act or deed, and in all courts and places, be deemed and held to have succeeded and shall become subrogated and shall succeed to all rights, obligations, properties, assets, investments, deposits, demands, contracts, agreements, court and private trusts and other relations to any person, creditor, depositor, trustor, principal or beneficiary of any court or private trust, obligations and liabilities of every nature, and shall execute and perform all such court and private trusts in the same manner as though it had itself originally assumed the relation of trust or incurred the obligation or liability."

o. 8860

IN THE 2

United States Circuit Court of Appeals

For the Ninth Circuit

ABBIE W. QUINN,

Appellant,

vs.

CENTRAL COMPANY (a corporation), as agent for
the shareholders of the Central National Bank
of Oakland, CENTRAL NATIONAL BANK OF OAK-
LAND (a national banking association in liquidation), and CENTRAL BANK OF OAKLAND (a
corporation),

Appellees.

BRIEF FOR APPELLEES.

IRA ABRAHAM,
Central Bank Building, Oakland, California,
*Attorney for the Defendants and Appellees, Central
Company (a corporation), as agent for the share-
holders of Central National Bank of Oakland, and
Central National Bank of Oakland (a national
banking association in liquidation).*

CLIFFORD BURNHILL,
Central Bank Building, Oakland, California,
Of Counsel.

FITZGERALD, ABBOTT & BEARDSLEY,
CHARLES A. BEARDSLEY,
M. W. DOBRZENSKY,
JAMES H. ANGLIM,
EDWARD B. KELLY,
CRELLIN FITZGERALD,
Central Bank Building, Oakland, California,
*Attorneys for the Defendant and Appellee, Central
Bank of Oakland (a corporation).*

FILED

FEB 14 193.

PERNAU-WALSH PRINTING CO , SAN FRANCISCO

Subject Index

Table of Authorities Cited

No. 8860

United States Circuit Court of Appeals
For the Ninth Circuit

ABBIE W. QUINN,

Appellant,

vs.

CENTRAL COMPANY (a corporation), as agent for the shareholders of the Central National Bank of Oakland, CENTRAL NATIONAL BANK OF OAKLAND (a national banking association in liquidation), and CENTRAL BANK OF OAKLAND (a corporation),

Appellees.

BRIEF FOR APPELLEES.

STATEMENT OF THE CASE.

Because the appellees believe that the "Statement of the Case" in the appellant's opening brief does not conform to the rules of this Court, the appellees present their statement of the case:*

---

*In this brief the plaintiff and appellant, Abbie W. Quinn, will be referred to either as the plaintiff or as the appellant. The defendant and appellee, Central National Bank of Oakland, will be referred to as the national bank. The defendant and appellee, Central Bank of Oakland (whose corporate name until April 22, 1933, was Central Savings Bank of Oakland), will be referred to as the savings bank. The defendant and appellee, Central Company as agent for the shareholders of the national bank, did not become a party to this suit until January 15, 1937, after the trial and prior to the entry of the decree, at which time it was substituted as a defendant in the place and stead of Joseph H. Grut, as receiver of the national bank. (R. 202-204.)

The plaintiff's alleged cause of action is apparently based upon the following series of transactions between her and the national bank:

1. The first of these series of transactions was between plaintiff and the bond department of the national bank, represented by Mr. Bothwell, an assistant cashier and the manager of the bond department, and involved the sales of bonds by the bond department to plaintiff from January 7, 1926, to September 24, 1929, the date upon which the instrument of trust was executed, a period of over three years and eight months.

2. The second of these series of transactions had to do with the preparation and execution of the instrument of trust on September 24, 1929, whereby plaintiff constituted the national bank her trustee.

3. The third of these series of transactions occurred after the execution of the instrument of trust and involved the purchase of certain securities by the trust department of the national bank from the bond department thereof for plaintiff's trust.

THE QUESTIONS INVOLVED AND THE MANNER IN WHICH THEY ARE RAISED.

1. What was the legal relationship existing between plaintiff and the national bank arising out of the purchases of securities from the bond department *prior* to the execution of the trust instrument on September 24, 1929? (*Infra,* pp. 9 to 46.)

(a) Did the parties intend that plaintiff should buy securities from the bond department and that it should *sell* to her securities which it either then owned or which it had contracted to purchase through participating in the underwriting thereof, in other words, did the parties intend that a buyer-seller relationship should exist, as the defendants contend and as was found by the District Court? (*Infra*, pp. 9 to 32.)

(b) Or, did the parties intend that the bond department should buy securities for plaintiff, and did she so direct, in other words, was the bond department constituted plaintiff's agent or broker for the purpose of purchasing securities for her, as plaintiff contended in her complaint and during the trial of the case? (*Infra*, pp. 9 to 32.)

(c) Or, was the relationship between the bond department of the national bank and plaintiff that of trustee and *cestui* during the period of three years and eight months *prior* to the execution of the instrument of trust, as is contended by plaintiff for the *first time* in her assignments of error and in her brief? (*Infra*, pp. 32 to 46.)

2. Was the national bank guilty of constructive fraud in the preparation and execution of the instrument of trust? (*Infra*, pp. 46 to 54.)

3. Is plaintiff entitled to rescind the instrument of trust by reason of the fact the trust department of the national bank purchased certain securities from the bond department thereof after the execution of the trust instrument? (*Infra*, pp. 54 to 73.)

The fourth question raised in appellant's brief (App's. Brief p. 48), namely, as to what liabilities, if any, the savings bank assumed when it purchased the trust department of the national bank, has become moot since the Court found that there were no liabilities on the part of the national bank to plaintiff. However, at pages 73 to 76 of this brief we shall show that it was not necessary for the Court to make a finding on this point since the findings otherwise made adequately support the decree of the District Court and therefore rendered unnecessary any finding on the question of whether or not there was any assumption of such alleged liabilities.

The fifth question raised in appellant's brief (App's. Brief, pp. 48-49) namely, as to whether or not the evidence supports the finding that prior to the commencement of the suit, the savings bank offered to permit plaintiff to revoke the trust and offered to agree that such revocation should not be a release or discharge of existing liabilities of the savings bank, if any, and, if so, whether such offer constituted a defense, will not be separately treated herein but will be dealt with in that portion of our argument wherein we discuss the question as to whether or not the national bank was guilty of any fraud in connection with the execution of the trust instrument by reason of the fact that the trust instrument contained a provision that upon revocation thereof a release should be given by plaintiff to the trustee. (*Infra,* pp. 46 to 54.)

THE EFFECT OF APPELLANT'S FAILURE TO COMPLY WITH THE RULES OF THIS COURT.

At the outset a question arises as to whether Rule 20 of the new rules of this Court, effective December 19, 1938, or Rule 24 of the old rules of this Court, which was in effect at the time the appeal was commenced, is applicable to the appellant's brief.

Rule 24, section 2, subparagraph (d) of the old rules required that each assignment of error be printed in full preceding the argument addressed to it unless the specified error was more than two printed pages in length, in which event it might be summarized before the argument addressed thereto. Twenty-seven of the assignments of error are less, and eight are more, than two pages in length.* While counsel have specified all thirty-five of their assignments of error as being relied upon (App's. Brief pp. 43-46), nevertheless in not a single instance has this provision of the old rules been complied with, in that none of the assignments of error has either been printed in full or in summarized form before any part of the argument directed thereto.

If, on the other hand, the new rules are held to be applicable, nevertheless counsel have not complied with Rule 20, section 2, subparagraph (d) thereof, which provides:

> "In equity * * * the specification shall state as particularly as may be, wherein the findings of fact and conclusions of law are alleged to be erroneous. * * *."

Nowhere do the specifications of error comply with this provision of the new rules. In addition to the specifications of error counsel have set forth in the briefest

---

*The Assignments of Error which are more than two pages in length are Assignment 8, R. 779-782; Assignment 17, R. 792-794; Assignment 18, R. 794-798; Assignment 20, R. 799-802; Assignment 21, R. 802-805; Assignment 22, R. 805-807; Assignment 23, R. 807-810; Assignment 32, R. 820-823.

Brief pp. 44, 49-52.)

A further violation of the rules appears. While counsel contend that certain of the findings are "contrary to the evidence" in not a single instance in their argument have counsel referred to the statement of evidence. (App's. Brief pp. 43 and 52.) In other words, in a case involving almost entirely questions of fact, no reference whatsoever is made in the argument to the pages of the record whereat the evidence involving the particular point under discussion can be found. This violates Rule 24, section 2, subparagraph (e) of the old rules as well as Rule 20, section 2, subparagraph (f) of the new rules.

A further neglect on appellant's part consists in the filing of a multitude of lengthy and confusing assignments of error. These assignments occupy 53 pages of the printed record. (R. 773-826.) Such practice defeats the very purpose of the requirement of assignments of error. In the case of *Local No. 167 of International Brotherhood of Teamsters v. United States* (1934), 291 U. S. 293, 54 Sup. Ct. Rep. 396, 78 L. ed. 804, the United States Supreme Court, while refraining from dismissing an appeal involving 250 confusing specifications, in view of the appellee's failure to object and the lack of precedent in point, nevertheless warned that such practice in the future would constitute grounds for dismissal. In *Cossack v. United States* (1936), 82 Fed. (2d) 214, 218 (C. C. A. 9), this Court not only condemned the practice of filing a multitude of unmeritorious assignments, but also declared that such practice was cause for dismissal in the future. In that case the assignments covered 18 printed pages, whereas here they cover 53 pages of the record.

In view of the fact the Court may choose to overlook the appellant's absolute non-compliance with the rules of this Court and undertake the task of determining whether any of the assignments indicates a material error, we shall, for that reason alone, and reserving our objection that all of the appellant's assignments of error have been abandoned, proceed to reply to the various arguments of counsel, and attempt to determine toward which assignment of error each argument of counsel is directed. The failure on appellant's part to observe said rules has greatly increased the burden imposed upon the Court as well as upon counsel.

ARGUMENT.
SUMMARY OF ARGUMENT.

The argument of the defendants and appellees may be summarized as follows:

1. Prior to the execution of the trust instrument on September 24, 1929, the relationship existing between plaintiff and the national bank was that of buyer and seller and not that of principal and agent or *cestui* and trustee. (*Infra*, pp. 9 to 46.) The contention of plaintiff that the relationship was that of *cestui* and trustee prior to the execution of the trust instrument is advanced for the first time on appeal and is unsupported by any evidence in the case. (*Infra*, pp. 32 to 46.) In fact the evidence shows, and the Court found, that it was not until

found that the securities which were retained on deposit with the bond department of the national bank after the purchases thereof by plaintiff were retained by the bank as depositary or bailee as a matter of accommodation to plaintiff. (*Infra,* pp. 35 to 42.) The fact that plaintiff may have reposed trust and confidence in the bond department of the national bank and in the manager thereof did not give rise to a trust relationship. (*Infra,* pp. 42 to 46.)

2. There was no fraud or wrong-doing in connection with the execution of the trust instrument. (*Infra,* pp. 46 to 54.)

3. The fact that after the execution of the trust instrument, the trust department of the national bank purchased certain securities from the bond department does not entitle plaintiff to rescind the instrument of trust or to secure the repayment of the moneys so invested, *first,* because even if it be conceded, which it is not, that such purchases constituted wrong-doing on the part of the trustee, nevertheless a trust cannot be rescinded or cancelled on account of subsequent wrong-doing on the part of a trustee, nor can the moneys so expended be repaid to plaintiff since such investments resulted in a substantial profit to the trust estate. (*Infra,* pp. 54 to 59.) *Second,* such purchases were proper and lawful (a) because plaintiff expressly directed the trust department to purchase such securities from the bond department with knowledge of all material facts (*infra,* pp. 59 to 68); and (b) because section 25 of the *California Bank Act* expressly authorized such purchases. (*Infra,* pp. 68 to 73.)

4. It was unnecessary for the District Court to make any finding or determination as to whether or not the savings bank would have assumed the liabilities of the national bank which are alleged by plaintiff to have arisen prior to the execution of the trust instrument since the finding that there were no liabilities rendered such question moot. (*Infra,* pp. 73 to 76.)

I. **PRIOR TO THE EXECUTION OF THE TRUST INSTRUMENT ON SEPTEMBER 24, 1929, THE RELATIONSHIP EXISTING BETWEEN PLAINTIFF AND THE NATIONAL BANK WAS THAT OF BUYER AND SELLER AND NOT THAT OF PRINCIPAL AND AGENT OR CESTUI AND TRUSTEE.**

1. **THE APPELLANT'S APPARENT THEORY OF THE RELATIONSHIP.**

In the first question stated by counsel, the issue is raised as to whether the instrument of trust should be rescinded in a suit brought by a depositor in the national bank who sustained an alleged relationship of trust and confidence toward it, for the reason that bonds *"were purchased for*"* the depositor *by the bank from itself,* prior to, but in contemplation of, the creation of a trust", without disclosing to plaintiff that the bonds were owned by the bank and were sold at a profit, and without disclosing that the bank could not lawfully purchase such securities from itself, and without advising plaintiff of her alleged legal rights of disaffirmance. (App's. Brief, pp. 46-47.)

The theory upon which counsel proceeded in the District Court was that plaintiff had constituted the bond department of the national bank her agent or broker for

---

*All italics are supplied by us, except where otherwise noted.

selling its own securities to her. Nowhere, prior to appeal, was any attempt made by plaintiff to argue or contend that the relationship between the parties was that of *cestui* and trustee prior to the time the trust instrument was actually executed on September 24, 1929. The Court can examine the complaint and the evidence in vain; it will find no allegation or evidence even hinting at the formation or creation of a trust prior to the time the trust instrument was actually executed. Now, for the first time, on appeal, counsel contend that the relationship between the parties was that of *cestui* and trustee *before* as well as after the execution of the trust instrument. (App's. Brief pp. 20-21, 52, 57 and 61.)

We assume that counsel's argument in this respect is directed in support of Assignments of Error Nos. 6, 7, 8 and 29. (R. 777-782, 816-818.)

———

2. THE DETERMINATION OF THE COURT THAT THE RELATIONSHIP WAS THAT OF BUYER AND SELLER IS WITHIN THE ISSUES AND IS SUPPORTED BY THE EVIDENCE.

With respect to the nature of the relationship prior to the execution of the trust instrument the District Court found that the securities "were in fact purchased by plaintiff from the national bank"; that the relationship "with respect to plaintiff's acquisition of said securities was that of buyer and seller and not that of a principal (on plaintiff's part) and an agent or broker to purchase securities (on the national bank's part)"; that plaintiff intended to buy securities from the national bank which it owned or had contracted to purchase and that the bank should sell its own securities to her; that it was not intended by plaintiff that the bank should purchase securities for her nor did she ever tell the national bank to do so. (R. 322-323.)

We now proceed to demonstrate that the matters so found were within the issues involved and that such findings were directly supported by the evidence.

(a) **The pleadings.**

In appellant's brief it is contended: The complaint does not allege plaintiff acted as purchaser and the national bank as seller (App's. Brief p. 19); nor does the complaint allege, either in terms or effect, that plaintiff, in any purchases prior to the execution of the trust instrument, acted in the capacity of principal and the national bank in the capacity of agent. (App's. Brief pp. 19-20.)

Let us turn to the complaint and to the answers of the defendants and see what issues the pleadings did in fact raise. In the complaint it is alleged:

> "* * * Bothwell * * * advised the plaintiff * * * to invest her funds * * * through the said Bond Department, in bonds; that the plaintiff * * * informed him that she * * * would invest her funds * * * through the said Bond Department, in bonds * * *." (R. 9-10.)
> "* * * that the plaintiff * * * approved the purchase *for her by the said Bank*, through Bothwell * * * of the said bonds and notes, * * *." (R. 11.)

Similar allegations appear in each instance of the purchase of securities prior to the execution of the trust instrument. (R. 12-16, 19-20.) It is further alleged (R. 20):

> "That, in each instance of the purchase aforesaid of the said bonds or notes *for the plaintiff* by the defendant * * * through the said E. D. Bothwell * * * the said bonds or notes were so purchased *for the plaintiff* by the said Bank *from itself* * * * and thereby the said Bank * * * was both *the purchaser* of the said bonds or notes *from itself,* in one capacity, *for the plaintiff,* and the seller, in another capacity, to the plaintiff, of the said bonds or notes so purchased; * * *."

From the foregoing, it definitely appears that plaintiff's theory of the relationship, prior to the execution of the trust instrument, was that she constituted the bond department her agent or broker *to purchase securities for her* but that in violation of its duties as such purchasing agent or broker, the bond department secretly sold its own securities to her and was thereby guilty of constructive fraud.

The answers of the defendants directly and unequivocally deny such allegations and such alleged relationship. Thus the answer of the savings bank provides:

> "* * * denies that * * * Bothwell advised plaintiff * * * to invest her funds * * * through the bond department in bonds * * *." (R. 102.) "* * * denies that plaintiff informed Bothwell that * * * she would invest her funds * * * through the bond department in bonds * * *." (R. 103.) "* * * Denies that plaintiff approved the *purchase for her* by the national bank * * * of said bonds or notes * * * and in this respect alleges that in none of the instances of the purchases of bonds or notes by plaintiff did the national bank, or Bothwell, or the bond department,

purchase bonds for plaintiff or act for plaintiff in the purchase thereof'' (save in four instances after the creation of the trust) "but instead, as plaintiff well knew, sold bonds to plaintiff * * * and that in all cases prior to the creation of the trust * * * plaintiff and the national bank were acting in the capacity of buyer and seller and not in the capacity of principal and agent.'' (R. 105-106.)

Similar denials appear in the answer of the national bank and Joseph H. Grut, the Receiver thereof. (R. 142-143, 145-146.)

The foregoing excerpts from the pleadings are typical of the allegations in the complaint and the denials in the answers on the subject as to whether or not plaintiff directed the national bank *to buy for her*. By denying these allegations the defendants put squarely in issue the question as to the nature of the relationship prior to the creation of the trust. Under such denials it was incumbent upon plaintiff to establish her theory of the relationship by evidence, and the way was open to the defendants to adduce evidence which not only rebutted her contention of agency, but which also showed what actually did transpire in the purchase of these securities by plaintiff. Furthermore, the answers explained the relationship by setting forth that it was that of buyer and seller. Counsel intimate that the allegations that plaintiff and the national bank "were acting in the capacity of buyer and seller and not that of principal and agent'' in the answers are outside the permissible scope of the pleadings. (App's. Brief pp. 19-20.) However, these allegations in the answers, being made by way of explanation, are permissible under Equity Rule 30, which provides:

"The defendant by his answer shall set out in short and simple terms his defense to each claim asserted in the bill, omitting mere statements of evidence and avoiding general denials, but specifically admitting, denying *or explaining* the facts upon which the plaintiff relies. * * *."

(b) The evidence.

The appellant has not even attempted to refer to any part of the evidence dealing with the nature of the relationship existing between the parties prior to September 24, 1929. As we shall proceed to show, plaintiff can hardly claim to have raised even a bare conflict in the evidence. Certainly the weight of the evidence establishes that plaintiff *intended to buy* securities from the national bank which the national bank owned and did not intend that the bank should act as agent or broker for the purpose of buying securities for her.

Plaintiff's evidence.

In response to a leading question, plaintiff answered as follows:

"Mr. Slack. Did he (Bothwell) ever make any purchases of any securities for you?" (R. 364.)

(Objection and objection overruled.) (R. 364-366.)

"Mrs. Quinn. A. Yes." (R. 366.)

Plaintiff then proceeded to testify that Bothwell said "they" would purchase bonds for her (R. 367); that Bothwell was to buy bonds for her trust fund (to be thereafter created). (R. 368.) The rest of plaintiff's testimony is substantially similar to the foregoing.

Counsel then introduced in evidence a letter dated February 28, 1928, addressed to plaintiff and signed by

Mr. Bothwell, the assistant cashier and manager of the bond department of the national bank. (Pl's. Ex. 1; R. 373, 539-540.) This letter will be referred to as the "Medford" letter. The material portions thereof are as follows:

"Dear Mrs. Quinn:

As requested in your letter of Feb. 26th, we are redeeming

$5000 Western States Gas and Electric
Company Bonds

as per bill herewith, *and confirming*

$5000 Medford Irrigation District Bonds,

as per bill enclosed. You will note that we secured the Medford Bonds at 97 which will give you a 6.22% yield. The difference of $350.00 has been credited to your commercial account.

The above transaction is subject to your **approval.**"

During the trial counsel for plaintiff placed great emphasis upon the fact that the letter provided: "You will note that *we secured* the Medford Bonds at 97 * * *". However, as Mr. Bothwell explained (R. 438):

"A. The word 'secured' could have been another word, 'confirmed', the word 'secured' being used was not in the sense that we went out and purchased the bonds. It was a matter of confirmation to her, the bonds at a price of 97."

That this explanation was fair and consistent is shown by Mr. Bothwell's letter to plaintiff dated August 17, 1929, which provides, so far as is material (Defs'. Ex. "I", R. 718-719):

"Dear Madam:

Referring to our recent conversation, we now take pleasure in *confirming sale to you* of:

$5,000 Central West Public Service Co. 7%,
in trade for:
$5,000 Rhodes Jamieson Company 7% bonds,
as per bills enclosed."

Furthermore, the "Medford" letter reads:
"* * * and *confirming*
$5000 Medford Irrigation District Bonds,
as per bill enclosed."

The word "confirming" is indicative of a sale, for example, "confirming the sale to you". Still more important, a bill was enclosed with the "Medford" letter and therefore was a part of the same communication. This bill (Defs'. Ex. "E", R. 423, 716) is similar in form to all of the other bills given to plaintiff and we therefore set it forth at length herein:

"Central National Bank   No. 6130
Bond Department

Sold to
    Abbie W. Quinn

Oakland, Calif., 2-28-28
as of 3- 1-28

Par Value	Security	Principal	Accrued Interest	Total
$ 5000.	Medford Irrig. Dist. 6% 1-1-56 at 97 6.22% basis Int. 2 mos.	$ 4850.00	$ 50.00	$
	INTERIM CERTIFICATE NUMBER			$4900.

Accrued interest on bonds is computed to date payment is made by the purchaser. If payment for the bonds figured on this statement is delayed beyond the above date include additional interest to date of payment.
All bonds listed on our offering sheets are carefully selected for their investment value. They carry our recommendation, but are not guaranteed."

This bill, which is, for all legal purposes, a bill of sale, clearly and unmistakably establishes that this was a sale by the bond department of the national bank to plaintiff. At pages 24 to 25 hereof, we shall establish the legal effect of a bill which is worded *"Sold to"* in supporting the defendants' theory of the buyer-seller relationship rather than plaintiff's theory of the principal and agent relationship.

The defendants' evidence.

The defendants' evidence on this point consists of the testimony of Mr. Bothwell and the witness Paul Anderson and certain documentary evidence.

Mr. Bothwell testified as follows: He became manager of the bond department of the national bank in 1920 or 1921 and continued as such until February, 1933 (R. 413-414); he recalled a conversation with plaintiff in January, 1926, in connection with the purchase of certain bonds when "Mrs. Quinn came to the bond department to buy bonds, and asked if we sold bonds, and I submitted an offering list, on which was listed the bonds that the Bank had for sale" (R. 415); she said "she had funds for investment, and that she wished to buy bonds, as she needed income". (R. 418.)

The defendants then offered and read in evidence, as an exemplar as to form, an offering list dated July 18, 1927. (Defs'. Ex. "A"; R. 419, 502, 705-707.) Mr. Bothwell testified that this offering list, with appropriate changes as to date and the list of securities, was a correct copy, as to form, "of the offering list which I showed to Mrs. Quinn on the occasion of her first visit in the Bond Department for the purpose of purchasing securities, on January 7, 1926''. (R. 419.) The offering lists were in the following form:

"Bond Department
Central National Bank, Oakland, Cal.

We offer subject to prior sale and change in price

July 18, 1927

Bond Dept. Phone Lakeside 5300

Security	Rate	Date	Price	Approx. Yield
(Example as set forth on Defs'. Ex. 'A')				
*	*	*	*	*
Hearst Magazines, Inc. Gold Deb.	6	Mar. 1-33	99.50	6.10
-	*	*	*	*	*	*

The above statements and statistics are derived from official sources, or those which we regard as reliable, or are carefully estimated. We do not guarantee, but believe them to be correct.''

Mr. Bothwell further testified that he told plaintiff at that time that "the bonds listed were bonds owned by the Bank, or contracted for, which we recommend and offer for sale" (R. 419); that when the purchases were made he gave plaintiff a bill (R. 420-421); on some occasions after the first purchase on January 7, 1926, plaintiff called personally at the bond department for the purpose of dealing in securities and on some occasions sales were made by mail; in the cases when plaintiff called personally at the bond department and a transaction was entered into resulting in the sale of a security a bill was given to her personally. (R. 422.) Mr. Bothwell denied that he told plaintiff the bank would purchase bonds for her. (R. 426.)

At a later session of the District Court counsel for plaintiff produced a package containing the original bills of sale which had been delivered to plaintiff on the occasion of each purchase; these were thereupon introduced in evidence as the Defendants' Exhibit "L". (R. 431, 722-725.) They covered all of the purchases prior to the execution of the trust instrument on September 24, 1929. It will be noted that each of these bills *is stamped as paid on the date it bears;* that each is in the form of the "Medford" bill set forth at page 16, *supra.* (R. 722-725.)

On none of these bills does there appear any charge for commission or brokerage. It appears from the record that all of the purchases prior to the execution of the trust instrument were made while plaintiff was personally present in the bond department except in the two instances of the purchases of the Medford Bonds and of the Central West Public Service Bonds. (Pl's. Ex. 1 and Defs'. Ex. "I"; R. 539-540, 718-719.)

Mr. Bothwell further testified that when plaintiff subsequently called at the bond department to purchase securities the same procedure was followed as on the occasion of the first purchases on January 7, 1926; the offering sheet was always exhibited where a person came in to purchase bonds; "the current offering list would be shown to her, and she would state that she now had funds for investment, and asked what we had to offer, and the securities would be secured from the offering sheet,— selected from the offering sheet. We would both be seated in my office, and the offering list would be between her and myself" (R. 433); in substance these subsequent conversations "would relate directly to the fact that Mrs. Quinn had additional funds, and asking what we had to offer". (R. 433-434.) "Offering lists were sent to her by mail. It was a custom to enclose offering lists in correspondence.'' (R. 434.)

Correcting an earlier error in his testimony (R. 422), Mr. Bothwell testified that ''Bills for the purchases were not sent to the Trust Department before the trust instrument was signed on September 24, 1929. After the instrument was signed, the bills were sent to the Trust Department''. (R. 434.)

On cross-examination, Mr. Bothwell testified that when plaintiff called in person the offering lists were on the desk, immediately before her; he may have handed her one; she may have picked it up and looked at it, or looked at it sitting alongside the desk; she looked at them on every occasion when she made a personal visit to purchase. (R. 436.) On every occasion when he wrote to her it was the custom, as was the case with respect to correspondence to all customers, to enclose the offering sheet with the letters. (R. 437.)

The witness further testified on cross-examination that when plaintiff first called at the bond department she said that ''she wished to buy bonds—I don't know the exact words, but the substance of whatever conversation took place was that she wished to buy bonds, and asked if the Bank had bonds for sale''. (R. 445.) He told her that the bank had, and exhibited the offering sheet. (R. 445.) The bonds were selected by plaintiff from the offering list. (R. 446.)

The defendants' witness, Paul C. Anderson, testified that he was employed in the bond department of the national bank from March, 1925, until it closed its doors in 1933; during this period the national bank bought and sold bonds as a regular practice and had offering lists of securities. (R. 501-502.)

Thereupon additional offering lists were identified and introduced in evidence. (Defs'. Exs. "Y", "Z", "AA" and "BB"; R. 503-504, 745-754.) He further testified that it was the practice of the bond department from the year 1926 down to the closing of the bank to mail offering lists at different intervals to customers of the bank and that it was the practice to exhibit offering lists to customers, or prospective customers, when they came into the bond department; "I know that was done. Mr. Bothwell always exhibited his offering lists when he had a prospective bond customer in his office". (R. 509-510.)

On rebuttal plaintiff testified (R. 533):

"Mr. Slack. Q. Mrs. Quinn, was there ever exhibited to you by Mr. Bothwell, or by any other official of the Bank, any offering list of securities? A. No, *not that I remember of.*"

The bills (Defs'. Ex. "L") were shown to her by her counsel and she was asked if she ever read the printed matter at the *bottom of the page* and she said "No". (R. 533.) She testified that no offering list was ever handed to her personally and that she did not remember if she ever received any by mail. (R. 534.)

(c) The surrounding facts and circumstances and all of the probabilities of the case establish that plaintiff intended to buy securities from the bond department of the national bank and that a buyer-seller relationship existed.

Plaintiff's mental capacity and her ability to understand business transactions.

Counsel complain of the finding (R. 322) "that at all times, both before as well as after the execution of the trust instrument, plaintiff had a highly developed business sense and was extremely able and alert mentally and was well able to understand, and did in fact understand, the nature of the transactions complained of in the complaint; plaintiff was accustomed to, and did in fact, exercise her independent judgment with respect to the transactions complained of in the complaint". Counsel contend that this finding has no support in the allegations of the complaint or in the evidence. (App's. Brief, pp. 58-59.) However, in the complaint it is alleged that at all times mentioned "plaintiff was, and she now is, a widow, and in poor health, * * *." (R. 8.) Obviously the purpose of this allegation was to show that plaintiff was ignorant of business transactions and was accustomed to rely upon other people. The finding above set forth is germane to this object of this allegation in the complaint. There is no requirement that findings comply *literally* with the wording of a pleading. (64 *C. J.* p. 1255, Sec. 1103.)

In order to evaluate the evidence properly it is necessary to appreciate plaintiff's mental capacity and the fact that she carefully read everything. There is abundant evidence establishing that plaintiff not only read over every paper submitted to her but had an understanding of business matters far surpassing that of the average individual. An outstanding example of this appears from

a letter dated May 21, 1930, sometime after the execution
of the instrument of trust, from plaintiff to Mr. Berven.
(Pl's. Ex. 16, R. 558.)   This letter reads as follows:

> "This day rec'd a letter from Mr. Bothwell in
> which he recommends California Cotton Mills Co.
> 1st mortgage bonds as a good re-investment of money
> from Reno, June 1st.   Will be glad if you will get
> same for me, in't due July 1st.   That will necessitate
> paying accrued in't.   *Why do I pay commission on
> accrued int.?   I noticed by last statement I rec'd less
> than a month's int. on bonds bought for me, but I
> was charged for the six months int., when all but a
> very small am't was my own money used to pay ac-
> crued int. and returned to me when int. came due.*
>
> In my case it wasn't so much, but I wanted to know
> if that is the way to do it?   As I will be in the same
> position with the June proposition and possibly many
> times in the future."

What plaintiff was complaining of in this letter was the
fact that the trust department's remuneration after the
trust was created consisted of a certain commission on
income received.   Plaintiff perceived that when securities
were purchased between interest dates she had to pay not
only principal but also for interest accrued from the last
interest date to the date of purchase, and that the trust
department had treated such accrued interest as income
upon which its commissions were in part based.   Not
only does the question raised by this letter show great
perspicacity on plaintiff's part, but the form thereof
shows that plaintiff had a clear and acute mind capable
of exercising independent business judgment.   Other ex-
amples of plaintiff's intelligence and acumen are to be
found in the Record.   (Pl's. Exs. 10 and 18, Defs.' Ex.
"R", R. 553, 560, 738.)

The bills of sale provided

"Sold to

Abbie W. Quinn".

The plaintiff appreciated the importance of these bills of sale as they were carefully retained by her and, after demand, were produced by her at the trial. (R. 431.) She did not deny that she read the bills of sale nor did she claim that she did not understand them. The only thing she denied was that she read the printed matter at the bottom. (R. 533.) There is no denial that she read the most important words *"Sold to"* nor did she testify that she did not know the meaning of these words.

We do not contend that the words "Sold to" are necessarily conclusive evidence of a buyer-seller relationship. For example, had the great weight of the evidence clearly established that plaintiff directed Bothwell to *buy* securities *for her,* the mere fact that Bothwell gave her a bill saying "Sold to" rather than "Bought for" probably would not have altered the legal relationship obviously intended by the parties. However, in the face of conflicting testimony as to whether a given relationship is that of buyer and seller or principal and agent, the words "Sold to" strongly corroborate the existence of the former relationship. Thus, in *Farr et al. v. Fratus* (1931), 277 Mass. 346, 178 N. E. 657, where the evidence was conflicting and where a confirmation slip was sent to the customer saying *"We confirm sale to you* of 50 Incorporated Investors, 77"*, the Court said:

> "The only construction which could reasonably be put upon what was said was that the plaintiffs contracted to sell the stock to the defendant. The testi-

mony as to the record of a direct sale *and the confirmation slips* point to the same conclusion. They refer to the transaction as a sale and there is nothing to indicate that any broker's commission was charged."

In an article in 43 *Yale Law Journal,* 46, 60, it is stated:

"Other courts have recognized the same distinctions and in general have employed the following differentiating characteristics or earmarks to distinguish the dealer from the agent.

(1) The form of the confirmation 'sold to you' rather than 'bought for your account' *is evidentiary of a dealer-customer relationship.*

(2) The fact that the customer *is not charged any commission* is likewise evidence that the 'broker' acted as dealer."

Two other highly significant matters of evidence which arise from the bills of sale, in addition to the words "Sold to", are that *no commission or brokerage was charged thereon and each bill of sale is stamped as paid on the date it bears.* (Defs.' Exs. "E" and "L", R. 716, 722-725.)

The fact that no commission or brokerage was charged plaintiff is strong evidence of a buyer-seller relationship.

It is inconceivable that plaintiff either intended, or could assume, that an agency existed, when, for a period of over three years, eight and one-half months prior to the execution of the trust instrument, no bill ever specified any brokerage or commission, no such charge was ever made to her, and she never thought she was paying any brokerage or commission since, to take her own testimony, she did not know the national bank was making any profit on these transactions. (R. 401.)

While it is possible to have a gratuitous agency, nevertheless an agent *usually* receives a commission or compensation. The fact a commission is charged connotes an agency, although it is not always conclusive. Thus in *Sloat-Darragh Co. v. General Coal Co.* (1921), 276 Fed. 502, 505 (C. C. A. 6), the Court said:

> "It is also true that the word *'commission' has a natural tendency to suggest an agency contract, as being compensation for services rendered; * * *.*"

Conversely, where no commission or compensation is charged, it would appear that a buyer and seller relationship is intended rather than that of principal and agent. For example, in *Yaeger v. Mechanics & Metals Nat. Bank* (1924), 122 Misc. Rep. 392, 204 N. Y. S. 38, 39, a given transaction was held a sale rather than an agency for the reason, among others, that no charge was to be made for services in buying certain bonds.

In *F. C. Adams, Inc. v. Elmer F. Thayer Estate* (1931), 85 N. H. 177, 155 Atl. 687, 689, the question arose as to whether a given transaction constituted a buyer-seller relationship or an agency to purchase. The Court pointed out that (155 Atl. 689):

> "Bills were sent the decedent for the prices he agreed to pay, *with no commission charged.*"

In holding the relationship to be that of buyer and seller, the Court emphasized the fact that the decedent was "to pay a named price for the stock" and that "no commission was charged". (155 Atl. 690.)

The fact that immediately upon the selection of a security plaintiff paid the bond department the price thereof and immediately received a bill of sale stamped ''Paid'' is consistent only with a buyer-seller relationship.

One of the most significant factors is the following: It requires time to execute an agency for purchase. However, in every instance of a purchase of securities by plaintiff when she was personally present in the bond department, she immediately paid the purchase price specified and the bills of sale, *which were receipted as "paid" on the very date each bore,* were given to her. (R. 420-422, Defs.' Ex. "L", R. 722-725.) Of necessity, therefore, plaintiff must have paid the purchase price of the securities at the time they were selected and before the bills of sale were delivered to her. If the bond department were acting in a brokerage or agency capacity toward plaintiff, she must have intended and understood that the bank was to purchase the securities from outside sources and that time would be required to place the "Buy" order with an outside dealer, outside seller, or with a bond exchange. She further must have known the obvious fact that the purchase price could not be ascertained until the "Buy" order was executed. On the contrary, where a buyer and seller relationship exists, one who pays for a security at the time of purchase receives a bill marked "Paid" at that time since no time is required to close the transaction since the bank would have the securities either on hand or contracted for.

The preponderance of the evidence together with the *probabilities* of the case are overwhelmingly in favor of the defendants' contention that plaintiff intended to, and did in fact, buy securities from the bond department. The bank had offering lists at the times in question. Is it likely that such offering lists, while used as a matter of course in the case of other customers, would not be used in plaintiff's case? If plaintiff had told Mr. Bothwell to buy bonds for her and had he wilfully and deliberately violated her instructions, would he not have told her that he would see if he could procure the securities for her, permitted a reasonable interval to elapse after her departure so as to cause it to appear that the bond department was purchasing securities for her, and would he not thereafter have sent her a statement which said "Bought for—Abbie W. Quinn", rather than "Sold to—Abbie W. Quinn"?

Why should the bond department have wilfully and deliberately violated plaintiff's instructions, in other words, committed a palpable fraud upon her? Fraud will never be presumed; evidence thereof must be clear and convincing. (12 Cal. Jur. p. 832, sec. 81.) If plaintiff's instructions were violated would not one seeking to perpetrate a fraud have attempted to cover up the transaction?

(d) The determination of the question as to whether a given relationship is that of buyer and seller or principal and agent is a question of fact and the finding of the trial Court in the case at bar is amply supported by the evidence.

The question whether parties occupy the relation of principal and agent, or buyer and seller, ordinarily involves a question of fact to be determined by the trial Court, whose decision is binding on the Appellate Court. Only where the evidence is clear and undisputed is it a question of law for the Court to decide. *(Bigelow v. Plummer et al.* (1937), 23 Cal. App. (2d) 441, 443-444, 73 Pac. (2d) 638; 55 *C. J.* p. 43, Sec. 8.) (See Appendix pp. i to ii for quotations from these authorities.)

It is not necessary for us to contend that any particular item of evidence, either direct or inferential, is, in and of itself, conclusive on this phase of the case. We do maintain, however, that on the direct testimony of the witnesses, the utmost that plaintiff can claim is a bare conflict in the evidence. The inferences to be drawn from the documentary evidence and the surrounding facts and circumstances overwhelmingly preponderate in favor of the defendants' contentions. We feel that we have demonstrated conclusively that the relationship between plaintiff and the bond department of the national bank prior to the execution of the trust instrument was that of buyer and seller and that it was so intended by plaintiff and the bond department. The Court so determined in its findings and conclusions after having heard the testimony and observed the witnesses. (R. 323, 348.)

It is well settled that findings of fact in an equity case will be taken as correct on appeal unless clearly against the weight of the evidence.

> *Hyland v. Millers Nat. Ins. Co.* (1937), 91 Fed (2d) 735, 737 (C. C. A. 9);
> *Ohio Casualty Ins. Co. v. Gordon* (1938), 95 Fed. (2d) 605, 610 (C. C. A. 10);
> *Tyronza Special School District v. Speer* (1938), 94 Fed. (2d) 825, 830 (C. C. A. 8); and
> *United States v. Sands* (1938), 94 Fed. (2d) 156, 161 (C. C. A. 10).

(e) Plaintiff's argument begs the question in assuming the very fact in issue, namely, that she directed the national bank to buy securities for her.

In the appellant's brief the very question at issue is begged, since it is assumed, without argument or even reference to the Record for supporting evidence, that the securities "were purchased for the depositor by the bank from itself * * * and, therefore, concealing from, the depositor the fact that the bonds and notes were owned by the bank, and were sold to the depositor at a profit * * *." (App's. Brief, p. 47.) Counsel also complain that the Court made no finding that "it was essential that plaintiff should have been fully informed of her legal rights concerning the transactions". (App's. Brief, p. 52.)

Like most fallacious arguments, this argument assumes the minor premise to be established in accordance with the appellant's theory, to the effect that the relationship was that of trustee and *cestui,* or agent and principal prior to the execution of the trust instrument. Thus after citing numerous cases (App's. Brief, pp. 52-55) it is argued at page 55 of appellant's brief:

"The rule applies with equal force to the multitude of cases in which an agent, authorized to purchase property for his principal, purchased the property from himself, frequently secretly, first taking the title to the property in himself. The law treats the relation between the agent and the principal very much the same as though the relation was that of a trustee and cestui que trust."

We have no quarrel with the proposition that an agent, employed to purchase property for his principal, cannot lawfully sell his own property to the principal without a full disclosure to the latter of all material facts, or at least showing that the principal had knowledge of all material facts. But the question involved with respect to the purchases prior to the execution of the trust instrument is whether or not such agency relationship did in fact exist. The Court found that no such agency relationship existed; that instead plaintiff intended to buy from the bank and the bank intended to sell its own securities and such finding is preponderately supported by the evidence. The only attack that could be directed at such finding is that it is unsupported by any evidence or contrary to the weight of the evidence. No such attack is made by counsel but instead the issue is adroitly sidestepped by assuming that the relationship was found to be that of principal and agent or *cestui* and trustee. An illustration of such evasion is found on page 56 of counsels' brief wherein, after referring to the rule governing the situation where an agent to purchase secretly sells his own property to the principal, it is said by counsel

> "There is no good reason why the rule should not be applied to the case of a seller and a buyer, if there is a fiduciary relation, as there may well be, from which a duty to disclose rests upon the seller (25 C. J. secs. 8-10, pp. 1118-20, tit. 'Fiduciary'); * * *."

No case has ever held that where a prospective buyer approaches a prospective seller, intending to buy the seller's own goods, the latter must inform the buyer "I am selling my own goods to you and I am making a profit on the sale". The fact that the buyer may have confidence in the seller does not in any manner alter the situation. It is human nature for one to patronize a merchant in whom one has trust and confidence, yet it has never been suggested until now that that gives rise to an agency, or fiduciary, or trust relationship. (See *infra*, pp. 42 to 46.)

---

3. **THE RELATIONSHIP OF THE PARTIES WAS NOT THAT OF CESTUI AND TRUSTEE PRIOR TO THE EXECUTION OF THE TRUST INSTRUMENT.**

(a) **Appellant's contention that the relationship was that of cestui and trustee prior to the execution of the trust instrument is raised for the first time on appeal and is contrary to the agency theory which appellant presented to the trial Court.**

The contention of plaintiff that the relationship between herself and the national bank was that of *cestui* and trustee *before* as well as after the execution of the trust instrument is advanced for the first time on appeal. (App's. Brief pp. 20-21, 52, 57 and 61.) This contention is outside the issues embraced in the pleadings and is contrary to the theory upon which plaintiff's case was actually presented to the trial Court. The assignment toward which counsels' argument is addressed is apparently Assignment No. 6. (R. 777-778.)

Nowhere in the complaint is any such allegation or contention made. In fact the contrary is directly and unequivocally asserted. Thus it is alleged that on the occasion of her first visit to the bond department plaintiff informed Bothwell "that she *would postpone the placing of her property in such a trust* with the said Bank until after the sale by her of her said parcel of real property, * * *". (R. 10.) This was on January 7, 1926. Again it is alleged that all of the securities purchased were held by the bank "*awaiting such time when* *the same would be assigned and transferred by her to the said Bank, as trustee of the trusts, in which she intended * * * to place her property* after the said parcel of real property, * * * had been sold by her, and pending such time, *and prior to the consummation of her said intention by the execution by her, on the said 24th day of September, 1929 * * * of the instrument of trust to and with the said Bank, * * *"* the securities were retained by the bank. (R. 16-17.) It is further alleged that due to poor health plaintiff did *not* immediately, after the sale of the real property on February 8, 1928, *"proceed to carry out her said intention of placing her property in the trust* aforesaid, with the defendant Central National Bank of Oakland, as trustee" (R. 18); that plaintiff was disinclined to attend to "the preparation of the instrument of trust, *whereby her property would be placed in trust* with the said Bank, as trustee * * *". (R. 18.) It is also alleged that shortly prior to September 24, 1929, plaintiff inquired "whether or not it was safe for her *to place her said property in trust"*. (R. 24.)

Certainly the foregoing portions of the complaint definitely negative any idea that there was a trust relationship prior to the actual execution of the trust instrument. Furthermore, the Court found that "Plaintiff did not intend to create a trust until approximately four (4) or five (5) months prior to September 24, 1929", the date of the execution of the trust instrument. (R. 323-324.) The evidence supporting this finding will be referred to at pages 35 to 42 of this brief.

Nowhere is there any evidence that plaintiff had constituted the national bank her trustee prior to September

24, 1929. Even taking her testimony at full face value it merely appears that she intended to create a trust later. (R. 367, 369.) Referring to her first conversation with Mr. Berven, the assistant trust officer, plaintiff testified that in her presence Mr. Bothwell told Mr. Berven, "that he would leave it to Mr. Berven to explain the matter to me and take the matter up and *later on* create the trust fund". (R. 391.) The plaintiff then testified that there was considerable delay between the time she sold her Reno property and the date upon which she actually executed the instrument of trust on September 24, 1929. (R. 391-396.)

(b) The mere intent subsequently to create a trust does not give rise to the relationship of trustee and cestui until such intent is executed.

Even if we assume that as early as the time of the first purchase on January 7, 1926, plaintiff intended to create a trust in the future (which we deny), the relationship of *cestui* and trustee did not arise until such intention was carried into effect by the execution of the trust instrument since "A manifestation of intention to create a trust *inter vivos at some time subsequent to the time of the manifestation does not create a trust*". (*Restatement of the Law, "Trusts"*, Vol. 1, p. 79, sec. 26.) Likewise "trust intent is lacking if the proof merely shows that the alleged settlor said *he intended to set apart a trust res later*". (*Bogert, Trusts and Trustees*, Vol. 1, p. 201, sec. 46.)

(c) The evidence shows that plaintiff did not intend to create
a trust until four or five months prior to the actual execution of the trust instrument. The securities which were
retained by the bank after the purchase thereof were
retained in a depositary capacity.

The District Court found that

"Plaintiff did not intend to create a trust until
approximately four (4) or five (5) months prior to
September 24, 1929. Plaintiff did not tell Bothwell
that she intended to create a trust until approximately four (4) or five (5) months prior to September 24, 1929; * * *." (R. 323-324.)

In response to the allegations in the complaint that
none of the bonds were delivered to plaintiff but were
held by the bank on deposit awaiting the time when she
would create the trust and that in the meantime money
collected on the interest coupons, which the bank clipped,
was deposited in plaintiff's bank account (R. 16-17), the
Court found that none of the securities purchased by
plaintiff were delivered to her but, at her request, were
held in safe-keeping by the national bank subject to her
order as a matter of accommodation to her; that said
securities were not held awaiting the time when the same
would be assigned or transferred by plaintiff to the bank
as trustee or until such time as she should create a trust.
At plaintiff's request the interest coupons were removed
and cashed by the bank and the proceeds were deposited
in plaintiff's commercial bank account. (R. 325.)

Both of the foregoing findings are supported by the
evidence. Thus Mr. Bothwell testified that plaintiff told
him of her intention to create a trust probably two or
three months before a contemplated trip to Rochester,

Minnesota, for a possible operation.* This was the only
time she mentioned to him her intent to create a trust.
(R. 416-417.) Mr. Bothwell on this occasion offered to
introduce plaintiff to Mr. Read, the trust officer of the
national bank, and upon hearing that she had already
met Mr. Read, he introduced her to Mr. Berven, the
assistant trust officer. (R. 417-418.)

The witness also denied that at or before the time
plaintiff made the first of her purchases of securities
she told him she wanted to put her property in a fund
(R. 425), or that he told her the bank would form a trust.
(R. 426.) He also testified that the bonds were not taken
away from the bond department but were left as undelivered bonds. This was pursuant to a conversation
with her, probably on the first visit, in the course of
which he said the bank would be glad to clip the coupons
and credit her account. The arrangement was made that
she would leave the bonds as undelivered bonds and that
the coupons would be clipped and credited to a commercial account, an ordinary banking commercial account,
subject to withdrawal on her checks. At some time mention was made that if bonds fell due or were redeemed,
the collection would be made and her commercial account
would be credited. This was an accommodation that was
extended to other customers of the bond department. (R.
426-427.)

He also testified that at the time of the first of the
purchases of securities by plaintiff the bank did not have
a record of bonds which were held in safe-keeping but
that more than a year later a safe-keeping file or record

*Plaintiff left on this trip on September 25, 1929, the day after the
execution of the trust instrument. (R. 534.)

system was inaugurated. (R. 429.) These records were then introduced in evidence as Defendants' Exhibits "K" and "M". (R. 429, 721, 726-729.) Three of the receipts were signed by plaintiff and the balance were not, but nevertheless 16 of these sheets were carefully preserved by plaintiff and were produced by her at the time of the trial. (R. 429.) These deposit sheets definitely show that the undelivered bonds were held by the bond department of the national bank *as a depositary, or bailee, and not as a trustee.* The following is the form of one of these receipts (Defs'. Ex. "M"; R. 726):

"Receipt for   S 112
Securities Deposited

Central National Bank of Oakland

Oakland, Calif. Aug. 15, 1928

Received
From ABBIE W. QUINN,
    c/o Mrs. Frank Musser
    Peralta Apartments   Cr. Com'l. a/c
  The securities listed below to be held by the Central National Bank of Oakland subject to the following conditions:
    1. The bank agrees to hold these securities **as depositary.**
    2. If this receipt is issued to more than one person, the receipt of any one of the persons to whom this is issued, without the receipt of the other or others, shall be sufficient to authorize the Bank to deliver the securities to such person so receipting for the same.
    3. This receipt is non-assignable and non-negotiable.

Description and Numbers	Maturity	Following and Subsequent Coupons Att'd.	Interest Payable

(Here follows contents of receipts describing the securities deposited.)

Central National Bank of Oakland
By Kirby Tharp, Teller.

This Receipt is
Non-Assignable and
Non-Negotiable."

It will be noted that the receipt is designated "Receipt for Securities Deposited". The undertaking of the bank is "to hold these securities *as depositary*".

customer does not give rise to a trust relationship, even in favor of one who intends at a later date to create a trust with the bank as trustee. In the case of *DeMott v. National Bank of New Jersey* (1935), 118 N. J. Eq. 376, 179 Atl. 470, wherein plaintiff sought an accounting from the defendant bank on the theory *that a certain custodian agreement evidenced an express trust,* or, in the alternative, if the custodian agreement was merely the evidence of the creation of an agency, *that the confidence reposed by plaintiff in the defendant's trust officer and the abuse of that confidence caused a constructive trust to arise,* it was held that no trust existed. In reaching this conclusion the Court emphasized the fact that the agreement, relied upon by plaintiff, was designated "Custodian Agreement" rather than a trust. Thus the Court said (179 Atl. 472):

> "It might be argued that it makes no difference what a given legal relation is termed; that the words 'bailment', 'agency', and 'trust' are merely labels. But a label necessarily imports the contents of the *package, and it is handled accordingly.* It is risky to tag a container of gasoline 'Water'; some one later may attempt to extinguish a fire with it. *So to carelessly call the 'Custodian Agreement' above set forth a trust agreement involves a train of consequences that were never intended by the parties, and which I refuse to thrust upon the defendant despite the strenuous insistment of the complainant that he regarded it as a trust agreement from the outset."*

In *State Y. M. C. A. v. Picher* (1934), 8 Fed. Supp. 412 (D. C. Maine), it was held that certain funds were not held in trust by a bank even though it received them knowing of the plaintiff's intention to create a trust and even though, at plaintiff's request, the trust officer of the bank had drafted a trust agreement satisfactory in form to plaintiff, where the bank failed before the actual signing of the trust instrument.

The foregoing two cases declare the following rules: (a) The holding of securities under a depositary arrangement does not constitute the depositary a trustee; (b) even an agency for the purpose of investing funds does not constitute the agent a trustee; (c) the receipt of property by a bank with knowledge of the depositor's intent to create a trust thereafter does not constitute the bank a trustee.

While plaintiff denied that she ever read the printed matter on the receipts for securities deposited (R. 533-534), nevertheless she carefully retained all of these receipts and produced them at the trial. Even if her testimony be given credence, nevertheless she did not testify that she was in any way prevented from reading these receipts. Furthermore, three of these receipts were signed by plaintiff. (*Supra*, p. 37.) In addition, they show the capacity in which the bank was acting with respect to the retained securities, namely, *as a depositary or bailee.*

Bothwell's testimony to the effect that plaintiff did not intend to create a trust until shortly prior to the actual execution of the trust instrument is further corroborated by correspondence passing between him and plaintiff wherein no mention was made that the retained

717-718.)

Mr. Berven testified that he first talked to Mrs. Quinn when she was introduced to him by Mr. Bothwell about three or four months before the trust was created and that they had a general conversation about creating a trust. (R. 465-466.) Later, and about a week before the trust was actually created "She came in, and *evidently had definitely decided to create a trust,* and gave me the information as to what she wanted in the trust". (R. 468.)

Thus the weight of the evidence irresistibly leads to the conclusion that plaintiff did not intend to establish a trust until shortly prior to September 24, 1929. Not only this, but plaintiff's alleged reasons for postponing the actual creation of the trust from January, 1926, to September, 1929, are not convincing. Thus she testified that at or prior to the occasion of her first visit to the bond department she explained to Mr. Bothwell that she wanted to put her property into a fund or an estate and that she informed him of what her property consisted, including real estate in Nevada; that Mr. Bothwell said they could not handle the real estate in Nevada and that the better thing was to first dispose of the real estate. (R. 366-368.) She further testified that the

Reno (or Virginia Street property as it was sometimes called), was sold on February 8, 1928 (R. 388) but that she hadn't sold her Sparks, Nevada, or her Oakland real estate (R. 392) and she wanted to dispose of these properties before she created the trust. (R. 394.) However, it appears from her testimony that on September 23, 1929, the day before the trust instrument was executed, no trouble was experienced in dealing with the Nevada property as Mr. Berven prepared for her a deed of gift to her daughter covering the Sparks property. (R. 396.)

Mr. Bothwell denied that plaintiff ever told him about her Nevada property (R. 415-416), or that he told her that her real property could not be handled in this state. In fact he did not know whether or not a trust company or a trust department in this state could act as trustee for real property situated in another state. (R. 425.)

Mr. Berven testified that when he first met plaintiff about three or four months before the execution of the trust instrument she mentioned one or two pieces of real estate in Sparks, Nevada, and he explained to her that the bank could not take title in trust to property situated in Nevada. He explained to her that she could dispose of that property by will or by a deed of gift. (R. 465-467.)

It is exceedingly unlikely that Mr. Bothwell, whose duties pertained solely to the bond department of the national bank (R. 413-414), would have known there was any question involved as to whether or not a national bank having its principal office in California could act as trustee in Nevada or with respect to Nevada real property.* Is it not far more likely that Mr. Berven, an assistant trust officer of the bank, was the one who appreciated the problem involved and therefore was the one who told Mrs. Quinn that the bank could not act as trustee with respect to Nevada real property? Furthermore, is it likely that the bank would have advised plaintiff to postpone the creation of her trust until the real property was sold? Would not the bank rather have advised her at the outset either to dispose of the Nevada real property by will, or by deed of gift to her daughter, as was ultimately done with respect to the Sparks property?

(d) The fact that plaintiff may have reposed trust and confidence in Mr. Bothwell and in the bond department of the national bank did not give rise to a trust relationship.

The Court found that plaintiff, as a depositor in the national bank, became well acquainted with Mr. Bothwell; "the acquaintanceship of plaintiff with Bothwell prior to the time of the first of her bond purchases on January 7, 1926 *was merely that of a depositor with a bank teller;* plaintiff reposed in Bothwell and in the bond department trust and confidence which Bothwell knew". (R. 321.)

Counsel do not assert with any degree of definiteness that they contend that such trust and confidence reposed in Mr. Bothwell and in the bond department, in and

---

*It is interesting to note that on September 9, 1929, the Supreme Court of Nevada, in the case of In re McGill's Estate (1929), 52 Nev. 35, 280 Pac. 321, held that under the particular wording of the Nevada statute, a foreign trust company or bank could do a trust company business in Nevada. This, apparently, was the first time this matter had ever been ruled upon by the Nevada courts.

of itself, operated to create a trust, prior to the actual
execution of the trust instrument, although such contention is hinted. (App's. Brief p. 57.) Nor does it appear
whether counsel intended to rely upon section 2219 of
the *Civil Code* which reads as follows:

> "Everyone who voluntarily assumes a relation of
> personal confidence with another is deemed a trustee,
> within the meaning of this chapter, not only as to
> the person who reposes such confidence, but also as
> to all persons of whose affairs he thus acquires in-
> formation which was given to such person in the like
> confidence, or over whose affairs he, by such confi-
> dence, obtains any control."

This section is not cited or even mentioned in the
appellant's brief although it is referred to in one of the
cases cited therein, namely, *Bank of America v. Sanchez*
(1934), 3 Cal. App. (2d) 238, 38 Pac. (2d) 787. (App's.
Brief p. 56.) Obviously this section requires much more
than the mere fact that one person reposes trust and confidence in another in order to give rise to a trust relationship since "it is not every case where parties trust
each other that the law recognizes as confidential". (*Brison v. Brison* (1888), 75 Cal. 525, 528, 17 Pac. 689.) It
is necessary that the one sought to be charged as trustee
"voluntarily assumes a relation of personal confidence".
Thus in the case of *Ruhl v. Mott* (1898), 120 Cal. 668,
678-679, 53 Pac. 304, where the trial Court had found
that by virtue of prior business dealings between plaintiff and defendant "plaintiff reposed *great confidence in
defendant, trusted him, and relied upon him* for advice"
(p. 678) and therefore had entered judgment in favor
of plaintiff, the Supreme Court reversed the judgment,

pointing out that this finding was insufficient to establish the confidential relationship defined in *Civ. Code*, sec. 2219, since the fact that plaintiff (120 Cal. 679)

> "* * * reposed confidence in the defendant did not cast any duty upon the latter, unless he 'voluntarily assumed a relation of personal confidence' with plaintiff, and this is not found".

A quotation from this case is set forth at pages iii to iv of the appendix to this brief.

This case was followed by this Court in the case of *Luette et al. v. Bank of Italy* (1930), 42 Fed. (2d) 9, 11 (C. C. A. 9), wherein this Court held that an allegation that the plaintiffs were inexperienced in business and relied upon the defendant for fair treatment, being accustomed to trust in and rely upon banks and bankers, was insufficient to establish a fiduciary relationship as there was no suggestion "that defendant voluntarily assumed a relation of personal confidence with plaintiff".

In *Jackson v. Gorman* (1929), 98 Cal. App. 112, 116, 276 Pac. 391, the Court said that there "must be something further than mere confidence in another's honesty and integrity to sustain the presumption of constructive fraud". (See Appendix pp. iv to v for a quotation from this case.)

Somewhat similar is the holding in *Meyer v. Zuber* (1928), 92 Cal. App. 767, 772, 268 Pac. 954, where the Court said that "mere friendship and affection existing between parties to a contract do not constitute a confidential relation".

To extend the doctrine declared in section 2219 to all situations wherein one person reposes trust and con-

fidence in another would tend to create a trust status in
most of the affairs of every day life.

> Doyle. et al. v. Murphy et ux. (1859), 22 Ill. 502,
> 508-509 (see Appendix pp. v to vi for a quota-
> tion from this case); and
>
> Steele et al. v. Clark (1875), 77 Ill. 471, 474.

Both of the foregoing cases were commented upon ap-
provingly by the California Supreme Court in the case
of *Brison v. Brison, supra,* page 43.

Even the fact that Mr. Bothwell knew that plaintiff imposed some degree of trust and confidence in him and in
the bond department of the national bank is immaterial
insofar as the creation of a trust thereby is concerned,
since it is necessary that the party sought to be charged
as trustee *must give his consent, either expressly or impliedly, to the changed relationship or status. Such consent cannot be implied from the bare carrying out of the
transaction,* after one party has declared his or her inexperience and reliance upon the other.

> Southern Trust Co. v. Lucas (1917), 245 Fed. 286,
> 288 (C. C. A. 8); and
>
> Hancock v. Anderson (1933), 160 Va. 225, 168 S.
> E. 458, 463.

Quotations from both the above cases are set forth at
pages vi to vii of the appendix.

In closing this portion of our brief we desire to call
to the Court's attention the fact that the District Court
found there was no fraud or misrepresentation on Mr.
Bothwell's part as to the type and value of the securities
sold to plaintiff. (R. 326-328.) It was also found that at
all times the securities sold by the national bank to plain-

tiff were sold at the fair market price and value thereof.
(R. 326.) The evidence not only supports these findings
(R. 430-431, 449) but also establishes that the same
securities were being sold by various reputable bond
houses in the community and were recommended by them
as sound investments at the time. (R. 514-515.) In fact,
during the trial of the case counsel for plaintiff conceded
"that no fraudulent representations were alleged in the
bill of complaint, * * * that there was nothing in the
bill of complaint in any way squinting at a fraudulent
representation in the purchase of any of the securities".
(R. 379-380.) The fact that many of the securities purchased by plaintiff prior to the execution of the instrument of trust, and, incidentally, prior to the market crash
of October, 1929, subsequently declined in value in common
with practically all other bond issues due to cataclysmic
and unprecedented economic conditions which suddenly
descended upon this country, of which the Court has
judicial knowledge, furnishes no evidence that the securities when previously sold to plaintiff, were not safe and
desirable. (*Mandelbaum v. Goodyear etc. Co.* (1925), 6
Fed. (2d) 818, 824 (C. C. A. 8).)

II. THERE WAS NO FRAUD OR WRONGDOING IN CONNEC-
TION WITH THE EXECUTION OF THE TRUST INSTRU-
MENT.

The third question stated by counsel is as to whether
the trust instrument should be rescinded because Article
VII thereof provided that if it were revoked the trustee
should be released and discharged of then existing lia-

bilities and obligations. (R. 73-74, App's. Brief p. 48.)
Counsel also complain that the District Court overlooked
the fact that Mr. Berven, in the preparation and submission of the trust instrument, was conclusively presumed to have had knowledge that plaintiff had reposed
great trust and confidence in the national bank and in
Mr. Bothwell in the prior purchases of bonds and notes
and that, as this trust and confidence had been violated,
it was Mr. Berven's duty to make a full disclosure of
these prior transactions, failing which he was guilty of
constructive fraud. (App's. Brief p. 60.)

The District Court found that Mr. Berven submitted
the trust instrument to plaintiff for her consideration
and approval; that plaintiff not only read it over, but
it was also read to her by Mr. Berven, and the provisions
thereof were explained to plaintiff paragraph by paragraph, and she stated she understood it. It was further
found that plaintiff asked Mr. Berven if she should submit the instrument of trust to an attorney of her own
selection for his advice, to which Berven replied that it
was proper she should do so, whereupon plaintiff stated
that her attorney was in Nevada and that as she was
about to leave for Rochester, Minnesota, she did not have
time to do so. (R. 332.) Therefore, the reason why, in
signing the instrument of trust, plaintiff did not seek or
obtain independent legal advice relating thereto, was
because of the fact that she was in a hurry to leave for
Rochester, Minnesota. (R. 333.)

In its conclusions of law the Court determined (R. 348):

"That the national bank was not guilty of any
fraud, concealment, or misrepresentation in connec-

tion with the execution of the instrument of trust dated September 24, 1929, and therefore plaintiff is not entitled to rescind the same.''

Apparently counsel are relying upon Assignment No. 21. (R. 802-805.)

At the outset may we briefly point out that at pages 10 'to 28 of this brief we have set forth the findings of the Court and supporting evidence to the effect that the relationship between plaintiff and the bond department prior to the execution of the trust instrument was that of buyer and seller, and was so intended by plaintiff, and that there was no wrong-doing in connection with the prior sales of securities. This being so, there was no prior wrong-doing about which plaintiff could have been informed by Mr. Berven or by anyone else at the time she executed the instrument of trust.

The fact that the trust instrument was executed by plaintiff without legal advice and that Article VII dealing with revocation provided that plaintiff should give a release of liability on the part of the trustee in the event of such revocation does not constitute constructive fraud or justify the rescission or cancellation of the trust instrument.

The evidence supports the findings which have previously been set forth herein. Plaintiff testified that Mr. Berven gave her one duplicate original of the trust instrument which she followed as he read from the other duplicate original. She did not recall that he made any statements as to any of the provisions as he read. (R. 398.) Nor did she ''remember that he made any statement to me, at the time he read over the instrument of trust to me and before I signed it, concerning the provisions of paragraph VII of the instrument''. (R. 399.)

Mr. Berven testified that he took one of the duplicate originals and plaintiff took the other. He read over the instrument paragraph by paragraph and explained each paragraph as he went along and asked her if there was any question as to each paragraph; she followed him with the duplicate; as he finished each paragraph he asked her if she understood it and her answer was ''Yes'', she was satisfied. (R. 471.)

The record also shows that plaintiff was not prevented from obtaining legal advice by any acts or conduct on the part of Mr. Berven or anyone connected with the national bank. In fact the evidence shows that Mr. Berven told plaintiff that it was proper that she should have legal advice. The following is the evidence on this point: Plaintiff testified that before she signed the trust instrument she asked Mr. Berven if it was necessary for her to have her attorney, or some attorney, look over the instrument for her; that he said ''No'', it would not be necessary, that it was a regular thing for the trust department to do, and that her interests were fully protected. (R. 400.)

Mr. Berven testified that plaintiff asked him if he thought she ought to take the trust instrument to her attorney and he told her it was perfectly proper that she should do so. She then said she wouldn't have time as she was going back East. She mentioned her attorney in Nevada. (R. 473.)

The District Court had an opportunity to observe the witnesses and its finding in accordance with Mr. Berven's testimony is determinative.

The general rule is that in the absence of fraud, mistake, undue influence, or other matters cognizable in equity, a trust will not be set aside where it has been voluntarily executed. It is immaterial that the settlor dislikes the trust and is sorry he created it. (65 *C. J.* p. 336, sec. 102.) Nowhere in the record does it appear that the national bank ever importuned or solicited plaintiff to create the trust. The idea originated with plaintiff.

We have been unable to find any case dealing with the effect of a provision providing for revocation on condition that the settlor give a release of liability to the trustee. However, such a provision presents a situation in nowise different than that presented where the trust instrument contains no provision permitting revocation. It is well settled that "The absence in a trust instrument of the power of revocation does not in itself render the trust invalid so as to warrant the Court in setting it aside". (65 *C. J.* p. 337, sec. 102.) This has been held to be true even where "the attention of the settlor was not called to that omission". (65 *C. J.* p. 346, sec. 119.)

In the case of *Whiteside v. Verity* (1920), 269 Fed. 227 (C. C. A. 6), suit was brought by the settlor, who was the sister of the trustee, to vacate a trust (or trust deed as it was termed by the Court) on the ground that she had had no independent legal advice, and, further, that the trust contained no provision permitting revocation. The bill was dismissed and this decree was upheld by the Circuit Court of Appeals, which held (p. 230):

"Plaintiff further insists that the deed was, as matter of law, improvident because of the combined effect of these circumstances: *She had no independent advice,* but relied upon her brother, the trustee, whose children were ultimate beneficiaries; *there was no power of revocation, and she was not explicitly cautioned as to this;* and the trustee had the power to suspend the income. We are satisfied that no one of these facts, nor all together, in the light of the whole record, raise any inference of law that the deed should be vacated. *Lack of independent advice is a circumstance which might well turn the scale,* if there were any reason to think that the trustee had taken an advantage; *but it will not of itself call for annulment.* Zimmerman v. Frushour, 108 Md. 115, 69 Atl. 796, 16 L. R. A. (N. S.) 1087, 15 Ann. Cas. 1128. The absence of power of revocation and of explicit caution thereon were once thought fatal (Everitt v. Everitt, L. R. 10 Eq. 405), *but it is now clear that they are only circumstances, and not of controlling force* * * *."

It is well settled that while "The lack of independent advice is a circumstance to be considered, * * * it will not of itself call for annulment of a trust". (65 *C. J.* p. 337, sec. 102.) Furthermore, the authorities go to the extent of holding that the mere lack of independent advice will not justify the setting aside of a *gift* even though a confidential relationship exists. (*Zimmerman v. Freshour* (1908), 108 Md. 115, 69 Atl. 796, 799 and *Farmer v. Associated Professors of Loyola College* (1934), 166 Md. 455, 171 Atl. 361, 364.)

In the third separate defenses of the savings bank (R. 135) and of the national bank (R. 173-174), it is pleaded that prior to the commencement of the suit, the savings bank, being then the successor trustee, offered to permit plaintiff to revoke the trust and the instrument of trust and to deliver all of the trust properties to plaintiff without any requirement that plaintiff should release existing liabilities. The District Court found that such offer was made. (R. 344.) Thus, even if it were the law, which it is not, that a trust or a trust instrument can be rescinded or cancelled if it provide that revocation can be effected only upon giving a release of liability to the trustee, this question has become immaterial in the instant case.

Counsel contend that this finding is unsupported by the evidence (App's. Brief pp. 45-46, 48, 63-65), and, in addition thereto, it is contended that this does not constitute a defense in any event. (App's. Brief pp. 31-32, 48-49, 64.) However, the evidence does clearly support this finding. Thus the witness, Charles A. Beardsley, testified that while he was representing the savings bank as its attorney, he had a number of conversations with Judge Slack in June or July, 1933 (prior to the commencement of this suit), and that in these conversations Judge Slack objected to the clause in paragraph VII of the trust instrument which provided that in the event of the termination of the trust it was necessary for plaintiff to release the trustee from all obligations thereunder. Mr. Beardsley further testified that he told Judge Slack that his client would prefer to have the trust terminated since Mrs.

Quinn was not satisfied with the operation thereof and would deliver to her the trust assets and "would waive the provisions in reference to her waiver of any claim which she might have against the trustee". This offer was not accepted. (R. 495-496.)

Counsel contend that since this was an offer only on the part of the savings bank, and not on the part of the national bank or its receiver, it was ineffective under any considerations. (App's. Brief pp. 31-32, 64.) No valid reason is advanced by counsel why such offer, even though made only on behalf of the savings bank, was not valid. The savings bank was then the successor trustee and had been such since April 22, 1933. (R. 81-84.) Plaintiff and the savings bank were the only parties concerned with a revocation of the trust instrument. If the savings bank chose to agree that notwithstanding such revocation plaintiff's rights against it should remain unimpaired, it is difficult to see how the acceptance of this offer by plaintiff would constitute a waiver of such rights, if any, as she might have against the national bank on account of antecedent liabilities of the national bank.

One further point that might be mentioned is that the contract for the sale of the trust department of the national bank to the savings bank expressly provided that the sale was "subject to the right of trustors and beneficiaries, after such transfers, to nominate another and succeeding trustee of the trusts so transferred, * * *". (R. 81.) This provision is also contained in section 31 of the *California Bank Act*. Therefore, the fact that the trust instrument provided that if it were revoked a release must be given, if ever material, became unimportant since, *first,* the offer was made to plaintiff to permit revocation without the giving of such release, and, *second,* because plaintiff could have appointed a new trustee of her own selection after the trust department of the national bank was sold to the savings bank pursuant to the contract for the purchase of the trust department and the provisions of the *California Bank Act,* and she then could have pursued such remedies as she desired.

III. THE FACT THAT AFTER THE EXECUTION OF THE IN-
STRUMENT OF TRUST, THE TRUST DEPARTMENT OF THE
NATIONAL BANK PURCHASED CERTAIN SECURITIES
FROM THE BOND DEPARTMENT DOES NOT ENTITLE
PLAINTIFF TO RESCIND THE INSTRUMENT OF TRUST.

1. EVEN IF IT BE CONCEDED, WHICH IT IS NOT, THAT SUCH
PURCHASES CONSTITUTED WRONGDOING ON THE PART OF
THE TRUSTEE, NEVERTHELESS A TRUST CANNOT BE RE-
SCINDED OR CANCELLED ON ACCOUNT OF SUBSEQUENT
WRONGDOING ON THE PART OF THE TRUSTEE.

The Court found that after the execution of the trust instrument on September 24, 1929, the following securities were purchased by the trust department, at the following dates and for the following amounts (R. 335):

Date of Purchase	Par Value	Description	Price
pril 8, 1930 as of			
pril 15, 1930	$1,000	Hearst Publications, Inc.	$ 985
une 5, 1930	1,000	California Cotton Mills Co.	850
une 27, 1930 as of			
uly 1, 1930	5,000	Federal Public Service Corporation	4,650
une 27, 1930 as of			
uly 1, 1930	6,000	Hearst Publications, Inc.	5,946
			12,431
uly 31, 1930	$2,000	Pacific Gas & Electric Co.	$ 2,205
uly 31, 1930	2,000	San Joaquin Light & Power Co.	2,290
anuary 20, 1932	5,000	East Bay Municipal Utility District	5,082.75
üly 11, 1932	5,000	Los Angeles Gas & Electric Corporation	4,925
		Total	$26,933.75

It was further found that of these purchases, only the first four blocks thereof were purchased by the trust department of the national bank from the bond department. The remainder, or the last four blocks of securities, were purchased from outside sources. (R. 335-336.) These findings are supported by the evidence. (Pl's. Ex. 5, R. 548.) Thus the evidence shows (Pl's. Ex. 8, R. 550-551):

"The last four items you will notice were purchased by the trust department direct from Weeden & Co., Dean Witter & Co. and Heller, Bruce & Co. The item listed under date of July 11, 1932 being $5000. Los Angeles Gas & Electric Corp. bonds were purchased from Heller Bruce & Co. with no profit accruing to the bond department."

The Federal Public Service Bonds which were purchased on June 27, 1930, as of July 1, 1937, were sold on July 16, 1930, for the principal price originally paid therefor by the trust estate, namely, $4650 principal, plus accrued interest to the date of resale. (Pl's. Ex. 5, R. 547, Pl's. Ex. 6, R. 548½.)

Therefore, the only securities with which we are concerned, which were purchased by the trust department from the bond department, are the two purchases of Hearst Publications Bonds and the single purchase of a California Cotton Mills Bond, three transactions in all. It is difficult to understand what complaint counsel have to find with these three transactions since an investment of $7781.00 resulted in a principal gain or profit or $254.00 to the trust estate with interest thereon (after deducting accrued interest at the time of purchase) of $1872.25, or an aggregate net gain to the trust estate of $2126.25. (Pl's. Ex. 9, R. 552; Pl's. Ex. 47, R. 645; Pl's. Ex. 48, R. 646½.)*

In the prayer of the Complaint and of the Supplemental Complaint, plaintiff asks that the trust instrument *be rescinded.* (R. 56, 189.)

---

*Thus the Hearst bond, bought on April 8, 1930, as of April 15, 1930, at a price of $985 was sold on April 6, 1935, at a price of $970, a principal loss of only $15 and in the meantime $338.89 interest was received thereon. The California Cotton Mills Bond bought on June 5, 1930, at a price of $850, was sold on November 6, 1935, at a price of $1065, a principal gain of $215 and in the meantime $150 interest was received thereon. The Hearst Publications bonds bought on June 27, 1930, as of July 1, 1930, at a price of $5946 matured in $3000 lots respectively on November 1, 1933, and November 1, 1934, at a total redemption price of $6000, a principal gain of $54 and in the meantime $1500 interest was received thereon. (R. 336, Pl's. Ex. 9, R. 552, Pl's. Ex. 48, R. 646½.) From the interest received, there should be deducted the aggregate accrued interest at the time of purchase, namely, $116.64. (Pl's. Ex. 47, R. 645.)

This involves solely the legal question as to whether a trust instrument, the execution of which is not procured through fraud, duress, or wrong-doing, *can be rescinded* by reason of a violation of the trust, technical or otherwise, thereafter occurring. Without the citation of any authorities, counsel assume that there can be such a rescission. This we deny. In such a case there may be a surcharge against the trustee in his accounts, or he may be removed, or under the contract for the sale of the trust department and the provisions of section 31 of the California Bank Act (*supra,* p. 53), there may be a substitution of trustees, but there cannot be a rescission of the trust instrument, an act which cancels the very existence of the trust itself, and which in many cases would destroy the right of remaindermen. Such rescission is radically different from a mere removal or substitution of trustees, in which case the trust continues to exist.

Thus in 65 *C. J.* p. 337, sec. 102, it is said:

"Under general rules equity ordinarily will not set aside a trust for nonperformance by the trustee, especially where the trust has been to a considerable extent performed."

Brower et al. v. Callender et al. (1882), 105 Ill. 88, 104:

"But if the trust were valid, the remedy for a breach of trusts, or a failure to perform his duty by the trustee, would be simply the removal of the old trustee and the appointing of a new one,—*not the setting aside of the deed of trust.*"

We do not concede that there was any breach of trust on the part of the national bank after the execution of the trust instrument. But even if there were, the only question left is what could or should be done with respect to the office of trusteeship. Since under the provisions of the contract for the purchase of the trust department and also the provisions of section 31 of the *California Bank Act,* the plaintiff could have substituted a new trustee in lieu of the savings bank (*supra,* p. 53), and since the savings bank offered to permit the revocation of the trust without any release of existing liabilities (*supra,* pp. 52 to 53), there would be no occasion for any *judicial* removal of the savings bank as trustee or a *judicial* substitution of a successor trustee.

In closing this portion of our brief may we call the Court's attention to an imaginary fear raised by counsel to the effect that if plaintiff does not have some form of judgment the jurisdiction of the District Court to enforce her rights under the trust instrument may be lost with the consequent "possibility that if a new action be instituted by her to enforce her legal rights, should she and the Central Bank be unable to agree, she may be met with the plea of res adjudicata". (App's. Brief, p. 60.) That this fear is entirely imaginary readily appears from an inspection of the decree of the District Court wherein the Court expressly provided that (R. 354-355):

> "* * * plaintiff may, if she so desires, revoke the instrument of trust dated September 24th, 1929, or appoint a new or successor trustee thereunder, and in the event of such revocation, or such appointment of a new or successor trustee, the defendant, Central Bank of Oakland, shall deliver to plaintiff or to such new or successor trustee, as the case may be, all trust assets, subject to such deductions as may be equitable and just for its compensation and expenditures * * *."

Then follows a general reference to the trust assets to be delivered either to plaintiff or to any successor trustee whom she might appoint. Thus it appears that the District Court was diligent in preserving plaintiff's right to a revocation of the trust instrument, if she so desired, and a recovery of the trust assets.

---

2. **THE EVIDENCE SHOWS THAT PLAINTIFF EXPRESSLY DIRECTED THE TRUST DEPARTMENT TO PURCHASE SECURITIES FROM THE BOND DEPARTMENT WITH KNOWLEDGE OF ALL MATERIAL FACTS.**

The second question stated by counsel is as to whether it was improper for the trust department to purchase securities from the bond department without disclosing that fact to plaintiff and that it could not do so without notifying plaintiff that it was improper to do so, whether with or without a profit to itself, and without notifying plaintiff of her rights in connection therewith. (App's. Brief, p. 47.) Again counsel complain that, as to these purchases, no finding was made that it was essential that plaintiff should have been informed of her legal rights in connection therewith. (App's. Brief, p. 52.) Counsel apparently rely upon Assignments Nos. 22, 23 and 32. (R. 805-810, 820-823.)

Numerous authorities are cited at pages 52 to 56 of the appellant's brief as sustaining the proposition that a trustee who would excuse himself for a breach of trust on the ground of *confirmation* by the *cestui* has the heavy burden of proving not only a full and fair disclosure of all material facts, but also that the beneficiary was fully advised of his rights, and *thereafter,* and with such knowledge, *confirmed* the breach. (App's. Brief, pp. 52-56.) We submit that the holdings of these authorities are not applicable to the instant case since they deal, in the main, with situations wherein, *after* the trustee has committed a breach of trust, he informs his beneficiary of what he has done, in some instances concealing from the beneficiary some of the material facts, and in other instances concealing from the beneficiary the latter's legal rights. Note that in those instances the trustee *has already committed a breach of trust* and knowledge thereof is obtained by the *cestui either contemporaneously with, or subsequent to, such breach.*

In fact it is conceded by counsel that the cases cited by them do not deal with a *prior direction* by the *cestui* to the trustee to act in a given manner, since they are professedly cited as dealing with a situation wherein a trustee "would excuse himself for a breach of trust on the ground of the *confirmation by the beneficiary of the breach* * * *". (App's. Brief, p. 52.) "Confirmation" of course is equivalent to *ratification* after the act.

But in the instant case there was no breach of trust since the only thing complained of is that the trustee *purchased* the securities for the *trust* from itself, and the record shows without any conflict whatsoever that plaintiff, *in advance, expressly authorized and directed the trust department to purchase from the bond department.**

---

*It appears that counsel do not complain of the making of a profit as an independent ground of relief, but merely that the making of such profit was incidental to and in aggravation of the purchase of securities from the bond department. Thus at page 21 of appellant's brief it is stated "the complaint alleged in aggravation of the unlawful act, that * * * in every instance of such purchases subsequent to the execution of that instrument, except the last four purchases made in 1930 and

The Court found, with respect to the subsequent purchases of securities from the bond department, that plaintiff

> "* * * *directed the trust department to purchase the same from the bond department; * * *in the instance of each of said purchases, plaintiff knew that the bond department of the national bank was the owner of the securities so suggested and submitted and, with knowledge of that fact and that the said bond department was making a profit thereon, nevertheless directed the trust department to make such purchases from the. bond department.* In the instances of said purchases plaintiff dealt directly with the bond department and directed the trust department to follow out her wishes in making such purchases." (R. 337.)

The evidence directly supports this finding. Mr. Berven testified that about two or three weeks before the trust instrument was executed plaintiff asked him "whether she could continue to deal with the Bond Department, and buy her securities, if she placed the property in trust with us. I told her I thought we could arrange that." (R. 468.) Again, about a week or ten days before the trust was created, plaintiff again came in and after Mr. Berven advised her that the type of securities bought by the trust department carried a lower rate of interest than those she already had so as to insure higher marketability and less fluctuation, she again wanted to know

---

1932, the National Bank made a profit on the transaction, which it concealed from plaintiff." Thus the making of a profit appears to be intended merely as matter in aggravation and not as an independent ground of relief. However, at pages 67 to 68 hereof we shall show that the record establishes plaintiff had knowledge of such profit.

62

"whether she could continue to buy her bonds, her securities, from the Bond Department." (R. 468-470.)

Not only this, but the documentary evidence relating to the three blocks of securities in question shows that plaintiff not only dealt directly with the bond department after the trust was created but also that *she expressly directed the trust department to purchase the securities in question from the bond department.*

The Hearst Publications bond purchased as of April 15, 1930.

On April 4, 1930, plaintiff wrote to Mr. Bothwell enclosing a trust department statement which showed that a bond had been called and requested information as to whether this meant the trust department was not placing the money in bonds when they were called, asking him to take the matter up with the trust department. (Pl's. Ex. 10, R. 553.) In reply he wrote to plaintiff on April 8, 1930, suggesting purchase of a Hearst Publications bond, stating that

"If this suggestion is agreeable to you, kindly sign and return the enclosed order and *we will confirm the bond, delivering the same to the Trust Department * * *.*" (Pl's. Ex. 12, R. 555.)

Thereafter plaintiff wrote to the trust department saying (Pl's. Ex. 13, R. 556):

"This will be your authority to charge my account $1012.78 and *pay a like amount to the Bond Department* against the delivery to you for my account of:
$1,000. Hearst Publications, Inc. 6¼% bond due 1940."

The California Cotton Mills bond purchased on June 5, 1930.

On May 20, 1930, Mr. Bothwell wrote the following letter to Mrs. Quinn (Pl's. Ex. 14, R. 556-557):

"Referring to *our recent conversation* when you were in Oakland, regarding the re-investment of $1000, which you expected to receive from Reno, we submit the following:

$1000 California Cotton Mills Co. 1st Mtge.
6% due July 1, 1940
at 85 to yield 8.20%.

$1000 Hearst Publications, Inc. 1st Mtge.
6¼% due Nov. 1, 1935
at 98.85 to yield 6.50%.

*　　*　　*　　*　　*　　*　　*

If either meet with your approval, kindly advise Mr. Berven, who will forward to you the necessary papers to sign."

On May 21, 1930, Mrs. Quinn sent to Mr. Berven the letter which is set forth on page 23 of this brief, requesting that he purchase the California Cotton Mills Bond for her (Pl's. Ex. 16, R. 558), and on May 26, 1930, she again wrote to him requesting that he purchase this bond for her. (Pl's. Ex. 15, R. 557.)

The Hearst Publications bonds purchased as of July 1, 1930.

On June 24, 1930, Mr. Bothwell wrote to plaintiff pointing out that she had $11,000 Washoe County Bonds falling due and suggesting $5000 Federal Public Service Corporation Bonds* and $6000 Hearst Publication Bonds. (Pl's. Ex. 17, R. 559.)

---

*It will be recalled that the Federal Public Service Corporation Bonds, although purchased, were sold shortly thereafter for the full price previously paid plus accrued interest. (Supra, p. 56.)

Plaintiff replied to Bothwell on June 25, 1930, stating in part: *"You* may reinvest the money as you have suggested * * *"* and calling his attention to the fact that Hearst Publications Bonds had previously been purchased. (Pl's. Ex. 18, R. 560.) On June 27, 1930, plaintiff wrote to the trust department directing them as follows (Pl's. Ex. 19, R. 560-561):

> "Out of the proceeds of the Washoe County bonds due July 1, 1930, *you are instructed to purchase from the Bond Department,* Central National Bank of Oakland, the following described securities as an investment for my trust account No. 604.
>
> Five (5) Federal Public Service Corp. 6% bonds due 12-1-47 at 93.
>
> Six (6) Hearst Publications 6¼% bonds three due 11-1-33 and 3 due 11-1-34 at 99.10."

———

The foregoing correspondence definitely and conclusively shows that in making the purchases of the securities in question, plaintiff dealt directly and exclusively with Mr. Bothwell of the bond department and her only dealings with the trust department were to direct it to purchase the securities offered to her by the bond department. For example, plaintiff directed the trust department to *"pay a like amount to the Bond Department"* (Pl's. Ex. 10), and instructed the trust department *"to purchase from the Bond Department * * *."* (Pl's. Ex. 19.)

The fact that the bond department *offered* these securities to plaintiff, and offered them *at a fixed price*—never at an uncertain price such as at market—*definitely brought*

*home to plaintiff the fact that these securities were owned
by the bond department.* It must be borne in mind that
plaintiff was a woman of acute perception and understanding. The record shows that she read everything
carefully and understood what she read. (*Supra,* pp. 22
to 23.) At no time did she testify that she did not
understand the foregoing correspondence relating to the
purchase of the securities in question.

In reference to the claim of counsel that it is not sufficient that the *cestui* ratifies the transaction upon being
informed that the trustee has purchased from itself, but
that the *cestui* must also be advised of her legal rights
to rescind, may we repeat, as previously stated, that the
situation presented by the authorities cited by counsel
is vastly different than the situation presented in the
case at bar. Here we are concerned with a situation
where *prior* to the purchase of securities by a trustee
from himself, the *cestui directed the trustee to purchase
from himself.* It is ridiculous to argue that in such a
case the trustee must say to the *cestui,* ''If you hadn't
given me such an authorization I could not purchase from
myself, and if I had purchased from myself without your
authorization, I would have acted in violation of my
duties as trustee and you could have rescinded the purchase''.

This in no wise resembles the situation where, *after*
a trustee has purchased securities for the trust which
he previously individually owned, he so advises the *cestui*
(but without likewise advising the latter that he can
rescind the transaction) who either expressly ratifies it,
or does not object.

This distinction was recognized in the case of *Ungrich v. Ungrich* (1909), 131 App. Div. 24, 115 N. Y. S. 413, 417-418, where a trustee with the prior consent of the adult beneficiary had purchased property from the trust. There the Court said:

"It was not necessary in view of the facts disclosed for the defendants to prove a ratification as though all that was done had been done without his knowledge and assent as the learned trial court appears to have assumed. *The rule that to fasten ratification upon a cestui que trust he must not only have been made acquainted with all the facts, but apprised also of the law, and how such facts would be dealt with by a court of equity, has no application to the situation presented. The plaintiff having sanctioned and assented to the transaction and concurred in the transfer of the property to his brother, and having understood all the facts and no deception having been practiced upon him, he is bound by such sanction, and cannot repudiate it notwithstanding the defendant Henry may have been guilty of a technical violation of his trust, and may by good fortune have largely benefited by the purchase.*"

This case was followed in the case of *In re Turner's Will* (1935), 156 Misc. 68, 281 N. Y. S. 452, 457, wherein the trustee had retained an investment which it was its legal duty to sell. It was held that the beneficiary could not complain because she had consented to the retention of the security in question, the Court saying (p. 457):

" 'It is likewise true that a cestui que trust cannot allege an act upon the part of his trustee to be a breach of trust which has been done *under his sanction or procurement or concurrence.*' "

In that case it did not appear that the trustee advised the beneficiary that it was legally improper to retain the investment or what her legal rights were concerning the transaction.

In answer to the contention of plaintiff that she did not know the bond department was making a profit on these purchases, and assuming counsel intend that such matter, if a fact, is regarded as constituting a new and independent ground of action, and not a matter *"in aggravation"* of the purchases by the trust department from the bond department allegedly without plaintiff's knowledge (*supra*, p. 60), the record supports the finding that plaintiff had knowledge of the making of such profit. This finding is set forth at page 337 of the record.

It will be recalled that prior to the time of the execution of the trust instrument on September 24, 1929, plaintiff told Mr. Berven that she desired to continue to deal with the bond department as before. (R. 468, 469-470.) The Court found that prior to the time plaintiff executed the instrument of trust she knew the bond department was making a profit (R. 326) notwithstanding her testimony to the contrary (R. 401), since such testimony was incredible in that no brokerage or commission was ever specified in the bills submitted to her at the time of each purchase. In other words, in order to give credence to plaintiff's testimony it would have been necessary to have assumed that she believed the bank was acting gratuitously in all of these prior transactions involving a great many thousands of dollars. Of necessity she must have known the bank was making a profit. Having this knowledge in mind prior to the time of the execution of the trust instrument, and desiring and inquiring if she could carry on her purchases from the bond department in the same manner, after the execution of the trust instrument, as before, she therefore had knowledge that the bond department was making a profit when she later directed the trust department to purchase from the bond department.

---

3. THE PROVISIONS OF SECTION 25 OF THE CALIFORNIA BANK ACT EXPRESSLY PERMIT A TRUST DEPARTMENT OF A BANK TO PURCHASE FROM ANOTHER DEPARTMENT THEREOF PROVIDED THAT THE PAIR VALUE OF THE SECURITIES BE PAID AND THE SECURITIES PURCHASED BE A LEGAL INVESTMENT FOR THE DEPARTMENT MAKING THE PURCHASE.

California Bank Act, sec. 25, provides:

> "* * * any bank having departments shall have the right to sell and transfer any bonds, securities or loans *from one department to another* upon receipt of the *actual value* thereof, if such bonds, securities or loans are, under the provisions of this act, a *legal investment* for the department purchasing the same."

In its conclusions of law the District Court determined, with reference to the purchases from the bond department after the execution of the trust instrument, that "the provisions of section 25 of the *California Bank Act* expressly permitted such purchases by the trust department from the bond department". (R. 350.)

It will be noted that section 25 of the *California Bank Act* contains but two requirements:

First. That the actual value of the securities be paid; and

Second. That the securities purchased be a legal investment for the department purchasing the same.

The Court found that in each instance the securities in question were sold by the bond department to the trust department at their fair value and were legal trust investments since the instrument of trust authorized the investment of the trust funds in "legals", *or otherwise;* that the words "or otherwise" were inserted in the trust instrument for that specific purpose.

These findings are supported by the evidence. Thus Mr. Bothwell testified that the securities were sold at their market value or price at the time of sale. (R. 430-431, 449.)

Section 105 of the *California Bank Act* provides that trust funds may be invested in securities which are legal for investment of the funds of a savings bank *or which are authorized by the trust instrument.* Article II of the trust instrument provides that "the trustee shall have full power to * * * invest * * * in such securities, properties, or investments of the character permitted by law for investment of trust funds, *or otherwise,* * * *". (R. 64-65.) Mr. Berven testified that in a conversation shortly before the execution of the trust instrument he told plaintiff that the high interest-bearing securities she had previously purchased were not of a type usually bought for trust investments; that they were required to buy securities considered legal for trust investments and that such securities had a higher marketability and less fluctuation and would naturally have a smaller rate of income, a rate not over five per cent, in response to which

Mrs. Quinn told him she would have to have at least six per cent. He thereupon told her that this could be done by inserting in the trust instrument a provision that they could buy securities legal for trust investments *or otherwise*. Such a provision was inserted in the trust instrument. (R. 469-470.) When the trust instrument was read over to her before it was signed, the purpose of the insertion of the words "or otherwise" was pointed out to her. (R. 472-473.)

Nowhere in that portion of counsel's brief designated "Argument" is there any criticism of the findings and the conclusions of law in question. In Assignments No. 21, subdivision 6 (R. 802-805), No. 23, subdivision 2 (R. 807-810), No. 32, subdivisions 4 and 5 (R. 820-823), apparently these findings and the conclusions are intended to be called into question as being unsupported by the evidence and also on the ground that the provisions of section 25 of the *California Bank Act* were not pleaded. We have already pointed to the sufficiency of the supporting evidence *which was admitted without any objection whatsoever*. These matters were directly put in issue by the pleadings. It is true that the answer did not state "The defendant relies on section 25 of the *California Bank Act*". Such pleading would probably have been improper, since the Court will take judicial notice of the provisions of the state law. Thus in *Cyc. Fed. Proc.*, Vol. 3, p. 627, sec. 855, it is said:

> "It is probably not necessary *that matters of which the court will take judicial notice be alleged in the answer,* but however that may be, an answer is not defective for so doing."

In the case of *Harpending v. Reformed etc. Church*
(1842), 16 Pet. 405, 41 U. S. 455, 10 L. ed. 1029, an
equity suit was commenced in the Federal Court. The
defendants prevailed on the ground that the statute of
limitations had barred plaintiffs. On appeal the plaintiffs contended that the statute had not been properly
pleaded. Thus (10 L. ed. 1041):

> "It is insisted that the act of limitations is not
> relied on *by express reference* to the statute of New
> York. We think it was unnecessary to rely *in terms*
> on the statute. It was more convenient not to do so.
> * * * *The court is judicially bound to take notice of
> the statutes,* when the facts are stated and relied on
> as a bar to further proceeding if they are found suf-
> ficient."

The only two requirements under section 25 of the
California Bank Act are that the *actual value* of the
securities be paid and that the securities be a legal investment for the department purchasing the same.

In the answers of the defendants it is alleged that in
each instance of the sales of bonds, they were sold at
then current market prices or the fair and reasonable
value thereof. (R. 106, 116, 146 and 155.) With respect to the requirement that the securities be a legal
investment for the department purchasing the same, it
expressly appears in the instrument of trust annexed to
the complaint as a part thereof, that the trust department was authorized to invest the trust funds in so-
called "legals", *"or otherwise"*. (R. 64-65.) Therefore, it was not necessary to plead this element in the
answers since it is not necessary to plead, by way of
defense, a matter appearing on the face of the bill of complaint.

In 21 *C. J.* p. 472, sec. 545, dealing with answers in cases in equity, it is said:

> "If, however, *facts appear on the face of the bill sufficient to defeat it, such facts need not be averred by way of defense.*"

Section 25 of the *California Bank Act* is applicable to national as well as to state banks. It also declares the policy of the State of California to be to permit the trust department of a bank to deal with another department thereof. Thus in *Estate of Smith* (1931), 112 Cal. App. 680, 687, 297 Pac. 927, it was held that where a national bank (Bank of America N. T. & S. A.) was executor of an estate and conducted three departments, commercial, savings and trust, and had deposited in its savings department, moneys it had received as executor, it was entitled to do so on the ground that section 25 of the *Bank Act* permitted such deposit.

Furthermore, that case recognized that there are natural and intrinsic differences between departmental banks as trustees and others acting in the same capacity. The Court also stated that since the legislature had spoken on the question of the departmentalization of banks the matter was not subject to review by the Courts. (This case is quoted from at page viii of the Appendix.)

Bogert, Trusts and Trustees, Vol. 3, p. 1544, section 489, takes the view that section 25 authorizes such purchases. Thus in footnote 72 it is said:

> "Cal. Gen. Laws 1931, Act. 652, sec. 25 (sale from department to department permitted); * * *."

It is well settled that national banks are entitled to conduct a trust business in competition with, and on the same basis as, state banks under the law of the state in which the national bank in question is located. (*First Nat. Bank v. Fellows* (1916), 244 U. S. 416, 37 Sup. Ct. Rep. 734, 61 L. ed. 1233; *Breedlove v. Freudenstein* (1937), 89 Fed. (2d) 324 (C. C. A. 5).)

It is respectfully submitted that the purchases in question were expressly authorized by section 25 of the *California Bank Act.* As the Court held in *Estate of Smith, supra,* in construing this section, there are natural and intrinsic differences between departmental trustees and other trustees due to the safeguards afforded by the *Bank Act.* The Court also pointed out that insofar as any question of public policy was concerned, the legislature had already spoken and the wisdom or unwisdom of such a statute was not open to judicial review.

———

IV. IT WAS UNNECESSARY FOR THE DISTRICT COURT TO MAKE ANY FINDING OR DETERMINATION AS TO WHETHER OR NOT THE SAVINGS BANK WOULD HAVE ASSUMED THOSE LIABILITIES OF THE NATIONAL BANK WHICH ARE ALLEGED BY PLAINTIFF TO HAVE ARISEN PRIOR TO THE EXECUTION OF THE TRUST INSTRUMENT HAD SUCH LIABILITIES BEEN FOUND TO EXIST, SINCE THE FINDINGS ACTUALLY MADE RENDER SUCH QUESTION MOOT.

In the findings of fact (R. 340-341) and in the conclusions of law (R. 350-351) the District Court expressly declined to make any determination as to whether or not the savings bank would have assumed and become liable for any liabilities of the national bank alleged to have arisen *prior* to the execution of the trust instrument on September 24, 1929, since it was determined that no such liabilities had been established and, therefore, the findings otherwise made rendered this question of any possible assumption of antecedent liabilities unnecessary to the decision of the case. The determination of the question of assumption or non-assumption of such alleged prior liabilities would only have been necessary had judgment been entered in plaintiff's favor, or if, on this appeal, the decree of the District Court should perchance be reversed, in which event, the savings bank, on the one hand, and the national bank and Central Company, as agent for the shareholders of the national bank, on the other hand, would seek to have the question as to the assumption or non-assumption of such liabilities determined.

Since it was conceded by the savings bank during the trial of the case that had any liabilities been established as arising out of, or relating or incidental to the purchase of securities by the trust department, or the conduct of the trust, *after* September 24, 1929, such liabilities would have been assumed by the savings bank, the Court so determined this hypothetical question with respect to such *subsequent* liabilities in accordance with such concession. (R. 341, 351.)

Counsel discuss this question in their appellant's brief. (pp. 48, 61-63.) In Assignments Nos. 24 (R. 810-813) and 33 (R. 823-825) counsel complain of the failure of the Court to find upon and determine these matters.

Equity Rule 70½ provides that the Court "shall find the facts specially and state separately its conclusions of law thereon; * * *". It is well settled that where findings are made upon issues which determine the case and thereby render other issues immaterial, it is not necessary to find upon such other issues. Thus in the case of

Parker v. St. Sure (1931), 53 Fed. (2d) 706, 708 (C. C. A. 9), this Court said:

> "The rule is well settled, in states where findings are required by law, *that it is not necessary to make findings on all defenses wherein findings actually made require a judgment in favor of either party.* We do not believe that the Supreme Court intended to extend this rule by Equity Rule No. 70½ so that in every case there must be specific findings upon every issue, regardless of the fact that findings actually made sustain a decree, * * *."

See, also:

> *Brown v. United States* (1938), 95 Fed. (2d) 487, 490 (C. C. A. 3);
>
> *Associated Industries Ins. Corp. v. Industrial Acc. Com.* (1927), 85 Cal. App. 184, 188, 259 Pac. 110;

and

> 64 *C. J.* pp. 1234-1235, sec. 1077.

In the case at bar since the Court found that no liability whatsoever had been established against any defendant, it was unnecessary to find whether the savings bank would have assumed such antecedent liabilities had they been found to exist. Had any such finding been made, based upon a hypothetical liability, then the issues involved on this appeal would have been greatly complicated in that the savings bank, on the one hand, and the national bank and the Central Company, on the other hand, while primarily opposing the plaintiff on this appeal, would nevertheless have been carrying on a secondary argument or cross-appeal, as it were, as between themselves. Had the District Court found that there was a liability established prior to the time of the execution of the trust instrument *then,* and only then, would

it have been necessary and proper to determine whether
or not the savings bank had assumed such liability.

Counsel comment (App's. Brief, pp. 13, 40-42) upon
the express declination of the District Court (R. 351) to
make any finding upon the special defenses of the statute of limitations pleaded in the answers of the savings
bank and of the national bank (R. 137, 175-176) and of
laches and plaintiff's waiver of her right to rescind,
pleaded in the supplemental answer of the national bank.
(R. 177-180.) The authorities last cited sustain the District Court in its declination since the finding and determination that plaintiff had not established any liabilities
whatsoever disposed of the case and rendered it unnecessary to find on special defenses which would have been
of value to the defendants only if liability had been found
to exist in the first instance.

CONCLUSION.

In closing we emphasize that the issues in this case
are simple and free from complexity, involving as they
do essentially questions of fact alone. Counsel have
criticized the findings of the District Court as being either
contrary to, or unsupported by, the evidence. It is significant that the appellant has not referred to the statement of evidence in a single instance in the argument in
her brief either to support her contentions, or to contradict the findings. This failure, together with the

neglect to comply in other respects with the requirements of the rules of this Court, even taken alone, justifies the affirmance of the decree.

This case falls into three chronological divisions: (1) the transactions occurring from the date of the first purchase of securities on January 7, 1926, to the date of the execution of the trust instrument on September 24, 1929; (2) the preparation and execution of the trust instrument; and (3) the transactions occurring after the execution of the trust instrument.

First. The Court found that prior to the execution of the trust instrument the intended and actual relationship existing between plaintiff and the national bank was that of buyer, on plaintiff's part, and seller, on the part of the national bank. The evidence overwhelmingly supports this finding. Plaintiff's apparent criticism of this finding is that the Court should, in addition thereto, have found that it was essential that plaintiff be informed of her legal rights in connection with these purchases. Such argument, which appears to be relied upon by counsel throughout their brief, is fallacious in that it assumes the very fact in issue to be as claimed by counsel, namely, that the relationship between plaintiff and the national bank prior to the execution of the trust instrument was either that of principal and agent or *cestui* and trustee. Since the issue was squarely joined in the pleadings and at the trial what the nature of this prior relationship was, and since the Court, determining in accordance with the convincing weight of the evidence, found that the relationship was not only that of buyer and seller but also that it was so intended by the parties, no duty arose, and it was in fact impossible, to notify plaintiff of alleged legal rights which were non-existent and which would have been existent only in the event the evidence established, and the Court found, that the relationship was that of principal and agent or *cestui* and trustee.

Second. With respect to the preparation and execution of the trust instrument on September 24, 1929, the evidence clearly shows, and the Court found, that there was no wrong-doing on the part of the national bank. As shown above, the prior relationship was intended by the parties to be, and was, that of buyer and seller, and therefore there was no breach of any alleged duty concerning which plaintiff could have been informed in regard to the prior purchases. Furthermore, it was definitely established by the evidence, and so found by the Court, that plaintiff was not in any manner prevented from obtaining legal advice with respect to the execution of the trust instrument, or in connection therewith.

Third. With respect to the purchases of securities by the trust department of the national bank from the bond department thereof after the execution of the trust instrument the Court found, and the evidence definitely shows, that the three purchases complained of were proper, first, because plaintiff, with knowledge of all material facts, expressly directed the trust department to do the very thing of which she now complains, namely, to purchase securities from the bond department of the national bank; and, second, because the provisions of Section 25 of the California Bank Act expressly permit a trust department of a bank to purchase securities from the bond department thereof. Furthermore, even if we assume for the purposes of argument, that the trust department of the national bank was guilty of technical wrong-doing in purchasing securities for plaintiff's trust from the bond department, which purchases incidentally resulted in a substantial profit to the trust, nevertheless the law is clear that such subsequent wrong-doing by a trustee is not a ground for rescinding the trust or cancelling the trust instrument but that the proper remedy would be a removal of the trustee. This question has become moot, since not only did the savings bank offer to permit a revocation of the trust instrument without a release of such liabilities as might have existed in favor of plaintiff, but, also, the provisions of the contract for the sale of the trust department from the national bank to the savings bank, and also the provisions of Section 31 of the *California Bank Act* expressly permitted plaintiff to appoint a new or successor trustee, thus rendering unnecessary any judicial removal of the trustee. Furthermore, the District Court was careful to provide in its Decree that plaintiff might, if she so desired, revoke the instrument of trust or appoint a new and successor trustee.

We submit that since this case involves questions of fact almost exclusively, the findings of the District Court, which are based upon the preponderance of the evidence, should be sustained. The District Judge having heard the testimony, having observed the witnesses, and having weighed the evidence in the light of all the surrounding facts and circumstances and of the inferences to be drawn therefrom, rendered judgment for the appellees. We therefore respectfully submit that the Decree should be affirmed.

Dated, Oakland, California,
February 14, 1939.

IRA ABRAHAM,
Attorney for the Defendants and Appellees, Central Company (a corporation), as agent for the shareholders of Central National Bank of Oakland, and Central National Bank of Oakland (a national banking association in liquidation).

CLIFFORD BURNHILL,
Of Counsel.

FITZGERALD, ABBOTT & BEARDSLEY,
CHARLES A. BEARDSLEY,
M. W. DOBRZENSKY,
JAMES H. ANGLIM,
EDWARD B. KELLY,
CRELLIN FITZGERALD,
Attorneys for the Defendant and Appellee, Central Bank of Oakland (a corporation).

(Appendix Follows.)

Appendix

The following authorities are referred to on page 29 of the appellees' brief in support of the argument that the determination of the question as to whether a given relationship is that of buyer and seller or principal and agent is a question of fact.

Bigelow v. Plummer et al. (1937), 23 Cal. App. (2d) 441, 443-444, 73 Pac. (2d) 638, 639 (cited on page 29):

"The question whether the parties occupied the relation (1) of principal and agent or (2) vendor and vendee is ordinarily a question of fact to be determined by the fact finder. Only where the evidence on the issue is clear and undisputed is it a question of law for the court to decide. (55 C. J. 43.) 'Where, as in this case, the facts and circumstances in evidence may reasonably authorize either one of two opposite inferences and the trial court has adopted one and rejected the other, its decision is binding upon the appellate court, the case being in substance the same as where the trial court decides upon the weight of contradictory evidence.' (*Boland v. Gosser,* 5 Cal. App. (2d) 700 (43 Pac. (2d) 559), and cases cited.)"

55 *C. J.* p. 43, sec. 8 (cited on page 29):

"The primary test as to the character of a contract, as to whether it constitutes a contract of sale or one of agency, is the intention of the parties gathered from the whole scope and effect of the language employed, and in doubtful cases the question must be determined upon a review of all that passed between the parties, before and contemporaneously with the dealings under consideration, and is generally a question of fact to be determined by a jury, except where the evidence on the issue is clear and undisputed, in which case it is a question of law for the court to decide. If by such ii

test it is apparent that it was the intention of the
parties that the one party is employed to purchase
goods on behalf of another, the transaction is an
agency to buy, as where one party, on the order of
another, secures and ships goods to him on a commission; but if it is intended that he is to purchase on
his own behalf and sell the goods to the other, the
transaction constitutes a contract to sell or sale.''

The following authorities are referred to at pages 43 to 45 of the appellees' brief in support of the argument that the fact plaintiff may have reposed trust and confidence in Mr. Bothwell and in the bond department of the national bank did not give rise to a trust relationship.

Ruhl v. Mott (1898), 120 Cal. 668, 678-679, 53 Pac. 304, 308 (cited on page 43):

"Nor can his ignorance be palliated or excused because of the alleged confidential relations which existed between plaintiff and defendant, or because of plaintiff's alleged weakness of mind.

The court does not find that he was of weak mind, and plaintiff's own testimony as to other land transactions, and the uniform financial success with which he met in his speculations negatives the idea that he was of feeble intellect. The confidential relationship is found by the court in the following language: 'One-half or more of all the business done by plaintiff came from the defendant, as manager of the firm of H. S. Crocker & Co., and, as a result of the relation between them, *plaintiff reposed great confidence in defendant, trusted him, and relied upon him for advice.'* But *this finding is not sufficient to establish the confidential relationship defined in section 2219 of the Civil Code, so as to charge the defendant with the high duties pertaining to a trustee,* and to shift the burden of proof to show the unfairness of the transaction from the plaintiff, where it naturally rests, to the shoulders of the defendant, and compel the latter to establish the fairness of the sale. It is to be remembered that plaintiff was himself a business man, had bought and sold real estate, and was contracting with the Crocker Company, of which defendant was a manager. *The fact that he reposed confidence in the defendant did not cast any duty upon the latter, unless he 'voluntarily assumed a relation of personal confidence' with* iv

plaintiff, and this is not found. Equity always views with strictness the business dealings of a man with one who stands in a position of dependence or confidence to him, when that relationship is either voluntarily assumed or is imposed by operation of law. But it would indeed be an anomaly if one dealing with a vendor of land should be allowed to shut his eyes and ears and making no use of his faculties in determining the value of the property he purchased, thereafter excuse himself by saying that he reposed confidence in the vendor. He may in fact have done so, but the fact does not establish a confidential relation as known to law, and for his trusting folly neither law nor equity can afford him redress.''

Jackson v. Gorman (1929), 98 Cal. App. 112, 116-117, 276 Pac. 391, 393 (cited on page 44):

"Friendly relations or even intimacy of relationship presents an entirely different question from what is understood as a confidential relation in law. *One may have confidence in another's integrity and honesty of purpose, and likewise believe that he will live up to any of his contracts, without having any confidential relations with such person that would void any agreements or transactions entered into between them, on the theory of constructive fraud or undue influence.* We think the record shows that the Harrises did have confidence in the honesty and integrity of the Jacksons, and believed that the Jacksons would comply with any agreements into which they entered, but there is absolutely no testimony showing anything further, or that there were any confidential business relationships, relationships existing between the Jacksons and the Harrises which would constitute a basis for a charge of constructive fraud. *There must be something further than mere confidence in another's honesty and integrity to sustain the presumption of constructive fraud.* (*In re Estate of Lavinburg,* 161 Cal. 536 (119 Pac. 915); *In re Estate of Higgins,* 156 Cal. 259 (104 Pac. 8).) As to what does constitute such relationship is well illustrated in the case of *Cox v. Schnerr,* 172 Cal. 371 (156 Pac. 509), where the person charged with fraud had been the confidential business agent, and for a long time transacted business for the one upon whom undue influence was alleged to have been exercised. What constitutes confidential relationship in law is also well illustrated in the case of *Piercy v. Piercy,* 18 Cal. App. 756 (124 Pac. 561), where a son had lived in the same house with his mother, managed her property as her agent, and also held a general power of attorney.''

Doyle et al. v. Murphy et ux. (1859), 22 Ill. 502, 508-509 (cited on page 45):

"It is urged, in connection with other grounds, for the reversal of the decree of the court below, that the court had no jurisdiction of the subject matter. While by the defendants in error, it is insisted that Maurice Doyle *was a trustee,* and being such, a court of equity has undoubted jurisdiction over the trust fund. That the court has such a jurisdiction in cases of strict trust, there is no doubt. But it does not therefore follow, that the court will assume jurisdiction in every case *where a mere confidence has been reposed,* or a credit given. The various affairs of life in almost every act between individuals in trade and commerce, *involve the reposing of confidence or trust in each other,* and yet it never has been supposed that because such a confidence or trust in the integrity of another has been extended and abused, that therefore, a court of equity would in all such cases assume jurisdiction. When one person sells property on credit, or loans

money to another, confidence is reposed and a trust is
entertained that the money will be paid by the debtor,
and yet no case has gone so far as to hold, that it
was such a trust, as gave to a court of equity jurisdiction under the head of trusts. If this were so, there
would be no case where property or money was obtained on a credit, in which the court would not have
jurisdiction.''

Southern Trust Co. et al. v. Lucas (1917), 245 Fed. 286,
288 (C. C. A. 8) (cited on page 45):

"It is true that one party cannot create a legal
obligation or status by pleading ignorance and inexperience to an opposing party in a business transaction. Those who have in the law's view been strangers
remain such, unless both consent by word or deed to
an alteration of that status. The communicated desire
or intention of one to impose upon the other a different status, involving greater obligations, is ineffective,
unless the other consents to the changed relation. It
is true that consent may find expression in acts as
readily as in words. *But such consent cannot be implied from a bare procedure with the transaction, after
one party has declared his or her inexperience and reliance upon the other.* The knowledge of this state of
mind in a party may be an important consideration
in determining the existence of fraud, as indicating
what effect might be anticipated from statements
made; but it cannot establish a confidential legal
status.''

Hancock v. Anderson (1933), 160 Va. 225, 168 S.E. 458,
463 (cited on page 45):

"Trust alone, however, is not sufficient. We trust
most men with whom we deal. There must be something reciprocal in the relationship before the rule can

be invoked. Before liability can be fastened upon one, there must have been something in the course of dealings for which he was in part responsible that induced another to lean upon him, and from which it can be inferred that the ordinary right to contract had been surrendered. If this were not true, a reputation for fair dealing would be a liability and an unsavory one an asset. A sale of bonds made by the Bank of England can be set aside no more quickly than a sale made by a 'bucket shop'."

The following authority is referred to on page 72 of the appellees' brief in support of the argument that the provisions of Section 25 of the California Bank Act expressly permit a trust department of a bank to purchase securities from another department thereof.

Estate of Smith (1931), 112 Cal. App. 680, 687, 297 Pac. 927, 930 (cited on page 72):

"It has been heretofore decided that where legislation affects banking corporations doing business as testamentary trustees as a class and such classification is not unreasonable, there is no valid constitutional objection to such legislation. (*Estate of Barnett,* 97 Cal. App. 138 (275 Pac. 453).) We find nothing unreasonable in such classification here and in our opinion there is a natural and intrinsic difference between departmental bank trustees and other trustees. The various sections of the Bank Act relating to capital, surplus, reserves, securities, inspection and the like (Bank Act, secs. 90, 96, 97, 98, 101, 103, 105, 106), surround every activity of departmental bank trustees with safeguards not required of trustees generally.

In arguing for affirmance counsel dwell at some length upon the policy involved in permitting departmental banks to deposit trust funds in their savings bank departments to be used in the same manner as other deposits. We deem it unnecessary to discuss the policy involved for it is upon this question of policy that the legislature has spoken and it acted within its province in so doing."

No. 8860

United States 3
Circuit Court of Appeals

For the Ninth Circuit

ABBIE W. QUINN,

Appellant,

v.

CENTRAL COMPANY, a corporation, as agent
for the shareholders of the Central National
Bank of Oakland, CENTRAL NATIONAL
BANK OF OAKLAND, a national banking
association in liquidation, and CENTRAL
BANK OF OAKLAND,

Appellees.

APPELLANT'S CLOSING BRIEF
AND APPENDIX J.

FILED

APR 1 _ 1939

UL P. O'BRIEN,
    CLERK

CHARLES W. SLACK,
EDGAR T. ZOOK,
    1101 Alaska Commercial Building,
    San Francisco, California,
        Attorneys for Appellant

PARKER PRINTING COMPANY, 545 SANSOME STREET, SAN FRANCISCO

TOPICAL INDEX

AUTHORITIES CITED

Note: Figures in italics refer to pages in Appendix J.

3. CASES.

No. 8860

United States
Circuit Court of Appeals

For the Ninth Circuit

ABBIE W. QUINN,

Appellant,

v.

CENTRAL COMPANY, a corporation, as agent
for the shareholders of the Central National
Bank of Oakland, CENTRAL NATIONAL
BANK OF OAKLAND, a national banking
association in liquidation, and CENTRAL
BANK OF OAKLAND,

Appellees.

APPELLANT'S CLOSING BRIEF

I.

THERE WAS A SUBSTANTIAL, IF NOT A COMPLETE, COMPLIANCE WITH THE RULES, OLD AND NEW, OF THIS COURT, RELATING TO THE SPECIFICATION OF ASSIGNED ERRORS.

Counsel for defendants and appellees, under a heading, (Reply Brief, p. 4), entitled, "The effect of appellant's failure to comply with the rules of this Court", argues, (Reply Brief, pp. 4-7), (but with obviously little confidence in the soundness of their argument), that counsel for plaintiff and appellant, in their opening brief, have "failed" and "neglected" to comply with, and have "violated", the provisions of paragraph (d), of subdivision 2, of former Rule 24, which require as follows:

> "A specification by number of such of the assigned errors as are to be relied upon, with reference to the pages of the record where the assignments appear. Thereafter each such assignment of error shall be printed in full preceding the argument addressed to it. Where the specified error is more than two printed pages in length, it may be summarized before the argument addressed to it, in which event the specified assignment must be printed in full in an appendix."

Observing, in this connection, (Reply Brief, p. 5), that

> "Twenty-seven of the assignments of error are less, and eight are more, than two pages in length";

and that

> "While counsel have specified all thirty-five of their assignments of error as being relied upon, (App's. Brief, pp. 43-46), nevertheless, in not a single instance has this provision of the old rules been complied with, in that none of the assignments of error has either been printed in full or in summarized form before any part of the argument directed thereto";

and consequently, and for the further reason, (Reply Brief, p. 6), that plaintiff has filed "a multitude of lengthy and confusing assignments of error", the appeal should be dismissed, (Reply Brief, pp. 6-7), or, (Reply Brief, pp. 76-7), the decree should be affirmed. But, notwithstanding that the severe penalty of the dismissal of her appeal or of the affirmance of the decree should be imposed upon plaintiff because of the negligence of her counsel, counsel for the defendants, nevertheless, states, (Reply Brief, p. 7), that "the Court may choose to overlook the absolute non-compliance with the rules of this Court", but in so doing,

> "The failure on appellant's part to observe said rules has greatly increased the burden imposed upon the Court, as well as upon counsel."

It may be observed, in passing, that, in the absence of any explanation and of any reason which might be conjectured, why this last quoted statement is true, the correctness of the statement is more than doubtful, and, therefore, it must be accepted as a fact that no burden whatever has been imposed either upon the Court or upon counsel for defendants because of any "failure on appellant's part to observe" the provisions above quoted of former Rule 24, even if it be conceded that counsel for plaintiff failed or neglected to comply with those provisions.

Moreover, the assignments of errors are printed in full, in Appendix H to plaintiff's opening brief, and for all practical purposes can be as readily referred to as if the assignments had been reprinted in full or in a summarized form preceding the arguments addressed to them, and, consequently, unnecessary repetition of them has been avoided.

Before answering the strictures of counsel for defendants, we here make mention of the following extraordinary sequence of events and their surrounding circumstances in the preparation and filing of plaintiff's opening brief:

The opening brief was prepared and in the hands of the printers during the latter part of the year 1938, and was served and filed on January 3, 1939. It was prepared in substantial conformity, as we believed at the time of its preparation, and as we still believe, with the provisions, above quoted, of paragraph (d), subdivision 2, of former Rule 24.

We were in ignorance at the time the opening brief was prepared and filed of the fact that these provisions had been materially changed by the provisions of paragraph (d), subdivision 2, of Rule 20 of the new rules, effective, according to the order of this Court, on *December 19, 1938,* or 15 days *prior* to the filing of the plaintiff's opening brief. If any notice of the adoption of the new rules had been given to the profession, by publication or in any other manner, such notice was not called to our attention until shortly after January 3, 1939, and, apparently, no such notice was given prior to that date. Later, and in the month of February, 1939, we learned from an unofficial source of the adoption of new Rule 20, and we shortly thereafter obtained from the office of the Clerk of this Court a typewritten copy of that rule. Still later, and on or about February 20, 1939, we obtained from the Clerk's office a copy of new Rule 19, relating to and entitled, "Printing Records", and of new Rule 20, relating to and entitled, "Briefs", preceded by a "Preamble", which provides that

> "The Federal Rules of Civil Procedure, whenever applicable, are hereby adopted as a part of the rules of this Court with respect to appeals in actions of a civil nature."

Moreover, it never occurred to us to inquire of the Clerk of this Court, either while the brief was under preparation, or at the time the brief was filed, or even at a later date, whether or not, by any possibility, the provisions of former Rule 24, relating to the preparation of briefs, had been materially changed.

The relevant provisions of paragraph (d), subdivision 2, of the new Rule 20 are as follows:

> "When the error alleged is to the omission or rejection of evidence the specification shall quote the grounds urged at the trial for the objection and the full substance of the evidence admitted or rejected, and refer to the page number in the printed or typewritten transcript where the same may be found. When the error alleged is to the charge of the court, the specification shall set out the part referred to *totidem verbis,* whether it be in instructions given or in instructions refused together with the grounds of the objections urged at the trial. In equity and admiralty cases, and at law when findings are made, the specification shall

state as particularly as may be wherein the findings of fact and conclusions of law are alleged to be erroneous."

Therefore, in equity cases, (as in the instant case in equity), the specification shall state, "as particularly as may be", wherein the findings of fact and conclusions of law are alleged to be erroneous. No greater particularity than this, consequently, is now required. And, if it be assumed that the above-quoted provisions of Rule 20 of the new rules are to govern the situation in hand, the requirements of those provisions have been fully met; and it is submitted that, in view of this fact, the Court surely would not inflict any penalty upon the plaintiff for the failure of her counsel to observe the requirements, (no longer in force), of former Rule 24.

The provisions of Rule 20, it may be further stated, are in harmony, as it seems to us, with the more reasonable provisions of Rule 52, subdivision (a), of the *Federal Rules of Civil Procedure,* the relevant provisions of which are as follows:

> "In all actions tried upon the facts without a jury, the Court shall find the facts specially and state separately its conclusions of law thereon and direct the entry of the appropriate judgment."

These provisions of Rule 52, subdivision (a), of the *Federal Rules of Civil Procedure,* which require the Court to find "the facts *specially* and state *separately* its conclusions of law thereon", have not been observed by counsel for defendants, since, in several instances, the facts found appear in the conclusions of law. But, what is of more importance, is that, in many instances, the facts found do not respond to the issues raised by the pleadings and on which the case was tried, and, in many instances, the facts found have no support whatever in any of the evidence, and, in many other instances, are contrary to the evidence, even where there is no conflicting evidence, and even where the evidence appears to be in conflict, but the conflict has been nullified by the finding, (Opening

Brief, p. 58), that "Plaintiff reposed in Bothwell and in the bond department trust and confidence, which Bothwell well knew."

It may also be observed, in passing, that the statement of counsel for defendants that plaintiff has filed "a multitude of lengthy and confused assignments of error", is, to say the least, somewhat extravagant, since the assignments of error are but thirty-five in all, and most of them are short, and none of them are of any great length, and none of them are "confused".

On the other hand, the findings of fact and conclusions of law are thirty-eight printed pages in length, (R pp. 317-355, App. F), and, to a large extent, are a disordered mixture of facts found with conclusions of law, and, in many instances, the findings are, (1), without any supporting evidence whatever, or, are, (2), contrary to the evidence, (even when the evidence, in any aspect, is not conflicting), or are, (3), without the issues raised by the pleadings and on which the case was tried, and, in some instances, there is a combination of one or both of the other of these offenses. So, also, in several instances, the confusion is accentuated because the conclusions of law have been erroneously drawn for the reason either that, (1), there is no evidence whatever to support the facts from which the conclusions are so drawn, or (2), the conclusions so drawn are without the issues, or (3), the conclusions are so drawn from facts found contrary to the evidence, or (4), the conclusions so drawn do not follow from the facts found.

It is an amazing fact, for which no explanation has been given by counsel for defendants, that of 35 assignments of error, 29 of the findings, so assigned as error, have either (1), no evidence whatever to support them, or (2), are contrary to the evidence, (even if it be assumed that, in some instances, the evidence, otherwise conflicting, has not been nullified by the findings last above quoted, as we have contended in our argument it has been, (Opening Brief, pp. 56-8)), or (3), are without the issues; and, in some instances, there is a combination of two, and sometimes three, of these many violations of elementary and well-settled rules of practice, (24 *Cal. Jur.,* p. 977, sec. 209, 24 *Id.,* p. 990, sec. 216, tit. "Trial", sub-tit. "Findings of fact and conclusions of law", 21 *C. J.,* pp. 583-5, sec. 720, tit. "Equity", sub-tit. "Findings", 64 *Id.* pp. 1232-3, sec. 1077, 64 *Id.* p. 1255, secs. 1102-3, tit. "Trial", sub-tit. "Findings of fact and conclusions of law"). The findings are of matters of vital substance, and they not only support nothing, but, on the contrary, they defeat themselves. Nor can they be lightly disposed of by counsel for defendants, (Reply Brief, p. 22), with the mere statement that

> "There is no requirement that findings comply literally with the wording of a pleading."

Tabulations, relating to the instances in which the findings (1), have no evidence to support them, (2), are contrary to the evidence, and (3), are without the issues, including listings, in some instances, under more than one heading, thus increasing the assignments of error, as numbered, (Opening Brief, p. 43), are set forth in Appendix J, (pages 1-2), to this brief.

It might be suggested, in closing this subject, that counsel for defendants, who have charged counsel for plaintiff with technical violations of rules of procedure, should not themselves have been guilty of violating rules of a substantial character.

II.

THE RELATION PRIOR TO THE EXECUTION OF THE IN-STRUMENT OF TRUST, ON SEPTEMBER 24, 1929, BETWEEN THE NATIONAL BANK AND PLAINTIFF, WAS SUBSTANTIALLY THAT OF TRUSTEE AND CESTUI QUE TRUST.

We quoted in our opening brief the finding of the District Judge, (App. F, Finding 7 of paragraph I), that "Plaintiff reposed in Bothwell and in the bond department trust and confidence, which Bothwell well knew", and, in that connection, made the statement, (the correctness of which has not been disputed by counsel for defendants in their answers to the complaint or in their reply brief), that the finding covered the period of more than ten years prior to the date of the first purchases of bonds and notes on January 7, 1926, for plaintiff from the National Bank, through Bothwell, the manager of its bond department, during all of which time Bothwell occupied the position of an executive officer of high rank, to-wit, that of an assistant cashier, besides the manager of the bond department, of the National Bank.

The relation between Bothwell and plaintiff during all the period of time extending from the time of the first purchases of bonds and notes to the time of the execution of the instrument of trust on September 24, 1929, was substantially that of trustee and cestui que trust for the reasons which follow, as established facts, (as we expect to demonstrate), from the last above quoted finding of the District Judge, to the effect that the relation between plaintiff and Bothwell, during many years prior to the date of the first of the said purchases of bonds and notes, was one of trust and confidence of plaintiff in Bothwell, and, therefore, through him as its agent, in the National Bank. These reasons, as established facts, are here summarized as follows:

(1), the intention of plaintiff, prior to the first purchases of bonds and notes, because of her ill health, (R 8, 215), of

placing her property in trust for her benefit, during her
lifetime, and for the benefit of her dependent daughter and
her grandson, after her death, (R 366-7, 368, 389, 394);

(2), the communication of this intention by plaintiff to Bothwell, with the inquiry by her of him as to whether or not
the National Bank could and would act as trustee of such
a trust, and his reply to plaintiff in the affirmative, (R 367,
368-9);

(3), the information by plaintiff to Bothwell of what her property consisted, including a parcel of improved business real
property, which she was desirous of selling, commonly
known as the "Virginia Street" property, situated in Reno,
Nevada, where she formerly resided, (R 367, 368, 388-9);

(4), the information by Bothwell to plaintiff that the National
Bank could not accept a conveyance to it of real property
situated in Nevada, and his consequent advice to plaintiff,
accepted by her, of investing her funds, available for investment, through the bond department of the National
Bank, in bonds, until after the sale by her of the said parcel
of real property, and, in the meantime, of investing her
funds, available for investment, through the bond department of the National Bank, in bonds, (R 367, 368-9);

(5), the statement of plaintiff to Bothwell that she did not have
any experience with bonds, and if such investments were so
made, she would have to depend on the bond department
of the National Bank to purchase for her safe and desirable
bonds, (R 369-70, 424);

(6), Bothwell's assurance to plaintiff that her funds would be
invested by the National Bank, through him, as the manager of its said bond department, in nothing but safe and
desirable bonds for her, just as secure as those of the
United States, and paying much more interest, (R 369-70);

(7), the purchases of bonds and notes, always selected and recommended by Bothwell to plaintiff as safe and desirable
investments, (R 371, 424);

(8), the reliance by plaintiff upon Bothwell's recommendations
and the approval by her, although, at times, with doubts,
which, however, were always dispelled by him, of their
safety and desirability, of the bonds and notes so selected

and recommended by him, and the purchases of the same, accordingly, for plaintiff by the National Bank, through him as the manager of its bond department, the initial purchase having been made on January 7, 1926, of bonds and notes of $25,000, par value, for $25,133.33, including accrued interest, (R 645, Plf's Ex. 47), and the total purchases of bonds and notes, prior to the execution of the instrument of trust, amounting to the sum of $82,000, at a cost to plaintiff of $80,642.50, (R 36-8);

(9), the retention by the National Bank in its possession of the bonds and notes so purchased before, (R 16-7, 215), as well as after, (R 35-6, 225), the execution of the instrument of trust, which, with the cost to plaintiff of $22,283.75 for bonds and notes purchased subsequent to the execution of the instrument of trust, made a total of $102,926.25 of her capital expenditures through the National Bank;

(10), the sale of the Virginia Street property on February 8, 1928, (R 388), and the removal by plaintiff from the Washoe County Bank, in Reno, Nevada, and the deposit by her with the National Bank, on February 2, 1929, (R 721, Defts' Ex. K), preparatory to the transfer of the same to the National Bank, as trustee of the trusts created by the instrument of trust, of $15,000, par value, Washoe County, County Roads and Highways Improvement and Construction bonds, and also, prior to June 1, 1929, (R 63, 389-90), the removal from the Washoe County Bank and depositing of the same with the National Bank of the promissory note and its securing mortgage, each dated June 1, 1923, executed to plaintiff by the Sparks Masonic Building Association, for the principal sum of $20,000. payable in installments, of which the sum of $6,000 had been paid, leaving as the balance of the principal unpaid the sum of $14,000, (R 63); and

(11), the introduction, (a), of plaintiff by Bothwell to said D. Read, the trust officer of the National Bank, through a letter or note of introduction from Bothwell to Read, and two interviews thereafter of plaintiff with Read, to whom plaintiff had been referred by Bothwell concerning the preparation for plaintiff of an instrument of trust, and the report by plaintiff to Bothwell that she could not seem to get Read interested in her affairs, (R 390-1), (b), the reply of Bothwell to plaintiff that he would introduce her to Berven, the assistant trust officer of the National Bank, and the accompanying by Bothwell to Berven's office and the introduction there by Bothwell of plaintiff to Berven, (R 391), (c), the statements by Bothwell to Berven that plaintiff wanted to create a trust, and that bonds had been purchased and were held for her by the National Bank for that purpose until such time when the trust would be created, (R 391), (d), the statement by Berven that plaintiff should sell her Virginia Street property, and later on they would create the trust for her,* (R 391), and (e), the subsequent preparation of the instrument of trust by the attorneys for the National Bank, with the assistance of Berven, (R 470-1), and the execution of the instrument by the National Bank and plaintiff, on September 24, 1929, with the execution by plaintiff of a deed from plaintiff to plaintiff's daughter of two unsold lots, owned by her and situated in Sparks, Nevada, (R 396), and also with execution by plaintiff of a deed to the National Bank of an unimproved lot of land, owned by her, situated in Oak-

---

*Note: Counsel for defendants states, (Reply Brief, p. 42, note), that on September 9, 1929, (or shortly before the instrument of trust was executed), the Nevada Supreme Court, in the case of *In re Gill's Estate*, 52 Nev. 35, 280 Pac. 321, (1929), had held "that under the particular wording of the Nevada statute, a foreign trust company or bank could do a trust company business in Nevada," and that "This, apparently, was the first time this matter had ever been ruled upon by the Nevada Courts." Such, however, is not an accurate statement of what the case holds. The case does not hold that "a foreign trust company or bank could do a trust company business in Nevada", but the case does decide that the Bankers' Trust Company, a Utah corporation, under the provisions of the Nevada Statutes, 1917, p. 355, c. 192, could be legally appointed as the administrator of an estate of a deceased person who was a resident of Nevada. The case, undoubtedly, was not called to the attention of either Bothwell or Berven, at the time of their conversation with plaintiff concerning the creation of her trust, even if it be assumed that it is an authority for a banking corporation or trust company, incorporated under the laws of another state, to transact a banking or trust business in Nevada without qualifying to do so under the laws of that state.

land, (R 59-60, 633-4), and also with the execution by plaintiff to the National Bank of an assignment of the note and its securing mortgage of the Sparks Masonic Building Association, (R 395-6, 631-2).

Counsel for defendants has advanced no direct argument in his reply brief to the contention which we have made, (Opening Brief, pp. 58-9), and which, to some extent, we have repeated under this heading, namely, that the finding of the District Judge, (App. F, Finding 7, of paragraph I), that "Plaintiff reposed in Bothwell and in the bond department trust and confidence, which Bothwell well knew", covering "a period of more than ten years prior to the date of the first purchases of bonds and notes on January 7, 1926", and that this finding completely nullified the findings, (and, of course, also completely nullified any evidence on which the findings may have been based to the contrary), including the finding that the relation between the National Bank and plaintiff in their dealings prior to the execution of the instrument of trust was that of seller and buyer, with no fiduciary relation existing between them.

Indirectly, however, counsel for the defendants has disputed the argument under the principal heading, (Reply Brief, p. 32), "The relationship of the parties was not that of cestui and trustee prior to the execution of the trust instrument", and under four sub-headings, as follows:

(a), (Reply Brief, p. 32), that "Appellant's contention that the relationship was that of cestui and trustee prior to the execution of the trust instrument is raised for the first time on appeal and is contrary to the agency theory which appellant presented to the trial Court";

(b), (Reply Brief, p. 34), that "The mere intent subsequently to create a trust does not give rise to the relationship of trustee and cestui until such intent is executed";

(c), (Reply Brief, p. 35), that "The evidence shows that plaintiff did not intend to create a trust until four or five months prior to the actual execution of the trust instrument. The securities which were retained by the bank after the purchase thereof were retained in a depositary capacity"; and

(d), (Reply Brief, p. 42), that "The fact that plaintiff may have reposed trust and confidence in Mr. Bothwell and in the bond department of the national bank did not give rise to a trust relationship".

A reply to each of these contentions of defendants, (which we now proceed to make), is deemed by us to be necessary.

1. **The assertions of counsel for defendants that plaintiff's contention that the relation between the National Bank and plaintiff prior, as well as subsequent, to the execution of the instrument of trust, has been advanced for the first time on appeal, is unsupported by the evidence, is without the issues, and is contrary to the theory on which the case was presented to the trial court, are incorrect.**

It is said by counsel for defendants, (referring, of course, to the relation between plaintiff and the National Bank, in their transactions prior to the execution of the instrument of trust), in his "Summary of argument", (Reply Brief, p. 7), that "The contention of plaintiff that the relationship was that of cestui and trustee prior to the execution of the trust instrument is advanced for the first time on appeal and is unsupported by any evidence in the case"; and later, under a heading, with some variations from the language just quoted, that, (Reply Brief, p. 32), that "Appellant's contention that the relationship", (again referring, of course, to the relation between plaintiff and the National Bank in their transaction prior to the execution of the instrument of trust), "was that of cestui and trustee prior to the execution of the trust instrument is raised for the first time on appeal and is contrary to the agency theory which appellant presented to the trial court"; and, still later, but with some variations from the language from both sentences just quoted, that, (Reply Brief, p. 32), "The contention of plaintiff that the relationship between herself and the national bank was that of cestui and trustee before as well as after the execution of the trust indenture is advanced for the first time on appeal", and that "This contention is outside the issues embraced in the pleadings and is contrary to the theory upon which plaintiff's case was actually presented to the trial Court", and that "Nowhere in the complaint is any such allegation or contention made", and "In fact the contrary is directly and unequivocally asserted".

We shall assume, however, in what we have to say in this particular, that counsel for defendants intends to include all of the items of his attack upon what he designates as plaintiff's "contention", namely, that the contention, (1), has been advanced for the first time on appeal, (2), is unsupported by any evidence, (3), is contrary to the agency theory which plaintiff presented to the trial court, and (4), is outside the issues embraced in the pleadings.

Counsel who, if we mistake not, is the author of the brief for defendants, (Reply Brief, p. 80), did not appear in the case until his principal, Mr. Abraham, counsel for defendant Central Company, as the agent of the stockholders of the National Bank, had been substituted as the attorney for the National Bank and its receiver, Grut, in the place of Mr. Richards, who was counsel, on the removal of the cause from the Superior Court of Alameda County to the District Court of the United States, in September, 1933, (R 85-99), and who later, on August 30, 1935, (after the complaint had survived numerous attacks upon it), signed and filed the answer on their behalf, (R 140-77), and still later, and on January 22, 1936, signed and filed a so-called "supplemental answer", (R 177-82), and who was present at and participated in the trial of the case until the introduction of the evidence was concluded on February 17, 1936, (R 514-7, 520-1, 534-5), (App. F, 2). Consequently, counsel for defendants may not have been as familiar with plaintiff's complaint and the evidence as he otherwise might have been.

It is true, as counsel for defendants says, (Reply Brief, p. 32), (referring to the relation between the National Bank and plaintiff, prior to the execution of the instrument of trust, as that of trustee and cestui que trust), that "Nowhere in the complaint is any such allegation or contention made". But the allegations of the complaint allege, completely and fully, the *facts* showing the existence of that relation, and, as we said in our opening brief, (p. 57), (but evidently what we said has been overlooked by counsel for defendants), that

> "The complaint does not allege, in so many words, that the relation between the National Bank and plaintiff, in their transactions, was that of trustee and cestui que trust, and had the relation been so alleged the allegation would have been a conclusion of law, which would not have added to or detracted from the facts, alleged in the complaint in detail".

What we thus said, it may be observed in passing, is in marked contrast with the allegation of the respective answers, repeated many times, that the relation between plaintiff and the National Bank in the purchases of the securities was that of *buyer and seller,* (App. B, 8, 9, 10, 11, 12, 13-4, 16, 17, 18, 34; App. C, 6-7, 9, 10, 11, 12, 15, 16, 31),—a conclusion to the support of which the answer contains no allegations.

Counsel for defendants is, therefore, mistaken when he stated that plaintiff's contention that the relation between herself and the National Bank was that of cestui que trust and trustee before, as well as after, the execution of the instrument "is advanced for the first time on appeal", that this contention "is outside the issues embraced in the pleadings and is contrary to the theory upon which plaintiff's case was actually presented to the trial Court", that "Nowhere in the complaint is any such allegation or contention made", and that "In fact the contrary is directly and unequivocally asserted." But if counsel for defendants had read, with even a small degree of care, the plain allegations of the complaint, (App. pp. 6-9, 15-6, 17-9, 23-4), from which he quotes, here and there, (Reply Brief, pp. 32-3), we do not believe that he would have stated, (Reply Brief, p. 33), that the portions of the complaint from which he has quoted, "certainly" "negative any idea that there was a trust relationship prior to the actual execution of the trust instrument."

Counsel for defendants, however, may be correct in his further statement, (Reply Brief, pp. 33-4), that "Nowhere is there any evidence that plaintiff had constituted the national bank her trustee prior to September 24, 1929," if he means, by the statement that no indenture of trust between plaintiff and the National Bank was executed by them prior to that date. And the sub-heading, (b), (Reply Brief, p. 34), that

> "The mere intent subsequently to create a trust does not give rise to the relationship of trustee and cestui until such intent is executed",—

states a proposition that we do not controvert. Nor do we controvert the quoted propositions, (Reply Brief, p. 34), that the mere

> "manifestation of intention to create a trust inter vivos at some time subsequent to the time of the manifestation does not create a trust";

nor that a trust intent may be lacking

> "if the proof merely shows that the alleged settler said he intended to set apart a trust *res* later."

But these propositions are vastly different from the proposition which we have formulated as the principal heading for the subject under consideration, namely, that "The relation prior to the execution of the instrument of trust, on September 24, 1929, between the National Bank and plaintiff, was substantially that of trustee and cestui que trust", and this because of the many established facts, above enumerated by us, culminating in the creation of the trust estate by the execution of the instrument of trust, which both plaintiff and the National Bank, at all times, commencing with the first purchases of bonds and notes for plaintiff by the National Bank down to the execution of the instrument of trust, intended to create. The trust, from its very inception, prior to the execution of the instrument of trust, had all the indicia which Professor Pomeroy, in 3 *Pomeroy, Equity Jurisprudence,* secs. 991, 992 and 997 (4th ed.) tit. "Express Private Trusts", says are required to create a voluntary, express and active, private trust, namely, a definite *res* or subject, an object, a trustee in which the *res* would vest, and cestuis que trustent.

The correctness of the first sentence in the subdivision (c), namely, that

> "The evidence shows that plaintiff did not intend to create a trust until four or five months prior to the actual execution of the trust instrument",

based upon the finding of the District Judge to that effect, (Finding 3, of paragraph II, assigned as error as contrary to the evidence, App. H, pp. 7-10), will be considered later in its relation to the finding that "Plaintiff reposed in Bothwell and in the bond department trust and confidence", extending during the entire period of time from the first purchases of bills and notes to the execution of the instrument of trust, and in its relation to the testimony of plaintiff compared with the testimony of Bothwell and Berven.

2.   **The receipts given by the National Bank to plaintiff for securities, purporting to have been as deposited for safe keeping by her with the National Bank, have no evidentiary value whatever in the determination of the question whether or not the relation between plaintiff and the National Bank was that of buyer and seller, and not that of principal and agent, or broker, or that of cestui que trust and trustee.**

The correctness of the second sentence in the subdivision (c), above quoted, namely, that

> "The securities which were retained by the bank after the purchase thereof were retained in a depositary capacity",

is challenged.

It is true, as counsel for defendants so states, in effect, (Reply Brief, p. 35), that the complaint alleges, (App. A, p. 15), that none of the bonds or notes purchased prior to the execution of the instrument of trust were ever delivered to plaintiff,

> "but, upon the respective said purchases thereof, the said bonds or notes were retained and held by the said Bank, on deposit with the said Bank, for the plaintiff, awaiting such time when the same would be assigned and transferred by her to the said Bank, as trustee of the trusts, in which she intended as aforesaid, to place her property after the said parcel of real property, situated in the said City of Reno, had been sold by her, and pending such time, and prior to the consummation of her said intention by the execution by her, on the 24th day of September, 1929, as hereinafter more particularly alleged, of the instrument of trust to and with the said Bank, the interest coupons on the said bonds and notes were removed therefrom by the said Bank, when and as the said interest coupons matured, and the money payable thereon was collected by the said Bank and deposited by the said Bank to the credit of the plaintiff in her said account with the said Bank."

It is true, also, as counsel for defendants so states, (Reply Brief, p. 35), that the District Judge found, and, it may be added that the same was assigned as error, (App. H, 10-1), that

> "None of the securities purchased by plaintiff from the national bank prior to September 24, 1929, were delivered to plaintiff, but at plaintiff's request were held in safe-keeping by the national bank subject to plaintiff's order as a matter of accommodation to plaintiff; said securities were not held by said bank awaiting the time when the same would be assigned or transferred by her to said bank as trustee or until such time as she should create a trust."

But, (contrary to finding in these respects), it is *not* true that the securities were held in safe keeping by the National Bank, either "at plaintiff's *request*", or as "a matter of *accommodation to plaintiff*", or that the securities "were not held by said bank awaiting the time when the same would be assigned or transferred by her to said bank as trustee or until such time as she should create a trust."

And it is *not* true, either, that the complaint alleges that the securities were held in safe-keeping by the National Bank "at plaintiff's *request*", or as "a matter of *accommodation* to plaintiff", *nor is it true* that the evidence is to that effect, but, on the contrary, the complaint contains *no* such allegations; and counsel for defendants is in error when he states, in effect, (Reply Brief, pp. 35-6), that the evidence supports the findings, in this particular, by the testimony of Bothwell, either standing alone, or in connection with the testimony of plaintiff. Neither the testimony of Bothwell, (R 426-7), nor the testimony of plaintiff, (R 367, 368-9, 391), supports the finding, that any *request* was made by plaintiff, that the securities were to be held "in safe-keeping by the national bank subject to her order as a matter of *accommodation to plaintiff*"; and if the securities, as found by the District Judge, "were not held by said bank awaiting the time when the same would be assigned or transferred by her to said bank as trustee or until such time as she should create a trust", for what purpose, it may be inquired, were they held by the National Bank? and why were the Washoe County bonds removed on February 2, 1929, (R 721, Pls' Ex. R), from the Washoe County Bank, in Reno, and why were the promissory note and its securing mortgage also removed from the same Bank, at or about the same time, and deposited with the National Bank, (R 63, 389-90), if it was not for the purpose, so intended by plaintiff and the National Bank, of transferring the same to the National Bank, as trustee of the trust estate created by the instrument of trust, executed on September 24, 1929?

The respective cases of *De Mott v. National Bank of New Jersey*, 118 N. J. Eq. 396, 179 At. 470, (1935), and *State Y. M. C. A. v. Picher*, 8 Fed. Supp. 412 (D. C., D. of Me., 1934), cited and commented upon by counsel for defendants,

(Reply Brief, pp. 38-9), have been summarized by us, in an appendix to this brief, (App. J pp. 139, 144), both as to the facts and the questions of law involved, and what the cases have decided, rather than what counsel for defendants states they have decided, have been included in the summarizations. No comments concerning them need here be made other than to say that neither of them is at all helpful to the cause of defendants, and both of them sustain plaintiff's contention that the relation between the National Bank and plaintiff, prior, as well as subsequent, to the execution of the instrument of trust, was that of trustee and cestui que trust.

We direct attention, in this connection, to what the court in the *Picher Case* designates as a leading case, and from which the court quotes at length, (8 Fed. Supp. 414), namely, the case of *Mississippi and Dominion Steamship Co. v. Swift*, 86 Me. 248, 29 At. 1063, 41 A. S. R. 545, (1924), and also to the case of *Keyes v. Paducah & Ill. R. Co.*, 61 Fed. (2d) 611, 86 A. L. R. 203, (C. C. A., 6th, 1932), from which the court quotes, (8 Fed. Supp. 415-6).

Considerable stress, however, is placed by counsel for defendants, (Reply Brief, pp. 36-7), on the "receipts for securities deposited", which were issued to plaintiff by the National Bank, from time to time, the undertaking of the National Bank, printed thereon, being "to hold the securities as depositary," (R 726-9, Defts' Ex. M), presumably for plaintiff, (although the receipts do not so state). 16 of these receipts were produced by counsel for plaintiff, as coming from plaintiff's possession, (R 429). The receipts were introduced in evidence by counsel for defendants, (Defts' Ex. M). Each of the first 12 of them is dated August 15, 1928, and were for blocks of bonds and notes purchased for plaintiff by the National Bank, extending from and including January 7, 1926, to and including March 30, 1928, (R 675, Plf's Ex. 47).

Each of these 12 receipts is signed, not by Bothwell, through whom the purchases were made, but by a person who wrote his name, (for example "Kirby Sharp"), above the printed word "Teller". No explanation was made by Bothwell, or by anyone else then connected with the National Bank, or by any other person, of the irregularities in that the receipts were dated August 15, 1928, whereas some of the purchases were made more than 2½ years, and the others were made more than 3 months, prior to that date; and it is to be noted in passing that the irregularities indicate that little or no importance is to be attached to them as giving notice to plaintiff of anything printed or written on the receipts.

Moreover, even Bothwell, evidently did not consider the receipts to be at all important for any purpose, except, perhaps, as memoranda for the National Bank, since, on April 8, 1930, or over 6 months *after* the execution of the instrument of trust, he wrote a letter to plaintiff, (R 555, Plf's Ex. 12), in which he "suggested" the reinvestment of funds held by the trust department of the National Bank, in 2 bonds, each of the denomination of $1,000, and in which he said that

> "If this suggestion is agreeable to you, kindly sign and return the enclosed order and we will confirm the bond, delivering same to the Trust Department *to be held in a safe keeping for your account.*"

And, apparently not having heard from plaintiff in response to his "suggestion", he again wrote to her, on *May 20, 1930*, (R 556-7, Plf's Ex. 14), in which he stated that "Both bonds *carry our recommendation*", and that "If either meet with your approval, kindly advise Mr. Berven, who will forward to you the necessary papers to sign." The "suggestion" was adopted, and the "recommendation" was approved, by plaintiff, since it appears, (R 645, Plf's Ex. 47), that one of the bonds was paid for on *April 8, 1930,* and, therefore, *on the date* on which Bothwell first wrote to plaintiff but "as of" *April 15, 1930,* and the other was paid for on *June 5, 1930,* or 15 days after he wrote his second letter; the irregularities thus again indicating that little or no importance is to be attached to the receipts as giving notice to plaintiff of anything written or printed on them.

It should be noted, in passing, that these 2 last mentioned bonds were purchased by the National Bank with trust funds, for the trust estate, from itself, through its bond department, by Berven, with the cooperation of Bothwell. The weight of the evidence, if any, to be given to all such documents, including bought and sold notes, bills of sale, accounts and so-called brokers confirmation "slips", will be discussed by us under a later heading of this brief.

Counsel for defendants say, however, (Reply Brief, p. 39), that.

> "While plaintiff denied that she ever read the printed matter on the receipts for securities deposited (R 533-4), nevertheless, she carefully retained all of these receipts and produced them at the trial"; that

> "Even if her testimony be given credence, nevertheless she did not testify that she was in any way prevented from reading these receipts. Furthermore, three* of these receipts were signed by plaintiff (Supra, p. 37)"; and that

> "In addition, they show the capacity in which the bank was acting with respect to the retained securities, namely, *as a depositary of bailee.* (Italics counsel's.)

---

*Note: We do not find the signature on any of the receipts here under consideration, (Defts' Ex. M), and since they were receipts "from Abbie W. Quinn", her signature to them would have no proper place. When, however, the bonds and notes which had been purchased for her by the National Bank, through Bothwell, as the manager of its bond department, were about to be transferred from the custody of the National Bank to the latter as the trustee of the trust estate created by the instrument of trust, and on September 24, 1929, the date of that instrument, she signed not *three*, but *thirteen*, receipts each entitled "Withdrawal from account of Abbie W. Quinn", (R 730-3, Defts' Ex. Q), for bonds and notes then held by the National Bank in its custody, and listed in that instrument, (App. A, 60-2), besides two "withdrawal" receipts for the $15,000, par value, Washoe County, County Roads and Highways Improvement and Construction bonds, (for which she had theretofore signed "deposit" receipts), dated February 2, 1929, (R 721, Defts' Ex. K). Why plaintiff signed "deposit"

If, under the circumstances above enumerated, the relation between the National Bank and plaintiff, prior to the execution of the instrument of trust, was not substantially that of trustee and cestui que trust, what, it may be asked, was the relation? and can there be any doubt that the answer to this question should be that the relation was substantially that of trustee and cestui que trust?

In concluding what we have to say under this heading, permit us to ask the following further questions, (supposititious, generally, it is true, but, nevertheless, as we believe them to be, potent and relevant questions to the solution of the principal problems in the instant case), namely:

Suppose that the National Bank became insolvent *prior* to the execution of the instrument of trust, but *subsequent* to the first purchases of securities for plaintiff, and particularly *after* the removal by plaintiff from the Washoe County Bank of her Washoe County bonds and of her promissory note and its securing mortgage, executed to her by the Sparks Masonic Building Association, would not plaintiff be entitled to have the securities, (the possession of which she never had), including the Washoe County bonds and the promissory note and its securing mortgage, delivered up to her? and, if so, would not the deliv-

---

receipts for bonds and notes theretofore purchased for her, when she never had the bonds and notes in her possession, but the same remained in the custody of the National Bank, and why she signed the "withdrawal" receipts for the Washoe County bonds, is one of the matters which should have, but which never has, been explained by the National Bank, or by Bothwell, or by any other of the National Bank's officials. It seems obvious that no explanation, or at least no plausible explanation, could be made. However this may be, if, as counsel for defendants contends, plaintiff had notice from the deposit and withdrawal receipts that the relation between the National Bank and plaintiff prior to the execution of the instrument of trust was that of seller and buyer, and not that of trustee and cestui que trust, as a consequence of the finding of a relation of trust and confidence between the parties, defendants have not sustained the burden of proof that she not only had full information of that fact, but also full information of her legal rights.

ery to her be on the ground that a trust relation existed between her and the National Bank?

Suppose, instead, that the National Bank, (as is the fact), became insolvent *after* the execution of the instrument of trust, and suppose that the business of the trust department of the National Bank had not been sold to the Central Bank, would not plaintiff be entitled to have the securities, then a part of the trust estate in the possession of the National Bank, as trustee of the trust estate created by the instrument of trust, delivered up to her? and, if so, would not the delivery to her be on the ground that a trust relation existed between her and the National Bank, if she chose to revoke the instrument, as she might do under paragraph VII thereof, (R 73-4)? and is there any doubt that these questions should be answered in the affirmative? and is there any substantial difference between the two supposititious cases, and, if so, what is the difference?

If, however, (as it might be thought), the relation between plaintiff and the National Bank, in the purchases of the securities *prior* to the execution of the instrument of trust, was that of principal and agent, instead of that of cestui que trust and trustee, the relation, nevertheless, according to the finding of the District Judge, (and even independently of that finding), was one of trust and confidence, and the purchases having been made with the intention of plaintiff and the cooperation of the National Bank, through Bothwell, as the manager of its bond department, with the particular purpose of transferring the securities to the National Bank, as trustee of the trust estate created by the instrument of trust, after plaintiff's Virginia Street property was sold, and that intention was thereafter accordingly consummated, *the result would be the same as if the relation were that of cestui que trust and trustee*, and the defendants are not at all aided by the theory. As said by Professor Pomeroy, in 2 *Pomeroy, Equity Jurisprudence,* sec. 959, p. 2055, (4th ed.), (quoted, Opening Brief, pp. 55-6),

> "Equity regards and treats this relation in the same general manner, and with nearly the same strictness, as that of trustee and beneficiary";

and, as also said in 1 *Cal. Jur.*, sec. 77, p. 788, tit. "Agency", citing many California cases,

> "It is an undisputed rule that equity regards and treats the relation of principal and agent in the same general manner and with nearly the same strictness as that of trustee and beneficiary."

And in the recent case of *Alexander v. State Capital Co.,* 9 Cal. (2d) 304, (1937), in which a suit was brought by the plaintiff against a building and loan association, in process of liquidation, after the California Building & Loan Commissioner had rejected the claims, (cited, Opening Brief, p. 56), the Court said, (p. 311), (citing with approval the case, (also cited, Opening Brief, p. 56), of *Bank of America v. Sanchez,* 3 Cal. App. (2d) 238):

> "The complaint alleged and the court found that the respondents relied upon the representations which we have been discussing and which we have concluded were actionable. The appellants contend that this finding is unsupported. The respondents testified that they relied upon the representations, which is the situation in practically every instance, or they testified that they were induced to convert their investments by the representations. Under the situation here existing, the finding is supported by the testimony. *It is true that the Building & Loan Association did not occupy any of the conventional or statutory relations which are declared to be fiduciary, but, nevertheless, there was evidence of the previous business relations of each respondent with the association and of confidence on the part of the respondent in the association and its officers.* In this respect, the case is not unlike that of *Bank of America v. Sanchez.* 3 Cal. App. (2d) 238 (38 Pac. (2d) 787), and strongly tends to confirm other testimony of reliance upon the representations". (Emphasis added.)

From all of which it therefore follows, (repeating, in substance, the last of the foregoing headings), that the receipts given by the National Bank to plaintiff for securities as deposited for safe keeping by her with the National Bank, and introduced in evidence by counsel for defendants, have no evidentiary value whatever in the determination of the question whether or not the relation between plaintiff and the National Bank was that of buyer and seller, and not that of principal and agent, or broker, or that of cestui que trust and trustee.

Attention is particularly called to those portions of the foregoing quotation, which, it will be noted, are quite in line with the rule formulated by us, (Opening Brief, p. 52), to the effect that, when a state of confidence is reposed by a principal in his agent, it is necessary for the agent to make a full and fair disclosure to the principal of all the material facts within the agent's knowledge, relating to the agent's breach of that confidence.

3. **The fact that it does not appear from the bills of sale that a commission was charged by the National Bank against plaintiff on the purchases of securities for her by the National Bank, through Bothwell, as the manager of its bond department, was, at most, but a circumstance which might indicate the relation between plaintiff and the National Bank to have been that of buyer and seller, and not that of principal and agent, or broker, or of trustee and cestui que trust, and that circumstance has no evidentiary importance in the instant case.**

Counsel for defendants states, (Reply Brief, p. 19), that

> "On none of these bills does there appear any charge for commission or brokerage. It appears from the record that all of the purchases prior to the execution of the trust instrument were made while plaintiff was personally present in the bond department except in the two instances of the purchases of the Medford Bonds and of the Central West

Public Service Bonds. (Pl's. Ex. 1 and Defs'. Ex. 'I'; R 539-540, 718-719.)" (Emphasis counsel's)

Counsel for defendants quotes from the article entitled "Stock 'Brokers' as Agents and Dealers", 43 *Yale Law Journal*, pp. 46, 60, as follows:

"(1) The form of the confirmation 'sold to you' rather than 'bought for your account' is evidentiary of a dealer-customer relationship.

"(2) The fact that the customer is not charged any commission is likewise evidence that the 'broker' acted as dealer."*

Counsel for defendants then states, (Reply Brief, p. 25), that

"Two other highly significant matters of evidence which arise from the bills of sale, are that *no commission or brokerage* was charged thereon and each bill of sale is

---

NOTE: The authors of the article add the following, which are not quoted by counsel for defendants, as additional "characteristics or earmarks recognized by courts to distinguish a dealer from an agent, in stockbroking transactions":

"(3) The 'broker' when acting as dealer usually acquires the stock at one price and transfers it to the customer at another.

"(4) If the 'broker' is selling from his inventory he is acting as a dealer.

"(5) He is nonetheless a dealer even though he had no inventory but was acquiring securities for his customer from any of several sources in the manner of any merchant. For a 'broker' to sell from his own inventory would establish that he acted as a dealer; but it is not true, conversely, that the absence of an inventory makes him an agent. That alone would not discriminate between an agent and a dealer, though it would be evidence to be weighed along with other of the criteria mentioned".

It does not appear, either from the foregoing quotations from the article in 43 *Yale Law Journal*, pp. 46, 60, or from anything that counsel for defendants has said, (Reply Brief, p. 25), that the quotations are "significant matters", much less *"highly* significant matters", "of evidence".

stamped as paid on the date it bears. (Defs'. Exs. 'E' and 'L', R 716, 722-5.)"*

Counsel for defendants further states, under the heading, (Reply Brief, p. 25),

"The fact that no commission or brokerage was charged plaintiff is strong evidence of a buyer-seller relationship",

that, (Reply Brief, p. 25),

"It is inconceivable that plaintiff either intended, or could assume, that an agency existed, when, for a period of over three years, eight and one-half months prior to the execution of the trust instrument, no bill ever specified any brokerage or commission, no such charge was ever made

---

*NOTE: The foregoing are all the references to the bills of sale that we have found in the Reply Brief of counsel for defendants.

Counsel for defendants has not, however, referred to *all* the bills of sale which were introduced in evidence, and a full list of them, as disclosed by the record, is as follows:

R 709, Defts' Ex. C; R 710, Defts' Ex. C R 711, Defts' Ex. C; R 711, Defts' Ex. C; R 712, Defts' Ex. C; R 713, Defts' Ex. C; and R 714, Defts' Ex. C.

It is a remarkable and curious fact that Defts' Ex. C, R 114, (4 in number, and to none of which counsel has made any reference whatever), are in the same form as the other bills of sale introduced, that is, they represent sales of securities by the "Central National Bank, Bond Department", to "Abbie W. Quinn", and they are respectively dated, and are for the respective securities, as follows: April 14, (as of April 15), $1,000, par value, Hearst Publications, R 713; June 5, 1930, $1,000, par value, California Cotton Mills, R 716; July 1, 1930, $5,000, par value, Federal Public Service Corporation, R 713; and July 1, 1930, $6,000, par value, Hearst Publications, R 714. These 4 sales, therefore, were made subsequent to the date, September 24, 1929, of the instrument of trust, and, although the bills indicate that the sales were made to plaintiff, they, of course, were made by the National Bank, through its bond department, not to plaintiff, but to the National Bank, for the trust estate created by the instrument of trust for the benefit of plaintiff and her daughter and her daughter's minor son, and were thus unlawfully made by the National Bank, in one capacity, to itself, in another capacity, as trustee of the trust estate created by the instrument of trust, and although they indicate charges for accrued interest, they, in common with the other bills of sale, did not indicate charges for commissions.

to her, and she never thought she was paying any brokerage or commission since, to take her own testimony, she did not know the national bank was making any profit on these transactions. (R 401.)"

But, after making these statements with considerable positiveness, counsel for defendants immediately continues with the statement, (Reply Brief, p. 26), as follows:

"While it is possible to have a gratuitous agency, nevertheless an agent *usually* receives a commission or compensation. The fact a commission is charged connotes an agency, although it is not always conclusive. Thus in *Sloat-Darragh Co. v. General Coal Co.* (1921) 276 Fed. 502, 505 (C. C. A. 6), the Court said:

"It is also true that the word *'commission' has a natural tendency to suggest an agency contract, as being compensation for services rendered; * * *"* (Emphasis counsel's),

to which we add the remainder, or omitted, portion of the sentence, namely, "but that is not its sole meaning"; and to which we also add another sentence from the opinion of the Federal Court, in the same connection, namely, (p. 505), that,

"But, even had the word 'commission' been a misnomer, it was not enough of itself 'to convert into an agency what was in fact a sale'."*

---

*NOTE: The case of *Sloat-Darragh v. General Coal Co.*, cited above by counsel for defendants, involved the question, (with other questions not material here), whether or not the plaintiff below, General Coal Company, (hereinafter called the plaintiff), was a seller to, or the agent of, Hamilton-Otto Coke Company, the predecessor in interest of the defendant below, Sloat-Darragh Company, (hereinafter called the defendant).

The plaintiff was engaged at Huntington, West Virginia, in buying and selling coal, and the defendant was a jobber in coal at Hamilton, Ohio.

The plaintiff sued for the purchase price of 100 tons of coal, alleged to have been sold to the defendant by the Carbon Hills Collieries Company, a producer of coal, at Huntington, basing its right of recovery upon a subrogation by virtue of an alleged payment by it of the indebtedness from the defendant to the Collieries Company for the purchase

As a case, on the other hand, of holding under quite an unusual combination of facts that the relation between the parties was one of principal and agent, and not one of seller and buyer, although no commission was charged, nor intended to be charged, is the comparatively recent case of *Kurtz v. Farrington,* 104 Conn. 257, 132 At. 540, 48 A. L. R. 259 (1926), summarized by us in Appendix J to this brief.

No explanation has been made by counsel for defendants why it was that bills of sale were rendered by the National Bank, through its bond department, to itself, through its trust depart-

---

price of the coal. The plaintiff, which was then the selling agent of the Collieries Company, wrote a letter of acknowledgment to the defendant of its "order for 100 cars of Eagle gas coal for the Hamilton-Otto Coke Company", the letter stating that, (p. 104),

> "We have instructed the C. and O. people to mail you promptly postal notices and our office will render you the invoices as per your suggestion which is absolutely in line with our ideas";

and an acknowledgment, as follows, was appended to the letter:

> "We thank you for your order No. 564 for 100 cars Eagle gas coal to be shipped at rate of three per day to the Hamilton-Otto Coke Company, * * * price $2.15 f.o.b. mines, less 10 cents per ton commission to you".

The defense was that the defendant was not the purchaser of the coal, but was merely the Collieries Company's agent, at Hamilton, which the defendant asserted was the Collieries Company's actual debtor. The question was submitted to a jury, which found for the plaintiff, and on appeal the judgment was affirmed.

The Court of Appeals held that the question was one for the jury, in view of the fact that, as requested in the order, the invoices were sent to the defendant, and the coal was charged to its account, and that the defendant had sent its check in payment of the first month's shipments, on which, however, it stopped payment on the bankruptcy of the Hamilton-Otto Coke Company, to which the coal had been delivered; since, so the Court of Appeals said, (p. 504),

> "It was not fairly open to question that there was sufficient evidence to justify submitting the contention that defendant, and not the Hamilton-Otto Company, was the real purchaser of the coal and was the Collieries Company's actual debtor".

The case, therefore, decides nothing more than that the question whether or not, in a transaction of sale and purchase, the fact that a commission is, or is not, charged, is a question of fact. The question, however, is of no importance where, as in the instant case, because the

ment, for the last purchases of bonds and notes made by the
National Bank, in 1930, namely, Hearst Publications, Inc.,
California Cotton Mills and Federal Public Service Corporation,
and, in the absence of any such explanation, it is fairly to be
presumed that no explanation, or at least no plausible explanation, can be made. At least, it may be said that the renditions
of the bills were irregularities, and that if it was the intention
of counsel for the Central Bank, in introducing the bills, which
were delivered to plaintiff for purchases made for her by
the National Bank prior to the creation of the trust, to charge

---

relation between the parties to the transaction is a relation of trust and
confidence, it was necessary for defendants to prove, as well as to allege,
that plaintiff had actual knowledge of the fact that no commission was
charged, and not that plaintiff was chargeable with notice of the fact
from the bill of sale or other document.

The case of *Yaeger v. Mechanics & Metals Nat. Bank*, 122 Misc. 392,
204 N. Y. S. 38, (1924), also ctied by counsel for defendants, (Reply
Brief, p. 26), is even less of an authority for defendants, (if that were
possible), than is the *Sloat-Darragh Company Case.*

In the *Yaeger Case*, the defendant bank agreed to purchase for the
plaintiff, Yaeger, for a stipulated price, namely, $5,012, (which Yaeger
paid in full), 28,000 marks, imperial German war loan bonds, and to
deposit the bonds, between certain dates, to Yaeger's account, in the
Deutsche Bank, Berlin, the German correspondent of the defendant
bank.

The action, which was brought by Yaeger against the defendant bank,
to recover damages because of the latter's failure to purchase the bonds
in accordance with the terms of the contract, in that, (as the Court
said, 204 N. Y. S. 38),

"The bonds were never purchased or deposited to the plaintiff's
account in the Deutsche Bank, although it is conceded that the defendant transmitted to Germany 28,000 marks for that purpose".

A verdict for Yaeger was directed, and on his motion for judgment
accordingly, as the Court said, (204 N. Y. S. 39), the case presented
the single question,

"whether the defendant by the terms of its contract agreed to act
as the agent for the plaintiff in the purchase of the bonds in
question or whether it agreed for the sum of $5012 to effect a sale
of the bonds to the plaintiff".

In a letter to the plaintiff's agent, the defendant advised the agent
that the total cost of the bonds amounted to $5,012, and requested
that a check for $12 be sent in order to make up the difference between

plaintiff thereby with knowledge of the fact that the purchases were made by the National Bank from itself, then defendants are subject to the well-settled rules, (which we shall elaborate hereafter), (1), that the burden was upon defendants of proving that plaintiff had such knowledge, (2), that the burden of proof was not sustained by the introduction in evidence of the bills, and (3), that even if the burden of proof had been sustained, in some other manner, *it was essential for defendants to prove that plaintiff had knowledge of the fact that the purchases were made by the National Bank from itself, and also, in addition, that plaintiff had knowledge of her legal rights, including her right to rescind the transactions.*

---

that amount and $5,000, which the defendant had already received. In commenting upon the letter, the Court said, (204 N. Y. S. 39):

> "It is clear from the letter just referred to that the defendant was not to look to the plaintiff for any additional costs in procuring the bonds, nor was any charge to be made by it for the services thus rendered. If the defendant consequent upon that letter had procured the bonds at a lower figure than that named by it, it would have profited by the transaction, since it was under no obligation to account to the plaintiff for any reduction in price. As soon as the money was paid to the defendant it became its property. *Legniti v. Mechanics & Metals National Bank,* 230 N. Y. 415, 130 N. E. 597, 16 A. L. R. 185. For the defendant to argue that its sole duty was to instruct its German correspondent to purchase bonds for the plaintiff and to deposit them to his account is to confuse the end agreed to be attained with the means proposed for attaining it".

The comment of counsel for defendants concerning this latter case is as follows, (Reply Brief, p. 26):

> "Conversely, where no commission or compensation is charged, it would appear that a buyer and seller relationship is intended rather than that of principal and agent. For example, in *Yaeger v. Mechanics & Metals Nat. Bank* (1924), 122 Misc. Rep. 392, 204 N. Y. S. 38, 39, a given transaction was held a sale rather than an agency, for the reason, *among others,* that no charge was made for services in buying bonds", (Emphasis added),

is not an accurate statement of what the Court decided, since there was but *one* reason why the relation was one of buyer and seller, and not one of principal and agent.

The case, consequently, as we have above said, is no authority for defendants, on the point, to which it has been referred, by counsel for defendants.

The remaining authority, namely, *Farr v. Fratus*, 277 Mass. 346, 178 N. E. 657, (1931), which is cited and quoted by counsel for defendants on the question of commissions, and in which, according to counsel for defendants, (Reply Brief, p. 24), "the evidence was conflicting", and in which a "confirmation slip was sent to the customer", with the statement that *"We confirm sale to you* of 50 Incorporated Investors, 77", and in which the Supreme Court of Massachusetts said, (Reply Brief, p. 24), (Emphasis counsel's), that

> "The only construction which could reasonably be put upon what was said was that the plaintiffs contracted to sell the stock to the defendant. The testimony as to the record of a direct sale *and the confirmation slips point to the same conclusion.* They refer to the transaction as a sale and there is nothing to indicate that any broker's commission was charged". (Emphasis counsel's).

The case was an action brought by the plaintiff, John Farr, Jr., and others, and in which exceptions to a denial to the defendant's motion for a directed verdict were sustained by the Supreme Judicial Court of Massachusetts, with a consequent judgment for the defendant.

We quote in full the paragraph of the opinion, (178 N. E. 657), of which the foregoing quotation by counsel for defendants is but a part:

> "The question in the case is whether upon the evidence the contract was one of purchase and sale and therefore within the statute of frauds, or whether it could have been found to be a contract by which the defendant employed the plaintiffs as his brokers. *The contract upon which the plaintiffs must rely was made by the telephone conversation. It did not appear that the defendant knew whether the plaintiffs owned any stock at the time the contract was made or that knowledge concerning that matter could affect his right to rely upon the contract which he made. In the telephone conversation nothing was said to indicate that the plaintiffs were being employed by the defendant as brokers to buy the stock for him.* The only construc-

tion which could reasonably be put upon what was said was that the plaintiffs contracted to sell ·the stock to the defendant. The testimony as to the record of a direct sale and the confirmation slips point to the same conclusion. They refer to the transaction as a sale and there is nothing to indicate that any broker's commission was charged. *A contract to sell shares of stock is a contract to sell a chose in action within the meaning of G. L. c. 106, sec. 6. Davis v. Arnold,* 267 Mass. 103, 109, 165 N. E. 885. The defendant's motion for a directed verdict should have been allowed." (Emphasis added)

We do not perceive how the case is an authority upon the question under consideration, namely, (Reply Brief, p. 25), that

"The fact that no commisison or brokerage was charged plaintiff was strong evidence of a buyer-seller relationship".

The question involved was whether or not a contract to well the shares of stock was within the Massachusetts statutes of frauds.

4.   The evidence does not establish the fact to be that any of the offering lists were ever "exhibited", "submitted", "presented", "shown" or "mailed" to plaintiff.

The evidence relating to the offering lists was obviously introduced on behalf of defendants for the purpose of charging plaintiff with knowledge, in the purchases, prior to the execution of the instrument of trust, of the bonds and notes from the National Bank, of the contents of the offering lists as indicating to plaintiff that the National Bank was the owner of the securities and was selling them to plaintiff, as such owner, and, therefore, that the assumed relation between the National Bank and plaintiff was that of seller and buyer and not that of agent and principal or of trustee and cestui que trust. The evidence consists entirely of the testimony of the two witnesses for defendants, namely, Bothwell and Anderson.

Bothwell's testimony may be summarized as follows: Although he variously testified on his direct examination that the offering lists were "exhibited", "submitted", "presented", "shown" or "mailed" by him to plaintiff, he never, on his cross-examination, testified positively that he ever "handed" a list to plaintiff, or that she ever "took a list in her hand", and all that he would say in this respect was that he "may" have "handed" "one" to her, or she may have "picked" one "up in her hand and looked at it", or she "may have looked at it" while "sitting alongside the desk". What he meant by exhibiting a list to her, so he testified on his cross-examination, is that the "offering sheets were always available on my desk". Nor did Bothwell testify positively that he ever "mailed" an offering list to plaintiff. The testimony of plaintiff and of Bothwell, in this particular, is respectively summarized in Appendix J, pages 3-26, 27-72, 73-96.

And the witness Anderson, having testified on his direct examination, (R 352-6), that the offering lists, which he identified and which were received in evidence, were in current use by the National Bank at or about the times when certain of the bonds and notes were sold by the National Bank, through its bond department, to plaintiff, was asked on his cross-examination, (R 380), whether he meant to say, of his own knowledge, that plaintiff ever received any of the offering lists, and he replied "not to my knowledge. I know nothing about that".

He was then asked, on his direct examination, (R 380), whether or not he knew that the "practice" of the bond department of the National Bank, from the year 1926 down to the time of the closing of the bank in 1933, was "to mail offering lists to customers" of the National Bank, to which he replied, "At different intervals, yes, it was", and also, (R 380), whether or not he knew that it was the "practice" of the bond department of the National Bank, "at that time to *exhibit* offering lists to customers when they came into the bond department", to which he replied, "I know that that was done. Mr. Bothwell always *exhibited* his offering lists when he had a prospective bond customer in his office". But after this general and indefinite testimony, his final testimony relating to the matter, on cross-examination, was as follows, (R 381):

> "Q. Of course, you cannot say, of your own knowledge, that any bonds or offering lists were ever *exhibited* to Mrs. Quinn by Mr. Bothwell? A. I was never in the office *when she was there with Mr. Bothwell, no.* Q. *So you cannot say that any bond lists or offering lists were submitted to her by Mr. Bothwell? A. I cannot say that, no".* (Emphasis added).

It is obvious that this testimony of Anderson did not prove, directly or indirectly, that plaintiff *read*, or even *saw*, any of the offering lists.

Although the purpose of Bothwell's examination by counsel for defendants was to charge plaintiff from the offering lists with knowledge of the fact that the National Bank was selling to her, through its bond department, its own bonds and notes, nevertheless, counsel for defendants did not ask Bothwell whether or not plaintiff *read* or even *examined* the lists, or that the lists *were read by him to plaintiff*, and although Bothwell testified, on his direct examination, that offering lists *were sent to plaintiff by mail*, and that "it was the custom to enclose offering lists in correspondence", on cross-examination, he could "not say that custom was followed with Mrs. Quinn". Plaintiff testified repeatedly, (R 411), that no offering list was ever handed to her personally by Bothwell or by any other official of the National Bank, and her best recollection was that she never received any offering list by mail.

Even if it be assumed that Bothwell had not been contradicted, and even if it be assumed that his testimony was candid and appeared to be truthful, it is obvious that his testimony proved nothing in the respect here under consideration; since, as in the case of Anderson's testimony, Bothwell's testimony did not, either directly or indirectly, prove that plaintiff *read*, or ever *saw*, any of the offering lists, or that any of the lists *were ever read to her*, or that any of the lists *were ever mailed to her*.

It follows, as a matter of course, that defendants completely failed to prove by the testimony of either Bothwell or Anderson the fact that plaintiff had any knowledge, or was chargeable with any knowledge, of anything contained in the offering lists, notwithstanding what counsel for defendants may say to the contrary, (Reply Brief, pp. 27-8).

Counsel for defendants, in what he says concerning the offering lists, (Reply Brief, pp. 27-8), has overlooked the well-settled rule that the burden rested upon defendants not only to allege, but to prove, that plaintiff had full knowledge of all the material facts, and had also full knowledge of her legal rights, in the transaction, a rule which will be discussed by us under a later heading of this brief.

It may be observed, in conclusion, that the bills confirming sales of bonds and notes to plaintiff by the National Bank, through Bothwell, as its manager, to which counsel for defendants devote considerable attention in their Reply Brief, pp. 14-7), are of less evidentiary weight, (if that were possible), than the evidentiary weight of the offering lists, which were never "exhibited, submitted, presented, shown or mailed to plaintiff."

5. The cases of Pence v. Langdon, 99 U. S. 578, 25 L. Ed. 420, (1879), Williams v. Bolling, 138 Va. 244, 121 S. E. 270, (1933), and Johnson v. Winslow, 155 Misc. 170, 279 N. Y. S. 147, (1935), involving relations of trust and confidence between agents, or brokers, and principals, or customers, in sales of securities, as evidenced by letters, bills of sale and confirmations of sales, including brokers "confirmation slips".

These three cases (respectively summarized in App. J 102-38), are considered by us to be the most important cases which we have been able to find, after an exhaustive search, involving relations of trust and confidence between agents, or brokers, and principals and customers, in sales of securities, as evidenced by letters, bills of sale and confirmations of sales, including brokers' "confirmation slips".

The object in these cases, as well as in the cases heretofore cited by counsel for defendants, and heretofore commented upon, by us, was to charge the principal, or customer, with knowledge, from the letters, bills of sale and confirmations of sale of the fact that the purchases of the securities were made by the principal, or broker, from himself, and, therefore, were unlawful, and that the principal, or customer, with full knowledge of the facts and of his legal rights, acquiesced in or ratified the sales.

III.

THE QUESTION OF THE EVIDENTIARY WEIGHT, IF ANY, TO BE GIVEN TO LETTERS, ORDERS FOR PURCHASES, BILLS OF SALE AND CONFIRMATIONS OF SALE, INCLUDING CONFIRMATION SLIPS, OF AGENTS, OR BROKERS, IS A QUESTION OF FACT, AND IS AN UNIMPORTANT QUESTION OF FACT.

The question of the evidentiary weight, if any, to be given to letters, orders for purchases, bills of sale, and confirmations of sale, or confirmation slips, is a question for the court, sitting without a jury, or for a jury, under proper instructions of the court, to determine.

In the foregoing cases of *Pence v. Langdon,* 99 U. S. 578, 25 L. Ed. 420, *Williams v. Bolling,* 138 Va. 244, 121 S. E. 270, *Johnson v. Winslow,* 155 Misc. 170, 279 N. Y. S. 147, and to which may be added the cases of *Hall v. Paine,* 224 Mass. 62, 112 N. E. 153, L. R. A., 1917C 737, and *Id.,* (on a subsequent hearing), 230 Mass. 62, 119 N. E. 664, *Leviten v. Bickley, Mandeville & Wimple, Inc.,* 35 F. (2d) 825, (C. C. A. 2d), and *McNulty v. Whitney,* 273 Mass. 494, 174 N. E. 121, the question of the evidentiary weight to be given to letters, orders for purchases, bills of sale and confirmations of sale, or confirmation slips, was decided, as it uniformly has been, in favor of the principal or customer. Consequently, the further question, whether or not the principal, or customer, was chargeable by the letters, orders for purchases, bills of sale and confirmations of sale, or confirmation slips, with knowledge that the agents, or brokers, had violated their obligations towards their principals, or customers, of the material facts relating to the transactions, and with knowledge of the legal rights of the principals, or customers, and the corresponding obligations of the agents, or brokers, obviously, was unnecessary for the decision in any of the cases.

If these conclusions are correct, as we submit they are, the evidentiary weight of the offering lists, of the orders for purchases, of the bills of sale and of the deposit receipts, introduced in evidence in the instant case, is much less, (if that were possible), than the evidentiary weight to be given to the letters, bills of sale and confirmations of sale, or confirmation slips, in the cases cited. In the language of *Johnson v. Winslow*, in 279 N. Y. S. 155, (referring to confirmations of sale), "there is nothing sacrosanct about" any such documents.

Our discussions of the subject under the preceding headings show, conclusively, (as we submit to be the fact), that the deposit receipts, the offering lists and the bills of sale introduced in evidence by defendants are without any evidentiary importance whatever for the purpose for which the same were introduced by defendants, namely, that of charging plaintiff with knowledge of the fact that the fiduciary, the National Bank, had violated its obligations to plaintiff, the beneficiary, in making the purchases of the securities, prior to the execution of the instrument of trust, for plaintiff, from itself, even if it be assumed in the case of the offering lists, against the fact, that plaintiff had seen and had read the offering lists, or that the offering lists had been read to her.

Furthermore, even if it be assumed, against the fact, that the deposit receipts, the offering lists and the bills of sale were of evidentiary value, it was necessary for defendants to allege in their answers, and to prove, (which defendants have failed to do), that plaintiff was chargeable with knowledge from the offering lists, orders for purchases, bills of sale and confirmations of sale or confirmation slips that the National Bank had purchased the securities for her from itself, and that she not only had full knowledge of that fact, but also had full knowledge of the legal obligations of the National Bank and of plaintiff's corresponding legal rights, and, in the absence of such allegations and proofs, the findings of the District Judge, had the same been made, would have been without the issues and could not be upheld.

IV.

THE APPLICATION OF THE PRINCIPLE THAT WHEREVER A RELATION OF TRUST AND CONFIDENCE EXISTS, WHETHER IT BE THE CONVENTIONAL RELATION OF TRUSTEE AND CESTUI QUE TRUST, OR THE RELATION BETWEEN A BOARD OF DIRECTORS, OR OFFICERS, OF A CORPORATION, AND ITS STOCKHOLDERS, OR THE RELATION BETWEEN AN AGENT AND PRINCIPAL, OR EVEN THE RELATION BETWEEN A SELLER AND BUYER, IT IS NECESSARY FOR THE FIDUCIARY, IN CONFESSION AND AVOIDANCE OF A TRANSACTION IN VIOLATION OF HIS OBLIGATIONS, TO ALLEGE, AND ALSO TO PROVE, THAT THE BENEFICIARY HAD FULL KNOWLEDGE OF ALL THE MATERIAL FACTS, AND ALSO HAD FULL KNOWLEDGE OF ALL THE LEGAL OBLIGATIONS OF THE FIDUCIARY AND OF ALL THE CORRESPONDING LEGAL RIGHTS OF THE BENEFICIARY, RELATING TO THE TRANSACTION.

In addition to the cases which we have summarized in Appendix J of this Reply Brief, the following cases are cited, (and some of them are quoted), in our Opening Brief, (pp. 52-5), namely: *Adair v. Brimmer*, 74 N. Y. 539, (App. J 97), *White v. Sherman*, 168 Ill. 589, 48 N. E. 128, 61 A. S. R. 132, (App. J 99), *Kershaw v. Julien*, 72 F. (2d) 528, (C. C. A., 10th), (App.

J 164), *Gates v. Megargel*, 266 Fed. 811, (C. C. A., 2d), (App. J 170), *Thompson v. Park Sav. Bank*, 96 F. (2d) 544, (C. A., D. of C.), and *Garrett v. Reid-Cashion Land & Cattle Co.*, 34 Ariz. 245, 270 Pac. 1044.

We also add the following authorities to the list of authorities cited in our Opening Brief, (pp. 52-6), the recent and well considered cases of *Johnson v. Winslow*, 155 Misc. 170, 279 N. Y. S. 147, and *In re Cook's Estate*, 20 Del. Ch. 123, 171 At. 730, which we have summarized in Appendix J, (pp. 121 and 150, respectively), and also 3 *Pomeroy, Equity Jurisprudence*, sec. 1083, p. 2491, (4th ed.), tit. "Powers, Duties and Liabilities of Express Trustees".

These authorities illustrate and apply the principle formulated in the foregoing heading.

This principle, which we have expressed, and, to some extent have discussed, in our Opening Brief, (pp. 52-9), is not directly attempted to be controverted by counsel for defendants. Counsel for defendants, however, in his discussion, in the light of such important cases as *Pence v. Langdon*, 99 U. S. 578, 25 L. Ed. 420, *Williams v. Bolling*, 138 Va. 244, 121 S. E. 270, (to neither of which counsel for defendants refers), and of the later case of *Johnson v. Winslow*, 155 Misc. 170, 279 N. Y. S. 147, as to the effect of the receipts of the National Bank to plaintiff for securities purporting to have been deposited for safe keeping by plaintiff with the National Bank, and of the bills of sale for securities sold by the National Bank to plaintiff, and of the offering lists to the public of securities for sale by the National Bank, have ignored that portion of the principle which imposes upon a fiduciary the necessity of alleging and of proving that the beneficiary had full knowledge of all the material facts relating to a transaction between the fiduciary and the beneficiary, which the beneficiary has attacked as in violation of the duties of the fiduciary, and also of alleging and proving that the beneficiary had full knowledge of all the legal obligations of the fiduciary and of all the corresponding legal rights of the beneficiary relating to the transaction.

As said by the distinguished judge who wrote the opinion in *Adair v. Brimmer*, 74 N. Y. 554, (App. J 98), (and quoted by the Chief Justice with approval in *Thompson v. Park Sav. Bank*, 96 F. (2d), 544, 549, (App. J 190)), "The maximum *'ignorantia legis excusat neminem'*, cannot be invoked in such a case", or, in other words, *the maxim cannot be invoked by the wrongdoing fiduciary.*

Moreover, it is incumbent upon the wrongdoing fiduciary, who contends that the beneficiary confirmed the violations of the fiduciary's obligations, to see to it that the beneficiary was fully informed of the violations and of his legal rights in relation thereto. *The fiduciary cannot impose upon the beneficiary the responsibility of informing the fiduciary of the violations of his obligations.* As the Chancellor said *In re Cook's Estate*, 171 At. 732, (App. J 152),

> "The cestui que trust is under no duty to act as adviser to his trustee. Consent, such as to foreclose the beneficiary from objecting, is not evidenced by failure to complain. Silence is not affirmation and approval."

Or, as said by Lord Justice Turner, in *Life Association of Scotland v. Siddal*, 3 DeG. F. & J. 58, 73, 45 Eng. Rep., (Full Reprint), 800, 806, a trustee cannot be permitted to escape from the liability incident to his duty as trustee

> *"by simply informing the cestui que trust that he has committed, or intends to commit, a breach of it"*, (Emphasis added),

nor can the trustee,

> "where the trust is clear, throw upon the cestui que trust the obligation of telling him what his duty is and of cautioning him to observe it, thus involving the cestui que trust in the burthen and expense of those duties which he has undertaken himself to perform."

The defendants have never accepted, nor have they even recognized, either in their pleadings, or in their evidnce, or in their arguments, the burden, as required by these authorities, of alleging and of proving that plaintiff had full knowledge of all the material facts relating to the purchases, both prior and subsequent to the execution of the instrument of trust, by the fiduciary, the National Bank, from itself, through its bond department, for the beneficiary, the plaintiff, of the bonds and notes in question, nor has the National Bank accepted the burden, as further required by these authorities, of alleging and of proving that plaintiff had full knowledge of the violations by the National Bank of its legal obligations to plaintiff and of the corresponding legal rights of plaintiff relating to the purchases.

The result of this failure of defendants to plead in confession and avoidance any of the questionable transactions between the National Bank and plaintiffs, of which plaintiff complains, or to prove the essential requirements of an otherwise possible complete defense, namely, that plaintiff had full knowledge of all the material facts, and also had full knowledge of all the obligations of the National Bank, and of the corresponding legal rights of plaintiff relating to the transactions, has been to render the defense incomplete and ineffective.

V.

NEITHER BOTHWELL NOR BERVEN WAS A CREDIBLE WITNESS.

There are two questions which materially affect the credibility of both Bothwell and Berven, namely: (1), when, with reference to the sale of plaintiff's Virginia Street property, on February 8, 1928, was the first conversation, if there was such a conversation, between plaintiff, Bothwell and Berven? and (2), when did Berven inform plaintiff that the type of securities which had been purchased for her was not the type of securities which the National Bank usually bought for trust investments?

The testimony of plaintiff and the testimony of Bothwell, relating and leading up to the conversations between them, involved in the first of these questions, are necessarily interrelated. An outline of plaintiff's testimony, followed by Bothwell's testimony, will be here presented.

Plaintiff testified that, (App. J 3, 4), she became acquainted with Bothwell about the time when she opened a savings account with the Central Bank, (under its then name of "Central Savings Bank"), in 1903, or 1904, and, therefore, several years prior to the organization of the National Bank on November 9, 1909. She did not recall when he was appointed to the position of manager of the bond department of the National Bank, (but which, according to his testimony, was in 1920 or 1921, (App. J 3, *Note*)). She, (App. J 4), "met him frequently in the Bank", and felt that she "was well acquainted with him". She talked with him about her financial, as well as her personal, affairs, in his private office in the Bank, more than once prior to the time of making the first purchases, on January 7, 1926, (App. J 4, *Note*). She told him who the immediate members of her family were, and explained to him that she wanted to put her property "in a fund, or some estate", where it would be cared for during her lifetime and for her heirs, who were a daughter and her grandson, on her death. She told him that she had 'real estate situated in Nevada and had some bonds and mortgages', the real estate consisting of a store, "commonly called the Virginia Street property", on Virginia Street, Reno, Nevada, lots in Sparks, a town near Reno, a lot in Oakland, a mortgage on the Masonic Temple, in Sparks, to secure a note executed to her by the Sparks Masonic Building Association, and bonds called the "Washoe County, County Roads and Highways Improvement and Construction bonds". Bothwell, (App. J 5), informed her that "they could handle the personal property, but the real estate in Nevada could not be handled by them" without complicating matters, and the better thing to do would be to dispose of that real estate and invest the proceeds in bonds, or something of that kind, "so it could be placed in the fund later on", which "he called a 'trust fund' ". She asked him "whether or not the Bank had a department to care for estates and for heirs", and he replied that "it had just the department of that kind to take care of estates for widows and orphans where they would be protected", and said that "the Bank would form a trust, or a trust would be formed by the Bank", and it would be cared for in the Bank, and in the meantime "they would purchase bonds for me, from time to time, as I acquired the money and sold the property to create the trust fund". She, (App. J 6), inquired of him as to whether or not he could place the property in the Bank, "in such a trust, or trust fund", as she described to him, so that she would be cared for during her lifetime and her daughter and her grandson after her death. She had more than one conversation with him, in which she told him of what her property consisted, and he told her "they could not manager the real estate in Nevada", and that I should sell it, and and "invest the money in bonds or in other personal property", and "This condition was to continue until I sold my Nevada real property", and "he was to buy bonds for my trust fund and hold them in the Bank until I could dispose of this property, and then, he advised me, that the better thing to do was to have a trust fund created".

She, (App. J 6-7), accepted his advice, and, in accepting the advice, it was her intention to create the trust after she had disposed of her Nevada real estate. She told him that she "did not have any experience in bonds, and that 'I just had to depend on such information I could get from the bond department' " of the National Bank, and he told her that the bonds to be purchased and held pending the creation of the trust were "to be substantial bonds", "reliable and safe bonds, and I would never lose my money", and that her money "would be placed in nothing but bonds which were safe and desirable". He selected, so she testified, all the bonds and securities for

the investment of her funds, and she "always approved of what
he suggested to me", "but at times I questioned them".*

Bothwell, on the other hand, testified, on his direct examination, (App. J 27-8), that he recalled a conversation between
plaintiff and himself, in January, 1926, in the Arcadia Building,
in which the National Bank was temporarily located, in connection with the first of the purchases of the bonds and notes; that
plaintiff "came to the bond department to buy bonds, and asked
if we sold bonds, and I submitted an offering list on which was
listed the bonds that the Bank had for sale"; that, (App. J 28),
plaintiff did not, at that time, tell him anything about the members of her family, nor did she tell him anything, at that time,
about owning real property in Nevada; that before that time
she never told him anything about members of her family, nor
had she ever told him about owning real property in Nevada;
that he could not recall the year, or the time, when he first
heard that she had a daughter, but it was after some accident
had happened, the nature of which he did not know, in which
her daughter was injured, and he had no recollection of having
heard that she had a daughter until after that accident, when
she mentioned to him that her daughter was in rather a bad
way on account of the accident; and that, (App. J 28), the first
time he heard that plaintiff ever owned any real property in
Nevada was after the instant action was commenced, "it was
after I left the Bank, I am pretty sure".

------

*Note: The first purchases of bonds and notes, made for plaintiff by
the National Bank, pursuant to this conversation between plaintiff and
Bothwell, were of the respective issues, par values, and prices, or costs,
including accrued interest, charged by the National Bank to plaintiff,
and were as follows, (Plf's Ex. 47, R. 645): $10,000, par value, so-
called "secured sinking fund gold bonds" of the Province of Buenos
Aires for $10,037.50; $5,000, par value, so-called "secured gold bonds"
of Miller & Lux, Inc., for $5,122.50; $5,000, par value, gold bonds of
Rhodes-Jamieson Co. for $5,122.50; and $5,000, par value, bonds of
Western States Gas & Electric Co. for $4,800, (App. A 10); or for the
total cost to plaintiff of $25,162.50, or a little less than 25% of the total
investment of plaintiff of $102,926.25, for bonds and notes, prior and
subsequent to the execution of the instrument of trust, (App. A 35-7).

That, (App. J 28-9), she made a statement to him as to her intention to create a trust, "probably two or three months", he did not know "just exactly how long, before a contemplated trip to Rochester, Minnesota", for the purpose of a possible operation; that he did not know "just when that trust instrument was executed", and had "no firsthand knowledge of that", but that, (App. J 29), was the only time that she mentioned to him that it was her intention, and she asked him if he thought it would be a good thing to do, "to create a trust", and he said he thought it would be, "under the circumstances", the circumstances being that she was to undergo an operation in Rochester; and that was "just two or three months before she went to Rochester", when she asked him if, in his opinion, "it would be a desirable thing to do", and he replied that he "thought it would be".

That, (App. J 29-30), he said, "I will introduce you to the trust officer", and she said that she "had already met Mr. Read", and he replied, "Well, I have nothing to do with the trust department. I better take you across and introduce you to a trust officer, or to Mr. Berven"; that, (App. J 30), he never, at any time, gave plaintiff a letter of introduction to Read, or to anyone else in the trust department; that he took plaintiff "over and introduced her to Berven", stating to the latter that plaintiff had been a client "and was a client of the bond department, and she was now contemplating making a trust, and asked him to take care of that"; and that he left immediately and went back to his office, and, therefore, was not present at the conversation between plaintiff and Berven.*

---

*Note: Notwithstanding this difference between the testimony of plaintiff on the one side and Bothwell and Berven on the other, *Read was not called by the defendants as a witness,* although he could have been readily so called, (App. J 85-6), had defendants so desired; and therefore, it is to be inferred that, had he been called, his testimony would have been unfavorable to defendants, (1 *Wigmore, Evidence,* sec. 584, (2d. ed.)), or, in other words, he would have testified had he been called, that plaintiff had interviewed him twice with reference to the creation of a trust, and, on both occasions, *prior to the sale of the Virginia Street property.*

On cross examination, Bothwell testified, (App. J 52-3), that he did not remember plaintiff prior to the time when she made the first purchases of bonds and notes, and the first time he remembered meeting her was "when she came to the bond department in the temporary quarters of the Bank", and he "recognized her as someone that I had seen but I did not know her name, and that was the reason, in order to avoid embarrassing questions, asking her who she was, why I asked her to sign a card on which I listed the securities that she purchased". Nevertheless, he later testified, on his cross examination, (App. J 63), in reply to a question whether he believed plaintiff had implicit confidence in him, that he "presumed" "she did in the Bank, she was buying bonds from the Bank, *because she had confidence in the Bank.* I don't know what confidence she had in me personally". (Emphasis added). Concerning this shifty reply, it may be observed, in passing, that his letters to plaintiff, almost immediately after her first purchases, on January 7, 1926, (R 735, Def's Ex. N, R 736, Def's Ex. O), belie the impression which he sought to create, that, at the time of the first purchases, plaintiff, whose name he did not know, was a stranger to him.

The District Judge, however, as stated in our Opening Brief, (p. 58), found (App. F, Finding 7, Paragraph I), that "plaintiff reposed in Bothwell and in the bond department trust and confidence which Bothwell well knew", and, as further stated in our Opening Brief, (p. 58), "This finding covers a period of more than ten years prior to the date of the first purchases of bonds and notes on January 7, 1926, during all of which time Bothwell occupied the position of an executive officer of high rank, of the National Bank, to wit, that of an assistant cashier, and the manager of the bond department, of the National Bank.

Therefore, Bothwell's testimony that she was practically a stranger to him, and that he did not even know her name when she first called upon him and made her first purchases of bonds and notes, can be characterized in no other manner than that of a premeditated falsehood, and the maxim *falsus in uno, falsus in omnibus,* is applicable. (2 *Wigmore, Evidence,* secs. 108, 113-4, (2d ed.); *Jones, Evidence in Civil Cases,* sec. 903). And, in that connection, it may not be inappropriate to state the applicability also of what was said in the case of *Blankman v. Vallejo,* 15 Cal. 638, 645, (1860), namely, that

> "We do not understand that the credulity of a court must necessarily correspond with the vigor and positiveness with which a witness swears";

or, in the language of Mr. Justice Field, who concurred, as a member of the California Supreme Court, in the case of *Blankman v. Vallejo,* in *Quock Ting v. United States,* 140 U. S. 417, 420, 35 L. Ed. 501, 502, (1921), (frequently cited elsewhere), that

> "There may be such an inherent improbability in the statements of a witness as to induce the court or jury to disregard his evidence, even in the absence of any direct conflicting testimony".

It is submitted that an inadmissible strain upon the credulity of the Court seems to have been attempted by Bothwell in this testimony, when it is recalled that plaintiff paid $25,116.50 for bonds and notes which he had selected and recommended to her as safe and desirable securities for the investment of her funds, (App. J 34-5, 44-5), and, therefore, that he should have explained, through counsel for defendants, who called him as a witness, why it was that his testimony ran counter to ordinary human behavior, when it is also recalled that the District Court found, (App. F, Finding 1, Paragraph II, Findings of Fact, although without the issues and contrary to the evidence, (App. H 4-5)), that

> "at all times, both before as well as after the execution of the trust instrument, plaintiff had a highly developed business sense, and was extremely able and alert, and was well able to understand and did in fact understand the nature of the transactions complained of in the complaint".

Notwithstanding, counsel for defendants have inconsequentially
argued, at considerable length, in support of the findings, (Reply
Brief, pp. 22-8), that "There is no requirement that findings
comply *literally* with the wording of a pleading". (Emphasis
counsel's).

We now turn to the testimony of Berven, who, called as a
witness for defendants, testified, on his direct examination, to
five conversations which he had with plaintiff.

The *first* conversation, so he testified, (App. J 73), was "approximately three or four months before the trust instrument
was executed on September 24, 1929". Bothwell, so Berven
testified, brought plaintiff in and introduced her to Berven and
said that plaintiff desired "to have some information regarding
a trust", and then Bothwell left. The conversation was "a
general conversation as to the creation of a trust", and, as near
as Berven recalled, was, (App. J 73):

> "Well, she wanted information as to creating a trust, as
> to the fees, and how a trust would operate, and discussed
> it in general".

Plaintiff, so Berven testified, (App. J 73), mentioned her
daughter. He asked plaintiff, (App. J 73-4), what property
she had, and she said she "had some bonds, and a piece of real
estate, and a mortgage, up in Nevada", and also, he thought,
"one or two pieces—one or two houses in Sparks, Nevada."
With reference to the property in Sparks, (App. J 74), he
"explained" to plaintiff that

> "we could not take title to property in trust in Nevada,
> and she wanted to know how she—she thought she could
> put up—she thought she could put all the property in, and
> wanted to know what she was going to do with that prop-
> erty. I explained to her that she could either dispose of
> that property by will or make a deed of gift".

The witness told plaintiff that

> "if she made a deed of gift she could give it to someone
> for delivery to her *daughter,* and she said she would give
> it to her *sister*". (Emphasis added).

She did not mention, so the witness testified, (App. J 74),

> "at that time, or at any other time, that she had property
> in Reno, Nevada. She did not mention anything about any
> property on Virginia Street, in Reno. She was not definitely
> committed to the idea of making a trust at that time. She
> was just seeking information. That, in general, was all the
> conversation, on that occasion, which I recall".*

The *second* conversation with plaintiff, so he testified, (App.
J 75),

Note: The impression is again here sought to be given by Berven
that plaintiff had never mentioned to him the creation of a trust until
"just two or three months" before a contemplated trip by her to
Rochester, Minnesota, for the purpose of undergoing an operation there
by Mayo Brothers. In other words, plaintiff had not formed or expressed
her intention, prior to the time of that conversation, of creating a trust,
(although she had invested, prior to the times of these purported conversations, through the bond department of the National Bank, of which
Bothwell was its manager, and on January 7, 1926, $25,000, par value,
bonds and notes, which he selected and recommended to her as safe and
desirable securities for the investment of her funds, and at a cost to her
of $25,162.50), and, consequently, the relation between the National
Bank and plaintiff in the purchases of bonds and notes for her, through
its bond department, was not one of trustee and cestui que trust, but
merely one of seller and purchaser. If such was the impression sought
to be given, and we submit that such was the impression sought, it
obviously runs counter to the finding of the District Judge, (App. F,
Finding 7, Paragraph I, Findings of Fact), that "Plaintiff reposed in
Bothwell and in the bond department trust and confidence which Bothwell well knew", this finding, (Opening Brief, p. 58), covering a period
of more than ten years prior to the date of the first purchases of bonds
and notes on January 7, 1926, (Opening Brief, p. 58) ; and that Bothwell, as well as Berven, should have explained, through counsel for
defendants, who called them as witnesses, why their testimony ran
counter to the ordinary human behavior of persons, including, in particular, plaintiff. The finding by the District Judge, (App. F, Finding 1,
Paragraph II, Findings of Fact, (App. H 4), as to plaintiff's mentality
was assigned, however as Error No. 4, as being without the issues and
contrary to the evidence).

"was shortly before the trust was created; I would say two
or three weeks before. She came in; just a short conversation. I recall it was just over the counter. She wanted to
know, at that time, whether she could continue to deal
with the bond department, and buy her securities, if she
placed the property in trust with us. I told her 'I thought
we could arrange that'. That, in substance, was all the
conversation which I had with her on that second occasion."

The next, or *third,* conversation, so the witness testified,
(App. J 75), was

"Well, it was just as I say, just about a week or a week
or ten days, before the trust was created. She came in, and
evidently had definitely decided to create a trust, and gave
me the information as to what she wanted in the trust.

"I wrote down with a pencil and a pad that I used there
the information which she gave me as to how she wanted
her property distributed, the income to her during her lifetime and a provision for her daughter and her grandson.
She either brought in a list, or I got a list, of her property
from the bond department at that time. I cannot recall.
I had the list before us. I do not know where the list is at
the present time.

"The list, as to the securities in it, was the same as the
list of securities which appear in the trust instrument."

The witness further testified, (App. J 75-6), in that connection, that he told plaintiff,

"at that time, that the securities that she had were not the
type of securities that we usually bought for trust investments; that we were required to buy securities that were
considered legal for trust investments; such securities had
a higher marketability and less fluctuation, and for that
reason they naturally would bring in a smaller rate of
income."

And, (App. J 76), that he told plaintiff the rate of income
such a type of security would bring, and said to her that she

"could not go approximately over 5 per cent.", and that plaintiff replied that "she would have to have at least 6 per cent. on her money." And that he also told plaintiff, (App. J 76),

> "we could not buy that type security, and she wanted to know, at that time, whether she could continue to buy her bonds, her securities, from the bond department. I told her, in order to do that, she could do it in two different ways, either have to make a partial revocation and buy her own securities and then make an addition to the trust after she purchased the new securities, or we could put that provision in the trust agreement, itself, where it provides we could purchase securities that were legal for trust investments or otherwise. In that way, she could direct us to buy securities as she desired."

He further testified, (App. J 76), that the trust instrument, when drawn up, contained such a provision, and that plaintiff did not give him any data in her own handwriting at that time, or at any other time, and that, (App. J 77),

> "after taking down the data from Mrs. Quinn as she gave it to me, as to the distribution clause, I took it up to the attorneys' office, Mr. Beardsley's office";

and that Mr. Abbott, of Mr. Beardsley's office, from the date, prepared the "distribution clause", the distribution clause including all of paragraph IV,

> "and furnished it to us, and we incorporated it with the usual standard clause, and after it was completed we submitted it to him again for his approval."

The *fourth* conversation, so Berven testified, which he had with plaintiff, (App. J 78), was after the instrument of trust had been prepared and was ready for execution. "Plaintiff came in on the date that the instrument bears", whereupon he took one of the duplicates and plaintiff took the other, and he

> "read over the instrument, paragraph by paragraph, and explained each paragraph as I went along, and asked her if there was any question as to each paragraph. She fol-

lowed me with her duplicate. As I finished each paragraph, I asked her if she understood it, and her answer was 'Yes', she was satisfied. I do not recall, offhand, the explanation I gave as to the various paragraphs of the instrument, or just what I did say after each paragraph".

After examining, at the request of counsel for the Central Bank, paragraph II of the instrument of trust, in answer to a question as to what, if anything, he told plaintiff concerning the provisions of that paragraph, he testified, (App. J 78-9),

"Well, I pointed out to her that the clause such as to securities, as the investments legal for trust investments, 'or otherwise', and pointed out to her that those two words, 'or otherwise', were put in there so she could direct her own investments in things other than were otherwise legal for the investment of trust funds".

To questions by counsel for the Central Bank as to what remarks, if any, he recalled were made by plaintiff during the conversation when the instrument of trust was executed, he testified that, (App. J 79), plaintiff "asked me if I thought she ought to take this to her attorney. I told her it was perfectly proper she should do so", that plaintiff replied, "Well, she said she wouldn't have the time, she was going back East", and that plaintiff said that her attorney was "up in Nevada".*

---

*Note: It does not appear from the record, either from plaintiff's testimony or otherwise, that plaintiff had an attorney, at the time, "up in Nevada". It does appear, however, from plaintiff's testimony, (App. J 17), as well as from her testimony here under review, that he successfully discouraged her from submitting the instrument of trust, (which he, together with the attorneys for the National Bank, had prepared), to some attorney of her own selection. And it is a fair inference from the fact—if it be the fact—that, since, so he testified, he shortly before criticized the "type" of securities in which the National Bank, through Bothwell, as the manager of the bond department, had invested her funds, the submission of the instrument by plaintiff to an attorney of her own choosing was the last thing which he desired; and it is also a fair inference that if the instrument had been submitted to an attorney of the plaintiff's own choosing, it would never have been executed by her, and the investments which had been made by the National Bank, through Bothwell as the manager of the bond department, would have been dis-

Continuing, he testified that he could not "recall just what conversation we had right after that; it was just that she was satisfied because the agreement was signed", and that he read to her the statement at the foot of the instrument of trust, and asked her if she understood that, and she replied that she did, "with all of the other paragraphs".

The last, or *fifth,* conversation, which he testified he had with plaintiff, was in his office, and was in regard to the letter, Defendants' Exhibit T, (R 741), referring to the default in the

---

approved, and steps, without a doubt, would have been taken for the repayment by the National Bank to plaintiff of the funds which she had entrusted to it for investment.

Even if it were true that plaintiff told him that she "would not have time" to consult an attorney, it was his duty to have insisted that she take the time to do so. Time was not of such importance to her that a delay of a few days for an examination by an attorney of her own selection of, perhaps, the most important instrument which she had ever signed, should not be made. He should have known, as, no doubt, he did, that she did not understand that she might be prevented, (so far as it was possible for adroit language to prevent her), from attacking the misdeeds of the National Bank through the provisions of paragraph II and through the provisions of paragraph III relating to the revocation of the instrument and by the declaration at the foot of the instrument. By the statement that, "she said she would not have time" to have the instrument examined by an attorney of her own selection, he not only stamped himself as an unscrupulous fiduciary, but, without doubt, testified to a thinly disguised untruth.

Attention is called in this connection to the fact that the District Judge, in Finding II, Paragraph 3, Findings of Fact, found, (App. F 17-8), that the firm of attorneys who were then the attorneys for the National Bank, and who continued to represent the National Bank as its attorneys until about May 20, 1933, "did not purport to represent plaintiff in connection with the preparation or execution of said instrument of trust but instead were acting for the national bank"; and that "Plaintiff was charged by the national bank, and thereafter paid to said bank, an acceptance fee in the sum of $100 for the acceptance by said national bank of the trusteeship under said instrument of trust"; and, therefore, while plaintiff, through the National Bank, *paid the attorneys* "an acceptance fee" for the services of the firm, nevertheless, Berven undoubtedly gave plaintiff the impression that the firm represented her also, (App. J 400), since he told her that her "interests were fully protected", and, consequently, the case was one in which the independent advice of an attorney of her own selection was needed by her as a victim of misplaced confidence.

payment of interest on bonds of Berkeley Terminal Properties, Inc., and that, (App. J 79-80), "The conversation was quite some time, two or three months, along in there, after the date of the letter", and that, as he recalled it, plaintiff asked him "Why did the bond department sell me those bonds", and he replied that "evidently they had figured they were good at the time they sold them to her, or they wouldn't have sold her those bonds".

After testifying that a list, on yellow paper, of plaintiff's securities had been prepared, either in the latter part of 1931 or in the early part of 1932, by one Bowell, who was working in the trust department at that time, and that he did not "know where the list is at the time", but he recalled that the "total of the then market values of the securities, as shown on that list, was approximately $75,000", whereupon, so he testified, (App. J 81), plaintiff "appeared to be quite angry about it", and said "I think I will have to see an attorney about this", to which the witness, so he said, made no comment.*

Berven, so he further testified, (App. J 81), in this connection, "did not say she should sell", but he told her that "I would

---

*Note: Berven's testimony, in this respect, namely, that plaintiff, when she was told by him that her securities then had a market value of approximately $75,000, "appeared to be quite angry about it", and that she thought that she would have "to see an attorney about this", does not accord with Bothwell's testimony, on cross examination, to the effect that, when plaintiff called to see him, shortly after her conversation with Berven, in the latter part of September or in the early part of the month of October, 1932, and handed him the list, Plaintiff's Exhibit 62, which she obtained from Cavalier & Company's office, (App. J 64),

"She came in and *she was in a very friendly attitude,* and, after the greeting, she said that she was very sorry that her bonds had gone down to such an extent as she had ascertained they had and presented the list and asked if I would look over the list and tell her approximately what they were worth at the present time";

but that, (App. J 66),

"she was not pleased with the showing of the way the securities had gone down but she always had a *very gracious manner* and she left feeling I presume that she would have to abide by the conse-

be glad to look over the securities and see if any of them, if I thought any of them, should be sold", and plaintiff replied, " 'Well, if I sell, look what a loss I will take'. She said, 'I don't mind so much if the market is down, but if I sell I won't get it back' ".

The witness also testified that, at this conversation, (App. J 81), plaintiff "asked me about Alameda Park Co. bonds", and

> quences or—I didn't know what was in her mind. She never told me that she contemplated any action at all";

and that her attitude

> "seemed to be just friendly, but disappointed";

and, to the question

> "just friendly, although the computations which you had computed showed she suffered a loss over the cost price of 66% or thereabouts she still was very, very friendly?"

he answered

> "I didn't say *she was very, very friendly,* but still appeared friendly".

It may be quite accurately stated, in this respect, that Berven's testimony was nearer the truth than was Bothwell's testimony. But, in another respect, his testimony does not bear the stamp of truthfulness, namely, he testified, on his direct examination, that, on the occasion of plaintiff's third visit, (App. J 75-6), about a week or ten days before the instrument of trust was executed, when she called on him, after she had definitely made up her mind to create a trust, that he told her

> "that the securities that she had were not the type of securities that we usually bought for trust investments",

and that

> "we were required to buy securities that were considered legal for trust investments",

and he accordingly recommended to her a method by which securities which were not of the type for legal investments could, nevertheless, be purchased by the National Bank, since it is quite accurate to say that, had she been informed by Berven, at that time, that her securities were not the type for legal investments, she would have immediately expressed her displeasure in no uncertain terms, and would have inquired why the National Bank had sold her securities of that sort. This would naturally have led to an investigation by an attorney of her own selection, with the result that the instrument of trust would never have been executed by her, and to a rescission of the transactions of purchases theretofore made for her by the National Bank, a consequence which both Berven and Bothwell would naturally wish to avoid.

that, "Well, she asked me what they were, and what they were
secured by, and I told her it covered the Neptune Beach property
over in Alameda, and that it was a short way over there, and
she could take a ride over and take a look for herself what the
property covered, what the securities are".*

Plaintiff also at this conversation, (App. J 81-2), "mentioned"
to him "the Alameda Investment Company bonds", and "I explained to her what they were secured by", and "I don't recall

---

*Note: Berven's character is well disclosed by this bit of his testi-
mony. The time had arrived, in the course of the unfortunate career of
the National Bank, when plaintiff was not so affectionately regarded by
the officials of the Bank as she had been during the time, prior to the
execution of the instrument of trust, when the Bank was investing her
funds in securities purchased from itself. She was then only a sickly old
woman, evidently much disturbed by the default in the payment of the
interest on the bonds of the Alameda Park Co., as well as in the default
in the payment of the interest on many other bonds and notes which had
been purchased for her by the National Bank, including the bonds of
the Alameda Improvement Company, and, consequently, she was apparently so much inclined to make trouble that Berven would be glad to
get rid of her. He knew, or should have known, that the Park Co. was
an amusement concern and depended for its support on the interest
which a fickle public might have and retain in the amusements which
the Park Co. afforded. He knew, or should have known, that the Park
Co. had mortgaged its property to the Bank, as trustee under the indenture of mortgage, to secure $8,000, par value, out of a total authorized
issue of $300,000, par value, of its bonds, and whether or not the bonds
were adequately secured would not be disclosed by any examination
which she might make, or, for that matter, any examination which might
be made other than by an expert in values. He knew, or should have
known, that the Bank and its officials, or both, occupied a dual position
as mortgagee under the indenture of mortgage and as a dealer in the
bonds secured by the indenture. He knew, or should have known, that
the property mortgaged by the indenture to secure the payment of the
principal of and the interest on the bonds issued under the indenture
consisted of parcels of land situated in the City of Alameda, and apparently, for the most part, tide lands on and in San Francisco Bay, and
included theater equipment of various kinds and a strange assortment
of other "personal property" embracing "pots, dishes, washing machines
and other equipment, laundry machinery, bathing suits and towels",
used by the public and quite likely more or less in disrepair. And he
knew, or should have known, that it was probable that investment in the
bonds would prove almost, if not quite, a complete loss.

her saying anything about that, just that I explained the securities to her".

On cross examination, Berven testified, (App. J 87-8), that his recollection about plaintiff's visits to his office and what occurred on the occasions of them had always been quite clear in his mind, so that he could not possibly be mistaken about any of them. Thereupon he was asked the question, (App. J 88), (referring to Mr. Edwards, the associate of the writer of this brief), whether he did not, in the presence of Edwards and Bothwell, in Mount's private office in the Central Bank Building, between the hours of two and three o'clock in the afternoon of January 23, 1933, (relating to the circumstances leading up to the execution of the instrument of trust), state to the writer of this brief, in reply to an inquiry by the writer, "that the subject was first mentioned" to him by plaintiff "about a year prior to the time" when he obtained from her the information of which he made a memorandum, and he replied that he did not "recall the statement".*

Berven was also asked the question, on his cross examination, (App. J 93-4), whether the writer of this brief did not, in the presence of Edwards, in his, (Berven's), office in the Central Bank Building, in the afternoon of December 13, 1932, call his attention to some of the bonds or notes in which plaintiff's funds had been invested, including, among others, the Province of Buenos Aires, the Province of Callao and the Fageol Motors Company bonds, and ask him if plaintiff was ever advised by the National Bank officials that her money should be invested in safer bonds, yielding a smaller return, and whether or not he replied that he "had so advised her", and that such advice had been given after the instrument of trust had been executed, and he replied "I cannot recall any such conversation".

*Note: "About a year prior to the time" when Berven obtained from plaintiff the information of which he made a memorandum, would make the time about September, 1928.

Later on, during the course of the trial, Mr. Edwards was called as a witness on behalf of plaintiff, and, after his attention was called to the foregoing respective questions propounded by the writer of this brief, he testified, (R 529-30), that the respective questions were asked and that Berven replied as above quoted.*

There is one further matter relating to Berven's veracity as a witness that may be here appropriately considered.

It will be recalled, (App. J 83, *Note*), that on July 16, 1930, Read wrote a letter to plaintiff, (Plf's Ex. 20, R 561-2), in which he advised plaintiff to sell the $5,000, par value, bonds of Federal Public Service Corporation, which had been purchased on June 27, 1930, by the National Bank, from itself, through Bothwell, for the trust estate, and to reinvest the proceeds in $3,000, par value, 6% bonds of Pacific Gas & Electric Company, at the price of $110½, and $2,000, par value, 6% bonds of San Joaquin Light and Power Corporation, at the price of $114¼, Read stating, in his letter that, (R 561), "The prices mentioned are taken from today's quotations and are of course subject to change without notice", and that, although the purchases so recommended would yield plaintiff considerably less than 5% per annum, she, nevertheless, wrote Read on July 26, 1930,

---

Note: It will be noted that to each of the respective impeaching questions Berven answered that he "did not recall" making the statements attributed to him. It is generally held that, if a witness testifies, in relation to impeaching questions, that he "does not recall" the statements, his answer is equivalent to a denial that he made them: 27 *Cal. Jur.*, p. 164, sec. 137, tit. "Witnesses"; 40 *C. J.*, p. 1120, sec. 1300, tit. "Witnesses"; *Jones, Evidence in Civil Cases*, sec. 849, (3d ed.).

It will also be noted that, according to the first of the foregoing impeaching questions, Bothwell was present at the conversation of January 23, 1933, between the writer of this brief and Berven, and that Bothwell was not called to the witness stand by counsel for defendants, either to corroborate or to deny the conversation. Therefore, it is a reasonable inference from his failure to take the stand, or, rather, from the failure of counsel for defendants to recall him to the stand, that his testimony, had he been recalled, would have been unfavorable to defendants.

(Plf's Ex. 23, R 564), without any complaint of the low rate of interest, "Please change bonds as you suggest if you deem it advisable. I certainly d*i*sire (sic) safe investments at all times", and the purchases were accordingly made, from third persons, on July 31, 1930, (Plf's Ex. 5, R 548).

Defendants have never explained why it was that the matter of purchases of bonds for the trust estate was suddenly taken by Read out of Bothwell's hands into his own hands. The person who in particular could make the explanation was Read himself, who, although available as a witness to counsel for defendants for the explanation, was never called as a witness, with the resulting implication that, if he had been called, his testimony would have been adverse to defendants, and with a probable explanation that Read had learned that the purchases up to that time, and both prior and subsequent to the execution of the instrument of trust, which had been made for plaintiff, or for the trust estate, by the National Bank, through Bothwell, as the manager of its bond department, were unlawful.

It may also be recalled that Berven testified, on his direct examination, (App. J 82-3), in connection with the introduction in evidence of an authorization, dated January 14, 1932, addressed to the trust department of the National Bank, and signed by plaintiff, (Defts' Ex. U, R 742), that he had a conversation with plaintiff, which occurred on the date of the authorization in the trust department in the National Bank, in regard to her signing the authorization, in which he told her that "she had a certain amount of funds in the trust account for investment", and in which he "suggested" to her "that she should get into some high grade bonds, and suggested the East Bay Municipal Utility as an investment for this fund she had on hand and she inquired as to what they would yield", whereupon, so he testified, he "told her that they would yield her approximately 4.80%", she being obliged to pay a premium on the bonds, and that she replied, "I cannot take such low interest", whereupon he told her "she should have bonds of that type in there, in her trust account, that she should not worry about it", to which she replied "I just hate to take such a low interest", but she finally signed the authorization.

Berven, in this testimony, had overlooked, or had forgotten, the fact that on July 30, 1930, or about eighteen months prior to the purchase of the bonds of the Utility District, $3,000, par value, Pacific Gas & Electric Company and $2,000, par value, San Joaquin Light and Power Corporation bonds were purchased at a high premium, with a consequent low yield in interest, not only without any questioning in that respect by plaintiff, but with her prompt approval, for the reason that she said that she certainly desired "safe investments at all times".

Wherefore, it is submitted, in the language of the foregoing heading of this portion of the brief, that neither Bothwell nor Berven was a credible witness; and this conclusion is aside from the fact that by the finding of the District Judge, to which we have referred in our Opening Brief, (p. 58), credence was given to the testimony of plaintiff against the testimony of both Bothwell and Berven.

VI.

PLAINTIFF NEVER DIRECTED OR CONSENTED TO THE PURCHASES BY THE NATIONAL BANK OF SECURITIES FOR THE TRUST ESTATE, CREATED BY THE INSTRUMENT OF TRUST, FROM ITSELF THROUGH ITS BOND DEPARTMENT; NOR DID THE PROVISIONS OF SECTION 25, OF THE CALIFORNIA BANK ACT, EXPRESSLY, OR BY IMPLICATION, PERMIT SUCH PURCHASES TO BE MADE BY THE TRUST DEPARTMENT FROM THE BOND DEPARTMENT OF THE NATIONAL BANK.

Berven, in his "second", or "short", conversation, "just over the counter", which he said he had with plaintiff, (App. J 75), testified, that "shortly before the trust was created",—he would say "two or three weeks before" the trust was created,—plaintiff "came in" and had "just a short conversation" with him, as he "recalled it", "just over the counter", "and wanted to know, at that time", whether she "could continue to deal with the bond department, and buy her securities, if she placed the property in trust with us", and he replied, so he testified, that he "thought we could arrange that." "That, in substance, was all the conversation which I had with her on that second occasion."

On this halting and vaguely inconclusive testimony, counsel for defendants contends, (Reply Brief, pp. 59, 61-2, 64, 65, 67-8, 78), that plaintiff *"expressly directed"* the trust department to purchase the securities in question from the bond department of the National Bank, for itself, as trustee of the trust estate, and from itself through its bond department; but, assuming, for the purpose of argument, that the testimony is to be understood as meaning, in the language of the allegations of the answers, that plaintiff dealt "directly", through Bothwell, with the bond department of the National Bank, that the purchases were made at the "express instance and request", or at the "express instance and direction", of plaintiff, and that in each of the instances of such purchases, (as also alleged in the answers), "plaintiff well knew that the trust department of the National Bank made said purchases from the bond department", nevertheless, neither the testimony nor the allegations can be, or should be, construed to mean that plaintiff *knew* that the National Bank, through its bond department, was purchasing the bonds and notes from itself.*

Note: It may be observed, in passing, that the testimony of Berven, (if it is to be believed), has the effect of proving from his own mouth that he knew *before* the instrument of trust was executed that the National Bank was purchasing bonds and notes from itself, through its bond department, and, therefore, since he failed to apprise plaintiff of that fact, he was guilty of *actual* concealed fraud, (as distinct from *constructive* concealed fraud), of which the Bank and its officials had conclusively imputable knowledge.

It may be conceded that it was possible for plaintiff to direct
or to consent that the purchases of the securities in question be
made by the National Bank, for the trust estate created by the
instrument of trust, from itself, through its bond department,
and for itself, through its trust department, as trustee of the
trust estate, with the qualification, however, that the direction
or consent, to be effective, was the plaintiff's full knowledge
of the facts and her full knowledge also of the violation by
the National Bank of its legal obligations, and with the further
qualification that the direction or consent be both alleged and
proved.*

---

*Note: Plaintiff alleged in her complaint, (App. A 33-4), that each
of the four purchases in question made subsequent to the execution of
the instrument of trust by the National Bank, namely, the purchase on
April 8, 1930, of $1,000, par value, of the so-called "first and collateral
trust" bonds of Hearst Publications, Inc., the purchase on June 5, 1930,
of $1,000, par value, bonds of California Cotton Mills Co., the pur-
chase on June 27, 1930, of $5,000, par value, bonds of Federal Service
Corporation, and the purchase also on June 27, 1930, of $6,000, par
value, additional bonds of Hearst Publications, Inc., was recommended,
in each instance, either by Bothwell, Read or Berven to plaintiff as a
safe and desirable investment for the trust estate, and that plaintiff
accordingly relied upon such recommendation and approved the purchase, and that in each of the instances of such purchase the bonds were
so purchased by the National Bank from itself, through Bothwell, as
the manager of its bond department, and were sold to itself, either
through Read, as the trust officer, or through Berven, as the assistant
trust officer, of the National Bank, "and thereby the said Bank was both
the purchaser of the said bonds from itself, in one capacity, for the
plaintiff, and the seller, in another capacity, to the plaintiff, of the said
bonds so purchased."

The complaint further alleged, (App. J 33-4), that in each of the
instances of purchase and sale the bonds were sold at a larger price
than the National Bank had originally paid for them, and thereby the
National Bank made a profit on each of the transactions, and the aggregate profits so made was the sum of $471; and that

"in violation of the great trust and confidence which the plaintiff
reposed, as aforesaid, in the said Bothwell and in the said Read
and in the said Berven, none of them disclosed to, but all of them
concealed from, the plaintiff the fact that through them, or some
of them, the said Bank had purchased from itself and sold to
itself, as aforesaid, the said bonds, and that the said Bank, in so
doing, had profited, as aforesaid, in each of the said instances of
the purchase and sale of the said bonds; and that the plaintiff had

Through no fault of the District Judge, except, perhaps, in
relying too much upon the attorneys in the preparation of the
findings, there has been a confusion in a combined finding on
two unrelated subjects, namely, (1), the provisions of the instrument of trust relating to investments for the trust estate,
and (2), the provisions of section 25 of the *California Bank
Act* relating to purchases for the trust estate by the trust de-

no knowledge of any of the said facts so concealed, and did not
discover any thereof, until the time and under the circumstances
hereinafter alleged."

The answer of the Central Bank alleges that in each of the instances
of the purchase and sale, (App. B 23-4),

"plaintiff dealt *directly* with Bothwell, as manager of the bond department, and *directed* the trust department of the National Bank
to purchase from the bond department said bonds and notes, and
in each of the said instances plaintiff *well knew* that the trust department of the National Bank was making said purchases of
bonds from the bond department"; and that,

"This defendant further alleges that it was at plaintiff's *express
instance and direction* that the trust department of the National
Bank made said purchases, and all of them, from the bond department"; with the conclusion that,

"due to plaintiff's own *wishes,* she *in effect* and *in reality* acted as
the principal in these transactions insofar as the trust department
of the National Bank was concerned, and *directed* said trust department as to the investments she desired it to make." (Emphasis
added throughout the foregoing).

The allegations of the answer of the National Bank and its receiver,
(App. C 21-2), are substantially the same as the foregoing allegations
in the answer of the Central Bank.

The District Judge, in Finding 2, Paragraph IV, Findings of Fact,
(App. F 22-3), found that Bothwell "suggested and submitted" the purchases to plaintiff, "without any other recommendation", and plaintiff,

"*relying in part* upon the said suggestion and submission, *and in
part* upon the relatively high rate of return, *directed* the trust department to purchase the same from the bond department; that
no recommendation was made by any officer of the trust department of said Bank in connection with said purchases; in the instance of each of said purchases plaintiff *knew* that the bond department of the National Bank was the owner of the securities so
suggested and submitted and, with knowledge of that fact and
that the said bond department was making a *profit* thereon, nevertheless *directed* the trust department to make such purchases from
the bond department. In the instances of said purchases plaintiff
dealt *directly* with the bond department and *directed* the trust department to follow out her wishes in making said purchases. The

partment from the bond department; and there has also been a commingling of conclusions of law with findings of fact, and a resulting confusion in the discussion of these subjects by counsel for defendants in his Reply Brief, (pp. 68-73).

We separate our consideration of these matters into the two headings following: (1), the findings relating to investments under the provisions of the instrument of trust; and (2), the findings relating to investments under the provisions of section

> *aggregate profit* made by the National Bank on such purchases was the sum of $471.00." And that, (App. F 23),
>
> "The National Bank did not *conceal* from plaintiff the fact that the trust department was purchasing bonds owned by the bond department, nor did it *conceal* from plaintiff that, in so doing, the Bank had profited in each of the instances of the purchase and sale of said bonds; that said bonds were in each case sold by the bond department to the trust department at the *fair value* thereof, and were *legal trust investments* for said trust department to make for plaintiff's trust *because* of the fact that the instrument of trust *authorized* the National Bank, as trustee, to invest the trust funds in securities or investments of the character permitted by law for the investment of trust funds, 'or otherwise'; that the said words 'or otherwise' were inserted in article II of the instrument of trust, (Exhibit "A" annexed to the complaint), in order to comply with plaintiff's *desire* that the trust funds be invested in securities having a return of not less than six per cent. (6%), and it was at the time of the execution of the instrument of trust explained to her that such words had that effect, *which was as plaintiff intended."* (Emphasis added).

The assignments of error, (Nos. 22 and 23, App. H 33-5), to the foregoing findings of fact are that the findings are contrary to the evidence and are without the issues raised by the complaint and the answers thereto.

The District Judge, in the Conclusions of Law, "3", (App. F 36), further found as follows:

> "That after the execution of the instrument of trust on September 24, 1929 the national bank, as trustee of plaintiff's trust, *was entitled to, and did lawfully, purchase the securities* which it did in fact purchase from the bond department *by reason of the fact* (*a*) that plaintiff *expressly authorized* and *directed* the trust department to make such purchases knowing that the bond department was then the owner of, and *intended* to sell to the trust department, said securities, and that the bond department would make a *profit* on such sales to the trust department, *and (b) the provisions of Section 25 of the California Bank Act expressly permitted such purchases by the trust department from the bond*

25 of the *California Bank Act* by the purchases by the National Bank from itself, through its bond department, for the trust estate.

1. The findings relating to investments under the provisions of the instrument of trust.

The contentions of counsel for defendants, supported by the finding referred to in the preceding note, (App. F 22-3), that the securities in question

---

department. Therefore, *plaintiff is not entitled to rescind any of the purchases of securities* made after the execution of the instrument of trust." (Emphasis added).

The assignments of error, (No. 32, App. H 48-51), to the last foregoing finding, are for the reasons, (1), that the findings are contrary to the evidence, and (2), in relation to the provisions of Section 25 of the *California Bank Act,* that, (a), do not expressly, or inferentially, permit the purchases in question to be made by the trust department from the bond department of the National Bank, and (b), that the provisions of Section 25 of the *California Bank Act* were not pleaded in the answers as a defense to the transactions of purchase and sale.

It is respectfully submitted, in this latter connection, that the facts should have been found, and should have been *separately* found, and not intermingled with conclusions of law, and that from the facts found appropriate conclusions of law should have been drawn. But, instead of observing this well-established rule of all codes of pleading and practice, (*Equity Rule,* 70½, as amended November 25, 1935, Rule 42, *Rules of Practice,* United States District Court, Northern District of California; *Equity Rule,* 70½, Rule 52, subdivision (a), *Rules of Civil Procedure,* and section 632, *California Code of Civil Procedure*), the conclusions of law are but conclusions upon conclusions. Moreover, the final conclusion of law that plaintiff "is not entitled to rescind any of the purchases" in question does not follow from any conclusions of law, or from any findings of fact, previously found. This is true for the reason that, even if it be assumed, against the evidence, that plaintiff "authorized" and "directed" "the trust department" of the National Bank to purchase the securities in question "from the bond department of the National Bank", that is, that plaintiff "authorized" and "directed" the National Bank to purchase the securities from itself, in one capacity, for itself, in another capacity, and even if it be further assumed, against the evidence, that plaintiff "knew that the bond department of the National Bank" was the owner of the securities, it does not follow that "plaintiff is not entitled to rescind any of the purchases of securities made after the execution of the instrument", *unless plaintiff had full knowledge, and had full knowledge from the National Bank,* at the time of such "authorization" and "direction" *of her legal rights* in relation to the purchases, and unless that fact be both alleged and proved, *which was not the case.*

"*were legal trust investments* for said trust department to make for plaintiff's trust *because* of the fact that the instrument of trust authorized the National Bank, as trustee, to invest the trust funds in securities or investments of the character permitted by law for the investment of trust funds, *'or otherwise'*," and the words *"or otherwise"* "were inserted in Article II of the instrument of trust" "in order to comply with *plaintiff's desire* that the trust funds be invested in securities having a return of not less than 6 per cent. and it was at the time of the execution of the instrument of trust explained to her that such words had that effect, *which was as plaintiff intended"*.

Counsel for defendants, in his Reply Brief, further states, that, (p. 69),

"The Court found that in each instance the securities in question were sold by the bond department to the trust department at their fair value and were legal trust investments since the instrument of trust authorized the investment of the trust funds in 'legals', *or otherwise;* that the words 'or otherwise' were inserted in the trust instrument for that specific purpose",

and also that, Reply Brief, (p. 69),

"These findings are supported by the evidence. Thus Mr. Bothwell testified that the securities were sold at their market value or price at the time of sale. (R. 430-431, 449.)" (Emphasis added throughout the foregoing).

Further along, and under a different heading, counsel for defendants states, in his Reply Brief, as follows, (pp. 71-2):

"In the answers of the defendants it is alleged that in each instance of the sales of bonds, they were sold at then current market prices or the fair and reasonable value thereof. (R. 106, 116, 146 and 155.) With respect to the requirement that the securities be a legal investment for the department purchasing the same, it expressly appears in the instrument of trust annexed to the complaint as a part thereof, that the trust department was authorized to invest the trust funds in so-called 'legals', *'or otherwise'*. (R. 64-65.) Therefore, it was not necessary to plead this element in the answers since it is not necessary to plead, by way of defense, a matter appearing on the face of the bill of complaint.

"In 21 *C. J.* p. 472, sec. 545, dealing with answers in cases in equity, it is said:

" 'If, however, *facts appear on the face of the bill suffi- cient to defeat it, such facts need not be averred by way of defense.' "* (Emphasis counsel's throughout the fore- going).

It is substantially true, as counsel for defendants further states in his Reply Brief, that, (p. 69),

"The Court found that in each instance the securities in question were sold by the bond department to the trust department at their *fair value* and were *legal trust invest- ments* since the instrument of trust authorized the invest- ment of the trust funds in 'legals', *or otherwise;* that the words 'or otherwise' were inserted in the trust instrument for that specific purpose". (Emphasis, throughout the foregoing, in part counsel's and in part added).

But it is *not* true, as counsel states in his Reply Brief, that, (p. 69), "These findings *are supported by the evidence";* al- though it is substantially true, as counsel further states, that

"Mr. Bothwell testified that the securities were sold *at their market value* or price at the time of sale". (Em- phasis added).

There is no evidence, however, to support the finding that the securities "were legal trust investments", for the reason given in the findings, that "the instrument of trust authorized the investment of the trust funds in 'legals', *or otherwise"*, because the words " 'or otherwise' were inserted in the trust instrument for that specific purpose", the only evidence, in this respect, being that of Berven, who testified that, (App. J 76), he told plaintiff, at the third conversation which he testified he had with her, after the instrument of trust had been prepared and was submitted by him to her, "that the securities that she had were not of the type of securities that we usually bought for trust investments", and that "we were required to buy securities that were considered legal for trust investments", and that he told her, in answer to her inquiry as to whether or not "we could not buy that type security", when she wanted to know, at that time, "whether she could continue to buy her bonds, her securities, from the bond department", "that she could do it in two different ways, either have to make a partial revocation and buy her own securities and then make an addition to the trust after she purchased the new securities, or we could put that provision in the trust agreement itself, where it provides that we could purchase securities that were legal for trust investments or otherwise", and "in that way she could direct us to buy securities as she desired"; but, on cross examination, he testified that, (App. J 91), "paragraph II of the trust instrument" contained *no* provision by which plaintiff would be permitted to direct the investment of the trust funds.

The result is, therefore, that there is no evidence to support either the allegations of the answer or the findings that the instrument of trust authorized the National Bank to purchase securities from itself for the trust estate, through its bond department.*

---

*Note: These conclusions cannot be lightly disposed of by such unfounded and unsupportable, and frequently confused and ambiguous, assertions, without argument, of counsel for defendants, as the following:

(Reply Brief, p. 14): "The appellant has not even attempted to refer to any part of the evidence dealing with the nature of the relationship existing between the parties prior to September 24, 1929"; and "As we shall proceed to show, plaintiff can hardly claim to have raised even a bare conflict in the evidence. Certainly the weight of the evidence establishes that plaintiff *intended to buy* securities from the national bank which the national bank owned and did not intend that the bank should act as agent or broker for the purpose of buying securities for her." (Emphasis counsel's).

(Reply Brief, p. 27): "The preponderance of the evidence together with the *probabilities* of the case are overwhelmingly in favor of the

2. The findings relating to investments under the provisions of section 25 of the California Bank Act by the purchases by the National Bank from itself, through its bond department, for the trust estate.

Counsel for defendants states his contention, in this respect, in the following heading of his Reply Brief, (p. 68):

defendants' contention that plaintiff intended to, and did in fact, buy securities from the bond department." (Emphasis counsel's).

(Reply Brief, p. 28): "The determination of the question as to whether a given relationship is that of buyer and seller or principal and agent is a question of fact and the finding of the trial Court in the case at bar is amply supported by the evidence".

(Reply Brief, p. 29): "It is not necessary for us to contend that any particular item of evidence, either direct or inferential, is, in and of itself, conclusive on this phase of the case. We do maintain, however, that on the direct testimony of the witnesses, the utmost that plaintiff can claim is a bare conflict in the evidence. The inferences to be drawn from the documentary evidence and the surrounding facts and circumstances overwhelmingly preponderate in favor of the defendants' contentions We feel that we have demonstrated conclusively that the relationship between plaintiff and the bond department of the national bank prior to the execution of the trust instrument was that of buyer and seller and that it was so intended by plaintiff and the bond department. The Court so determined in its findings and conclusions after having heard the testimony and observed the witnesses. (R. 323, 348.)"

(Reply Brief, p. 29): "It is well settled that findings of fact in an equity case will be taken as correct on appeal unless clearly against (the weight of the evidence)."

(Reply Brief, p. 30-1), (referring to the purchases in question made prior to the execution of the instrument of trust, and to the "argument" of counsel for plaintiff, as "begging the question", and as "most fallacious"): "The Court found that no such agency relationship existed; that instead plaintiff intended to buy from the bank and the bank intended to sell its own securities and such finding is preponderately supported by the evidence. The only attack that could be directed at such finding is that it is unsupported by any evidence or contrary to the weight of the evidence. No such attack is made by counsel but instead the issue is adroitly sidestepped by assuming that the relationship was found to be that of principal and agent or *cestui* and trustee."

(Reply Brief, p. 40): "the weight of the evidence irresistibly leads to the conclusion that plaintiff did not intend to establish a trust until shortly prior to September 24, 1929. Not only this, but plaintiff's alleged reasons for postponing the actual creation of the trust from January, 1926, to September, 1929, are not convincing".

(Reply Brief, p. 76): "In closing we emphasize that the issues in this case are simple and free from complexity, involving as they do

"The provisions of section 25 of the *California Bank Act* expressly permit a trust department of a bank to purchase from another department thereof provided that the fair value of the securities be paid and the securities purchased be a legal investment for the department making the purchase".

And he follows this heading with the further statement that, Reply Brief, (p. 68),

essentially questions of fact alone. Counsel have criticized the findings of the District Court as being either contrary to, or unsupported by, the evidence. It is significant that the appellant has not referred to the statement of evidence in a single instance in the argument in her brief either to support her contentions, or to contradict the findings."

(Reply Brief, p. 77), (referring to the finding of the District Judge that the relation between the National Bank and plaintiff prior to the execution of the instrument of trust was that of *seller and buyer*), "The evidence overwhelmingly supports this finding. Plaintiff's criticism of this finding is that the Court should, in addition thereto, have found that plaintiff be informed of her legal rights in connection with these purchases."

(Reply Brief, p. 77-8), (referring to the question whether or not the relation between plaintiff and the National Bank prior to the execution of the instrument of trust was that of *principal and agent or of cestui que trust and trustee*): "Such argument, which appears to be relied upon by counsel throughout their brief, is fallacious in that it assumes the very fact in issue to be as claimed by counsel, namely, that the relationship between plaintiff and the national bank prior to the execution of the trust instrument was either that of principal and agent or *cestui* and trustee."; and "Since the issue was squarely joined in the pleadings and at the trial what the nature of this prior relationship was, and since the Court, determining in accordance with the convincing weight of the evidence, found that the relationship was not only that of buyer and seller but also that it was so intended by the parties, no duty arose, and it was in fact impossible, to notify plaintiff of alleged legal rights which were non-existent and which would have been existent only in the event the evidence established, and the Court found, that the relationship was that of principal and agent or *cestui* and trustee."

(Reply Brief, pp. 79-80): "We submit that since this case involves questions of fact almost exclusively, the findings of the District Court, which are based upon the preponderance of the evidence, should be sustained. The District Judge having heard the testimony, having observed the witnesses, and having weighed the evidence in the light of all the surrounding facts and circumstances and of the inferences to be drawn therefrom, rendered judgment for the appellees."

> *"California Bank Act,* sec. 25, provides: * * * any bank having departments shall have the right to sell and transfer any bonds, securities or loans *from one department to another* upon receipt of the *actual value* thereof, if such bonds, securities or loans are, under the provisions of this act, a *legal investment* for the department purchasing the same". (Emphasis counsel's).

And further states, Reply Brief, that (p. 68),

> "In its conclusions of law the District Court determined, with reference to the purchases from the bond department after the execution of the trust instrument, that 'the provisions of section 25 of the *California Bank Act* expressly permitted such 'purchases by the trust department from the bond department'. (R. 350.)
>
> "It will be noted that section 25 of the *California Bank Act* contains but two requirements:
>
> *"First.* That the actual value of the securities be paid; and
>
> *"Second.* That the securities purchased be a legal investment for the department purchasing the same".

Followed by the following statement, Reply Brief, that, (p. 69),

> "Section 105 of the *California Bank Act* provides that trust funds may be invested in securities which are legal for investment of the funds of a savings bank *or which are authorized by the trust* INSTRUMENT Article II of the trust instrument provides that 'the trustee shall have full power to * * * invest * * * in such securities, properties, or investments of the character permitted by law for investment of trust funds, or otherwise, * * *'. (R. 64-65)". (Emphasis added).*

Note: Sections 25 and 105, and also section 104, of the *California Bank Act,* have been reprinted, from 1 *Deering, General Laws of California, 1937,* in Appendix J, 195-200, to this Reply Brief.

Section 25, referring to banks which maintain different departments, provides, (App. J 195), as follows:

> "No department, shall receive deposits from any other department of the same corporation; except that the savings department

Under the preceding heading V, "Neither Bothwell nor Berven was a credible witness", we have set forth substantially the testimony of the three principal witnesses in the case, namely, plaintiff, Bothwell and Berven, and, in doing so, we confidently believe that we have demonstrated the fact to be that, in the language of the heading, "Neither Bothwell nor

or the commercial department of any bank may receive deposits from the trust department of the same corporation or association and may set aside, as required by section 105 of this act, bonds or securities of any kind in which savings banks are permitted by law to invest; provided, however, that any bank having departments shall have the right to sell and transfer any bonds, securities or loans from one department to another upon receipt of the actual value thereof, if such bonds, securities or loans are, under the provisions of this act, a legal investment for the department purchasing the same."

Section 105, (App. J 199-200), provides as follows:

"any trust department of any bank doing a departmental business may deposit such funds so held by it with the savings department or the commercial department of the same corporation or association; provided, however, that no such funds so held awaiting investment shall be deposited by any trust department of a departmental bank with the savings department or the commercial department of the same corporation or association or of any corporation or association holding or owning the whole or any part of the capital stock of the trust company making such deposit unless such corporation or association shall first set aside, as security for such deposit, bonds or securities of the kind in which savings banks are permitted to invest and which bonds or securities so set aside shall have a value not less than the funds so deposited; provided, further, that no security shall be required in case of any such part of any such deposits as is insured under the provisions of any law of the United States."

In a later part of his Reply Brief, (pp. 70-1), counsel for defendants makes the following statements:

"Nowhere in that portion of counsel's brief designated 'Argument' is there any criticism of the findings and the conclusions of law in question. In Assignments No. 22, subdivision 5 (R. 802-805), (No. 23, subdivision 2 (R 807-810)), No. 32, subdivisions 4 and 5 (R. 820-823), apparently these findings and the conclusions are intended to be called into question as being unsupported by the evidence and also on the ground that the provisions of section 25 of the *California Bank Act* were not pleaded. We have already pointed to the sufficiency of the supporting evidence *which was admitted without any objection whatsoever.* These matters were directly put in issue by the pleadings. It is true that the

Berven was a credible witness", and that both of them have been thoroughly discredited. The case, therefore, insofar as the testimony on the vital questions of fact involved in the testimony are concerned, stands for its support alone upon the testimony of plaintiff, and the case of the plaintiff is not only unimpaired, but, on the contrary, is strengthened, by the docu-

---

answer did not state 'The defendant relies on section 25 of the *California Bank Act'*. Such pleading would probably have been improper, since the Court will take judicial notice of the provisions of the state law. Thus in *Cyc. Fed. Proc.*, Vol. 3, p. 627, sec. 855, it is said:

" 'It is probably not necessary *that matters of which the court will take judicial notice be alleged in the answer,* but however that may be, an answer is not defective for so doing.' (Emphasis counsel's).

"In the case of *Harpending* v. *Reformed etc. Church* (1842), 16 Pet. 405, 41 U. S. 455, 10 L. ed. 1029, an equity suit was commenced in the Federal Court. The defendants prevailed on the ground that the statute of limitations had barred plaintiffs. On appeal the plaintiffs contended that the statute had not been properly pleaded. Thus (10 L. ed. 1041):

" 'It is insisted that the act of limitations is not relied on *by express reference* to the statute of New York. We think it was unnecessary to rely *in terms* on the statute. It was more convenient not to do so. * * * *The court is judicially bound to take notice of the statutes,* when the facts are stated and relied on as a bar to further proceeding if they are found sufficient.'

"The only two requirements under section 25 of the *California Bank Act* are that the *actual value* of the securities be paid and that the securities be a legal investment for the department purchasing the same". (Emphasis, throughout the foregoing, counsel's).

We further quote as follows from the Reply Brief, (p. 72):

"Section 25 of the *California Bank Act* is *applicable to national as well as to state banks. It also declares the policy of the State of California to be to permit the trust department of a bank to deal with another department thereof.* Thus in *Estate of Smith* (1931), 112 Cal. App. 680, 687, 297 Pac. 927, it was held that where a national bank (Bank of America N. T. & S. A.) was executor of an estate and conducted three departments, commercial, savings and trust, and had deposited in its savings department, moneys it had received as executor, it was entitled to do so on the ground that section 25 of the *Bank Act* permitted such deposit.

mentary evidence, which, in view of our discussion of the documentary evidence, supports, in every respect, the case for plaintiff. If, in the petulant language of counsel for defendants, there has been any conduct on our part which "begs" a disputed question, or if there has been any "failure" in any of our arguments, or if we have "adroitly sidestepped" any disputed

---

"Furthermore, that case recognized that there are natural and intrinsic differences between departmental banks as trustees and others acting in the same capacity. The Court also stated that since the legislature had spoken on the question of the departmentalization of banks the matter was not subject to review by the Courts. (This case is quoted from at page VIII of the Appendix.)

"*Bogert, Trusts and Trustees,* Vol. 3, p. 1544, section 489, *takes the view that section 25 authorizes such purchases.* Thus in footnote 72 it is said:

"'Cal. Gen. Laws 1931, Act. 652, sec. 25 (*Sale from department to department permitted*); * * *.'

"It is well settled that national banks are entitled to conduct a trust business in competition with, and on the same basis as, state banks under the law of the state in which the national bank in question is located. (*First Nat. Bank* v. *Fellows* (1916), 244 U. S. 416, 37 Sup. Ct. Rep. 734, 61 L. Ed. 1233; *Breedlove* v. *Freudenstein* (1937), 89 Fed. (2d) 324 (C. C. A. 5).)" (Emphasis, throughout the foregoing, in part, counsel's, and, in part, added).

(The case of *Estate of Smith*, (or *In re Smith's Estate*), 112 Cal. App. 680, 292 Pac. 927, (1931), which counsel for defendants cites, (Reply Brief, p. 73), arose under provisions of *section 105* of the *California Bank Act*, and it was held that where the Bank of Italy had funds of a trust estate awaiting investment, the Bank was authorized to deposit those funds in its savings bank deposits to the credit of itself, as executor of the estate, and it should be chargeable with interest at its customary rate of four per cent, per annum, compounded semi-annually, and that it was consequently error for the lower court to charge the Bank with the legal rate of seven per cent., from the time of deposit up to the date of its final account. The case decides nothing more, and counsel for defendants is in error when he "submits", (Reply Brief, p. 373), "that the purchases in question were expressly authorized" by the section.)

These statements are confused and either inaccurate or incorrect in the following particulars:

(1). The statement, (Reply Brief, p. 70), that "Nowhere in that portion of counsel's brief designated 'Argument' is there any criticism of the findings and conclusions of law in question" is incorrect.

(2). The statement, (Reply Brief, p. 70), that the assignments of

question, it was incumbent upon counsel for defendants to point out to the Court and to counsel for plaintiff wherein the reprehensible "begging", or the equally reprehensible "failure", or "sidestepping", existed, and this counsel for defendants has completely failed to do.

---

error to the findings of fact and conclusions of law, to which counsel refers, "are intended to be called into question as being unsupported by the evidence", is neither accurate nor correct. There is but one of the three errors assigned as such, namely, No. 32, subdivisions 4 and 5, (App. H 51), and that assignment is as follows: "(4), that the provisions of Section 25 of the *California Bank Act* did not, and do not, expressly, or inferentially, permit any such purchases to be made by the said Trust Department, (or, more accurately, the said National Bank), from the said Bond Department, (or, more accurately, the said National Bank), and, moreover, the provisions of Section 25 of the said *California Bank Act* were not pleaded either by the said Central Bank, or by the said National Bank, or its receiver, the said J. H. Grut, as a defense to the said transactions of purchase and sale; (5), that, consequently, the conclusions of law contained in the said above quotation, (referring to the purchases of the said bonds), that the said National Bank 'was entitled to, and did lawfully, purchase the securities which it did in fact purchase from the bond department', is erroneous, and, on the contrary, the fact is that the said National Bank unlawfully purchased the said bonds, and, for that reason, the plaintiff was and is entitled to a decree rescinding and setting aside the said purchases and rescinding and setting aside the said instrument of trust, as prayed for in the bill of complaint and in the amendments and supplements to the bill of complaint, filed in this action".

(3). We have been unable to find in his Reply Brief, (p. 70), that counsel for defendant ever "pointed to the sufficiency of the supporting evidence"; and, if it be assumed, for the purpose of argument, that any such evidence was admitted, the fact that it was "admitted without any objection whatsoever" would neither add to, nor detract from, the weight of the evidence.

(4). The statement, (Reply Brief, p. 70), that "These matters were directly put in issue by the pleadings" is incorrect. The "matters" were not pleaded, and, consequently, they could not be either "directly", or indirectly, "put in issue by the pleadings".

(5). It is true "that the answer did not state 'The defendant relies on Section 25 of the *California Bank Act'*", and we may agree with counsel for defendants, (Reply Brief, p. 70), that "Such pleading" would not only "probably have been improper", had it been made in the form quoted, but it would have been *unconditionally* improper, not, however, for the reason given by counsel for defendants, that "the Court will take judicial notice of the provisions of the state law", but for the reason that the pleading would have tendered no issue.

Attention has ben directed to the fact that the provisions of section 25 of the *California Bank Act,* under which, so it is contended by counsel for defendants, the National Bank was authorized to purchase securities, prior to the execution of the instrument of trust, from itself, through its bond department, for the trust estate, and that such fact was neither pleaded, nor even referred to, in the answers, and, therefore, no issue was presented by the pleadings on which the District Judge was justified in finding, in Finding No. 32, (App. H 51), and that, in this connection, counsel for defendants, while admitting that the provisions of the section were not pleaded, nevertheless, counsel for defendants, in his Reply Brief, (p. 70), states that "We have already pointed to the sufficiency of the supporting evidence, *which was admitted without any objection whatsoever",* and that "These matters were directly put in issue by the pleadings", (emphasis counsel's), for the reason, (expressed somewhat doubtfully), that the Court would take "judicial notice of the provisions of the state law", referring, in this connection, to 3 *Cyclopedia Federal Procedure,* sec. 855, p. 627, and to *Harpending v. Reformed etc. Dutch Church,* 16 Pet. 405, 10 L. Ed. 1029, (1842).

But, in the first place, we are not aware of any authority, (and certainly counsel for defendants has cited none), that because the evidence—assuming, against the fact, that there was any evidence—was admitted without any objection, the mere admission of the evidence without objection would present any issue on which the Court would be justified in making a finding; and, while it is true, as counsel for defendants states in his Reply Brief, (p. 70), that the answers did not state that "defendant relies on section 25 of the *California Bank Act",* it is also true that if the answers had contained any such allegation, the pleading, without question, would not have been in proper form to raise an issue. We believe, however, that the defense, if it was a defense, should have been pleaded by the allegation, for example, that "the purchases were authorized under the provisions of the section". We believe, also, that such an allegation would be supported by the two authorities cited by counsel for defendants, namely, 3 *Cyclopedia Federal Procedure,* sec. 855, p. 627, and *Harpending v. Reformed etc. Dutch Church,* 16 Pet. 405, 10 L. Ed. 1029. But this discussion is purely theoretical, since the provisions of the section were not, in any manner, pleaded as an authorization for the otherwise unlawful purchases.

Counsel for defendants further states, as we understand counsel, that if the provisions authorized the purchases, the National Bank would be bound to recognize the authorization as valid. But this conclusion by no means follows, since it is well settled that, while national banks are subject, in many respects, to legislative enactments of the states, yet a state cannot, by any legislation, impair the powers, rights or duties of national banks, as provided by the enactments of the Congress. Nevertheless, an enactment of a state legislature which provided that a corporate trustee might lawfully purchase with trust funds securities owned by it, from itself, for the trust estate, would obviously be so subversive of good morals and of sound public policy that it is more than doubtful if either the Congress, or the administrative officers of the Federal government, or the Federal courts would be bound by such an enactment:

> *Davis v. Elmira Savings Bk.,* 161 U. S. 275, 283, 40 L. Ed. 700, 701, (1896);
>
> *Easton v. Iowa,* 188 U. S. 220, 238, 47 L. Ed. 452, 459, (1903);
>
> *First National Bank of San Jose v. State of California,* 262 U. S. 366, 369, 67 L. Ed. 1030, 1035, (1923);
>
> *Jennings v. United States Fidelity & Guaranty Co.,* 294 U. S. 216, 225-6, 79 L. Ed. 869, 875-6, (1935).

As was said in the first of these cases, Mr. Justice White, (afterwards Chief Justice White), writing the opinion:

"National banks are instrumentalities of the Federal government, created 'for a public 'purpose, and as such necessarily subject to the paramount authority of the United States. It follows that any attempt by a state to define their duties or control the conduct of their affairs is absolutely void, wherever such attempted exercise of authority expressly conflicts with the laws of the United States and either frustrates the purpose of the national legislation *or impairs the efficiency of these agencies of the Federal government to discharge the duties, for the performance of which they are created.* These principles are axiomatic and are sanctioned by the repeated adjudications of this court". (Emphasis added).

We have no doubt that if the state had enacted such a provision, whether in the *California Bank Act,* or otherwise, the comptroller of the currency, through his examiners, would not have approved of an investment by a national bank of trust funds in securities, or other property, which the bank itself owned, either wholly or in part.

We may add, in this connection, that the state courts do not favor enactments which permit, or apparently permit, corporate trustees to invest trust estate funds in securities, such as so-called "participating" securities, owned by the trustees:

> *St. Paul Trust Co. v. Strong,* 85 Minn. 1, 9, 88 N. W. 256, 258, (1901);
> *Kelly v. First Minneapolis Trust Co.,* 178 Minn. 215, 217, 276 N. W. 696, (1929);
> *In re Schmidt's Estate,* 163 Misc. 156, 297 N. Y. S. 328, (1937).

In the case of *Kelly v. First Minneapolis Trust Co., supra,* (Chief Justice Wilson writing the opinion), it was said:

> "When a statute which is intended to make an innovation upon the common law is susceptible of more than one construction, it is not to be construed as altering the common law further than the language of the statute clearly and necessarily requires. This fundamental proposition

arises out of the rule that statutes in derogation of the common law are to be strictly construed".

And it was further said that

"the statutory law regulating trust companies was enacted for the protection of their patrons. It is stringent. The relaxation contended would be a rather fundamental departure. We construe the intention of the legislature to depart from a thoroughly established doctrine of the common law, especially when supported by principles and morals, only when it has clearly expressed such intention. All doubtful language must be construed against the intention to make such change".

We have heretofore, under heading IV, in this brief formulated and discussed that wherever a relation of trust and confidence exists, whether it be the conventional relation of trustee and cestui que trust, (as in the instant case), or the relation between a board of directors, or officers, of a corporation, and its stockholders, or the relation between an agent and principal, or, (notwithstanding what counsel for defendants may say to the contrary), even the relation between a seller and buyer, it is necessary for the fiduciary to allege, and also to prove, that the beneficiary had full knowledge of all the material facts, and also had full knowledge of all the legal obligations of the fiduciary, and of the corresponding legal rights of the beneficiary, relating to the transaction, and, moreover, it is incumbent upon the fiduciary to see to it that the beneficiary has such full and complete knowledge. Defendants have not even attempted to support this burden.

But, says counsel for defendants, in a somewhat lengthy argument, (Reply Brief, pp. 64-8), the principle is not applicable to a case in which a cestui que trust previously consents to what would otherwise be a violation of the obligations of the trustee, but only in a case in which the cestui que trust ratifies or acquiesces in the trustee's unlawful transaction subsequent to the transaction. If counsel for defendants, however, had examined the cases which we have cited in our Opening Brief, (pp. 52-9), with only a slight degree of care, he would have ascertained that the cases make no such distinction, and that one of the cases first cited by us in our Opening Brief, (p. 53), is the case of *McAllister v. McAllister,* 120 N. J. Eq. 407, 414, 180 At. 723, 728, (aff'd. 121 N. J. Eq. 264, 190 At. 52), (1936), in which the beneficiary consented in advance to what would otherwise be a violation on the part of the trustees of the obligations imposed upon them by the law. Moreover, there is no reason, (and none has been suggested by counsel for defendants), for any distinction between a consent by a beneficiary whether prior or subsequent to the otherwise unlawful transaction.*

Note: The case of *Ungrich v. Ungrich,* 131 App. Div. 24, 115 N. Y. S. 413 (1909), on which counsel for defendants has placed considerable stress, (Reply Brief, p. 66), as a case in which, so counsel says, the "distinction was recognized", that is, the "distinction" between a precedent consent, and a subsequent ratification or acquiescence, by a cestui que trust of what would otherwise have been an unlawful purchase by a trustee of property belonging to the trust estate, does not "recognize" any such "distinction" at all, but holds, as expressed in an accurate and precise paragraph, (115 N. Y. S. 414), of the syllabus to the case, that "Where a cestui que trust sanctioned and assented to a purchase by his trustee of the trust estate, the trustee to hold title was not required to show that the cestui que trust ratified the transfer after having been informed of the facts and the law." The quotation by counsel for defendants from the opinion in the case, (Reply Brief, 67), leads to the belief that counsel did not understand the facts of the case and that he has misunderstood what the court decided. The case is not an authority for defendants, but, on the contrary, it is an authority for plaintiff. The facts of the case are, substantially, as follows:

The father, Henry Ungrich, of two sons, Henry Jr. and Martin Louis, died leaving a will by which he gave to his three executors and trustees, who were his two sons, Henry, Jr. and Martin, and a nephew, all his property, consisting largely of real estate, apparently situated in New York City, in trust, to sell the property, at their discretion, and to convert it into cash, and to pay the one-half part to Henry, Jr. absolutely, and to hold the other one-half part to the use of Martin, during the latter's lifetime, and, on his death, to pay the principal to Henry, Jr., if living, or to his issue, in the event of his death, and, in default of issue, to certain designated persons. Until a sale of the property was made, one-half of the net income therefrom was to be paid to Martin. Quarterly statements of the income of the property and of the disburse-

But there is nothing in any of the sections of the *California Bank Act,* namely, sections 25, 105 and 104, which provides, either expressly or by implication, the startling proposition that a bank, such as the National Bank, might lawfully purchase from itself, through its bond department, securities for the investment of funds of a trust estate of which it was the trustee, and it is doubtful, if any of the sections did so provide,

---

ments connected therewith were rendered by the executors and trustees, and one-half of the net rentals from the property were paid by the executors and trustees to Martin, (who, as just mentioned, was, himself, one of the executors and trustees), for something over a year.

Shortly after his father's death, Martin, (who was an architect by profession), complained to his co-executors and trustees, (some of the complaints being in his own letters, written while he was away on a vacation), of the uncertainty of the income and of the amounts expended on the property, and indicated a desire, (because of descriptions of the property, which he requested and which were sent to him, and from which he could prepare diagrams for use of appraisers of the property), that the property be sold. Martin, apparently, had either suggested to Henry, Jr., or had requested him, to purchase all the property; but Henry, Jr., had expressed a desire to purchase only one of the parcels of the property. Apparently, however, Henry, Jr., finally offered to purchase all of the property for between $140,000 and $150,000, of which $7,500 was to be paid in cash, and the balance secured by a mortgage of the property, but Martin thought the price too low. Finally after numerous communications and conferences between Martin and Henry, Jr., they met with their co-executor and trustee, and with the attorney for the estate, in the office of the latter, with the result that, acting on the advice of the attorney, an appraisal of the property was made by a competent and disinterested appraiser, agreed upon, at the total sum of $152,000, and the property was sold to Henry, Jr. for the sum (above the appraisal), of $157,000, of which one-half, or the sum of $78,500, was paid in cash, and the remainder secured by purchase money mortgages on the various parcels of the property, with interest at 4% per annum.

The attorney had informed the executors and trustees that the property could not be sold by them to one of themselves, but Martin replied, (115 N. Y. S. 416), that if he and Henry, Jr. were "satisfied," "he did not see who could object" to Henry, Jr. buying the property, but he "insisted that the price should be $5,000 more than the appraisal, making it $157,000, and that the interest on the mortgage should be more than 4 per cent., and that if Henry, Jr. bought any, he should buy all, and not select the best, and that personally he thought the property should be held"; but "Henry insisted that, by reason of the income from

that the provisions would be valid against the rule, founded upon good morals and a wise public policy, that a trustee cannot deal with itself in a case, such as the instant case, of a national bank.

---

the property, he would not pay more than 4 per cent. on the mortgages, and his appraisal was less than the price proposed to be given."

It was finally agreed that the property would be purchased by Henry, Jr. for the total price of $157,000, and, to overcome the objection of the attorney, that the property could not be purchased by Henry, Jr., (one of the executors and trustees), a deed of the property would be made to one Davenport, who was a clerk in the attorney's office, who would execute back purchase money mortgages bearing interest at the rate of 4% per annum for the deferred payments of one-half of the purchase price, distributed over the various parcels of the property. A contract, in duplicate, to this effect, was prepared and executed, after Martin had said, in reply to a question, that the contract "was satisfactory to him", and the deed of the property was executed by the executors and trustees to Davenport for an expressed consideration of $157,000, who, in turn, executed to the executors and trustees purchase money mortgages for $78,000, or for one-half of the purchase price, with interest at the rate of 4% per annum, and who also executed to Henry, Jr. a deed of the property, subject to the mortgages, Henry, Jr. apparently having paid to his co-executors and trustee the remaining one-half of the purchase price.

The attorney, after Martin had expressed himself as satisfied with the contract, wrote on each of the duplicates of the contract the words "contract approved by me", under which Martin wrote his name. In addition to the contract, and to the "approval", which Martin signed, "a formal paper", (which Martin signed and acknowledged on the same day when the deed to Davenport and the latter's conveyances to Henry, Jr. were executed), was drawn, reciting, (115 N. Y. S. p. 416), that Henry, Jr. had "proposed to purchase all the real property for the consideration of $157,000" at Martin's request and with his consent and approval and full knowledge."

About one year thereafter, Martin and his wife executed to Henry, Jr., at the latter's request, and because his title to the property was questioned, three deeds to the property. A settlement of the personal property of the estate was arranged at the time, or shortly after, the execution of the deed to Davenport, and the execution by him of the purchase money mortgages, and of the deed subject to the mortgages, from him to Henry, Jr. of the property, and for four years thereafter Martin accepted, without complaint, the interest from the mortgages, and accountings in the surrogate's court were had by the executors, of which Martin had notice.

Henry, Jr. thereafter, and after he had made certain improvements on some of the parcels of the property, sold the same at a loss, but, on the

It is, therefore, submitted that, as stated in the heading for this discussion, plaintiff never directed or consented to the purchases by the National Bank of securities for the trust estate, created by the instrument of trust, from itself, through its bond deparment; nor did the provisions of section 25 of the *California Bank Act,* expressly or by implication, permit such purchases to be made by the trust department from the bond department of the National Bank.

---

other hand, sold one of the parcels at a profit of upwards of $100,000. Upon learning of this latter transaction, Martin brought the instant action, (apparently on the theory that, in addition to his consent to the purchase of the property by Henry, Jr. before the purchase was made, *a ratification of the purchase by him was necessary),* to declare the purchase by Henry, Jr. to be unlawful, as in contravention of his duty as trustee, and to impose a trust in Martin's favor upon one-half of the profits, which had been made by Henry, Jr., and for the removal of the latter as trustee and for the substitution in his place of another trustee.

The appellate court, in reversing a judgment in Martin's favor, besides holding as reported in the paragraph of the syllabus above quoted, held, as reported in another paragraph of the syllabus, (115 N. Y. S. 414), as follows:

> "Where a cestui que trust assented to a purchase by the trustee of the trust estate, and the evidence showed that the price paid by the trustee was adequate, and there was nothing to show representations as to rents produced by the property or of anything in connection with the property except its value, and the cestui que trust had knowledge of the value of buildings and building sites, and he understood the effect of the instruments executed by him in the transfer to the trustee, the cestui que trust could not set aside the sale, though the trustee made large profits by his purchase."

The case, therefore, presents the remarkable contention, in effect, of a cestui que trust, that, although he had formally, and in most carefully prepared writings, consented to the otherwise unlawful purchase by the trustee of property of the trust estate, the formal writings amounted to a *ratification,* which required a repetition by the trustee to the cestui que trust of all the facts, previously consented to by the cestui que trust, relating to the purchase prior to its consummation, and of all the legal obligations of the trustee and the corresponding rights of the cestui que trust relating thereto,—a contention, it is submitted, that is nothing short of an absurdity.

VII.

**IT IS IMMATERIAL THAT A TRUSTEE OR OTHER FIDU-
CIARY DID NOT PROFIT, OR THAT THE CESTUI
QUE TRUST OR OTHER BENEFICIARY DID NOT
SUSTAIN A LOSS, OR EVEN THAT HE BENEFITED,
OR THAT THE TRUSTEE, OR OTHER FIDUCIARY,
ACTED IN GOOD FAITH, IN THE VIOLATION BY
THE TRUSTEE OR OTHER FIDUCIARY OF HIS
DUTY OF GOOD FAITH AND LOYALTY TO HIS
CESTUI QUE TRUST OR OTHER BENEFICIARY.**

It is alleged in the complaint that in each of the transactions
of purchase of securities, prior to the execution of the instrument of trust, by the National Bank for plaintiff from itself,
through Bothwell, as the manager of its bond department, as
well as in the first four purchases of securities subsequent to the
execution of the instrument, in the year 1930, by the National
Bank from itself, through Bothwell, as the manager of its bond
department, for the trust estate, the National Bank made a
profit, which the Bank concealed from plaintiff. These allegations were made solely as allegations of constructive fraud, in
aggravation of the wrongdoing of the National Bank. Notwithstanding this fact, some stress seems to be placed by counsel
for defendants, (Reply Brief, p. 56), upon the fact that in certain instances of purchases, in particular those which were made,
in the year 1930, and, therefore, subsequent to the execution of
the instrument of trust, by the National Bank, through its bond
department, for the trust estate, the profits were small.

This fact that the profits were comparatively small in those
instances was and is of no importance, in the absence of allegations of actual, as distinct from constructive, fraud, other
than as matters in aggravation of the charges by plaintiff against
the National Bank of the unlawful character of the purchases.
On the whole, however, while the profits to the National Bank
from this source were considerable, and were increased from
interest on the securities and gains over the purchases on sales,

redemptions and maturities of securities, from time to time, the aggregate gains were small when compared with the losses both of principal, as well as interest, in many instances, (R 505-6, 645-646½, Plf's Exs. 47 and 48; R 506-9, 526-7, 754-6, Defts' Exs. CC, DD and EE); and the losses indicate gross careless-ness, to say the least, on the part of the National Bank, not only in the initial investment of plaintiff's funds, but in looking after plaintiff's investments after the same had been made.*

*Note: (1), schedules "A" and "B", (Pl's Ex. 47, and Pl's Ex. 48, R 645-646½) prospectus, (Pl's Ex. 58, R 656), and 4 letters, namely, of August 24, 1934, from Berven to the writer of this brief, (Pl's Ex. 54, R 652), of August 29, 1934, from the writer of this brief to Berven, (Pl's Ex. 55, R 653), of September 12, 1934, from Berven to the writer of this brief, (Pl's Ex. 56, R 654), and of September 13, 1934, from the writer of this brief to Berven, (Pl's Ex. 57, R 655), all relating to the "7½% Secured Sinking Fund Gold Bonds" of the *Province of Buenos Aires, Argentine;* (2), prospectus of January 1, 1927, (Pl's Ex. 59, R 661), all relating to the so-called *"Guaranteed and Secured* Sinking Fund 7½% Gold Bonds" of the *Province of Callao, Peru;* (3), circular letter of the National Bank, Bond Department, addressed to the "Holders of *Medford Irrigation District* 6% Bonds", (Pl's Ex. 24, R 565), and letter of August 16, 1933, from Geo. T. Petersen, assistant trust officer of the Central Bank, addressed to the writer of this brief, enclosing circular letter of August 22, 1933, addressed to the "Bond Holders of *Medford Irrigation District"*, signed by E. D. Bothwell and others, (Pl's Ex. 25, R 568); (4), descriptions, *if any,* of properties mortgaged, or trans-ferred in trust, in the various documents, (Pl's Ex. 28-31, R 579-612), of the so-called "Chattel Mortgage and Trust Indenture", or "Trust Agreement", of the *Jackson Furniture Company,* the so-called "Chattel Mortgage and Trust Indenture", or "Trust Indenture of Mortgage", of *Alameda Park Co.,* the so-called "Chattel Mortgage and Trust Inden-ture", or "Trust Indenture", of *Alameda Investment Company,* and the so-called "Trust Indenture" of *Berkeley Terminal Properties, Inc.,* re-spectively.

It will be readily seen from the foregoing exhibits that the so-called "bonds" of the *Province of Buenos Aires* and of the *Province of Callao* are not bonds, but are unenforceable obligations of governmental subdi-visions or agencies; that the so-called "bonds" of the *Medford Irrigation District,* likewise, were not bonds, but were mere obligations of the Dis-trict, the payment of which was dependent upon the collection of assess-ments, practically unenforceable, against the lands of the District; that the so-called "Sinking Fund Gold Notes" of the *Jackson Furniture Com-pany* were not bonds, but were, as they were called, "notes", and that the "notes" were not secured by any property whatever, the only obliga-tions of the Company being "promises", some of which being that it

The authorities which support the rules formulated by us in the foregoing heading VII are very numerous, and, from the numerous authorities, the following have been selected as supporting the rules:

> 2 *Pomeroy, Equity Jurisprudence*, sec. 958, (4th ed.), tit. "Constructive Fraud", (Trustee);
>
> 2 *Id.*, sec. 959, (Agent);
>
> 3 *Bogert, Trusts and Trustees*, sec. 484, tit. "Constructive Fraud".
>
> 1 *Restatement, Trusts*, sec. 170, subsection (1), p. 431, and comments (a) and (b) on subsection (1), pp. 431-2;
>
> 2 *Restatement, Agency*, sec. 389, comment c, p. 474;
>
> 2 *C. J.*, p. 703, sec. 361, tit. "Agency";
>
> 2 *Am. Jur.*, p. 213, sec. 265, tit. "Agency";
>
> 25 *Cal. Jur.*, p. 136, sec. 13, tit. "Trusts";
>
> *Magruder* v. *Drury*, 235 U. S. 106, 59 L. Ed. 151, (1914);
>
> *Gates* v. *Plainfield Trust Co.*, 121 N. J. Eq. 460, 191 At. 304, (1937);
>
> *In re Bender's Estate*, 122 N. J. Eq. 192, 192 At. 718, (1937);
>
> *Tracy* v. *Central Trust Co.*, 327 Pa. 77, 192 At. 809, (1937).

---

would "not" do certain things, (R 579), and the fact that the Company paid the notes in full, (Defts' Ex. DD, R 755), was due more to good fortune than to the sagacity and propriety of the officials of the National Bank in investing plaintiff's funds in the "notes"; that the so-called "Collateral Trust Gold Bonds" of the *Alameda Investment Company* are not bonds, but are mere obligations of the Company to pay, and are secured by no property other than promissory notes and mortgages or deeds of trust, and the payment of the obligations of the Company depends upon the collectability of the notes, which, thus far, apparently, has not been conspicuously successful; that the so-called "Gold Bonds" of the *Alameda Park Co.*, an amusement resort "at Neptune Beach", Alameda, (Plf's Ex. 29, R 586), are secured by real estate in the City of Alameda, considerable portions of which are "Salt Marsh and Tide Lands", and the personal property securing the bonds actually includes a ludicrously miscellaneous assortment of "cafeteria equipment, consisting of pots, dishes, washing machines and *other* equipment", and "bathing suits and towels"; that the so-called "Sinking Fund Gold Bonds" of the *Berkeley Terminal Properties, Inc.* is secured by real estate on which the "Properties, Inc." promised to erect buildings with some of the moneys ob-

These propositions are aside from the rule that if a relation of trust and confidence exists, whether it be the conventional re-

tained by the sale of the bonds, (Plf's Ex. 31, R 612-4, 623-4) ; and that in each of the "Indentures" of the 4 mentioned corporations the National Bank is named as the trustee, and thus the National Bank occupied a dual position towards the companies and towards their bondholders, including plaintiff, to whom it sold, through its bond department, large blocks of bonds.

It will also be readily seen from the foregoing schedules, "A" and "B", and from a circular letter, dated April 7, 1933, (Pl's Ex. 33, R 625), addressed by the "Bond Holders Committee, *Fageol Motors Company*", to the "Non-Depositing Bond Holders" of that Company, and from the 4 letters, (Pl's Exs. 26, 34-6, R 571, 628-30), that the only security for the payment of the obligations of the Company is a royalty sales contract of motor vehicles, in which, for the $10,000 of plaintiff's money invested, liquidating dividends of the Company, in bankruptcy, amounting to less than $3,000, have been paid, with very little prospects of other liquidating dividends; that the *St. Louis Gas and Coke Company* and the *Southern United Gas Company* have been in default in their respective interest payments since 1932, (schedule "B") ; and, likewise, that the *Central West Public Service Company* has been in default in its interest payments since 1932, (Plf's Ex. 48, R 646-646½), and the mortgage securing the Company's obligations is a second mortgage, with probably sufficient property only to pay off the obligations under the first mortgage, (Pl's Ex. 26, R 572).

It should have been perfectly obvious to Berven, at the time of the preparation of the instrument of trust by him, (with the assistance of one of the National Bank's attorneys), that the bonds and notes which had been purchased for plaintiff by the National Bank, through its bond department, were not of the type in which plaintiff's funds should have been invested, and, particularly so, in the four instances in which the National Bank occupied the dual position towards the National Bank, on the one hand, and the bondholders, on the other. Moreover, the care and skill which the National Bank, as a compensated corporate trustee, held itself out to the world as possessing, namely, that which an individual of ordinary prudence would use, not in the management of his own property, but in the management of a trust estate committed to his care, did not cease with the acceptance of the trust, but continued during the constantly changing conditions requiring the dispositions of the bonds and notes, or some of them, and the reinvestment of the proceeds. The stark fact, however, was, that neither Berven nor Read, (who were charged with knowledge of the situation, even if they had not actually been informed of it), had the courage of insisting that many of the bonds and notes should be at once disposed of and the proceeds of such disposition be reinvested in bonds and notes of a different type. Temporizing by them had the inevitable result that the situation did not improve, that

lation of trustee and cestui que trust, or the relation between a board of directors, or officers, of a corporation, and its stockholders, or the relation between an agent and principal, or even the relation betwen a seller and buyer, it is necessary for the fiduciary, in confession and avoidance of a transaction in violation of his obligations, to allege, and also to prove, that the beneficiary had full knowledge of all the material facts, and also had full knowledge of all the legal obligations of the fiduciary, and of all the corresponding legal rights of the beneficiary, relating to the transaction.

It is sufficient, in support of the rule formulated in the last above heading, to quote from one of the foregoing authorities, namely, 1 *Restatement, Trusts,* sec. 170, subsection (1), and comments (a) and (b) on subsection (1), pp. 431-2, as follows:

> *"Sec. 170. Duty of Loyalty.*
>
> "(1) The trustee is under a duty to the beneficiary to administer the trust solely in the interest of the beneficiary.
>
> "(2) The trustee in dealing with the beneficiary on the trustee's own account is under a duty to the beneficiary to deal fairly with him and to communicate to him all material facts in connection with the transaction which the trustee knows or should know.
>
> *"Comment on Subsection* (1):
>
> *"a. Fiduciary relation.* A trustee is in a fiduciary relation to the beneficiary and as to matters within the scope of the relation he is under a duty not to profit at the expense of the beneficiary and not to enter into competition with him

---

Read resigned, and that Bothwell lost his position with the National Bank.

In addition to the case of *In re Cook's Estate,* 20 Del. Ch. 123, 171 At. 730, reproduced in full in Appendix J 150, to this brief, the following are cited on the questions here under immediate consideration: 1 *Restatement, Trusts,* sec. 227, pp. 645-59; 3 *Bogert, Trusts and Trustees,* sec. 611, pp. 1938-50; *United States Nat. Bank & Trust Co. v. Sullivan,* 69 F. (2d) 412, C. C. A. 7th, (1934); *Tannenbaum v. Seacoast Trust Co.,* 16 N. J. Misc. 234, 198, 855 (1938); and *Marshall v. Frazer,* 80 P. (2d) 12, (Oreg., 1938).

without his consent, unless authorized to do so by the terms
of the trust or by a proper court.

"*b. Sale of trust property to the trustee individually.*
A trustee with power to sell trust property is under a duty
not to sell to himself either by private sale or at auction,
whether the property has a market price or not, and whether
or not the trustee makes a profit thereby. It is immaterial
that the trustee acts in good faith in purchasing trust property for himself, and that he pays a fair consideration".

In the case of *Magruder* v. *Drury, supra,* the rule formulated
in the last preceding heading, to the effect that it is immaterial
that a fiduciary did not profit, or that the beneficiary did not
sustain a loss, or even that the beneficiary benefitted, or that the
fiduciary acted in good faith, in the violation by the fiduciary
of his duty of good faith and loyalty to his beneficiary, was applied with much severity. The facts of the case are as follows:

Two persons, namely, Samuel Maddox and Samuel A. Drury,
had been appointed by the Supreme Court of the District of
Columbia the trustees for two minors, namely, Alexander R.
Magruder and Isabel R. Magruder, who were the beneficiaries
of trusts created by the will of their grandfather, William A.
Richardson, deceased.

Drury was a member of Arms & Drury, a firm of real estate
brokers. The firm made loans, from time to time, of the firm's
own moneys on promissory notes, secured by real estate, charging, for their services, the borrowers a commission of from one
to two per cent., dependent upon the circumstances, for the making of the loans. As the loans were paid off, the notes were
taken over by the firm at their face value, with accrued interest.

Drury invested the trust funds in the purchase of certain of
the notes, paying therefor the face value thereof, with accrued
interest, without any profit to the firm on the sales.

Reports, made by the trustees, were referred by the Supreme
Court of the District to an auditor to state the final account of
the trustees. The beneficiaries excepted to the account of the

auditor, which allowed the commissions. The Supreme Court of the District, however, allowed the commissions, and the allowance was approved by the Court of Appeals of the District.

The United States Supreme Court, while affirming, on appeal, the decree of the lower courts in other respects, reversed the decree as to the commissions, on the ground that a trustee can make no profit out of his trust, although no injury was intended, and none was, in fact, done, to the trust estate.

The United States Supreme Court first quoted from the auditor's report, as follows, (235 U. S. 118, 59 L. Ed. 156):

" 'No profit was made by the firm of Arms & Drury on the sales of the notes to the trustees. . . . *The transactions of Arms & Drury, with the trustees were in the regular course of their business, in which they had their own monies invested. They cost the estate not a penny more than if the transactions had been with some other firm or individual.* If the firm of Arms & Drury, out of their own monies, made loans on promissory notes, upon which loans were paid by the borrower the customary brokerages, those were profits on their own funds, in which this estate could have no interest, and in which it could acquire no interest by reason of the subsequent purchase of those notes by the trustees for their real value, any more than could any of the purchasers of such notes from Arms & Drury claim such an interest. *No charge of malfeasance or misfeasance is made against the trustees or that by reason of these transactions the trustees benefitted in any manner out of the money of this estate.* On the contrary, the relation of the firm of Arms & Drury to Drury and Maddox, trustees, benefitted the estate, by enabling the trustees at all times to make immediate re-investment of its funds, without loss of income, and by enabling the trustees to at all times readily procure reinvestments without payment of brokerage, a brokerage not uncommonly charged the lender for placing his money, as well as the borrower for procuring his loan in times of stringency. *The application of the well known rule in equity should rather, therefore, be in favor of the trustees than against them with respect to these transactions.* The objection narrows itself to a claim that Drury by reason of his position as trustee, should in addition to the benefit of his valuable services, commercial knowledge, and business acumen, made the estate a gift of profits on his individual monies, to which the estate is in no wise entitled, and to which it could not make a semblance of reasonable claim, had the trustees been other than Drury or the agents of the estate been other than Arms and Drury.' " (Emphasis added).

The United States Supreme Court continued, (235 U. S. 119, 59 L., Ed. 156):

"*It is a well settled rule that a trustee can make no profit out of his trust. The rule in such cases springs from his duty to protect the interests of the estate, and not to permit his personal interest to in any wise conflict with his duty in that respect. The intention is to provide against any possible selfish interest exercising an influence which can interefere with the faithful discharge of the duty which is owing in a fiduciary capacity.* 'It therefore prohibits a party from purchasing on his own account that which his duty or trust requires him to sell on account of another, and from purchasing on account of another that which he sells on his own account. In effect, he is not allowed to unite the two opposite characters of buyer and seller, because his interests, when he is the seller or buyer on his own account, are directly conflicting with those of the person on whose account he buys or sells'. *Michoud* v. *Girod*, 4 How. 503, 555, (11 L. Ed. 1076, 1099).

"*It makes no difference that the estate was not a loser in the transaction or that the commission was no more than the services were reasonably worth. It is the relation of the trustee to the estate which prevents his dealing in such way as to make a personal profit for himself.* The findings show that the firm of which Mr. Drury was a member, in making the loans evidenced by these notes, was allowed a commission of one to two per cent. This profit was in fact realized when the notes were turned over to the estate at face value and accrued interest. The value of the notes when they were turned over depended on the responsibility and security back of them. When the notes were sold to the estate it took the risk of payment without loss. *While no wrong was intended, and none was in fact done to the estate, we think, nevertheless, that upon the principles governing the duty of a trustee, the contention that this profit could not be taken by Mr. Drury owing to his relation to the estate, should have been sustained".* (Emphasis added.)

---

*Note: It will be observed that the beneficiaries did not ask that the transactions in the purchases of the notes for the trust estate be *rescinded*, as they might have done, *but asked, as they had the right to do, that the profits on the transactions, in the commissions received by the firm, or rather Drury's share of the commissions, be accounted for by, and be charged against, the trustees.*

VIII.

A CORPORATE TRUSTEE, SUCH AS THE NATIONAL
BANK, COULD NOT, AND CANNOT, LAWFULLY PUR-
CHASE SECURITIES FROM ONE OF ITS DEPART-
MENTS FOR ANOTHER OF ITS DEPARTMENTS,
SINCE THE DEPARTMENTS ARE NOT, IN ANY
SENSE, SEPARATE AND DISTINCT ENTITIES, BUT
ARE MERE INSTRUMENTALITIES FOR THE CON-
VENIENT TRANSACTION OF BUSINESS BY THE COR-
PORATION. NOR CAN A CORPORATE TRUSTEE
LAWFULLY PURCHASE SECURITIES FROM AN-
OTHER CORPORATION IN WHICH IT IS INTER-
ESTED AS A STOCKHOLDER.

The first of these propositions applies to the purchases of
securities by the National Bank, both prior and subsequent to
the execution of the instrument of trust, for plaintiff, or for the
trust estate, as the case may be, from itself, through its bond
department, and is well sustained by eminent authority of
1 *Restatement, Trusts,* sec. 170, p. 431, comment i, and illustrations 3, 4 and 5, p. 436, from which we quote as follows:

> "*i. Sale to trust by corporate trustee.* A corporate trustee
> violates its duty to the beneficiary if it purchases property
> for the trust from one of its departments, as where it pur-
> chases for the trust securities owned by it in its securities or
> banking department. A corporate trustee cannot properly
> purchase for the trust property owned by an affiliated or
> subsidiary corporation in which it has the entire interest or
> a controlling interest or an interest of such a substantial
> nature that there would be a temptation to consider its own
> advantage in making the sale and not to consider solely the
> advantage to the beneficiaries of the trust. The rule is the
> same where the shares of the selling corporation are owned
> by the shareholders of the corporate trustee. So also, a
> corporate trustee cannot properly purchase property for the
> trust from one of its officers or directors.

"*Illustrations:*

"3. *A, a trust company, is trustee for B. A purchases bonds for the trust from its own securities department. A commits a breach of trust in so doing.* (Emphasis added).

"4· A, a trust company, is trustee for B. A owns all the shares of C, a corporation dealing in securities. A as trustee purchases bonds from C. A commits a breach of trust in so doing.

"5· The facts are the same as in Illustration 4, except that the shares of C are held in trust for the shareholders of A and the beneficial interests in the shares of C are transferable only with the shares of A. A commits a breach of trust in purchasing for the trust property owned by C".

The second of the foregoing propositions is well illustrated by the case of *In re Jones' Estate,* 155 Misc. 315, 280 N. Y. S. 521, (1935), which was a proceeding in a surrogate's court, of New York, for an accounting by the receiver, in liquidation, of the First National Bank & Trust Company of Yonkers, as testamentary trustee of Ellen Major Jones, deceased.

The First National Bank of Yonkers was named in the will of the decedent as trustee of trusts created by the will. This bank qualified and continued to act as such trustee until it was succeeded, as such trustee, by merger with the First National Bank & Trust Company.

Objections to the account of the successor trustee, (the First National Bank & Trust Company), was filed by the adult life beneficiary of the trusts, and also by the guardian for the infant remainderman, on the ground that the Bank & Trust Company had unlawfully invested funds of the trust estate, to the extent of the sum of $8,000, in a mortgage participation certificate, which had been issued by the Bank & Trust Company in a mortgage held by it in its individual capacity upon land of one of its affiliates, namely, the Yonkers Safe Deposit Company.

The mortgage had been made by the Esemes Realty Corporation to the First National Bank of Yonkers, on July 25, 1928, and was upon improved real property situated in Yonkers. On October 18, 1928, the property was conveyed by the Esemes Realty Corporation to the Yonkers Securities Corporation. And the participation certificate was issued by *the successor trustee,* on June 16, 1930, at which time the property, subject to the mortgage to the First National Bank, was owned by the Securities Corporation.

The principal of the mortgage was past due at the time the certificate was issued, and the mortgage had not been extended. Previously, and on January 24, 1930, a second mortgage, which had been placed upon the property, was assigned to the Safe Deposit Company. The first mortgage, (of which the $8,000 certificate formed a part), was held by the Bank & Trust Company, and the second mortgage was held by the Safe Deposit Company.

One Palmer was the president, and one Snodgrass was the vice president, of all three corporations, namely, the Bank & Trust Company, the Securities Corporation and the Safe Deposit Company, and one Bright was the cashier and the trust officer of the Bank & Trust Company, and the secretary of the two other corporations. The same three men were the directors of the Securities Corporation, and were three of the five directors of the Safe Deposit Company. These three men, and the other principal officers of the Bank & Trust Company, owned the controlling stock interest of the Bank & Trust Company. The Bank & Trust Company owned 995 of the 1,000 issued shares of the Safe Deposit Company, and the five directors thereof each held one share, in all five shares being held by the same three men and two other officers of the Bank & Trust Company. The Securities Corporation was, in turn, owned by the Safe Deposit Company and the stockholders of the Bank & Trust Company. These affiliates, or subsidiary corporations, never had officers or clerks separate from those of the Bank & Trust Company, and they operated as part of the Bank & Trust Company, and the

Safe Deposit Company operated its vaults in the main office of the Bank & Trust Company.

As the surrogate said, (280 N. Y. S. 523):

> "It would appear that the securities corporation and the safe deposit company were more than affiliates of the bank. *They were used as departments of the bank itself. The ownership and the control of the mortgaged property in question were in the hands of the same individuals through the medium of corporations all in the interest of the accountant trustee. Impartial judgment, action, or discretion with respect to the trust estate was impossible. A situation of inconsistent fidelity on the part of the trustee is created as it may be influenced by the duality of control and loyalty"*. (Emphasis added).

In deciding that the investment by the Bank & Trust Company in the participation certificate contravened, under the circumstances, "public policy and the law of the state", the surrogate said, (280 N. Y. S. 523):

> "This is a case where we may lift the corporate veil, disregard the corporate entity, and squarely raise the question as to the extent of the liability of the trustee, sweep away the act of legerdemain, and impose the concepts of justice and equity. *We are confronted with the condition of a trustee dealing with itself, buying for the trust estate part of its own mortgage upon its own property. This contravenes public policy and the law of the state. Matter of Peck's Estate, 152 Misc. 315, 273 N. Y. S. 552, and cases cited, an opinion by this court"*. (Emphasis added).

The surrogate, after further holding, (280 N. Y. S. 524), that

> "After October, 1928, the property was not self-sustaining as disclosed by the stipulation. *The allocation of participation certificates in such a mortgage was imprudently and negligently made. Durant v. Crowley, 197 App. Div. 540, 189 N. Y. S. 385, affirmed 234 N. Y. 581, 138 N. E. 455. It is required of a trustee with regard to a trust fund*

*that it should exercise such diligence and prudence in the
care and management of such funds as in general prudent
men of discretion and intelligence employ in the handling
of their own like affairs.* This principle was stated in *King
v. Talbot,* 40 N. Y. 76. 85, many years ago and it still
holds in New York state",— (emphasis added).

finally held that the participation certificate was the property of
the Bank & Trust Company, and that its account should be sur-
charged with the sum of $8,000, (or the amount of the trust
funds which it had invested in the certificate), with interest
from the date of the certificate, less income paid to the life
beneficiary.

———

IX.

COUNSEL FOR DEFENDANTS HAS OVERLOOKED THE WELL SETTLED DISTINCTION BETWEEN ACTUAL FRAUD AND CONSTRUCTIVE FRAUD.

Counsel for defendants, in closing the portion of the brief
under the heading, (Reply Brief, p. 42), namely, "The fact
that plaintiff may have reposed trust and confidence in Mr.
Bothwell and in the bond department of the national bank did
not give rise to a trust relationship", stated, (Reply Brief, p.
45), that he desired

> "to call to the Court's attention the fact that the District
> Court *found there was no fraud or misrepresentation* on
> Mr. Bothwell's part as to the type and value of the securi-
> ties sold to plaintiff", (R 326-328) (emphasis added);

and that, (Reply Brief, p. 45),

> "It was also found that at all times the securities sold
> by the national bank to plaintiff were sold at the fair
> market price and value thereof (R 326). The evidence
> not only supports these findings (R 430-431, 449), but
> also establishes that the same securities were being sold
> by various reputable bond houses in the community and

were recommended by them as sound investments at the time";

and that, (Reply Brief, p. 46),

"In fact, during the trial of the case counsel for plaintiff conceded 'that no fraudulent representations were alleged in the bill of complaint, * * * that there was nothing in the bill of complaint in any way squinting at a fraudulent representation in the purchase of any of the securities' ".

Counsel for defendant, in omitting all that was said by counsel for plaintiff, overlooked the well settled distinction between actual fraud and constructive fraud.*

---

*Note: This does not purport to be a complete statement of what occurred between counsel for plaintiff and counsel for defendants during the argument between counsel, (R 378-80). The following is a complete statement, no material part of which should, of course, have been omitted:

Mr. Slack replied that Mr. Kelly's argument went to the weight of the evidence offered and not to its admissibility, and that the weight of the evidence was a matter for the Court to decide. Mr. Slack further stated that the said letter showed the character of the territory in Oregon covered by the Medford bonds and what that territory was used for.

Counsel for defendants further objected to the introduction of the said letter in evidence, on the ground that its introduction constituted an attempt to show that the subsequent decline in value of the bonds, or the difficulty into which the Medford District got, was some evidence that, at the time the bonds were purchased, Bothwell had made a misrepresentation when he said, five years before and at the time the bonds were purchased, that he believed the bonds contained all of the elements to make them a safe and desirable investment.

In reply to this further objection, Mr. Slack stated that the allegations of the complaint, concerning the safety and desirability of the bonds which had been sold to Mrs. Quinn, were allegations in aggravation, and that no relief concerning the allegations was prayed for.

In answer to a question of Mr. Slack by Mr. Kelly that he had understood that Mr. Slack did not claim any fraudulent representation, Mr. Slack replied that the allegations of the bill of complaint were plain and spoke for themselves, and that no fraudulent representations were alleged in the bill of complaint, but, as the bill of complaint alleged, there was a concealment on Bothwell's part, chargeable to the National Bank, in that Bothwell had not disclosed to Mrs. Quinn, as he should have done, because of the confidential relation which existed between the National Bank, through himself, and Mrs. Quinn, the fact that the

Two intermingled findings of fact and conclusions of law were found by the District Judge, one referring to the purchases of securities prior to the execution of the instrument of trust, for plaintiff, by the National Bank, through its bond department, and the other referring to the purchases of securities subsequent to the execution of the instrument, for the trust estate, by the National Bank, also through its bond department, (App. F 34-5), (omitting, (App. F 35-6), from the end of the second paragraph following, the descriptions of the "trust assets to be so delivered" and the "instruments to be so executed"), which, for convenient reference, are reproduced in the footnote.*

National Bank had purchased the bonds from its bond department, always at a profit to itself, and the National Bank had thus acted in a dual capacity of both seller and purchaser, and that, also, at the time the instrument of trust was executed, there was a concealment on Berven's part, likewise chargeable to the National Bank, in that Berven was conclusively chargeable with notice of the same set of facts, and failed to disclose to Mrs. Quinn, as it was incumbent upon him so to do, that the National Bank had purchased the bonds from its bond department, always at a profit, and had thus acted in a dual capacity.

Mr. Slack further stated, in reply to the objections, that there was nothing in the bill of complaint in any way squinting at a fraudulent representation in the purchase of any of the securities.

*Note: "1· That prior to the execution of the instrument of trust on September 24, 1929 the relationship existing between plaintiff and the national bank was that of buyer and seller and *no fraud, concealment, or misrepresentation was practiced upon plaintiff* by the national bank either with respect to said relationship, or with respect to the value or desirability of the securities purchased or their market value, or with respect to the fact that said national bank was making a profit on such sales, or with respect to the fact that said bank was selling its own securities to plaintiff, and therefore plaintiff is not entitled to rescind any of the purchases of securities made by her from the bond department of the national bank prior to the execution of the instrument of trust." (Emphasis added).

"2. That the national bank was not guilty of any fraud, concealment, or misrepresentation in connection with the execution of the instrument of trust dated September 24, 1929, and therefore plaintiff is not entitled to rescind the same. However, in view of the fact that the savings bank (Central Bank of Oakland), the successor trustee under said instrument of trust, prior to the commencement of the action, and in its answer, *offered to permit plaintiff to revoke said instrument of trust,* plaintiff

The assignments of error in relation to these two so-called Conclusions of Law, (No. 29, No. 30 and No. 31, App. H 44-6, 46-7, 47-8), also for convenient reference are respectively reproduced in the footnote.*

---

may, if she so desires, revoke said instrument of trust, or appoint a new, or successor trustee, as provided for by the provisions of paragraph 1 of the contract dated April 22nd, 1933, relative to the purchase of the trust department of the national bank by the savings bank." (Emphasis added).

*Note: "29. The said Court erred in finding, as a fact, intermingled with, and misplaced in, the Conclusions of the Law found by the said Court

'That prior to the execution of the instrument of trust on September 24, 1929, the relationship existing between the plaintiff and the national bank was that of buyer and seller, and no fraud, concealment, or misrepresentation was practiced upon plaintiff by the national bank either with respect to said relationship, or with respect to the value or desirability of the securities purchased or their market value, or with respect to the fact that said national bank was making a profit on such sales or with respect to the fact that said bank was selling its own securities to plaintiff;'

from which the erroneous conclusion of law is found by the said Court, to wit,

'and therefore plaintiff is not entitled to rescind any of the purchases of securities made by her from the bond department of the national bank prior to the execution of the instrument of trust;'

for the reason that the evidence shows the facts to be that the relation existing between the plaintiff and the said National Bank, prior to the execution of the said instrument of trust, was not that of buyer and seller, but was that of cestui que trust and trustee; and for the further reason that the said National Bank, through the said Bothwell, as the Manager of the said Bond Department, failed to disclose to, and concealed from, the plaintiff the facts that the securities sold, prior to the execution of the said instrument, to the plaintiff by the said National Bank were owned, in each instance of such sales, by the said National Bank, and that, in each instance of such sales, the said National Bank made a profit thereon, and further failed to disclose to, and concealed from, the plaintiff that, because of such facts, the plaintiff had the legal right to disaffirm such sales, and, further, that, because of such concealment, the said National Bank had perpetrated, and was guilty of, a fraud, upon the plaintiff.

"30. The said Court erred in finding as a fact, likewise, as aforesaid, intermingled with, and misplaced in, the Conclusions of the Law found by the said Court,

It will be readily seen, from the foregoing quotations from the Reply Brief of counsel for defendants, that counsel, in the language of the foregoing heading, here under consideration, "has overlooked the well settled distinction between actual fraud and constructive fraud", the distinction being nowhere better

> 'That the national bank was not guilty of any fraud, concealment, or misrepresentation in connection with the execution of the instrument of trust dated September 24, 1929',

from which the erroneous conclusion of law is found by the said Court

> 'and therefore plaintiff is not entitled to rescind the same;'

for the reason that the evidence shows the facts to be that the said National Bank, through the said Berven, the Assistant Trust Officer of the said Trust Department, failed to disclose to, and concealed from, the plaintiff the facts that, in each instance of the sale of the said securities to the plaintiff, by the said National Bank, through the said Bothwell, as the Manager of the said Bond Department, the said securities were owned by the said National Bank, and that, in each instance of such sales, the said National Bank made a profit thereon, and further failed to disclose to, and concealed from, the plaintiff that, because of such facts, the plaintiff had the legal right to disaffirm such sales, and to rescind and set aside the said instrument of trust, and, further, that, because of such concealment, the said National Bank had perpetrated, and was guilty of, a fraud upon the plaintiff; and, further, also, that irrespective of her said right of rescission, the plaintiff was and is entitled to a decree in this action rescinding and setting aside the said instrument of trust in order that her rights, consequent upon such rescission and setting aside of the said instrument of trust, might, and should be, judicially determined, as set forth in the prayer of the said bill of complaint, and in the prayer of the amendments and supplements to the said bill of complaint, filed in this action.

"31. The said Court erred in finding as a fact, also, likewise, as above, intermingled with, and misplaced in, the Conclusions of the Law found by the said Court, that,

> 'in view of the fact that the savings bank (Central Bank of Oakland), the successor trustee under said instrument of trust, prior to the commencement of the action, and in its answer, offered to permit plaintiff to revoke said instrument of trust, plaintiff may, if she so desires, revoke said instrument of trust, or appoint a new, or successor trustee, as provided for by the provisions of paragraph 1 of the contract dated April 22nd, 1933, relative to the purchase of the trust department of the national bank by the savings bank, and in the event of such revocation, or such appointment of a successor trustee, the savings bank shall deliver to plaintiff or to such successor trustee, as the case may be, all trust assets, subject to such deductions as may be equitable and just for its compensation and

stated than in section 1572 and section 1573 of the *California Civil Code,* as follows:

> *"Section 1572. Actual fraud, what.* Actual fraud, within the meaning of this chapter, consists in any of the following acts, committed by a party to the contract, or with his connivance, with intent to deceive another party thereto, or to induce him to enter into the contract:
>
> 1. The suggestion as a fact, of that which is not true, by one who does not believe it to be true;
>
> 2. The positive assertion, in a manner not warranted by the information of the person making it, of that which is not true, though he believes it to be true;
>
> 3. The suppression of that which is true, by one having knowledge or belief of the fact;
>
> 4. A promise made without any intention of performing it; or,
>
> 5. Any other act fitted to deceive."
>
> *"Sec. 1573. Constructive fraud.* Constructive fraud consists:
>
> 1. In any breach of duty which, without an actually fraudulent intent, gains an advantage to the person in fault, or anyone claiming under him, by misleading another to his prejudice, or to the prejudice of anyone claiming under him; or,

---

expenditures as set forth in the letter dated June 10, 1933, and shall execute such instruments as may reasonably be necessary to effect the foregoing.'

The said Court so erred for the following reasons: (1), that it is not the fact that the said Savings Bank, either prior to, or since, the commencement of this action, offered to permit the plaintiff to revoke the said instrument of trust; and (2), it is respectfully submitted that the said Court, as a court of equity, should have determined, by its findings and its decree in this action, (as it was incumbent upon the said Court so to do, by a well settled rule of equity practice and procedure), all the rights and duties of the respective parties to the action, and should not leave open and undetermined, as has been done, by the above quoted finding, for the determination hereafter, without the intervention of the said Court, questions of the future conduct, (which may be disputed), of the parties to the action, as set forth in the prayer of the bill of complaint, and in the prayer of the amendments and supplements to the bill of complaint filed in this action."

2. In any such act or omission as the law specially declares to be fraudulent, without respect to actual fraud."

It will also be readily seen that the findings of fact and conclusions of law, above quoted, likewise overlooked the well settled distinction between actual fraud and constructive fraud.

There is nothing in the complaint, (and naturally there would be nothing in the answer, either of the Central Bank or of the National Bank), which charges any actual fraud, either in misrepresentations, or in concealments, by Bothwell, Berven, or Read, in any manner relating to the purchases of the securities in question, or in any other respect, either prior, or at the time, or subsequent to the time of the execution of the instrument of trust; and such being the fact, and the unquestionable fact, it is obvious that the findings of the District Judge to the contrary are without the issues presented by the pleadings and the evidence.

The evidence, however, leading up to, and immediately relating to, the execution of the instrument of trust, as set forth and discussed by us, under the heading "V. Neither Bothwell nor Berven was a credible witness", and, in particular, relating to the second and third conversations which Berven testified that he had with plaintiff, (*ante,* pp. 50-8), need not here be repeated, in detail. Suffice it to say, however, that such evidence shows, quite clearly, that Berven was guilty of actual fraud in several particulars, notably in the particular of discouraging plaintiff from seeking independent advice in the submission of the instrument of trust to an attorney of her own selection, (*ante,* this Brief, pp. 54-5, *note*), and in the particular of plaintiff finally signing the instrument because he told her "it was not necessary" for her to submit the instrument to an attorney of her own choosing. We do not contend that it is necessary, under all circumstances, or even that it is important, for the beneficiary of a trust to have independent advice in relation to the signing of an instrument of trust, but we do contend that it was an important element to the validity of the instrument of trust in the instant case that plaintiff should have had independent advice. (See: 2 *Black, Rescission and Cancellation*, sec. 244, pp. 693-5, sec. 362, p. 979, (2d ed.); 12 *Cal. Jur.*, sec. 13, pp. 775-6, sec. 16, pp. 779-80, sec. 17, pp. 780-2, tit. "Cancellation of Instruments").

X.

THE KNOWLEDGE OF BOTHWELL, THE ASSISTANT CASHIER OF THE NATIONAL BANK AND THE MANAGER OF ITS BOND DEPARTMENT, OF THE PURPOSE FOR WHICH THE SECURITIES WERE PURCHASED, PRIOR TO THE EXECUTION OF THE INSTRUMENT OF TRUST, FOR PLAINTIFF, BY THE NATIONAL BANK, THROUGH ITS BOND DEPARTMENT, WAS CONCLUSIVELY IMPUTED TO THE NATIONAL BANK, AND, BEING SO IMPUTED, WAS CONCLUSIVELY IMPUTED TO ALL OTHER OFFICERS OF THE NATIONAL BANK, INCLUDING BERVEN, ITS ASSISTANT TRUST OFFICER, AND READ, ITS VICE PRESIDENT AND TRUST OFFICER.

The proposition formulated in this last foregoing heading is well sustained:

> 3 *Fletcher, Cyclopedia Corporations*, sec. 795, pp. 38-9;
> *Curtice v. Crawford County Bank*, 118 Fed. 390, 394, (C. C. A., 10th, 1902);
> *Sanders v. McGill*, 9 Cal. (2d) 145, 153-5, 70 P. (2d) 159, 163-4, (1937).

Thus, in the case of *Curtice v. Crawford County Bank, supra*, it was held, substantially as stated in one of the headnotes, (namely, the second headnote), to the case, that where the president, one Turner, of the defendant bank, to whom a pledgee, the plaintiff Curtice, of one Hynes, the cashier of the bank, had exhibited the certificate therefor held by Curtice, in order to ascertain with certainty that the certificate had been regularly issued, stating to the president of the bank the fact of the pledge, received such information while acting in his official capacity, the bank was thereby conclusively charged with knowledge of the pledge, so as to render the lien on the shares of the capital stock which the State of Arkansas had conferred upon the bank, for a loan subsequently made by the bank by the pledgor, Hynes, although the loan was made some two or three years after the transaction between the president and the pledgee, subject to the rights of the pledgee, whose debt had not been paid.

Again, in the case of *Sanders v. McGill, supra,* it was similarly held, substantially as stated on one of the paragraphs of the syllabus, (namely, paragraph 7), to the case, that knowledge by an officer of a bank, within the scope of his duties, was imputable to the bank, and, therefore, where the bank was the payee of the note involved in the case, and such officer had knowledge that the bank held shares of the capital stock of a water company as security for the payment of the balance due on the note, such knowledge was conclusively imputed to the bank, and the bank could not successfully contend that a sale of the note was made under a mistake, because the officer of the bank who negotiated the sale had no such information and dealt without any notice of the true status of the shares of the capital stock.

XI.

THE OBLIGATIONS AND LIABILITIES OF THE NATIONAL BANK, ARISING FROM THE PURCHASES OF SECURITIES, PRIOR TO THE EXECUTION OF THE INSTRUMENT OF TRUST, FOR PLAINTIFF, BY THE NATIONAL BANK, THROUGH BOTHWELL, AS THE MANAGER OF ITS BOND DEPARTMENT, AS WELL AS PURCHASES SUBSEQUENT TO THE EXECUTION OF THE INSTRUMENT OF TRUST, FOR THE TRUST ESTATE, BY THE NATIONAL BANK, FROM ITSELF, THROUGH BOTHWELL, AS THE MANAGER OF ITS BOND DEPARTMENT, WERE ASSUMED BY THE CENTRAL BANK, UNDER THE CONTRACTS BETWEEN THE NATIONAL BANK AND THE CENTRAL BANK, RELATING TO THE SALE TO THE CENTRAL BANK OF THE WHOLE OF THE BUSINESS OF THE TRUST DEPARTMENT OF THE NATIONAL BANK.

This proposition is fully discussed by us in our Opening Brief, (pp. 60-3), and has not been answered by counsel for the Central Bank, other than to state, (Reply Brief, pp. 73-6), that the declination of the District Judge to find on the question was unnecessary, because "moot", (App. F 36-7, in Conclusion of Law numbered 4, assigned as error No. 33. (App. G 51-2). We assume, therefore, that counsel for the Central Bank have conceded the correctness of the proposition, and that no further discussion of the subject is necessary. Nevertheless, we may add that the proposition is strengthened by Finding No. 7, paragraph I, (App. F 7), to the effect that plaintiff "reposed in Bothwell and in the bond department trust and confidence, which Bothwell well knew", and by Finding No. 4, in Conclusions of Law, (App. F 36-7), to the effect that "Had any liabilities been established as arising out of, or relating or incidental to, the purchase of the securities by the trust department, or the conduct of said trust, after the execution of the trust instrument on September 24, 1929, such liabilities would have been assumed by the savings bank"; and that that finding was an admission that the obligations and liabilities of the National Bank, which resulted from the purchases of the securities from itself for the trust estate, through Bothwell, as the manager of its bond department, were assumed by the National Bank, and stand on precisely the same footing as the obligations and liabilities of the National Bank, which resulted from the purchases of the securities from itself for plaintiff, through Bothwell, as the manager of its bond department, and, consequently, were trust department obligations and liabilities of the National Bank.

XII.

NO OFFER WAS EVER MADE BY THE CENTRAL BANK, AS ALLEGED IN ITS THIRD SEPARATE DEFENSE, PRIOR TO THE COMMENCEMENT OF THE INSTANT ACTION, TO PERMIT PLAINTIFF TO REVOKE THE TRUST AND THE INSTRUMENT OF TRUST AND TO DELIVER ALL THE TRUST PROPERTIES TO PLAINTIFF, NOR WAS AN OFFER EVER MADE TO PLAINTIFF, PRIOR TO THE COMMENCEMENT OF THE INSTANT ACTION, TO AGREE THAT SUCH REVOCATION SHOULD NOT BE A RELEASE OR DISCHARGE OF EXISTING LIABILITIES AND OBLIGATIONS OF THE CENTRAL BANK, IF ANY.

Notwithstanding that the facts are substantially as stated in the foregoing heading of this brief, counsel for defendants state, (Reply Brief, pp. 52-3), that "the evidence clearly supports the finding and that Mr. Beardsley made the offer which was not accepted." On the contrary, as stated in our Opening Brief, p. 64, in the first place, there is no evidence whatever to support the allegations of the defense. The testimony of Mr.

Beardsley, called by the Central Bank as a witness, is as follows, (R 495-6):

> "In substance, Judge Slack, in one or more of the meetings in my office, called attention to paragraph VII as one of the clauses of the trust instrument to which he objected because of the fact 'that it provided that in the event of the terminaion of the trust it was necessary for Mrs. Quinn to release the trustee from all obligations under the trust instrument, and I told Judge Slack that, as far as that was concerned, the Central Bank, whom I represented, would prefer to have the trust terminated and to turn over to Mrs. Quinn whatever we had belonging to her, since she was not satisfied with our operation of the trust, and we would waive the provisions in reference to her waiver of any claim which she might have against the trustee, and were perfectly willing to enter into a stipulation or agreement saving any rights that she might have against the Central Bank in the event of the termination of the trust.
>
> "I do not recall definitely the response which Judge Slack made to that except I know that nothing of that kind was done."

In the next place, even if there were evidence to support the allegations, the following analysis of the offer was sufficient to demonstrate its absurdity as a defense, in whole or in part, namely: The offer was, (1), to revoke the trust and the instrument of trust and to deliver all of the properties to plaintiff, and (2), "to agree that such revocation should not be a release or discharge of the *existing* liabilities and obligations of the *Central Bank,* 'if any', to plaintiff"; with a prayer that because plaintiff "refused such offer", plaintiff be penalized by decree that she "take nothing by her complaint"; that is, because plaintiff, (so it is alleged), refused the offer to enter into an agreement with the Central Bank, (the terms of which were not defined), to release or discharge "the existing liabilities and obligations" of the *Central Bank only,* and not those of the National Bank, to plaintiff, plaintiff is to "take nothing by her complaint",—not even her costs against either the Central Bank or the National Bank and its receiver, and that even under such provisions as those of section 1997, of the *California Code of Civil Procedure,* and under similar statutory provisions in other jurisdictions, (15 *C. J.,* secs. 133-4, p. 75, sec. 138, tit. "Costs"), the penalty for the refusal by plaintiff of the offer of defendant relates only to certain of plaintiff's costs.

Finally, it is evident that the finding of the District Judge in relation to the offer is not supported either by the pleadings or by the evidence.

———

WHEREFORE, it is again respectfully submitted, that the decree of the District Court should be reversed, with instructions to enter a decree in favor of plaintiff against the Central Bank and the National Bank, in accordance with the prayer to the amendments and supplements to the complaint, (App. D 6-8).

CHARLES W. SLACK and
EDGAR T. ZOOK,
*Attorneys for Plaintiff
and Appellant.*

(Appendix Follows)

Appendix

Appendix J

Appendix J.

1. Findings which have no evidence to support them.

Find. 1, Par. II, (App. H, pp. 4-5);

Find. 5, Par. II, (App. H, pp. 18-9);

Find. 5, Par. II, (App. H, pp. 19-20);

Find., Par. VII, (App. H, pp. 43-4).

2. Findings which are contrary to the evidence
(14 not conflicting, and 9 conflicting)*

Find. 4, Par. I, (App. H, p. 1), *not* conflicting.

Find. 5, Par. I, (App. H, pp. 1-3), *not* conflicting.

Find. 7, Par. I, (App. H, pp. 3-4), *not* conflicting.

Find. 1, Par. II, (App. H, pp. 4-5), *not* conflicting.

Find. 1, Par. II, (App. H, p. 5), *not* conflicting.

Find. 2, Par. II, (App. H, pp. 5-6), *conflicting*—Bothwell.

Find. 2, Par. II, (App. H, pp. 6-7), *not* conflicting.

Find. 3, Par. II, (App. H, pp. 7-8), *conflicting*—Bothwell.

Find. 3, Par. II, (App. H, pp. 10-1), *conflicting*—Bothwell.

Find. 4, Par. II, (App. H, pp. 11-2), *not* conflicting.

Find. 4, Par. II, (App. H, pp. 13-4, second portion), *not* conflicting.

Find 5, Par. II, (App. H, pp. 14-5), *not* conflicting.

Find 5, Par. II, (App. H, pp. 15-6), *conflicting* — Bothwell and Berven.

**Note:* The references in this tabulation to testimony as "conflicting", or as "not conflicting", are not intended to convey the impression that the testimony of Bothwell, or of Berven, or of both, really conflicts or not, in certain instances, with plaintiff's testimony, in relation to the same subject matter, but are inended to mean that the testimony would be conflicting if it were not for the fact that the testimony had been nullified by the finding of the relation of trust and confidence existing between plaintiff and the National Bank prior to the execution of the instrument of trust.

26-7), *conflicting*—Bothwell.

Find. 2, Par. III, (App. H, pp. 27-30), *conflicting*—Bothwell and Berven.

Find. 2, Par. VI, (App. H, pp. 41-2), *conflicting*—Berven.

Find. Par. VII, (App. H, pp. 43-4), *not* conflicting.

3. Findings which are without the issues raised by the pleadings.

Find. 7, Par. I, (App. H, pp. 3-4).

Find. 1, Par. II, (App. H, pp. 4-5).

Find. 1, Par. II, (App. H, p. 5).

Find. 2, Par. II, (App. H, pp. 6-7).

Find. 4, Par. II, (App. H, p. 13, first portion).

Find. 5, Par. II, (App. H, pp. 18-19).

Find. 5, Par. II, (App. H, pp. 19-20).

Find. 5, Par. II, (App. H, pp. 20-1).

Find. 5, Par. II, (App. H, pp. 20-2).

Find. 2, Par. IV, (App. H, pp. 33-5, in part).

Testimony, respectively, as summarized, of Abbie W. Quinn, plaintiff, witness E. D. Bothwell, former manager of the bond department of the National Bank, and witness S. Berven, assistant trust officer of the National Bank, and later trust officer of the Central Bank.

1. The testimony of Abbie W. Quinn, Plaintiff.

Plaintiff testified, on her direct examination, (R 364), that she opened a savings account with the Central Bank, under its then name of the Central Savings Bank, (R 44), in 1903 or 1904, and became a depositor of the National Bank, on its organization in 1909, (R 364); that she could not state when she became acquainted with Bothwell, but it was about the time she opened an account with the Central Bank; that Bothwell's occupation at that time was that of a teller of one of the Banks; that, (R 364, 365), she did not recall when he was appointed to the position of manager of the bond department of the National Bank.*

---

*NOTE: Bothwell testified (R 413) that he entered the employ of the Central Bank on May 26, 1909, "as a general utility clerk assisting at the teller's windows", and "continued in that general utility work" until the organization of the National Bank on August 9, 1909, [not on *November* 9, 1909, as erroneously appears in the record, (R 413)], when he ceased to be employed by the Central Bank and became a paying teller of the National Bank; that he continued as a paying teller of the National Bank for approximately two years, when he was appointed an assistant cashier of the National Bank, and he continued to be an assistant cashier of the National Bank up to the time when he left the employment of the National Bank in February, 1933; and that he became the manager of the bond department of the National Bank in 1920 or 1921.

Plaintiff, so she testified, (R 364), became acquainted with Bothwell about the time when she opened an account with the Central Bank; that she *"met him frequently in the Bank"*, and *"felt that I was well acquainted with him"*; that she talked with him about her financial, as well as her personal, affairs more than once prior to the time of his making the first purchases for her; that, (R 365, 366), she could not fix the exact date in 1926 when the first securities were bought, but thought it was in February, March or April;* that she talked with him in his private office in the Bank, she thought, more than once prior to the time of making the first purchases; that, (R 367), she told him who the immediate members of her family were, and explained to him that she wanted to put her property "in a fund, or some estate", where, (R 367, 368), it would be cared for during her lifetime, and for her heirs, who were a daughter and her grandson, on her death; that, (R 367, 368), she had "real estate situated in Nevada, and had some bonds and mortgages"; that, (R 368), the real estate was a store, commonly called the "Virginia Street property", on Virginia Street, Reno, Nevada, lots in Sparks, a town near Reno, a lot in Oakland, a mortgage on the Masonic Temple in Sparks to secure a note of the Sparks Masonic Building Association, and bonds called the "Washoe County, County Roads

---

*NOTE: The first purchases of securities was made on January 7, 1926, (R 375; R 548½, Plf's Ex. 6; R 645, Plf's Ex. 47).

and Highways Improvement and Construction
Bonds''; that, (R 367),

> "He said they could handle the personal property,
> but the real estate in Nevada could not be han-
> dled by them, without complicating matters, that
> in funds of that sort, they could not handle real
> estate, and that the better thing to do would be
> to dispose of the real estate and put it in bonds,
> or something of that kind, so it could be placed
> in the fund later on. *He called the fund a 'trust
> fund'* ''. (Emphasis added).

Plaintiff further testified, (R 367), that when she
first asked him "whether or not the Bank had a department to care for estates and for heirs", he replied
that "it had just the department of that kind, to take
care of estates for widows and orphans, where they
would be protected". He said

> "the Bank would form a trust, or a trust would
> be formed by the Bank, and it would
> be cared for in the Bank, and, in the meantime,
> they would purchase bonds for me, from time to
> time, as I acquired the money and sold the prop-
> erty, to create this trust fund."

Plaintiff further testified, (R 368), that her "condition of health at that time was very poor", and it
"has continued to be poor up to the present time, and
at times I am very ill from acute attacks"; and that
she had consulted many physicians, including Mayo
Brothers, of Rochester, Minnesota, but had never been
operated upon at any time to relieve her condition,
because the doctors said it was unwise to do so.

Plaintiff, further continuing her testimony, said that (R 368)

> "I inquired of Mr. Bothwell as to whether or not I could place my property in the National Bank in such a trust, or trust fund, as I described to him, so that I would be cared for during my lifetime and my child and my grandson after that";

that, (R 368), she had more than one conversation with him, in which she told him of what her property consisted, (R 367, 368), and he said that (R 368),

> "they could not manage the real estate in Nevada, and I should sell it and invest the money in bonds or in other personal property. This condition was to continue until I sold my Nevada real property. He was to buy bonds for my trust fund, and hold them in the Bank until I could dispose of this property, and then, he advised me that the better thing to do was to have a trust fund created."

Plaintiff accepted, so she testified, (R 369), *his advice, and, in accepting the advice, it was her intention to create the trust after she had disposed of her Nevada real estate.* (Emphasis added).

Plaintiff told him, she testified, in continuing her testimony, that, (R 369), *"I did not have any experience in bonds",* and that *"I just had to depend on such information I could get from the bond department"* of the National Bank. The bonds to be purchased and held pending the creation of the trust "were to be substantial bonds", he said, "reliable and safe bonds, and I would never lose my money." He always told her, (R 370), that her money "would be placed in nothing but bonds which were safe and desirable." (Emphasis added).

She asked him, (R 370), what he thought about investing her money in United States bonds, but he said she "would have to have some unlimited means to have any revenue from Government bonds, that they would pay so little." He said that he "could give me bonds that would be just as secure and would obtain me much more interest", and that she would not lose any of her principal. He did not explain to her, plaintiff continued, (R 370), the difference between so-called bonds and so-called notes, or between so-called bonds and so-called debenture bonds, or between so-called bonds and so-called collateral bonds. Nothing was so explained to her by Bothwell or Berven, or anyone else connected with the National Bank. She did not know at any time during the making of the investments by Bothwell whether or not the bonds or notes, if secured at all, were adequately secured. "I did not know anything about it. He just told me that they were well secured."

He selected all the bonds or securities for the investment of her funds, so she testified, (R 371). I "always approved of what he suggested to me, but at times I questioned them."

When he made the selection of Fageol Motors bonds as an investment for her, (R 371),

> "I asked him about what they were and he told me that they were real first-class bonds and were secured by some company in the east."

He always asked plaintiff, so she testified, (R 371), for her approval. He spoke to her verbally, instead of writing to her, about certain bonds. *She always approved of the purchases which he recommended.* (Emphasis added).

She remembered, so she testified, (R 371-2), that she raised a question with him concerning the bonds of California Cotten Mills Company, but he said "they were very good bonds, that the automobile industry alone would take much of their product", and that "there was no doubt they would be good bonds", and accordingly she approved the purchase of them.

She also raised the question as to the propriety of investing her funds, so she testified, (R 372), in bonds of the Medford Irrigation District, of Alameda Investment Company, and of Alameda Park Company, and, so she testified, (R 372),

> "I felt perhaps they were not so good," but he said "they were good, that the Bank thought they were good, they used them in the bank for their security, and that they considered them good substantial bonds."

Concerning the Medford Irrigation District bonds, so she testified, (R 372),

> "I asked him if he considered irrigation bonds were good bonds, and he said yes, he did, that the Bank bought them, invested their money in them."

She received the letter, (R 539, Plf's Ex. 1), dated February 28, 1928, addressed to her as "Dear Mrs.

Quinn", and signed by him as "Assistant Cashier, Manager Bond Dept.", and reading as follows:

"As requested in your letter of Feb. 26th, we are redeeming $5000 Western States Gas and Electric Company Bonds as per bill herewith, and confirming $5000 Medford Irrigation District Bonds, as per bill enclosed. You will note that we *secured* the Medford Bonds at 97 which will give you a 6.22% yield. The difference of $350.00 has been credited to your commercial account.

"The above transaction is subject to your approval.

"We have handled several hundred thousand dollars of Medford Irrigation District Bonds, *and believe they contain all of the elements to make them a safe and desirable investment.*

"We are sorry you are ill, and trust that you will soon be in good health again. With very kindest regards, and thanking you for this favor, we remain, Yours very truly, E. D. Bothwell, Assistant Cashier, Manager Bond Dept." (Emphasis added).

Plaintiff recalled, so she said, that the Medford Irrigation District bonds were purchased for her after he had written that letter to her.

She recalled also, so she testified, (R 373), the purchase with her funds of bonds of the Province of Buenos Aires and bonds of the Province of Callao, Peru, and she asked him how the bonds of the Province of Buenos Aires were secured, and he said they were secured by the Province of Buenos Aires and were a perfectly safe investment, and he also told her that the bonds of the Province of Callao "were a safe investment and well secured."

Plaintiff, continuing her testimony, further testified, (R 388-9), that the Virginia Street property was sold on February 8, 1928, for about $22,000 over and above commissions and expenses; that she deposited the money which she received for the property in a bank in Reno, in which she had an account and where she was at the time; and that she wrote checks on the Reno bank to pay for the bonds purchased by Bothwell for her.

She recalled that (R 389), some of the bonds purchased were sold and some of the bonds were redeemed, both before and after the execution of the instrument of trust; that the money so obtained on such sales and redemptions was paid to the National Bank; and that she never received any money from the bonds so sold and redeemed, except the interest.

Plaintiff further testified, (R 389), that the condition of the health of her daughter, Ruth Quinn Osborne, who was born in 1897, since she was a young girl, was and is now very poor; that her daughter was dependent upon her for support; and that she told Bothwell, at her first interview with him, when she talked with him as to what she wanted done with her property, that her daughter was dependent upon her.

She further testified, (R 389), that she owned the Washoe County, County Roads and Highways Improvement and Construction bonds quite a while be-

fore she talked with Bothwell about her affairs; that
she explained to him that she had those bonds and also
the mortgage on the Masonic Building, in Sparks, on
deposit in the Washoe County Bank, in Reno, and
she testified, in this connection, (R 389-90), that she
removed the bonds and mortgage from the Washoe
County Bank and deposited them with the National
Bank before the creation of the trust, and this she
knew, because the National Bank collected the first
June payment on the bonds of the Masonic Building
Association before that time.

Plaintiff, continuing her testimony, testified, (R
390), that she was acquainted with Daniel Read, who
sometimes signed his name as D. Read; that she first
met him, after talking with Bothwell, with reference
to the creation of a trust fund; that Bothwell asked
her to go and talk with Read about the matter, and he
gave her a letter, or a note, of introduction to Read,
but that she could not remember how long that was
before the creation of the trust, although it was quite
some time; that she had a talk with Read, pursuant
to the letter, or note, of introduction, and told him
that she wanted to talk with him about the matter and
get what information she required; that he did not
seem to be very much interested, and it was very hard
for her to talk with him; that when she first called on
him, he seemed to be busy at the time, and "I felt that
he was indifferent and did not seem to be interested
in me."

Plaintiff, so she testified, (R 390), made a second
call on Read concerning the matter, with the same

result. She could not remember how long it was after the first call, but it was quite a little while, perhaps two or three months. She was very ill at the time, and there would be months at a time when she was not out and did not go down to the Bank.

Further continuing her testimony, plaintiff testified, (R 390-1), that later on she went back to Bothwell's office and told him that she could not seem to get Read interested in her affairs, and that he did not seem to have time for her, or seemed indifferent, or something of that sort; that Bothwell then said that he would introduce her to Berven, and he went with her to Berven's office and introduced her to Berven and explained to Berven what she desired to do with her estate; that she told Berven, (R 391), that she "wanted to create a trust fund, and that they were purchasing bonds for me for the trust fund, and that the bonds were held in the Bank with my other investments until such time as I would accumulate all that I wished to put in the trust fund"; that Bothwell said he would leave it to Berven to explain the matter to her and take the matter up and later on create the trust fund; that, (R 391), *those present at the conversation were Bothwell, Berven and herself;* that the conversation was at Mr. Berven's office in the Central Bank Building; that Berven said, (R 391), that

> "I should sell my Virginia Street property and accumulate—get what I wanted first in a fund in the Bank, or in these bonds, *and later on they would create a trust fund for me.*" (Emphasis added).

Plaintiff further continuing her testimony, testified, (R 391-2), that *she called on Berven a second time, after the Virginia Street property had been sold—* some time about April or May or June of 1928,—it must have been in 1929, because, so she said, she had her property in Sparks and in Oakland that she wanted to sell first, and, (R 392-3), there was quite a delay between the first and second conversations because "they told me that nothing could be done, I would have to sell the property and use the money for investing in bonds"; that, (R 394), she was ill a great deal of the time, and had acute attacks of illness during that period, and at the second visit they talked about the preparation of the instrument of trust and that she contemplated a trip to see the Mayo Brothers at Rochester, Minnesota. (Emphasis added).

Plaintiff, further continuing her testimony, testified, (R 395), that she gave Berven a memorandum of the provisions which she wanted inserted in the instrument of trust, and was informed by Berven when the instrument was prepared and ready for execution.

She recognized her signature at the foot of the instrument of trust, ("Exhibit A" to the complaint), the duplicate original of which was shown to her, (R 395). She did

"not know where whoever prepared that instrument got the description in the instrument of my Oakland property, nor where they got a list of the other properties in the instrument, including the Washoe County, County Roads and Highways Improvement and Construction bonds and the note and mortgage of the Sparks Masonic Building Association.''

She ''did not have the possession of either the Washoe County bonds or the note and mortgage of the Sparks Masonic Building Association. The Bank had possession of them.''

She remembered, so she testified, (R 395), that an installment of principal, of $1,000, of the note of the Sparks Masonic Building Association, fell due in June before the instrument of trust was signed, and was collected by and held in the National Bank in her funds.

She recalled signing the assignment shown to her and marked ''Plaintiff's Exhibit 38'', (R 631-33), from herself to the National Bank of the note and mortgage of the Sparks Masonic Building Association, but, (R 396), did not recall her notarial acknowledgment to the assignment. She did not know who prepared the assignment. It was presented to her for her signature on the date of the execution of the instrument of trust.

She had not succeeded, so she testified, (R 396), in selling her Oakland lot nor in selling her lots in Sparks before the execution of the instrument of trust.

She recognized her signature, (R 396), to the instrument dated September 23, 1929, and designated as ''Deed of Gift'', which was shown to her and marked ''Plaintiff's Exhibit 39'', (R 633-4),* from herself

---

*Note: Plaintiff's Exhibit 39, is obviously erroneously designated in the record, (R 396), as Plaintiff's Exhibit *38*, (R 633-4).

to her *daughter,* of her lots in Sparks. She did not know who prepared that instrument. It was handed to her for her signature by Berven and was signed by her in the Bank. Berven told her she could leave it with her papers to be handed to her daughter, who, at the time, was in New York.

She did not recall, so she testified, (R 396), signing in the Bank, on the occasion of the execution of the instrument of trust, any papers other than the instrument of trust, (which was executed in duplicate), the assignment of the note and mortgage of the Sparks Masonic Building Association, and the deed of gift to her daughter.

She thought, so she testified, (R 397), that she first saw the instrument of trust on the day she signed it. Berven told her that Mr. Abbott, the attorney for the National Bank, had prepared it. She never consulted Mr. Abbott, or any other member of his firm, about the preparation of the instrument, or anyone else, other than Berven, connected with the National Bank. She never met Mr. Abbott, or any other member of the firm of Fitzgerald, Abbott and Beardsley.

Counsel for the Central Bank thereupon produced an assignment of the note and mortgage dated April 22, 1933, from the National Bank to the Central Bank, and the same was introduced and read in evidence by counsel for plaintiff, and marked "Plaintiff's Exhibit 40", (R 635-6).

It was admitted by counsel for the respective parties, (R 397), that no other assignment was executed,

and that there was no other release or any receipts
given by the Central Bank to the National Bank on
the sale by the National Bank to the Central Bank of
the business of the trust department of the National
Bank, Mr. Beardsley, one of the counsel for the Central Bank, stating, in that connection, that, (R 397):

> "We treated the contract and the formal ap-
> proval by this Court and the consent of the Comp-
> troller of the Currency as a transfer of all the
> assets of the trust department, and we only made
> separate instruments where it was deemed desir-
> able for the purpose of recording. I will say that
> the details of the sale were handled by me and
> they were described under the provisions and
> terms of the statute, and the execution of the
> agreement, which was itself a transfer, and the
> assets were turned over, and then for these in-
> struments of record, like this mortgage, why, we
> had a separate instrument to be recorded in order
> to make the record clear."

Plaintiff, continuing her testimony, testified, (R
398), that Berven retained one of the duplicate originals and gave her the other duplicate original of the
instrument of trust. He read from the duplicate original, which he retained, and she followed it as he read
it. She did not recall, (R 399), that he made any statement to her when he so read the instrument as to any
of the provisions of the instrument. He made no statement to her as to the provisions of paragraph I of the
instrument. She did not remember, (R 399), that he
made any statement to her at the time he read over
the instrument to her and before she signed it, con-

cerning the provisions of paragraph VII of the instrument.

She did not recall, so she testified, (R 400), that Berven read over to her the statement, or said anything to her about the statement, at the foot of the instrument of trust.

Plaintiff, continuing her testimony, testified, (R 400), that before she signed the instrument of trust she asked Berven

> "if it was necessary for me to have my attorney, or some attorney, look over the instrument for me, and he said 'no', it wouldn't be necessary, that it was a regular thing for the trust department to do, and that my interests were fully protected."

Plaintiff further testified, (R 400), that *she signed the instrument without any advice from any attorney, "Because he told me it was not necessary."* (Emphasis added).

Plaintiff paid the trust department, so she testified, (R 401), $100, which they charged her on the execution of the instrument of trust. She did not know what the charge was for.

Plaintiff further testified, (R 401), that Berven did not say anything to her at the time, or before the time, of the execution of the instrument about the character of the bonds and notes that are listed in the instrument, nor did he say anything to her at that time, (R 401), in any manner relating to the purchases of bonds and notes which had been made prior to the execution of the instrument, nor, (R 401), did any other official of the Bank say anything to her at that time, or before that time, about the kind of bonds that she bought through Bothwell, nor did she know up to that time that the National Bank was making any profit on the purchases by her of the notes and bonds.

She did not recall, so she testified, (R 402), but thought it was in 1932, when the first default in the payment of interest occurred on the bonds and notes that had been purchased for her. She did not remember whether or not, about that time, there was more than one default. She remembered a number of defaults occurring, (R 646, Plf's Ex. 48). She called upon Bothwell and had a conversation with him, (R 402), concerning the defaults, and he told her that some of the defaulted bonds and notes "would eventually come back again and would be good bonds", and he told her, (R 402), not to worry about it, that "I would not lose my principal".

She informed Berven, (R 402), at the time, or about the time, of the execution of the instrument of trust, and before the instrument was executed, of the contemplated trip to Mayo Brothers. She left on that trip on the morning of September 25th, or the next day, after the instrument was executed. She was in a hurry at the time she made her departure, and Berven knew it. On the arrival at the end of her journey, she consulted with Dr. Charles Mayo, the younger of the Mayo Brothers. He gave advice, but did not perform any operation.

Plaintiff further testified, (R 402), that she did not come to know Read better after her interviews with him, except that he wrote her the letter, Plaintiff's Exhibit 20,* about changing some of her investments. That letter, (R 561), dated July 16, 1930, addressed to plaintiff, at Los Angeles, as "Dear Madam", and signed "Daniel Read, Asst. Vice-President", is as follows:

"On July 3, 1930 we purchased for your trust account, in accordance with your instructions of June 27, 1930, $5,000.00 par value Federal Public Service Corporation 6% Bonds due 1947 at 93.

Information has since reached us which leads us to believe that it would be advisable for you*r* (sic) to dispose of these holdings and reinvest the proceeds in something else. We suggest reinvestment in the following bonds:

$3,000 par value Pacific Gas & Electric First and Refunding 6% Bonds due 1941 at 110½.

$2,000 par value San Joaquin Light & Power Company, Unifying and Refunding 6% Bonds due 1952 at 114¼.

The prices mentioned are taken from today's quotations and are, of course, subject to change without notice.

Please let us hear from you on this subject, at your earliest convenience."

Before replying to this letter, and on July 24, 1930, plaintiff, from Santa Cruz, wrote a letter, addressed to Berven, (R 562, Plf's Ex. 21), in which she stated that

*Note: Erroneously referred to, in the record, as "Exhibit *19*."

she had been away from Los Angeles since July 13th, and expected to be in Oakland for a day soon. Read, on July 25th, replied to this letter to Berven, and enclosed a copy of his letter to her of July 16th, addressing her as "Dear Madam", and signing the letter, "Daniel Read, Asst. Vice President," and in which he stated, (R 563, Plf's Ex. 22), as follows:

> "We are in receipt of your favor of July 24, 1930 in which you state that you have been away from Los Angeles since the 13th, and expect to be in Oakland for a day soon.
>
> We enclose herewith copy of our letter of July 16, 1930 addressed to you at Los Angeles, in case the original has not yet reached you.
>
> We would ask you to kindly give this matter your early attention."

To this last letter, plaintiff replied by letter, (R 564), Plaintiff's Exhibit 23, dated July 26, 1930, and addressed "Dear Sir", as follows:

> "Your letter of 25th inst is just rec'd.
> Please change bonds as you suggest, if you deem it advisable. I certainly disire (sic) safe investment at all times."

It was stipulated by counsel for the respective parties to the action, (R 404-5), that Plaintiff's Exhibit 48, (R 646), Schedule B, was made as of December 4, 1935; that on the said Schedule B the small letter "c" means called; that the small letter "s" means sold; the small letter "x" means a partial payment; the small letter "n" means a note; the small letter "p"

means payments on certificates of deposit; the small
letter "x" also means liquidating payments, such as
in the case of Fageol Motors, Inc.; the small letter
"m" means maturity, that is, paid at maturity; the
word "called" means calls anticipating maturity at a
certain price; and the word "default" is expressed
either by the abbreviation "Def.", or by the word
"Default". A partial default is indicated in the case
of the bonds of the Province of Callao as "Partial
def.", and, in the case of the Province of Buenos
Aires, although "Default" is used, it means only a
partial default.

Plaintiff, continuing, testified as follows, (R 405-6),
that she did not know, at any time prior to the execution of the instrument of trust, that the bonds and
notes which Bothwell was purchasing for her from
the bond department of the National Bank were owned
at the times of the purchases by that Bank; that she
did not ascertain the fact that the bonds and notes so
purchased were owned at the times of their purchases
by the Bank until after she called at the office of her
counsel and he informed her that they had been so
purchased; that she did not know at any time after
the execution of the instrument of trust, and up to the
times when the last four purchases of bonds were made
by the trust department of the National Bank that the
bonds and notes so purchased were owned at the times
of purchase by the Bank; that she was not told of that
fact, or informed of it, until she consulted her counsel;
and that was true also of the information concerning

the profits, that is, that the Bank had made a profit on those transactions.

Further continuing, the plaintiff testified, (R 407), that she did not think of any property reserved by her, or not transferred by her to the National Bank in trust under the instrument of trust, except some money to defray her expenses, some Nevada fire insurance stock, and the Sparks lots.

Plaintiff further continuing, testified, (R 409-10), that she called on Berven at his office in the Central Bank Building after the receipt by her from him of Plaintiff's Exhibit 61, (R 673-4), in the latter part of October or in the first part of November, 1932; that no person, other than Berven and herself, was present when she called on him. Berven said that he thought that she should sell the Alameda Investment Company bonds and reinvest the money in other securities because he felt she should change those bonds into better securities; that he did not say what bonds were the better securities into which he thought she should change. She thought that it would be a great loss, the way he explained it to her, and she thought that she did not want to dispose of them at such a loss. She did not remember that he had a list of the bonds before him at the time of the conversation, but he gave her a list of her securities; that when she declined to have the bonds sold, or to have them changed, at a great loss, he asked her if she would go with him down to Cavalier & Co., and talk over the matter; that she hesitated about going because she told Berven she would not gain anything by leaving the Bank and going to a brokerage office; that Berven said he would like to have her go down and talk with Goodwin, at Cavalier & Co.'s office, on 14th Street, near Franklin, in Oakland, where she went with Berven, and where she met Goodwin; and that Goodwin looked over the list and said that she should sell the bonds.

Plaintiff further continuing, testified (R 410-11), that on the following day, after her talk with Goodwin, she called on Bothwell at his office in the National Bank; that no one besides Bothwell and herself was present on that occasion; that she asked Bothwell if he would look over the list and figure out just what she had, what those securities were worth; that she did not know in whose handwriting the pencilling on the list was, but she did know that Bothwell figured the securities for her in pencil on the list.

It was thereupon, (R 411), stipulated by counsel for the respective parties to the action that the pencil notations on the right of the center of the page, (Plaintiff's Exhibit 62, R 675-6), were made by Bothwell, as was also the case with the pencil notations on the left of the page, down to the figures, "28,860"; that the figures on the list below the figures, "28,860", were in plaintiff's handwriting.

Plaintiff, continuing her testimony, testified, (R 411), that the figures on the list below the figures, "28,860", were in her handwriting, and that she added those in there the day she left the Bank to get a balance for herself.

Plaintiff, continuing her testimony, testified, (R 411-12), that she remembered telling him that,

> "I felt greatly hurt to think that my bonds were in such a condition, and that I did not,—I declined to have them sold at that price, and that I felt that I needed legal advice."

Plaintiff went home, and in a day or two came to her counsel's office and consulted him. She brought along with her her duplicate original of the deed of trust, and also, (Plaintiff's Exhibit 62, (R 675-6)), the list of bonds with the tabulations and figures on them. Addressing her counsel, she testified, (R 412):

> "You were my attorney before that time. I cannot remember when that was, but I think it must have been 30 years ago."

She recalled receiving information from her counsel as to the sale of the business of the trust department by the National Bank to the Central Bank in April, 1933.

The testimony of plaintiff, as above summarized, is her testimony on her direct examination. She was not cross-examined.

Plaintiff was later *recalled* in her behalf *in rebuttal*, and testified, (R 532), that she did not remember asking Berven, at any time before the execution of the instrument of trust, if she could continue to deal with the bond department of the National Bank if she placed her property in trust with the Bank, and her best recollection is that no such conversation ever occurred.

She further testified, (R 532-3), that Berven never said to her, at any time before the execution of the instrument of trust, that the type of security in which her funds had been invested was not the type of security that the National Bank would buy for trust investments, nor did he ever say to her, (R 533), that the rate of income on such a type would not go over 5%, nor did she ever say to him that she should have at least 6%, nor was there ever exhibited to her by Bothwell, or by any other official of the National Bank, any offering list of securities, nor did she ever read the printed matter at the bottom of any of the various bills of sale, Defendants' Exhibit L, (R 722), nor did anyone in the Bank ever call her attention to the matter at any time, nor, (R 533), did she ever read any printed matter at the bottom of the receipts for securities deposited which had been introduced in evidence, Defendants' Exhibit K, (R 721), nor did anyone in the National Bank ever call her attention to such printed matter; and she further testified, (R 534), that no offering list was ever handed her personally by Bothwell, or by any other official of the Bank, and that she did not remember that she ever received, by mail, any offering list of the National Bank, and her best recollection was that she never received any offering list by mail.

She further testified, (R 534), that she never told Berven, at the time the instrument of trust was executed, that she would not have time to take the instrument to a lawyer because she was going back east; and that she left for the east the next day after the instrument was executed, but could not remember that she had her transportation at the time of the execution of the instrument of trust.

On cross-examination by Mr. Richards, counsel for the National Bank and its receiver, she answered to the respective questions put to her, (R 534-5), as follows:

> "*Q.* Mrs. Quinn, you stated that you did not say to Berven that you wanted 6% interest? *A.* I don't remember setting any price for interest. *Q.* You might have said it, however? *A.* I don't know. *Q.* You were interested in a high rate of interest? *A.* With safety."

2. The testimony of E. D. Bothwell.

Bothwell, a witness for defendants, testified, (R 414), that he recalled meeting plaintiff, in connection with the purchase of bonds, in the early part of the year 1926; that at that time, the National Bank and also the Central Bank, (Savings Bank), were located at the corner of 14th and Franklin Streets, Oakland, in what was known as the "Arcadia Building"; that the Banks were located there for several months, probably four, five or six months after January 1, 1926; that the bond department of the National Bank was located on the main floor, and the trust department of that Bank was located in a balcony, of the Arcadia Building; that about the middle of the year 1926, both Banks changed their location to the building known as the "Central Bank Building", at 14th Street and Broadway, Oakland, approximately a block away from the Arcadia Building; that the bond department was located on the ground floor and the trust department on the mezzanine floor of the Central Bank Building; and that the bond department of the National Bank continued to be located on the ground floor for about six months, when that department was moved to the mezzanine floor, where it continued to be located.

He recalled, (R 415), a conversation with plaintiff in January, 1926, in connection with the purchase of certain bonds, including, among others, bonds of the Province of Buenos Aires; that such conversation took place in the Arcadia Building; and that plaintiff

"came to the bond department to buy bonds, and asked if we sold bonds, and I submitted an offering list, on which was listed the bonds that the Bank had for sale."

Plaintiff did not, at that time, (R 415),

"tell me anything about the members of her family, nor did she tell me anything, at that time, about owning any real property in the State of Nevada."

"Before that time',' as he testified, (R 415), "she had never told me anything about members of her family, nor had she ever told me about owning real property in Nevada."

He could not, (R 415),

"recall the year or the time when I first heard that Mrs. Quinn had a daughter, but it was after some accident had happened, the nature of which I do not know, in which her daughter was injured, that is, I have no recollection of having heard that Mrs. Quinn had a daughter until after that accident, when she mentioned to me that her daughter was in rather a bad way on account of the accident."

He thought that, (R 415-6), the first time he heard that plaintiff ever owned any real property in Nevada was

"after the action was commenced, that is when— well it was—I think it was—it was after I left the Bank, I am pretty sure."

Plaintiff made a statement to him, (R 416),

"as to her intention to create a trust." "Probably two or three months, I don't know just exactly

how long, before a contemplated trip to Rochester, Minnesota."

She told him, (R 416), that the purpose of that trip
was a possible operation.

"*Q.* When, in relation to the date of the creation of the trust instrument, on September 24,
1929, did the plaintiff make mention to you of her
intention to create the trust? *A.* Well, I didn't
know just when that trust instrument was executed. I had no first-hand knowledge of that, but
that was the only time that she mentioned about
it, that it was her intention, and she asked me if
I thought it would be the thing to do to create a
trust, and I said I thought it would, under the circumstances."

The "circumstances" were, that she was to undergo
an operation in Rochester, at the Mayo Brothers.

"*Q.* How long after the first of her purchases,
the record showing the first of the bonds purchased on January 7, 1926, was it that she mentioned to you her intention to create a trust?
A. Well, at the time I mentioned, just two or
three months before she went to Rochester, Minnesota. *Q.* What did she say to you at that time
in regard to creating a trust? *A.* She asked me
if, in my opinion, it would be a desirable thing to
do. *Q.* What did you say? *A.* I said I
thought it would be. *Q.* Did you offer to introduce her to anyone? *A.* I did. I said, 'I will
introduce you to the trust officer'.

"She said that she had already met Mr. Read,
and I said, 'Well, I have nothing to do with the

trust department. I better take you across and introduce you to a trust officer or to Mr. Berven'."

He never at any time, (R 417), gave plaintiff a letter of introduction to Read, or to anyone else in the trust department. He took the plaintiff over and introduced her to Berven.

"*Q.* State, to the best of your recollection, what was said by you to Mr. Berven at that time. *A.* I introduced Mrs. Quinn to Mr. Berven, stating that she had been a client, and was a client, of the bond department, and she was now contemplating making a trust, and asked him to take care of that."

He left immediately, and went back to his office.

The witness then testified that he recalled, in general, the substance of what was said at the time, when she first came to the bond department. It was, (R 418), "that she had funds for investment, and that she wished to buy bonds, as she needed income."

"*Q.* Now, at that time, did Mrs. Quinn make any mention to you of the amount of interest she wanted to receive on the bonds? *A.* Only when the offering sheet was exhibited she said that she needed at least six per cent, and more if she could get it. *Q.* Did you make any statement to Mrs. Quinn as to the type of bonds that bore six per cent, or more? *A.* Just that one statement, that interest was compensation for risk taken, and the higher the interest the greater the risk."

Counsel for the Central Bank thereupon offered and read in evidence, (R 419), as an exemplar to show the form, an offering list dated July 18, 1927, and the same was marked "Defendant's Exhibit A." (R 705-7).

The witness, then continuing his testimony, testified, (R 419):

"That instrument, omitting from it the date and the list of securities, is a correct copy, as to form, of the offering list which I showed Mrs. Quinn on the occasion of her first visit in the bond department for the purpose of purchasing securities, on January 7, 1926."

He recalled the statement which he made to plaintiff at that time, (R 419-20), namely, "that the bonds listed were bonds owned by the Bank, or contracted for, which we recommend and offer for sale."

"*Q.* What, if anything, did Mrs. Quinn say to you at that time, if you recall? *A.* Well, I cannot just recall just the exact conversation, but the substance of it was that certain bonds on the list, some of them were lower rates of interest, others were higher rates, and, if the Bank recommended all on the list, why not the higher rate of interest? *Q.* Is that what she said to you? *A.* In substance, yes. *Q.* Do you recall what, if any, response you made to that? *A.* Well, the usual statement, that interest was the compensation for risk taken, and the higher the interest the greater the risk."

The attention of the witness was then called to the offering list, (R 420), "Defendants' Exhibit A", and he was asked the question, whether or not the offering list which he had and exhibited to plaintiff on

January 7, 1926, contained a statement of the rate
of interest that the various issues bore, to which the
witness answered, "It would, yes. It contained the
market price and approximate yield."

The witness then stated, (R 420-1), that when plaintiff made the purchases, he gave her a bill for the
purchase.

Thereupon, counsel for the defendants offered and
read in evidence, as an exemplar, a form of bill, which,
as the witness testified, (R 421), was given by him to
plaintiff on the occasion of the first purchase of bonds
she made, and the same was marked "Defendants'
Exhibit B", (R 708). Thereupon, counsel for defendants also offered in evidence, (R 421), bills for
the purchases made by plaintiff from the National
Bank commencing with the purchases of January 7,
1926, and ending with the purchases of June 27, 1930,
and the same were together marked "Defendants'
Exhibit C", (R 709-14).

Bothwell, then continuing his direct testimony, testified, (R 422):

"On some occasions, after the first purchase on
January 7, 1926, Mrs. Quinn called personally at
the bond department, for the purpose of dealing
in securities. On some occasions, sales were made
by mail. In the cases when Mrs. Quinn called
personally at the bond department and a transaction was entered into resulting in the sale of a
security, a bill, in the form of 'Defendants' Exhibit B', was given to Mrs. Quinn personally,
with the descriptions as to purchases that are set

forth in the various bills which are a part of 'Defendants' Exhibit C.' I think that on all purchases made by mail, the bills were turned over
to the trust department against the payment.''

Bothwell then, further continuing his direct testimony, testified, (R 422), that he received the letter
shown to him by counsel for the Central Bank, dated
Reno, Nevada, February 26, 1928, and signed "Abbie
W. Quinn", in which she acknowledged the receipt of
the notice of Western States Gas and Electric Company bonds being called for redemption, and in which
she requested, (R 715),

"Will you please collect same for me, and I will
want to reinvest the money, and will be glad if
you will select bonds (not foreign) which you
consider a good investment".

The letter was thereupon introduced in evidence
by counsel for the Central Bank, and marked Defendants' Exhibit D, (R 715).

Further continuing his direct examination, Bothwell testified, (R 423), that

"Plaintiff's Exhibit 1 was sent by me to Mrs.
Quinn in reply to her letter to me of February
26th, Defendants' Exhibit D. The bill, dated February 28, 1928, as of March 1, 1928, which is a
part of Defendants' Exhibit C, (R 709), was sent
to Mrs. Quinn with Plaintiff's Exhibit 1, and the
bill was in the form of Defendants' Exhibit B''.

Thereupon counsel for the Central Bank introduced
in evidence the bill, (on white paper), last shown to

the witness, and the same was marked Defendants'
Exhibit E, (R 716).

The witness, further continuing his direct examination, (R 423), testified that "After the first purchase, Mrs. Quinn came in again"; that he could not
state whether or not the offering list, Defendants'
Exhibit A, was exhibited to plaintiff on the occasion
of her first visit to the bond department; that, (R 423),

> "A new offering list would be put out at ir-
> regular intervals, sometimes two days might
> elapse, other times three or four or five days, or
> might be a week, depending on how active the
> sales were";

and that, (R 423-4), he could not state definitely
whether or not the offering list, Defendants' Exhibit
A, was the offering list which was in force or which
was current on the occasion of plaintiff's second series
of purchases.

The witness, after testifying that he was familiar
with the prospectus of the bonds of the Province of
Buenos Aires, Plaintiff's Exhibit 58, (R 656), testified,
in answer to questions, as follows, (R 424-5):

> "Q. Do you recall, in general, what, if any,
> words of recommendation you used to Mrs. Quinn
> in connection with her purchase of bonds? A.
> That all bonds offered by the Bank were consid-
> ered sufficiently safe for the Bank to place its
> money in them."

> "Q. Were there any other words of recom-
> mendation which you used to Mrs. Quinn, that

you now recall, in connection with purchases of securities? *A*. I usually stated that—I presume I did with Mrs. Quinn,—they were considered satisfactory, while I might have said 'safe and desirable' ".

"*Q*. What did you say, what words of recommendation, such as those which you have just now indicated? *A*. The prospectus and the reputation of the underwriting house".

The witness then testified, (R 424), that

"In the instance of the Province of Buenos Aires bonds, the underwriting house was Blair & Co., and that house enjoyed a good reputation. J. & W. Seligman & Co., of New York, were the underwriters of the issue of the Province of Callao bonds, and that house enjoyed a good reputation at the time".

The witness, after testifying, (R 424), that he had been "sitting here in Court throughout the trial", and had "noticed Mrs. Quinn testifying", and had "heard her testimony", denied, categorically, the testimony of plaintiff, (R 425-6): that she talked to him about her affairs prior to the time that she made any purchases; that she talked to him about the members of her family prior to or at the time she made any purchases of bonds; that, at or before the time she made the first purchase of bonds, she told him that she wanted to put her property in a fund; that he made such a statement to her as that the Bank could manage her personal property, but that the real estate could not be handled in this State; that he ever knew whether or not a trust company or a trust department in this State could act as trustee for real property situated in another State; that he told plaintiff that the Bank could not act as trustee or take charge of real property situated in Nevada; that he ever told plaintiff that the Bank had a department to take care of estates for widows and orphans, but he told her, that the Bank would form a trust; that he ever told her that the Bank would form a trust, and that, in the meantime, the Bank would purchase bonds for her, from time to time; that he ever had any conversation with her about United States Government bonds; and that he ever told her that she would never lose any money on the bonds that were then being sold to her.

Further testifying, on his direct examination, Bothwell said, (R 426-7), that the bonds purchased on January 7, 1926, were not taken away from the bond department by plaintiff; and that the same

"were left with the bond department as undelivered bonds. I had a conversation with her, probably on the first visit, although I cannot fix the time definitely, about what would be done with those bonds that were left with the bond department. In the course of that conversation, I said that we would be glad to clip the coupons and credit an account. At that time, I did not know that she did not have an account, and the arrangements were made that we should leave the bonds as undelivered bonds and that the coupons would be clipped and credited to a commercial account, —an ordinary banking commercial account,—subject to withdrawal on her checks, which the first coupons would open. At some time, mention was made that if bonds fell due or were redeemed, the collection would be made and her commercial account would be credited. That was an accommodation that was extended to other customers of the bond department".

"The letter, copy of which you now show me, dated February 27, 1926, addressed to Abbie W. Quinn, is a copy of a letter which was sent to Mrs. Quinn".

Thereupon, after identification of the same as a copy of a letter which the witness had sent to plaintiff, the copy was introduced in evidence by counsel for the Central Bank, and marked Defendants' Exhibit F, (R 717).

Thereupon, after identification of the same as a copy of a letter which he sent to plaintiff, the copy was introduced in evidence by counsel for the Central Bank, and marked Defendants' Exhibit G, (R 717), the same being dated August 27, 1926, addressed to Abbie W. Quinn, and stating that

"We enclose duplicate deposit tag covering coupons due Sept. 1, 1926, clipped from—

"Rhodes Jamieson Co. bonds $175.

which we are holding subject to your order".

Counsel for the Central Bank also thereupon introduced in evidence another letter, dated March 28, 1927, which the witness identified as a copy of a letter which he had written to plaintiff, and the same was marked Defendants' Exhibit H, (R 718), and which stated that

"We enclose herewith duplicate deposit tag for $325, covering coupons due Apr. 1, 1927 clipped from

"Miller & Lux	$175.00
"Western States G. & E.	150.00
	$325.00

which we are holding subject to your order".

Counsel for the Central Bank also introduced in evidence, as Defendants' Exhibit I, a copy of a letter, dated August 17, 1929, addressed to plaintiff and signed by Bothwell, (R 718), as "Assistant Cashier, Manager Bond Dept."

Counsel for the Central Bank thereupon also introduced in evidence a letter, dated December 1, 1929, addressed to S. Berven from plaintiff, and the same was marked Defendants' Exhibit J, (R 719-20), the letter referring to a difference between the money in her account and the Bank's balances.

The witness, continuing his testimony on his direct examination, testified, (R 429), that

"The bond department of the Bank, at the time of the first of the purchases, did not then have any record of bonds which were held in safe keeping. More than a year afterwards, a safe keeping file or record system was inaugurated".

Counsel for the Central Bank thereupon introduced in evidence four sheets, three of them signed by plaintiff. Two of the three sheets, which were dated February 2, 1929, referred to the Washoe County, County Roads and Highways Improvement and Construction bonds. The remaining of the said three sheets, which was dated July 9, 1929, referred to the Southern United Gas Company bonds. The fourth sheet, which was dated August 23, 1929, referred to the Central West Public Service Company bonds, and was not signed by plaintiff, but it was stipulated by counsel for the respective parties to the action that the last mentioned bonds were received by the National Bank from plaintiff. The said four sheets, together, were marked Defendant's Exhibit K, (R 721).

Counsel for plaintiff then produced, (R 429), as coming from plaintiff's possession, 16 sheets, none of them signed by plaintiff, referring to the deposit of bonds by plaintiff with the National Bank, and the same were introduced in evidence by counsel for the Central Bank, and, together, were marked Defendants' Exhibit M, (R 726-29).

The witness, further testifying on his direct examination, said that, (R 429-30): "The safe keeping records were kept in the bond department of the National Bank"; that the list, Plaintiff's Exhibit 62, was not prepared by the witness; that he did not ask anyone to prepare it for him or for Mrs. Quinn; that the pencilled matter appearing on Plaintiff's Exhibit 62, on the right side of the first page, and on the left side of the first page, thereof, down to and including the figures "28,860", was in the witness' handwriting; that the figures below the figures "28,860" were not in his handwriting; and that plaintiff brought the exhibit to him, but he could not recall the date when she did so, but it was her only visit to him or to his office after the trust was created.

The witness was then questioned by counsel for the Central Bank, and testified, as follows, (R 430):

"*Q.* Do you recall what conversation, if any, you had with Mrs. Quinn on the occasion on which she brought that list to you? *A.* She came in with the list, in a very friendly attitude, and said that she was very sorry that her securities were going the way they were, meaning defaults, and asked if I would look over this list, which I did, and pencilled what was just then considered to be the market price, just to determine approximately what they were worth at that time".

The witness further testified, on his direct examination, that, (R 430-1): he commenced the bond business with the Liberty Loan drives in the years 1917 and 1918, and possibly also in the year 1919; that from that time on he was, and is now, in the bond business; that he was familiar with the going prices of securities which were sold to plaintiff at the time they were sold; that "The securities which were sold to her were sold at prices which were the going prices for those securities. At the time those securities were sold to her, the securities had a going or a market value"; and that "The securities which were sold to her were sold to her at the then going market prices".

Counsel for plaintiff thereafter, (R 431), handed to counsel for the Central Bank a package, with the

statement by counsel for plaintiff that the package
had been handed to him by plaintiff that morning, and
that it contained original bills, on white paper, of
which the bills on yellow paper, introduced in evidence
and marked Defendants Exhibit C, (R 709-12), were
copies or duplicate bills. Thereupon counsel for the
Central Bank introduced in evidence the said white
sheets, or original bills, and the same, together, were
marked Defendants' Exhibit L, (R 722-25).

The record contains a tabulation, (R 431-2), inserted in the record, for convenient reference, of the
respective bonds, and their respective par values, and
the dates of the said respective bills, —the originals on
white paper and the duplicates on yellow paper, —introduced in evidence.

The witness, continuing his direct examination,
testified that, (R 433), in his testimony, theretofore
given, he referred to a certain offering list, which he
testified was presented to plaintiff on the occasion of
her first visit to the National Bank, in the bond department; that, after that first visit, which occurred
in January, 1926, plaintiff called at the bond department of the National Bank, from time to time; that
the procedure which occurred on the occasion of her
subsequent visits to the bond department was similar
to that on her first visit; that the offering sheet always
was exhibited where a person came in to purchase
bonds; that, as he also had testified, an offering sheet
would come out at irregular intervals, sometimes one
would be three or four days, or possibly a week, after
another; that, on the occasion of plaintiff's subsequent

42

visits to the bond department, the current offering sheet would be shown to her,

"and she would state that she now had funds for investment, and asked what we had to offer, and the securities would be secured from the offering sheet, —selected from the offering sheet. We would both be seated in my office, and the offering list would be between her and myself".

On subsequent visits, so the witness testified, (R 433-4), "The conversations usually were not of long duration, but would relate directly to the fact that Mrs. Quinn had additional funds, and asking what we had to offer"; and that "We would just mention by name those that we had to offer, and, if there were any questions regarding where a particular company was located, they would be answered"; but that he did not recall any instances of plaintiff's asking him about particular companies; that "She did not make inquiry, in a general way, about companies listed on various offering lists"; and that "Offering lists were sent to her by mail. It was a custom to enclose offering lists in correspondence".

The witness further testified that, (R 434),

"Bills for the purchases were not sent to the trust department before the trust instrument was signed on September 24, 1929. After that instrument was signed, the bills were sent to the trust department".

On *cross examination,* Bothwell testified as follows, (R 434-5):

"I stated, in my direct examination, that it was our custom to include offering lists in mailing correspondence. That custom, as I recall, extended from shortly after we entered the new building until the bond department was discontinued.

"The first conversation that I have related on my direct examination between myself and Mrs. Quinn, concerning the purchase of bonds, occurred in the premises in the Arcadia Building temporarily occupied by the two Banks. As I testified on my direct examination, some months later, I think six months, the two Banks removed back to the premises known as the 'Central Bank Building', on the corner of 14th Street and Broadway. That building was in the course of construction at the time we were temporarily in the Arcadia Building. The premises occupied by the two Banks, before their removal to the Arcadia Building, was at 14th Street and Broadway, on the same lot where the present building is now located.

"There is no reference to an offering list in Plaintiff's Exhibit 1, (R 539-40), dated February 28, 1928, which you now show me, with the request that I examine the exhibit.

"*Q.* Do you know why it was omitted? *A.* It was not customary to refer to it. It was just simply our custom to put it in all correspondence. We did not refer to it, as we did not—that is, we did not communicate with prospects at any time on securing business. We just dropped them in just to show what we were offering.

(R 436). "*Q.* Well, Mrs. Quinn was not a 'prospect' at that time, she was a customer?

A. Yes, she was a customer. *Q.* A pretty steady one for a long time, a number of years? *A.* She had been in a number of times, yes.

"*Q. Do I understand you to testify that, when she came in person to call on you, concerning the purchase of bonds, that you handed her an offering sheet? A. The offering sheets were on the desk, immediately before her.* (Emphasis added).

"*Q. Did you, when she was calling on you, personally, concerning purchases, hand her an offering sheet? A. I may have handed her one, or exhibited one to her. On all occasions, one was exhibited to her whether she took it in her hand or not, I could not at this time say, but on every occasion the offering sheet was exhibited to her. She may have picked it up in her hand and looked at it, or looked at it sitting alongside the desk.* (Emphasis added).

(R 436-7). "*Q.* Well, that is not very definite. Will you say she did that sort of thing, or you did that sort of thing, hand it to her, or that she took the offering sheet from the pile on your desk, and looked at it? *A. She looked at them, yes. Q. Always? A. On every occasion when she made a personal visit to purchase. Q. On every occasion, it was her custom, is that your answer? A. Yes. Q. And on every occasion when you wrote to her, all that you can say is that that was your custom with all customers to put the offering sheet in with your letters; is that right? A. That was the custom, yes. Q. You cannot say, in this particular case, that that custom was followed with Mrs. Quinn? A. I cannot, no.* (Emphasis added).

"Q. What do you mean in your direct testimony by saying you 'exhibited' to her an offering sheet when she called? A. The fact that the offering sheets were always available on my desk, a dozen or more, depending on the number we had, were there. They were always exhibited to every client who came in to purchase bonds, and Mrs. Quinn stopped in. Q. Is that what you would have his Honor, and myself, and the counsel to understand, that you meant by the word 'exhibiting', which was repeatedly asked you in that form, 'Did you exhibit to her an offering sheet'? A. I did. Q. That is what you mean by 'exhibition', is it? A. Yes." (Emphasis added).

"There is no reference at all to an offering list in Plaintiff's Exhibit 12, (R 555), which you now show me and have requested me to read. You have called my attention to the word 'secure', in the sentence in Plaintiff's Exhibit 1, (R 539), (referring to Mrs. Quinn), 'You will note that we secured the Medford bonds at 97, which will give you a 6.22% yield' ".

(R 438). "Q. Did you have any difficulty in securing those bonds from yourself? A. The word 'secured' could have been another word, 'confirmed', the word 'secured' being used was not in the sense that we went out and purchased the bonds. It was a matter of confirmation to her, the bonds at a price of 97.

"Q. Mr. Bothwell, this was a very important transaction, involving an offering to her of $5,000 par value bonds, which you said you 'secured' at 97, and I am asking you what did you mean by 'secured' them, when you had them already?

A. Just as I have just now explained. *Q.* That is the only explanation you can make? *A.* Yes, that is the only explanation I can make".

(R 438-9). "*Q.* What was the object of enclosing an offering list in a letter in which you recommended certain bonds, like the two exhibits which I have just shown you, Plaintiff's Exhibit 1 and Plaintiff's Exhibit 12, (R 555)? *A.* In case the recommendations should not be satisfactory, the list of bonds we had for sale at the time would be on this offering list.

"*Q.* But, Mr. Bothwell, you always recommended bonds to her, did you not? *A.* No specific recommendation, other than that contained in our offering list. *Q.* That is not my question. You always recommended to her—do you understand the question? *A.* Yes. *Q.* An investment in certain bonds, didn't you? *A.* Not without the discussion, when she was present, regarding the list of bonds. *Q.* Well, when you recommended, as you did in one of the two letters, Plaintiff's Exhibits 1 and 12, which I just showed you, those particular bonds as safe and desirable investments for her funds, when you did that, you made a recommendation to her positively? *A.* I did, because she was absent.

"*Q.* Did she ever turn down any recommendation you made of those bonds, disapprove them, in other words? *A.* In reply to a request that I keep her advised of attractive bonds that might be offered, I sent her, on two occasions, a suggestion for investments, which were not followed".

(R 440). "*Q.* What are the two occasions, can you refer to them? *A.* Well, I cannot just recall them at the moment".

Thereupon counsel for the Central Bank produced copies of two letters, which he introduced in evidence as Defendants' Exhibits N, (R 735), dated January 26, 1926, and Defendants' Exhibit O, (R 736), dated February 6, 1926, and addressed respectively to Abbie W. Quinn, and signed by Bothwell, as "Assistant Cashier, Manager Bond Dept.", or "Manager Bond Department".

By counsel for plaintiff, (R 440). "I am showing you copies addressed to her by, I presume, yourself, although the copies don't contain the signature. One is dated January 26, 1926, and the other is dated February 6, 1926".

The witness, to counsel for plaintiff. "Those are the two letters I referred to. I did not hear from her in regard to them, as far as I can recall. I do not recall having received any reply to them. I always mailed to the last address known to us, and I did not know whether she had difficulty in getting those letters or not. I do not know whether or not she received the letter of January 26, 1926, and all I testify to in that regard is that, as far as I know, I had no answer to the letter".

Defendants' Exhibit N, (R 735), addressed to "My dear Mrs. Quinn", states as follows:

"We are enclosing herewith a circular descriptive of a new issue of Rheinelbe Union Bonds, which are being offered today.

"We consider this one of the most attractive of the Foreign Issues that have been offered. The splendid earnings of the combined companies, together with the past dividend record has been exceptionally good.

"Application will be made to list the bonds on the New York Stock Exchange, which will give them a wide marketability. Principal and interest is payable in United States gold coin. The present price of 94 and accrued interest will yield over 7.55%.

"We could recommend $5000 of these bonds as a conservative investment for your account.

"With very kindest regards, we remain".

Defendants' Exhibit O, (R 736), addressed to "Dear Mrs. Quinn", states as follows:

"We are enclosing herewith a circular descriptive of Cities Service Company Bonds.

"This company is one of the largest Public Utility Holding Companies in the country.

"We particularly call your attention to the splendid earning statement which shows that for the year 1925 they earned nine times the amount required to cover all bonds outstanding. For the past seven years, they have averaged seven times requirements and in no one year has the amount been less than six times.

"The bond has marketability, being regularly quoted in New York.

"We recommend them as a safe and conservative investment".

The witness further testified that, (R 440-1):

"The pencillings on the right-hand margin of the first page of Plaintiff's Exhibit 62, (R 675-6), which you have handed me, are in my handwriting, and the pencillings on the left-hand margin of the first page, down to and including the figures '28,860', are also in my handwriting. The figures in pencil immediately below the figures '28,860' are not in my handwriting.

"The abbreviations in the first column, on the right-hand margin of the first page, of the list, '@10', '@14' and '@11', respectively, mean 'at $10', 'at $14' and 'at $11', respectively, per hundred; and the figures having a total of $1,850, carried out in the second column, on the right-hand margin of the first page, '500', '700' and '550', respectively, mean dollars, for $5,000, par value, of the bonds of Central West Public Service Company, $5,000, par value, of the bonds of Southern United Gas Company, and $5,000, par value, of the bonds of St. Louis Gas & Coke Company, respectively. The abbreviation 'Def.', in the first column, on the right-hand margin of the first page, means 'default' in the payment of interest".

(NOTE: The witness made a mistake in the addition. The total is "$1750", instead of "$1850".)

(R 441-2). "The figures, in pencil, made by me, on the first page of the list, first and second columns, on the right-hand margin, represent my estimate of the market prices, at the time, of the specific bonds indicated, including the prices of the bonds of Medford Irrigation District, Province of Buenos Aires and Province of Callao. At the time that this list was exhibited to me, when Mrs. Quinn was present in the office, it represented my estimate of the then market values. I do not recall whether or not I consulted any books or publications as to what the market prices were at that time. I may have done so, but I don't remember. I was more or less familiar with the going quotations.

"We had, at the time, publications of different concerns of market quotations of stocks and bonds, Moody's Manual Service, and also, I believe, Fitch's Quotation Service. Those publications are used quite generally by dealers in bonds and stocks, including bond houses, throughout the country, and, from the statistical and historical standpoints, are relied upon and followed by dealers as being correct.

"I am familiar, from year to year, with the ratings of bonds as contained in Moody's publications, and have examined a great number of them, and am familiar with Moody's ratings. The rating of bonds as "Aaa" means bonds of high grade, or highest grade. The rating refers to such securities as those of our own government, and would be the best bond ratings of governmental bonds. The rating 'Aa' is a rating not quite so good as that of 'Aaa', but still considered high grade. The rating 'A' is not quite so good as high grade, but, I believe, its meaning is excellent or sound, but not so good as 'Aaa' or 'Aa'. In other words, 'A' would mean a sound security, but not quite as good as 'Aa' or 'Aaa' ''.

(R 443). "The Moody rating 'Baa' means a good hazard of safety. The rating 'Ba' would not be quite so good, and the rating 'B' would be the rating above the best of speculatives, but the low-

est of semi-investments. It would not mean a
speculative security, but the lowest of semi-investments. The Moody rating 'Caa', 'Ca' and 'C'
are not as good as the Moody ratings 'Baa', 'Ba'
and 'B'.

"I recognize the sheet which you show me,
issued in 1931, as a sample of a sheet issued by
Moody in that year, and is usually inserted in the
front of Moody's Manual Service".

Counsel for plaintiff thereupon introduced in evidence the sheet so referred to, and the same was
marked Plaintiff's Exhibit 63, (R 677-95).

The witness, further continuing his cross-examination, testified as follows, (R 443-4):

"Reading from that sheet, the rating of 'B'
bonds is as follows:

" 'Bonds carrying the B rating are always
characterized by speculative features, being well
down the scale in our statistical formula. Usually
their asset value is somewhat uncertain, their
earning power is weak or of a fluctuating character and their stability is comparatively poor. Very
often a bond issue of the B class, in the course
of time, rises to a higher plane, but almost as frequently it turns out poorly and slips to' a still
lower grade. A bond at present in default, or of
a company in receivership, with considerable
assets as yet unliquidated may be given this rating.
Or this rating may indicate such probabilities.
Intelligent selection is absolutely essential' ".

(R 444). "I do not recall that I ever looked
up the rating of such a bond as that of Fageol

Motors Company in either Moody's Service or Fitch's Service.

"I believe that Moody's Service rates the bonds of the Province of Buenos Aires and also the bonds of the Province of Callao. I did not look at the ratings in these publications for either of those bonds before I recommended those bonds to Mrs. Quinn. We relied upon the prospectuses of the underwriting houses, and the ratings were not usually available until some time after the offerings were made. Some of the bond houses on which we relied did not turn out to be reliable".

The witness then, continuing his cross examination, testified, in respective answers to respective questions, as follows, (R 444):

"*Q. What was the extent of the acquaintance, Mr. Bothwell, you had with Mrs. Quinn, if any, prior to the time when she made the first purchase of bonds and notes? A. I don't remember Mrs. Quinn before that time. Q. You don't have any recollection about her at all? A. None*". (Emphasis added.)

The witness, continuing his cross examination, testified as follows, (R 444-5):

"*I became assistant cashier and general manager of the bond department of the National Bank about 1920 or 1921. I do not recall exactly the exact time. The first time I remember meeting Mrs. Quinn was when she came to the bond department in the temporary quarters of the Bank. I recognized her as someone that I had seen, but I*

*did not know her name, and that was the reason,
in order to avoid embarrassing questions, asking
her who she was, why I asked her to sign the card
on which I listed the securities that she purchased.*
(Emphasis added.)

"I do not recall that she had ever been to my
office, for any purpose, before the first time to
which I testified, when she called to buy bonds. To
the best of my recollection, she never called at my
office before that time".

The witness, further continuing his cross examination, was asked the following questions, and gave the
following answers, respectively, (R 445-6):

*"Q. When she came and called on you, on that
first occasion, as you testify, what did she say to
you? A. That she wished to buy bonds—I don't
know the exact words, but the substance of whatever conversation took place was that she wished
to buy bonds, and asked if the Bank had bonds
for sale. Q.* What did you tell her? *A.* That
the Bank had, and exhibited the offering sheet.
Q. That was the time when you said that you
exhibited to her this offering sheet? *A.* Yes.
Q. With that explanation which you have of
Defendants' Exhibit A? *A.* Yes. *Q.* At that
time, did you recommend to her any bonds as a
desirable and safe investment for her? *A.* Just
the entire list, or bonds recommended by the
Bank". (Emphasis added.)

(R 446). "(Mr. Slack): That is not an answer
to my question. (To the reporter: Read the question, please. Question read by the reporter).

"*A.* That entire list of bonds were recommended by the Bank, and they were considered by the Bank as safe and desirable.

"*Q.* I will put the question again: Did you recommend to her these bonds that were purchased by her on that occasion? *A.* They were included in the general recommendation.

"*Q.* That is still not an answer, I submit, may it please your Honor. Did you recommend any specific bonds to her? I will put it in that way: Did she select them from the list? *A.* They were selected by her. *Q.* Selected by her? *A.* From the list. *Q.* From the list? *A.* Yes".

(R 446). The attention of the witness was directed by counsel for plaintiff to a photostatic copy of Schedule A, Plaintiff's Exhibit 47, (R 645), and to the four blocks of bonds purchased from the National Bank, bond department, according to the legend at the heading on the Schedule, on January 7, 1926, namely, Province of Buenos Aires, par value, $10,000, Miller & Lux, Inc., par value, $5,000, Rhodes-Jamieson Co., par value $5,000, and Western States Gas and Electric Co., par value, $5,000.

Bothwell, in that connection, was interrogated on his cross examination and answered as follows, (R 447):

"*Q.* She selected, you mean to say, those bonds? *A.* She did. *Q.* And you had no hand in it?

"*A.* It was a mutual selection from the list. In other words, she would point out—she first of all stated that she needed the higher rate of in-

terest, and a rate of interest above six per cent.,
and that was the reason for the selection by her
of those bonds, on the ground that, if they were all
recommended by the Bank, the lists were recommended by the Bank, then one might be as good
as another, but, if they were recommended, then
the higher rate of interest would also be satisfactory. I told her that, in my opinion, high interest
represented an additional risk, but that, as the
Bank recommended all these bonds, they probably
were considered as satisfactory as any bond having an interest rate of that kind".

Continuing his testimony on cross examination,
Bothwell was asked the question by counsel for plaintiff, (R 447), why he used the word "probably" in his
"answer this time", and did not use it, as counsel recalled it, in his direct examination, whereupon he answered and was questioned as follows, (R 447):

"*A.* Well, whether the word 'probably' was
used or not, I could not say definitely. *Q.* You
could not state—— *A.* I could not state positively. *Q.* Could not state positively? *A.* No.
But that was my usual custom, where high rates
of interest were selected on our offering lists. We
had lower rates of interest, as well as high".

(R 448). "*Q.* Did you warn her, at that time,
that there was a decidedly speculative character
in an offering by a department of a government,
or by a government, of any other bonds of any
government, or any department of a government,
a decidedly speculative character, if the bonds
carried $7\frac{1}{2}\%$ or 7% even? *A.* I did not. *Q.* Why

didn't you do it? *A*. Because they were not considered at that time highly speculative. *Q*. Didn't she ask you, didn't she say she wanted to invest funds in bonds? *A*. Yes. *Q*. She didn't ask you to pick out speculative bonds for her, or to help her in the selection of them? *A*. They were not considered speculative. *Q*. She did not ask you that? *A*. No, *she did not ask for speculative bonds.*"

The witness, on cross examination, continued as follows, (R 448):

"The rating on the Province of Buenos Aires bonds at that time was the rating 'A'. I cannot give you the rating on the Province of Callao bonds without referring to the record".

(R 448). "In the first interview which I had with Mrs. Quinn, when she came to me stating that she wanted to buy bonds, she did not say anything about owning any bonds. She did not mention the Washoe County bonds, or how she acquired them, nor did she mention the Sparks Building note and mortgage and how she obtained those securities".

(R 449). "The bonds and notes were always sold to Mrs. Quinn at the market price at the time of the sale. I do not recall any fluctuations from day to day in the market price of the bonds sold to her. There was not fluctuating market on bonds at that time. Practically all of the bonds were in what was termed a 'syndicate', and were sold at a fixed offering price. If the Bank was a member of a syndicate, it was bound by the terms

of the syndicate agreement and had to sell at a
certain price, so that, if there were any fluctuations in the price of a bond during the particular
day on which it was sold, that was not material,
since the Bank was bound by what the syndicate
terms of the agreement might be''.

(R 449-50). "The legend 'Member of Syndicate', on the extreme right of Schedule A, Plaintiff's Exhibit 47, (R 645), refers to the respective
bonds of the Province of Buenos Aires, Miller &
Lux, Inc., Rhodes-Jamieson Co., Western States
Gas & Electric Co., California Cotton Mills Co.,
Jackson Furniture Co. and Province of Callao,
purchased in 1926 and 1927. The first four of
these, under the preceding legend 'How Payment
Was Made', appear as 'Not Recorded'. I do not
know positively how Mrs. Quinn paid for those
bonds. For the next three bonds, namely, those of
California Cotton Mills Co., Jackson Furniture
Co. and Province of Callao, under the said legend
'How Payment was Made', appears the statement
'Check on 94-1, Reno, Nevada'. As to the first
four bonds on Schedule A, indicated as 'Not Recorded', there would be a record, but I believe the
records were not available at the time when
Schedule A was prepared, but there would be of
necessity some record. They were not paid in cash,
and must have been paid by a check. The check
might have been on a deposit which Mrs. Quinn
had in one or the other, or in both, of the two
Banks, that is, in the National Bank and in the
Savings Bank. I know that the actual cash was
not given to me, because I would have remembered
that''.

(R 450-1). "The bonds of the Fagoel Motors Company appear on the extreme right of Schedule A as having been in a 'Selling Group'. A selling group was a secondary group. A syndicate participated usually in a definite commitment. A selling group would be allowed to take down and pay for a certain number of bonds with the privilege, in a great many cases, of obtaining additional bonds, if the selling orders exceeded what we considered were our requirements. When, we will say, the house of J. & W. Seligman & Co. had, or was in the prospects of acquiring, quite a block of bonds, perhaps the entire issue, that house would request of various dealers information as to whether or not they would take a certain number of the bonds. We usually received a lengthy wire describing the issue and stating that the bonds were offered, and, in some cases, they would say they were reserving for us a certain number, which were left open, and, if we wished to participate, we would wire back that we would take down a certain number of bonds, and, in that way, they could place most of the bonds, if not all of them".

(R 451). "The National Bank, as indicated on the second sheet of Plaintiff's Exhibit 9, (R 552), now shown to me, paid, on February 27, 1928, for the $10,000 par value bonds of Fageol Motors Company, $9,500, and, on the same day, namely, February 27, 1928, the National Bank sold the said bonds to Mrs. Quinn for $10,000, or at a profit to the Bank of $500".

(R 451). "I am somewhat familiar with the Medford Irrigation District situation. The National Bank was the largest dealer in the bonds of the District, and bought bonds at the time they were offered at whatever price the Bank could get for them. The Bank set the market price for the bonds. The last three items, all relating to bonds of the District, appearing on the first sheet of Plaintiff's Exhibit 9, show, (1), that on March 22, 1926, the National Bank purchased $1,500, par value, and on September 6, 1927, purchased $2,500, par value, of the District bonds from Dr. E. A. Majors, at par, in each instance, and (2), that on February 2, 1928, the National Bank purchased $1,000, par value, of the District bonds from A. W. Maher at the price of $777.50; or for a total cost to the Bank of $4,777.50; and that on February 27, 1928, the Bank sold all the said bonds to the plaintiff for the price of $4,850, or at a profit of $72.50.''

(R 451-2). "I presume that Dr. Majors was a customer of the National Bank at the time. I have seen him, but not in connection with these purchases of the bonds from him. All I know about the purchases of the bonds from him is when the bonds came into the bond department inventory, and then I ascertained, for the first time, that the bonds had been purchased from him in two separate transactions, one for $1,500, par value, and the other for $2,500, par value. I was never informed why it was that somebody in the Bank, other than myself, had arranged these transactions with Dr. Majors for the bond department, and was not informed at that time or later of any indebtedness of Dr. Majors to the Bank. I knew nothing of that''.

(R 452-3). "The only explanation that I can give about the purchase by the Bank from A. H. Maher of $1,000, par value, bonds of the District is that it was a 'distressed' bond that was offered at the price and the Bank purchased it. I don't know that such was the fact, nor do I know that the bond was not salable outside of the bank. We were the market for the bonds of the District, and the Bank was probably at that time the only bidder for the bond. I would not say that Mr. Maher could not have marketed his bond other than at the Bank, or that the bond was not worth what he could get for it outside of the Bank, because I don't know whether he attempted to sell it anywhere else. I could not say definitely that I had the transaction with him, but it was in the bond department. I don't recall just how the purchase from him was transacted or anything about it".

The witness, continuing his cross examination, was questioned, and answered, as follows, (R 453-4):

"*Q.* Why do you call it a 'distressed' bond? *A.* Well, I just used that word 'distressed'. Frequently, people were in need of funds and were willing to sacrifice in order to get funds quickly. We might have taken an order to dispose of a bond and when it was disposed of, to give the owner of the bond the dividends, but, if the owner wanted cash immediately, we would designate it as a 'distress' bond, and say, 'Well, we will pay so much for it now'.

"I don't know that the bond was a 'distressed' bond when we came to purchase it from Mr. Maher. When I called it a 'distressed' bond, I meant to say that it might have been a 'distressed' bond. I don't know what Mr. Maher's necessities were at the time that the bond was purchased''.

"Q. When you came to sell it to Mrs. Quinn, it was not a 'distressed' bond? A. It was one of quite a number. Q. Well, it wasn't a 'distressed' bond when you came to sell it to Mrs. Quinn. Look at the price you got for these three lots, $5,000 altogether, par value, for Mrs. Quinn? A. Yes. Q. How much did you get? A. $4,850''.

(R. 454). "Q. You did not charge her on the basis of the 'distressed' bond, we will call it, but on a basis which you fixed? A higher basis than that? A. It was fixed by the Bank. It was not fixed by me personally. I had orders to sell at the price which was obtained. The price was fixed by one of the executive officers, Mr. Carlston, who was the President of the Bank. Mr. Carlston died after leaving the Bank. He was supplanted, as President of the Bank, by Mr. Mount''.

Continuing, the witness further testified, on his cross examination, (R 454):

"It is the fact that at or about the time the bonds of the Medford District began to decline very sharply in the market. That was general of irrigation bonds. I did not know at the time of the sale to her that the bonds of the District were on the decline. The fact that one of the bonds was purchased by the Bank from Mr. Maher for $777.50 did not excite my suspicions at all that there must have been something wrong with the bond, or with the bonds generally of irrigation districts''.

(R. 454). "One of the officers of the Bank,
named Hassler, visited the District to attend a
convention, and I understand that a message was
sent to the Bank calling attention to the attrac-
tiveness of the District, and the bond department
was then advised to purchase bonds of the District when they came into the market at prices
which would be submitted before they were purchased. Mr. Hassler was a cashier of the Bank
at the time, but is not now with either of the
Banks".

Further, the witness testified, on cross examination,
with questions and answers as follows, (R 455):

"*Q*. Those two lots, referring to the first two
blocks of Medford District bonds purchased by
the National Bank from Dr. Majors, hadn't moved
very rapidly, had they, if the Bank held them
during that length of time? *A*. The Medford
Irrigation District bonds were traded in by the
Bank, and accumulation was irrespective of the
number of the bonds or the purchase date, the
price they were placed in the inventory, and it
was just a coincidence that those particular bonds
were taken out at that time. They were not sold
again before the time of purchase, but just simply taken out of the inventory at that time.

"*Q*. The point is, they did not move very
rapidly? *A*. The bonds were sold right along.

"*Q*. But the Bank held those two blocks of
bonds for quite a considerable length of time
before they were disposed of to Mrs. Quinn.
A. That is true.

"The Court: 'So I may follow the testimony on
these Medford Irrigation bonds, the net to the

National Bank was $72.50?' Mr. Slack: 'Yes, that is correct'. Mr. Kelly: 'On $5,000 worth'.

"*Q.* During all of the times of the purchases, beginning with the very first and down to the end, when you had any connection with the matter, that is down to the four last purchases, you understand to what I refer— *A.* Yes''.

The witness, still further testifying on his cross examination, with questions and answers, as follows, (R 456):

"*Q. Did you believe that Mrs. Quinn had implicit confidence in you? A.* I did not know that she had. *Q.* Did you believe it? I am attempting to get your state of mind. *A. I had no thought on the matter at all. In reference to that, I presume she did in the Bank, she was buying bonds from the Bank, because she had confidence in the Bank. I don't know what confidence she had in me personally*''.

(R 456). "*Q.* Well, I will take your answer as far as it goes, Mr. Bothwell. You were on quite friendly terms with her during this period of time? *A.* Nothing, except just on business. I never met Mrs. Quinn outside, unless I said 'How do you do' on the street as we would pass each other. I do not recall that in my letters to her I addressed her as 'My dear Mrs. Quinn', nor that she addressed me as 'My dear Mr. Bothwell'. If it is in the letters, they were so addressed. That was the customary form''.

(R 456-7). "*Q.* Calling your attention to the visit which Mrs. Quinn made at your office in the latter part of the month of September, or in the early part of the month of October, 1932, when she had with her and handed you this exhibit, Plaintiff's Exhibit 62, (R 675-6), what did she first say to you?

"*A.* I do not recall the opening of the conversation. She came in and she was in a very friendly attitude, and, after the greeting, she said that she was very sorry that her bonds had gone down to such an extent, as she had ascertained they had, and presented the list, and asked if I would look over the list and tell her approximately what they were worth at the present time."

(R 457). "*Q.* Then what did you do? *A.* I made the pencil memorandum on the sheet. *Q.* Then handed back the document or paper that she handed you, the list of bonds, Plaintiff's Exhibit No. 62, with your pencillings? *A.* I did, yes. *Q.* What did she say then? *A.* I do not recall the conversation in its entirety. *Q.* Can you give us your best recollection of what she said when you showed that the loss on the bonds over the cost price to her was $28,860? *A.* I do not recall".

(R 457-8). "*Q.* Your mind is blank on that? "*A.* Well, I recall her coming in and talking with me, but just what the conversation was, other than that the price of the bonds and of the—of what I thought of the future prospects might be, I said it would be impossible to tell, that in all probability some of them would show appreciation over a period of time, but we could not guess at that time what the ultimate outcome would be; probably words to that effect. I had

not only Mrs. Quinn, but others asking similar
questions many clients of the Bank and outsiders
coming in to me constantly.

"I don't recall anything in that respect about
the Medford Irrigation District bonds".

(R 458). "*Q*. Well, can't you tell by what she
said when she saw those figures, your computations? *A*. I do not recall. She had already, from
some source which I do not know, ascertained
approximately what the value was, because she—
when she approached me she said that she was
sorry that the bonds had gone down so much, so
she had evidently ascertained from some other
source".

"*Q*. Well, we will leave that aside. I am directing your attention to what, if anything, you can
recall she said when you handed back this tabulation to her, this tabulation with your pencillings
upon it? *A*. I do not recall anything definitely".

"*Q*. Didn't she say to you that she felt very
much hurt? *A*. She may have said so, although
I do not recall. *Q*. Is it your best recollection
that she said something of that kind to you?
A. I do not recall.

"I said nothing about disposing of the bonds.
She never said to me that she would not dispose
of her bonds but would consult a lawyer about
the matter".

(R 458-9). "*Q*. She said to you, so you said,
both on your direct examination and you have
repeated it now, in substance, as I read from your
direct examination, as follows: 'She came in with
the list, in a very friendly attitude, and said that

she was very sorry that her securities were going
the way they were, meaning defaulting', is that
right? *A.* Yes. *Q.* Did she leave in a very
friendly attitude? *A.* I thought so.

(R 459). "*Q.* You thought she was pleased
with the showing, did you?

"*A.* No, she wasn't pleased with the showing of the way the securities had gone down,
but she always had a very gracious manner, and
she left feeling, I presume, that she would have
to either abide by the consequences or—I didn't
know what was in her mind. She never told me
that she contemplated any action at all.

"*Q.* When you said that you presumed she left
—what did you mean by 'presume'? *A.* Well,
that was my own presumption. *Q.* But not her
attitude at the time? *A.* It seemed to be just
friendly, but disappointed. *Q.* Just friendly, although the computations which you had computed
showed she suffered a loss over the cost price of
66%, or thereabouts, she was still very, very
friendly? *A.* I did not say she was very, very
friendly, but still appeared friendly".

On *redirect examination,* Bothwell testified as follows, (R 460):

"Cavalier & Co. underwrote the bonds of Alameda Investment Company and of the Alameda
Park Co."

Counsel for plaintiff admitted that during the
months of January and February, 1926, the plaintiff
had, as her address, Peralta Apartments, Oakland.

The witness, continuing his testimony on his re-direct examination, testified as follows, (R 460) :

"The original of the letter, copy of which you now show me, dated January 26, 1926, addressed to Mrs. Abbie Quinn, was sent by me to her".

Thereupon counsel for the Central Bank introduced in evidence the said copy of the letter last referred to, shown to the witness, and the same was marked Defendants' Exhibit N, (R 735).

The witness, continuing his testimony on his re-direct examination, testified as follows, (R 460):

"Mrs. Quinn did not buy the bonds referred to in that letter, that is, the Rheinelbe Union bonds. I did not hear from her about that bond issue.

"The original of the letter, copy of which you now show me, dated February 6, 1926, addressed to Mrs. Abbie W. Quinn, was sent by me to her".

Thereupon counsel for the Central Bank introduced in evidence the said copy of the letter last referred to, shown to the witness, and the same was marked Defendants' Exhibit O, (R 736).*

---

*NOTE: The letter, which was addressed to "Dear Mrs. Quinn", and was signed by the witness as "Assistant Cashier, Manager Bond Department", stated as follows:

"We are enclosing herewith a circular descriptive of Cities Service Company Bonds.

"This company is one of the largest Public Utility Holding Companies in the country.

"We particularly call your attention to the splendid earning statements which shows that for the year 1925 they earned nine times the amount required to cover all

The witness, continuing his testimony on his redirect examination, testified as follows, (R 460-1) :

"I am familiar with the rating which Medford Irrigation District bonds had in Moody's at the time of the sale thereof to her. The rating was 'A' rating. Moody's rating of the bonds in 1931 was substantially the same as the 'A' rating in 1928, when the bonds were sold to her".

Counsel for the Central Bank then read from Plaintiff's Exhibit 63, (R 677, 680-1), as follows:

"Bonds carrying the A rating are also well up the scale as regards such tests as asset value, earning power and stability. While necessarily on a lower plane in these weighted averages, their classification as high grade investments is fully demonstrated. Many bonds suitable for general investment purposes fall in the A class. They are entirely sound obligations of representative companies, but, lacking the higher degree of protection obtainable in bonds of the Aaa and Aa grades, they are more apt to reflect changing conditions by price fluctuation".

The witness, continuing his testimony on his redirect examination, testified as follows, (R 461):

bonds outstanding. For the past seven years, they have averaged seven times requirements and in no one year has the amount been less than six times.

"The bond has marketability, being regularly quoted in New York.

"We recommend them as a safe and conservative investment".

"Moody's rating of the bonds of Province of Buenos Aires, sold to Mrs. Quinn in January, 1928, I believe was Baa".

Counsel for the Central Bank thereupon again read from Plaintiff's Exhibit 63, (R 677, 681), as follows:

"Bonds carrying the Baa rating generally make a good showing in the test of asset value, earning power and stability, but they warrant more discrimination than those of higher rating. Many unseasoned issues of strong companies are given this rating, as well as the junior bonds of large corporations with several funded obligations. Occasionally a Baa bond represents an issue of a representative corporation where the outlook is uncertain, and a once prime investment, while still sound, has acquired a speculative tinge. For investors who do not require the higher grade bonds, Baa issues will frequently afford a larger income return than the Aaa, Aa or A classes, and in the course of time such issues may enter a higher class, if the corporation maintains good earning power, conservative and efficient management and a sound financial position".

The witness, continuing his testimony on his redirect examination, testified as follows, (R 462-4):

"I could not say definitely what was the rate of interest which bonds of Moody's Aaa rating would bring in the year 1926, but the rating would be somewhere between 4 and 5%. There would not be such a great change in the interest yield of bonds having a Moody Aa rating. Probably the yield would be from 4½% to 5¼%.

"I cannot tell you definitely whether the National Bank was a member of a syndicate, or of a selling group, for the disposition of the bonds of the Fageol Motors Company. The Bank appears to have been a member of a selling group. Members of a selling group have a price below which they cannot sell to the public. I do not recall the offering price in the case of the bonds of Fageol Motors Company, but think it was at par. The bonds were sold to Mrs. Quinn at that price. Selling group members buy bonds or get bonds below the price at which they are sold to the general public.

"The market value today of the bonds of California Cotton Mills Company, I believe, is 114. The present price is approximately 6½ times higher than the market price indicated on Plaintiff's Exhibit 62".

(NOTE: The price of these bonds, of $114 per hundred, would be slightly more than 8 times, instead of 6½ times, higher than the market price of $14 per hundred, indicated on Plaintiff's Exhibit 62).

The witness, continuing his testimony on his redirect examination, testified as follows, (R 463):

"The $6,000, par value, bonds of Hearst Publications, Inc., maturing in 1933, sold to Mrs. Quinn, have been paid off at par. The present bid for Hearst Publications, Inc., bonds, maturing in 1940, is 102.

"The $5,000, par value, bonds of Jackson Furniture Company, sold to Mrs. Quinn, were called by the Company and paid at 101, on January 1, 1936.

"The bonds of Miller & Lux, Inc., maturing in 1935, are still in default. I am not certain what the present market value is, but it is somewhere in the neighborhood of 70 to 75.

"The market value at the present time of the $10,000, par value, bonds of Province of Buenos Aires, sold to Mrs. Quinn, is between 55 and 60. The $5,000, par value, bonds of Medford Irrigation District, sold to Mrs. Quinn, have been sold at 40''.

The witness, continuing his testimony on his re-direct examination, testified as follows, (R 464):

"The depression of 1929 affected the bond market in general. There was a general decline in the market price of bonds from 1929 to 1932. The first year after 1929, the decline was not so great. The decline accelerated as time went by until it culminated in about 1932, in probably the low point. It would be difficult to determine at what time in 1932 was the low point because various classes of bonds reached a low point at one time, others at another. The industrials were probably the first to reach a low point.

"Generally speaking, since 1932, there has been a trend upward, and, at the present time, the prime grade bonds are holding in a high position and the intermediate bonds are trending up''.

On *recross examination,* Bothwell testified as follows, (R 464-5):

"The Rheinelbe Union bonds were issued in the Rhein-Elbe country of Germany. In my letter to Mrs. Quinn, copy of which has been introduced in evidence as Defendants' Exhibit N, (R735), I recommended those bonds to her on January 26, 1926, as a 'conservative investment' for her account.

"The Cities Service Company bonds I recommended to her in my letter to Mrs. Quinn of February 6, 1926, a copy of which has been introduced in evidence as Defendants' Exhibit O (R 736), as 'a safe and conservative investment'. The President of that Company was Mr. E. L. Dougherty. I cannot verify that his name has occupied the front pages of many of the papers for a considerable period past, and I wouldn't express an opinion that the references to him in the papers have not been in a very complimentary way".

(R 465). "When I recommended to Mrs. Quinn such bonds as those of the Province of Callao, we sold or recommended the bonds by prospectuses and did not take into consideration the career politically of the Republic of Peru".

3.   The testimony of S. Berven.*

The witness Berven testified, (R 465), that

"The *first* time I ever met Mrs. Quinn was approximately three or four months before the trust instrument was executed, on September 24, 1929"; and that, (R 466), Bothwell brought her in and introduced her to Berven. "*Q.* What was said by Mr. Bothwell to you? *A.* Just merely introduced me and said Mrs. Quinn desires to have some information regarding a trust".

"*Q.* Did you then have a *conversation* with Mrs. Quinn? *A.* I did. *Q.* Did Mr. Bothwell make any statement to you and Mrs. Quinn at that time, other than as you have just testified? *A.* No. Just merely introduced me to her". And Bothwell then left.

"*Q.* What conversation did you have with Mrs. Quinn at that time? *A.* A general conversation as to the creation of a trust. *Q.* Well, what did she say, as near as you recall? *A.* Well, she wanted information as to creating a trust, as to the fees, and how a trust would operate, and discussed it in general".

Plaintiff, so the witness testified, (R 466), mentioned her daughter. He asked her what property she had, and

---

*NOTE: Berven testified, in this connection, (R 465), that, for a number of years prior to March, 1933, he was the assistant trust officer of the National Bank; that he became the assistant trust officer of that Bank some time in May, 1936; that he was now employed in the trust department of the Central Bank, and held the position now in that Bank as trust officer; and that he was never connected with or employed by the Central Bank prior to the closing of the National Bank in March, 1933.

"She said she had some bonds, and a piece of real estate, and a mortgage, up in Nevada, and that she had, I think, one or two pieces—one or two houses in Sparks, Nevada. *Q.* Did you make any mention to her about her property in Sparks, Nevada? *A.* Yes, I did. *Q.* What did you say? *A.* I explained to her that we could not take title to property in trust in Nevada, and she wanted to know how she—she thought she could put up— she thought she could put all the property in, and wanted to know what she was going to do with that property. I explained to her that she could either dispose of that property by will or make a deed of gift.

"*Q.* Did you have any conversation with her about making a deed of gift at that time? *A.* Yes. I told her that if she made a deed of gift she could give it to someone for delivery to her *daughter,* and she said she would give it to her *sister*".

"She did not mention", so the witness testified, (R 467), "at that time, or at any other time, that she had property in Reno, Nevada. She did not mention anything about any property on Virginia Street, in Reno. She was not definitely committed to the idea of making a trust at that time. She was just seeking information. That, in general, was all the conversation, on that occasion, which I recall".

"I saw her once", so the witness continued, (R 467-8), "I would say several months, before that time. It would not be longer than maybe three or four months. I saw her going into Mr. Read's office. Mr. Read was then the trust officer of the National Bank.

"My *second conversation*", so the witness testified, (R 468), with her "was shortly before the
trust was created; I would say two or three weeks
before. She came in; just a short conversation. I
recall it was just over the counter. She wanted
to know, at that time, whether she could continue
to deal with the bond department, and buy her
securities, if she placed the property in trust with
us. I told her 'I thought we could arrange that'.
That, in substance, was all the conversation which
I had with her on that second occasion".

The next, or *third conversation,* so the witness testified, (R 468-9), was

"Well, it was just as I say, just about a week
or a week or ten days, before the trust was created.
She came in, and evidently had definitely decided
to create a trust, and gave me the information as
to what she wanted in the trust.

"I wrote down with a pencil and a pad that I
used there the information which she gave me as
to how she wanted her property distributed, the
income to her during her lifetime and a provision
for her daughter and her grandson. She either
brought in a list, or I got a list, of her property
from the bond department at that time. I cannot
recall. I had the list before us. I do not know
where the list is at the present time.

"The list, as to the securities in it, was the
same as the list of securities which appear in the
trust instrument".

(R 469) "*Q.* Did you make any remark to
Mrs. Quinn at that time about the securities which
she then had? *A.* Yes. *Q.* What did you say?

A. I told Mrs. Quinn, at that time, that the securities that she had were not the type of securities that we usually bought for trust investments; that we were required to buy securities that were considered legal for trust investments; such securities had a higher marketability and less fluctuation, and for that reason they naturally would bring in a smaller rate of income.

"*Q.* Did you tell her the rate of income such a type of security would bring? *A.* Yes. *Q.* What was that? *A.* I said she could not go approximately over 5 per cent. *Q.* What, if anything, did Mrs. Quinn say in reply to that? *A.* She said she would have to have at least 6 per cent. on her money.

(R 469-0) "*Q.* What else was said by either you or Mrs. Quinn at that conversation? *A.* Well, I told her we could not buy that type security, and she wanted to know, at that time, whether she could continue to buy her bonds, her securities, from the bond department. I told her, in order to do that, she could do it in two different ways, either have to make a partial revocation and buy her own securities and then make an addition to the trust after she purchased the new securities, or we could put that provision in the trust agreement, itself, where it provides we could purchase securities that were legal for trust investments or otherwise. In that way, she could direct us to buy securities as she desired.

(R 470) "*Q.* When the trust instrument was drawn up, did it contain such a provision? *A.* It did.

"She did not give me any data in her own hand-writing at that time, or at any other time."

(R 470) Thereupon the witness produced, at the request of counsel for the Central Bank, a duplicate original of the trust instrument, which the witness identified as the trust instrument to which he had previously testified, and the same was introduced and read in evidence by counsel for the Central Bank, and marked "Defendants' Exhibit P".*

The witness, then continuing, (R 470),

"*Q.* Will you briefly state how that instrument was prepared, and by whom? *A.* Well, after taking down the data from Mrs. Quinn as she gave it to me, as to the distribution clause, I took it up to the attorneys' office, Mr. Beardsley's office".

The witness, further continuing, (R 470-1), testified that the man in the attorneys' office to whom he gave the data was Mr. Abbott,

"and from that information he [Mr. Abbott] prepared the distribution clause, and furnished it to us, and we incorporated it with the usual standard clause, and after it was completed we submitted it to him again for his approval";

and that the distribution clause includes all of paragraph IV, and

"That was the paragraph prepared by Mr. Abbott. The rest of the trust instrument, including

---

*NOTE: "Defendants' Exhibit P" was omitted from the transcript of Berven's testimony, because a copy of the same is annexed to the complaint, as "Exhibit A" thereto, (App. A 58-75).

the acknowledgment at the bottom, was prepared by me, typed under my supervision in the trust department'';

and that, (R 471),

"The other duplicate of the trust instrument was given to Mrs. Quinn, complete as to signatures and acknowledgments".

The witness, further continuing his testimony, testified (as the *fourth* of the conversations which he had with plaintiff), (R 471), that

"After the trust instrument was prepared and ready for execution, Mrs. Quinn came in on the date that the instrument bears, namely, September 24, 1929. I took one of the duplicates and Mrs. Quinn took the other, and I read over the instrument, paragraph by paragraph, and explained each paragraph as I went along, and asked her if there was any question as to each paragraph. She followed me with her duplicate. As I finished each paragraph, I asked her if she understood it, and her answer was 'Yes', she was satisfied. I do not recall, off hand, the explanation I gave as to the various paragraphs of the instrument, or just what I did say after each paragraph".

The witness, after examining, at the request of counsel for the Central Bank, paragraph II of the instrument of trust, was asked, (R 472), the following questions, to which he gave the following answers:

"*Q.* I will ask you to examine paragraph II and state what, if anything, you told Mrs. Quinn concerning the provisions in that paragraph. *A.* Well, I pointed out to her that the clause such as to securities, as the investments legal for trust investments, 'or otherwise', and pointed out to her that those two words, 'or otherwise', were put in there so she could direct her own investments in things other than were otherwise legal for the investment of trust funds.''

The witness was further interrogated by counsel for the Central Bank and answered, (R 473), as follows:

"*Q.* What remarks, if any, do you recall were made by Mrs. Quinn during this conversation when the trust instrument was executed? *A.* She asked me if I thought she ought to take this to her attorney. I told her it was perfectly proper she should do so. *Q.* What did she say then? *A.* Well, she said she wouldn't have the time, she was going back East. *Q.* Did she say who her attorney was? *A.* Yes. She mentioned her attorney up in Nevada. *Q.* What, if anything, did you say in response to that? *A.* I cannot recall just what conversation we had right after that; it was just that she was satisfied because the agreement was signed. *Q.* Did you read to her the acknowledgment, or the statement, at the foot of the trust instrument? *A.* Yes, I did. *Q.* Did you ask her if she understood that? *A.* Yes, I did, with all of the other paragraphs''.

The witness, further continuing his testimony, testified, (as the *fifth* conversation which he had with plaintiff), (R 474-5), that he had a conversation with plaintiff, at his office, in regard to the letter, Defendants' Exhibit T (R 741), referring to the default in the payment of interest on the bonds of Berkeley Terminal Properties, Inc.; that

> "The conversation was quite some time, two or three months, along in there, after the date of the letter";

that, as he recalled it, (R 474), plaintiff asked him "Why did the bond department sell me those bonds", and he replied that

> "I told her evidently they figured they were good at the time they sold them to her, or they wouldn't have sold her those bonds";

that, (R 474-5), he did not have any further conversation with plaintiff at the time about her securities; and that

> "A list of her securities was prepared, whether she asked us to prepare it, or I prepared it expecting her to come in, I know the list was prepared. It was prepared either in the latter part of 1931 or the early part of 1932. The list was prepared by Mr. Bowell, who was working in the trust department, either the latter part of 1931 or the early part of 1932. I have not the list at the present time. The list was in pencil, on a yellow piece of paper. I do not know where the list is at the time. I recall that the total of the then market values of the securities was, as shown on that list, approximately $75,000. I showed the list to Mrs. Quinn at that time".

The witness, continuing, was then questioned, and answered, as follows, (R 475-6):

"*Q.* Did she make any statement in regard to the valuations as they then appeared? *A.* She appeared to be quite angry about it. *Q.* What did she say? *A.* She said, 'I think I will have to see an attorney about this'. *Q.* What did you say? *A.* I made no comment on it.

"*Q.* Did you say anything to her at that time in regard to selling any of those securities? *A.* Yes, I did not say she should sell. I told her I would be glad to look over the securities and see if any of them, if I thought any of them, should be sold, and she said, 'Well, if I sell, look what a loss I will take'. She said, 'I don't mind so much if the market is down, but if I sell I won't get it back'.

(R 476). "*Q.* Did Mrs. Quinn at that conversation make specific reference to any of the bonds on the list which you then showed her? *A.* Yes, she asked me about Alameda Park Co. bonds. *Q.* What did she say about Alameda Park Co. bonds? *A.* Well, she asked me what they were, and what they were secured by, and I told her it covered the Neptune Beach property over in Alameda, and that it was a short way over there, and she could take a ride over and take a look for herself what the property covered, what the securities are.

"*Q.* Was anything said at that conversation by Mrs. Quinn about any other bond on the list? *A.* Yes. She mentioned the Alameda Investment Company bonds. *Q.* What did she say about those bonds? *A.* I explained to her what they were secured by. *Q.* What did Mrs. Quinn say about that to your statement as to what they were secured by? *A.* I don't recall her saying anything about that, just that I explained the securities to her.

"I do not know whether or not, at or after that time, Mrs. Quinn saw an attorney until she saw Judge Slack".

"The list", so Berven testified, (R 476), to which the witness said he referred as having been prepared by Bowell, was not the list, Plaintiff's Exhibit 62, which had been introduced in evidence during plaintiff's direct examination, (R 409-12).

Thereupon, (R 477-8), counsel for the Central Bank introduced in evidence an authorization, dated January 14, 1932, addressed to the trust department of the Central National Bank, and signed by plaintiff, and the same was marked Defendants' Exhibit U, (R 742); and, in that connection, the witness testified, (R 477-8):

"I had a conversation with Mrs. Quinn in regard to her signing that authorization in connection with the purchase of $5,000 or $5,500, par value, of the bonds of East Bay Municipal Utility District. That conversation occurred on the date of the authorization, namely, January 14, 1932, and took place in the trust department in the National Bank".

"*Q.* State what was said by you to Mrs. Quinn in regard to the execution of that authorization? *A.* Well, she had a certain amount of funds in the trust account for investment. I suggested to Mrs. Quinn that she should get into some high grade bonds, and suggested the East Bay Municipal Utility as an investment for this fund she had on hand, and she inquired as to what they would yield. *Q.* What did you tell her? *A.* I told her they would yield her approximately 4.80 percent. *Q.* Did she have to pay a premium on those bonds? *A.* Yes. *Q.* What did she say in respect to that? *A.* She said 'I cannot take such low interest'. I told her she should have bonds of that type in there, in her trust account, that she should not worry about''.

"*Q.* Did she say anything then? *A.* She said, 'I just hate to take such a low interest'. *Q.* She finally signed? *A.* Finally she agreed to sign''.*

The witness, continuing, testified, (R 478):

"I recall sending to Mrs. Quinn the letter dated September 12, 1932, Plaintiff's Exhibit 60, (R 673), asking her to call at her early convenience with reference to the bonds of Alameda Invest-

---

*NOTE: Prior to this time, Read wrote a letter to plaintiff, (R 561-2, Plf's Ex. 20), dated July 16, 1930, in which he advised plaintiff to sell the $5,000, par value, bonds of Federal Public Service Corporation, which had been purchased June 27, 1930, by the National Bank from itself, through Bothwell, for the trust estate, and to reinvest the proceeds in $3,000, par value, 6% bonds of Pacific Gas and Electric Company, at the price of $110½, and $2,000, par value, 6% bonds of San Joaquin Light and Power Corporation, at the price of $114¼, and, although the purchases would yield plaintiff considerably less than 5% per annum, she wrote Read, on July 26, 1930, (Plaintiff's Exhibit 23, R 564), without any complaint of the low rate of interest, "Please change bonds as you suggest, if you deem it advisable. I certainly disire (sic) safe investments at all times", and the purchases were accordingly made from third persons on July 31, 1930, (Plf's Ex. 5, R 548).

ment Company, and also recall sending her the
letter dated October 29, 1932, Plaintiff's Exhibit
61, relating to the same subject. She came in to
see me in response to the letter of October 29,
1932. I don't recall when she came in, but it seems
within a very few days. I had a conversation with
her when she came in".

"*Q.* What was that conversation? *A.* Well, I
pointed out to Mrs. Quinn that we thought that
either half the securities, or a portion of the securities, or maybe all of them, should be sold at
that time. *Q.* Of what securities? *A.* Of the
Alameda Investment Company. *Q.* Did you tell
Mrs. Quinn about what price she could obtain
for the Alameda Investment bonds if she sold at
that time. *A.* Yes. *Q.* Approximately what price
was that? *A.* Approximately 40".

"*Q.* What, if anything, did Mrs. Quinn say in
respect to your suggestion that some of those
bonds be sold? *A.* 'Well, see what a loss I would
take'. She said she wouldn't get it back if she
sold them now. *Q.* What did you say to her?
A. Well, I explained to her that we thought they
should be sold, and that there was a possibility of
a default, that she should decide maybe to sell
half of them, and maybe the other half would
come up and she would average the price".

The witness, further continuing, testified, (R 479-
80), as follows:

"She wanted to know if there was anyone else
outside the Bank that was familiar with the Alameda Investment Company securities that she
could talk to. I told her I thought Cavalier &

Co. were familiar with that issue, and mentioned Mr. Goodwin. I recall I was just going out to lunch, and took her into Cavalier's and introduced her to Mr. Goodwin. I merely introduced her to him and told him she wanted to talk to him about the Alameda Investment Company bonds. I knew that Cavalier & Co. had underwritten those bonds, and I knew that Mr. Goodwin was in charge of their bond department, and that was the reason why I took her to see Mr. Goodwin in connection with those bonds. I did not stay and hear any conversation between her and Mr. Goodwin.

"I never saw Plaintiff's Exhibit 62, (R 675), prior to the time of the trial of this action. I do not know who prepared that list. I did not bring that list to Mr. Goodwin. I do not know that Mrs. Quinn brought the list to him. I did not see any list presented. The list did not come off any of the typewriters in the trust department.

"That was the last conversation I had with her. She did not come back to my office from the office of Cavalier & Co."

Thereupon counsel for the Central Bank offered in evidence an authorization, dated July 8, 1932, addressed to the Trust Department, Central National Bank, and signed by plaintiff, relating to the purchase of General Refunding Mortgage, 6%, bonds of Los Angeles Gas & Electric Corporation, and the same was marked Defendants' Exhibit V, (R 742).

On *cross examination* by counsel for plaintiff, Berven testified as follows, (R 480-1):

"Mr. Read left the National Bank, I believe, on January 1, 1933. He entered into the employment of the East Bay Municipal Utility District. I believe that he was, and still is, the treasurer of the District, and that his office is in the City of Oakland."

"As I testified on my direct examination, *I met Mrs. Quinn, for the first time,* three or four months, maybe in June or July of 1929, before the trust instrument was executed. That was the time, as I testified on my direct examination, when she was brought to my office by Mr. Bothwell, who simply introduced her and left the office." (Emphasis added.)

(R 481) "As I also testified on my direct examination, I had a general conversation with her at that time, as to the creation of a trust, but she was not, I think, definitely committed to the idea of making a trust, and was just seeking information. As I also testified on my direct examination, I had seen her three or four months prior to that time, that is, before I first met her, and I had seen her going into Mr. Read's office prior to that time, that is, before I met her."

"As I also testified on my direct examination, *my next conversation with Mrs. Quinn* was two or three weeks before the trust instrument was executed, *and my second conversation with her was merely a short conversation,* in which she wanted to know whether she could continue to deal with the bond department of the Bank and buy her securities if she placed the property in the trust with the Bank, and I told her that I thought we could arrange that." (Emphasis added.)

"You are not to infer from my testimony that there might be some difficulty in making that arrangement. I had no doubt about the fact I could make the arrangements so her securities, after a trust was created, or rather trust securities, could be purchased through the bond department of the Bank.''

(R 481-2) ''As I also testified on my direct examination, *the next, or third, conversation which I had with Mrs. Quinn* was just about a week or ten days before the trust instrument was created, at which time, as I expressed it on my direct examination, she had evidently 'definitely decided to create a trust'; and, on that occasion, as I also testified on my direct examination, she gave me the information about the trust, and, as I also testified on my direct examination, we had a list of her property before us. I am not certain, and I do not know, where that list came from. It was not prepared under my direction, because I did not have the list, and I did not know where her securities were at that time. It might have been prepared by someone in the Bank, but not in the trust department, and it might have been prepared by someone in the Bank at my direction.'' (Emphasis added.)

(R 482) ''*Q.* You have a clear recollection, have you not, about these three visits of Mrs. Quinn to your office? *A.* Yes, I have. *Q.* A clear recollection, am I right? *A.* Yes. *Q.* Including the approximate times or dates of the visits? *A.* Yes.''

(R 482-3) ''*Q.* Your recollection about the three visits, and what occurred at them, the occasions of them, and about the times or dates of the visits, had always been quite clear in your mind, hasn't it? *A.* Yes. *Q.* So that you could not possibly be mistaken about any of them? *A.* No."

The witness Berven, to counsel for plaintiff, continuing, (R 483) :

"I have met Mr. L. V. Edwards, your associate, on several occasions. I saw him in the office several times when you and he were there. I remember that on one occasion you were together. I don't recall the date, but it was sometime along in January, shortly before the National Bank closed. I cannot say, and have no ideas, at what time of the day it was."

(R 483) "*Q.* Did I not, in the presence of Mr. Edwards and Mr. Bothwell, in Mr. Mount's private office of the Central Bank, in the Central Bank Building, between the hours of two and three o'clock in the afternoon of January 23, 1933, inquire of you about the circumstances leading up to the execution of the trust instrument, and did you not state to me, in reply to my inquiry, that the subject was first mentioned to you by Mrs. Quinn about a year before, about a year prior to, the time when you obtained from her the information of which you made a memorandum? *A.* I don't recall making that statement."

(R 483-4) "I testified on my direct examination, in answer to a question as to what was said by either myself or by Mrs. Quinn on the occasion of the third visit, in connection with the type of securities she had, as follows: 'Well, I told her we could not buy that type security, and she wanted to know at that time whether she could continue to buy her bonds, her securities, from the bond department. I told her in order to do that she could do it in two different ways, either have to make partial revocation and buy her own securities, and then make an addition to the trust after she purchased the new securities, or we could put a provision in the trust agreement, itself, where it provided that we could purchase securities that were legal for trust investments, or otherwise. In that way, she could direct us to buy securities if she desired'. And then the question was asked, when the trust instrument was drawn up, did it contain such a provision, and the answer was 'It did'. That conversation took place on the occasion of Mrs. Quinn's third visit, when I took the memorandum from her."

"*Q.* Yes, it was at that time, that is perfectly clear, you are perfectly clear about that? *A.* Yes. *Q.* There could be no mistake concerning it? *A.* No. *Q.* As to the time and place? *A.* No."

(R 484-5) "*Q.* Now, Mr. Berven, I direct your attention to an earlier call upon you by Mr. Edwards and myself, during the afternoon of December 13, 1932, at your office in the Central Bank Building: Did I not, in the presence of Mr. Edwards, upon that occasion, in your office, in the Central Bank Building, between the hours of two and three o'clock, in the afternoon of December 13, 1932, inquire of you concerning the type of securities to which your attention was directed; do you recall such an occasion as that? *A.* I remember you called, but I don't remember exactly the conversation."

(R 485) *"Q.* Do you remember my asking you at that time, or at some time, anything about your statement to her about the type of securities that she was placing in the trust, or desired to place in the trust? *A.* I don't recall such a conversation, no."

"As I testified on my direct examination, after I had taken down the data, as Mrs. Quinn gave it to me, as to the distribution clause, I took the data to Mr. Abbott, of Mr. Beardsley's office, and from the data Mr. Abbott prepared the distribution clause and furnished it to us and we incorporated it in the trust instrument, with the usual standard clauses, and, after the trust instrument was completed, we submitted it to him again for his approval."

"The distribution clause, prepared by Mr. Abbott, includes all of paragraph IV of the trust instrument. The rest of the trust instrument, including the acknowledgment at the bottom, was prepared by me, and was typed under my supervision, in the trust department."

"The 'usual standard clauses', to which I have referred, are various clauses in the trust instrument, such as clauses relating to investments, and to the payment of inheritance taxes and revocation."

(R 486) "With the exception of the words 'or otherwise' in the investment clause, paragraph II of the trust instrument is one of the usual clauses. I inserted the words 'or otherwise' in that clause and submitted the instrument as so changed to Mr. Abbott".

"Paragraphs III, V, VI and VII of the trust
instrument are the usual standard clauses".

The attention of the witness Berven was then again
directed by counsel for the plaintiff to the provisions
of paragraph II of the trust instrument, and, in answer to the following respective questions, testified as
follows (R 486):

"*Q.* Is it not a fact, Mr. Berven, that paragraph II of the trust instrument contains no provision by which Mrs. Quinn would be permitted
to direct the investment of the trust funds? Would
you like to look at the trust instrument? *A.* Yes.
Q. I would like you to look at Defendants' Exhibit P, that is the Bank's copy, original duplicate
of—or duplicate original of the trust instrument,
and direct your attention to paragraph II of that
exhibit. *A.* No, it contains no such provision."

The witness Berven, on further cross-examination,
continuing, (R 486-7):

"I referred Mrs. Quinn to the properties themselves covered by the deed of trust of Alameda
Park Co., and, as I testified on my direct examination, the properties were the Neptune Beach
properties in Alameda, and I told her she could
take a ride over there and take a look for herself
what the securities were. What I meant to say
was that she could take a look for herself at the
properties. It should not be 'what the securities
are', but 'what the securities behind the bonds
were'. She could tell what the properties looked
like, and what properties were over there."

(R 487) "*Q.* So you did not think it worth while for you to accompany her and point out the properties, and explain what they were? *A.* The question did not come up at all about going over with her."

"Mr. Slack: I will put the question again. Read it, Mr. Reporter. (Question read by the reporter.) *A.* I never thought of going over there."

(R 487) "The securities of Mrs. Quinn, which I valued at $75,000, embraced all the bonds in the trust at that time. I could not say exactly if it embraced the four last purchases, namely, the bonds of Pacific Gas & Electric Company, San Joaquin Light & Power Corporation, East Bay Municipal Utility District and Los Angeles Gas & Electric Corporation. It embraced any securities that she had before that time, which was the latter part of 1931, or the early part of 1932, when the list was made up, and some of the securities, like the East Bay Municipal Utility District bonds, were purchased in 1932."

(R 488) "The East Bay Municipal Utility District bonds were purchased on January 20, 1932, according to Schedule A, Plaintiff's Exhibit 47, (R 645), so those bonds might not have been included in the list. The bonds of Los Angeles Gas & Electric Corporation might not have been included, but the bonds which they replaced may have been on the list."

The attention of the witness Berven was called by counsel for the plaintiff to his cross-examination of the witness in relation to the conversation which the witness testified occurred between the witness and the plaintiff on the occasion of the plaintiff's call upon the witness in response to the letter of the witness to the plaintiff, dated October 29, 1932, Plaintiff's Exhibit 61, (R 673), and, in answer to the following respective questions of counsel for the plaintiff, testified as follows:

"*Q*. Now, have you related, or did you relate, Mr. Berven, all the conversation between you and Mrs. Quinn on that occasion? *A*. As far as I can recollect, yes. *Q*. You can think of nothing further? *A*. No."

"*Q*. Was anything said, if you can recall, about reinvesting any money which would be obtained from a sale of all or a portion of the Alameda Investment Company bonds? *A*. No discussion at that time that I can recall."

(R 488-9). "*Q*. No discussion at that time. What was the object of selling all or a portion of them if there was no discussion of a reinvestment of the proceeds in other securities? *A*. We had to decide on selling first before we could think of reinvesting. *Q*. But there was, to the best of your recollection, nothing said about reinvesting? *A*. No."

"*Q*. Did I not, in the presence of Mr. Edwards, in your office in the Central Bank Building, in the afternoon of December 13, 1932, call your attention to some of the bonds or notes in which Mrs. Quinn's funds had been invested, including, among others, the Province of Buenos Aires, the Province of Callao, and the Fageol Motor Company, and ask you if Mrs. Quinn was ever advised by the National Bank officials that her money should be invested in safer bonds, yielding a smaller return, and did you not reply that you had so advised her, and that such advice had been given after the trust instrument had been executed. *A.* I don't recall that exact conversation. *Q.* Well, if there was no exact conversation, what conversation was there, if any, upon that subject which you do recall, Mr. Berven? *A.* I cannot recall a conversation."

(R 489-90) "*Q.* I am directing your attention particularly to the time referred to in this connection, when, as stated in what I inquired of you in the question, Who advised her, and if such advice had been given after the trust agreement had been executed; you say there was no such conversation. *A.* I cannot recall any such conversation."

The witness Berven, (*questioned by Mr. Richards,* counsel for the defendants National Bank and Joseph H. Grut, its receiver), continuing, (R 490):

"*Q.* Mr. Berven, as I understand your testimony, you were, or have been, in charge of the Trust Department for the Central Bank since the receivership, or since March 14, 1933. *A.* I have been the Assistant Trust Officer. *Q.* You have been the Assistant Trust Officer. Prior to that time, and for a number of years, you were the Assistant Trust Officer of the National Bank? *A.* Yes. *Q.* Are you now in charge of that Department? *A.* I am. *Q.* And have been for how long? *A.* Trust Officer since January 8th of this year."

(R 490-1). "*Q.* Since January 8th of this year. Has the so-called Abbie W. Quinn trust been directly under your charge? *A.* Yes. *Q.* Since the appointment of Mr. Grut, one of the defendants, as the receiver of the National Bank, which appointment was on May 8, 1933, have you, or has the Central Bank, through your department, sold certain of the bonds that were in the Abbie Quinn trust? *A.* Yes. *Q.* And have you received interest for Mrs. ·Quinn? *A.* Yes."

(R 491). "*Q.* And have generally taken charge of that trust, is that so? *A.* Yes. *Q.* Right to date? *A.* Yes."

"*Q.* Now, have you ever advised Mr. Grut, his office, or my office, as his attorney, of any of these transactions, such as the collection of interest and sale of bonds of the Quinn trust, which took place subsequent to the appointment of Mr. Grut? *A.* No. *Q.* And Mr. Grut has never consulted with you, or consented, as far as you know, to any of those transactions; that is correct, isn't it? *A.* That is correct."

(R 491-2). "*Q.* Now, Mr. Berven, can you state what bonds have been sold by the Central Bank, without the authorization or consent of the receiver of the National Bank? *A.* I have a list there in my portfolio. *Q.* Would you give it to me, please? *A.* Yes. *Q.* You just read from it and give me the list of bonds that were sold since May 8, 1933, to date. *A.* On August 17, 1933,

$10,000, par value, Alameda Investment Company
bonds, for the net proceeds of $3,996; on April
2, 1935, there was a sale of $4,000, par value,
Miller and Lux, Inc., 7%, bonds, for the net proceeds of $3,038.40; on April 6, 1935, $1,000, par
value, Hearst Publications, Inc. 6¼%, bond, for
$970 net; and on November 6, 1935, $6,000, par
value, California Cotton Mills bond, for $6,390
net. That is all the sales.''

(R 492). "Q. Now, Mr. Berven, since the sale
of any of these bonds which you have just referred to, do you know whether or not the market
price of those bonds, or any of them, has increased? A. Just from what I heard yesterday
on some bonds. Q. Well, what do you know
about it; what is the fact?''

(R 493-4). "A. Just from what I heard yesterday on market value on some of these is the
only way I can repeat that. Q. Yes. A. The
California Cotton Mills bonds brought $106, and
I heard yesterday they were selling for $114; I
was informed that the Alameda Investment bonds
were selling, there is no exact amount, between
$32 and I would say $35. They were selling in
1933 for $40; Hearst Publications, Inc. bonds
we sold for $97, and I heard yesterday they were
selling up to $102; and Miller and Lux, Inc. bonds
we sold for $76, and I heard yesterday they esti-
mated the value as between $70 and $76.''

Adair v. Brimmer,
74 N. Y. 539, (1878).

This was an appeal to the Court of Appeals from the judgment of the Supreme Court affirming the decree of a Surrogate in an accounting by the executor trustees of the will of James S. Wadsworth, deceased.

The appeal involved the question of the ratification, claimed to have been made by the adult beneficiaries, (namely, three daughters of the testator), of an unauthorized investment by the executor trustees of funds of the estate in the stock of a corporation formed for the purpose of developing and working coal lands in which the testator had an undivided interest.

The opinion does not disclose the facts relating to the claimed ratification. But, inferentially, while the executor trustees, on whom the burden of proving the ratification was held to have rested, apprised the daughters of the facts, the executor trustees did not prove that the beneficiaries were apprised of their legal rights, that is, the beneficiaries were not informed as to how those facts would be dealt with by a court of equity, aside from the question that the rights of the issue of the daughters in remainder could not be so barred.

The Court, (Mr. Justice Rapallo writing the opinion), used the following frequently quoted language, (pp. 553-4):

"To establish a ratification by a cestui que trust, the fact must not only be clearly proved, but it

must be shown that the ratification was made with a full knowledge of all the material particulars and circumstances, and also in a case like the present that the cestui que trust was fully apprised of the effect of the acts ratified, and of his or her legal rights in the matter. Confirmation and ratification imply to legal minds, knowledge of a defect in the act to be confirmed, and of the right to reject or ratify it. *The cestui que trust must therefore not only have been acquainted with the facts, but apprised of the law, how these facts would be dealt with by a court of equity. All that is implied in the act of ratification, when set up in equity by a trustee against his cestui que trust, must be proved, and will not be assumed. The maxim 'ignorantia legis excusat neminem', cannot be invoked in such a case. The cestui que trust must be shown to have been apprised of his legal rights. (Cumberland Coal Co. v. Sherman,* 20 Md. R., 151; S. C., 30 Barb., 575; *Lammot v. Bowly,* 6 H. & J., 526.)" (Emphasis added).

White v. Sherman,
168 Ill. 589, 48 N. E. 128, (1897).

The case of *White v. Sherman* involved, principally, investments made by a trustee, in his own name, of trust funds, in fluctuating and speculative railroad stocks. It was claimed, on behalf of the trustee, that the investments, although not legally made, had been approved by the beneficiaries, but the evidence of the approval, as the Court said, was unsatisfactory.

The reports of the trustee to the beneficiaries, which were relied upon to show their approval, concealed the fact that the stocks had been purchased in the name of the trustee, and also concealed the fact that the stocks were steadily declining in value at the time the reports were made. The *earlier* reports did not show whether the stocks were purchased with the trust funds or the trust funds had been loaned on the stocks. The *later* reports showed, however, that the trust funds had been invested in the stocks, and one of the later reports stated what the trustee had done, but did not request the beneficiaries to advise him what he should do about the matter; and there was no evidence, except *inaction* on the part of the beneficiaries, to show that they approved of the acts of the trustee.

There was evidence of the receipt by the trustee of dividends upon the stocks, but there was no evidence that the dividends had been paid to any of the beneficiaries, although it appeared that the dividends might have been applied, with other moneys, in the payment of a mortgage on real property constituting a part of the trust estate.

The Court, in affirming the judgment of an appellate court, holding that the evidence did not support a ratification by the beneficiaries of the unlawful transactions of the trustee, said, (48 N. E. 132):

"In order to bind a cestui que trust by acquiescence in a breach of trust by the trustee, it must appear that the cestui que trust knew all the facts, *and was apprised of his legal rights,* and was under no disability to assert them. Such proof must be full and satisfactory. The cestui que trust must be shown, in such case, to have acted freely, deliberately and advisedly, with the intention of confirming a transaction which he knew, or might or ought, with reasonable or proper diligence, to have known to be impeachable. *His acquiescence amounts to nothing* if his right to impeach is concealed from him, *or if a free disclosure is not made to him of every circumstance which it is material for him to know.* He cannot be held to have recognized the validity of a particular investment, unless the question as to such validity appears to have come before him. *The trustee setting up the acquiescence of the cestui que trust must prove such acquiescence.* The trustee must also see to it, that all the cestuis que trust concur, in order to protect him from a breach of trust. If any of the beneficiaries are not sui juris, they will not be bound by acts charged against them as acts of acquiescence. *The trustee cannot escape the liability merely by informing the cestuis que trust, that he has committed a breach of trust. The trustee is bound to know what his own duty is, and cannot throw upon the cestuis que trustent the obligation of telling him what such duty is.* Mere knowledge and noninterference by the cestui que trust before his interest has come into possession do not always bind him as acquiescing in the breach of trust."

Pence v. Langdon,
99 U. S. 578, 25 L. Ed. 420 (1879).

The case of *Pence v. Langdon* is the pioneer case upon the subject, and, of course, is of controlling importance here. The action, brought by the plaintiff and appellee, Langdon, against the defendant and appellant, Pence, was based upon a unilateral rescission of a purchase of 7,500 shares of mining stock.

Langdon resided in Minnesota, and Pence resided in California, where he was engaged in mining operations, in which one Watson was interested; and, therefore, the transaction relating to the purchase of the shares was through letters between the parties. These letters, as the Supreme Court said, (99 U. S. 580, 25 L. Ed. 421), "Properly construed, show clearly the agency of Pence as claimed by Langdon", the agency having been disputed by Pence.

To a letter which Langdon wrote Pence, that he had seen Watson and made inquiries of Watson about the mining interests of Pence and Watson, Pence replied by letter, in which, referring to the mine in which he and Watson were interested, Pence stated that

> "There is an eighth, that is 7,500 shares, that can be bought if taken at once, at the same I paid and the same Watson paid, after looking and prospecting for five weeks";

that "The price is" "$8,368.75 gold"; that

> "Should you conclude to buy, you must telegraph me here on receipt of this letter";

and that

> *"This will put you on the ground floor with us,*
> or better than I am, as I have spent about $600
> to find this mine, prospect it and have title looked
> up". (Emphasis added).

Langdon thereupon bought the shares and paid to
Pence the price asked by the latter for them.

Pence thereafter, on January 28, 1875, wrote a
letter to Langdon, from San Francisco, in which he
stated that

> "There have been not less than ½ doz. after
> the 7,500 *shares of stock I sold you,* and all were
> astonished to find themselves too late; and still
> more astonished when I told them there was no
> more to be had at present, as we have the con-
> trolling interest, and propose to run the mine as
> we think best", (emphasis the court's);

that

> "The stock I have deposited in the Nat. Gold
> Bank and Trust Co. of this city";

and that

> "I would like to have you come out after the
> roads get good and weather pleasant in the spring".

This letter enclosed a bill, commencing "Hon. R.
B. Langdon, Mina., *to J. W. Pence, dr.",* (emphasis
added), and in which the stock was charged and the
amount paid credited.

Two persons, Linton and Shepherd, were interested
with Langdon in the purchase, and they, together

with Langdon and Pence, later, on June 20, 1875, visited the mine and, on that occasion, claimed that they learned, for the first time, that Pence had sold them his own stock, and that the stock was worth much less than they had paid for it.

On the day following the visit to the mine, Langdon and the persons interested with him notified Pence that they rescinded the transaction, and demanded the refund of the money which had been paid for the stock. Linton and Shepherd transferred their interests to Langdon, who brought the action, based upon the rescission, and, for present purposes, Langdon may be considered as the only party interested on his side of the case.

The certificate for the stock remained in the bank, in which it had been deposited by Pence, so that Langdon never had the possession of it.

The case was tried before a jury, and it is to be inferred from the instructions to the jury, (to which the defendant Pence excepted), that Pence relied principally upon three points for the reversal of the judgment, namely: (1), that he acted in the transaction as the owner of the stock, and not as the agent of Pence for the purchase of it; (2), that Langdon was chargeable with knowledge of the fact that the stock sold belonged to Pence, by the statement in Pence's letter to Langdon of January 28, 1875, that several persons were "after the 7,500 *shares of stock I sold you*", and by the fact that the bill to Langdon for the stock was *"to J. W. Pence, dr."*, and that

Langdon, therefore, had acquiesced in the sale; and
(3), laches or delay in the rescission of the transaction.

The judgment in Langdon's favor, on the verdict
of the jury, was affirmed, on a writ of error, by the
Supreme Court.

The four instructions to the jury, which the Supreme Court said were respectively "exactly right",
and there could be no "doubt as to the soundness"
thereof, and as an entirety "were clear, accurate, and
well expressed", were as follows:

"1· In deciding this question of fact, you must
take the letters and telegrams and all of them,
and looking at them in the light of the previous
relations of the parties, and of what each of the
writers knew, placing yourselves in the writers'
place and situation in order better to ascertain
their meaning and purpose, and in the light shed
upon this question of fact by these letters and
telegrams, and by the history of the whole transaction, you must determine whether the defendant did undertake to act as the plaintiff's agent
for the purchase of the stock from others."

"2· It is not enough to charge the plaintiff
with knowledge of the mal-character of the transaction, that the language used was such as might
have caused some persons to suspect it. He might,
in view of previous friendly relations, have no
suspicion of bad faith, and might naturally regard expressions as inaccurately used, rather than
put upon them a construction which would show
bad faith on the part of the defendant, which he
had no reason to anticipate."

"3. Before the plaintiff was required to affirm or rescind the contract, he must be shown to have had actual knowledge of the imposition practiced upon him. It is not enough to show that he might have known or suspected it from data within his reach."

"4· If the jury believe that the plaintiff had no actual knowledge or belief that defendant had put his own stock upon them, until June, 1875, at the mine, then his repudiation of the transaction, if made then, was sufficient."

The Supreme Court said, (Mr. Justice Swayne writing the opinion), (99 U. S. 579, 25 L. Ed. 421):

"Acquiescence and waiver are always questions of fact. There can be neither without knowledge. The terms import this foundation for such action. One cannot waive or acquiesce in a wrong while ignorant that it has been committed. *Current suspicion and rumor are not enough. There must be knowledge of facts which will enable the party to take effectual action.* Nothing short of this will do. But he may not wilfully shut his eyes to what he might readily and ought to have known. When fully advised, he must decide and act with reasonable despatch. He cannot rest until the rights of third persons are involved and the situation of the wrongdoer is materially changed. Under such circumstances he loses the right to rescind, and must seek compensation in damages. *But the wrongdoer cannot make extreme vigilance and promptitude conditions of rescission. It does not lie in his mouth to complain of delay unaccompanied by acts of ownership, and by which he has*

not been affected. The election to rescind or not to rescind, once made, is final and conclusive.

"*The burden of proving knowledge of the fraud and the time of its discovery rests upon the defendant.*

"Here Langdon was lulled into security by his relations to Pence, and by Pence's letters.

"There is no proof that he had the slightest knowledge or even suspicion of any foul play until he visited the mine. His action then was prompt and decided". (Emphasis added).

It will be noted that the case involved both letters and a bill of sale. And if, as the Supreme Court held, the questions, in view of the letters, and, particularly, the letter of Pence to Langdon, of January 28, 1875, and in view of the bill of sale for the stock, enclosed in that letter, whether or not Pence undertook to act as the agent of Langdon, in the purchase of the stock, and, if so, whether or not Langdon was chargeable by the letters and the bill of sale with knowledge of the fact that Pence was the owner of the stock, and, as such owner, sold the stock to Langdon, were questions of fact, and, as such were properly submitted by the trial court to the jury, *a fortiori,* the question whether or not, in the instant case, the National Bank, through its bond department, acted as an agent of the plaintiff in making the purchases of the bonds and notes, prior to the execution of the instrument of trust, and, if so, whether or not the plaintiff was chargeable with knowledge, by the bills of sale, of the fact that the bank was making the purchases from itself, as the owner of the bonds and notes, and that the plaintiff, with such knowledge, acquiesced in the unlawful purchases, were, likewise, questions of fact, which, in the absence of a jury, the court must decide. But, as we have elsewhere pointed out, because of the failure of the defendants to *plead the facts as a defense, no findings in favor of the defendants, can be upheld.*

It is respectfully submitted that the case of *Pence v. Langdon* is a binding authority upon this Court; and that, since the decision in that case was in favor of the principal, Langdon, so the decision of this Court, in the instant case, on the like questions, (aside from the fact that the defendants failed to plead the defense), must be in favor of plaintiff, and particularly so, since there is no evidence whatever, (in the language of the Supreme Court), *that plaintiff "wilfully shut her eyes to what she might readily and ought to have known".*

It is also respectfully submitted that these questions of fact should be decided with reference to all the other circumstances of the case, and with the assumption, (for the purpose of such decision), that the relation between the National Bank and plaintiff, in the making of the purchases, was that of trustee and cestui que trust. Among the facts to be considered are the facts that plaintiff was and is an unlettered, (R 553, Pl's Ex. 10, R 558, Pl's Ex. 16; R 560, Pl's Ex. 18; R 564, Pl's Ex. 23), sickly and aging woman, (R 363, 368), and lacking in experience in such transactions as the purchases of bonds and notes, (R 369, 370), who placed herself in the hands of Bothwell, the manager of the Bond Department of the National Bank, and also including, among the circumstances, paraphrasing the language of the Supreme Court, that

> "There is no proof that the plaintiff had the slightest knowledge or even suspicion of any foul play until she was told, in effect, by Berven, the assistant trust officer of the Bank, that her money should have been invested in 'better securities' ".

And it is respectfully submitted that since the decision in *Pence v. Langdon* was in favor of Langdon, so the decision of this Court, in like questions, (aside from the fact that defendants failed to plead the defense), should be in favor of plaintiff, and particularly so, *since there is no evidence whatever,* (the burden of introducing which, if it existed, rested upon defendants), *that plaintiff, (paraphrasing the language of the Supreme Court), "wilfully shut her eyes to what she might readily and ought to have known."*

Notwithstanding the fact that this case is conclusive upon the questions here under discussion, we deem it to be advisable, in view of the importance of the questions, to consider, at some unavoidable length, the 2 remaining cases above cited, in the order in which they are cited, as well as according to their chronology.

Williams v. Bolling,
138 Va. 244, 121 S. E. 270, (1923).

The case of *Williams v. Bolling,* next to the case of *Pence v. Langdon,* is one of first importance. The facts, which resemble, in their essentials, several of the facts in the instant case, are quite lengthy, and are somewhat involved, and condensation, to any considerable extent, seems to us to be practically impossible.

The case was that of a suit in equity, commenced in December, 1917, by the plaintiff and appellee, Bolling, against the defendants and appellants, Williams and others, for the rescission, (apparently because of fraud), of certain transactions between the parties, involving the sale by the defendants for the plaintiff of 100 shares of stock of Atlantic Coast Line Railway Company, and the purchase by the defendants for the plaintiff of $10,000, par value, first mortgage bonds, with 40 shares of the preferred stock and 60 shares of the common stock, of Georgia & Florida Railroad Company.

The defendants were dealers, at Richmond, Virginia, in investment securities. The plaintiff resided in different places in Virginia, at some distance from Richmond, and during a number of years prior to the transaction in question, had purchased, through the defendants, stocks and other investment securities, often at the suggestion or advice of the defendants. Most of the transactions between the parties, including the transactions in question, had been conducted by written correspondence.

The plaintiff had previously, and in September, 1907, (121 S. E. 271), purchased, through the defendants, the 100 shares of stock of the Atlantic Coast line Railway Company, which the defendants held as collateral security for advances made by them to the plaintiff. The defendants had also previously, and in March, 1907, informed the plaintiff by letter that they were organizing the Georgia & Florida Railroad Company, (a circular concerning which they enclosed), and in such organization, so the letter stated, (121 S. E. 274), the

> "syndicate subscribers *receive* for every $1,000 invested $1,000 first mortgage 5 per cent. 50 years gold bonds, $400 6 per cent. preferred stock, and $600 common stock",

and recommended to the plaintiff the sale of some of his securities and the investment of the proceeds of the sale in the bonds of that company.

This recommendation was not acted upon by the plaintiff at the time when it was made. But, considerably later, namely, on January 14, 1909, (121 S. E. 271), the plaintiff wrote the defendants requesting a further advance up to $1,000, and inquired of the defendants if it would not be better to close out the stock instead of waiting for better prices therefor.

To this letter, the defendants replied on January 15, 1909, (121 S. E. 272), informing the plaintiff that he could draw on them for $1,000, if desired, and suggested to the plaintiff that he sell the Atlantic Coast Line Railway stock at 109 or 110, and buy

$10,000 of the Georgia & Florida Railroad bonds "at par and interest in the bankers' syndicate", carrying a bonus of $4,000 in preferred, and $6,000 in common, stock of the company.

To this letter of the defendants, the plaintiff replied ou the following day, namely, January 16, 1909, (121 S. E. 272), stating that "in regard to change of investment", "I am guided by your greater knowledge and experience, and authorize you to sell my 100 shares as you suggest at 109 or 110", and buy Georgia & Florida Railroad bonds, "at par and interest, receiving as bonus preferred and common stock", and referred to the defendants "as old and tried friends", and "What you decide upon will meet my approval".

Upon the receipt of this letter from the plaintiff, the defendants, on January 20, 1909, (121 S. E. 272), credited the plaintiff's account with the sale of 100 shares of the Atlantic Coast Line Railway stock, at $10,925, (or at 109¼ per share), and charged the plaintiff with the purchase of $10,000 Georgia & Florida Railroad bonds, at par, with accrued interest, or a total of $10,111.11; and, on January 21, 1909, wrote the plaintiff as follows:

"We have sold for you 100 shares of A. C. L. common stock at 100½, and we charge you by the cost of $10,000 Georgia & Florida first mortgage 5 per cent. bonds at par and interest, carrying a bonus of $4,000 in preferred stock and $6,000 in common stock".

Adding, (121 S. E. 276):

"We have given you this participation in the Bankers' Syndicate, as we feel that it is very safe

and should bring you good profits during the next
12 months''.

And advising that they were not recommending that
the plaintiff hold them for at least 12 months.

Accompanying this letter was a memorandum statement, which, without an alteration to be presently
noticed, read as follows, (121 S. E. 272):

"We have to-day sold you:
10,000 Ga. & Fla. Synd. sub. 100........ ....$10,000
Int. 5% from Nov. 1, '08................................. ...   111.11
                                                            _____
                                                             $10,111.11
$10,000 Ga. & Fla. Ry. 1st mortg. 5's.
 4,000 Ga. & Fla. Ry. Pref. Stk.
 6,000 Ga. & Fla. Ry. Com. Stk.''

This statement was on a printed form, for "bought"
and "sold" securities, (121 S. E. 275), on which the
words "We have to-day . . . *for* you" were printed.
The word "for" in the statement, as filled out, had
a line drawn through it, in pencil, so that the statement, as filled out, read, "We have to-day *sold*
~~for~~ you". The plaintiff testified *that he never noticed
the wording of the statement* until his counsel, in preparing the papers for the suit, called his attention to
it, whereupon, (121 S. E. 276), he "was utterly sur-
prised".

The Georgia & Florida Railroad Company paid
the interest on its bonds for a few years, and then,
apparently, defaulted. Most, if not all, of the interest
so paid was from a fund set aside for the purpose,
and was not paid from the earnings of the road.

The bonds and stocks of the Georgia & Florida Railroad Company, apparently, were held by the defendants as collateral security for the indebtedness of the plaintiff to the defendants; and, at the time of the trial, they appear to have passed from the possession of the defendants into the possession of the plaintiff.

It appeared from the evidence, or from the defendants' answer, (121 S. E. 272), that the defendants had not sold the 100 shares of Atlantic Coast Line Railway stock, on January 20, 1909, as they had reported, on January 21, 1909, to the plaintiff they had done, but, on January 20, 1909, had sold only 35 of the shares, and had transferred the remaining 65 shares to their own stock account, (*or, in other words, the defendants had sold 65 shares to themselves*), and, at the same time, had transferred from their own bond and stock account the $10,000, par value, bonds, and the 40 shares of preferred, and the 60 shares of common, stock, of the Georgia & Florida Railroad Company, *or again, in other words, the defendants had sold to the plaintiff the bonds and stock of the latter company belonging to themselves.*

It also appeared from the evidence, (121 S. E. 272), that the defendants had sold, of the 65 shares of Atlantic Coast Line Railway Company's stock, on February 5, 1909, 10 shares, at 109½, on February 9, 1909, 10 shares, at 109¾, and the remaining 45 shares, several months later, at a considerable advance.

The plaintiff, upon the filing by the defendants of the answer, on April 8, 1918, knew, for the first time,

(121 S. E. 274), that the defendants had taken over the 65 shares to their own stock account; and, unless the plaintiff was chargeable with knowledge, by the memorandum statement, of the fact, the plaintiff did not know, prior to the time of the preparation of the papers for the suit, that the bonds and stock of the Georgia & Florida Railroad Company had been transferred from the defendants' own bond and stock account to the plaintiff's account.

It is to be noted, in passing, that the stock of the Atlantic Coast Railway Company was either sold, or taken over, by the defendants, and the bonds and stock of the Georgia & Florida Railroad Company were purchased by the defendants themselves, on January 20, 1909, and that the suit was not commenced, (evidently for want of knowledge by the plaintiff of the facts), until some time in December, 1917, or nearly 9 years after the transactions.

The trial court, in a learned and exhaustive opinion, ordered a decree for the plaintiff setting aside the transaction, (121 S. E. 275), and (1), charging the defendants with the 65 shares of the Atlantic Coast Line Railway Company's stock, at the prices at which the defendants sold the shares, with interest from the dates of sales, (2), crediting the defendants with the plaintiff's indebtedness to them, with charges against them for money which they had received, and (3), the re-delivery by the plaintiff to the defendants of the bonds and stock of the Georgia & Florida Railroad Company.

The Supreme Court affirmed the decree, on appeal therefrom, adopting the opinion of the trial court as a part of its opinion.

The opinion of the trial court quotes at length from the opinion in other cases, particularly the opinions in two other well-considered cases decided by the Virginia Supreme Court, namely, *Ferguson v. Gooch,* 94 Va. 1, 26 S. E. 397, 40 L. R. A. 234, (1896), and *Cardozo v. Middle Atlantic Immigration Co.,* 116 Va. 342, 82 S. E. 80, (1914). The opinions from these two cases deal largely with the rules relating to the obligations, (to which we need not particularly here refer), of good faith and loyalty of agents towards their principals.

It appears from the opinion of the trial court, (121 S. E. 275), that the defendants claimed, "with great confidence", that in the memorandum statement, which accompanied their letter of January 21, 1909, to the plaintiff,

> "the plaintiff was told in language as plain as language can convey that defendants sold their own bonds to plaintiff";

but the trial court answered this claim of the defendants as follows, (121 S. E. 275):

> "Their letter of January 21, 1909, inclosing this statement to plaintiff, and in which they would naturally have given plaintiff full information of how they as his agents had executed the trust conferred on them by him, *does not contain the information of the true facts.* It does not tell plaintiff they had taken themselves 65 shares

of his A. C. L. stock they were instructed to sell, *nor does it tell him that the bonds* they were instructed to buy, and which the letter says they charged his account with the cost of, *were their own bonds.*

"The plaintiff says in his evidence, in testifying about this memorandum statement spoken of, and of the words, 'We have to-day sold you', that he never noticed those words until the counsel, in preparing the papers for this suit, called his attention to it. *If the defendants, as they do, rely on ratification of plaintiff of the agents' acts, the burden of proof is on defendants to show that plaintiff ratified their acts after full knowledge of all the facts. I do not think the defendants have met such burden".* (Emphasis added).

It also appears, from the opinion of the trial court, (121 S. E. 275), that

"the defendants claim that they were mere instruments in the performance of an appointed service, and not fiduciaries in the performance of trust, and having sold the stock at a price authorized by the plaintiff, he has sustained no legal damage".* (Emphasis added).

In answer to this claim of the defendants, the trial court observed, (121 S. E. 275), that "it is sufficient to say", in the language of *Ferguson v. Gooch,* 84 Va. 8, 26 S. E. 400, 40 L. R. A. 237, that

" 'The rights of the principal will not be changed, nor the capacity of the agent enlarged, by the fact that the agent is not invested with a discretion,* but simply acts under an authority to purchase a particular article at a specified price, or to sell a particular article at the market price' ". (Emphasis added).

The Supreme Court, in discussing the same subject of ratification, (121 S. E. 276), quotes from the case of *Cardozo v. Middle Atlantic Immigration Co.,* 116 Va. 360, 361, 82 S. E. 80, 87, as follows:

" 'It is not enough for the broker or agent to say he thought the principal was advised as to all the facts, *nor is it sufficient if he is able to point out circumstances from which an inference might be drawn that the principal knew or had means of knowledge'."* (Emphasis added).

Continuing, the Supreme Court said, (121 S. E. 276):

"For the communication from the principal to be held to convey by inference the information in question in such case, the inference must be so obvious that it is apparent that the principal 'wilfully shut his eyes to what he might readily and ought to have known'. See *Pence v. Langdon,* 99 U. S. 578, 25 L. Ed. 420, in which the communications from the agent contained language *more strongly warranting the inference in question than in the instant case".* (Emphasis added).

It was also contended by the defendants in the Supreme Court, (121 S. E. 277), (a contention which will be discussed by us later), that consideration was not given by the trial court to the fact that the memorandum *"showed that no commission was charged on the purchase of the mortgage bonds and stock therewith, which should, as it is claimed, have informed appellee that it was not a purchase for him, as he supposed, but a sale to him by appellants personally".* (Emphasis added).

But the Supreme Court disposed of this contention, adversely to the defendants, in the following language, (121 S. E. 277):

"We do not think that it can be said that appellee should have reasonably expected that such a memorandum would set out the commissions charged if it had been a purchase for him, and that the inference must be drawn, from its not stating any commissions as charged, that it conveyed the information aforesaid. He would naturally expect the information as to commissions charged or not charged to appear in a different character of document, such as an account rendered by appellants".

To the argument of the defendants that they acted in good faith, and with honest and upright intentions, particularly in the sale to the plaintiff of the bonds and stock of Georgia & Florida Railroad Company, *the Supreme Court, while apparently sympathizing with the defendants, said,* (121 S. E. 277):

"But, for the reasons of public policy set forth in the opinion of the court below, which we have adopted as aforesaid as a part of this opinion, we feel constrained to adhere to the established rule on the subject, which is also set forth in such opinion, the importance of which, as a matter of public policy, is so great that it transcends in importance and supersedes all consideration of any individual interests involved in any particular case *in which it does not affirmatively appear that the agent has in fact made the disclosure aforesaid to his principal which the rule as aforesaid requires"*. (Emphasis added).

The following conclusions, applicable to the instant case, are to be drawn from this case:

(1) Nothing will defeat the right of a principal to repudiate and rescind a transaction of purchase or sale because of the fact that the agent dealt with himself, except the ratification of the transaction, after full knowledge, by the principal, of all the facts; *and the burden rests upon the agent to prove that the principal was fully informed of all the facts within the agent's knowledge.*

(2) It is not sufficient for the agent to say that he thought the principal was advised as to all the facts, *nor is it sufficient for the agent to point out circumstances from which an inference might be drawn that the principal knew, or had means of knowledge, of the facts, unless the inference is "so obvious that it is apparent that the principal"*, in the language of the Supreme Court in *Pence v. Langdon,* *"wilfully shut his eyes to what he might readily and ought to have known"; and, therefore, since it did not appear that the principal, Bolling, "wilfully shut his eyes to what he might readily and ought to have known", the letter and the memorandum statement were not, in themselves, sufficient to charge the principal, Bolling, with knowledge of the unlawful acts of his agents.*

Johnson v. Winslow,
155 Misc. 170, 279 N. Y. S. 147, (1935).

The action in this case was brought by the plaintiff, Elinore I. Johnson, against the defendants, members of a firm of stock brokers, with their main office in New York City, for the conversion of bonds belonging to the plaintiff.

The plaintiff, by a writing, guaranteed the defendants that the account of her son-in-law, Charles E. Van Vleck, with the defendants, should at all times meet the "marginal requirements" of the defendants, and authorized the defendants, without "prior notice or demand on" the plaintiff, "to use and apply any and all collateral" that the defendants might "hold or have in any account or accounts" for the plaintiff "to make good any deficit in your marginal requirements".

The plaintiff, on August 28, 1931, deposited with the defendants, pursuant to her guaranty, some $379,-000 of bonds, ($20,000 of which were Liberty bonds), and, at various times, from January 14, 1932, to May 11, 1932, made similar deposits of bonds, aggregating $175,000, the defendants, apparently, (279 N. Y. S. 151), obtaining the bonds for that purpose from the Florida National Bank of Jacksonville, which had custody of the bonds for the plaintiff, and which attended to the preparation of the plaintiff's income tax returns. Apparently, some, if not most, of the bonds so deposited were unlisted on stock exchanges.

The defendants, at various times, from May 14, 1932, to April 1, 1933, (279 N. Y. S. 151), made sales, pursuant to the guaranty, of the bonds so deposited, crediting the plaintiff's account from the sales with the sum of $388,495.55. The entire debit balance of the account was thus satisfied and the securities held by the defendants for Van Vleck's account were released to him, or to his order.

The plaintiff understood and believed, (so she claimed), that, under her transactions with the defendants, and in the making of the sales by the defendants of her bonds, the defendants were acting as her brokers, or, in other words, that the defendants were acting as her agents, and this was the view, (279 N. Y. S. 160, 166), taken by the Court of the relation.

The plaintiff claimed, (279 N. Y. S. 152), that it was not until on or about August 7, 1934, after making inquiries of the defendants in regard to the particulars concerning the sales of her bonds, *that she learned, for the first time, that the bonds were not sold by the defendants for her account, but that the defendants had purchased the bonds for their own personal account.*

The plaintiff thereupon, (apparently, (279 N. Y. S. 152), on August 17, 1934), demanded that the defendants deliver the bonds to her, offering to pay the defendants at the time of such delivery any indebtedness due the defendants. This demand the defendants refused.

The plaintiff claimed that, at the time of the demand, the bonds had a market value of $451,412.20, and, for the difference between this amount and the amount of $388,495.55, which the defendants had credited to her account, namely, $62,916.65, with interest thereon from August 17, 1934, the plaintiff demanded judgment.

The Court directed that judgment be entered as prayed, (279 N. Y. S. 168), namely, for $62,916.65, with interest thereon from August 17, 1934, to the date of entry, plus the amount then due the plaintiff for damages for the conversion, together with costs.

The Court, in a lengthy opinion, came to the conclusion, (279 N. Y. S. 152), that

> "Under the facts of this case, and all the de· cisions, there was an undoubted conversion by defendants of plaintiff's securities by reason of their having sold bonds of plaintiff to themselves without her knowledge".

There were two principal contentions of the defendants, namely:

(1), *that the plaintiff had knowledge, at the time, of the fact that the defendants had sold her bonds to themselves, and ratified what the defendants did;* and

(2), that there was a custom among stockbrokers to sell to themselves unlisted securities held by them as collateral on margin accounts of customers.

The first of these contentions, in the language of the Court, (279 N. Y. S. 153-4),

> "is that the transactions must be considered as trades between themselves as dealers and the plaintiff because at the time of each purchase by themselves of plaintiff's securities they notified

the plaintiff and her agent* by sending written printed confirmations of such purchases reading, 'We confirm purchase *from you*' instead of sending the plaintiff the form reading 'We have sold *for your account*'." (Emphasis added).

The Court, continuing, said (279 N. Y. S. 154):

"*Defendants have the burden of proving that plaintiff knew that defendants had themselves bought her securities. They have not done so.* In *Williams v. Bolling,* (1923) 138 Va. 244, 259, 121 S. E. 270, 273, the court adopted the opinion of the court below, to the following effect: 'As will be seen, from the above authorities, *nothing will defeat the principal's right of remedy except his own confirmation after full knowledge of all the facts. But the burden of proof is on the agent, in a transaction of this character, to prove that the principal was fully informed of all the facts within the agent's knowledge. Jackson v. Pleasanton,* 95 Va. (654) at p. 658, 29 S. E. 680.' In this case there was one dissenting opinion, but upon application for a rehearing the decision as formerly announced was adhered to.

"In the case at bar defendants notified plaintiff ou the 30th day of December, 1931, *by circular letter that they would continue to do a 'strictly commission' business. This was enough to prevent any suspicion at that time from arising that they would participate as principals in a trade with their customers.* Later, after the plaintiff's securities had been bought by defendants themselves,

* NOTE: The word "agent" undoubtedly here refers to the Florida National Bank of Jacksonville, to whom confirmation slips had been sent by the defendants.

they sent her a so-called 'confirmation slip' which read: 'We confirm purchase from you.' *This must be considered first in litera.* It simply says that 'we confirm purchase from you.' *It does not say,* 'We confirm purchase by ourselves from you,' *nor does it say,* 'We confirm purchase from you by ourselves.' It might apply to any purchase. It did appear from forms used in an ordinary purchase by others than an agent (broker) that a different form was used, which said, 'We confirm purchase for your account.'

"The court can see no real difference in the meaning of these two confirmations judged merely by their words. Suppose the confirmation had read, 'We confirm purchase for your account'; how could that have thrown any light on who the buyer was? In the opinion of this court a confirmation is, as between a layman and a broker, in effect, merely a question mark of report. If there was a proper purchase or sale, it needs no confirmation further than a memorandum of the exact date, price and kind of securities. *A confirmation can add nothing to a transaction.* By a confirmation it is intended to call attention to a transaction in order that there may be no mistakes made. After a trade has occurred, where it is not claimed there was any mistake made by either party, it is merely a questionnaire sent to the customer which, in effect, says 'It is our understanding that the purchase or sale is such and such.' 'If our understanding is not correct, let us know and we will both straighten it out.' "

The Court, continuing, said (279 N. Y. S. 155):

"But if acquiescence in such a trade covered by such a questionnaire is invoked, the question it asks must be so definite that it cannot be misunderstood. There are some hundreds of pages of stock exchange and clearing house rules and the layman cannot be expected to give any paper any more effect than it carries on its face. Both the plaintiff and the employee of the custodian bank swear that it conveyed no intimation to either of them that the securities had been bought by defendants themselves.

"The courts have held that there is nothing sacrosanct about 'confirmations,' and in the case of *Porter v. Wormser* (1884) 94 N. Y. 431, 447, the opinion reads: 'The principle is undeniable that an agent to sell cannot sell to himself, for the obvious reason that the relations of agent and purchaser are inconsistent, and such a transaction will be set aside without proof of fraud. The claim that the defendants purchased the bonds themselves is based upon certain notices in writing, sent by the defendants to the plaintiff, of the several alleged sales, headed 'Bought of D. M. Porter, Esq., by I. and S. Wormser,' containing a statement of the particular amount of bonds sold and the price and accompanied in each instance except one, by a letter signed by the defendants, referring to the notice enclosed. The defendant Nathan testified that the bonds were sold by the defendants, between the calls, at the offices of the different dealers in government bonds, and there is no evidence to the contrary, except the notices referred to, which the witness said, in answer to a general question, represented the transaction therein referred to. It is insisted that these notices, which the counsel characterizes as 'purchase notes,' conclusively determine the point that the defendants were the purchasers of the bonds, and that parol evidence was inadmissible to show that they sustained any other relation to the transaction, or that in fact the bonds were sold to third persons. We think the defendants were not precluded from showing the real transaction, and that the rule that parol evidence is inadmissible to change or vary written contracts has no application. The notices were simply reports by an agent to his principal of his proceedings in the execution of the agency. The plaintiff impeaches the agent's transaction, because upon the face of the reports the agent appears to have undertaken to execute an agency to sell, by selling to himself. It was, we think, admissible for the defendants to show the actual transaction, and that by mistake or inadvertence it was misrepresented in the written advices.'

"In the above case it was also held that the headings to the notice of sale by defendants to plaintiff indicated that the bonds were bought of plaintiff by defendants; plaintiff claimed that defendants, as his agents, could not purchase, and so that the sales were void; defendants, however, proved that the sales were made to others. Held, that defendants were not precluded by the notices from showing the real transaction." (Emphasis added).

The Court, commenting upon *Meyer, Law of Stock Brokers and Stock Exchanges,* said, (279 N. Y. S. 156):

"Meyer in his excellent treatise on the 'Law of Stock Brokers and Stock Exchanges,' section 43a

of the Supplement of 1933, at page 32, points out
the difference between the relationship of a
broker and his customer, and the relationship of
vendor and vendee. He says: 'There is nothing in
the law which prevents a person from engaging
in the business of buying and selling securities
for his own account as principal. Such a person
is a security dealer as distinguished from a
broker. His rights and duties have been before
the courts for adjudication repeatedly.' He quotes
from the case of *Coolidge v. Old Colony Trust
Co.,* 259 Mass. 515, 156 N. E. 701 as follows: 'If
one of his customers wanted one of the real estate
stocks in which Burroughs (the dealer) special-
ized he quoted a price, intended to be sufficiently
above the price at which he could buy to insure
himself a satisfactory profit. When his customer
accepted the price quoted Burroughs then went
into the market and bought the stock as cheap as
he could and kept the difference. If he could not
get the stock at a price that gave him a profit he
would go back to the buyer and get him to raise
his bid. When a customer wanted to sell the
method was reversed. The practice was to get as
wide a spread as possible between the bid and
asked prices and to conceal from each customer
the price paid or received by the other. In only
rare cases was stock bought or sold on a commission basis. The relation between Burroughs and
his customers was that between buyer and seller
or debtor and creditor.' Meyer's book continues:
'He (the broker) sells to his customers, at price
which usually affords him a profit, securities
which he has purchased for his own account elsewhere, or buys from his customers securities for

his own account with a view of disposing of them elsewhere at a profit.' In the case at bar the brokers had already sold plaintiffs securities at a certain price before they bought them. Meyer continues: 'Among those who ordinarily act as stock dealers rather than stock brokers are 'over the counter' houses which deal in securities not listed on exchanges. . . .' Meyer further points out: 'However, a stock broker may also become a stock dealer toward his customer in any one transaction, even though he has acted as broker in other transactions,' and he quotes the case of *McNulty v. Whitney,* 273 Mass. 494, 174 N. E. 121, to the effect that:

" 'Where the course of dealings between the parties has established a relationship of customer and broker, the customer is justified in assuming that that relationship will continue, and will not become one of buyer and seller, unless he is notified by the broker of the latter's intention to change the relationship.' He continues: (1) 'Transactions are usually confirmed by stock dealers to customers in language somewhat as follows: 'We are pleased to confirm sale to you,' or 'We are pleased to confirm purchase from you.' Stock brokers, on the other hand, usually couch their confirmations in language somewhat as follows: 'We have this day bought for your account and risk . . .' (2) A stock dealer ordinarily charges no commission, whereas a stock broker usually does make such a charge. (3) A stock dealer usually sells to his customer at a price different from that at which he has purchased the securities elsewhere, or buys from his customer at a price different from that at which he resells elsewhere. A broker, on the other hand, must confirm the purchase or sale to his customer at the exact price at which he himself buys or sells. He is not permitted by law to make a secret profit; nor is he permitted to supply his own stock in fulfillment of a purchase made for a customer, or take for his own account stock which he has sold for a customer. The presence of these three circumstances in any particular transaction is strong evidence that the relationship between the parties was that of stock dealer and customer rather than that of stock broker and customer. . . . In the last analysis, the question to be determined is the relationship which the parties intended to assume and the intention of the parties, if not disclosed by an express agreement, must be gathered from all of the facts and circumstances of the particular case.' Meyer further points out: 'However, a stock broker may also become a stock dealer towards his customer in any one transaction, even though he has acted as broker in other transactions,' and he again quotes the case of *McNulty v. Whitney*, 273 Mass. 494, 501, 174 N. E. 121, 124. In that case the court said:

" 'There was nothing in the form of the order for the Nonquitt Spinning Company stock to indicate that the transaction was not to be executed by the defendants as brokers in accordance with arrangements made when they undertook to buy stock for the plaintiff on margin. He had a right to assume that in all the transactions concerning the buying and selling of stock the defendants would continue to act as brokers unless notified in some way that the relationship had changed. He testified that he was not so notified.' In regard

to the legal effect of the slips, the court said: 'To
maintain the contention that they bound the
plaintiff with knowledge that he was buying the
defendant's property, it must appear not only
that he read or should have read them but also
that if read they would give him notice of a direct sale. The absence from the slips of a charge
for commission could not be ruled to be notice of
a direct sale, especially in view of the answer received by the plaintiff when he directed the attention of the defendant's agent to this omission.
It cannot be said as matter of law that the words
'Sold to' on the slips concerning the stock in
question, either when the slips are considered by
themselves or in connection with other slips representing purchases by the defendants as brokers,
bound the plaintiff with notice that the defendants were selling him their own stock. See *Met-
calf v. Williams,* 144 Mass. 452, 454 (11 N. E.
700); *Greenburg v. Whitney,* 245 Mass. 303, 306
(139 N. E. 844). The words are not necessarily
inconsistent with the interpretation that the
brokers were selling property of another customer as in *Hall v. Paine,* 224 Mass. 62, 74, 76
(112 N. E. 153, L. R. A. 1917 C, 737). It was for
the jury to say under all the circumstances
whether the confirmation slips were notice to the
plaintiff that he was buying directly from the defendants, or should have put him upon inquiry to
ascertain if that was so. *Picard v. Beers,* 195
Mass. 419, 428 (81 N. E. 246).' So in the instant
case the confirmation slips, 'We confirm purchase
from you,' did not of themselves put the plaintiff
upon inquiry to ascertain whether or not the defendants were actually purchasing the bonds

themselves instead of selling the same to third parties. More than that, the defendants wrote the plaintiff that they did a strictly commission business, and the other communications from defendants to plaintiff referred to the purported transactions as sales for her account.''

The Court then continued (279 N. Y. S. 158) as follows:

"With all of the above quotations I agree, but I add to the very clear statement of the law that in order to show that the relationship has changed from that of customer and broker for a particular transaction there must be evidence that the parties agreed to such change for the particular transaction, or that the conduct of the parties was such as to imply acquiescence and consent after full knowledge by the customer. It may be that among dealers and brokers in that line of business a confirmation that 'we confirm purchase from you' would be sufficient to bring home knowledge that the relationship of dealer and customer existed, but where, as here, the relationship that existed between them from the start was that of customer and broker, the mere sending of the confirmation referred to did not and could not thereby change the relationship from that of customer and broker to that of dealer and customer. The customer has the right to assume that the same relationship continues until it is changed by agreement or by such conduct on the part of the customer as ratifies the new relationship. The court has given considerable time and study to the issues of law and fact presented here, and it seems to me that there should be some rule

adopted by the Stock Exchange and/or by authority of government control which would pro-
hibit a condition of affairs which this case discloses, to the effect that no broker will be permitted to buy in his own name or to sell his own
stock to a customer, where the relationship is that
of broker and customer, without the consent and
authority of the customer in writing. The writing
should contain such information to the customer
as to inform him that the relationship of dealer
and customer is one which permits the broker to
sell stocks of his own to the customer and also
permits the broker to purchase the securities himself and sell to third parties after such purchase.
In any event, the broker should after the purchase notify the customer of the price which he
has obtained in the sale of the securities or
stocks. When the broker sells his own stock to a
customer, he should with such sale inform the customer of the amount of such stock he owns or
controls and the price which he paid for it and
the date when he purchased or obtained control
of such stock. The rule should apply not only to
listed, but unlisted, securities and stocks.

"In the instant case the plaintiff was a layman,
and was not fully acquainted with all the technicalities of the street or dealings on the Exchange.
She had a right to assume that the relationship
of customer and broker, a fiduciary, would protect her, to the end that in acting for her, they
would do all in their power to protect her account with them, and that in so doing she would
get the full advantage of the knowledge of the
defendants as such brokers in the management

and care of the account. This she had a right to assume, and this she was entitled to.

"The defendants claim that the confirmations were also sent to her agent, to wit, the Florida National Bank of Jacksonville, and that such confirmations found their way to one Harold I. Clayton, an employee of said bank. There was no proof in the case which would establish such agency on the part of the bank by the broker as to impute knowledge to the plaintiff. Even if we assume that the bank was an agent of the plaintiff, I cannot hold that the mere fact that the confirmations were sent to them as such agent is absolute knowledge that there was an existing agreement or understanding between the plaintiff and defendants, whereby the relationship was that of dealer and customer and not that of customer and broker. There was no agreement established by the defendant to show the relationship of dealer and customer either express or implied. It was, however, established by the plaintiff that the relationship existing between the parties was that of customer and broker. The bank was employed by the plaintiff not as agent but merely to be the custodian of her securities and to prepare her income tax returns. In accordance with this employment it was necessary that the bank receive various letters, statements of account, and confirmations.

"The plaintiff and the employee of the bank both testified that the confirmations sent did not inform them that the defendants had purchased any of the securities in question, and while the words 'We confirm purchase from you' were on the confirmations, the words either were not looked at or were not completely observed, and in any event they did not mean anything to them. I believe this testimony to be true and hold that the mere sending of the confirmations under the relationship of customer and broker did not and could not change such relationship except after full knowledge of such change attempted by the defendants.

"No proof has been submitted to me whereby any ratification was made by the plaintiff or even her agent so-called after full knowledge had been given. No agreement either express or implied has been given to change the existing relationship of that of customer and broker. The law is well settled that the fiduciary relationship between the customer and broker requires full faith and confidence be given to the acts of the brokers in the belief that they would at all times be acting for their customer in all his dealings, and the plaintiff had a right to assume and to rely upon the fact that they were acting for her benefit at all times during the existence of such relationship."

The Court further continuing, (279 N. Y. S. 160), said:

"A broker must fully inform his customer concerning material facts of a transaction. *Am. Cotton Mills v. Monier* (1932) 61 F. (2d) 852, Circuit Court of Appeals, 4th Circuit. A stockbroker employed by a customer cannot, without the knowledge and consent of the customer, fill the order with stock owned by himself. *In re B. Solomon & Co.* (1920) 268 F. 108, Circuit Court of Appeals, 2d Circuit. The evidence here is not seriously disputed that the defendants at the time of the alleged purchase from plaintiff in each instance had, before themselves buying plaintiff's bonds, sold to a customer of their own, and in every instance the price they paid the plaintiff was below the prices which they had obtained.

"They assert that there was a *custom* as to unlisted securities, whereby they were authorized and justified in their conduct by first getting a customer for their own account and then purchasing from the customer at two or three points lower than what they had sold them for. Defendant, however, failed to prove such a custom. If there be such a custom where the relationship existed between parties as dealer and customer, such custom has no relevancy in the instant case, for there is no proof here to establish the existence of such relationship between the parties. The testimony is very pointed on this issue. Defendant's counsel on the trial said: 'We should not have done it. We have done it for years and we made a mistake.' Allen, one of the defendants, referring to the fact that defendants in selling out a customer would purchase his unlisted securities, said, 'That was our usual practice and the way we did business.' The witness Allen testified that this was the way of defendants doing business, even though he had never heard of any other brokerage firm 'ever buying the securities from a customer when the customer is forced to sell pursuant to a margin call.' The person in charge of defendants' trading department admitted that the easiest part of the business in his department, which always made money, was 'to make money out of buying your customers' securities and reselling them.' After a close study of the evidence and the minutes which

have been furnished me, I have arrived at the conclusion upon the whole evidence that there is
nothing in the record from which the witness,
Allen, or the defendants could assume that the
plaintiff had knowledge of the technicalities of
the brokerage business, or that she knew the different relationships that exist between customer
and broker and that of dealer and customer. The
evidence satisfies me that she had no technical
knowledge, nor did the bank who was her custodian, and not her agent, as the defendants contend it was.

"The plaintiff has fully and completely established the fact that the relationship between her
and the defendants was that of customer and
broker and that the defendants' duty as a fiduciary in that regard required them to sell the
securities for her and to give her credit for the
proceeds of such sale. The relationship of customer and broker did not permit them to purchase the securities and to make a profit without
asking her. I have concluded that the purchases
by the defendants were illegal and voidable and
in the circumstances the defendants were chargeable with possession of the bonds when the plaintiff discovered the illegal acts of the defendant,
though it was some time after the transactions
between the parties had terminated. It matters
not how long a time existed between the actual
transaction and the discovery thereof unless the
plaintiff can be charged with knowledge of the
facts so as to amount to ratification, which the
evidence here does not show. She was wholly without knowledge of the acts of the defendant until

demand was made by her for the return of the bonds.''*

---

* NOTE: Three questions, of importance in the case in hand, were decided in *Johnson v. Winslow,* namely: (1), that a seller, or broker, of securities, who sells the securities for a principal or customer, and between whom there is a fiduciary relation, cannot lawfully sell the securities to himself; (2), that the burden of proving that the principal or customer had full knowledge of the facts and of his legal rights, and, with such full knowledge, he ratified or acquiesced in the unlawful act, rests upon the broker; (3), that the principal or customer is not chargeable with such knowledge by "confirmation" notices of sales given by the agent or broker to the customer; and (4), that if there was a custom as to unlisted securities, by which the defendants were authorized to purchase for the account of the plaintiff the unlisted securities at from two to three points lower than the price charged by them to plaintiff, that custom had not been proved.

It might be noted, in passing, that if the custom, or, more properly, the "usage", (3 *Williston, Contracts,* (Rev. ed.), sec. 649), as contended for by the defendants, had been proved, the usage would not have been valid,—a rule which has been frequently applied, (as in *Johnson v. Winslow,* 155 Misc. 186-7, 279 N. Y. S. 164-5), in cases in which the relation between the parties was that of agent, or broker, and principal, or customer: *Meyer, Stock Brokers and Stock Exchanges,* p. 164-6, sec. 27, and cases cited; *Day v. Holmes,* 103 Mass. 306, 309, (1869); *Hall v. Paine,* 224 Mass. 62, 72-4, 112 N. E. 153, 158-9, L. R. A. 1917C, 737, 744-5, (1916); *Ferguson v. Gooch,* 94 Va. 1, 9, 26 S. E. 397, 400, 40 L. R. A. 234, 237, (1896); *Bradley v. Davidson,* 47 App. D. C. 267, 282, (1918). *The defense of usage, therefore, defeated itself.*

It might also be noted, in passing, that such a usage, (as is demonstrated in this brief), *must be pleaded,* as it was in the so-called "ninth and separate defense", in the supplemental answer of the National Bank and its receiver (App. E, 4-5).

De Mott v. National Bank of New Jersey,
118 N. J. Eq. 396, 179 At. 470 (1935).

The question involved in this case, (which was a
suit for an accounting), was whether or not the defendant Bank was liable to the complainant, John H.
De Mott, for three items of purchases, made by the
Bank, and claimed by De Mott to have been unauthorized by him, of a total of 3,845 shares of common
stock voting certificates of the Consolidated Chemical
Company, a corporation, at a cost of $96,125, appear-
ing in an account, designated as "Custodian Account",
which had been set up on its books by the Bank for
De Mott.

The account was so set up pursuant to a letter addressed to the Bank by De Mott, (179 At. 471-2), and
forming an agreement between the parties, in which
De Mott authorized the Bank "to hold any securities
or other property deposited" with the Bank "for such
account", subject to instructions, which were to remain in force until revoked by De Mott, or by his
legal representatives.

The letter directed the Bank "to collect whatever
income and principal may become due on such property and the proceeds of sale of any thereof and remit
principal upon instructions", from De Mott, and to
"remit income monthly with statement". The letter
further authorized the Bank to have any securities
held for the account transferred into the name of a
nominee of the Bank, "in order to facilitate the collection of income", but provided that the Bank's

"responsibility" to De Mott "shall not be thereby impaired". The letter also further authorized the Bank to execute, "as agents", in De Mott's name, "all necessary certificates of ownership that may be required under the Federal Income or other Tax Regulations now or hereafter in effect, inserting on such certificates" De Mott's name "as the owner of the security, but without claiming thereon any personal exemption on securities".

The letter further provided as follows: (1), that it was understood the Bank would use its "best efforts" for De Mott's "account and risk to make purchases and sales of securities and other property and to reinvest the proceeds of such sales", as De Mott might, from time to time, "direct" the Bank in writing, but that the Bank "shall be under no responsibility for failure so to do", if it "shall have acted in good faith"; (2), that the Bank "shall be under no duty to take any other action with respect to any property deposited" by De Mott, "unless specifically agreed to" by the Bank in writing, or "to appear in or defend any suit with respect thereto unless requested" by De Mott in writing and indemnified to the Bank's satisfaction; (3), that, as compensation for the Bank's "services hereunder", the Bank "shall be entitled to receive 5% on income"; and (4), that De Mott shall "be responsible for all expenses incurred" by the Bank "in connection with this account and any taxes or other charges required to be paid" by the Bank in connection therewith, and the Bank was "authorized to charge" the account "for all such expenses, taxes and charges".

The account was carried in the trust department of the Bank under the direct supervision of one Rohde, the trust officer of the Bank.

De Mott had previously created two trusts, with the Bank as trustee. The first so created was an irrevocable trust, known as the "John H. De Mott Personal Trust", wherein there were transferred by De Mott to the Bank, as such trustee, certain securities, the income of which was to be paid by the Bank to De Mott for life, with dispositions over at the time of his death. The second trust was known as the "Sarah Jane Winifred De Mott Trust", and was created for the purpose of providing a property settlement, in lieu of alimony claimed by De Mott's wife, the beneficiary of the trust.

The complaint was framed and the case was tried on the theory, (179 At. 471), that the letter "evidences an express trust, or in the alternative", that if it was "merely the evidence of the creation of an agency, then that agency, coupled with the confidence reposed" by De Mott in Rohde, the Bank's trust officer, "and the abuse of that confidence by him, caused a constructive trust to arise".

The Vice Chancellor found, (179 At. 471), that De Mott had ratified and confirmed the three questioned investments.

The Vice Chancellor further held, (179 At. 472), *that De Mott had not intended to, and did not, set up a trust for himself by means of the "custodian agreement", and that there was no constructive trust be-*

cause De Mott had ratified and confirmed the questioned investments. The Vice Chancellor, therefore, advised a decree allowing the disputed items.

There should be no question, (179 At. 474), (it may be stated in passing), that the "custodian" agreement created the relation of principal and agent between De Mott and the Bank.

The Vice Chancellor, therefore, held, (1), that the "custodian" agreement created the relation of principal and agent between De Mott and the Bank, represented by the trust officer Rohde, (2), that the parties did not intend to create an express trust, and (3), that, assuming there was a breach of confidence reposed by De Mott in the Bank, represented in the matter by the trust officer, a constructive trust did not arise from that breach of confidence.

We agree with counsel for defendants, in referring to the foregoing case of *De Mott v. National Bank of New Jersey,* and to the case next summarized in this Appendix J, of *State Y.M.C.A. v. Picher,* as "declaring the following rules", (Reply Brief, p. 39), that

"(a) The holding of securities under a depositary arrangement does not constitute the depositary a trustee; (b) even an agency for the purpose of investing funds does not constitute the agent a trustee; (c) the receipt of property by a bank with the knowledge of the depositary's intent to create a trust thereafter does not constitute the bank a trustee";

but with the qualifications, namely, (1), that the rules are abstract and have no relevancy whatever either to the *De Mott Case* or to the *Picher Case;* (2), that rules (a) and (b) are not at all involved in the *Picher Case*, in which no "securities" whatever were deposited by the plaintiff's representatives with the defendant bank, and in which no "agency" whatever for the "purpose of investing funds" ever existed between the plaintiff, as the principal, through its representatives, with the defendant bank, as the agent, much less a relation of cestui que trust and trustee; (3), that rule (c) is not at all involved in the *De Mott Case* for the reason that the "custodian agreement" in that case was never intended by the parties to be an express trust with the plaintiff, as the cestui que trust, and the defendant bank, as the trustee, but was intended, (either by its express provisions, or by implication), as an agency, in which the plaintiff was the principal and the defendant bank was the agent, and as an agency the terms of which had never been violated, as contended by the plaintiff.

The cases, therefore, are not at all helpful in the solution of any of the problems involved in the instant case.

State Y. M. C. A. v. Picher,
8 F. Supp. 412, (D. C., D. of Me., 1934).

This was a suit in equity, instituted by the State Young Men's Christian Association, a corporation, against the defendant Picher, as the receiver of People's Ticonic National Bank, an insolvent national bank of the State of Maine, to secure priority of payment from the assets of the Bank in the hands of the receiver, of the sum of $17,000, on the theory that the Bank held the money, at the time it closed its doors, in trust for the Association. The case involved two principal questions, which were decided in favor of the defendant, namely, (1), was the relation of debtor and creditor between the Bank and the Association changed by a concluded, as distinct from a contemplated, contract between the parties, into the relation of trustee and beneficiary? and (2), conceding that the contract was so concluded, could the trust fund be identified and traced into the receiver's possession, thereby increasing the funds in the hands of the receiver for distribution to general creditors?

The Association, prior to February 10, 1933, had received a gift of $30,000, in the form of a check on a New York bank. The Association, through its officers, namely, Brown, its treasurer, and Smith, its secretary, having charge of its business affairs, determined to use $13,000 of the amount for the current needs of the Association, and to reserve the remaining $17,000 for use of the Association during the following year.

The president of the Bank, who was consulted, on February 10th, by the two named officers of the Asso-

ciation about the matter, offered to collect the check,
through the facilities of the Bank, and to consider,
and later advise, how best to protect the proposed reserve sum of $17,000. The offer was accepted, and the
check was accordingly endorsed and left with the Bank
for collection, and for the deposit of the amount of
the check to the credit of the Association in the regular checking account of the Association with the Bank.
The amount of the check was entered, shortly afterwards, in the regular passbook of the Association with
the Bank. The president, being satisfied that the
maker of the check was solvent, gave credit to the
Association at once for the $30,000, and permitted the
Association to draw at once on the account to the
amount of several thousand dollars. The check was
sent by the Bank to New York for collection, and the
amount of it was credited to the Bank by its correspondent.

*No part of the amount was ever segregated from
the assets of the Bank.* No one, on behalf of the
Association, ever asked for any different arrangement, or for any part of the amount in cash, or that
any part of the amount be kept separate from the
rest. *The entire amount was left to the credit of the
Association with the Bank, in the regular checking
account of the Association, with other amounts* deposited by the Association before and after, the total
of which was drawn against, from time to time as required, until, at the time the Bank closed its doors,
the balance in the account to the credit of the Association was about $21,000.

Both the passbook of the Association and the usual deposit slip, made out by a clerk at the time, showed simply a deposit of $30,000 to the credit of the Association, in the usual course of business. This was understood by all parties at the time. The officers of the Association expected to make a division of the money later and to lay aside and specially safeguard $17,000 of the amount for future use, and the president of the Bank understood that such was the intention.

"The transaction", so the Court said, (p. 413), participated in by all the parties, at the conclusion of the conversations on February 10, cannot be differentiated from that of an ordinary deposit in a bank to the credit of the depositor's checking account. Mr. Brown, the treasurer, and Mr. Smith, the secretary, were content at the time to leave all the money in the bank to the credit of the plaintiff for the short period they thought would elapse before arrangements would be made to take $17,000 from the account and secure it in some way to be agreed upon".

The situation so remained for several days, while the officers of the Association and the president of the Bank were discussing what measures should be taken in regard to the amount of $17,000, which the Association's officers intended to reserve for later use. Finally, the president proposed that the Bank should hold that amount in trust. A discussion of the terms of the proposed trust followed, and the president offered to have his trust officer draw up a written agreement. One was drawn and submitted to the Association's officers, but was not satisfactory and was re-

jected. Shortly after, another agreement was submitted, and at a special meeting of the executive committee of the Association, held on February 28th, "the
trust agreement that had been prepared for safe-
guarding the balance of cash on hand", was described
by Smith, and a vote was passed "allowing Mr. Brown
and Mr. Smith to *complete* the agreement" with the
Bank. According to the proposed contract, the money
turned over to the Bank was *to be invested by the
Bank as the Association should direct, and, until invested, the Bank was obligated to pay the Association 4 per cent. interest, and to secure the repayment
of the principal, which was to be on deposit, by bonds.*

The next morning, on March 1st, Brown told the
trust officer of the Bank that the executive committee
of the Association had accepted the proposed arrangement and were ready to go ahead. "Prior to this
time", as the Court said, (p. 413), "the negotiations
between the parties had resulted in no complete agreement." The trust officer asked Brown to bring his
copy of the proposed agreement to the Bank, so that
another copy could be made for both parties to sign.
At that time, Smith was out of town, and, on his return, on March 3d, an appointment was made with the
Bank officials to meet on Saturday, March 4th, at
noon, to sign the agreement. On arriving at the Bank,
at the appointed time, the officials of the Association
found that the Bank was closed, and had been so for
two hours. As the Court said, (p. 414): "No agreement was signed. Nothing had been done in pursuance
of its terms. This receivership followed".

The Court, in decreeing that the bill of complaint be dismissed, held, (among other matters, not material here), (pp. 414, 415): (1), *"the initial relationship between the Bank and the plaintiff was that of debtor and creditor in the usual course of the commercial banking business, and such relationship continued until the closing of the Bank, unless changed by agreement of the parties"*; (2), *no contract was concluded between the parties, and, for that reason, the original status of the Association "as a depositor or creditor remained unchanged"*; (3), *since it was contemplated that the contract should be in writing, no contract, binding upon the parties, came into existence, or was complete, until the writing was executed by the parties*; (4), *the proposed contract, even if signed by the parties, and the sum of money turned over to the Bank did not create a trust*, since, according to its provisions, the money was to be invested by the Bank as the Association might direct, and, until invested, the Bank was obligated to pay the Association 4 per cent. interest and to secure the repayment of the principal, on demand, by bonds. "On the contrary, the definite status of debtor and creditor was established, changed from the previous relationship only in that the creditor, who was previously unsecured, became a secured creditor and was to be paid interest. The bank was to have the use of the money"; and (5), *in any event, there could be no priority payment by the receiver to the Association,* "because there was never placed in the hands of the bank, as supposed trustee, any property which can be identified and traced to the receiver's possession, and which increased the funds under his charge to be distributed to general creditors''.

The case, therefore, has no relevancy to the facts of the instant case, for the reason that a trust relation was never created because an instrument creating the trust, intended to be drawn by one of the officers of the Bank, was never drawn.

In re Cook's Estate,
20 Del. Ch. 123, 171 At. 730 (1934).

To the first and final account of the trustee under the last will of William H. Cook, deceased, exceptions were taken by Harold L. Cook, the beneficiary of the trust estate.

The exceptions challenged the propriety of certain investments made by the trustee.

The will did not confer upon the trustee any special liberty of judgment in the management of the trust estate.

Under a statute of Delaware, trustees were not absolutely required to invest trust funds in the so-called "legals" enumerated in the statute, but such investments were permitted by the statute, and if the trustees kept within the categories of investments named in the statute, the statute afforded, so the Chancellor said, a protection to them against surcharges due to loss, "which, had they stepped outside the authorized classes of investment, they might well be made to bear."

The investments to which the exceptions were taken were 4 in number,—none of them falling within any of the classes permitted by the statute. The question, therefore, was, what degree of care and skill was to be exacted of the trustee under the circumstances?

The Chancellor made two observations, the first being that the standard of care and skill which a trustee was expected to exercise was that which a man of ordinary prudence would exercise in dealing with his own property, that is, such care and skill as an ordinary prudent man would exercise "if he were minded to make an investment for the benefit of other people for whom he felt morally bound to provide," and the next observation being that the primary object to be attained by a trustee in investing trust funds was their safety.

All 4 investments were made in bonds, one of them being in bonds of Equitable Office Building, the owner and operator of an office building in New York City, and the same was secured by a second mortgage.

The other 3 investments were made in bonds of the American Water Works Company, a utility holding company, in bonds of the Atlantic Coast Line, a railroad company, and in bonds of the Childs Company, the operator of a chain of restaurants, and all 3 of these bonds were unsecured, except those of the Equitable Office Building, which were second mortgage bonds.

The bonds of the 4 issues were selected by the trustee largely upon the recommendation of a broker.

The bonds of the Childs Company and of the American Water Works Company were given only a fourth rating by standard investment appraisers, while the bonds of the Equitable Office Building were given a sixth rating. As to these bonds, the Chancellor held, (171 At. 732), that the trustee, in the purchase of them,

> "did not exercise that degree of care which an ordinarily prudent man would have exercised in

the investment of funds belonging to another. The safety of the principal, which should have been the first consideration, was unreasonably exposed to jeopardy."

As to the bonds of the Atlantic Coast Line, the Chancellor said that (171 At. 732):

"while they were without the protection of security, yet they appear to have been highly regarded at the time they were purchased. They enjoyed the most favorable rating. My conclusion with respect to them is that the trustee should not be taxed with their shrinkage in value."

Evidence was introduced at the hearing that the beneficiary knew of the investments made by the trustee, and made no objection thereto, and, as the Chancellor said, this circumstance was shown "in order to raise an estoppel against the beneficiary based on consent", and, as to this, the Chancellor continued (171 At. 732) as follows:

"That consent of a beneficiary, under some circumstances, may afford protection to a trustee against the consequences of a breach of duty, may be conceded. But before exonerating consent can be made out, it must appear that the *cestui que trust* knew all the facts, was apprised of his legal rights, was under no disability and acted freely, deliberately and advisedly with the intention of confirming the transaction which he knew, or might or ought, with reasonable or proper diligence, to have known to be impeachable. *White v. Sherman,* 168 Ill. 589, 48 N. E. 128, 61 Am. St. Rep. 132. A trustee cannot relieve himself of the responsibility of an investment by the simple expedient of informing the beneficiary that the investment had been made. The *cestui que trust* is under no duty to act as adviser to his trustee. Consent, such as to foreclose the beneficiary from objecting, is not evidenced by failure to complain. Silence is not affirmation and approval. *Life Association of Scotland v. Siddal*, 3 DeG. F. & J. 58, 45 Eng. Reprint, 800; *Phillipson v. Gatty*, 7 Hare, 516, 68 Eng. Reprint, 213."

Kurtz v. Farrington,
104 Conn. 257, 132 At. 540, 48 A. L. R. 259, (1926).

This was an action brought by the plaintiff and appellee, Anna J. Kurtz, against the defendant and appellant, Daniel T. Farrington, to recover the sum of $2,000, and interest, as damages for the alleged fraud of the defendant, in the purchase of certain real property, situated in Waterbury, Connecticut, and which had been advertised for sale by the owner, one Strong.

The plaintiff recovered judgment against the defendant for the amount claimed, namely, $2,000, plus $192, interest; and, on appeal, the judgment was affirmed.

The findings of the trial court were held by the Supreme Court, in affirming the judgment, to be supported by the evidence.

The disputed question was whether or not the defendant, as the plaintiff claimed, acted in the transaction as her agent, and, therefore, occupied a fiduciary relation to her, or, on the other hand, whether as the defendant claimed, the relation was that of seller and purchaser.

The action was brought on the theory that the defendant was the plaintiff's agent.

The facts are as follows, (132 At. 543):

The defendant had long been engaged as a real estate agent in Waterbury. The plaintiff had previously purchased, through him, or through his agency, several pieces of real property in that city.

In all these transactions, he had acted as the agent of the sellers, and not as the agent for the plaintiff, and had received his commissions from the sellers.

In the instant case, the defendant received no compensation from the plaintiff; and it did not appear whether the plaintiff expected to pay the defendant for his services or not.

On October 12, 1923, the defendant, in response to Strong's advertisement of the property, which appeared in a local paper, telephoned Strong for an appointment, and, on October 13th, began negotiations for the purchase of the property for himself.

The plaintiff, on October 13th, also saw the advertisement, and, on October 14th, attempted, without success to see Strong with a view to a possible purchase of the property. The plaintiff, failing to find Strong, went directly to the defendant's office, and there told the defendant of the property, showed him the advertisement, and told him of her thought of possibly buying the property.

Although the defendant was then negotiating with Strong for the purchase of the property, *he did not disclose that fact to the plaintiff, but told her he would find out about the property.*

The defendant, thereafter, on October 14th, telephoned the plaintiff that he had found out about the property, and asked her to call to see him, which she did on October 15th.

The defendant thereupon took the plaintiff for an inspection of the property, showed her a map, gave her information about the property lines, and the terms of purchase, saying to her that the lowest price at which the property could be bought was $30,000.

She thereupon decided to buy the property, requested the defendant to undertake to get the property for her, and turned over to him $1,000 on account of the purchase price.

In the language of the Court, (132 At. 543),

"So far as the plaintiff was concerned, it is clear that she depended entirely upon the defendant to this point, and, so far as appears, she had no information whatsoever which put her upon inquiry as to his real position in the matter. His service for her was such as would be expected of an agent who was accustomed to act in behalf of customers seeking their services. The plaintiff took no further active part in putting the transaction through. She employed no counsel or other assistance throughout, but the defendant took charge of the matter for her, and saw to it that all the deeds were prepared at the office of his own counsel, met her at the bank where the necessary cash was obtained by a mortgage of the property to the bank, and delivered to her the final papers."

Continuing, the Court said (132 At. 543):

"The finding shows that all this time, while her interests had thus been looked after by the defendant, she was unaware, and he concealed from her the fact, that he had an interest personally in the transaction as a buyer and a seller of the property. He not only permitted, but induced, her to believe that he was acting for her and solely in her interest, and on the facts disclosed by the finding she was fully justified in so supposing."

The defendant, during this time, (apparently), (132 At. 540-1), had closed his negotiations with Strong for the purchase of the property for $29,000, concealing that fact from the plaintiff; and thus profited, by the deal, the difference between $31,000, or what the plaintiff paid, and $29,000, or what the defendant paid.

The Court, in conclusion, held (132 At. 544):

(1), that, under the circumstances, *the fiduciary relation of principal and agent existed between the plaintiff and the defendant, which the law did not allow to be violated by the defendant to the damage of the plaintiff;*

(2), *that the relation of principal and agent need not arise from an express appointment and acceptance,* but was often established by the words and conduct of the parties and the circumstances of the particular case;

(3), (132 At. 543), *that compensation was not a necessary element to the relation of principal and agent;* and

(4), (132 At. 544), *that the defendant was estopped by his conduct from denying the relation.**

---

* NOTE: The following is the language of the Court, in these foregoing respects, (132 At. 543):

"While an agency is thus generally the result of contract, express or implied, *it is not always necessary to find all the elements of a contract in order to establish the relation.* Even where one undertakes to act for another without compensation, and the element of consideration necessary for a contract is lacking, *if he does in fact enter upon the undertaking, the relation of agency between him and the party for whom he is acting is created.* 2 *Corpus Juris,* 419, and citations.

"When the plaintiff visited the defendant on the 15th of October, and requested him to undertake to get the property for her, and the defendant, by his concealment of his knowledge of the matter, led her to believe that he was free to act in her behalf, and did so by pretending to look up the matter for her, and telephoned her the following day that he had done so, she was justified in believing that he was in fact representing her, and his subsequent conduct down to the consummation of the sale, so far as this was disclosed to her by him, was properly a confirmation of that belief on her part, and she acted upon that belief throughout. *Under these circumstances, a fiduciary relation was created which the law does not allow the defendant to violate to the damage of the plaintiff. It is not necessary to enter into meticulous definitions of the relation, or seek to determine whether it arose by an express or implied contract between the parties, or whether the defendant should be treated as estopped by his conduct from denying that the relation existed. The relation need not arise from an express appointment and an acceptance, but is often established from the words and conduct of the parties and the circumstances of the particular case.*

"The defendant, in brief and argument, dwells upon the contention that the plaintiff 'must have known' that the defendant 'was not her hired agent', and argues from this that there could not have been an agency by express or implied contract. *There is, as we have seen, nothing to show whether she expected to pay the defendant for his services or not, but compensation is not a necessary element.*

"*Neither can we concur in the claim of the defendant that the essential elements of an estoppel, many of which were presented in Herzog v. Cooke,* 121 A. 868, 99 Conn. 366; *C. & C. Electric Motor Co. v. D. Frisbie & Co.,* 33 A. 604, 66 Conn. 67; *Goldberg v. Parker,* 87 A. 555, 87 Conn. 99, 46 L. R. A. (N. S.) 1097, Ann. Cas. 1914C, 1059; *Monterosso v. Kent,* 113 A. 922, 96 Conn. 346; *Lewis v. Lewis,* 57 A. 735, 76 Conn. 586, and other cases in this state cited by him, *are wanting in this case.* In fact, the statement the defendant quotes from the opinion in the *Frisbie Case* applies with rather striking effect to the circumstances disclosed by the finding in this case, viz.:

" '*When one person by anything which he does or says, or abstains from doing or saying, intentionally causes or per-*

mits another person to believe a thing to be true, and to act
upon such belief otherwise than but for that belief he would
have acted, *neither the person first mentioned nor his repre-*
sentative in interest is allowed, in any suit or proceeding
between himself and such person or his representative in
interest, to deny the truth of that thing.'

"Our conclusion is not only that there was a fiduciary
relation between the plaintiff and defendant, but that the
facts show agency by contract. In any event, the defendant
is now estopped by his conduct from denying the fiduciary
relation." (Emphasis added).

Carr v. National Bank and Loan Company of Watertown,
167 N. Y. 375, 60 N. E. 649, 82 A. S. R. 725, (1901).

This case, cited in our Opening Brief, p. 55, was an action brought by the plaintiff against the defendant bank for the rescission of transactions in which certain bonds belonging to the defendant were sold to the plaintiff by one Sherman, the president and manager of the bank.

The plaintiff recovered a judgment entitling her to disaffirm the transactions and declaring the bonds to be the property of the defendant, subject to the payment of the amount of the plaintiff's recovery for the face value of the bonds and unpaid interest, and therefore the action was one in equity.

The plaintiff, upon the death of her husband, came into possession of moneys from insurance policies issued on his life. Sherman induced her to allow him to invest the moneys on his representations that he could do so in sound and safe securities yielding 6% annually. She assented, and as the insurance moneys were paid to her, turned the moneys over to Sherman, who deposited them with the bank.

From time to time during the years 1892 and 1893, Sherman withdrew the moneys and paid them to the bank in the purchase by him from the bank of the bonds in question, which had theretofore been acquired by the bank, whereupon the bonds were transferred to the plaintiff and kept in the bank for her.

In these transactions, Sherman acted as the plaintiff's personal friend, and she relied wholly upon his

representations and judgment, taking no active part
in the purchase of the bonds and having no knowledge
in relation to them, or as to their ownership.

Sherman stated to the plaintiff, in response to her
inquiries, that the bonds were "first mortgage bonds,
first-class security, as good as gold and that he had
gotten them expressly for her." The bonds, however,
were in fact second mortgage bonds, and were not
"first-class securities", nor had they been expressly
procured for plaintiff's investment, as Sherman had
said they were.

The plaintiff, in 1896, discovered the falsity of Sherman's representations and that he had been acting for
the bank in selling the bonds at a profit to the bank
of 5%.

Defaults occurred in the payment of the interest
coupons on the bonds, but the coupons were taken up
and cashed by the bank, and the plaintiff was informed that the defaults were due to temporary causes,
and further representations of a reassuring character
were made, the falsity of which were discovered by her.

Upon the plaintiff's discovering the falsity of Sherman's representations and the bank's interest in the
bonds, the plaintiff tendered the bonds to the bank and
demanded their face value, which she had paid with
interest.

The Court of Appeals held against the contentions
of the bank, (1), that actual fraud in a transaction
was not essential to the granting of the relief which
the plaintiff demanded, and (2), that the bank, retain-

ing the benefit of the transactions, could defend on the ground of Sherman's lack of authority or on ground of want of power as a national bank to engage in the business of buying and selling securities, the Court saying (167 N. Y. 379):

"The appellant argues that the facts did not establish any actual fraud on the part of the defendant. But that was not essential to the granting of the relief which plaintiff demanded. There was shown to have been such a condition of things, in the situation of the parties and in the ignorance in which the plaintiff was kept of material facts, by ways of suppression, or of misrepresentation, as, in equity, to warrant her in wholly repudiating the transaction. It is quite immaterial that there may have been no intention to actually defraud. (*Hammond v. Pennock,* 61 N. Y. 145.) The plaintiff supposed that she had enlisted the disinterested services of Sherman in the investment of her moneys, and, relying upon what he told her, confided them to him; whereas, in fact, he was acting for the bank, of which he was president and manager, in disposing, at a profit, of a series of securities, which it had acquired. He was acting for the defendant as a seller of the bonds and for the plaintiff as an intending purchaser, and a fraudulent motive was not necessary to be proved, either on the defendant's part, or on that of the common agent, for, in the view of a court of equity, there was such fraud in law as to make the contract a voidable one, at the election of the plaintiff. The plaintiff has been made to suffer her loss through misplaced confidence in one whom she believed to be devoted to her interests, while, at the time, he

was acting for the defendant's, and the legal
theory of her right to equitable relief, by the way
of rescission, rests upon the basis that Sherman
undertook to act as the agent of both parties in a
matter where their interests were, for obvious
reasons, to be regarded as conflicting. In such
cases equity will, upon the seasonable application
of a party, avoid the transaction and this right is
conceded, without reference to any actual fraud.
A binding transaction requires the free and con-
scious action of the party's mind upon its subject.
The general equitable doctrine should be regarded
as well settled."

The judgment in the case was affirmed by the Supreme Court of the United States, in *National Bank
and Loan Company v. Carr,* 189 U. S. 426, 47 L. Ed.
881 (1903), on the authority of a companion case,
namely, *National Bank and Loan Company v. Petrie,*
189 U. S. 423, 47 L. Ed. 879 (1903), involving the
question whether or not the appellant as a national
bank was liable under the circumstances.

The opinion by Mr. Justice Holmes in the *Carr Case*
is as follows (189 U. S. 426, 47 L. Ed. 882):

"This case is similar in substance, pleading and
argument to the foregoing, with the additional
fact that the president of the bank acted as the
confidential adviser of the defendant in error and
did not reveal to her that the bonds belonged to
the bank or that he was on both sides of the transaction and interested against her. As soon as she
found out that the bank was the seller she repu-
diated the sale."

Kershaw v. Julien,
72 F.(2d) 528, (C. C. A., 10th), (1934).

The facts in this case furnish an excellent illustration of the victimizing of an aged and infirm widow by the president of a bank, in whom the widow, unfortunately for her, placed great trust and confidence, and, in that respect are somewhat similar to those of the instant case.

This case involved a proceeding by the plaintiff and appellee, Helen H. Julien, as executrix of the will of Florence M. Hershey, deceased, against the defendants and appellants Kershaw, as receiver of the Commercial National Bank, and Security National Bank, both of Independence, Kansas.

The decedent, Mrs. Hershey, had lived for a number of years in Independence, where she was a customer and depositor of the Commercial Bank. She was well along in years, crippled, deaf and in poor health. From time to time she purchased real estate mortgages from the Commercial Bank and from Guernsey, its president. Apparently about the time she began to make the purchases, in 1923 or 1924, Guernsey assured her that any mortgages which she purchased would be "first-class loans"—"first-class in every way".

Mrs. Guernsey moved to California about 1923, but remained a customer and depositor of the Commercial Bank and continued to purchase, by correspondence, mortgages from that bank. In the correspondence, the bank, at all times, described the mortgages so continued to be purchased by her as "desirable" or "choice".

During the year 1927, and until his death in November of that year, one Lockwood was a customer and depositor of the Commercial Bank. He was hopelessly insolvent, and his indebtedness to the bank was a matter of concern to it. One of his notes, namely, a note for $10,000, had been charged off, and other notes were precariously secured. At the time of his death, he owed the bank upwards of $17,000, in addition to an indebtedness of $12,500 on the mortgage in controversy.

Guernsey, in October, 1926, owned a sheriff's certificate of sale to 320 acres of land near Independence. There were no improvements of any consequence on the land. Half of the land was covered with scrub oak trees and was without grass or water, and afforded slight pasture for but a few head of stock during the summer. Of the remainder of the land, 130 acres were cultivated, but part of the land was hardpan and part of it was white alkali. The fair market value of the land in 1927 was $4,000.

Guernsey transferred the certificate to Lockwood, and Lockwood, in 1926, gave a mortgage on the land to the Commercial Bank for $12,500, and later, namely, on September 8, 1927, a sheriff's deed of the land was executed to Lockwood.

The bank, in August, 1927, assigned the mortgage without recourse to Mrs. Hershey, who then resided in California, charging her account with the bank with $12,757.17, the face value of the mortgage and accrued interest, and kept the proceeds, crediting the amount on Lockwood's indebtedness to the bank.

Mrs. Hershey assumed that the mortgage was a "first-class mortgage", with a reasonable margin of value over the encumbrance. Lockwood paid no interest, but the bank paid the interest regularly, thus lulling Mrs. Hershey into inaction, until the bank failed in 1930. Mrs. Hershey, on the failure of the bank, discovered that she had been victimized, and filed a claim with the receiver of the bank for $7,757.17, the difference between the price she had paid for the mortgage and $5,000, which, for some reason, she considered to be the value of the mortgage. The receiver rejected the claim, whereupon this action followed.

The National Security Bank was apparently made a defendant because of the fact that it had purchased from the receiver certain assets of the Commercial Bank. Apparently, however, the Security Bank in such purchase did not assume any liabilities of the Commercial Bank.

The facts were alleged with appropriate allegations of fraud practiced upon Mrs. Hershey. The prayer was for a prior and preferred claim against the assets of the Commercial Bank in the hands of the receiver and against the assets purchased by the Security Bank.

The answer of the Commercial Bank, (characteristically in such cases), denied the fraud and alleged that Guernsey was the agent of Mrs. Hershey and not of the Commercial Bank, and that the Commercial Bank had no lawful authority to act as her agent in the investment of her funds.

The trial court found that Mrs. Hershey had been defrauded, allowed the claim against the receiver, further decreed that the receiver should accord the claim priority over unsecured creditors of the Commercial Bank, and impressed a trust upon the assets acquired by the creditor bank from the Commercial Bank.

The Circuit Court of Appeals held against the contentions of the appellants, as follows: (1), that the evidence, although in part circumstantial, "established the fault beyond the shadow of a doubt", and that Guernsey's testimony that he was deceived in relying upon an appropriate appraisal of the land by a person with whom he had many business relations, and, consequently, "believed the mortgage was well secured", was too incredible for belief; (2), that Guernsey's representations at the time when Mrs. Hershey began purchasing the securities from him and from the Commercial Bank, that the mortgages would be "first-class in every way", "need not be reiterated with every offering" of the mortgages; (3), that the statements relating to the value of the mortgages were representations of fact and not expressions of opinion, since a statement by an experienced banker to a confiding customer that a note is aptly secured when he knows that it is not is more than an expression of opinion— it is a deliberate misrepresentation of the fact; (4), that the hypothesis that the Commercial Bank was liable only if it affirmatively misrepresented a material fact was not sound, since the rule applied "when those upon an equal footing deal at arm's length", and did not apply to a situation where, as in the case in hand, the bank sustained a relation of confidence towards a customer with whom it dealt, and when, because of such confidence, a duty was imposed upon it to disclose every material fact within its knowledge; and (5), that the claim that Guernsey was the agent of Mrs. Hershey instead of the Commercial Bank found no support, since the bank, "acting through its president and acting managing officer", "took and retains the proceeds of the mortgage", and, "having done so", it is not in a position to deny either the authority of its president or its power to sell a mortgage.

The Court of Appeals, however, held that the decree was erroneous in that, (1), the claim had no priority over other unsecured securities of the Commercial Bank, and (2), the Security Bank was not liable, since that bank had not assumed the liabilities of the Commercial Bank.

The decree, therefore, was modified as to the receiver by the limitation of the preference and as to the liabilities of the Security Bank, but otherwise the decree was affirmed.

Concerning the fourth of the foregoing rulings, the Court of Appeals (Circuit Judge McDermott writing the opinion), said, (p. 530):

> "Furthermore, the hypothesis that the bank is liable only if it affirmatively misrepresented a material fact is not sound. That rule applies when those upon an equal footing deal at arm's length. *The situation here put upon the bank the obligation to disclose all facts known to it which were*

material to the transaction. Mrs. Hershey had been
a customer of the bank for years; she had bought
many mortgages from it; she had been assured
that investments offered her would be first class
in every way; she had purchased mortgages from
the bank through the years in reliance upon such
assurance. *Having gained her confidence by such
course of conduct, it may not escape responsibility
for its abuse by invoking a rule applicable between
strangers. When such a state of confidence exists,
it is the duty of him in whom the confidence is
reposed to disclose every material fact within his
knowledge. Bacon v. Soule,* 19 Cal. App. 428, 126
P. 384. When there is a duty to speak, the suppression of the truth is as reprehensible and as
actionable as the utterance of the false. *The Kal-
farli* (C. C. A. 2) 277 F. 391, 400; *Copper Process
Co. v. Chicago Bonding & Ins. Co.* (C. C. A. 3)
262 F. 66, 73, 8 A. L. R. 1477; *New York Life
Ins. Co. v. Gay* (C. C. A. 6) 36 F. (2d) 634, 638;
Nairn v. Ewalt, 51 Kan. 355, 32 P. 1110. In *Tyler
v. Savage,* 143 U. S. 79, 98, 12 S. Ct. 340, 346, 36 L.
Ed. 82, the Supreme Court held that 'This suppression of a material fact, which Tyler was bound
in good faith to disclose, was equivalent to a false
representation.' So here; the gross inadequacy of
the security and the insolvency of the makers were
material facts which the bank knew and sup-
pressed although bound in good faith to disclose.''
(Emphasis added).

Gates v. Megargel,
266 Fed. 811, (C. C. A., 2d, 1920).

This was a suit brought by Herman B. Gates and others against Roy C. Megargel and another, co-partners doing business under the firm name of R. C. Megargel & Co.

There was a decree in favor of certain of the plaintiffs and interveners and against certain others of the plaintiffs and interveners, from which certain of the defendants, against whom the decree was rendered, appealed.

Many of the plaintiffs and interveners did not appeal, or, having appealed, abandoned their appeals after a settlement out of court, thus leaving before the appellate court a portion only of the defendants.

The suit arose out of a so-called "syndicate agreement", contained in a letter written by the defendants, to many persons, including the plaintiffs and interveners, whom the defendants believed might be interested in the stock of a corporation, called the "Glenrock Oil Company".

The letter was dated August 17, 1917, and emanated from the office of the defendants, in New York City, and informed those to whom it was addressed that the Oil Company had been recently incorporated under the laws of the State of Virginia, with a total authorized capital stock of $10,000,000, divided into 1,000,000 shares, of the par value of $10 each.

The letter stated that the Oil Company was formed for the purpose of acquiring, by direct purchase or through controlling interests in other corporations, producing and prospective oil properties located in the State of Wyoming and elsewhere.

The letter also stated that Megargel & Co. were "negotiating for the purchase of certain shares of the capital stock of the Oil Company", and were

> "forming a syndicate to acquire from us a portion of said stock to the extent of not exceeding 100,000 shares, when, as and if, acquired by us, at a price of $7.00 per share".

The letter also stated that

> "We are to be managers of the syndicate, and may *be members* thereof, notwithstanding our relations as vendors thereto and managers thereof, and as such managers we shall have full power to determine, within the limit above stated, the amount of stock to be purchased from us by the syndicate, and with full power to sell, purchase, resell and repurchase for account of the syndicate, at public or private sale, any shares of stock at such prices and on such terms as we may deem fit; to pay the usual brokerages, as well as such commissions for effecting sales or purchases for account of the syndicate as we may deem proper; to charge the syndicate reasonable commissions and the usual brokerages for sales or purchases effected by us; to make advances to the syndicate, charging interest thereon; to make or procure loans and secure the same by pledge of syndicate stock or otherwise, to such amounts and in such manner as from time to time we may deem expedient; and generally to act in all respects as in our opinion may be to the interest of the syndicate".

The letter also stated, (p. 813), that

> "*We shall not be liable under any of the provisions of this letter or for any matter connected therewith, except for want of good faith,* and no obligation not herein expressly assumed by us shall be deemed to be implied".

The letter also stated, (p. 813), that

> "The syndicate managers may purchase, sell, or otherwise dispose of, or be interested in, the purchase, sale or other disposition of, any stock or other securities of said corporation or its subsidiary companies, or contract in any respect with it or them, without restriction and without responsibility therefor to the syndicate".

The letter also stated, (pp. 813-4), that

> "All expenses incurred in the acquisition of such stock for the syndicate, in the marketing of the same, and all other expenses incurred by us as syndicate managers shall be charged against the syndicate. *We shall make no charge to the syndicate for acting as syndicate managers,* other than reasonable commissions and the usual brokerages for sales or purchases offered by us, *being otherwise compensated in our purchases of said stock*".

Those who accepted the offer contained in the letter, including the plaintiffs and interveners, did so, (p. 814), by signature thereto, as was required, merely by acknowledging receipt of "your letter dated August 17, 1917", "offering us a participation" in "the syndicate aforesaid", *"which we hereby accept upon the terms therein stated".*

The Oil Company was organized on the morning of August 17, 1917, (p. 815), with a dummy board of directors, "who did nothing except the formal matters of adopting the sale and by-laws and things of that kind". They subsequently resigned, and thereupon the "real board of directors" was chosen, including one Collins, "from whom were, in a sense derived", the 100,000 shares of the capital stock of the Oil Company, mentioned in the agreement. Collins, on August 10, 1917, as the representative of sundry existing oil companies located or operating in Wyoming, agreed with the defendants that the Oil Company should be organized with a capital stock of $10,000,000, eight-tenths of which, (p. 815), should be "issued or reserved for issue to acquire if possible a controlling interest in", (inter alia), the existing corporations represented by him.

Thus, as the Court said, (p. 815), Collins, in exchange for the shares of existing oil companies, would acquire "many shares of the Glenrock Oil Company when formed", and, on August 10, 1917, "he agreed in writing with the defendants that if he should so acquire 242,500 shares, he would sell, and Megargel would buy, 100,000 shares thereof at the price of $3.50 per share".

Contemporaneously with the execution of the Collins-Megargel agreement, the defendants made a contract with one Taylor, (who subsequently became a director of the Oil Company), (p. 815), to purchase, on a six months option, 44,000 shares of the Oil Company at the same price of $3.50 per share.

The Taylor-Megargel contract provided, (p. 815), that the defendants would "use their best efforts to form a syndicate to purchase from them not exceeding 100,000 shares" of the Oil Company, "when, as and if, acquired" by the defendants, "and to use their best efforts, by means of said syndicate and otherwise, to create and establish a market for shares of the capital stock" of the Oil Company.

The Collins-Megargel agreement also provided that the defendants would "use their best efforts to form the syndicate above mentioned, and by means of said syndicate and otherwise to create a market for the shares" of the Oil Company.

The defendants, (p. 815), ultimately took and paid for the 100,000 shares of the Oil Company, and made such payments after they had collected from, and practically with the money furnished, by the syndicate subscribers; and the defendants, having obtained the 100,000 shares, transferred the same to the syndicate, or to themselves as syndicate managers, on their books.

The defendants, (p. 815), then attempted to market the syndicate stock on the New York Curb, buying as well as selling, "supporting" the prices by such purchases. Their efforts were not wholly successful, although the quoted prices were maintained above the syndicate prices until December 10, 1917. Thereafter, the stock fell almost continuously until December 20,

1917, when it reached less than $5 per share, and, on that day, this suit was commenced.

The reason for the suit, (p. 816), was the discovery by the original plaintiffs, or some of them, that the defendants had paid but $3.50 per share for the syndicate stock, paid for by the syndicate at $7 per share. On this point, as the Court said, (referring to Megargel), (p. 816),

> "the principal defendant testified that he had 'never told anybody what I was paying for the stock; I never told anybody who subscribed to the syndicate until long after the syndicate was formed'."

The record, as the Court said, (p. 816),

> "is, for the most part, devoted to explaining how and with what knowledge or notice, or means of acquiring knowledge, the various parties complainant joined the syndicate".

To those who proved to the satisfaction of the lower court that they had been actually deceived, either by the language of the syndicate letter, or, dehors that letter, by the defendants' words, the lower court awarded decrees, excepting those who, with knowledge of the price paid by the defendants, agreed to enter a *second syndicate,* which, on or about November 1, 1917, the defendants "sought to form to carry forward the affairs of the first syndicate, which, by that time, promised to fall". *Nothing,* so the Court said, (p. 816), *ever came of this second effort to syndication.*

The complainant appellants were those who did not prove any deception personally practiced on them by the defendants, or who were debarred from the fruits of such deception by their transactions in respect of the attempted second syndicate.

The theory of the suit, as the Court said, (p. 816), (Circuit Judge Hough writing the opinion), *was that the syndicate agreement was valid, and made Megargel the plaintiffs' trustee, and that Megargel, "while otherwise executing his fiduciary duties, (1), deceived them in respect of the price to him of the syndicate stock, and (2), made a secret profit out of such deception,"* "and, therefore, the bill calls him to account for his stewardship".

"The action was not based on fraud, but on breach of duty; and it is not described in the list of remedies given in *Heckscher v. Edenborn,* 203 N. Y. at page 220, 96 N. E. 441, and is like *Yale Gas, etc. Co. v. Wilcox,* 64 Conn. 101, 29 Atl. 303, 25 L. R. A. 90, 42 Am. St. Rep. 159".*

Contrary to the defendants' contention that the breach of the fiduciary duty dated only from the day when the syndicate was formed, and the business of "creating a market" for the Oil Company's stock began, the Court held, (pp. 817-8), *that the fiduciary relation existed between plaintiffs and Megargel, the*

---

*Note: The case of a promoter, who procured subscriptions to the capital stock of a corporation, which he organized and controlled, to acquire patents, having a secret contract with the owner of the patents by which the purchase price of the patents, payable by the corporation, was to be divided between the promoter and the owner of the patents.

subscribers and the syndicate maker, when, (in legal contemplation), the latter invited the former to come into his scheme; and, although, in one sense, the relation could not fully exist until there was a cestui as well as a trustee, yet, *"if one asks another to trust him, he assumes the position of a trustee for many purposes by the asking,"*, and if, therefore, Megargel, on August 17, 1917, *"assumed a portion of trust quoad possible subscribers now represented by these appellants"*, it was his duty to inform them that he was making a profit.

"Under the facts", the Court further held, (p. 819),

> *"the whole transaction must be regarded as unitary, and defendant held as a fiduciary ab initio, because he agreed to take stock only to pass it along to himself as trustee".*

And, (pp. 819-20),

> *"Since liability grows out of duties equitably imposed by a voluntarily assumed relation, it may be said generally that one who seeks or creates an agency or trusteeship or any fiduciary position, for the purpose and with the intent of secretly profiting therefrom, is not acting in good faith, and from the time he forms the intent occupies such a position* 'that any profits resulting from his dealings with' the concern whose agency he seeks must be accounted for".

On the question of estoppel urged against such of the present appellants as consented to go into "the inchoate and futile second syndicate, after learning of the defendants' secret profit," *the Court held,* (p. 820, *that "estoppel is mostly a question of intent", and "certainly no intent to ratify their trustee's breach has been shown in respect of these appellants.* But on the holding now made, *"that these appellants were cestui que trustent and were dealing with their trustee, it is plain law that a cestui who has been wronged by his trustee can only be held to have ratified when he not only knows the facts, but is informed of his rights under the law." In re Long Island, etc. Co.,* 92 App. Div. 1, 87 N. Y. Supp. 65. *The present case falls far short of meeting this requirement".**

The result was that so far as the decree appealed from affected the present appellants, the decree was reversed and the cause remanded for further proceedings not inconsistent with the opinion.

---

*Note: In other words, the Court held on the question involved in the instant case, prior to the creation of the trust estate by the instrument of trust, on September 24, 1929, (1), that, although the relation of trustee and cestui que trust had not been completed by the creation of a *res,* nevertheless, the relation existed to such an extent that the trustee was accountable to the cestui que trust for the unlawful profits which the trustee had made, and (2), that *in order to charge the cestui que trust with an estoppel by reason of his conduct, it was necessary for the trustee to prove that the cestui que trust not only knew the facts but that he was informed of his rights under the law,*—the rule, substantially, as contended by us.

Garrett v. Reid-Cashion Land & Cattle Co.,
**34 Ariz. 245, 270 Pac. 1044, (on petition for
rehearing, 34 Ariz. 482, 272 Pac. 918, 1928).**

This was an action brought by non-consenting
minority stockholders of the Garrett Sheep Company,
a corporation, to set aside the merger of that corporation with the defendant corporation, Reid-Cashion
Land & Cattle Company, and to have the assets of the
Sheep Company retransferred to it by the Land &
Cattle Company, or, in lieu of such transfer, for the
value of the plaintiff's shares of stock in the Sheep
Company at the time of the merger.

From a judgment against certain of the plaintiffs,
the latter appealed to the Supreme Court, which
reversed the judgment, with directions to the trial
court to take evidence of the value of the plaintiffs'
shares in the Sheep Company, as of the time the
assets were transferred, on the merger, to the Land
& Cattle Company, and to enter judgment for the
plaintiffs for that value, with legal interest thereon,
(as for a conversion of the assets), from that time.

Four individuals, namely, Cashion, Sullivan, Reid
and Markham, were the owners of the majority of
the shares of capital stock of the Sheep Company,
and controlled its board of directors. These same
individuals were also the owners of a majority of
the shares of the capital stock of the Land & Cattle
Company, and, likewise, controlled its board of
directors.

The merger of the Sheep Company with the Land
& Cattle Company, and the transfer of the assets of

the former to the latter, were accomplished by these same individuals, against the objections of the minority stockholders, *who, however, and in ignorance of their rights, surrendered their certificates for stock in the Sheep Company, and accepted, in lieu thereof, certificates of stock in the consolidated Land Company.*

In other words, as the Court said, (270 Pac. 1052):

"The question, then, it seems to us, reduces itself to this: *Have the cestuis que trustent, who have accepted certificates of stock of the consolidated company, the right under the circumstances to tender such certificates back and receive the value of their property as of the time of its conversion by the trustee?* The evidence is undisputed that the former were not trained in business and did not know the legal effect on their rights of the transaction absorbing the Garrett Sheep Company by the Reid-Cashion Land & Cattle Company— that, indeed, they believed they were bound by the action of the majority stockholders, and acted under that belief in accepting such stock—that it was 'half a loaf' or nothing. The yardstick employed to measure the rights of parties dealing at arm's length is not the proper measure of the rights growing out of fiduciary relations. If it were, perhaps these minority stockholders would be remediless. The trustee owes certain duties to his cestui que trust that he must observe, and among them is the duty not to sell to himself the trust property. This duty was breached. Reid, Cashion, Sullivan, and Markham were in fact both companies, since, as majority stockholders and managing and directing officers, they bodily took over the exercise of their functions. *They*

were in contemplation of law both the seller and
purchaser. As trustees of the minority stockhold-
ers, they owed it to such stockholders to disclose,
not only all the facts, but to inform them, espe-
cially in view of their being women without busi-
ness experience or familiarity with corporate law,
of their legal rights".

The Court, in condemning the transaction, as a
breach of trust, said, (270 Pac. 1050):

"Plainly stated, Cashion, Sullivan, Reid, and
Markham, as the owners of the majority of the
stock of the Garrett Sheep Company, as its board
of directors, president, secretary, treasurer and
general manager, sold and conveyed not only
their interests in such company, but the interests
of the minority stockholders, to the Reid-Cashion
Land & Cattle Company, their own personal corporation, for a price fixed by themselves, to be
paid, not in cash, but in shares of stock of the
purchasing corporation, upon an adjustment of
values determined by them. These individuals
were both the sellers and purchasers of the assets
of the Garrett Sheep Company, dealing, as one
may, with his own but not with trust property.
The power these individuals had over the Garrett
Sheep Company was not without limitations. It
should have been exercised within the law and
with due regard for the interests of the minority.
Such interests cannot be ignored or treated as
common prey by the majority".

On the question that there was a relation of trust
and confidence between the parties, (which the Court
treats, in the foregoing quotations, as a relation of

trustees and cestuis que trustent), the Court cites a number of cases, and quotes from two of them, namely, *Jones v. Missouri-Edison Electric Co.,* 144 Fed. 765, (C. C. A., 8, 1906), and *Alabama Fidelity Mortgage & Bond Co. v. Dubberly,* 198 Ala. 545, 73 So. 911, (1916).

We, in turn, quote from these cases, as follows:

In the case of *Jones v. Missouri-Edison Electric Co.,* in holding that the relation of the holders of the majority of stock of a corporation and that of its directors to the holders of the minority of the stock is fiduciary, that a corporation is the trustee for its stockholders, and, therefore, that where the holders of the majority of the stock of a corporation combine, elect and control its directors to execute a preconceived scheme, and use the powers of the corporation to carry it out, they put themselves in the place of the corporation and become trustees for the holders of the minority of the stock, the Court said, (p. 771, Circuit Judge Sanborn writing the opinion):

> "*The fraud or breach of trust of one who occupies a fiduciary relation while in the exercise of a lawful power is as fatal in equity to the resultant act or contract as the absence of the power. The relation of a stockholder to his corporation, to its officers and to his co-stockholders is a relation of trust and confidence. The corporation holds its property in trust for its stockholders who have a joint interest in it. The officers of the corporation, if not technical trustees for the stockholders, are such in so real a sense that any use by them of the property of the corporation for their own profit*

*to the detriment of any of the stockholders is a
breach of their trust and their duty, which is
actionable in equity. The stockholders of a corporation are jointly interested in the same property and in the same title.* Community of interest
in a common property or title imposes a community of duty and mutual obligation to do nothing
to impair the property or the title. It creates
such a fiduciary relation as makes it inequitable
for any of those who thus share in the common
property to do anything to or with it for their
own profit at the expense of others who have the
same rights. *Jackson v. Ludeling,* 21 Wall. 616,
622, 22 L. Ed. 492; *Booker v. Crocker,* 132 Fed. 7,
8, 65 C. C. A. 627, 628.

"A combination of the holders of a majority or
of three-fifths of the stock of a corporation to
elect directors, to dictate their acts and the acts
of the corporation for the purpose of carrying
out a predetermined plan places the holders of
such stock in the shoes of the corporation and
constitutes them actual, if not technical trustees
for the holders of the minority of the stock. The
devolution of power imposes correlative duty. The
members of such a combination become in practical effect the corporation itself because they
draw to themselves and use the powers of the corporation. In a sale of its property, in a consolidation of the corporation with another, in every
act and contract of the corporation which they
cause they make themselves the trustees and
agents of the holders of the minority of the stock
because it is only through them that the latter
may act or contract regarding the corporate property or preserve or protect their interests in it.

Such a majority of the holders of stock owe to the minority the duty to exercise good faith, care, and diligence to make the property of the corporation in their charge produce the largest possible amount, to protect the interests of the holders of the minority of the stock and to secure and deliver to them their just proportion of the income and of the proceeds of the property. Any sale of the corporate property to themselves, any disposition by them of the corporation or of its property to deprive the minority holders of their just share of it or to get gain for themselves at the expense of the holders of the minority of the stock, becomes a breach of duty and of trust which invokes plenary relief from a court of chancery." (Citing many cases). (Emphasis added).

In the case of *Alabama Fidelity Mortgage & Bond Co. v. Dubberly,* the Supreme Court of Alabama, in holding that, if the same persons, as directors of two different corporations, represent both in a transaction in which their interests are opposed, that transaction may be avoided by either company or by a stockholder, without regard to the question of advantage or detriment, said, referring to the fiduciary relation existing between the parties, (73 So. 914, Mr. Justice Somerville writing the opinion):

"It is the settled law of this state that if the same persons, as the directors of two different companies, represent both companies in a transaction in which their interests are opposed, such transaction may be avoided by either company, or at the instance of a stockholder in either company, without regard to the question of advantage or detriment to either company. (Citing cases).

"This doctrine is founded upon that rigorous rule of morality, to be found, perhaps, in every enlightened system of jurisprudence, which recognizes one of the commonest of the infirmities of human nature, and sternly forbids the unequal conflict between duty and self-interest. *'The value of the rule of equity, to which we have adverted, lies to a great extent in its stubbornness and inflexibility. Its rigidity gives it one of its chief uses as a preventive or discouraging influence, because it weakens the temptation to dishonesty or unfair dealing on the part of trustees, by vitiating, without attempt at discrimination, all transactions in which they assume the dual character of principal and representative'. Munson v. Syracuse G. & C. R. R. Co.,* 103 N. Y. 58, 74, 8 N. E. 355, 358. In the administration of trusts this is one of the master principles of equity".

Concerning the question as to the ratification of the transaction by the minority stockholders, in the acceptance by them of the new certificates, the Supreme Court of Arizona, in holding that there was no ratification, said, (270 Pac. 1052):

"A claim of ratification by the cestuis que trustent, here based on the mere fact that they accepted the proffered stock in the consolidated company, is not founded in justice, and we believe has no support in the law.

"The rule that we think should be applied to the facts of this case is as stated in *Adair v. Brimmer*, 74 N. Y. 539, loc. cit. 553, 554, and is as follows:

" 'To establish a ratification by a cestui que trust, the fact must not only be clearly proved, but it must be shown that the ratification was made with a full knowledge of all the material particulars and circumstances, and also in a case like the present that the cestui que trust was fully apprised of the effect of the acts ratified, and of his or her legal rights in the matter. Confirmation and ratification imply to legal minds, knowledge of a defect in the act to be confirmed, and of the right to reject or ratify it. *The cestui que trust must therefore not only have been acquainted with the facts, but apprised of the law, how these facts would be dealt with by a court of equity. All that is implied in the act of ratification, when set up in equity by a trustee against his cestui que trust, must be proved, and will not be assumed.* The maxim, *'ignorantia legis excusat neminem',* cannot be invoked in such a case. *The cestui que trust must be shown to have been apprised of his legal rights. Cumberland Coal Co. v. Sherman, 20 Md. 151; S. C., 30 Barb. 575; Lammot v. Bowly, 6 H. & J. (Md.) 526' ".* (Emphasis added).

Thompson v. Park Sav. Bank,
96 F.(2d) 544, (C. A., D. of C., 1938).

This was a second appeal from a decree of dismissal in a class suit, brought in the United States District Court for the District of Columbia, by the plaintiffs, Joseph W. Thompson, and others, as depositors and creditors of the Park Savings Bank, against the Bank, one Moran, as the receiver of the Bank, (appointed by the Comptroller of the Currency), the Comptroller of the Currency, and the directors of the Bank, as defendants.

The Bank was incorporated, as a banking corporation, on August 30, 1909, under the laws of Alabama. The life of the Bank was limited, by its charter, to 20 years, with the privilege of extension. From its incorporation to March 6, 1933, the Bank was engaged exclusively in a general banking business in the District of Columbia. Most of the stockholders, directors and officials of the Bank lived in the District.

On October 11, 1928, a little less than a year before the expiration of its charter, an amendment to the articles of incorporation of the Bank, increasing the Bank's capital stock, was approved by the proper officials of Alabama.

The Bank was closed by order of the President, on March 6, 1933, and, on March 9, 1933, a conservator for the Bank was appointed, who, in turn, was succeeded by the receiver, the defendant Moran, who took over the Bank's assets under the direction of the Comptroller of the Currency.

The object of the suit was to hold the directors liable for losses to the depositors, growing out of the Bank's failure. The suit was based on the contention that the directors were trustees as to some of the depositors, and partners as to others.

The bill charged as follows: that, under the Alabama laws, the Bank's charter had expired on August 30, 1929, and that, after that time, the Bank ceased to have corporate power to engage in any business except the liquidation of its affairs; that, under the Alabama laws, the directors of the Bank became trustees for the sole purpose of winding up the Bank's affairs; that, instead of liquidating, the directors, in the name of the Bank, continued its banking business, the same as it had done before; and that, as before, dividends had been paid, reports had been made to the Comptroller of the Currency, and the Bank's affairs had been examined by the Comptroller.

The bill also charged the liability as existing on August 30, 1929, of the directors of the Bank as liquidating trustees of the assets of the Bank, and as partners as to transactions subsequent to that date.

The bill prayed for the appointment of a receiver of the Bank, in the place of Moran, who had been appointed the receiver by the comptroller. Later, by permission of the trial court, Moran, as receiver, filed a cross-bill, praying, on his own behalf, the same relief sought by the plaintiffs in the bill.

On motion of the defendant directors to dismiss the bill and the cross-bill, the trial court held as follows:

that, after the expiration of its charter, the Bank continued in existence as a de jure corporation with limited powers; that the directors were not liable as partners, or otherwise, for losses resulting from the conduct of the business of the Bank after August 30,
1929; but that the bill stated a cause of action against
the directors, as trustees, as to the depositors on August 30, 1929, who thereafter left their balances in the
Bank.

Pursuant to its ruling, the trial court entered a
decree dismissing the bill and the cross-bill as to those
parties who charged the defendant directors with liability, either as co-partners, or otherwise, on account
of transactions after August 30, 1929, but refused a
dismissal as to the part of the bill and the cross-bill
which charged the directors as liquidating trustees of
the Bank's assets, which did, or should have, come into
the hands of the directors, as such trustees, at the expiration of the Bank's charter on the latter date.

This action of the trial court affected specifically
the plaintiff, Thompson, who had become a depositor
of the Bank after August 30, 1929.

On appeals, by Thompson, and also by Moran, the
receiver, the Appellate Court affirmed the decree,
under the Alabama laws, as applied by that Court. On
this second appeal, the Appellate Court said, (Chief
Justice Groner writing the opinion) in the Appellate
Court's own language, (p. 547), that

"the only question which we have to decide on
this appeal is whether the depositors in the bank

on August 30, 1929, whose money has not since been paid to or withdrawn by them are entitled to maintain this suit".

And also, again in the Court's own language, (p. 547), that

"The liability sought to be imposed in this suit is not the liability of the bank, its officers, or its directors at the time it failed, but the liability of the directors who were such in 1929, as trustees of a fund which by operation of law should have come into their hands on the day in question; and in that view it is equally of no importance whether the bank by consent of the trustees mistakenly continued to use the fund and to commingle it with other funds in the operation of the banking business".

And further, (again in the Court's own language), (p. 547), that

"The question is rather whether the depositors in their subsequent dealings and by their conduct waived their right to an accounting, or (as the trial judge thought) they are now equitably estopped to demand it".

The Appellate Court, therefore, holding, (pp. 547-8):

"If, under the Alabama statutes, failure of the bank's stockholders to renew the charter dissolved the corporation and created out of its then assets a trust fund in the hands of the directors for the benefit of its then stockholders and creditors, and of this there can be little, if any, doubt, then necessarily the liability of the directors at that instant accrued for the faithful discharge of the statutory duty. A right of action then arose in favor of, and enforceable by, the depositors who were such at that time, unless such depositors by their conduct or otherwise have lost all right to require the directors to account".

The Appellate Court, referring to its opinion on the first appeal, (p. 548), in which the Court said that—

"after the expiration date of the charter and the continuation of the business, the persons who thereafter dealt with the bank as depositors were charged with constructive knowledge of the terms of the charter and of the laws of the state of Alabama. If we apply this rule, we have a situation in which, in the absence of a direct showing that either the plaintiff depositors on the one hand or the defendant directors on the other had actual knowledge of the expiration of the charter of the bank, all were presumed to have knowledge of the happening of that event; and so we get back to the question whether the depositors by continuing to deal with the bank after the charter expired are precluded from asserting their original right to look to the directors for an equitable distribution of the fund which by the terms of the statute it was their duty to distribute in liquidation of the bank's obligations. In other words, whether the directors in the circumstances can escape their liability as trustees by claiming either waiver, ratification or estoppel. We think the question must be answered in the negative".

The Appellate Court then proceeded to say that the laws of Alabama, on the dissolution of the bank, (p. 548), created

"an express trust as to which the directors were trustees and the depositors the cestui que trustent";

and the question was whether or not the rule should be applied that, (p. 548),

"to establish waiver or ratification by a cestui que trust it must be shown that the waiver or ratification was made with full knowledge of all the material particulars and circumstances, and that the cestui que trust was fully apprised of the effect of the acts ratified, and of his or her legal rights in the matter". (Emphasis added).

The Appellate Court continuing, (pp. 548-9):

"Confirmation and ratification, (and this is true also of waiver) it was said by the Court of Appeals of New York in *Adair v. Brimmer*, (74 N. Y. 539, 553, 554), imply to legal minds, knowledge of a defect in the act to be confirmed, and of the right to reject or ratify it. The cestui que trust must, therefore, not only have been acquainted with the facts, but apprised of the law, how these facts would be dealt with by a court of equity. All that is implied in a case of waiver or in the act of ratification, when set up in equity by a trustee against his cestui que trust, must be proved, and will not be assumed. *The maxim ignorantia legis excusat neminem cannot be invoked in such a case. The cestui que trust must be shown to have been apprised of his legal rights.* The same rule was approved in *Cumberland Coal & Iron Co. v. Sherman*, 20 Md. 117, 151, and *Schroeder v. American Nat. Red Cross*, 215 Wis. 54, 254 N. W. 371. Judge Hough, likewise, in *Gates et al. v. Megargel*, 2 Cir., 266 F. 811, 820, said it is plain law that *a cestui who has been wronged by his trustee can only be held to have ratified when he not only knows the facts, but is informed of his rights under the law.* Here, admittedly, the depositors had no actual knowledge of the expiration of the charter or their legal rights in that case.

"Nor, as we think, are the directors in any better condition under the doctrine of estoppel, for in the case of estoppel the party alleging it—in this case the directors—must show that he has done something or omitted to do something in reliance upon the other party's conduct by which he will now be prejudiced if the facts are shown to be different from those upon which he relied. Where the parties have equal knowledge or opportunity of knowledge, or where the facts are known equally to both, or both have equal means of ascertaining them, there can be no estoppel." (Citing several authorities). (Emphasis added).

The Appellate Court concluded, (p. 549), as follows:

"In this view we think the lower court was wrong in holding, as it did, that there is no difference between the situation of the depositor who dealt with the bank after the 30th of August, 1929, and the depositor whose money was in the bank when the charter expired and the trust arose. As to the latter, the obligation of the directors as trustees came into being by the statute, and plaintiffs and others in like situation, upon a showing

that they are in that class, are entitled to the
benefits of the trust to the extent of their deposits
as of August 30, 1929, and except to the extent
that their deposits as of that date were withdrawn
after that date".

Consequently, the case was remanded to the lower
court, (p. 549),

"with instructions to set aside the former decree
and refer the case to an auditor for an accounting
to determine which depositors of the bank as of
August 30, 1929, continued as such, and to determine what part of their deposits as of that day
remained in the bank during the ensuing period".

SECTIONS OF THE CALIFORNIA BANK ACT

SEC. 25 OF THE CALIFORNIA BANK ACT.

(1 Deering, General Laws of California, 1937, p. 232, Article I, General Provisions):

"Sec. 25. *Departmental reserves: Inter-department transactions.* Every bank shall maintain for each department total reserves equal in amount to that required by this act for the respective business conducted, and shall keep separate and distinct the total reserves of any department from that of any other department; and all deposits made with other banks, whether temporary or otherwise, shall be assets of the respective departments by which they were made, and shall be so carried on the books of such other banks, and shall be repaid only upon the order of the department to whose credit they stand. No department shall receive deposits from any other department of the same corporation; except that the savings department or the commercial department of any bank may receive deposits from the trust department of the same corporation or association and may set aside, as required by section 105 of this act, bonds or securities of any kind in which savings banks are permitted by law to invest; provided, however, that any bank having departments shall have the right to sell and transfer any bonds, securities or loans from one department to another upon receipt of the actual value thereof, if such bonds, securities or loans are, under the provisions of this act, a legal investment for the department purchasing the same. (Amended

196

by Stats. 1913, p. 151; Stats. 1915, p. 1109; Stats. 1921, p. 1372; Stats. 1931, p. 341.)

Annotation: See 4 Cal. Jur. 128.

This section in so far as it permits the trust department of a bank acting as executor of a decedent's estate to deposit funds of the estate in its savings department, with the right to mingle the funds with other funds, is not unconstitutional upon the ground that it creates a discriminatory preference in favor of departmental bank trustees and other trustees: *Estate of Smith,* 64 Cal. App. Dec. 1117, 297 Pac. 927.''

SEC. 104 OF THE CALIFORNIA BANK ACT.

(1 Deering, General Laws of California, 1937, p. 287, Article IV, Trust Companies):

"Sec. 104. *Issuance of participation certificates: Title to underlying security: Purpose of section.* (a) Any trust company may issue participation certificates approved as to form by the Superintendent of Banks on a trust deed or mortgage and the debt secured thereby which is a legal investment for savings banks, and which is owned by such trust company or by any department of a departmental bank of which such trust company is a department; and such trust company shall issue said certificate to the department owning such trust deed or mortgage and debt, and the department owning and holding any such participation certificate may sell and transfer the same to any department of the bank, and it may be held therein, anything in this act to the contrary notwithstanding. Any trust company, the whole or any part of the capital stock of which is owned by departmental bank, shall, for the purposes of this section, be deemed a department of such bank, and shall have the right to sell to such bank any such participation certificate and to buy from said bank any such certificate for itself. The amount of participation certificates issued and outstanding at any time shall not exceed the face value of the trust deed or mortgage and debt upon which the same are predicated.

(b) *Title to underlying security.* The full legal title in such trust deed or mortgage and debt (hereinafter referred to as security) shall be held by the trust company issuing such certificates as trustee of an express trust, with all powers necessary to extend, renew, enforce, collect and liquidate the same, acquire title to the property covered thereby either through foreclosure or by voluntary conveyance; manage, lease, sell (either for cash or upon deferred payments), exchange, or otherwise realize upon such security or property and distribute the net proceeds thereof. All sums so realized shall, as and when received by said trustee, after payment of its compensation and all costs, charges and expenses, including brokers' commissions and advances for taxes and assessments, incurred or made in connection with the protection, administration and liquidation of said security or property, be distributed to the trusts or persons who are beneficiaries of said trust, as their interests may appear therein. The rights and interests therein of any such beneficiary failing to contribute on demand its or his pro rata of sums advanced, expended or required by said trust company in the protection, administration or liquidation of such trust shall be subject to a lien for all sums, with legal interest thereon, advanced, expended or required for any of such purposes by such trustee or by any other beneficiary of such trust.

(c) Such trust in said security or property shall continue in such trust company so long as any of said certificates are outstanding, irrespective of any distribution of said certificates from the trust in which the same are held.

(d) *Purpose of section.* The purpose of this section is to define and clarify the rights and obligations of trust companies and of all persons and trusts interested in participation certificates issued under subsection (a) of this section, whether heretofore or hereafter issued. If any provision herein shall be determined to be unconstitutional, such decision shall not affect the validity of the remaining portions of this section. The Legislature hereby declares that it would have enacted this section and each subsection, sentence, clause and phrase thereof irrespective of the fact that any one or more of the other subsections, sentences, clauses or phrases be declared unconstitutional. (Former section repealed by Stats. 1913, p. 183; New section added by Stats. 1925, p. 526; Amended by Stats. 1933, p. 1190; Stats. 1937, p. 778.)"

SEC. 105 OF THE CALIFORNIA BANK ACT.

(1 Deering, General Laws of California, 1937, p. 288, Article IV, Trust Companies):

"Sec. 105. *Trust companies' investments: Deposit in banks: Holding of trust property.* Except as otherwise provided by law every trust company shall invest its capital and surplus and any trust funds received by it in connection with its trust business, in accordance with the provisions of this act relative to the investment or loan of funds deposited with savings banks, unless the terms or provisions of the trust of which such funds constitute a part contain a specific agreement or provision to the contrary or unless it is otherwise ordered by the court in connection with any court trust.

Deposit in banks. Any trust company holding funds awaiting investment or distribution may deposit such funds with any State or National bank which has been designated as a depositary by the Superintendent of Banks, or in which such deposit will be fully insured under the provisions of any law of the United States, and any trust department of any bank doing a departmental business may deposit such funds so held by it with the savings department or the commercial department of the same corporation or association; provided, however, that no such funds so held awaiting investment shall be deposited by any trust department of a departmental bank with the savings department or the commercial department of the same corporation or association or of any corporation or association holding or owning the whole or any part of the capital stock of the trust company making such deposit unless such corporation or association shall first set aside, as security for such deposit, bonds* or securities of the kind in which savings banks are permitted to invest and which bonds or securities so set aside shall have a value not less than the funds so deposited; provided, further, that no security shall be required in case of any such part of any such deposits as is insured under the provisions of any law of the United States.

Holding of trust property. Every trust company may hold, during the life of the trust, all property, real and personal, received by it into the trust from any source, though such property be not legal for the investment of trust funds, in the same manner and upon the same conditions as if such property were legal for the investment of trust funds, unless the terms of the instrument creating or declaring the trust specifically provide to the contrary. (Amended by Stats. 1913, p. 183; Stats. 1927, p. 1804; Stats. 1931, p. 356; Stats. 1933, p. 1191; Stats. 1935, p. 1650.)''

---

*Note: This word appearing as "bond", singular, in 1 Deering, General Laws of California, p. 288, is "bonds", plural, in *California Statutes, 1935*, p. 1650, and, obviously, the plural form of the word is correct.

No. 8886

United States

Circuit Court of Appeals

For the Ninth Circuit.

TAFT BUILDING LAND TRUST, TRUST NO.
B-7620, TITLE INSURANCE AND TRUST
COMPANY, Trustee,

Petitioner,

vs.

COMMISSIONER OF INTERNAL REVENUE,

Respondent.

Transcript of the Record

Upon Petition to Review a Decision of the United States
Board of Tax Appeals.

PARKER PRINTING COMPANY. 545 SANSOME STREET. SAN FRANCISCO

No. 8806

United States

Circuit Court of Appeals

for the ___ Circuit.

TAFT BUILDING LAND TRUST TRUST TO
FIRST EXCHANGE INSURANCE AND TRUST,
LONGHAM Trust,

Petitioner.

vs.

COMMISSIONER OF INTERNAL REVENUE,

Respondent.

Transcript of the Record

Upon Petition to Review a Decision of the United States
Board of Tax Appeals

No. 8886

United States

Circuit Court of Appeals

For the Ninth Circuit.

TAFT BUILDING LAND TRUST, TRUST NO.
B-7620, TITLE INSURANCE AND TRUST
COMPANY, Trustee,

Petitioner,

vs.

COMMISSIONER OF INTERNAL REVENUE,

Respondent.

Transcript of the Record

Upon Petition to Review a Decision of the United States
Board of Tax Appeals.

PARKER PRINTING COMPANY, 545 SANSOME STREET, SAN FRANCISCO

INDEX

The references in this index are to the page where the particular matter is first mentioned, and although the subject may be treated in detail, page numbers thereafter are omitted. Where possible, the reference is made to the question by which a matter is introduced.

INDEX.

[Clerk's Note: When deemed likely to be of an important nature, errors or doubtful matters appearing in the original certified record are printed literally in italic; and, likewise, cancelled matter appearing in the original certified record is printed and cancelled herein accordingly. When possible, an omission from the text is indicated by printing in italic the two words between which the omission seems to occur.]

APPEARANCES:

For Taxpayer:
  GEO. M. THOMPSON,
  M. D. HALL, Esq.,
  JOHN T. RILEY.

For Comm'r:
  S. B. PIERSON, Esq.

Docket No. 87480

TAFT BUILDING LAND TRUST, TRUST NO.
B-7620, TITLE INSURANCE TRUST COM-
PANY, TRUSTEE,

Petitioner,

vs.

COMMISSIONER OF INTERNAL REVENUE,

Respondent.

DOCKET ENTRIES

1936

Dec. 14—Petition received and filed. Taxpayer
    notified. (Fee paid).

Dec. 14—Copy of petition served on General
    Counsel.

1937

Feb. 5—Answer filed by General Counsel.

Feb. 10—Copy of answer served on taxpayer.

July 20—Hearing set week beginning Sept. 27,
    1937, Los Angeles, Calif.

1937

Sept. 29—Hearing had before Mr. Mellott on merits. Submitted. Petitioner's brief due 11/13/37. Respondent's 12/13/37. Reply 12/28/37.

Nov. 1—Transcript of hearing of Sept. 29, 1937.

Nov. 10—Brief and proposed findings of fact filed by taxpayer. 11/11/37 copy served on General Counsel.

Dec. 13—Memorandum Reply brief filed by General Counsel.

Dec. 27—Reply brief filed by taxpayer. 12/27/37 copy served on General Counsel.

  1938

Mar. 31—Memorandum findings of fact and opinion rendered. Arthur J. Mellott. Div. 11. Judgment will be entered that there is a deficiency.

Mar. 31—Decision entered, Arthur J. Mellott, Div. 11.

May 28—Supersedeas bond in the amount of $5,452.72 approved and ordered filed.

June 4—Petition for review by United States Circuit Court of Appeals, Ninth Circuit, with assignments of error filed by taxpayer.

June 4—Proof of service filed by taxpayer.

June 4—Praecipe filed by taxpayer, with proof of service thereon. [1*]

---

*Page numbering appearing at the foot of page of original certified Transcript of Record.

U. S. Board of Tax Appeals

United States Board of Tax Appeals

Docket No. 87480

TAFT BUILDING LAND TRUST, TRUST NO.
B-7620, Title Insurance and Trust Company,
Trustee,

Petitioner,

vs.

COMMISSIONER OF INTERNAL REVENUE,
Respondent.

PETITION

The above named Petitioner hereby petitions for
a redetermination of the deficiency set forth by the
Commissioner of Internal Revenue in his notice of
deficiency, symbols IT:E:4, HAK-90D, dated October 20, 1936, and as a basis of its proceeding
alleges as follows:

(1) The Petitioner designated Taft Building
Land Trust, Trust B-7620, is a trust, Title Insurance
and Trust Company, Trustee, address 433 South
Spring Street, Los Angeles, California. The Trustee
is acting in a fiduciary capacity for the several
beneficiaries designated in a certain Declaration of
Trust executed on the 15th day of July, 1927.

(2) The notice of deficiency (a copy of which is
attached and marked "Exhibit A") was mailed to
the Petitioner on October 20, 1936.

(3) The taxes and penalties in controversy are income taxes for the calendar year 1933 as follows:

Deficiency	Penalty
$2,726.36	$681.59

(4) The dtermination of tax set forth in the said notice of deficiency is based upon the following errors:

(a) Respondent has erroneously and illegally determined Petitioner to be an association taxable as a corporation and has erroneously and illegally failed to treat Petitioner as a trust the income of which is taxable under Section 161 of the Revenue [2] Act of 1932.

(b) Respondent has erroneously and illegally assessed a 25 per cent penalty for delinquency in filing income tax return in the sum of $681.59.

(5) The facts upon which the Petitioner relies as a basis of this proceeding are as follows:

(a) Under date of July 15, 1927, an agreement and Declaration of Trust was executed by Mitchum Tully & Company, a corporation organized and existing under the laws of the State of California, as Party of the First Part, as Trustor, Title Insurance and Trust Company, a corporation duly organized and existing under the laws of the State of California and authorized to accept and execute trusts, Party of the Second Part, as Trustee, and Harry L. Dunn and Albert Parker, Parties of the Third Part as beneficiaries. The agreement and Declaration of Trust was actually executed on the 15th day of July, 1927 but for convenience was dated as of the 15th day of June, 1927. A certified copy of said agreement and Declaration of Trust is attached hereto and made a part hereof.

(b) The Trustor by grant deed dated July 12, 1927, conveyed to the Trustee real property in the City of Los Angeles, County of Los Angeles, State of California, described as

The Westerly one hundred twenty (120) feet of Lots one (1) and two (2) and the Northerly twenty (20) feet of the Westerly one hundred twenty (120) feet of Lot three (3), in Block eleven (11) of Hollywood, as per map recorded in Book 28, Pages 59 and 60, Miscellaneous Records of said County; together with the buildings thereon and appurtenance thereto.

(1) The real property described was improved [3] with a twelve story store and office building that was erected in 1924.

(2) Article 5 of said Declaration provided: "It being understood that it is the intention of the Trustee as soon as may be after the execution of this Agreement and Declaration of Trust to execute a lease of the above described property to Sun Realty Co., a California corporation, as lessee, said lease to be dated July 15th, 1927, and to be expressed to run for a period of ninety-eight (98) years

and six (6) months and to provide for the
payment by the lessee to the Trustee as lessor,
of a yearly rental of Forty-two thousand
Dollars ($42,000) in addition to the payment
of taxes, insurance premiums, etc.; said lease
to contain an option allowing said lessee to
purchase said property, upon sixty (60) days'
prior notice, upon any December 15 or June
15 for the purchase price of Seven Hundred
Twenty-five Thousand Dollars ($725,000.) if
such purchase be completed on or before June
15, 1952; and for the purchase price of Seven
Hundred Fifty Thousand Dollars ($750,-
000.00) on any December 15 or June 15 thereafter, but within the time which may be
specified in said lease, said lease to contain
such further terms, provisions and conditions
as the Trustee may approve.''

(c) The Trustee executed a lease with the
Sun Realty Co. as provided for in the foregoing
portion of Article 5 of said Declaration of Trust
and said lease is still in full force and **[4]**
effect. A certified copy of said lease is attached
hereto as Exhibit C and by reference made a
part hereof.

(d) The land and building hereinbefore referred to that is subject to the lease expressed
to run for a period of 98 years and 6 months
from July 15, 1927, constitutes the sole asset
of the trust estate.

(e) The activities of the Trustee are limited to the collection of 12 monthly checks and making distribution of the income received pursuant to the terms of the trust.

(1) The only expenses incurred and paid by the Trustee are Trustee's fees in the sum of $500.00 per annum and a small amount each year for postage stamps.

(f) The Petitioner has been treated as a trust, taxable under Section 161 of the Revenue Act of 1932 and similar provisions of prior Acts for the years 1927 to 1932, inclusive.

(g) Petitioner filed an income tax return for the calendar year 1933 on Form 1040 for amounts not distributed until after December 31, 1933, and paid a tax in the sum of $62.51 and penalty in the sum of $15.63. The said return ou Form 1040 was filed on or about April 12, 1934. Form 1041 was filed on or about April 12, 1934, showing net income distributed to beneficiaries of Petitioner during the calendar year 1933. The returns were prepared in sufficient time to file on or before March 15, 1934, but inadvertently became attached to other papers and were misfilled in the rocrds of the Trustee. Immediately upon discovery, the returns were filed with the Collector.

(6) Petitioner prays for relief from the deficiency asserted by the [5] Respondent on the following and each of the following particulars:

(a) The Petitioner is not taxable as an association within the meaning of the Revenue Act of 1932 but any income realized is taxable pursuant to the provisions of Section 161 of the Revenue Act of 1932.

(b) Petitioner's failure to file income tax return on or before the prescribed date was due to reasonable cause and the 25 per cent penalty should not be asserted.

Wherefore, Petitioner prays that this Board may hear and redetermine the deficiency herein alleged.

(Signed) GEORGE M. THOMPSON
(Signed) JOHN T. RILEY
(Signed) MARSHALL D. HALL
Counsel for Petitioner,
505 Title Insurance Building,
Los Angeles, California.

State of California
County of Los Angeles—ss:

E. H. Booth, Jr., being duly sworn, hereby deposes and says that he is Asst. Trust Officer of Title Insurance and Trust Company, Trustee under Trust No. B-7620, and that he is duly authorized to verify the foregoing Petition; that he has read the foregoing Petition or had the same read to him and is familiar with the statements contained therein and that the facts stated are true except as to those facts stated to be upon information and belief and those facts he believes to be true.

(Signed) E. H. BOOTH

Subscribed and sworn to before me this 8th day of December, 1936.

[Seal]   (Signed) **W. J. WOOD**
Notary Public In and for the County of Los Angeles
State of California. [6]

EXHIBIT A

Treasury Department
Washington

Oct. 20, 1936.

Office of
Commissioner of Internal Revenue

Taft Building Land Trust, Trust No. B-7620
Title Insurance & Trust Co., Trustee,
433 South Spring Street,
Los Angeles, California.

Sirs:

You are advised that the determination of your income tax liability for the taxable year 1933 discloses a deficiency of $2,726.36 plus penalty of $681.59, as shown in the statement attached.

In accordance with section 272 (a) of the Revenue Act of 1932, as amended by section 501 of the Revenue Act of 1934, notice is hereby given of the deficiency mentioned. Within ninety days (not counting Sunday or a legal holiday in the District of Columbia as the ninetieth day) from the date of the mailing of this letter, you may file a petition with the United States Board of Tax Appeals for a redetermination of the deficiency.

Should you not desire to file a petition, you are requested to execute the enclosed form and forward it to the Commissioner of Internal Revenue, Washington, D. C., for the attention of IT:C:P-7. The signing and filing of this form will expedite the closing of your return by permitting an early assessment of the deficiency and will prevent the accumulation of interest, since the interest period terminates thirty days after filing the form, or on the date assessment is made, whichever is earlier.

Respectfully,

(Signed) GUY T. HELVERING,

Commissioner.

By (Signed) .... SHERWOOD,

Deputy Commissioner. **[7]**

STATEMENT

IT:E:4

HAK-90D

In re: Taft Building Land Trust, Trust B-7620,
Title Insurance & Trust Co., Trustee,
433 South Spring Street,
Los Angeles, California.

INCOME TAX LIABILITY

Year—1933.

Income Tax Liability—$2,788.87.

Income Tax Assessed—$62.51.

Deficiency—$2,726.36.

Penalty—$681.59.

Net Income

Net income reported in return
    (form 1040) $ 2,562.66

Add:
1. Distribution to beneficiaries as
    reported in form 1041   38,970.00

                                    $41,532.66

Deduct:
Depreciation on building   21,250.00

Net income corrected $20,282.66

Explanation of Change

1. Under date of January 18, 1936, it was held by the Bureau that the trust was an association taxable as a corporation. This action was sustained in a conference in this office under date of April 23, 1936.

Depreciation deducted in the return   None
Depreciation allowable (see below) $21,250.00

Income decreased   · $21,250.00

Your protest with respect to depreciation has been conceded in part as follows: [8]

Depreciation allowable on building, 2½% on $850,-000.00 equals $21,250.00. Information on file in this office indicates the adjustment for depreciation is acceptable to you.

Your protest with respect to excess-profits tax is conceded to the extent that a recomputation discloses no excess-profits tax liability.

Computation of Tax

		Penalty
Net income	$20,282.66	
Income tax liability at 13¾% of $20,282.66	2,788.87	$697.22
Income tax assessed (form 1040) account, No. April 200278	62.51	15.63
Deficiency of income tax and penalty	$ 2,726.36	$681.59

Section 291 of the Revenue Act of 1932 provides that in case of any failure to make and file a return within the time prescribed by law or prescribed by the Commissioner in pursuance of law, 25 per centum of the tax shall be added to the tax.

A copy of this letter has been mailed to your representative, Mr. George M. Thompson, 505 Title Insurance Building, Los Angeles, California, in accordance with the authority contained in the power of attorney executed by you and on file with the Bureau. [9]

EXHIBIT B

This Agreement and Declaration of Trust actually executed this 15th day of July, 1927, but for convenience dated as of the 15th day of June, 1927, between Mitchum, Tully & Co., a corporation duly organized and existing under the laws of the State of California (hereinafter sometimes called "Trustor"), party of the first part, Title Insurance and Trust Company, a corporation duly organized and existing under the laws of the State of California and authorized to accept and execute trusts (hereinafter sometimes called "Trustee"), party of the second part, and Harry L. Dunn and Albert Parker and such persons, partnerships, associations and/or corporations as may become parties hereto by the acceptance of certificates issued hereunder (hereinafter sometimes called "Beneficiaries"), parties of the third part,

Witnesseth:

Whereas, Mitchum, Tully & Co. have conveyed to Title Insurance and Trust Company by Grant Deed dated July 12th, 1927, the real property in the City of Los Angeles, County of Los Angeles, State of California, described as:

> The Westerly one hundred twenty (120) feet of Lots one (1) and two (2) and the Northerly twenty (20) feet of the Westerly one hundred twenty (120) feet of Lot three (3), in Block eleven (11) of Hollywood, as per map recorded in Book 28, Pages 59 and 60, Miscellaneous Records of said County; together with the buildings thereon and appurtenances thereto.

Subject to taxes for the fiscal year of 1927-1928 and subject to existing leases, whether recorded or unrecorded.

and,

Whereas, no consideration for said property or any part thereof has been paid by the Trustee, said property having been purchased and paid for by the Trustor and then conveyed and transferred to the Trustee to be leased, held, sold and conveyed upon the terms, trusts and conditions herein contained; and

Whereas, it is the intention of the parties hereto that Harry L. Dunn and Albert Parker be the original Beneficiaries hereunder and that certificates representing the beneficial rights hereunder be issued to said persons as Beneficiaries as hereinafter provided, and

Whereas, the Trustee has agreed to execute this Agreement and Declaration of Trust upon the terms: provisions and conditions herein contained; and

Whereas, the Trustee now holds the said property in trust and it is the desire of the parties hereto to set forth herein the terms, trusts and conditions upon which the same shall be held, leased, sold and conveyed, and the rentals, profits, proceeds and avails thereof paid, applied and distributed;

Now, Therefore, the Trustor and the Trustee and Harry L. Dunn and Albert Parker do hereby declare as follows, and said parties and the holders of certificates issued hereunder do hereby agree with each other and in such manner as to bind their respective heirs, executors, administrators and successors and assigns, and do make this Agreement and Declaration of Trust with respect to the said property, and the rentals, profits, proceeds and avails thereof and the right to collect, receive and pay and apply the same: [10]

Article 1.

The Trustee shall hold as trustee upon the trusts hereinafter set forth for the benefit of Harry L. Dunn and Albert Parker and their respective successors and assigns, as owners of the undivided beneficial rights or interest provided for herein, represented by the certificates issued hereunder (hereinafter sometimes called "Land Trust Certificates"), all the title, right and interest in and to the real property above described acquired by the Trustee by and under that certain corporation grant deed as of July 12th, 1927, but in fact executed and delivered simultaneously herewith, from Mitchum, Tully & Co., a California Corporation.

Article 2.

The beneficial right or interest (hereinafter generally called "beneficial interest") existing hereunder shall be represented by Land Trust Certificate or Certificates to be issued hereunder by the Trustee as hereinafter provided. For convenience such beneficial interest shall be deemed to consist of six hundred and sixty-five (665) equal fractional undivided parts, each of which is and shall be a one-six hundred and sixty-fifth (1/665th) interest in the whole. The owner or the respective owners of said six hundred and sixty-five fractional parts (hereinafter generally called "beneficial interests" or "fractional rights"), as represented by Land Trust Certificate or Certificates issued hereunder, shall receive payments hereunder as, and only as, hereinafter provided. For convenience in the making of such payments each of said six hundred and sixty-five beneficial interests shall be given a serial number and this serial number shall be set forth upon the Land Trust Certificate representing the same. Said Land Trust Certificate shall, except as hereinafter provided, vary only as to dates of the respective certificates, the serial number, or numbers, set forth thereon, the names of the respective beneficiaries, and the number of fractional parts represented by the respective certificates, said certificates and the endorsements thereon to be in form substantially as follows:

(Form of Land Trust Certificate)

United States of America

State of California

City of Los Angeles.

Taft Building Land Trust Certificate No............

Beneficial interests numbered............

....( )

This certifies that... is, on the books of the undersigned (hereinafter sometimes called the "Trustee"), registered as the owner of...( ) of

the Six hundred and sixty-five (665) equal fractional undivided beneficial interests provided for
under that certain Agreement and Declaration of
Trust dated June 15, 1927, and executed by the undersigned, covering the property known as the
"Taft Building," located at the southeast corner of
Vine Street and Hollywood Boulevard in the City
of Los Angeles, State of California, which Agreement and Declaration of Trust is known on the
records of the Trustee as its Trust No. B-7620. The
particular beneficial interest, or interests, represented by [11] this certificate carry the serial number, or numbers, hereinabove set forth in the caption of this certificate.

This certificate is issued under and pursuant to
the above mentioned Agreement and Declaration of
Trust and reference is hereby made thereto for a
statement of the rights of the holder of this certificate and of the holders of other certificates
issued thereunder and for a statement of the terms
and conditions of said Agreement and Declaration
of Trust, including the duties and immunities of
the Trustee thereunder, to all of which rights, terms
and conditions the holder of this certificate by the
acceptance hereof assents, and to which Agreement
and Declaration of Trust by such acceptance such
holder becomes a party, as fully to all intents and
purposes as if said holder had signed the same.

As provided in said Agreement and Declaration
of Trust, the owner of each of the Six hundred and
sixty-five (665) undivided beneficial interests there-

under, as represented by this and similar certificates, is and shall be entitled to receive periodically, after the payment of the expenses of the trust, his proportionate share of the rentals and revenues received by the Trustee under and pursuant to said Agreement and Declaration of Trust, it being provided and agreed, however, that unless and until redemption payments shall have been made in respect of each of said Six hundred and sixty-five (665) beneficial interests as provided in said Agreement and Declaration of Trust the amount which the holder of each one-six hundred sixty-fifth (1/665th) interest shall receive through such periodical prorata payments in any six month period ending December 15 and June 15 shall be limited to Thirty Dollars ($30.00) United States gold coin, and that such prorata payments shall be made on or as of December 15 and June 15 of each year unless and · until such dates be changed as provided in said Agreement and Declaration of Trust. The right to such payments of Thirty Dollars ($30.00) in respect of each of such six-month periods shall be considered cumulative so that if in or in respect of any such six-month period the full amount of Thirty Dollars ($30.00) shall not for any reason have been paid or set aside in respect of any beneficial interest entitled thereto, then the owner of such beneficial interest shall be entitled to receive the amount of such deficiency, without interest thereon, upon the next periodical payment date from any funds then available for distribution through the Trustee.

As provided in said Agreement and Declaration of Trust any surplus of rentals and revenues from said property remaining after such payments have been made at the rate of Thirty Dollars ($30.00) for each six-month period then elapsed shall be set aside and applied as therein provided to the making of additional or redemption payments to owners of said beneficial interests. The particular serial number or numbers of beneficial interests in respect of which such payments shall from time to time be made may be selected by the Trustee, in its discretion, from certificates offered to it, or the Trustee may select by lot the serial numbers of the beneficial interests to be paid and thereupon shall give thirty (30) days' notice thereof and on the next semi-annual or other periodical payment date shall set aside the moneys for such payment to the credit of the owners of such beneficial interests, all as provided in said Agreement and Declaration of Trust. Prior to the receipt of any such redemption payment the owner, or owners, of the fractional beneficial interests so affected shall surrender his certificate or certificates to the Trustee and the same shall be stamped "Redemption payment made," or with some other appropriate legend approved by the Trustee, and thereupon returned to said holder or holders, or at the option of the Trustee, a new certificate conforming in substance to the terms hereof and to the [12] terms of said Agreement and Declaration of Trust, insofar as the same may be applicable, shall be returned to said holder or holders.

The holder or holders of such certificates upon which such payment has been made or in respect of which such funds have been set aside (and of certificates issued in lieu thereof) shall not thereafter (whether the same shall have been stamped or not) be entitled to any further payments from the funds of the trust until after redemption payments shall have been made in respect of all other of the Six hundred and sixty-five (665) beneficial interests, or funds set aside for that purpose, after which time, however, the holders of all such beneficial interests shall share prorata in all future payments and distributions made under said Agreement and Declaration of Trust. Redemption payments shall be made in respect of each one-six hundred and sixty-fifth (1/665th) beneficial interest in such amounts as the Trustee may in its discretion determine; provided, however, that no such payment in respect of any one-six hundred sixty-fifth (1/665th) beneficial interest shall be more than One Thousand Fifty Dollars ($1050) United States gold coin if made on or before June 15, 1937; nor more than One Thousand Thirty Dollars ($1030) if made thereafter and on or before June 15, 1947; and shall not be more than One Thousand Ten Dollars (1010) if made thereafter and on or before June 15, 1957; and shall not be more than One Thousand Dollars ($1000) if made thereafter; in the event, however, of the exercise by the lessee of the option to purchase provided for in the original long term lease mentioned in Article 5 of said Agreement and Declaration of Trust, re-

demption payments shall be made at the rate of
One Thousand Eighty Dollars ($1080) each, in
respect of each fractional beneficial interest upon
which such redemption payment has not been previously made. In each case there may be added to the
amount of any redemption payment, regardless of
the amount of such redemption payment, an amount
equal to such fraction of the above mentioned Thirty
Dollar ($30) semi-annual payment which shall have
accrued in respect of such fractional beneficial
interest from the last semi-annual payment date to
the date of the making of such redemption payment.
Whenever beneficial interests are selected by lot by
the Trustee for call and redemption payment after
thirty (30) day's notice as above provided, the
amount of such payment shall be the then prevailing maximum amount as above specified.

Unless and until changed as provided in said
Agreement and Declaration of Trust said semi-
annual or periodical payments shall be made by the
Trustee to the holder or holders of certificates registered as such on the Trustee's transfer books on
the fifth day prior to the date fixed for such payments. Redemption and other payments shall, however, be made to the holder or holders of the respective certificates registered as such on the Trustee's
transfer books at the time the respective certificates
are surrendered for stamping thereon the appropriate legend as hereinbefore provided.

This certificate is not a promise, agreement and/or
guarantee on the part of or by Title Insurance and

Trust Company for the payment of any sum or sums herein mentioned, or interest thereon; the same being payable solely from moneys which may be received by Title Insurance and Trust Company, as Trustee, under the provisions of the aforesaid Agreement and Declaration of Trust, and if, as and when available for payment and/or distribution under the terms and provisions of said Agreement and Declaration of Trust.

The fractional beneficial interest represented by this certificate, or parts thereof in full fractional parts of one-six hundred and sixty-fifth (1/665th) each of the full beneficial interest, or multiples thereof, may be transferred and assigned upon surrender of this certificate, the appropriate forms provided on the reverse hereof having been duly executed and payment of any stamp and other taxes and charges payable upon such surrender having been made, and the transferee shall by accepting [13] this certificate or any certificate which may hereafter be issued in place hereof become forthwith a party to said Agreement and Declaration of Trust and be bound thereby and entitled to all rights of a beneficiary thereunder. Until such transfer shall have been made upon the books of the undersigned, the registered holder hereof may be treated as sole owner of the fractional part or parts of beneficial interest represented hereby, and the undersigned and all other parties to said Agreement and Declaration of Trust shall be fully protected and under no liability whatsoever in recognizing such registered holder as such owner, any notice to the contrary notwithstanding.

In Witness Whereof, Title Insurance and Trust Company, a California corporation, with its principal place of business in the City of Los Angeles, as Trustee under said Agreement and Declaration of Trust, has caused these presents to be signed in its corporate name by its President or Vice-President, and its corporate seal to be hereunto affixed and attested by its Secretary or Assistant Secretary this ....day of ...., 19................

TITLE INSURANCE AND
TRUST COMPANY,

as Trustee as Aforesaid

By... -

Vice-President.

Attest:

....

Assistant Secretary

(Form of Assignment to be placed on
Back of Certificate)

Assignment

For value received, the undersigned, (a single person) (a married person) (a corporation), being the owner of the within certificate issued by Title Insurance and Trust Company of Los Angeles under the Agreement and Declaration of Trust mentioned in said certificate, and of the undivided fractional interest or interests therein described and evidenced by said certificate, does hereby assign, grant and transfer unto... all right, title and interest represented by the within certificate and all right, title and interest of the undersigned in and to said undivided fractional interests.

By accepting said certificate and in consideration therefor, the undersigned became a party to and agreed to the within mentioned Agreement and Declaration of Trust and directed that the terms and conditions thereof be carried out as therein provided, and as provided in said Agreement and Declaration of Trust this assignment and transfer is made to become effective only upon the acceptance and ratification by the above named assignee, grantee and transferee of all of the terms and conditions of [14] said Agreement and Declaration of Trust; and acceptance by said assignee, grantee and transferee of the within certificate, or of any certificate or certificates which may be issued in lieu thereof or the assertion of any rights under said Agreement and Declaration of Trust or to the property covered thereby shall be deemed to be and shall constitute a complete acceptance and ratification by said Agreement and Declaration of Trust. The undersigned makes no promise, representation, guaranty or warranty for or in respect of the payment of any money under, or the carrying out of the terms of said Certificate or Agreement and Declaration of Trust.

And the undersigned..
spouse of said owner consents to and joins and con-
curs in said assignment, grant and transfer.

[Seal]   ....

[Seal]   ....

Executed in the presence of

....

(If the owner be married person the last paragraph of the foregoing form will be completed accordingly and said form signed by the spouse of
such owner. If the owner be a single person or corporation strike out said paragraph.) [15]

In the sole and absolute discretion of the Trustee
upon proof satisfactory to it that the name of the
building now on said premises has been changed, the
words "Taft Building" appearing in the above
form of certificate may be omitted from, and such
other words as in the opinion of the Trustee appropriately designate the title of said building may
be inserted in any certificate issued hereunder. No
recitation herein or in the caption of any certificate
outstanding hereunder of any name of any building
shall constitute, or be taken to constitute, any representation of fact as to the actual name of any building located upon said premises.

In the sole and absolute discretion of the Trustee
the form of said certificates and/or of the endorsements thereon may be changed or amended if the
same be necessary or desirable in the opinion of the
Trustee or counsel employed by it in order more

effectively to carry out the terms and conditions of this Agreement and Declaration of Trust or more accurately to express the then status of the trust and of the property subject hereto.

Article 3.

The Trustee is authorized and agrees, upon receipt of permit therefor from the Commissioner of Corporations, to issue a Land Trust Certificate or Certificates representing the entire Six hundred and sixty-five (665) beneficial interests in the names of Harry L. Dunn and Albert Parker, or to issue Land Trust Certificates in their respective names in such proportions and manner as said Harry L. Dunn and Albert Parker may jointly in writing direct the Trustee. The beneficial interest existing hereunder or parts thereof, in full fractional parts of 1/665th each, or multiples thereof, may be transferred, granted and assigned by the execution of the forms endorsed on the Land Trust Certificate or Certificates representing the same and the acceptance of such transfer by the transferee therein named and such certificate or certificates may thereupon be transferred upon the books of the Trustee upon surrender of the certificate or certificates, the appropriate forms on the reverse thereof having been duly executed and any stamp and other taxes payable upon such transfer having been paid. The Trustee may also charge not more than one dollar ($1.00) as a transfer fee in respect of each transfer on its books of a Land Trust Certificate and may require the transferee to pay the same as a condition of transfer. The Trustee may also, in connection with any application for transfer following the death of any certificate holder, or following any judgment or decree in any action at law or in equity, affecting such certificate, require the applicant to make payment of any expenses incurred by the Trustee in connection with such application and transfer and the examination of such proceedings.

The transferee by accepting such certificate or any certificate which may be issued in place of any such certificate or by asserting any rights to the interest transferred, shall become forthwith a party to this Agreement and Declaration of Trust and be bound hereby and entitled to all the rights of a beneficiary hereunder. Until such transfer shall have been made upon the books of the Trustee the registered holder of any such certificate may be treated as sole owner of the fractional part or parts of beneficial interests represented thereby and the Trustee and all other parties hereto shall be fully protected in recognizing such registered holder as such owner, and shall not be affected by any notice to the contrary.

Pending the preparation of definitive Land Trust Certificates, the Trustee may, if desired, execute and deliver temporary Land Trust Certificates substantially of the tenor of the certificates herein provided for, which shall be exchangeable at the principal office of the Trustee for definitive Land

Trust Certificates to be issued hereunder, and upon any such exchange such temporary certificates shall be [16] forthwith cancelled by the Trustee and shall be of no further force and effect. Until such exchange holders of such temporary certificates shall be entitled to all of the rights of Land Trust Certificate holders hereunder.

In case any Certificate issued hereunder shall become mutilated, or be destroyed, stolen or lost, the Trustee may thereafter in its discrection issue in lieu thereof a new certificate representing the interest represented by such mutilated, destroyed, stolen or lost certificate in exchange and substitution for the certificate mutilated upon cancellation thereof or in lieu of and substitution for the certificate destroyed, stolen or lost, upon the registered holder's filing with the Trustee evidence satisfactory to the Trustee that such certificate was destroyed, stolen or lost and of such holder's ownership thereof and furnishing the Trustee with indemnity, satisfactory to the Trustee for the benefit of all interested parties. The Trustee may, in the event that any unusual service or investigation is required in connection with any application and/or issue of such new certificate, require the applicant therefor to make payment of the expenses of the Trustee incurred in connection with such matter.

The Trustee shall keep a register of the names of the holders of certificates issued hereunder, and proper transfer books in respect of such certificates. The Trustee shall also keep books of account showing the receipts and disbursements of the trust estate. Such register shall be conclusive evidence in favor of the Trustee of the ownership of certificates issued hereunder, and of the interests represented thereby, and the Trustee and all the parties hereto may consider and treat the registered holders of certificates as sole owners and holders thereof despite notice to the contrary. Such books of account shall at all reasonable times be open to the inspection of any holder of any certificate issued and at the time outstanding hereunder or his agent duly appointed in writing.

No holder of any certificate issued hereunder shall have as such any estate or interest in the real property subject to this trust but may as owner and holder of the beneficial interest or right or fractional part or parts thereof existing hereunder enforce the performance of the trust and of this agreement. No such owner or holder shall have any right to call for any partition of the real property covered by this Agreement and Declaration of Trust during the continuance of this trust and agreement. No transfer by operation of law of the interest of any holder of any certificate issued hereunder during the continuance of this trust and agreement shall operate to terminate said trust or agreement nor shall it entitle the successors of such holder to an accounting or to take any action in the courts or otherwise against the trust estate or Trustee, but the successors of such holder shall succeed to all his right under this Agreement and Declaration of

Trust upon production of evidence of such transfer
in form satisfactory to the Trustee and upon transfer of such certificate on the books of the Trustee
and should it be held that any such right of such
holder ceases or terminates upon any such transfer,
then a new right equivalent to that held by such
holder shall ipso facto be created and exist as and
from that time, in favor of such successor or successors. In the event of the death of any such holder
the person or persons entitled by law shall succeed
to the rights of such holder under this Agreement
and Declaration of Trust, but the Trustee shall be
fully protected in paying and accounting to the administrator or executor of such decedent for all
moneys otherwise payable to such decedent hereunder, until the person or persons entitled by law
shall establish to the satisfaction of the Trustee
their succession to such interest and cause to be
transformed in his or their names on the books of
the Trustee the certificate or certificates representing the same.

Article 4.

No assessments shall ever be made upon the
holder of any certificate [17] issued hereunder.

Article 5.

Among the express purposes of this trust and
among the purposes and powers of the Trustee
under this Agreement and Declaration of Trust is
and shall be the purpose and power to rent and
lease the real property hereinabove described, or

any part thereof, as soon as may be after the execution of this Agreement and Declaration of Trust, upon a long term lease for the benefit of the Trustor, and for the benefit of Harry L. Dunn and Albert Parker as the original beneficiaries hereunder and their respective successors as owners of the beneficial interests hereunder and holders of the Land Trust Certificates herein provided for, it being understood that it is the intention of the Trustee as soon as may be after the execution of this Agreement and Declaration of Trust to execute a lease of the above described property to Sun Realty Co., a California corporation, as lessee, said lease to be dated July 15th, 1927, and to be expressed to run for a period of ninety-eight (98) years and six (6) months and to provide for the payment by the lessee to the Trustee as lessor, of a yearly rental of Forty-two Thousand Dollars ($42,000) in addition to the payment of taxes, insurance premiums, etc.; said lease to contain an option allowing said lessee to purchase said property, upon sixty (60) days' prior notice, upon any December 15 or June 15 for the purchase price of Seven Hundred Twenty-five Thousand Dollars ($725,000) if such purchase be completed on or before June 15, 1952; and for the purchase price of Seven Hundred Fifty Thousand Dollars ($750,000.00) on any December 15 or June 15 thereafter, but within the time which may be specified in said lease, said lease to contain such further terms, provisions and conditions as the Trustee may approve.

Article 6.

It is expressly understood and agreed by and between all parties hereto that such payment or other considerations, if any, as may have been or may be received by the Trustor and/or by the initial beneficiaries and certificate holders referred to or named herein, in respect of the execution or agreement to execute or negotiations for the execution of the above mentioned lease to Sun Realty Co., is not and shall not become or be deemed rental, income, revenue or proceeds under said lease, and is not and shall not become subject to or a part of this trust and agreement, such payment and/or other consideration having been, or being or to be, taken and retained by the Trustor and/or said beneficiaries in their respective individual and separate capacities (as distinguished from their respective capacities as Trustor and beneficiaries and holders of certificates hereunder) as part of the consideration for the establishment of this trust and execution of this Agreement and Declaration of Trust, and each future beneficiary hereunder, by the acceptance of a Certificate or the assertion of any rights hereunder, not only releases, waives and relinquishes to said Trustor and/or said original beneficiaries in their individual capacities, all right, title and interest, if any, in and to the payment or other consideration mentioned in this Article, but also relieves and discharges said Trustee hereunder of and from any and all duty, liability, obligation and/or responsibility for or in connection with any payment or other consideration or any other matter heretofore in this Article 6 mentioned.

Article 7.

In the event that Sun Realty Co., or any other lessee under the above mentioned long term lease, or any successor lessee, shall make default in any of the provisions thereof, the Trustee shall have full authority to take such [18] steps and do such things as may to it seem advisable and proper and if in the opinion of the Trustee it shall become necessary or advisable to terminate said lease the Trustee may take such steps as may be necessary and proper so to terminate it. In such event or in the event that such lease shall be terminated for any reason or shall expire by limitation, the Trustee shall have full authority to do any and all such things as in its opinion may be necessary or proper for the best interests of the holders of certificates issued and at the time outstanding hereunder with respect to leasing, operating, selling, conveying or otherwise disposing of said property; and in the event of any other lease or leases being executed with respect to said property, or any part thereof under the power herein conferred upon it, such lease or leases may be for any period or periods of time, within or extending beyond the life and continuation of this trust and agreement, up to but not exceeding ninety-nine (99) years from the date of the execution of such lease or leases, or such other maximum period as may at the time of such execution be lawful, and may be upon such terms, conditions, limitations and covenants and for such rent and in such form as the Trustee may deem advisable.

The Trustee shall have full power to enforce any lease or leases made by it hereunder and to receive and pay and distribute and apply the rents, revenues and proceeds thereunder and therefrom for the benefit of the original beneficiaries hereunder and their respective successors as holders of the Land Trust Certificates herein provided for, and the carrying out and accomplishment of the same shall be among the express purposes of this trust. The Trustee shall further have full power with the concurrence of the lessee or lessees under any such lease or leases, to enter into, execute and deliver any agreements or instruments in writing modifying or supplementing any such lease or leases, if and when, in the discretion of the Trustee, it shall appear advisable in the interest of the beneficiaries hereunder so to do; provided, however, that no such modification or supplement shall have the effect of decreasing the amount of rental and payments or option price specified in said original lease to Sun Realty Co.

Article 8.

The Trustee shall, subject to the provisions of Article 9 and of Article 12 hereof, in each year distribute the rentals and income thereof pro rata among the owners of the Six hundred and sixty-five (665) fractional interests represented by Land Trust Certificates issued hereunder. Such distribution shall, so long as the above mentioned original long term lease is in force and in good standing (and thereafter so long as in the opinion of the Trustee the same is convenient and desirable), be made on or as of December 15 and June 15 in each year to the holders of Land Trust Certificates issued hereunder whose names are registered as such on the books of the Trustee on the fifth day prior to the date of distribution above fixed. Such distribution shall be made by check by the Trustee or by such other means as the Trustee may in its opinion consider convenient and desirable. Unless and until redemption payments shall have been made in respect of all of said Six hundred and sixty-five (665) fractional beneficial interests as hereinafter in Article 9 provided, the amount which shall be distributed in respect of each of said Six hundred and sixty-five (665) fractional interests in any six-month period ending December 15 and June 15 through such periodical prorata payments, shall be limited to Thirty Dollars ($30.00) United States gold coin. The right to such payments of Thirty Dollars ($30.00) in respect of each of such six-month periods shall be considered cumulative so that if in or in respect of any such six-month period the full amount of Thirty Dollars ($30.00) shall not for any reason have been paid or set aside in respect of any beneficial interest entitled thereto, then the owner of such beneficial interest shall be entitled to receive the amount of such de- [19] ficiency without interest upon the next periodical payment date from any funds then available for distribution through the Trustee hereunder, such payment to be made to the person who is or was the holder of the Land Trust Certificate representing such beneficial interest on the transfer books of the Trustee five (5) days prior to said periodical payment date. If on any semi-annual or other periodical payment date all such Thirty-Dollar ($30.00) payments have been made or set aside in respect of all beneficial interests entitled thereto and no such deficiency exists, and there then remains in the hands of the Trustee any further funds, the Trustee shall apply the same to redemption payments to be made to the holders of Land Trust Certificates in the manner, times and amounts as hereinafter in Article 9 provided.

Article 9.

As and when moneys become available for use under this Article the Trustee may make further payments, in addition to the $30.00 payments provided for in Article 8, upon condition that the holder of certificates representing fractional beneficial interests in respect of which such payments are made shall surrender the same so that the words "Redemption payment made" may be endorsed thereon and so that thereafter no further payments shall be made in respect of such fractional beneficial interest until after redemption payments shall have been made in respect of all of said Six Hundred and Sixty-five (665) beneficial interests. If in any case it should be desired to make such a payment in respect of one but not all of the fractional beneficial interests represented by any one Land Trust Certificate, then such Land Trust Certificate shall be surrendered for exchange and a new certificate with the legend "Redemption payment made," stamped thereon shall be returned in respect of the fractional beneficial interest or interests so paid and a second certificate without such legend returned in respect of the fractional interest or interests not so paid. At the time of making any semi-annual payment or other periodical payment under Article 8 hereof, the Trustee shall mail or deliver to the holders of certificates upon which redemption payments have not been made, a notice specifying the approximate number of beneficial interests upon which the Trustee is prepared to make redemption payments and inviting offers of certificates to be made to it for that purpose. The Trustee shall thereafter apply such monyes as are available for that purpose to the making of such redemption payments at such time and in such amounts as it in its discretion may determine, provided, however, that the Trustee shall in every case accept the lowest offer or offers at the time available, and provided further that no such redemption payment in respect of any one of said six hundred and sixty-five (665) fractional beneficial interests shall be more than One Thousand Fifty Dollars ($1050) United States Gold Coin, if such payment be made on or before June 15, 1937; nor more than One Thousand Thirty ($1030) Dollars if such payment be made thereafter and on or before June 15, 1947; nor more than One Thousand Ten ($1010) Dollars if such payment be made thereafter and on or before June 15, 1957, and shall not

be more than One Thousand ($1,000) Dollars if
such payment be made thereafter; it being understood, however, that the Trustee may in addition to
said amounts apply in connection with the making
of such redemption payments, an amount equal to
such fraction of the semi-annual $30.00 payment
which shall have accrued in respect of such fractional right from the last semi-annual payment date
to the date of such application. If at any time not
more than forty (40) days nor less than thirty (30)
days prior to any semi-annual or other regular disbursement date, the Trustee shall have on hand
funds available for application under this Article
and sufficient in amount to make redemption payments at the above specified then prevailing maximum rate on one or more of said fractional beneficial interests then the Trustee shall prior to a date
thirty (30) days preceding such disbursement date,
draw by lot the serial number or numbers of fractional beneficial interests in respect of which redemption payments have not [20] been made
(selecting a sufficient number of said fractional
beneficial interests to exhaust the available funds
then in its hands) and shall send by mail a notice
to the registered holder of each such fractional beneficial interest or interests so selected addressed to
his address as standing upon the transfer books of
the Trustee which notice shall state that said beneficial interest is and has been called for redemption
payment upon said next disbursement date and that
thereafter the holder of said beneficial interest shall

be entitled to no other payments in respect thereof
until all of said Six Hundred and Sixty-five (665)
fractional beneficial interests shall have been so
paid. Such notice having been so mailed, the Trustee
shall set aside such amount of money from said
funds as will be sufficient to make redemption payments in respect of each said beneficial interest or
interests at the above specified then prevailing maximum rate and after said disbursement date the
holder of said fractional beneficial interests shall
(whether or not a certificate or certificates representing such fractional right or rights shall have at
that time been stamped "Redemption payment
made") receive no further payments in respect
thereof, nor any interest whatsoever, until after redemption payments shall have been made in respect
of all of said Six Hundred and Sixty-five (665)
fractional interests, after which time, however, the
owner of each such 1/665th fractional interest, as
represented by outstanding Land Trust Certificates,
shall share pro rata in full further funds, less expenses, fees, advances and disbursements of the
Trustee hereunder and of these trusts, as and when
the same are available for distribution hereunder
through the Trustee. No redemption payments shall
be made under this Article 9 except upon the surrender for stamping or endorsement as above provided of the certificate or certificates representing
the fractional beneficial interests, or any thereof, in
respect of which such payments are to be made but
after such payment and stamping or endorsement

said certificate or certificates shall be returned to
the holder or holders thereof and may thereafter be
assigned and transferred on the books of the Trustee
in the same manner as if no such redemption payment had been made except that any certificate or
certificates issued in lieu thereof upon such transfer
shall likewise be stamped or endorsed "Redemption
payment made." In its sole discretion the Trustee
may, if in its opinion or in the opinion of its counsel
such course is desirable, adopt some other appropriate legend for stamping or endorsement upon certificates so surrendered. In its sole discretion the
Trustee may, if in its opinion or in the opinion of its
counsel such course is desirable, take up and permanently cancel such certificates and in lieu of re-
turning the same to the holders thereof with such
legend endorsed or stamped thereon, deliver to such
holder or holders, a new certificate or certificates, in
such form and containing such terms not inconsistent with the provisions and conditions hereof as
the Trustee may in its discretion adopt, entitling
each such holder to his proportionate share in all
funds received and available for distribution
through the Trustee after such time when redemption payments shall have been made in respect of
all of said Six Hundred Sixty-five (665) beneficial
interests.

Article 10.

Among the express purposes of this trust and
among the purposes and powers of the Trustee
under this Agreement and Declaration of Trust, is

and shall be the purposes and powers to sell and convey and/or to assign, transfer and set over the [21] trust estate.

Subject to the existence of the option hereinafter mentioned and to the terms and conditions of this Article 10, full power and authority are vested in the Trustee in respect of the sale of said properties constituting the trust estate, absolute discretion being given it as to how and when the same shall be put upon the market, the manner, method and terms of sale and the price or prices to be realized therefor.

In the event the lessee under the above described lease to Sun Realty Co. shall exercise the option to purchase the premises hereinbefore described as provided in said lease, the Trustee shall, upon receipt of the purchase price in said lease set out, have full authority to complete said sale and execute any necessary conveyances without securing any consent from the holders of certificates issued hereunder.

The Trustee may, at any time, sell and convey the premises hereinbefore described and all of the trust estate without securing any consent from the holders of certificates issue hereunder provided that there be realized from said sale and conveyance and made available for distribution among the beneficiaries hereunder at least One Million Two Hundred and Fifty Thousand Dollars ($1,250,-000.00).

Upon receipt of consents in writing signed by the registered holders (or their duly authorized agents or attorneys) of certificates representing at least two-thirds (2/3) of the Six hundred and sixty-five (665) fractional beneficial interests provided for herein (which consents must include consents from the holders of certificates representing at least two-thirds (2/3) of the fractional beneficial interests upon which redemption payments shall not at the time have been made as provided in Article 9 hereof), the Trustee may at any time, but shall not be obligated to, sell and convey the premises hereinbefore described upon such terms as may be provided for in such consents.

Any conveyance made by the Trustee hereunder and pursuant to the authority herein provided shall be effective to divest and to convey all right, title and interest in said premises vested in the Trustee and/or in the owners of beneficial interests hereunder and/or in the holders of certificates issued hereunder, and the Grantee named in such conveyance shall not be required to see to the application of the purchase money by the Trustee.

Upon any sale of the above described premises as herein provided the proceeds of such sale shall after payment or setting aside of the compensation, expenses and disbursements of the Trustee and other expenses of such sale and conveyance, be applied first to the payment of the then prevailing maximum amount specified in Article 9 hereof to the holders of certificates representing fractional beneficial interests upon which redemption payments have not theretofore been made or set aside, as provided in said Article 9; provided however, that in the event of the exercise by the Lessee of the option to purchase provided for in the lease to Sun Realty Co., hereinabove mentioned, and the receipt by the Trustee of such purchase money, redemption payments shall be made from such moneys at the rate of One Thousand eighty dollars ($1080) in respect of each beneficial interest in respect of which redemption payment has not theretofore been made; and there shall be added to the amount of said last mentioned redemption payment an amount equal to such fraction of the Thirty Dollar ($30.00) semi-annual payment which shall have accrued in respect of such fractional beneficial interest from the last semi-annual payment date to the date of the making of such redemption payment; and any moneys [22] then remaining shall then by the Trustee be set aside for distribution and as soon as reasonably possible distributed pro rata and share alike in respect of each of said Six hundred and sixty-five (665) fractional rights to the holders of Land Trust Certificates representing the same.

Notice of the time and place of such final distribution shall be mailed by the Trustee to the holders of the Land Trust Certificates at their several addresses as the same appear upon the transfer books of the Trustee fifteen (15) days prior to the date fixed for such distribution. If after notice has been given as aforesaid the holders of any certificates shall fail or neglect to present the same as in the said notice specified, the Trustee shall place to the credit of each outstanding certificate the distributive share to which the holder thereof is entitled and shall be subject to no further duty to the holder or holders of the same except to pay such distributive share upon demand and surrender of said certificate, such payment to be made to or the order of the person so registered as the holder thereof at the time of the surrender of such certificate. The Trustee shall not be required to pay interest upon any funds so credited. No such final distribution shall be made, however, except upon surrender to the Trustee for complete cancellation of the certificate or certificates in respect of which the payments are to be made. Upon such distribution and/or credit this trust shall be deemed terminated.

Article 11.

Any moneys received by the Trustee hereunder in connection with proceedings in condemnation, expropriation or eminent domain and any other moneys received by the Trustee hereunder, the disbursement of which is not herein expressly provided for, shall, if and to the extent that the same are not in the opinion of the Trustee required to meet any ordinary or extraordinary charges, payments or disbursements hereunder, be by the Trustee applied as provided in Article 9 hereof. After redemption payments have been made or set aside in respect of all said Six hundred and sixty-five (665) Fractional beneficial interests then any balance of such moneys remaining in the hands of the Trustee shall be distributed pro rata, share and share alike, to the holders of said Six hundred and sixty-five (665) fractional beneficial interests in the manner provided in Article 10 hereof, provided, however, that if upon any such distribution under said Article, any part of the real property hereinabove described shall still remain in the ownership of the Trustee that the Trustee at the time of making such distribution shall endorse a legend upon each certificate representing beneficial interests or rights in respect of which such payment is made stating that an additional payment of a specified amount has been made in respect of the fractional rights represented by such certificate and such certificate shall be thereupon returned to the holder thereof.

Article 12.

As partial consideration to Title Insurance and Trust Company for its execution of this Agreement and Declaration of Trust and its acceptance of the same and for the performance of its duties hereunder and its agreement to perform the same, the Trustor and Harry L. Dunn and Albert Parker, as original beneficiaries and owners of all beneficial interests and holders of all certificates representing the same existing hereunder, hereby agree to and do assign and transfer to Title Insurance and Trust Company in its separate and individual capacity (as distinguished from its capacity as Trustee) all their right, title and interest in and to one undivided fifty-sixth (56th) part of the rents and profits and current income of the real property hereinabove described and/or any and all rentals and current income accruing under any of the leases hereinabove provided for including the right [23] to collect and receive the same, and Title Insurance and Trust Company shall have and enjoy the same in its individual and separate capacity and for its own uses and purposes but only for so long as said Title Insurance and Trust Company continues to exercise its functions as provided in this Agreement and Declaration of Trust, and upon the resignation of said Title Insurance and Trust Company said one undivided fifty-sixth (56th) part shall be assigned and transferred to and ipso facto vested in the successor to said Title Insurance and Trust Company hereunder, likewise in its individual and separate capacity. Said Title Insurance and Trust Company hereby agrees, however, that it will return for payment and application hereunder to holders of Land Trust Certificates hereunder on each June 15 and December 15 (except as hereinafter in this paragraph provided), all amounts received by it as such owner and holder of said one fifty-sixth (56th) undivided part during the then preceding period of six (6) months in excess of the sum of $250.00; provided, however, that after June 15, 1937 and prior to June 16, 1962, only such amounts in excess of the sum of $312.50 need be so returned, and after June 15, 1962, only such amounts in excess of $375.00 need be so returned. The above provision that if at any time Title Insurance and Trust Company or its successors hereunder be called upon to and shall complete any sale, execute any conveyance, or lease (other than the above mentioned lease to Sun Realty Co.), initiate, defend or take part in any litigation or like proceeding or perform any

other unusual or extraordinary service hereunder,
or make necessary or authorized advances or disbursements hereunder, that then said Title Insurance and Trust Company, or its successors shall be
entitled to reasonable compensation, and its costs,
fees, and expenses in connection therewith, including attorneys' fees, and/or reimbursement therefor
and/or in connection therewith and this may be retained by said Title Insurance and Trust Company,
or its successors, out of said one fifty-sixth (56th)
undivided part in excess of said sums so specified,
or out of any other moneys or funds coming into
the custody or possession of said Title Insurance
and Trust Company or its successors hereunder;
and for any such moneys in excess of said one
fifty-sixth (56th) undivided part to which the Title
Insurance and Trust Company, or its successors,
may be so entitled, said Title Insurance and Trust
Company, or its successors, shall have a lien and
claim on the trust estate and its income and proceeds superior to any rights of the holders of any
certificates issued hereunder. All amounts which
Title Insurance and Trust Company or its successors are entitled to receive and retain pursuant to
the provisions of this paragraph shall be deemed
to constitute the "expenses, disbursements and compensation of the Trustee" as said phrase is used
and appears elsewhere in this Agreemnt and Declaration of Trust. The transfer and assignment to
Title Insurance and Trust Company provided for
in this paragraph shall take effect immediately after

this Agreement and Declaration of Trust shall have been executed and become effective.

. Article 13.

Title Insurance and Trust Company has agreed to and does accept the trust hereunder and execute this Agreement and Declaration of Trust and has agreed and does hereby agree that during the continuance of this trust and agreement or until it shall resign hereunder it will collect and receive and pay and apply and distribute rentals and other moneys and perform the duties prescribed for it herein, and such acceptance and agreement is made upon condition and in consideration of the transfer of title to the above described property to Title Insurance and Trust Company, and of the execution of this Agreement and Declaration of Trust by the Trustor and by Harry L. Dunn and Albert Parker and of the agreement by said parties on their own behalf and on behalf of their successors and assigns to all of the terms and conditions hereof and of their specific agreement to cause to be transferred to Title Insurance and Trust Company, fractional beneficial interest No. 1 consisting of one six hundred and sixty-fifth (1/665th) of the whole beneficial interest existing hereunder and including that proportionate share of the [24] rentals and proceeds accruing hereunder; provided, however, that if a successor should replace Title Insurance and Trust Company hereunder prior to the termination of this trust that then Title Insurance and Trust Company shall transfer said beneficial Interest No. 1 to the successor Trustee on receipt by Title Insurance and Trust Company of the then value of said beneficial interest No. 1 as fixed by current sales of similar interests or by private agreement or by arbitration by the senior United States District Judge for the Southern District of California, it being understood that said beneficial interest No. 1 and the certificate representing the same, shall be held by Title Insurance and Trust Company, or its said successor, in its individual capacity and not as Trustee hereunder so that such Trustee holding the same may receive for its own use and purposes free from any obligations as Trustee hereunder any payments made thereon while it remains such holder. Notwithstanding any provision in any part of this Agreement and Declaration of Trust contained to the contrary, said beneficial interest No. 1 and the certificate representing the same shall not be called for a redemption payment and no redemption payment shall be made upon the same until after redemption payments have been made in respect of all other beneficial interests outstanding hereunder or simultaneously with such payments. And as partial consideration for such acceptance and such agreement by the Trustee and as an essential condition of the same and to protect Title Insurance and Trust Company, and its successors, as owner in its own right of said beneficial interest No. 1 and of the one individed fifty-sixth (56th) interest in the rents and profits provided for in Article 12 hereof, and to further

secure to the Trustee and its successors the right,
power and authority to receive, collect, distribute
and apply and pay rents and profits and other
moneys as above provided during the continuance
of this trust and agreement and as long as any Land
Trust Certificates are outstanding, and to carry out
the terms and conditions of this Agreement and Declaration of Trust, the Trustor and Harry L. Dunn
and Albert Parker and all owners of beneficial interests and holders of certificates representing the
same, now or hereafter parties hereto, do hereby
transfer and assign to Title Insurance and Trust
Company and to its successors hereunder, any and
all right, title and/or interest which each and every
of them may now or hereafter have in and/or to the
rents, profits and avails and proceeds of the real
property hereinabove described and/or coming due
or payable under any of said leases or this Agreement and Declaration of Trust, and not hereinabove
in this Agreement and Declaration of Trust disposed of, and the right to collect and receive the
same, all to be held and used by said Title Insurance and Trust Company and its successors, in trust
and in order that the purposes and intent of this
Agreement and Declaration of Trust may be completely executed and carried out and rentals and
moneys received, distributed, paid and applied to
and for the use and benefit of Harry L. Dunn and
Albert Parker and their respective successors as
holders of the Land Trust Certificates issued or to
be issued as above provided, said payments, applica-

tion and distribution to be made in the manner and
at the time and in the amounts all as herein provided; said right, title and interest to cease, however, and pass from said Title Insurance and Trust
Company at such time as it may cease to be Trustee
hereunder, and then to pass ipso facto and be vested
in its successor or successors upon like conditions
and trusts.

To induce and in consideration of the execution of
this Agreement and Declaration of Trust by Title
Insurance and Trust Company, and in order that
the purposes and provisions hereof may be more
effectually carried out, said Trustor and all owners
of beneficial interests and holders of certificates representing the same now or hereafter parties to this
Agreement and Declaration of Trust do hereby
agree that Title Insurance and Trust Company and
its successors hereunder shall have and exercise
until the termination of this trust and agreement
and of the completion of all of the purposes herein
set forth full and irrevocable right, power and
authority to collect and receive and pay and apply
and distribute the [25] rents, profits and income
accuring hereunder and/or under any of said leases
together with all other moneys, funds and proceeds
accruing hereunder and to pay, apply and distribute
the same to the respective owners of beneficial interests existing hereunder as represented by the holders
of Land Trust Certificates, all in the manner, at the
times and in the amounts herein elsewhere provided,
and to execute leases, sales and conveyances all as

herein elsewhere provided, and such right, power and authority as may be necessary or desirable in order that said Title Insurance and Trust Company and its successors may perform and carry out said functions as Trustee, lessor, agent and/or contracting party hereto has been and is hereby expressly and irrevocably granted and delegated to Title Insurance and Trust Company and its successors hereunder.

The transfer and assignment to Title Insurance and Trust Company provided for in this Article 13 shall take effect immediately after the taking effect of the transfer and assignment to Title Insurance and Trust Company hereinabove provided for in Article 12, provided, however, that if for any reason said transfer and assignment mentioned in Article 12 shall not promptly have become effective as therein provided, that then the transfer and assignment provided for in this Article 13 shall forthwith become effective immediately after this Agreement and Declaration of Trust shall have been executed and become effective, it being understood and agreed, however, that the Land Trust Certificate representing beneficial interest No. 1 shall first be issued in the name of and be delivered to Harry L. Dunn and/or Albert Parker, and then assigned and transferred to Title Insurance and Trust Company.

Article 14.

After termination of the above mentioned original long term lease to Sun Realty Co. the Trustee may, in its discretion, if such course appears to it to be advisable, change the dates of making semi-annual periodical payments hereunder, provided, however, that such payments shall be made at least twice in each twelve month period from June 15 to June 14, inclusive, if sufficient funds be available therefor. In the event that the Trustee shall desire to do so, it may, in its own absolute discretion, at any time seek the advice of the holders of the Land Trust Certificates issued hereunder. If the holders of certificates representing a majority of the six hundred sixty-five beneficial interests (including a majority of the fractional beneficial interests upon which redemption payments shall not at the time have been made as provided in Article 9 hereof) shall notify the Trustee in writing of their agreement upon the course which they desire to have taken, not inconsistent with any of the express provisions hereof, the Trustee may in its discretion (but shall not be obligated to do so) endeavor to effectuate the same, and in the event that it does so, shall be fully protected in so doing. Afer redemption payments shall have been made as hereinabove provided in respect of all of the six hundred sixty-five (665) fractional beneficial interests, the Trustee may, in its discretion, propose the modification or elimination of any of the terms, conditions, trusts or provisions hereof and/or the addition hereto of any new terms, conditions, provisions and/or trusts, and in the event that such propoal be consented to in writing by the then registered holders of Land Trust Certificates representing three-quar-

ters (¾) of the six hundred sixty-five (665) fractional beneficial interests of any of the terms,
conditions, trusts or provisions hereof and/or the
addition hereto of any new terms, conditions, provisions and/or trusts, and in the event that such
proposal be consented to in writing, by the then
registered holders of Land Trust Certificates representing the three-quarters (¾) of the six hundred sixty-five (665) fractional beneficial interests
hereunder, the Trustee may, in its discretion, but
shall not be obliged to, make effective such changes,
eliminations and/or additions by the execution of an
instrument supplemental hereto; provided, however,
that no [26] such elimination, change, alteration or
addition shall have the effect of giving the owner of
any fractional beneficial interest as such any preference or advantage over the holder or owner of
any other fractional beneficial interest. Nothing
herein provided, however, shall be construed to
qualify or limit the discretion of the Trustee to
pursue such course of action consistent with the then
existing provisions hereof, as may in its opinion be
necessary or advisable for the best interests of the
certificate holders.

Article 15.

The Trustee does not warrant its title as owner
of the premises hereinbefore described, nor does it
warrant the validity of the lease hereinbefore described, nor the validity and/or enforceability of
the option to purchase therein contained, nor of
any other lease of said premises which may here-

after be made, nor guarantee the performance of the covenants thereof by the lessee or lessees thereunder, nor does it make any representations or assume any liability in respect of the title to the property or the legal effect of the certificates by it issued hereunder; nor does it make any promise, agreement and/or guarantee as to the payment of any sum or sums mentioned in this Agreement and Declaration of Trust, or any interest thereon, the same being payable solely from moneys which may be received by said Trustee under the provisions of said Agreement and Declaration of Trust, and if, as and when available for payment and/or distribution under the terms and provisions thereof. The Trustee undertakes only to exercise ordinary care in collecting the rental under the lease hereinbefore described and any future lease of said premises executed pursuant to the terms hereof and in enforcing the provisions thereof, to the extent that it shall deem it for the best interest of the certificate holders so to do, and in distributing moneys hereunder if, as and when available hereunder therefor, as provided herein, or in carrying out any sale of said premises and distributing the net proceeds among the holders of certificates issued and at the time outstanding hereunder, as the case may be, and shall not be liable for any act performed by it in good faith hereunder.

Except as otherwise provided in this instrument, the Trustee shall have the exclusive right to manage and control the trust estate as it may deem for the best interests of the holders of certificates issued and at the time outstanding hereunder and shall not be subject to any obligation to the holders of certificates issued hereunder other than such as are expressly assumed hereunder.

The Trustee accepts, and shall have, no obligation to fulfill or carry out the obligations of the lessor under said lease or any future lease except at the expense of the trust estate. In no event shall the Trustee have any individual liability in respect thereof.

The Trustee shall have full power to compromise and settle claims either in contract or tort made by it or against it or against the trust estate and to charge the expense thereof against the proceeds and/or income derived from the trust estate.

The Trustee, in acting hereunder or under the aforesaid lease or any other lease of the above described premises, shall be protected in relying upon any notice, request, consent, affidavit, certificate, assignment, note or other paper or document believed by it to be genuine and to be signed by the proper party.

The Trustee shall be entitled to indemnity and to be paid from the trust estate for any personal liability by it incurred in the administration of this trust, except such as may arise from its personal and willful default. [27]

The Trustee shall not be liable for any error of judgment or for any loss arising out of any act or omission in the execution of this trust, including its acts and omissions as lessor under the aforeaid lease or any other lease of the above described premises, so long as it acts in good faith; nor shall it be personally liable for the acts or omissions of any attorney, agent, servant or employee appointed by or acting for it (reasonable care having been used in his selection), and it shall not be obliged to give any bond to secure the due performance of this trust by it.

The corporation or other entity which may at any time be Trustee hereunder may acquire, own and dispose of fractional parts of the beneficial interest hereunder to the same extent as if it were not Trustee.

Among the express purposes of this trust and among the purposes and powers of the Trustee under this Agreement and Declaration of Trust is and shall be the purposes and powers, in its discretion, to mortgage or otherwise bind or charge the real property hereinabove described and all the assets of the trust for the purpose of providing funds to meet any exigency arising in connection therewith and for the benefit of the beneficiaries hereunder. The Trustee shall have power, in order to meet any exigency existing hereunder to borrow money upon any usual terms, either from the corporation which is at the time Trustee hereunder or from any other person or corporation, and give notice or any other security therefor, or to cause notes to be given and to pledge and/or hypothecate the trust estate as security for the payment thereof, but no such obligation and no such mortgage obligation or other hypothecation shall bind personally any beneficiaries or holders of certificates issued hereunder nor the Trustee. The Trustee shall have power and authority in order to make payments of interest or principal in respect of any such borrowings or mortgages or other hypothecation to apply such moneys as may, from time to time, be available hereunder and such payments and applications may be made in preference and with priority to any claims of beneficiaries hereunder to periodical or other payments in respect of any fractional beneficial interests owned by them.

The Trustee may advise with legal counsel selected by it, and any action taken or omitted to be taken by it in good faith in accordance with the opinion or advice of such counsel shall be conclusive on the holders of Land Trust Certificates issued hereunder, and the Trustee shall be fully protected and shall not be subject to any liability in respect thereof.

In every written contract made by the Trustee in connection with the trust estate, reference may be made to this instrument, and every person or corporation contracting with the Trustee shall look to the funds and property of the trust for payment of any debt, note, judgment or decree, or of any money that may otherwise become due and payable by reason of the failure on the part of the Trustee to perform such contract in whole or in part, or for any other cause, and neither the Trustee nor the holders of certificates issued hereunder, present or future, shall in any event be personally liable therefor.

Article 16.

In the event that the Trustee or any successor hereafter appointed, shall wish to resign, the Trustee shall give four weeks' notice thereof to all the then holders of certificates issued hereunder, either by registered letter sent to their last address*ed* as the same shall appear on the books of the Trustee, such notice to be deemed to commence with the mailing of said letter or by publication once a week for four weeks in a newspaper published and of general circulation in the City of Los Angeles, California. If the holders of Land Trust Certificates representing a majority of the six hundred [28] and sixty-five (665) beneficial fractional interests upon which redemption payments have not been made, shall within two weeks after the expiration of the period of notice above provided, request the Trustee in writing to convey the trust estate to a specified Trustee who is willing to accept the trust, the Trustee shall, upon the making of such conveyance and upon accounting for all funds which have previously come into its possession, and the assignment and transfer to its successors, upon the terms herein provided, of the one undivided fifty-sixth part of the rents and profits provided for in Article 12, and of the beneficial interest No. 1, and of its interest in rents and revenues and funds received under Article 13, be discharged from further liability hereunder. In the event of the failure or neglect of the holders of a majority in interest of the certificates to express their choice of a successor within the period above provided or if in the opinion of the Trustee such choice is unsuitable, the Trustee may request the person who at the time shall be the Federal Judge designated in and for the District of the United States wherein the premises hereinbefore described are located, or if there be more than one such person, then the one senior in office, to designate a successor Trustee which shall be a bank or trust company qualified to accept such trust and to act hereunder. Upon conveying the trust estate to a successor Trustee chosen by any of the methods above provided and upon accounting for all funds which have previously come into its possession, the Trustee shall be discharged from further liability.

In the event of the consolidation or merger of the corporation which is for the time being acting as Trustee hereunder, with any other corporation such consolidated corporation shall succeed to the title and rights of the original Trustee, subject to the terms and conditions of this Agreement and Declaration of Trust. The purchase of the assets and the assumption of the liabilities of the corporation which is for the time being acting as Trustee hereunder shall be treated as a merger or consolidation within the meaning of this paragraph.

Each and every successor Trustee appointed in accordance with the terms hereof shall, in respect of the trust estate and the conduct and management thereof, and in respect of the sale thereof under any of the provisions hereof, have and enjoy each and every right, power, authority and discretion by the terms hereof reserved to or vested in said Title Insurance and Trust Company as Trustee hereunder.

Article 17.

Unless sooner terminated as elsewhere in this instrument provided, the trusts in this Agreement and Declaration of Trust defined shall terminate upon the death of the last to die of the following named persons:

Bertha Abrams, Hertha J. Abramson, Newton Bissinger, Gutave Brenner, Julius Brownstein, Sophia J. Coffer, Minnie Cooper, and Isador Earl Cooper, Sidney Ehrman, Donald Lawrence Eisner, and Harry Eisner, all of the City of San Francisco, California.

George M. Adair, Rose Harris Adler, H. A. Allen, Stuart D. Anderson, D. Antink, Sadie L. Armer, C. W. Arnold, Sarah H. Bachman, Robert Baker, Donald L. Bantock and Ada I. Bantock, I. A. Allen, Wesley M. Barr, Nannie Barrie, J. S. Barrie, R. M. Barton, Milton Baruch, J. Y. Baruh, Irene Bastheim, Claud Beelman, Geo. S. Behrendt, Sadie M. Behrendt, Trustee, Sadie M. Behrendt, Sam Behrendt, Glen Behymer, L. E. Behymer, Sylvia O. Behymer, H. A. Belcher, L. B. Belcher, H. B. Bendtsen, Doris M. Benjamin, C. E. Berlin, Minerva Berman, Frank W. Black, Abe Bloom, James C. Bogart, Ester H. Bowers, Flora E. Bradley, George Bradley and Frances Bradley, Alexander Brick, Lenore Brick, Minnie Brick, Aleck Brownstein, Chas. Brownstein, Elsie H. Brownstein, Robert Grant Brownstein, [29]

Patsy Bufano, Thomas Burkofsky, Jennie Burris, Rozellia O. Butler, O. O. Chism, Daniel Clarke, Amelia B. Cline and W. H. Cline, Morris Cohn, Louis M. Cole, Ysidora Louis Cole, John T. Cooper, Aleck Curlett, Frank C. Curtis and Minnie A. Curtis, Robert L. Cuzner, Milton L. Davidson, Norman G. Davidson, Kate L. Day, F. S. DeVoin, S. F. DeVoin, Wm. H. Dickson, Jane Stimson Dulin, Dr. D. W. Edelman, A. R. Edson, A. Eisner, Bluma Eisner, I. Eisner, all of the City of Los Angeles, California.

E. M. Asher, of the City of Beverly Hills, California.

Lockwood R. Bantock and Margaret Bantock of the City of Arcadia, California.

Frances Marion Devereux of the City of Cincinnati, Ohio, Rosabelle H. Baeder, Irma Benjamin, Flora W. Bernhard, Henry Bernhard, Mollie Bernhard, Fannie S. Block, Elizabeth S. Block, Herman W. Block, Sylvan Cole, and Walter E. Deutsch, all of the City of New York, New York;

Alfred G. Carter, Pearl V. Carter, of the City of South Pasadena, California;

Rev. William ` Corr, of the City of Pasadena, California;

. Ruth Dawson, of the City of Long Beach, California;

Robert C. Devereux, of the City of Alhambra, California;

Francis S. Devereux, of the City of St. Petersburg, Florida;

Mary Drysdale, Mina Drysdale, of the City of Hollywood, California.

Faith Whitney, daughter of Marcus B. Whitney and Vera Whitney, his wife, of the City of Mount Vernon, State of New York; James Stillman, Timothy Stillman, Calvin Stillman, John Stillman and Dora Stillman, all children of Ernest G. Stillman and Mildred Whitney Stillman, his wife, all of the City of New York, State of New York;

Ralph H. Spotts, Jr., and Victor J. Spotts, both children of Ralph H. Spotts and Delpha V. E. Spotts, his wife, of the City of Beverly Hills, County of Los Angeles, State of California; and Eugene Dunn, son of Henry W. Dunn and Laura Mae Dunn, his wife, of the City of Long Beach, California;

John Francis Jones, Richard Welton Jones, George Earle Jones, Jr., all children of George E. Jones and Frances Jones, his wife, of the City of South Pasadena, State of California;

Thomas Tully and Robert Tully, children of Jaspar Tully and Leslie Tully, his wife, of the City of Berkeley, California;

Allen Mitchum, son of Colis Mitchum and Eleanor Mitchum, his wife, of the City of Berkeley, California;

Elizabeth Witter and Barbara Witter, both children of W. Guy Witter and Helen Witter, his wife, of the City of Pasadena, California;

Porter Bruck and Barbara Bruck, both children of Porter Bruck and Dodothy Bruck, his wife, of the City of South Pasadena, California;

George Crane and Peter Crane, both children of William Crane and Catharine Crane, [30] his wife, of the City of Pasadena, California;

Peter Edwards and William Edwards, both children of William A. Edwards and Josephine Edwards, his wife, of the City of Santa Barbara, California;

John Van Alst Austin and Miriam Austin, both children of John Van Alst Austin and Margaret Austin, his wife, of the City of Santa Barbara, California;

Serena Kamper, daughter of Gustave Anthony Kamper and Margaret Kamper, his wife, of the City of Honolulu, Territory of Hawaii;

Edwin Sill Fussell, Paul Fussell, Jr., and Florence Elizabeth Fussell, all children of Paul Fussell and Wilma S. Fussell, his wife, of the City of Pasadena, California;

Harry L. Dunn of the City of Pasadena, California;

Albert Parker, of the City of Los Angeles, California;

Robert Eisner Lissner, Richard Louis Lissner, Aline M. Lissner, Richard James Lauter, Herbert M. Baruch, Jr., Edith Blum, Ruth Davidson, Harriett Davidson, Alvin Robert Stitch, Janice Ethelyn Stitch, Harriet Green, Arthur McClane, George Newmark Behrendt, Patricia Meyer, Nancy Frank, Blanche May, Doris E. Nerenberg, Marvin L. Nerenberg, and Albert Parker, all of the City of Los Angeles, California;

Harry L. Dunn and Louise R. Dunn, both of the City of Pasadena, California.

Upon such termination of said trust by lapse of time the Trustee shall sell and convey the trust estate, in such manner and upon such terms as it, in its discretion, may consider most desirable in the interests of the beneficiaries hereunder, or, if at the time of such termination redemption payments have been made as provided in Article 9 hereof in respect of all the six hundred and sixty-five fractional beneficial interests hereunder, then the Trustee may, in its absolute discretion, upon the payments of its costs, fees, expenses, advances, (if any) with interest thereon, transfer and convey title to the trust estate, subject to any then existing encumbrances and leases to the then owners of such beneficial interests, as represented by Land Trust Certificates then outstanding, according to the records of the Trustee as tenants in common in the proportions of the beneficial interests owned by each. Prior to the making of such transfer and conveyance, the Trustee may require the surrender of all outstanding certificates.

Upon the completion of any sale under the provisions of this Article, the Trustee, after the payment of costs and expenses and reimbursing itself for any authorized disbursements or advances made hereunder, shall make redemption payments as provided in Article 9 hereof to the owners of any beneficial interests in respect of which redemption payments have not previously been made, and shall then

distribute any balance remaining pro rata to the
owners of the six hundred sixty-five (665) fractional
beneficial interests hereunder, as represented by the
holders of the Land Trust Certificates issued hereunder; such distribution to be made as provided in
Article 10 for final distribution of the proceeds of
sale thereunder and upon making such transfer and
distribution and accounting for all funds which have
come into its hands the Trustee shall be discharged
and free of further liability hereunder. [31]

Article 18.

The term "Trustee" shall be deemed, unless the
context shall otherwise indicate, to contemplate the
Trustee for the time being, and said term shall include said Title Insurance and Trust Company and
each successor to said Title Insurance and Trust
Company which may hereafter be Trustee under
any of the provisions of this instrument and such
Trustee as shall at the time be acting as Trustee
hereunder shall have full power to execute, issue
and transfer certificates hereunder; and said term
"Trustee" shall be deemed to and shall include Title
Insurance and Trust Company and its successors
hereunder in its and their individual capacity (as
distinguished from trust capacity) in such references as are shown by the express words of the
context hereof to mean or include such individual
capacity.

Article 19.

It is the understanding of the parties hereto that
all of the purposes, provisions, conditions, covenants

and agreements contained in or provided for in this Agreement and Declaration of Trust are legal and valid but if any one or more of said purposes, provisions, conditions, covenants or agreements be in fact contrary to law or illegal or void, then such purpose, provision, covenant, condition or agreement only shall be null and void and shall be deemed separable from the remaining purposes, provisions, conditions, covenants and agreements contained in or provided for herein, and the same shall in no way effect or impair the validity of the remaining purposes, provisions, conditions, covenants or agreements contained in or provided for in this Agreement and Declaration of Trust and all of the parties hereto hereby declare that they would have executed and agreed to this Agreement and Declaration of Trust irrespective of the fact that any one or more of said purposes, provisions, conditions, covenants or agreements be contrary to law, illegal or void.

Article 20.

The Trustee will deposit all funds received by it hereunder, less its costs, fees, advances, if any, and expenses, in a bank or banks of its selection, which bank or banks shall be located in the City of Los Angeles, California. Any interest which may be paid by such bank or banks upon such deposit or deposits shall be added to, distributed, applied and paid hereunder in the same manner as the funds upon which such interest may have been earned.

Article 21.

If the property covered hereby, or any portion thereof, or the income, proceeds or avails thereof, and/or the beneficial interest, or any part thereof, hereunder, become liable for the payment of any inheritance, income or other tax whatsoever, the Trustee is authorized to withhold and pay such tax out of any moneys in its possession, or which may come into its possession, for the account of the person or persons whose interest or interests hereunder are so liable, unless such tax shall have been paid by such person or persons or by some one in his or their behalf, or by some other person.

Provided, if any such tax be not so paid, and there are not sufficient moneys available under this Trust, and payable or applicable to the payment to the account of such person or persons, to pay the same, then the Trustee, at its option (but shall not be obligated so to do) may advance a sufficient sum or sums to pay such tax, which advancement with interest thereon at the rate of seven per cent. (7%) per annum from date of advancement to date of repayment shall constitute a first lien upon the interest or interests under this Trust of the person or persons whose said interests hereunder are so liable. [32]

Article 22.

By acceptance of any certificate issued hereunder or the assertion of any right thereunder or hereunder, the original or any successive holder shall be deemed to become a party hereto and to assent

and agree to all of the terms, conditions and provisions contained in this Agreement and Declaration
of Trust and to direct and authorize the carrying
out and completion of the same.

The terms, provisions and conditions hereof shall
bind said Trustor and said Trustee and their respective successors and assigns, and all beneficiaries
hereto and hereunder and their respective heirs,
legatees, devisees, administrators, executors, successors and assigns, whether or not the same be holders of Land Trust Certificates hereunder. The
terms, conditions and provisions hereof shall inure
to the benefit of said Trustor and said Trustee and
their respective successors and assigns, and to the
benefit of said Harry L. Dunn and Albert Parker
and their successors as holders of Land Trust Certificates hereunder.

Article 23.

The Trustee may record this Agreement and Declaration of Trust at any time that it may deem
advisable; and furthermore, it is understood and
agreed that the Trustee may disclose any of the
records and/or communications of or in connection
with this Trust to any person as freely as if all
such records and communications were matters of
public record.

Said Mitchum, Tully & Co., as Trustor, and Harry
L. Dunn and Albert Parker, as original beneficiaries
and initial holders of all of the six hundred and
sixty-five fractional rights provided for hereunder,
and Louise R. Dunn, as wife of Harry L. Dunn,

join herein to signify their respective assents and agreements to the terms hereof.

In Witness Whereof, Said Title Insurance and Trust Company and said Mitchum, Tully & Co. have caused this instrument to be signed in their respective names by their respective presidents or vice-presidents, and their respective seals to be hereunto affixed and attested by their respective secretaries or assistant secretaries, and said Harry L. Dunn, and Louise R. Dunn, his wife, and Albert Parker, a single man, have hereunto affixed their hands and seals, all at the City of Los Angeles, on the 15th day of July, 1927.

[Corporate Seal]   MITCHUM, TULLY & CO.

By (Signed) C. E. JONES
Vice-President

By " Assistant Secretary

TITLE INSURANCE AND TRUST COMPANY

[Corporate Seal]

By (Signed) STUART O'MELVENY
Vice-President.

By "   E. H. MOORE
Assistant Secretary.

[Seal]   ALBERT PARKER

[Seal]   HARRY L. DUNN [33]

State of California,
County of Los Angeles—ss.

On this 15th day of July, 1927, before me, P. L. Bishop, a Notary Public in and for the County of Los Angeles, State of California, personally appeared Harry L. Dunn, known to me to be the person whose name is subscribed to the within instrument and acknowledged to me that he executed the same.

In Witness Whereof, I have hereunto set my hand and affixed my official seal the day and year in this certificate first above written.

(Signed) P. L. BISHOP

Notary Public in and for the County of Los Angeles,
    State of California.

My commission expires January 12th, 1929.

State of California,
County of Los Angeles—ss.

On this 15th day of July, 1927, before me, P. L. Bishop, a Notary Public in and for the County of Los Angeles, State of California, residing therein, duly commissioned and sworn, personally appeared Louise R. Dunn, wife of Harry L. Dunn, known to me to be the person whose name is subscribed to the within instrument, and acknowledged to me that she executed the same.

In Witness Whereof, I have hereunto set my hand and affixed my official seal the day and year in this certificate first above whitten.

(Signed) P. L. BISHOP

Notary Public in and for the County of Los Angeles,
    State of California.

My Commission expires January 12th, 1929. [34]

State of California,
County of Los Angeles—ss.

On this 15th day of July, 1927, before me, P. L. Bishop, a Notary Public in and for the County of Los Angeles, State of California, personally appeared Albert Parker, known to me to be the person whose name is subscribed to the within instrument and acknowledged to me that he executed the same.

In Witness Whereof, I have hereunto set my hand and affixed my official seal the day and year in this certificate first above written.

[Seal]   (Signed) **P. L. BISHOP**
Notary Public in and for the County of Los Angeles,
    State of California.

My commission expires January 12th, 1929.

State of California,
County of Los Angeles—ss.

On this 15th day of July, 1927, before me, P. L. Bishop, a Notary Public in and for said County of Los Angeles, State of California, residing therein, duly commissioned and sworn, personally appeared Stuart O'Melveny, known to me to be the Vice President, and E. H. Moore, known to me to be the Assistant Secretary, respectively, of Title Insurance and Trust Company, one of the corporations that executed the within and foregoing instrument, known to me to be the persons who executed the within and foregoing instrument on behalf of the said corporation, and acknowledged to me that such corporation executed the same.

In Witness Whereof, I have hereunto set my hand and affixed my official seal the day and year in this Certificate first above written.

[Seal]   (Signed)   P. L. BISHOP

Notary Public in and for the County of Los Angeles,
    State of California.

My commission expires: January 12, 1929. [35]

State of California,
County of Los Angeles—ss.

On this 15th day of July, 1927, before me, P. L. Bishop, a Notary Public in and for said County of Los Angeles, State of California, residing therein, duly commissioned and sworn, personally appeared G. E. Jones, known to me to be the Vice President, and M. Fitch, known to me to be the Assistant Secretary, respectively, of Mitchum, Tully and Co., one of the corporations that executed the within and foregoing instrument, known to me to be the persons who executed the within and foregoing instrument on behalf of the said corporation, and acknowledged to me that such corporation executed the same.

In Witness Whereof, I have hereunto set my hand and affixed my official seal the day and year in this certificate first above written.

[Seal]   (Signed)   P. L. BISHOP

Notary Public in and for the County of Los Angeles,
    State of California.

My commission expires: January 12th 1929.

I, the undersigned, do hereby certify the above Agreement and Declaration of Trust to be a true and correct copy of the original dated and signed as above, presented to me this 9 day of December, 1936.

[Seal]   JOYCE BENT
Notary Public in and for the County of Los Angeles,
     State of California.

My Commission Expires April 15, 1940. [36]

EXHIBIT C

This Indenture of Lease, dated the 15th day of July, 1927, by and between Title Insurance and Trust Company, a Corporation organized and existing under and by virtue of the laws of the State of California, with its principal place of business in the City of Los Angeles, County of Los Angeles, State of California, hereinafter sometimes called the Lessor, and Sun Realty Co., a corporation organized and existing under and by virtue of the laws of the State of California, with its principal place of business in the City of Los Angeles, County of Los Angeles, State of California, hereinafter sometimes called the Lessee;

Witnesseth:

That for and in consideration of the covenants and promises of Lessee, and subject to the terms, provisions and conditions of this lease, Lessor hereby leases, demises and lets unto Lessee, and

Lessee, subject to said terms, provisions and conditions, hereby takes and leases from the Lessor, all that certain real property situated in the City of Los Angeles, County of Los Angeles, State of California, more particularly described as follows:

The Westerly One Hundred Twenty (120) feet of Lots One (1) and Two (2), and the Northerly Twenty (20) feet of the Westerly One Hundred Twenty (120) feet of Lot Three (3), in Block Eleven (11) of Hollywood, in the City of Los Angeles, County of Los Angeles, State of California, as per map recorded in Book 28, Pages 59 and 60, Miscellaneous Records of said County. Together with the buildings thereon and appurtenances thereto.

Subject to taxes for the year 1927-28, and rights under existing leases, whether recorded or unrecorded.

Article I.
Term

The term of this lease shall commence July 15th, 1927, and shall end at midnight on January 14, 2026, being ninety-eight (98) years, six (6) months in all.

Article II.
Rentals

The Lessee covenants to pay to the Lessor a net monthly rental in the sum of Thirty-five Hundred Dollars ($3500.00) per month for each and every month during said Ninety-eight (98) year and Six (6) months' period. All rentals required to be paid under the provisions of this lease shall be paid

to Lessor monthly in advance, on or before
the first day of each calendar month after date
(payments for the portion of each calendar month
at the commencement and end of the term hereof to be reduced proportionately, and payment
of rent for such first fractional period being hereby
acknowledged), at the principal office of said Lessor
at Title Insurance Building in the City of Los Angeles, State of California, or at such other place in
[37] the City of Los Angeles, State of California
as may be designated in writing by the Lessor to
Lessee from time to time, in gold coin of the United
States of America, of the present standard of weight
and fineness. Until the holders of the record title to
more than an undivided one-half interest in the
reversion of said demised premises, if at any time
there shall be more than one such holder of said
record title, shall in writing notify Lessee to make
such payments to some other person in the City of
Los Angeles, Lessee may make said payments to
Lessor at said office at said Title Insurance Building
in Los Angeles, and after a designation in the
manner aforesaid to make said payments to a different person, may make said payments to said person so designated; and the holders of the record
title to more than an undivided one-half interest
in said reversion, may from time to time, designate
a different person in the City of Los Angeles as the
person to whom to make said payments, but until
such notice thereof has been given to Lessee, Lessee
may continue to make such payments to the last person designated.

It is expressly understood and agreed that by the word "dollar" wherever used in this lease, is meant a United States of America gold coin composed of 25.8 grains of gold .900 fine, which is the present standard of weight and fineness of said United States of America gold coin; provided, however, that should it be difficult or inconvenient for Lessee to obtain the said gold coin with which to make any payment herein required to be made, any such payment may be made in other lawful money of the United States of America in an amount which shall be equivalent in market value to the market value of such payment in said gold coin at the time and place where such payment is required to be made hereunder.

Lessee shall pay such rentals without any deduction or abatement whatsoever, and said net monthly rental shall be over and above all costs, repairs, rates, taxes, assessments, charges and expenses of any and every nature and decription which Lessee, under the provisions of this indenture, is required to make at the cost and expense of Lessee.

No acceptance by Lessor of any currency, legal tender, check, coin, money or value whatever, in lieu of such standard gold coin of the United States of America, or its equivalent in market value in other lawful money of the United States as aforesaid, as hereinbefore specified, shall be construed as a waiver on the part of Lessor of the right to demand the payment of any other unpaid installment or installments of rent in such standard of gold coin of the United States of America, or its equivalent in market value in other lawful money of the United States as aforesaid.

In the event that any installment of rent is not paid when due, Lessee covenants that said installment shall bear interest at the rate of Seven per cent (7%) per annum from the date when it becomes due until paid.

Article III.

Taxes and Assessments

During the entire term of this lease, Lessee covenants to pay, bear and discharge, in addition to the net rentals in this instrument reserved, all taxes, assessments, impositions, payments, charges and levies, license fees and penalties of every kind, for revenue or otherwise, of any governmental or legal authority whatsoever, whether general or special, ordinary or extraordinary, of every kind and description, including in the foregoing (without in anywise limiting the generality of the above language) water, gas and electricity rates, assessments for street, sidewalk, sewer and other improvements, which may be `taxed, assessed, im- [38] posed, charged, levied or become a lien against and/or upon the premises demised, or any part thereof, or upon any or all buildings and improvements at any time thereon, or upon the leasehold estate created by this indenture, or upon the reversionary estate, or any of them.

The taxes, assessments, impositions, payments, charges and levies, license fees and penalties to be paid, borne or discharges by Lessee hereunder, shall not include taxes, assessments, impositions, payments, charges or levies, license fees or penalties which may at any time be taxes, assessed, imposed, charged or levied upon or against any real or personal property of Lessor other than that hereby demised, even though the same might from time to time be levied or charged or become a lien against the premises demised, including in the foregoing (without in anywise limiting the generality of the above language) all taxes, assessments, impositions, payments, charges and levies, license fees and penalties, upon or against income, income profits, gifts, and inheritance, and succession and estate taxes of, upon or against Lessor, or any successor or assignee of Lessor and any franchise, license or capital stock taxes upon or against any corporate Lessor, and any poll, excise, occupation or other taxes, assessments, impositions, payments, charges or levies, license fees or penalties, that may be personal to Lessor, or to any successor or assignee of Lessor. Lessee covenants and agrees, however, that if land trust certificates, or certificates of beneficial interest under a trust or agreement covering the reversionary estate in the demised premises are issued, and if taxes shall be assessed, imposed, charged or levied upon the rights, interest or estates evidenced by such land trust certificates or certificates of beneficial interest, (whether the same be regarded as real property or

as personal property), and the amount of taxes
which would otherwise be assessed against or payable by the Lessee be for that reason decreased, that
then Lessee will pay, bear and discharge said taxes
so assessed, imposed, charged or levied upon said
rights, interest or estate evidenced by such certificates or reimburse the person paying the same to
the extent of such decrease, such reimbursement to
be effected by depositing amounts equal to those so
paid, limited as aforesaid, with the trustee of the
trust under which said certificates were issued; provided, however, that, notwithstanding anything in
this Article III contained, the aggregate of all the
taxes to be paid by the Lessee during any tax
period shall not exceed the total tax for such period
which would have been levied and assessed upon
the entire fee simple absolute estate in the land and
improvements constituting the demised premises
hereunder if no such trust certificates or certificates
of beneficial interest had been issued.

The first regular state, county and municipal taxes
to be paid by Lessee as aforesaid, and which taxes
Lessee agrees to pay, are eleven-twelfths (11/12)
of such taxes for the first half of the fiscal year
1927-28, and the last of such taxes to be paid by
Lessee shall be one-twelfth (1/12) of the last half of
such taxes for the fiscal year 2025-26. The intention hereof is that Lessee shall pay all taxes for the
term of this lease under whatever system of taxation may be in force.

The land covered by this lease and any buildings

or improvements at any time thereon shall always be assessed for the purpose of taxation in the name of Lessor, provided the same is permitted under the laws or regulations relating thereto, and each payment or installment of such taxes or assessments of every kind, levies, rates, duties, tolls, imposts, license fees, costs and penalties to be paid by Lessee hereunder must be paid at least five (5) days before the same become delinquent, and in the name of Lessor; and the original or duplicate receipts showing payments of such taxes, assessments and all other charges above described shall be deposited with the Lessor, at the place where the last preceding installment of rent was payable, at least five (5) days before such delinquency. As between the parties [39] hereto Lessee alone shall have the duty *to* attending to, making and filing any statement or report which may be provided or required by law as the basis, or in connection with the determination, equalization, reduction or payment of any and every obligation which has to be borne or paid which may become payable by Lessee hereunder, and more particularly hereinbefore specified and enumerated. Lessor shall not in anywise be or become responsible therefor, nor for the contents of any such statement or report so prepared or filed by Lessee, nor shall Lessor be obligated to make, join in, or become a party to any protest or objection to any law, order, proceeding or determination which might impose any obligation or liability upon Lessor hereunder or increase the same, but in all of the aforesaid matters and things Lessee shall have and Lessor hereby irrevocably grants to Lessee the necessary power and authority to act therein in the name of Lessor wherever the same is permitted or required by law, but without any cost, expense or liability upon Lessor. In making payment of such taxes and assessments and other charges above enumerated, Lessee has no obligation to make any more definite specification of the name of Lessor than that Lessee makes such payment on behalf of the person under whom Lessee holds the demised premises, and Lessee has no obligation to obtain or deliver receipts for such payments in the name of any person other than that appearing on such bills, as Lessor may, at Lessor's option, have delivered to Lessee at least fifteen (15) days prior to the date on which such taxes or assessments or other charges respectively become delinquent.

Either party may, in its own name and behalf, or if appropriate, in the name and on behalf of the other, and at its own cost and expense, exercise any and all rights, claims, remedies or defenses against, or to prevent the collection or enforcement of said taxes, assessments, impositions, payments, charges or levies, license fees or penalties, or any of them, by any claim, protest, objection, contest, defense, action or suit, before any or all persons, bodies, commissions, tribunals or courts, provided that notice of intention so to do shall be given to the other party at least five (5) days before delinquency occurs; and after payment may claim, recover or obtain the repayment or return of any and all moneys paid in satisfaction of said taxes, assessments, im-

positions, payments, charges or levies, license
fees or penalties from the other party hereto, who by the terms hereof should have paid
such taxes, assessments, impositions, payments,
charges or levies, lecense fees or penalties. It is the
intention hereof that either party may take any appropriate step or proceeding whatever, whether
herein enumerated or not, to secure to itself its
rights and remedies in the premises, and it is understood that in the event of non-payment, as a condition to taking and prosecuting such appropriate
steps, the party taking and prosecuting the same
shall procure, preserve and maintain such a stay
of all proceedings for the enforcement or collection of such taxes, assessments, impositions, payments, charges or levies, license fees or penalties
as will fully protect and preserve the title and rights
of both parties in and to the demised premises and
shall provide for payment of the contested tax or
charge, together with all penalties, interest, costs
and expenses, by a deposit of a sufficient sum of
money, or by a good and sufficient undertaking, as
may be required or permitted by law to accomplish
such stay. In the event of any such contest or proceedings hereunder, the party taking the same agrees
within five days after the final termination thereof,
adversely to the party contesting said tax, assessment,
imposition, payment, charge or levy, license fee or
penalty, to pay and discharge the amount involved
therein or affected thereby, together with all penalties, fines, interests, costs and expenses that may
accrue thereon or may result therefrom.

Should either party within the times herein limited be in default in the payment or discharge *or* any of said taxes, assessments, impositions, payments, charges or levies, license fees or penalties to be paid, borne or discharged by [40] it, the other party, except in cases of contest and stay of proceedings as above provided, may, at its option, without notice to or demand upon the party so in default, pay or discharge, or redeem, or in anywise compromise or adjust the same, or any part thereof, together with any penalties, fines, interest, costs or expenses which may be added thereto by reason of such default, and in any and every one of such instances, the lagality and validity of any such payment to the full amount so paid or expanded, and the regularity of all proceedings had in respect thereto, or toward enforcement thereof, shall, as between the parties hereto, conclusively be deemed to exist. Any amount so paid hereunder shall be repaid by the other party within thirty (30) days after notice to the party for whom payment was made, together with interest thereon at the rate of Seven Per Cent (7%) per annum from the date of such payment.

Article IV.

Present Building.

Lessee may, at Lessee's option, at any time during the term of this *lease* lease, add additional stories to the present building upon the demised premises and make any other additions, changes, or alterations in said present building, structural or otherwise, provided such additions, changes or alterations can be made without impairing the strength or substantially depreciating the value of said building and can be lawfully made; and provided, further, that said building shall be at all times a "Class A" building as defined in the Building Ordinances of the City of Los Angeles in force at the date of this lease, and shall be a store, bank, hotel, loft, and/or office building. As to the construction of such additional stories and as to the making of any of said additions, changes or alterations, the work thereof shall be done strictly in accordance with all laws, ordinances or governmental regulations which may then be in force with reference thereto, and provided that in the event that the cost thereof shall be in excess of twenty-five thousand dollars ($25,000.00), Lessee shall, prior to the commencement of any such work, procure for the benefit of Lessor, a suitable surety bond satisfactory to Lessor, to protect Lessor and said property against all mechanics' liens or materialmen's liens or liens of like nature which may be created by reason of the doing of such work.

Lessee convenants to hold Lessor and the property hereby leased, harmless from, and to indemnity Lessor from all loss or liability of any and every kind, nature or description accruing or happening during the term of this lease, and caused directly or indirectly by Lessee in the removal of such existing building or structure, the excavation for and construction of any new building, or by any subsequent work of repair, alteration, restoration or reconstruction, additions or changes, and particularly from all loss or liability of any and every kind to any adjacent landowner in the withdrawal of lateral support to adjacent lands by reason of the excavation for any new building or by reason of severance of prior building.

Lessee covenants that Lessor shall not be obligated or required to repair or to reconstruct or to maintain or to make additions to, or alterations of any building or other improvement whatsoever at any time situated upon the demised premises or to bear the expense of any work, repair, reconstruction, damage or maintenance whatsoever in or about the demised premises.

Lessee shall have the right to join or connect the present building upon the demised premises with any other structure or structures upon any adjoining or adjacent lands so as to permit the use of said structure or structures in conjunction with and/or as a part of said present building, and for that purpose shall [41] have the right to remove connecting walls or portion thereof in said present building; but any such joinder *of* connection shall be made and shall be at all times during the term hereof maintained in such manner that such joinder and connection may be broken and terminated and each of said buildings or structures separated from the other and proper walls erected without any injury to said present building.

Lessee agrees that at the expiration of the term of this lease, whenever and however occurring, (it

being hereby specifically understood that the holder
of the Lessee's interest hereunder at the time of
such termination shall be bound by and not relieved
from this covenant notwithstanding such termination, and that the owner of the Lessee's interest at
the time of such joinder shall be bound by and not
relieved from this covenant notwithstanding any assignment hereof as herein expressly permitted) to
wall up any of the sides of said present building
which are then being used or which may theretofore have been used in connection with another
building, and to pay Lessor any costs, damage or expense to Lessor arising out of the separation of said
present building from any adjoining building.

Article V.
Mechanics' and Materialmen's Liens.

Lessee further covenants to pay, or cause to be
paid, all the expenses of every kind, character or
description, including bills for labor and materials
incurred in connection with the construction, demolition, excavation, removal, maintenance, repair or
other physical action required or permitted under
this lease in respect of any building or improvement whatsoever at any time or times upon said
demised premises.

Lessee covenants to keep all of the demised
premises and the improvements at any time or times
thereon at all times during the term of this lease,
free and clear of mechanics' liens, materialmen's
liens and other liens of like nature, and that Lessee
will at all times fully protect and indemnity Lessor

(7%) per annum from the time of payment by Lessor until repaid by Lessee, and such sums shall be repaid by Lessee to Lessor as so much additional rent at or before the next ensuing rent day after payment by Lessor.

The payment, adjustment or compromise by Lessor of any such claim, lien or judgment in the manner above described, or the payment and making of such redemption in the manner above described, shall be deemed conclusive evidence of the validity of such claim, lien, judgment or sale, as between the parties hereto.

Should any liens be filed against the property covered by this lease or the improvements thereon, or should any action of any character affecting the title to any of said property, or any interest or estate of Lessor or Lessee therein, be commenced, each party hereto shall give to the other written notice thereof as soon as notice of such lien or actions comes to the knowledge of such party.

Lessor, or Lessor's agents, shall at all times have the right to go upon and inspect the demised premises and also to post and keep posted thereon notices provided for by Section 1192 of the Code of Civil Procedure of California, or by any other law of said State *or which* Lessor may deem to be for the protection of Lessor and said property from mechanics' liens or liens of a similar nature.

Notice is hereby given by Lessor that any mechanics' liens or other liens shall in no way, manner or degree affect the claims or rights of Lessor on any building or improvements place on said property, or attach to said property, or diminish or suspend said claims or rights in any manner whatsoever.

Article VI.

Insurance and Casualties.

It is expressly covenanted and agreed that the destruction or partial destruction of any building or improvements now or at any time situated upon the demised premises from any cause whatsoever, either human or divine, shall not release Lessee from this lease or from any of the obligations of Lessee hereunder, whether for the payment of rent or otherwise. [43]

In the event of any destruction, whether partial or total, of the present building upon the demised premises, or any substitute therefor, addition thereto or replacement thereof, from any cause whatsoever, either human or divine, during the term of this lease, the Lessee covenants with all reasonable diligence, at the cost and expense of Lessee, to repair, restore or reconstruct said building as the case may require, so as to place the same in substantially the condition it was in immediately before the casualty, or to repair, restore or reconstruct said building or to construct a new building so that the building so repaired, restored, reconstructed or newly constructed, shall be a "Class A" building as hereinbefore defined of store, bank, loft, hotel and/or office type, and, in the case of a newly constructed building or of a loft building whether newly constructed or not, of a value not less than the undepreciated reproduction value of the building so destroyed, immediately before such destruction, (and if, in whole or in part, of hotel type, of a value of not less than One Million Dollars ($1,000,000) and the Lessee shall have all such work of repair, restoration, reconstruction, or construction completed and the building so repaired, restored, reconstructed or newly constructed, ready for occupancy, free from all mechanics' liens or other liens of a like nature, as soon after such casualty as practicable and in any event within twenty-four (24) months after such casualty, and shall pay all costs and expenses of such repair, restoration, reconstruction or construction; provided, however, that Lessee shall not be required to repair, restore, reconstruct or construct any building so long as it may be prevented from so doing by governmental or military authority. Lessee shall also promptly, at its own cost and expense, repair any and every damage that may be done to any and every building constructed, restored, reconstructed, rebuilt or maintained on said demised premises during the term of this lease, except as hereinafter expressly provided.

If any said building is either seriously damaged or destroyed during the last ten years of the term hereby created, Lessee, at Lessee's option, may, if not in default in any of Lessee's obligations under this lease, be relieved of the obligation to reconstruct or repair the same upon Lessee releasing to Lessor any and all insurance moneys which may be due or payable or collected on account of the insurance carried on account of said improvements, buildings or structures, then on the property, and at the same time delivering the possession of the leased premises and every part thereof to Lessor; provided, however, that the Lessee shall pay all rent, taxes and other charges accruing hereunder up to the date of such surrender of possession.

Lessee covenants at Lessee's own expense to keep the present building, or any replacement thereof, substitution therefor or addition thereto, insured against loss and/or damage by fire in some insurance company or companies (which so long as the distinction is used in the said County of Los Angeles, shall be of the class known as "board" companies or that organization commonly referred to as "Affiliated Underwriters" (Ernest W. Brown, Inc. being its present atorney-in-fact), or such other companies as may from time to time be expressly approved by Lessor in writing), at all times during the life of this lease, such fire insurance to be in an amount not less than eighty per cent (80%) of the full insurable value of such building, or in an amount as near thereto as can be obtained. Such fire insurance shall be so written as not to include the so-called "fallen building clause."

Lessee covenants, at Lessee's own expense, to keep the present building or any replacement thereof, substitution therefor, or addition thereto, insured against loss and/or damage by earthquake in some insurance company or companies approved in writing by the Lessor (provided, however, that no approval shall be required of that organization commonly referred to as "affiliated underwriters," Ernest W. Brown, Inc., being its present attorney-in-fact, or of London Lloyds or [44] any company of the class known as "board" companies, said companies being hereby approved), at all times during the life of this lease, said earthquake insurance to be in an amount not less than eighty percent (80%) of the full insurable value of such building, or in an amount as near thereto as can be obtained. If, however, it should be determined as hereinafter provided that the cost of such earthquake insurance is exorbitant then while such cost remains exorbitant the amount of such earthquake insurance so required may be reduced to such amount as can be obtained at a cost equal to the cost of earthquake insurance in an amount not less than eighty percent (80%) of the full insurable value of such building for the last period during which such cost shall be determined not to have been exorbitant. If however, such reduced amount of earthquake insurance is less than the maximum provable amount of damage, determined as hereinafter provided, which said building would suffer in event of earthquake, then the lessee will provide and cause to be deposited with the trustee for insurance hereunder security (of a character determined, as hereinafter provided, to be satisfactory) for the payment to such trustee in case of damage by earthquake to such building of an amount equal to the difference between the reduced amount of earthquake insurance so required to be carried and the amount of the maximum provable damage (as so determined). Provided, however, that in the event the cost of such earthquake insurance is determined to be exorbitant, as aforesaid, the Lessee may, at its option, in lieu of earthquake insurance and/or in lieu of the security herein provided for, carry in favor of the Lessor, so called single interest insurance or other insurance, written by solvent insurance companies qualified to do business in the State of California in form satisfactory to the Lessor or determined by arbitration as hereinafter provided to be satisfactory, insuring the restoration of the building as by this lease required after injury or destruction by earthquake, the same to be in principal amount equal to the amount of other earthquake insurance by the terms hereto required and not at said time being carried. If at any time and from time to time Lessor or Lessee shall allege that cost of earthquake insurance is exorbitant or not exorbitant or shall desire to have fixed or revised the estimate of the maximum probable amount of damage which would be suffered by said building or buildings in event of earthquake or should desire to have decided the sufficiency or insufficiency of security provided for hereunder, then the Lessor or the Lessee, as the case may be, may serve on the other a written request to have any or all of said questions (the same to be specified in such request) so raised determined by arbitration as herein provided. The party making such request shall designate therein the name and address of an arbitrator selected by it to represent it in such arbitration. Any request for arbitration made as aforesaid by either party hereto shall be duly executed in behalf of said party, and under its corporate name and seal, by its president or vice president, and by its secretary or assistant secretary, and shall be accompanied by a certified copy of a resolution of the board of directors of the party authorizing and directing the making of such request, and authorizing the appointment of the arbitrator therein designated. Within five (5) days after the service of any such request and designation, Lessor or Lessee, as the case may be, on whom such request is served, shall designate an arbitrator to represent it in such arbitration, and shall notify the other party in writing of the name and address of the arbitrator so designated, and within three (3) days after such last mentioned notice Lessor and/or Lessee shall notify said two arbitrators of their designation and appointment as such arbitrators, and shall instruct them to proceed with the arbitration. Within ten (10) days after either Lessor or Lessee shall have given such notice, said two arbitrators shall designate a third arbitrator. If at the expiration of said ten (10) day period, said two arbitrators shall have failed to designate as such third arbitrator a person who shall have accepted such appointment, then, upon the request of either arbitrator, Lessor or Lessee, the person acting as the presiding judge of the Superior Court of the State of California, in and for the County of Los Angeles, may designate such third arbitrator. The three arbitrators so selected shall constitute a board of arbitration for the pur- [45] pose of determining the question so raised. Any arbitrator designated either by Lessor or Lessee may or may not be an officer or employee of Lessor or Lessee, as the case may be, making such designation.

Within twenty (20) days after the selection of such third arbitrator said board of arbitration shall determine and answer the question or questions so raised, and shall notify Lessee and Lessor in writing of the determination so made. For the purpose of making any such determination, and for all other purposes in connection with any such arbitration, the decision of any two of the members of the said board of arbitration shall be binding upon the parties hereto; and from and after any such determination the Lessee covenants and agrees to comply therewith until such determination is revised, amended or revoked by arbitration in accordance with the provisions hereof.

All expenses of every kind and nature whatsoever in connection with any such arbitration, including among other things the compensation of said arbitrators and all expenses incurred by said arbitrators in connection with said arbitration, shall be paid by the Lessee; and in no event shall the Lessor be required to designate any arbitrator as aforesaid, pursuant to any request for arbitration made by the Lessee, until and unless the lessee shall have furnished to the Lessor indemnity satisfactory to the Lessor against any and all liability and/or expense which may be incurred by the Lessor in connection with any such arbitration (but the Lessor shall not unreasonably or arbitrarily reject any such proposed indemnity). Should any request for arbitration be served as aforesaid by the Lessor, the Lessee forthwith shall furnish to the Lessor indemnity satisfactory to the Lessor against any and all liability and/or expense which may be incurred by the Lessor in connection with such arbitration (but the Lessor shall not unreasonably or arbitrarily reject any such proposed indemnity). Should the Lessee fail to furnish the Lessor with indemnity as aforesaid, the Lessor may, nevertheless, but shall not be required to, proceed with such arbitration, but this provision shall not be construed to relieve the Lessee from its default in failing to furnish such indemnity, nor from the consequences of any such default, and any moneys expended by the Lessor in connection with such arbitration shall be repaid to the Lessor by the Lessee upon demand, together with interest from the date the same were expended by the Lessor to the date of repayment by the Lessee at the rate of ten per cent (10%) per annum.

Should Lessor or Lessee, as the case may be, upon whom any such request for arbitration is served, fail to designate an arbitrator within the time and in the manner herein provided, then, at the option of the party making such request, the arbitrator designated by such party shall be vested with full power and authority to determine the questions so raised, and any such determination by any such sole arbitrator shall have the same effect as any arbitration made as aforesaid by a board of arbitration created as aforesaid.

For the purpose of determining the questions so raised, any such board of arbitration or any such sole arbitrator shall be vested with absolute discretion as to the manner and method of making such determination and as to the matters which are properly to be considered in the making of such determination; and without limiting the effect of the foregoing general language, it is expressly understood and agreed that any such board of arbitration and/or any such sole arbitrator may, but shall not be required to, take into consideration any or all of the following matters;

(a) Estimates by architects and/or engineers and/or contractors of the probable damage that would be done to said improvements by earthquake. **[46]**

(b) The cost of said insurance in relation to the protection gained.

(c) The probable ability of Lessee to restore any such building or improvement in event of damage by earthquake without the use of earthquake insurance money.

By agreement between Lessor and Lessee, the time within which anything is required to be done under the provisions of this section may be extended.

In the event of any arbitration as herein provided, Lessor and Lessee shall each cooperate with the other and with the board of arbitration and/or sole arbitrator, as the case may be. In particular, Lessee covenants and agrees to furnish to any such board of arbitration and/or sole arbitra*tion* any and all financial information, statements and all data relative to the financial condition of Lessee as such board of arbitration or such sole arbitrator may request; and Lessee further covenants and agrees that any such board of arbitration and/or sole arbitrator shall have full access to all books, records and accounts of Lessee.

If any arbitrator is unwilling or unable to act, a successor shall be appointed by the same person or persons and in the same manner herein provided for the appointment of the arbitrator whose place is to be filled.

In the event of any arbitration as herein provided, the arbitrator or arbitrators acting therein shall be entitled to a reasonable compensation for their services in connection with such arbitration, which compensation shall be paid as aforesaid by Lessee. In the event of any arbitration as herein provided, the board of arbitration or sole arbitrator, as the case may be, shall have the right, at the expense of Lessee, to obtain such estimates, appraisals, audits, opinions and/or other data, and for all or any such purposes to employ such attorneys, valuers, surveyors, engineers, accountants, and/or other experts and/or such other reasonable means as such board of arbitration or sole arbitrator may deem necessary.

Should Lessee fail to keep said building and improvements insured as herein provided, or to obtain and maintain any other insurance for which provision is herein made, Lessor at its option may procure such insurance and keep said property so insured, and any sums paid out by Lessor for such insurance shall be paid by Lessee to Lessor as so much additional rent at or before the next ensuing rent day after the payment thereof by Lessor, together with interest thereon at the rate of ten percent (10%) per annum from the date of payment by Lessor until repaid by Lessee.

As long as the board of fire underwriters for the District in which the premises are situated shall exist and make such certification the full insurable value of said building shall be deemed to be the sum certified as such by said board of fire underwriters.

All policies covering said insurance shall be in such form that the loss, if any, shall be payable to Title Insurance and Trust Company, of Los Angeles, as trustee, or to some other bank or trust company in the City of Los Angeles, authorized to carry on a trust company business, approved by Lessor, as trustee, for the benefit of Lessor and Lessee as their respective interests may appear, and said policies shall, as soon as issued, be delivered to said trustee and thereafter be held by the trustee. Said company or its successor in trust, or other

ed,
he
ole
see
rd
all
la-
ch
re-
iat
ra-
nd

et,
on
ed
ice

:o-
in
'or
)n,
by
in
ra-
he
p-
'or
ys,
'or
as

bank or trust company agreed upon, is made and
constituted a trustee to hold such insurance policies
and to receive any money that may become due or
paid thereunder and authorized to do any and all
acts necessary for collection, said moneys to be held
by said trustee as security for the performance by
Lessee of lessee's agreement to repair, [47] rebuild,
and reconstruct any and every injury and damage
or destruction to said building, and to pay out the
same as herein provided: it being understood, however, that such trustee shall be in no manner obligated hereunder, except to receive and pay out any
moneys that may be received by it as such trustee,
together with such interest as may be paid by said
trustee at the time upon like trusts of similar size,
and is authorized to retain from said trust fund
the necessary expenses incidental to the collection
of any of said funds and a reasonable amount for
its services in connection with this trust. Should
said Title Insurance and Trust Company, of Los
Angeles, or its successors as to this trust, be unwilling or unable, owing to the laws and regulations
then in force, to act as herein provided, then in any
event the said insurance moneys shall be payable
to some other bank or trust company in Los Angeles, California, authorized to transact a trust
business, to be approved by Lessor, and in such
manner as may be permitted by said laws and
regulations, in such a way that all moneys paid or
recovered on account of such policies, or any of
them, shall constitute a trust fund as herein provided.

All insurance moneys collected by said trustee shall be paid to Lessee in four (4) equal installments as the injury done by any casualty insured against is repaired by Lessee, and the repairs paid for; the first instalment to be paid when one-quarter ($\frac{1}{4}$) in value of such repairs has been made and paid for; another instalment when one-half ($\frac{1}{2}$) in value of such repairs has been made and paid for; another quarter when three-quarters ($\frac{3}{4}$) in value of such repairs has been made and paid for; and all of the balance of said moneys shall be paid to Lessee, or said Lessee's order, when such repairs have been completed and paid for, and there has been furnished said trustee a certificate or guarantee of Title Insurance and Trust Company, Los Angeles, or Title Guarantee and Trust Company, Los Angeles, or of some other Title company satisfactory to Lessor that the time for filing of mechanics' or other like liens has expired and that no such liens are outstanding. If said certificate of such title company shows that the time for filing of mechanics' or other like liens has expired and that no such liens are outstanding except certain specifically enumerated liens, then such trustee is hereby authorized to pay to Lessee or Lessee's order all of the balance of said moneys, except such part thereof as the trustee shall deem expedient to retain for the purpose of protecting said property against such liens, including interest, attorneys' fees, costs and other charges in connection therewith.

All such repairs or reconstruction shall be made under the supervision of a certified architect and no instalment of said insurance moneys shall be paid to Lessee, or Lessee's order, until there has been filed with said trustee a sworn statement of said architect in charge of said repairs to the effect that the required pro rata proportion of such repairs as above provided has been made and paid for. The sworn statement, when filed with the trustee shall be conclusive proof of the repairs and payments so made, so far as said trustee is concerned.

In the event of any default of Lessee regarding any of the terms, agreements, covenants or conditions in this lease to be by Lessee performed, which shall result in *an* termination of this lease by Lessor in the manner hereinafter specified, all insurance moneys and policies shall be forthwith assigned and delivered to Lessor.

Lessee agrees to provide, pay for and maintain any and every kind of insurance that may, at any time during the term of this lease, be required by any law, ordinance or governmental regulation to be carried or maintained by the owner of all or any part of the leased premises or of any building that may be erected thereon, or by the owner of the reversionary estate thereon, or by the owner or holder of this lease or of the leasehold estate created hereby; and any [48] sub-lease shall provide that the tenant therein and every sub-tenant and occupant of said leased premises, or of any part thereof, shall provide, carry and maintain all of such insurance that may at any time be required of them or any of them by any law, ordinance or governmental regulation pertaining thereto; and Lessee agrees to hold and save Lessor free and harmless from all liability, loss, damage or expense which may accrue by reason of the failure of Lessee, or any other person or persons above designated, to provide, carry or maintain all or any part of such insurance.

The Lessee further covenants to procure at the cost and expense of the Lessee, and to maintain in force during the term of this lease, in addition to all other insurance mentioned herein, public liability insurance in an amount not less than twenty-five thousand dollars ($25,000.00) to any person, and one hundred thousaid dollars ($100,000.00) in any one accident, and adequate boiler insurance and elevator insurance in an amount not less than twenty-five thousand dollars ($25,000.00) to any one person, and one hundred thousand dollars ($100,000.00) in any one accident, and adequate insurance against liability for workmen's compensation, and also during any periods of construction or alteration work during the term of this lease adequate insurance against liability arising on account of injuries to workmen and employees, pedestrians, and any other persons or property, caused directly or indirectly by any building, construction or alteration work under the provisions of this lease. All insurance policies mentioned in this paragraph shall be written in standard and solvent insurance companies doing business in California. The Lessee agrees that nothing in this section of the lease contained, nor the fact that the amount of such insurance hereinabove mentioned is or may be insufficient to fully protect the Lessor and the Lessee, and each of them, and the said premises, and building and improvements, free and harmless from all liability, shall limit or in any manner relieve the Lessee from said Lessee's obligations to indemnity and save and hold harmless the Lessor, as in this lease provided.

Lessee agrees, from time to time, to keep Lessor advised of all insurance which Lessee has procured under the requirements of this lease, and that within thirty (30) days after the same has been procured or renewed, Lessee will deliver to said trustee the original or original duplicate receipt or receipts for all insurance premiums on such insurance.

Should Lessee fail to keep said building and improvements insured as herein provided, or obtained and maintain any other insurance as herein provided, Lessor, at lessor's option, twenty-four (24) hours after written notice to Lessee of its intention so to do, may procure such insurance and keep said property so insured, and any sums paid out by Lessor for such insurance shall be paid by Lessee to the Lessor at or before the next ensuing rent date after the payment thereof by Lessor, together with interest thereon at the rate of seven per cent (7%) per annum, from date of payment by Lessor until paid by Lessee.

Lessor shall not be required to repair or to reconstruct or to maintain the present building or improvements upon the demised premises, or to bear any expense of any repair, reconstruction or maintenance, or to repair or to reconstruct or maintain any new building or improvements placed or to be placed therein at any time whatsoever, or to bear the expense of any repair, reconstruction or maintenance in, upon or about the demised premises, or any improvements thereon.

In the event of any destruction, whether partial or total, of the present building upon the demised premises or any substitute therefor, addition thereto or replacement thereof, from any cause whatsoever either human or divine, during the term of this lease, the Lessee shall before commencing any work of repair, restoration, reconstruction or new construction, cause to be filed with the trustee [49] for the holding of insurance moneys a certificate of a certified architect under whose supervision such work is to be done, stating the amount of the contract price, or if there is no contract price then the estimated cost, of such work. If the amount so certified be more than the amount of insurance moneys then in the hands of such Trustee, Lessee covenants and agrees that it will forthwith, and prior to the commencement of such work, either (a) deposit with such trustee the amount of such excess cost either in cash or in marketable securities under a deposit agreement satisfactory to such trustee or (b) deliver to Lessor a bond, inuring to the sole benefit of

Lessor, in the amount of such excess cost with Lessee as principal and either individual surety or sureties satisfactory to Lessor, or a corporate surety company, as surety, guaranteeing the completion of such work, within the time provided under this lease, free from all liens of mechanics, materialmen or other like liens.

Article VII.

Hypothecation by Lessee.

Nothing in this indenture contained shall be construed to prevent Lessee from encumbering the whole or any part of its leasehold interest in the demised lands by mortgage, pledge, trust deed, bond issue, or otherwise; but the rights of any mortgagee, pledgee, trustee, beneficiary, bondholder, assignee, or trustee under any bond issue, shall at all times be subject to the rights of Lessor to exercise any of the rights, options and remedies in this lease or by law provided, including the right to terminate this lease in case of default as herein provided, and shall in no wise alter, be secured by, affect or diminish the reversionary interest, or any interest or estate, of Lessor, to the lands and premises herein described, or in or to any buildings or improvements now placed or which may be hereafter placed thereon. The purchaser at foreclosure or other sale of said leasehold interest or any part thereof under any such assignment, mortgage, pledge, trust deed, bond issue or other instrument, shall assume, and by virtue of such purchase shall be deemed to have assumed, personally, payment of rentals, and performance and observance of all obligations of Lessee set forth under this lease, and such purchaser shall be obligated at Lessor's request to execute and acknowledge, by way of further assurance, an instrument in writing expressly accepting and assuming all said obligations and agreeing to and with Lessor that purchaser shall be bound by all of the covenants, agreements, restrictions and conditions of this lease, subject, however, to being released therefrom as in the case of other assignees as hereinafter provided.

Article VIII.

Notices.

All notices or demands or documents of any kind which either party may be required, or may desire, to serve upon or deliver to the other under the terms of this lease, may be served upon, or delivered to such party by delivering said notice, demand or document personally to the president, vice-president, secretary or treasurer of such party (or, if an individual, then to said person), or by mailing the same or a copy thereof by registered mail, postage prepaid, to said party at its address, in the City of Los Angeles, California, filed in writing with the party giving such notice, which address may be changed to any other address in said City of Los Angeles, California, from time to time, by a writing filed with the other party. Until such time as either party hereto, or its assignee, files in writing with the other party any other address in the City of Los Angeles, California, *then that give* below, Lessor's address is hereby fixed at Title Insurance Building, Los Angeles, California, and Lessee's address is hereby fixed at 720 Roosevelt Building, 727 West 7th Street, Los Angeles, California. [50]

In the event that the record interest of either Lessee or Lessor shall be vested in more than one person, no address shall be deemed to be effectively changed until a new address is designated in writing, as aforesaid, by the record holders of more than an undivided one-half interest thereof, and any such new address designated by the record holders of more than an undivided one-half interest shall be deemed to be an effective change of address hereunder.

In the event of service by registered mail, such service shall be deemed complete forty-eight (48) hours after the deposit of the same in the Post Office in the City of Los Angeles, California, addressed as herein permitted. If either party shall be required or may desire to serve any such notice or demand, or deliver any document upon or to any co-partnership or association of persons other than a corporation, service of such notice or demand or delivery of said document to any one of such co-partners or members of such association in any of the manners as aforesaid shall be sufficient as a personal service thereof.

In the event that Lessee shall execute a mortgage or deed of trust of Lessee's interest hereunder, to secure an issue of bonds, or one or more notes, Lessee or the mortgagee or trustee mentioned in said mort-

gage or deed of trust, may furnish, and upon written
request of Lessor shall furnish, to Lessor within
thirty (30) days after the execution thereof a copy
of said mortgage or deed of trust, and may designate, in a written instrument concurrently delivered
to Lessor, a place in the City of Los Angeles, here
designated as the place of business where notice
may be served upon the mortgagee or trustee in such
mortgage or deed of trust described; and, in that
event, Lessor agrees that if Lessor shall give notice
to Lessee upon which Lessor shall rely for any termination of Lessee's interest hereunder, Lessor,
within three (3) days after service of said notice,
shall serve a notice of similar import on said trustee, or mortgagee, by leaving the same at the place
of business so designated.

Until notified in writing to the contrary by the
person specifically named herein as Lessor, Lessee
shall be entitled to assume such person is the only
owner upon whom Lessee shall serve any notice or
deliver any copy of instruments, and service upon
the owner specifically named in this indenture, and
then in being, actually having a place of business
in the County of Los Angeles, State of California,
shall be good and sufficient notice to Lessor and all
persons, if any, claiming under Lessor; and provided further that in the event that land trust certificates or certificates of beneficial interest under
any trust or agreement covering the reversionary
estate in the demised premises are issued, any notice which the Lessee shall be required or desires to

serve upon the Lessor shall be sufficient if served
upon the then trustee under the trust or agreement
under which such land trust certificates or certificates of beneficial interests shall have been issued.

Article IX.

Use of Premises and Indemnity

Lessee covenants at all times during the term of
this lease (subject only to the express provisions
elsewhere contained in this indenture), at the cost
and expense of Lessee, to keep any building and
other improvement erected upon the demised premises during the term of this lease in first-class condition and repair, and in a good, safe and secure
condition, Lessee further covenants at all times during the term of this lease to keep all other appurtenances unto the said demised premises belonging
and the sidewalks steps and excavations under [51]
the sidewalks, in good repair and in good, safe and
secure condition and to conform to all municipal
ordinances, and all laws and governmental regulations affecting said premises and appurtenances and
the sidewalks and streets in front of and adjoining
said premises.

Lessee covenants that the demised premises and
all buildings thereon at the commencement of the
term of said lease and thereafter erected shall,
during the term hereof, be used only and exclusively
for proper and legitimate purposes; that Lessee will
not use, or suffer or permit any person to use, in
any manner whatsoever, the demised premises, or
any building or other improvements at any time

thereon or any part thereof for any extra-hazardous purpose, or for any purpose or use in violation of the laws of the United States or of the State of California, or of the ordinances of the County or City of Los Angeles, or rules or regulations of any duly constituted Board or Commission of the City of Los Angeles, the County of Los Angeles, or the State of California, or for any unlawful purpose whatsoever, or for any trade or business that may be unlawful, and that Lessee will not use, or suffer or permit any person to use the demised premises, or any building or improvement at any time thereon or any part thereof, for the purpose of conducting a saloon, even though the same might be from time to time lawful during the term of this lease.

All sub-leases made by Lessee shall contain the same provisions as are contained in this lease as to restrictions on the use of said premises. Should any sub-tenant engage in any unlawful business or use the premises in a manner forbidden by this lease, Lessee shall promptly dispossess him, but if the sub-lease contains the required provisions, Lessee shall not be deemed in default for delay involved in legal proceedings being taken and had against the sub-lessee with all due diligence and dispatch; provided, that Lessee shall in no event be excused from any of the obligations of Lessee to indemnity and save and hold harmless Lessor.

Lessee further covenants at all times during the term of this lease, at the cost and expense of Lessee, to make such alterations, additions and changes in and about the demised premises, appurtenances thereto, and improvements at any time thereon as may be required to be made by any legal or governmental authority or by the laws, ordinances or regulations of any governmental authority. Lessee covenants not to make or permit any addition, change or alteration of any improvement or building at any time on the demised premises except in accordance with the provisions herein expressly contained.

Lessee covenants to indemnify and keep and save Lessor harmless from any penalty or damage or charges imposed for any violation of any of said laws, ordinances or regulations, whether occasioned by neglect, omission or wilful act of Lessee, or any person on said premises holding under Lessee, or the former owners of said premises. Lessee covenants to indemnify and save and keep harmless Lessor against and from any loss, cost, damage, claim, expense, or liability arising out of any accident or other occurrence causing injury to any person or property whomsoever or whatsoever and due directly or indirectly to the use or disuse of said premises, or any part thereof by Lessee or by any person or persons holding under Lessee, or the former owners of said premises, or arising out of any failure of Lessee in any respect to comply with the requirements and provisions of this lease, as well as all costs and attorneys fees incurred in any proceeding, action or suit growing out of or in connection therewith.

In the event that, during the term of this lease, under any present or future law or statute of the United States, the State of California, or the County or City of Los Angeles, or under any rule, order or regulation of any duly constituted Board, Commission or Official of any of said Governmental units, any order of abatement or any order or judgment preventing the use of the demised premises by Lessee shall be made upon the ground that the demised premises, or any part thereof, consti- [52] tute a nuisance or are used or have been used in violation of law, Lessee covenants that Lessee shall not be relieved thereby, or by reason of Lessee's loss of the possession of the demised premises of the payment of rentals or of any other of Lessee's liabilities or obligations under this indenture.

Article X.

Assignment

Lessee covenants that it will not assign all or any share of said leasehold interest or estate in the demised premises, at any time during the term hereof, except in strict accordance with the covenants, agreements, provisions and conditions of this Article X, but nothing herein contained shall prevent Lessee from sub-leasing the whole or any part of the demised premises at any time. Such subleasing, however, shall not release Lessee from its obligations and/or responsibilities under this lease, but Lessee (or its assignee, as herein permitted) shall at all times in such event remain primarily respon-

sible and liable for each and all of such obligations
and responsibilities.

It is expressly covenanted and agreed and notice
is hereby given to all persons that any assignment
of all or any share of said leasehold estate or interest of Lessee made otherwise than in strict accordance with the covenants, agreements, provisions
and conditions of this article, shall be wholly null
and void; provided, however, that this article shall
not be construed to nullify the rights of any trustee
under any trust deed, mortgage or pledge, or any
trustee, bondholder or beneficiary under any bond
issue, or any person claiming under or through
them, as specified and defined in Article VII hereof
entitled "Hypothecation by Lessee."

Lessee covenants and it is hereby expressly provided and conditioned that any such assignment
(other than an incumbrance of the Lessee's leasehold
interest by mortgage, pledge, trust deed, or otherwise
as herein permitted) shall be evidenced by an instrument in writing duly executed and acknowledged
by both parties thereto and recorded in the Recorder's office in the County of Los Angeles, State of
California and that in any such instrument the
assignee shall expressly accept and assume all of
the obligations contained in this lease to be kept
and performed by Lessee, and shall agree to and
with Lessor that the assignee shall be bound by all
the covenants, agreements, provisions and conditions
hereof; and that an executed original of said instrument shall be delivered to Lessor before any such
assignment shall become valid or effective.

Notwithstanding anything to the contrary contained in this indenture, Lessee may, in accordance
with this Article X, assign the whole or any part
of Lessee's leasehold interest or estate in the entire
demised premises, at any time after the first one
year of the term of this lease, provided that Lessee
shall not at the time of said assignment be in default in respect to any of the terms or provisions
hereof. In the event of any such assignment of the
whole of said interest after the first year of the
term of this lease Lessee shall be released from all
obligations thereafter accruing hereunder, subject,
however, to the exception contained in Article IV
hereof and to the following exception, to-wit: That
if prior to the time of such assignment there has
been any destruction, whether partial or total, of
the present building upon the demised premises, or
any substitute therefor, addition thereto or replacement thereof, from any cause whatsoever, either
human or divine, then Lessee shall not be released
from any of its obligations hereunder, unless and
until all work of repair, restoration, reconstruction
or new construction required under this lease has
been completed, free from all liens of mechanics,
[53] materialmen or other like liens. The assignee
of Lessee and all subsequent assignees, in the event
of assignment of the aforesaid leasehold interest in
strict compliance with the aforesaid provisions and
limitations, shall after any such assignment be released and discharged from obligations thereafter
accruing in the same manner as in the case of the

original assignment, but subject to the same exception hereinbefore in this paragraph stated.

Lessee further covenants, and it is hereby provided and conditioned, that the provisions, conditions, covenants and agreements of this Article X shall not be deemed to have been waived or exhausted by one or more assignments, but that each and every of said conditions, restrictions, covenants, agreements and provisions shall apply to and bind, not only Lessee herein named, but each and every assignee and succeeding assignees and successors in interest and legal representatives of any of them in the same manner as Lessee.

Article XI.
Forfeiture by Default, and Redemption

1. Should Lessee at any time during the term hereof be in default in the payment of the rental or other moneys herein agreed or required to be paid by Lessee, or commit or suffer a breach or default in respect to the performance of any other of the covenants, promises, undertakings, agreements, obligations or conditions in this instrument contained or any part or portion of any such covenants, promises, undertakings, agreements, obligations or conditions, and *may* such default or breach shall continue for a period of thirty (30) days after written notice thereof by Lessor to Lessee, then in any such event, Lessor at said Lessor's option, may, at any time after the expiration of said thirty (30) days' period, immediately terminate this lease and the leasehold

interest or estate hereby created, and Lessor may, at any time after the expiration of said thirty (30) days' period, enter upon said demised premises and the building and improvements thereon, either with or without process of law, and remove all persons therefrom, and all buildings and improvements situated on said premises at the time of making such default by Lessee, and any additions to said building or improvements shall remain on said premises and become absolutely the property of Lessor; and no compensation therefor shall be allowed or paid Lessee; and without the necessity of any other or further notice or demand whatsoever, all right, title and interest of Lessees therein or thereto, whether in law or equity, shall immediately cease and terminate, except as hereinafter provided in section 2 of this Article XI.

Without in any wise limiting the generality and the effect of the paragraph preceeding this, Lessee covenants and agrees upon the termination of said demised term at such election of Lessor, or by the lapse of time, or in any other way, that Lessee will surrender and deliver up the above described premises and property peaceably to Lessor, Lessor's agents or attorneys, immediately, in good condition and repair, reasonable wear and tear thereof excepted, and if Lessee, Lessee's agents, attorneys or tenants hold the premises or any part thereof one day after the same shall have been surrendered according to the terms of this lease, Lessee shall be deemed guilty of unlawful detainer of said premises under the statutes of the State of California, and shall be subject to eviction and removal with or without process of law.

2. Should Lessor terminate this lease as herein provided, Lessee or any trustee under any trust deed, mortgage, pledge, or any trustee, bondholder or beneficiary under any bond issue covering Lessee's interest hereunder, may, at any time within one hundred eighty (180) days after such termination, redeem and revive [54] this lease from any forfeiture or termination by the payment of all sums due at the time of such redemption and revival, together with interest thereon at the rate of seven per cent (7%) per annum, and by curing any other default in any other of the terms or conditions hereof which may then exist; provided, however, that where such other default is of such a nature that it cannot be cured without first obtaining possession of the demised premises from Lessor, and provided further that the party redeeming as herein permitted be not then in possession of said premises, then such other default, for the purpose of the redemption as herein permitted (but not for any other purpose) shall be deemed to be cured by the delivery to Lessor of adequate security for the curing of such other default; and thereupon this lease shall be and become in full force and effect as if it had not been so terminated by Lessor.

Article XII.

Ownership of New Building

The present building now on the demised premises, as well as any building or buildings substituted, reconstructed, rebuilt or placed at any time on said premises, and all additions thereto, shall remain on said land and shall become the absolute property of the Lessor without cost to Lessor, upon any termination of this lease, whether by lapse of time or by forfeiture or otherwise. Nothing in this article or in article numbered XI and headed "Forfeiture by Default, and Redemption," or elsewhere in this lease, and no other fact or matter, shall be construed as placing the title of said present building, or any such other building, or any addition to any such present or other building, in Lessee; but said present building and all other buildings and additions above enumerated shall be a part of the land over and upon which it is built, and the title to the same shall at all times be in Lessor, subject to the leasehold interest of Lessee in the same manner as the land itself.

Article XIII.

Policy of Title Insurance and Waiver of Warranty

Concurrently with the execution hereof Lessor has caused to be made and delivered to Lessee by Title Insurance and Trust Company, of Los Angeles, California, a leasehold policy of title insurance in which the liability of said Title Company has been fixed at the amount of Five Hundred Seventy-two Thousand One Hundred Dollars ($572,-

100), insuring and guaranteeing to and for the sole benefit of Lessee that the title to the real property hereinbefore described was, at the date of such policy vested in Lessor and that the leasehold estate hereby created is a first lien thereon, subject only to some or all of the matters hereinbefore stated following the description of said real property. Said policy of title insurance is furnished to Lessee and received by it in lieu of and in discharge of any and every express or implied warranty, guaranty, covenant or representation by Lessor as to Lessor's title to the premises demised and as to Lessor's right to make this lease, and any express or implied warranty of quiet enjoyment other than the warranty against unlawful acts of the Lessor. It is expressly understood that the Lessor does not in any way or to any extent make any warranty, guaranty, covenant or representation as to Lessor's title to the premises demised nor as to Lessor's right to make this lease, nor as to the quiet and peaceable enjoyment by the Lessee, its successors or assigns, of the demised premises; nor does Lessor undertake that said policy of title insurance is correct. [55]

Article XIV

Replacement of New Building

Having in mind that at some time or times during the long term of this lease it may be deemed advisable to replace the present building on the leased premises with what may then be a more modern building, it is agreed, therefore, between the

cost and be reasonably worth when completed not
less than four hundred fifty thousand dollars ($450,-
000), exclusive of all carrying charges, and shall
be constructed and completed with all reasonable
diligence after the removal of the other building
on said premises, and in a first class manner in
every particular, and according to complete plans
and specifications therefor, which must be submitted
to and approved by Lessor.

At the time of the deposit of such four hundred
fifty thousand dollars ($450,000) in cash or securi-
ties with such banking institution or institutions,
a proper and sufficient written agreement shall be
made between the parties hereto, or their successors
in interest, and such banking institution or institutions as trustee, said agreement to provide that the
four hundred fifty thousand dollars ($450,000) in
cash or securities shall be released to Lessee in four
equal installments pro rata, as such more modern
building is constructed and paid for, but the last
installment shall not be released until the construction of said more modern building has been fully
completed and fully paid for and said premises are
free and clear from all mechanics' liens or other
such liens for services, supplies, equipment or material and the time for filing same shall have expired and all rents and other payments accruing
prior to such time under the provisions of this lease
have been paid and all other covenants, agreements,
obligations, conditions and provisions of this lease
provided to be performed by Lessee up to said time

have been fully performed in the manner herein provided.

Said agreement shall also provide that in the event the demolition of the then existing structures upon said leased premises has been begun as in this paragraph contemplated, and Lessee shall fail thereafter, after thirty (30) days' written notice requiring it to do so, to proceed with the work of removing the then existing building and the construction of the new and more modern building with due diligence until the same is completed and paid for, that then and in that event said banking institution or institutions, as trustees, shall deliver to Lessor the cash or securities, or cash and securities, which may have been deposited with such bank- [56] ing institution or institutions under the terms of this paragraph, and such cash and securities may be retained by Lessor as liquidated damages on account of the failure of Lessee to complete the demolition of the then existing structures upon said leased premises and the construction of the new and more modern building, as herein contemplated. It is understood, however, that the provisions of this paragraph shall not be deemed to apply wherever, by the terms of this lease, it would be incumbent upon Lessee to rebuild or reconstruct said building or repair the same after the destruction of a substantial part thereof by fire or earthquake.

In lieu of depositing the sum hereinbefore in this article mentioned in cash or securities, Lessee may, prior to commencing the removal of any existing building, execute and deliver to Lessor a bond, inuring to the sole benefit of Lessor, with liability in the sum of not less than four hundred fifty thousand dollars ($450,000), with the Lessee as principal and either individual surety or surieties satisfactory to the Lessor, or a corporate surety company, as surety, guaranteeing the removal of such existing building and the completion within two years from the commencement of work for the removal of such existing building of a new building as hereinbefore provided in this article, free from liens of mechanics, materialmen and other like liens; provided, however, that the time for the completion of such new building shall be extended to correspond with any delay occasioned by reason of strikes, lockouts or labor conditions, acts of God or the public enemy, mob violence, general conflagration, destruction or partial destruction of said building while in course of construction or any cause beyond the control of the lessee whether similar or dissimilar to those herein enumerated, not including, however, any delay caused by financial trouble or financial inability of the lessee.

Article XV

Option to Purchase

In consideration of the promises and of the mutual covenants and agreements herein contained, and the sum of Ten Dollars ($10) paid to Lessor by Lessee, receipt of which is hereby acknowledged, Lessor hereby gives and grants to Lessee an option to purchase the aforesaid leased property upon the following terms and conditions, of which time shall be of the essence;

The purchase price which Lessee shall pay to Lessor for said property under said option is and shall be the sum of Seven Hundred Twenty-five Thousand Dollars ($725,000), if the consummation of said purchase be made on or before June 15, 1952, or the sum of Seven Hundred Fifty Thousand Dollars ($750,000) if the consummation of said purchase be made thereafter during the term of this lease. In either case, said purchase price shall be paid in gold coin of the United States of America, of the standard of weight and fineness as hereinbefore defined, or its equivalent in market value as aforesaid. Any such purchase pursuant to this option shall be consummated on some June 15 or December 15, provided, however, that the Lessee may at its election fix any other date for the consummation of such purchase by paying to and depositing with the Lessor in addition to the above mentioned purchase price such amount of the rental as would accrue hereunder up to and including the June 15 or December 15 (whichever be the earlier) next succeeding the date of consummation of such purchase.

Lessee shall, if it elects to exercise said option, give notice in writing to Lessor, which notice shall state that Lessee has elected to purchase said property and the date on which Lessee intends to consummate said purchase, which date shall not be less than sixty (60) and not more than ninety (90) days from the giving of said notice, and shall concurrently with the giving of such [57] notice deposit in escrow with Title Insurance and Trust Company, of Los Angeles, California, or such other title insurance company as Lessor and Lessee shall approve, the sum of Fifty Thousand Dollars ($50,000), in gold coin as aforesaid or in its equivalent in market value as aforesaid.

Lessor covenants and agrees that at least thirty (30) days before the date specified in said notice as the date on which Lessee intends to consummate said purchase, Lessor will execute to Lessee or its nominee, and deposit in escrow with the same escrow holder, a good and sufficient grant deed conveying to Lessee or its nominee the real property hereinbefore described, subject only to any taxes and assessments, some or all of the matters hereinbefore stated following the description of said real property, and matters done, made or suffered by Lessee; and upon the deposit of said deed Lessor covenants to order a search of title of said property to be made by said title company, and to order a policy of title insurance or guarantee of title from said title company. Lessor further covenants and agrees, at the close of said escrow to furnish Lessee a policy of title insurance or guarantee of title of said company or of some other responsible company, in such amount as Lessee may designate, not in excess of the purchase price of said property, showing title to said property vested in Lessee, free and clear of all encumbrances except taxes and assessments, some or all of the matters hereinbefore stated following the description of said real property, and matters done, made or suffered by Lessee.

Lessee covenants and agrees that within ten (10) days after notice from the said title company that, had said deed been recorded at the time stated in said notice, it could then have issued its policy of title insurance or guarantee of title showing title to said property vested of record in Lessee or its nominee, free and clear of all incumbrances except as aforesaid, Lessee will deposit in said escrow the full remainder of the purchase price of said property as hereinbefore set forth; provided, however, said additional money need not in any event be deposited by said Lessee in said scrow prior to the date specified in said notice from Lessee to Lessor as the date on which Lessee intends to consumate said purchase.

Upon the deposit in escrow of said additional money as aforesaid said escrow shall be closed by the recordation of said deed and the delivery of the money representing the entire purchase price to Lessor. The escrow fee in connection with said transaction shall be paid one-half by Lessee and one-half by Lessor. The full cost of said policy of title insurance or guarantee of title shall be paid by Lessor.

In the event Lessee gives notice to Lessor of Lessee's election to purchase said property, and such intended purchase is not consummated on the

date set by reason of any default or failure of
Lessee, Lessee covenants and agrees that it will
pay Lessor as liquidated damages and not as a
penalty the sum of Fifty Thousand Dollars ($50,-
000), it being recognized that from the nature of
the case it would be impossible or extremely difficult
to determine the actual amount of damage to
Lessor, and Lessee further covenants and agrees
that Lessee shall have no right to exercise the aforesaid option at any subsequent time; it being intended and hereby provided that Lessee may exercise said option once and once only, and that if
Lessee, having given notice of its exercise of said
option, fails or makes default in consummating said
purchase, said option and all rights of Lessee under
this Article XV shall be and be deemed to be
exhausted and terminated. [58]

Lessor's obligations under this article shall be
merely to convey, and cause said policy of title
insurance or guarantee of title to be furnished in
respect of, the real property hereinbefore described,
and any building or other improvement thereon, in
the then condition of such real property, building
or other impromevent. If a portion of the land hereinbefore described should be taken after the date
of this lease and prior to the consummation of said
purchase by proceedings in condemnation or eminent domain, Lessor shall have no obligation in
respect of the part of the land so taken, or for
any building or other improvement taken or damaged by such taking, but the purchase price to be

paid by Lessee shall be reduced by the amount actually received by Lessor as the result of such proceedings and then applicable for such reduction as hereinafter provided in Section 12 of Article XVI, less the attorney's fees and other expenses and costs of Lessor in such proceeding, but no credit shall be accorded to Lessee on account of any interest whatsoever on such amount.

Subject to the provisions of this Article XV said option may be exercised at any time during the term of this lease provided Lessee be not then in default in respect of any of the terms, covenants or conditions in this indenture contained. This option shall, however, unless it may legally and validly extend and be effective during the whole term of this lease, terminate and cease and become null and void upon the death of the last survivor of the following persons:

Bertha Abrams, Hertha J. Abramson, Newton Bissinger, Gustave Brenner, Julius Brownstein, Sophia J. Coffer, Minnie Cooper and Isador Earl Cooper, Signey Ehrman, Donald Lawrence Eisner, and Harry Eisner, all of the City of San Francisco, california;

George M. Adair, Rose Harris Adler, H. A. Allen, Stuart D. Anderson, D. Antink, Sadie L. Armer, C. W. Arnold, Sarah H. Bachman, Robert Baker, Donald L. Bantock and Ada I. Bantock, I. A. Allen, Wesley M. Barr, Nannie Barrie, J. S. Barrie, R. M. Barton, Milton Buruch, J. Y. Baruh, Irene Basthein, Claud Beelman, L. E. Behymer, Geo. S.

Behrandt, Sadie M. Behrendt, Trustee, Sadie M. Behrendt, Sam Behrendt, Glen Behymer, Sylvia O. Behymer, H. A. Belcher, L. E. Belcher, H. B. Bendteen, Doris M. Benjamin, C. E. Berlin, Minerva Berman, Frank W. Black, Abe Bloom, James C. Bogart, Ester H. Bowers, Flora E. Bradley, George Bradley and Frances Bradley, Alexander Brick, Lenore Brick, Minnie Brick, Aleck Brownstein, Chas. Brownstein, Elise H. Brownstein, Robert Grant Brownstein, Patsy Bufane, Thomas Burkefaky, Jennie Burris, Rozellia C. Butler, O. C. Chism, Daniel Clarke, Amelia B. Cline and W. K. Cline, Morris Cohn, Louis M. Cole, Yaidora Louis Cole, John T. Cooper, Aleck Curlett, Frank C. Curtis and Minnie A. Curtis, Robert L. Cuzner, Milton L. Davidson, Norman C. Davison, Kate L. Day, F. S. DeVoin, S. F. DeVoin, Wm. H. Dickson, Jane Stimson Dulin, Dr. D. W. Edelman, A. R. Edson, A. Eisner, Bluma Eisner, I. Eisner, all of the City of Los Angeles, California;

E. M. Asher, of the City of Beverly Hills, California; Lockwood R. Bantock and Margaret Bantock of the City of Arcadia, California;

Frances Marion Devereux of the City of Cincinnati, Ohio;

Rosabelle H. Baeder, Irma Banjamin, Flora W. Bernhard, Henry Bernhard, Mollie Bernhard, Fannie S. Block, Elizabeth S. Block, Herman W. Block, Sylvan Cole, and Walter B. Deutsch, all of the City of New York, New York;

Alfred G. Carter, Pearl V. Carter, of the City of South Pasadena, California; [59]

Rev. William Corr, of the City of Pasadena, California;

Ruth Dawson, of the City of Long Beach, California;

Robert C. Devereux, of the City of Alhambra, California;

Francis S. Devereux, of the City of St. Petersburg, Florida;

Mary Drysdale, Mina Drysdale, of the City of Hollywood, California.

Faith Whitney, daughter of Marcus B. Whitney and Vera Whitney, his wife, of the city of Mount Vernon, State of New York;

James Stillman, Timothy Stillman, Calvin Stillman, John Stillman and Dora Stillman, all children of Ernest G. Stillman and Mildred Whitney Stillman, his wife, all of the City of New York, State of New York;

Ralph H. Spotts, Jr., and Victor J. Spotts, both children of Ralph H. Spotts and Delpha V. R. Spotts, his wife, of the city of Beverly Hills, California, County of Los Angeles, State of California; and

Eugene Dunn, son of Henry W. Dunn and Laura Mae Dunn, his wife, of the city of Long Beach, California;

John Francis Jones, Richard Walton Jones, George Erle Jones, Jr., all children of George E. Jones and Frances Jones, his wife of the City of South Pasadena, State of California;

Thomas Tully and Robert Tully, children of Jaspar Tully and Leslie Tully, his wife, of the City of Berkeley, California;

Allen Mitchum, son of Colis Mitchum and Eleanor Mitchum, his wife, of the City of Berkeley, California;

Elizabeth Witter and Barbara Witter, both children of W. Guy Witter and Helen Witter, his wife, of the City of South Pasadena, California;

Porter Bruck and Barbara Bruck, both children of Porter Bruck and Dorothy Bruck, his wife, of the City of South Pasadena, California;

George Crane and Peter Crane, both children of William Crane and Catharine Crane, his wife of the City of Pasadena, California;

Peter Edwards and William Edwards, both children of William A. Edwards and Josephine Edwards, his wife, of the City of Santa Barbara, California;

John Val Alst Austin and Miriam Austin, both children of John Van Alst Austin and Margaret Austin, his wife, of the City of Santa Barbara, California;

Serena Kamper, daughter of Gustave Anthony Kamper and Margaret Kamper, his wife, of the City of Honolulu, Territory of Hawaii;

Edwin Sill Fussell, Paul Fussell, Jr. and Florence Elizabeth Fussell, all children of Paul Fussell and William S. Fussell, his wife, of the City of Pasadena, California; [60]

Harry L. Dunn of the City of Pasadena, California;

Albert Parker, of the City of Los Angeles, California;

Robert Eisner Lissner, Richard Louis Lissner, Aline M. Lissner, Richard James Lauter, Herbert M. Baruch, Jr., Edith Blum, Ruth Davidson, Harriett Davidson, Alvin Robert Stitch, Janice Ethelyn Stitch, Harriet Green, Arthur McClane, George Newmark Behrendt, Patricia Meyer, Nancy Frank, Blanche May, Doris E. Nerenberg, Marvin L. Nerenberg, and Albert Parker, all of the City of Los Angeles, California;

Harry L. Dunn and Louise R. Dunn, both of the City of Pasadena, California.

It is expressly understood, anything herein contained to the contrary notwithstanding, that the Lessor makes no warranty, guaranty, covenant or representation as to the validity of the aforesaid option to purchase, nor as to its enforceability by the Lessee against the Lessor, or its successor or successors in interest in said demised premises. If said option to purchase shall at any time be declared and held to be void for any reason by any court of competent jurisdiction, such decision shall not affect the validity of the remaining portions of this lease. And the Lessee hereby declares that it would have entered into said Lease irrespective of the fact that any one or more or all of the provisions thereof relating to said option to purchase be declared and held invalid and/or void and/or unenforceable.

Article XVI

Miscellaneous

1. It is specifically understood and agreed that any and all sub-leases which may hereafter be made or executed by Lessee and/or any sub-tenancies of any nature whatsoever hereafter created by Lessee, shall be subject and subordinate to this indenture of lease and to each and all of the terms, conditions and covenants hereof, and that any and all instruments or documents by which any such sub-lease or other tenancy is created or affected shall contain a provision to such effect and shall likewise contain a provision that the continuance of the term of any such sub-lease and/or tenancy is dependent upon the continuance of the term of this lease.

2. It is understood that Lessor reserves and has and shall have, at all times during the term hereof, the right and power, subject to this lease, to mortgage, pledge, hypothecate or otherwise encumber and/or sell or otherwise deal with or dispose of its reversionary interest in the demised premises and/or the fee title thereto, or any part thereof, and/or Lessor's interest under this lease by mortgage, trust deed, pledge, hypothecation, assignment, deed or otherwise.

3. Wherever in this lease any words of obligation or duty regarding any of the parties are used, such words or expressions shall have the same force and effect as though in the express form of covenants.

4. Each and all of the various rights, powers, options and remedies of Lessor contained in this lease shall be considered as cumulative, and no one of them as exclusive of the other or as exclusive of any remedies allowed by law.

5. If Lessor shall, without any fault on Lessor's part, be made a party to any litigation commenced by or against Lessee, or Lessor, involving the enforcement of any of the rights or remedies of Lessor against Lessee, or arising on account of the default of Lessee in respect of any of the obligations of Lessee under [61] this indenture, then Lessee will pay on demand all costs and reasonable attorney's fees incurred by or against Lessor in such litigation, and Lessee shall also pay costs and such attorney's fees incurred by or against Lessor in enforcing the covenants, terms and provisions of this lease.

6. Lessor shall not be obligated to pay any charge whatsoever to any corporation or person who shall act at any time in any trust capacity hereunder for any services of such trustee performed under this indenture, but said trustee shall be entitled to take out of any trust funds collected or deposited with such trustee its charges, costs and reasonable compensation. Until changed upon five (5) day's notice in writing from Lessor to Lessee, Title Insurance and Trust Company, of Los Angeles, is selected as and shall be the Trustee under this lease. The charges and compensation of any trustee acting as such under the terms hereof shall be paid by Lessee but this provision shall not obligate

Lessee to pay any trustee or agent acting under any trust or Agreement (other than this Indenture of Lease) covering the reversionary estate in the demised premises for any charges for services rendered by it under such trust or agreement.

7. No waiver of a breach of any of the covenants, agreements, restrictions and conditions of this lease shall be construed to be a waiver of any succeeding breach of the same or other covenants, agreements, restrictions and conditions, nor shall any delay of Lessor in enforcing any right, remedy, privilege or recourse accorded to Lessor, nor any number of recoveries thereunder, affect, diminish, suspend or exhaust such rights, remedies, privileges or recourses.

8. Lessor hereby assigns to Lessee but without warranty express or implied, the Lessor's interest in all leases, whether recorded or unrecorded, existing immediately prior to the time of delivery of this lease, covering all or any part of the property hereby demised, together with the right to all rentals which may hereafter become due on such existing leases. At the end of the term of this lease (whenever and however occurring) Lessee shall execute and deliver to Lessor such appropriate instrument of assignment or otherwise as Lessor shall deem satisfactory for the purpose of vesting in Lessor all rights of the Lessor under all such leases, and in all subleases executed by the Lessee, including the right to receive all rentals which may thereafter become due on such leases. Nothing herein contained shall, however, authorize the execution of subleases except

subject to the terms of this lease and to the rights of the Lessor hereunder, nor shall authorize the execution of subleases running beyond the term of this lease.

9. Each and every of the terms, covenants and conditions of this lease shall inure to the benefit of and shall bind (as the case may require) not only the parties hereto, but each and every of the successors, assigns and legal representatives of the respective parties hereto; and wherever in this lease a reference is made to any of the parties hereto, such reference shall be deemed to include, wherever applicable, also a reference to the successors, assigns and legal representatives of such party, the same as if in every case expressed; and all of the covenants, agreements and restrictions and conditions contained in this lease shall be construed as conditions, covenants and restrictions running with the land.

10. The language in all parts of this indenture shall in all cases be construed simply according to its fair meaning and not strictly for or against Lessor or Lessee.

11. Lessee covenants and agrees that during the continuance of this lease it will give written notice to the Lessor of any construction, demolition, [62] excavation, removal and/or alteration of, in or affecting the building or buildings now upon or which may hereafter be placed or erected upon the premises hereby leased, if the total contract price or estimated cost thereof $5,000.00, at least five (5) days before the commencement of such work in or-

der that Lessor may give necessary notices, etc., to protect its reversionary or other interests from liens.

12. Should the Lessee at any time during the continuance in force of this lease be permanently deprived of substantially the whole of the demised premises by condemnation or any other proceedings having for their object the taking of the property or any part thereof for public use or under the laws of eminent domain, then it is agreed that this lease and the option herein provided for shall thereupon terminate and the Lessor and Lessee each shall be entitled to receive such judgment as may be awarded to it for its respective interest. If, however, anything less than substantially the whole of said premises shall be taken the Lessee shall not thereby be released from any of the obligations of the Lessee hereunder and the amount of rentals thereafter due shall not thereby be decreased; provided, however, in such event that if there shall have been included in the award to Lessee any amount as equivalent to the value of the sum of rents payable in future or the value of the sum of any portion of the rents so payable, then Lessee covenants that on written demand of Lessor all of such amount so awarded the Lessee on account of such rents or portion of such rents shall forthwith be paid directly to Lessor and thereafter, such payment having been made, Lessee shall receive on account of each installment of rental a credit equal to the proportion of such installment or rental, for the value of which said sum was so awarded, it being understood and

agreed, however, that in the event that this lease be terminated for any reason prior to the date of termination originally fixed herein Lessor shall be under no further obligation to make credits to Lessee on account of the payment of such moneys received through such award. Provided, further, however, that in the event the Lessee shall exercise the option herein in Article XV provided, the unconsumed portion of any amount paid on account of rents or portion of rents, i. e., the then value of the rents or portion of rents payable in the future and for which credit is to be given hereunder, shall be credited as if paid on account of, and be deducted from, the said option price, the amount of such credit to be in no instance, however, more than the amount of the award paid to Lessor by Lessee as hereinabove provided. It is, however, understood and agreed that Lessor shall have the option, in its discretion, of making or not making the above demand and that if Lessor makes no such written demand upon Lessee as hereinabove provided within ten (10) days of the receipt of Lessee of such award that then Lessee shall retain such amount so received by it and shall receive no credit on rentals as hereinabove provided.

It is further understood, that in any such condemnation proceedings, Lessee shall receive no damages on account of the value of the option in Article XV provided, save and unless the same shall have been exercised prior to the time that the award shall become final, but in the event Lessee shall exercise said option, then there shall be credited, as if paid on account of the option price in addition to any sum hereinbefore required to be so credited, such amount as the Lessor shall have been awarded in such condemnation proceedings as damages to said Lessor acruing.

In Witness Whereof, Title Insurance and Trust Company, as Lessor, and Sun Realty Co., as Lessee, have caused this indenture of lease to be executed on their behalf by their respective officers thereunto duly authorized and their respective corporate seals hereunto to be affixed, all at Los Angeles, California, as of the day and year in this indenture first above written. [63]

TITLE INSURANCE AND
TRUST COMPANY,
By STUART O'MELVENY,

(RHS)   President.

[Seal]   By E. H. MOORE,

Assistant Secretary.

Lessor.

SUN REALTY CO.,
By I. EISNER,

President.

[Seal]   By DAVE ANTINK,

Secretary,

Lessee.

(Add acknowledgments). [64]

State of California,
County of Los Angeles—ss.

On this 15th day of July, 1927, before me, P. L. Bishop, a Notary Public in and for said County of

Los Angeles, State of California, residing therein, duly commissioned and sworn, personally appeared Stuart O'Melveny, known to me to be the Vice President, and E. H. Moore, known to me to be the Assistant Secretary, respectively, of Title Insurance and Trust Company, one of the corporations that executed the within and foregoing instrument, known to me to be the persons who executed the within and foregoing instrument on behalf of the said corporation, and acknowledged to me that such corporation executed the same.

In Witness Whereof, I have hereunto set my hand and affixed my official seal the day and year in this certificate first above written.

[Seal]   P. L. BISHOP,
Notary Public in and for the County of Los Angeles, State of California.

My commission expires January 12th, 1929.

State of California,
County of Los Angeles—ss.

On this 15th day of July, 1927, before me, Louis M. Lissner, a Notary Public in and for said County of Los Angeles, State of California, residing therein, duly commissioned and sworn, personally appeared I. Eisner, known to me to be the President, and Dave Antink, known to me to be the Secretary, respectively, of Sun Realty Co., one of the corporations that executed the within and foregoing instrument, known to me to be the persons who executed the within foregoing instrument on behalf of the said corporation, and acknowledged to me that such corporation executed the same.

In Witness Whereof, I have hereunto set my hand and affixed my official seal the day and year in this certificate first above written.

[Seal]   LOUIS M. LISSNER,
Notary Public in and for the County of Los Angeles,
    State of California.

My commission expires August 31, 1927.

Mitchum, Tully & Co., a corporation and Harry L. Dunn and Louise R. Dunn, his wife, and Albert Parker, a single man, do hereby, for the purpose of subjecting any interest which they or either of them may or might have in and to the property described in said foregoing Lease, to the terms thereof, and without implying any necessity therefor, hereby consent to and join in the execution of the same on behalf of the Lessor, agreeing, however, that all payments shall be made and covenants [65] performed and notice given by the Lessee to and upon the Lessor named in said lease, its successors and assigns, as therein provided, and not to the undersigned by virtue of anything herein contained, and further that the undersigned shall not be deemed to assume any liability or obligation or to make any warranty hereby.

In Witness Whereof, Mitchum, Tully & Co. has caused this instrument to be executed in its behalf by its vice president and assistant secretary, and its corporate seal to be hereunto affixed, and said Harry L. Dunn, Louise R. Dunn and Albert Parker have hereunto affixed their hands and seals as of the 15th day of July, 1927.

                    MITCHUM, TULLY, & CO.,
[Seal]   By GEORGE E. JONES,
                                   Vice President.
                    By M. FITCH,
                                   Assistant Secretary.
[Seal]   ALBERT PARKER.
[Seal]   HARRY L. DUNN.
[Seal]   LOUISE R. DUNN. [66]

State of California,
County of Los Angeles—ss.

On this 15th day of July, 1927, before me, P. L. Bishop, a Notary Public in and for the County of Los Angeles, State of California, personally appeared Harry L. Dunn, known to me to be the person whose name is subscribed to the within instrument and acknowledged to me that he executed the same.

In Witness Whereof, I have hereunto set my hand and affixed my official seal the day and year in this certificate first above written.

[Seal]   P. L. BISHOP
Notary Public in and for the County of Los Angeles,
     State of California.

My commission expires January 12, 1929.

State of California,
County of Los Angeles—ss.

On this 15th day of July, 1927, before me, P. L. Bishop, a Notary Public in and for the County of

Los Angeles, State of California, residing therein, duly commissioned and sworn, personally appeared Louise R. Dunn, wife of Harry L. Dunn, known to me to be the person whose name is subscribed to the within instrument, and acknowledged to me that she executed the same.

In Witness Whereof, I have hereunto set my hand and affixed my official seal the day and year in this certificate first above written.

[Seal]   P. L. BISHOP

Notary Public in and for the County of Los Angeles,
    State of California.

My commission expires January 12th, 1929. [67]

State of California,
County of Los Angeles—ss.

On this 15th day of July, 1927, before me, P. L. Bishop, a Notary Public in and for the County of Los Angeles, State of California, personally appeared Albert Parker, known to me to be the person whose name is subscribed to the within instrument and acknowledged to me that he executed the same.

In Witness Whereof, I have hereunto set my hand and affixed my official seal the day and year in this certificate first above written.

P. L. BISHOP

Notary Public in and for the County of Los Angeles,
    State of California.

My commission expires January 12th, 1929.

State of California,
County of Los Angeles—ss.

On this 15th day of July, 1927, before me, P. L. Bishop, a Notary Public in and for said County of Los Angeles, State of California, residing therein, duly commissioned and sworn, personally appeared George B. Jones, known to me to be the Vice-President, and M. Fitch, known to me to be the Assistant Secretary, respectively, of Mitchum, Tully & Co., the corporation that executed the within and foregoing instrument, known to me to be the persons who executed the within and foregoing instrument on behalf of said corporation, and acknowledged to me that such corporation executed the same.

In Witness Whereof, I have hereunto set my hand and affixed my official seal the day and year in this certificate first above written.

[Seal]   P. L. BISHOP
Notary Public in and for the County of Los Angeles,
    State of California.

My commission expires January 12th, 1929.

I, the undersigned, do hereby certify the above Indenture of Lease to be a true and correct copy of the original dated and signed as above, presented to me this 9th day of December, 1936.

[Seal]   JOYCE BENT
Notary Public in and for the County of Los Angeles,
    State of California.

My commission expires April 15, 1940.

[Endorsed]: U. S. B. T. A. Filed Dec. 14, 1938.

[68]

[Title of Board and Cause.]

ANSWER

The Commissioner of Internal Revenue, by his attorney, Morrison Shafroth, Chief Counsel, Bureau of Internal Revenue, for answer to the petition of the above-named taxpayer, admits and denies as follows:

(1) Admits that petitioner's address is 433 South Spring Street, Los Angeles, California, but denies the remaining allegations contained in Paragraph (1) of the petition.

(2) Admits the allegations contained in Paragraph (2) of the petition.

(3) Admits the allegations contained in Paragraph (3) of the petition.

(4)-(a) and (b). Denies that the Commissioner erred as alleged in sub-paragraphs (a) and (b) of Paragraph (4) of the petition.

(5)-(a) to (f), inc. For lack of full and complete information, denies the allegations of fact contained in sub-paragraphs (a) to (f), inc., of Paragraph (5) of the petition.

(g) Admits that petitioner filed an income tax return for 1933 on Form 1040; that Form 1041 was filed which purported to show the net income distributed; but denies the remaining allegations of fact contained in sub-paragraph (g) of Paragraph (5) of the petition. [69]

(6) Denies generally and specifically each and every allegation contained in taxpayer's petition and not hereinbefore admitted, qualified or denied.

Wherefore, it is prayed that taxpayer's appeal be denied.

(Signed) MORRISON SHAFROTH
Chief Counsel,
Bureau of Internal Revenue

Of Counsel:

    CHESTER A. GWINN

    HUGH BREWSTER

        Special Attorneys,

        Bureau of Internal Revenue.

vc-2/5/37.

[Endorsed]: U. S. B. T. A. Feb. 5, 1937. [70]

[Title of Board and Cause.]

George M. Thompson, C. P. A., John T. Riley, Esq., and Marshall D. Hall, Esq., for the petitioner.

Stanley B. Pierson, Esq., and Freeman Paulson, Esq., for the respondent.

MEMORANDUM FINDINGS OF FACT
AND OPINION

Mellott: The commissioner determined a deficiency in petitioner's income tax for the year 1933 in the amount of $2,726.36 and added a delinquency penalty of 25 percent, or $681.59, for failure to file a return within the time prescribed by law. It is alleged that he erred (1) in failing to treat the petitioner as a trust and in determining it to be an association taxable as a corporation; and (2) in assessing the 25 percent penalty.

Findings of Fact

The petitioner was created by an agreement and declaration of trust (a true and correct copy of which is attached to the petition) executed July 15, 1927 (but for convenience dated June 15, 1927) between Mitchum, Tully & Co., a California corporation, as trustor or grantor, Title Insurance and Trust Company, a California corporation, as trustee, and Harry L. Dunn and Albert Parker and "such persons, partnerships, associations and/or corporations as may become parties hereto by the acceptance of certificates issued hereunder" as beneficiaries.

The declaration of trust provides, among other things, that the trustee shall hold in trust for the benefit of Dunn and Parker, and their respective successors and assigns, as owners of the undivided beneficial rights or interest represented by certificates, all the title, right and interet in and to certain described real property located at the southeast corner of Hollywood Boulevard and Vine Street in Los Angeles, California; that the beneficial interest in the trust shall consist of 665 equal, fractional, undivided, parts and shall be represented by certificates to be issued by the trustee, the certificates being transferable by the execution of the assignment on the reverse side thereof and transfer on the books of the trustee; that the trustee shall issue a certificate or certificates for the entire 665 beneficial interests to Dunn and Parker; shall keep a register of the names of the holders of certificates, proper transfer books in respect of such certificates, and books of account showing the receipts and disbursements of the trust estate; shall have the power to rent and lease the trust estate, or any part thereof, to Sun Realty Co., a California corporation, under a lease dated July 15, 1927, for a period of 98½ years for a yearly rental of $42,000 in addition to the payment of taxes, insurance premiums, etc., with the option to purchase the property for $725,000 prior to June 15, 1952, and for $750,000 within the time specified in the lease, which may contain such further terms, provisions and conditions as the trustee may approve; that in the event the Sun Realty Co., or [71] any other lessee under the above mentioned long term lease or any successor lessee, shall default, or in the event such lease shall be terminated for any reason or shall expire by limitation, the trustee shall have full authority to terminate the lease or to take such steps as in its opinion may be necessary and proper for the best interests of certificate holders with respect to leasing, operating, selling, conveying or otherwise disposing of the trust property; to enforce any lease or leases made by it, to execute and deliver any agreement in writing, modifying or supplementing any lease or leases if and when in its discretion it shall appear advisable, providing no such modification shall decrease the amount of the rentals and payment or option price specified in the original lease to Sun Realty Co.; that, in the event the Sun Realty Co. shall exercise its option to purchase, the trustee shall, upon receipt of the purchase price, have full authority to execute the necessary conveyance without securing the consent from certificate holders; that the trustee may, subject to the option of Sun Realty Co., sell and convey all of the trust property at its discretion without the consent of the certificate holders provided the sale will make available for distribution among the beneficiaries at least $1,250,000; that upon the receipt of written consents of ⅔ds of the 665 interests, including ⅔ds of the unredeemed certificates outstanding, the trustee may at any time, but shall not be obligated to, sell and convey the trust property upon such terms as may be provided in such consents; that the trustee shall have full power to compromise and settle claims either in contract or tort made by it or against it or the trust estate and to charge the expense against the income of the trust; that it, in its discretion, may mortgage and otherwise bind or charge the trust estate for the purpose of providing funds to meet any exigency arising in connection therewith and for the benefit of certificate holders; borrow money upon any usual terms, giving notes or other security therefor, and apply moneys, as available from time to time, for the payment of principal or interest in respect to any borrowings or mortgages or other hypothecation, in preference and with priority to any claims of beneficiaries to periodical or other payments in respect to their fractional interests; distribute semi-annually rentals and income, less its fee as determined in the trust agreement and ex-

penses, pro rata to the holders of certificates whose
names are registered as such on the books of the
trustee, not exceeding, however, $30 for each frac-
tional beneficial interest, which semi-annual distribution shall be cumulative without interest, the remaining rentals and income to be applied to the redemption of certificates; that, except as otherwise
provided, the trustee shall have the exclusive right
to manage and control the trust estate and shall not
be subject to any obligation to the certificate holders
except as expressly assumed; that the trustee, in its
own absolute discretion, may seek the advice of the
certificate holders, and if notified in writing, by a
majority of the 665 beneficial interests, including a
majority of the interests upon which no redemption
payments have been made, of their agreement upon
a course which they desire to be taken, not inconsistent with any of the express provisions of the
trust agreement, may endeavor to effectuate the
same but shall not be obligated to do so; that as
and when moneys in excess of the semi-annual distributions and expenses become available the trustee may redeem the certificates by inviting offers
of certificate holders for such purposes and applying such moneys for such redemption payments,
which shall not be more than $1,050 on or before
June 15, 1937, nor more than $1,030 thereafter and
on or before June 15, 1947, nor more than $1,010
thereafter and on or before June 15, 1957, and thereafter not more than $1,000, together with accrued
semi-annual distribution to date of redemption;

that the certificates so redeemed by payment shall have an endorsement thereon "Redemption Payment [72] Made," and the certificate holders thereafter shall receive no further payments nor any interest whatsoever until after redemption payments have been made upon all of the 665 interests, after which time the owner of each 1/665th interest, as represented by outstanding certificates, shall share pro rata in all further funds, less expenses, fees and disbursements of the trustee, as and when available for distribution; that, when all certificates have been redeemed, the trustee may, in its discretion, propose the modification or elimination of terms, conditions, trusts or provisions of the trust agreement, or any additions thereto, and, if consented to by ¾ths of the certificate holders, the trustee may, in its discretion, but shall not be obligated to, make effective such changes, provided such change shall not have the effect of giving to any certificate holder any preference or advantage over any other certificate holder; that the trustee shall not be liable personally in acting as trustee except for its personal and willful default; that no holder of any certificate shall have, as such, any estate or interest in the trust property but may enforce the performance of the trust and trust agreement; that no transfer by operation of law of the interest of any certificate holder shall operate to terminate the trust nor entitle the successors of such holder to an accounting or to take any action in the courts or otherwise against the trust estate or trustee; that in the event of death of any certificate holder the person or persons entitled by law shall succeed to the rights of such holder; that no assessment shall ever be made upon the holder of any certificate; that neither the trustee nor the certificate holder shall in any event be liable personally upon any contract or obligation made or entered into by the trustee in connection with the trust estate; that the trustee may resign upon giving 4 weeks' written notice to the certificate holders who may select its successor, and, in the event of their failure or neglect so to do, the trustee may request the Federal Judge of the District Court in and for the district in which the property is located to designate a successor trustee; and that unless sooner terminated as provided in the agreement, the trust shall terminate upon the death of the last to die of numerous persons named in the trust agreement.

Mitchum, Tully & Co., grantor in the trust agreement, was, during the time herein involved and prior thereto, engaged in business as investment bankers and underwriters. It had purchased the trust property and negotiated and arranged for the lease with Sun Realty Co. prior to the execution of the trust agreement. The improvements on the property consisted of a 12-story building, having stores on the ground floor and offices above. The trustee executed the Sun Realty Co. lease on July 15, 1927, at or about the same time that it executed the trust agreement.

The lease (a true and correct copy of which is attached to the petition) provides in part for a term of 98½ years commencing July 15, 1927, at a net monthly rental of $3,500 and requires the lessee to pay all taxes, general or special, which may be levied against the property or the leasehold, to keep the property insured against damage by fire and earthquake and to repair and maintain the premises leased.

After the execution of the trust agreement the trustee issued eight certificates representing the 665 beneficial units to Dunn and Parker, who assigned them to Mitchum, Tully & Co., who in turn assigned or sold them to others. During 1933 all of the 665 beneficial units were outstanding and unredeemed certificates were held by 222 persons. Of the 665 units outstanding 17 had been redeemed as provided in the trust agreement by [73] the end of 1933. However, the interest of the holders of beneficial units was not extinguished by redemption. Such holders merely relinquished their right to receive any further distributions until all units had been similarly redeemed.

During the course of a year the activities of the trustee consisted of collecting the monthly rental and depositing the same, making two distributions a year, paying Federal and state (effective in 1937) income taxes and its own fees, the entry thereof in its books of account, and the performance of ordinary duties of any real estate trust, such as ascertaining whether proper insurance was carried by the lessee and the like.

No meetings were ever held which were attended by the trustee or beneficiaries of the trust in connection with the management of the affairs of the trust. The rent provided for under the Sun Realty Co. lease was always paid although the rent was delinquent at the time the lessee's interest in the trust property was foreclosed under a bond issue. However, the receiver appointed at that time paid the delinquent rent within the 30-day period specified in the lease. At that time the trustee had some discussions as to the status of the lease with a trust company which took over the management of the property.

The fiduciary return of income for the calendar year 1933 was received in the office of the collector of internal revenue (6th Calif.) Los Angeles, California, on March 20, 1934, five days later than the date prescribed by law for the filing of such returns. Subsequently, the assistant trust officer of the Title Insurance and Trust Company filed with the collector his affidavit, in which it is stated that the delinquency in filing "was due to no intent to violate the law, but was occasioned by purely an oversight by the Trustee, that said Return was prepared in due time but became misplaced among other papers." Under the circumstances it is found that the failure to file the return was due to reasonable cause and not due to willful neglect.

OPINION.

The petitioner reported its income as a trust and contends that it is taxable as such since, in the language of its brief, it was "formed for the purpose of holding title to one piece of real estate * * *, to collect the monthly rental * * * and to distribute same to the beneficiaries * * *." Respondent contends, and determined the deficiency upon the theory, that petitioner is taxable as a corporation because of the provisions of section 1111 (a) (2) of the Revenue Act of 1932, which defines the term "corporation" as including "associations, joint stock companies and insurance companies." The question for our determination, therefore, is whether petitioner is such an "association" or whether it is a "pure trust."

We have attempted to set out in our findings the substance of the 48-page trust agreement, which not only was attached to the petition but which also was formally introduced in evidence. There is no substantial disagreement between the parties as to the facts so the question is entirely one of law. We think that respondent's construction is correct and in harmony with the construction placed upon similar agreements in the group of cases decided by the Supreme Court December 16, 1935. Morrissey et al v. Commissioner, 296 U. S. 344; Swanson et al v. Commissioner, 296 U. S. 362; Helvering v. Coleman-Gilbert Associates, 296 U. S. 369; and Helvering v. Combs et al, 296 U. S. 365. [74]

In the Morrissey case a trust was created for the development of a tract of land through the construction and operation of golf courses, club houses, etc., and the conduct of incidental businesses. Provision was made for the issue of beneficial interests and those who took them became shareholders in the common undertaking to be conducted for their profit. They were found to be "associates" and the entity was held taxable as an association because of its "resemblance" to a corporation, though "identity" was lacking. "The arrangement provided for centralized control, continuity, and limited liability, and the analogy to corporate organization was carried still further by the provision for the issue of transferable certificates."

The Swanson case involved a trust created by two landowners who had constructed an apartment house on property which they owned. The property has been conveyed to trustees, who were given complete control and management of it, and the trust instrument provided for the issuance of 1,000 "receipts" to evidence the interests of the beneficiaries, each of the shares or "receipts" having a par value of $100. The receipts were evidence of the ownership of personal property and not real estate, and they might be transferred by assignment. The trust had succession, could sue and be sued, and neither the trustees nor the beneficiaries could be held personally liable, all persons dealing with the trustees being required to look only to the property of the trust. It was held that the trust constituted an association and that it was taxable as a corporation; that "The limited number of actual beneficiaries did not alter the nature and purpose of the common undertaking. Nor did the fact that the operations of the association did not extend beyond the real property first acquired change the quality of that undertaking,"

In Helvering v. Coleman-Gilbert Associates five co-owners of apartment houses had conveyed the property to themselves as trustees. The trust was to continue for fifteen years and the trustees were given full power and authority to hold, improve, and dispose of the property for the benefit of the persons named as beneficiaries; also to invest and reinvest the trust property, including its income. The trustees were to have no power to bind the beneficiaries personally and were to be held responsible only for willful default and breach of trust. The terms of the trust instrument authorized a wide range of activities by the trustees in the purchase, improvement and sale of properties. The court held that while "weight should be given to the purpose for which the trust was organized, * * * that purpose is`found in the agreement of the parties * * * and (they) are not at liberty to say that their purpose was other or narrower than that which they formally set forth in the (trust) instrument * * *."

In Helvering v. Combs et al it was held that a trust created to finance and drill an oil well, the beneficiaries being "all persons who may own or

acquire portions of the whole beneficial interest"
and the certificates being transferable, was taxable
as a corporation, though the beneficiaries did not
hold any meetings, the trust had no office, no seal,
by-laws or official name and the operations of the
trustees were confined to the one lease they acquired.

It is true that the trustee in the instant case performed compartively few duties. Its chief activities
consisted in collecting the rent, keeping the necessary records, seeing that the lessee complied with all
of the terms of the lease and distributing the net
income in accordance with the trust instrument.
However, in determining whether the trust is a
"pure trust" or an "association" the terms of the
trust instrument, rather than [75] a particular
year's activity, must be considered. Helvering v.
Goleman-Gilbert Associates, supra. Under the trust
agreement the trustee had full power to lease, operate, mortgage, sell, or otherwise dispose of the
trust property, subject only to the existing lease
and the option given to the lessee therein to purchase it. Nor does the fact that the enterprise was
limited to one piece of property justify the conclusion that the operating entity was a trust rather
than an association. Cf. Swanson et al v. Commissioner, supra.

It would serve no useful purpose to discuss all the
cases cited by the parties upon brief. Suffice it to
say that many of them were decided prior to the
decisions in the cases cited above and the others,
we think are distinguishable upon their facts. We

have expressed the opinion, and now hold, that the respondent did not err in taxing petitioner as a corporation.

Section 291 of the Revenue Act of 1932 provides for the assessment and collection of an additional tax of 25 percentum of the tax due in case of any failure to make and file a return within the time prescribed by law. It provides, further, however, that "when a return is filed after such time and it is shown that the failure to file it was due to reasonable cause and not due to willful neglect no such addition shall be made to the tax." We have found that the failure to file the return within time was due to reasonable cause and not to willful neglect; so we decline to approve the imposition of the penalty.

Judgment will be entered that there is a deficiency in income tax for the year 1933 in the amount of $2,726.36.

Entered Mar. 31, 1938. [76]

United States Board of Tax Appeals
Washington
Docket No. 87480.

TAFT BUILDING LAND TRUST, TRUST No.
B-7620, TITLE INSURANCE AND TRUST
COMPANY, TRUSTEE,

Petitioner,

v.

COMMISSIONER OF INTERNAL REVENUE,

Respondent.

DECISION.

Pursuant to the determination of the Board, as set forth in its Memorandum Findings of Fact and Opinion, entered March 31, 1938, it is

Ordered and decided: That there is a deficiency in income tax of $2,726.36 for the year 1933, and no penalty.

Entered Mar. 31, 1938.

[Seal]   (Signed) ARTHUR J. MELLOTT,

Member. [77]

[Title of Board and Cause.]

PETITION FOR REVIEW OF DECISION OF THE UNITED STATES BOARD OF TAX APPEALS.

To the Honorable, the Judges of the United States Circuit Court of Appeals for the Ninth Circuit:

Taft Building Land Trust, Trust No. B-7620, Title Insurance and Trust Company, Trustee, in support of this its petition filed in pursuance of the provisions of Section 1001 of the Act of Congress approved February 26, 1926, entitled "The Revenue Act of 1926" as amended by Section 603 of the Act of Congress approved May 29, 1928, entitled "The Revenue Act of 1928" and as further amended by Section 1101 of the Act of Congress approved June 6, 1932, entitled "The Revenue Act of 1932" for the review of the decision of the United States Board of Tax Appeals, a final order of determination having been entered on March 31, 1938, respectfully shows to this honorable court as follows:

I.

Statement of the Nature of the Controversy
Brief Statement of Facts.

The question presented in this appeal is whether the petitioner is taxable for the calendar year 1933 as an association or as a trust within the meaning of the Revenue Act of 1932.

The Petitioner was created by an Agreement and Declaration of Trust executed July 15, 1927 (but

for convenience dated June 15, 1927) between
Mitchum [78] Tully & Company, a California corporation, as Trustor, Title Insurance and Trust
Company, a California corporation, as Trustee, and
Harry L. Dunn and Albert Parker and such persons, partnerships, associations and/or corporations
as may become parties thereto by the acceptance of
certificates issued thereunder as beneficiaries.

The Trustor (Mitchum Tully & Company) by
grant deed dated July 12, 1927, conveyed to the trustee the real property located at the corner of Hollywood Boulevard and Vine Street in the City of
Los Angeles improved with a twelve story building
containing stores on the ground floor and offices
above. Prior to the execution of the Agreement and
Declaration of Trust, Mitchum Tully & Company
had negotiated and arranged for the lease of the
trust properties with Sun Realty Company. The
Agreement and Declaration of Trust, provided,
as among its express purposes, for the execution by the Trustee of a lease (previously negotiated by the Trustor) with the Sun Realty Company and this lease was executed by the Trustee
on July 15, 1927, at or about the same time as it
executed the trust agreement. The lease was for a
period of 98½ years commencing July 15, 1927, and
provided for a net monthly rental of $3,500.00 and
required the lessee to pay all taxes, general and
special which may be levied against the property of
the leasehold and to keep the property insured
against damage by fire and earthquake. The lease

contained an option to purchase the property for $725,000.00 prior to June 15, 1952, and for $750,-000.00 thereafter until the expiration of the lease.

The beneficial interest in the trust consisted of 665 equal fractional parts represented by certificates issued by the trustee. The certificates were transferred by the execution of the assignment on the reverse side thereof and transferred on the books of the trustee. The Declaration of Trust provided that the trustee shall keep a register of the names of the holders of certificates, proper transfer books in respect of such certificates and books of [79] account showing receipts and disbursements of the trust estate. The activities of the Trustee during the year consisted of receiving twelve monthly checks and depositing the same, making two distributions a year to the beneficiaries and the performance of ordinary duties such as ascertaining whether proper insurance was carried by the lessee and the like.

The Trustee filed a Fiduciary Return of Income for the calendar year 1933. The Commissioner of Internal Revenue determined that the Petitioner was an Association taxable as a Corporation and proposed a deficiency in the amount of $2,726.36.

II.
Statement of Proceedings Heretofore Held.

The Commissioner of Internal Revnue, Respondent herein, on the 20th day of October, 1936, mailed to petitioner what is termed a deficiency letter wherein the Commissioner proposed a deficiency of taxes for the year 1933 in the sum of $2,726.36 (and a penalty in the amount of $681.59 eliminated by the Board decision). In due course of time and within the ninety day period, petitioner filed its appeal with the United States Board of Tax Appeals wherein it alleged that Respondent had erroneously determined petitioner to be an association taxable as a Corporation and had erroneously failed to treat the petitioner as a trust the income of which is taxable under Section 161 of the Revenue Act of 1932. Thereafter the Board of Tax Appeals entered its order determining a deficiency in tax against petitioner in the sum of $2,726.36.

III.

Declaration of Court of Review.

The petitioner being aggrieved by the findings of fact, opinion, decision and order, and being a resident of the City of Los Angeles, State of California, desires a review thereof in accordance with the provisions of the Revenue Act of 1926 as amended by the Revenue Act of 1928 and as further amended by the [80] Revenue Act of 1932 by the United States Circuit Court of Appeals for the Ninth Circuit, within which circuit is located the office of the Collector of Internal Revenue to which the said petitioner made its income tax return for the year 1933.

IV.

Assignments of Error.

The petitioner, as a basis of review, makes the following assignments of error:

1. The Board of Tax Appeals erred in determinging a deficiency in tax against the petitioner for the year 1933 in the sum of $2,726.36.

2. The Board of Tax Appeals erred in determining that petitioner is an association taxable as a corporation under the provisions of Section 1111 (a) (2) of the Revenue Act of 1932.

3. The Board of Tax Appeals erred in failing to hold that petitioner is a trust taxable under the provisions of Section 161 of the Revenue Act of 1932.

4. The Board of Tax Appeals erred in failing to find that petitioner was not "doing business."

5. The Board of Tax Appeals erred in failing to find as a fact that petitioner was not doing business in an organized capacity.

6. The Board of Tax Appeals erred in that the opinion and decision of the Board based upon its findings of fact are contrary to law.

7. The Board of Tax Appeals erred in that there are no findings of fact to sustain the Board's conclusion of law as set out in its opinion and decision.

8. The Board of Tax Appeals erred in that the conclusions of law set forth in its opinion are con-

trary to and not in harmony with the Board's findings of fact.

(Signed) JOHN T. RILEY
Counsel for Petitioner,
505 Title Insurance Building,
Los Angeles, California. [81]

State of California
County of Los Angeles—ss:

John T. Riley, being first duly sworn, says that he is counsel of record in the above-named cause; that as such counsel he is authorized to verify the foregoing petition for review; that he has read the said petition and is familiar with the statements contained therein; and that the statements made are true to the best of his knowledge, information and belief.

(Signed) JOHN T. RILEY

Subscribed and sworn to before me this 26 day of May, 1938.

[Seal]   (Signed) EDRENA ROGERS
Notary Public in and for the County of Los Angeles
State of California.

My commission expires Sept. 15, 1941.

[Endorsed]: U.S.B.T.A. Filed June 4, 1938. [82]

[Title of Board and Cause.]

PRAECIPE FOR RECORD

To the Clerk of the United States Board of Tax
  Appeals:

You are hereby requested to prepare and certify
and transmit to the Clerk of the Circuit Court of
Appeals for the Ninth Circuit with reference to
petition for review heretofore filed by the petitioner
in the above cause, a transcript of the record of the
above cause, prepared and transmitted as required
by law and by the rules of said Court, and to include
in said transcript of record the following documents
or certified copies thereof, to wit:

(1)   The docket entries of all proceedings before
the Board of Tax Appeals.

(2)   Pleadings before the Board of Tax Appeals,
as follows:

(a)   Petition for redetermination, including
  exhibits.

(b)   Answer of the respondent.

(3)   The findings of fact and opinion of the
Board of Tax Appeals.

(4)   The decision of the Board.

(5)   The petition for review, filed by the petitioner in the above cause.

(6)   This Praecipe.

(Signed) JOHN T. RILEY
                    Attorney for Petitioner,
                    505 Title Insurance Building,
                    Los Angeles, California. [83]

Personal service of a copy of the within Praecipe is hereby admitted this 4th day of June, 1938.

J. P. WENCHEL

Chief Counsel,

Bureau of Internal Revenue,

Counsel for Respondent.

[Endorsed]: U.S.B.T.A. Filed June 4, 1938. [84]

[Title of Board and Cause.]

CERTIFICATE

I, B. D. Gamble, clerk of the U. S. Board of Tax Appeals, do hereby certify that the foregoing pages, 1 to 84, inclusive, contain and are a true copy of the transcript of record, papers, and proceedings on file and of record in my office as called for by the Praecipe in the appeal (or appeals) as above numbered and entitled.

In testimony whereof, I hereunto set my hand and affix the seal of the United States Board of Tax Appeals, at Washington, in the District of Columbia, this 23rd day of June, 1938.

[Seal]   B. D. GAMBLE

Clerk, United States Board of

Tax Appeals.

[Endorsed]: No. 8886. United States Circuit Court of Appeals for the Ninth Circuit. Taft Building Land Trust, Trust No. B-7620, Title Insurance and Trust Company, Trustee, Petitioner, vs. Commissioner of Internal Revenue, Respondent. Transcript of the Record. Upon Petition to Review a Decision of the United States Board of Tax Appeals.

Filed July 11, 1938.

PAUL P. O'BRIEN,

Clerk of the United States Circuit Court of Appeals for the Ninth Circuit.

TOPICAL INDEX.

TABLE OF AUTHORITIES CITED.

CASES.   PAGE

STATUTE.

No. 8886.

In the United States
Circuit Court of Appeals
For the Ninth Circuit.

TAFT BUILDING LAND TRUST, TRUST No. B-7620, TITLE
INSURANCE AND TRUST COMPANY, Trustee,

Petitioner,

vs.

COMMISSIONER OF INTERNAL REVENUE,

Respondent.

BRIEF FOR PETITIONER.

Opinions Below.

The opinion of the Board of Tax Appeals in this case
[R. 158-162] is a memorandum opinion.

Jurisdiction

The petition for review involves a deficiency of income
tax for the calendar year 1933 in the sum of $2,726.36.
The petition for review, filed June 4, 1938 [R. 169], is
taken from the decision of the United States Board of
Tax Appeals entered March 31, 1938 [R. 163], pursuant
to the provisions of Sections 1001-1003 of the Revenue
Act of 1926, c. 27, 44 Stat. 109-110; as amended' by

Section 603 of the Revenue Act of 1928, c. 852, 45 Stat. 873; as further amended by Section 1101 of the Revenue Act of 1932, c. 209, 47 Stat. 286; and by Section 519 of the Revenue Act of 1934, c. 277, 426, 48 Stat. 760, 926.

The allegation showing the existence of the jurisdiction of the Board of Tax Appeals and of this Court are contained in the petition filed with the Board [R. 3-8] and the petition for review [R. 164-167].

Question Presented.

Is the income of the petitioner for the calendar year 1933 subject to tax as the income of an association under Section 1111(a)(2) or as a trust under Sections 161 and 162 of the Revenue Act of 1932?

Statutes Involved.

See appendix, pages 29-30.

Statement of the Case.

The issue in this case involves the determination of whether or not the petitioner during the calendar year 1933 was an association taxable as a corporation within the purview of the Revenue Act of 1932. [R. 164.]

The petitioner was created by an agreement and declaration of trust executed July 15, 1927 (but for convenience dated June 15, 1927), between Mitchum Tully & Company, a California corporation, as trustor, Title Insurance and Trust Company, a California corporation, as trustee, and Harry L. Dunn and Albert Parker and such persons, partnerships, associations and/or corporations as may become parties thereto by the acceptance of certificates issued thereunder as beneficiaries. [R. 150.]

The trustor (Mitchum Tully & Company), by grant deed dated July 12, 1927, conveyed to the trustee the real property [R. 13] located at the corner of Hollywood boulevard and Vine street in the city of Los Angeles, improved with a twelve-story building, containing stores on the ground floor and offices above. [R. 155.] Prior to the execution of the agreement and declaration of trust Mitchum Tully & Company had negotiated and arranged for the lease of the trust properties with Sun Realty Company. [R. 155.]

The agreement and declaration of trust (article 5) provided, as among its express purposes, for the execution by the trustee of a lease (previously negotiated by the trustor) with the Sun Realty Company. [R. 30-31.]

Article 5 of the agreement and declaration of trust reads as follows:

> "*Among the express purposes of this trust* and among the purposes and powers of the trustee under this agreement and declaration of trust is and shall be the purpose and power to rent and lease the real property hereinabove described, or any part thereof, as soon as may be after the execution of this agreement and declaration of trust, upon a long term lease for the benefit of the trustor, and for the benefit of Harry L. Dunn and Albert Parker as the original beneficiaries hereunder and their respective successors

as owners of the beneficial interests hereunder and holders of the Land Trust Certificates herein provided for, *it being understood that it is the intention of the trustee as soon as may be after the execution of this agreement and declaration of trust to execute a lease of the above-described property to Sun Realty Co.,* a California corporation, as lessee, said lease to be dated July 15th, 1927, and to be expressed to run for a period of ninety-eight (98) years and six (6) months and to provide for the payment by the lessee to the trustee as lessor, of a yearly rental of forty-two thousand dollars ($42,000) in addition to the payment of taxes, insurance premiums, etc.; said lease to contain an option allowing said lessee to purchase said property, upon sixty (60) days' prior notice, upon any December 15 or June 15, for the purchase price of seven hundred twenty-five thousand dollars ($725,000) if such purchase be completed on or before June 15, 1952; and for the purchase price of seven hundred fifty thousand dollars ($750,000.00) on any December 15 or June 15 thereafter, but within the time which may be specified in said lease, said lease to contain such further terms, provisions and conditions as the trustee may approve." (Italics supplied.) [R. 30-31.]

This lease was executed by the trustee on July 15, 1927, at or about the same time as it executed the trust agreement. [R. 155.] The lease was for a period of 98½ years, commencing July 15, 1927, and provided for a net monthly rental of $3,500.00 and required the lessee to pay all taxes, general and special, which may be levied against the property of the leasehold and to keep the property insured against damage by fire and earthquake and to repair and maintain the premises leased. [R. 156.]

The lease granted to the lessee an option to purchase the property for $725,000.00 prior to June 15, 1952, and for $750,000.00 thereafter until the expiration of the lease. [R. 126-127.]

That in the event the lessee (Sun Realty Co.) shall exercise its right to purchase, the trustee shall, upon receipt of the purchase price, have full authority to execute the necessary conveyance without securing consent from certificate holders; that the trustee may, subject to the option of Sun Realty Co., sell and convey all of the trust property at its discretion with the consent of the certificate holders, providing the sale shall make available for distribution among the beneficiaries at least $1,250,-000.00, and that the trustee may at any time, upon obtaining the written consent of two-thirds (⅔) of the six hundred and sixty-five (665) interests, sell and convey the property upon such terms as may be provided in such consents, but that the trustee was not obligated so to do. [R. 152.]

Upon any sale of the trust property, the trustee was to make distribution of the proceeds as provided in the declaration of trust, after deducting any expenses, and the trust was to terminate. [R. 40-44.]

Upon termination by lapse of time (unless sooner terminated) the trustee could transfer the property to the then beneficiaries as tenants-in-common in the proportions of the beneficial interests owned by each, or could sell the properties and distribute the proceeds to the beneficiaries. [R. 61-66.]

The beneficial interest in the trust consisted of 665 equal fractional parts, represented by certificates issued by the trustee. After the execution of the trust agreement the trustee issued eight certificates, representing the 665 beneficial units, to Dunn and Parker, who assigned them to Mitchum Tully & Company (trustor), who, in turn, assigned or sold them to others. During 1933 all of the 665 beneficial units were outstanding and unredeemed certificates were held by 222 persons. [R. 156.] The certificates were transferable by the execution of the assignments on the reverse side thereof and transfer on the books of the trustee. The declaration of trust provided that the trustee shall keep a register of the names of the holders of certificates, proper transfer books in respect of such certificates and books of account showing receipts and disbursements of the trust estate. [R. 150-151.]

The activities of the trustee during a year consisted of receiving twelve monthly checks and depositing the same, making two distributions a year to the beneficiaries, and the performance of ordinary duties, such as ascertaining whether proper insurance was carried by the lessee and the like. [R. 156-157.]

No meetings were ever held which were attended by the trustor or beneficiaries of the trust in connection with the management of the affairs of the trust. [R. 157.]

The rent provided for under the Sun Realty Co. lease was always paid, although the rent was delinquent at the time the lessees' interest in the trust property was foreclosed under a bond issue. However, the receiver appointed at that time paid the delinquent rent within the thirty-day period specified in the lease. [R. 157.]

The trustee filed a fiduciary return of income for the calendar year 1933. The Commissioner of Internal Revenue determined that the petitioner was an association, taxable as a corporation, and proposed a deficiency in the amount of $2,726.36. [R. 149.]

The Commissioner of Internal Revenue, respondent herein, on the 20th day of October, 1936, mailed to petitioner what is termed a deficiency letter, wherein the Commissioner proposed a deficiency of taxes for the year 1933 in the sum of $2,726.36 (and a penalty in the amount of $681.59 eliminated by the Board decision). In due course of time and within the ninety-day period, petitioner filed its appeal with the United States Board of Tax Appeals, wherein it alleged that respondent had erroneously determined petitioner to be an association, taxable as a corporation, and had erroneously failed to treat the petitioner as a trust, the income of which is taxable under Section 161 of the Revenue Act of 1932. Thereafter the Board of Tax Appeals entered its order determining a deficiency in tax against petitioner in the sum of $2,726.36. [R. 162.]

Assignments of Error.

The petitioner relies upon the following assignments of error:

1. The Board of Tax Appeals erred in determining a deficiency in tax against the petitioner for the year 1933 in the sum of $2,726.36. [R. 168.]

2. The Board of Tax Appeals erred in determining that petitioner is an association, taxable as a corporation, under the provisions of Section 1111(a)(2) of the Revenue Act of 1932. [R. 168.]

3. The Board of Tax Appeals erred in failing to hold that petitioner is a trust, taxable under the provisions of Section 161 of the Revenue Act of 1932. [R. 168.]

4. The Board of Tax Appeals erred in failing to find that petitioner was not "doing business". [R. 168.]

5. The Board of Tax Appeals erred in failing to find as a fact that petitioner was not doing business in an organized capacity. [R. 168.]

6. The Board of Tax Appeals erred in that the opinion and decision of the Board, based upon its findings of fact, are contrary to law. [R. 168.]

7. The Board of Tax Appeals erred in that there are no findings of fact to sustain the Board's conclusion of law, as set out in its opinion and decision. [R. 168.]

8. The Board of Tax Appeals erred in that the conclusions of law set forth in its opinion are contrary to and not in harmony with the Board's findings of fact. [R. 168.]

Summary of Argument.

The petitioner was not taxable as an association under Section 1111(a)(2) of the Revenue Act of 1932 for the calendar year 1933 for the following reasons:

(1) Petitioner was not "doing business" at any time during the calendar year 1933.

(2) The trustee was bound by the agreement and declaration of trust to execute a lease for a period of 98 years and 6 months at the time it accepted the trust estate. The lease had previously been negotiated by the trustor. The trustee did execute this lease at or about the same time it executed the trust agreement on July 15, 1927. This lease from date of execution to the present time is and has been in full force and effect.

(3) The activities of the trustee consisted of collecting twelve monthly checks during a year and making two semi-annual distributions to the beneficiaries of the trust.

(4) The purpose for which the trust was formed, as shown by the findings and declaration of trust and its actual operations, show that this petitioner is not an association, but is a trust, taxable under the provisions of Section 161 of the Revenue Act of 1932.

(5) The findings of fact of the Board of Tax Appeals show that the petitioner was not "doing business" and the Board should have so found.

(6) The opinion and the decision of the Board, based upon its findings of fact, are contrary to law.

(7) The Board of Tax Appeals to sustain its decision should have found as a fact that the petitioner *was* "doing business".

ARGUMENT.

I.

The Petitioner Was Not an Association Taxable at Corporate Rates.

The following are the assignments of error to which this point is directed:

(1) The Board of Tax Appeals erred in determining the deficiency of tax against the petitioner for the year 1933 in the sum of $2,726.36. [R. 168.]

(2) The Board of Tax Appeals erred in determining that petitioner is an association, taxable as a corporation under the provisions of Section 1111 (a)(2) of the Revenue Act of 1932. [R. 168.]

(3) The Board of Tax Appeals erred in failing to hold that petitioner is a trust, taxable under the provisions of Section 161 of the Revenue Act of 1932. [R. 168.]

The Revenue Act does not purport to tax all trusts as associations, as the Revenue Act of 1932, in Sections 161 and 162, provides for the taxing of trusts that are not taxable as associations. Trusts that constitute an association for the purpose of carrying on a business are taxable as an association at corporate rates. Other trusts that are *not* "doing business" are treated as true trusts, taxable under Sections 161 and 162 of the Revenue Act of 1932.

The Board of Tax Appeals in its opinion [R. 158] agrees with the Commissioner's interpretation that the petitioner is an association within the meaning of the provisions of Section 1111(a)(2) of the Revenue Act of 1932 and states that such construction is in harmony with the construction placed upon similar agreements in the group of cases decided by the Supreme Court December 16, 1935:

> *Morrissey et al. v. Commissioner,* 296 U. S. 344;
>
> *Swanson et al v. Commissioner,* 296 U. S. 362;
>
> *Helvering v. Coleman-Gilbert Associates,* 296 U. S. 369; and
>
> *Helvering v. Combs et al.,* 296 U. S. 365.

Petitioner respectfully submits that this construction is in error and that the cases cited by the Board in its opinion are not controlling in this case for the reason that in all of these cases the trusts involved were *doing business,* while petitioner submits that it is *not doing business* and the Board of Tax Appeals did not find that petitioner was doing business. The Supreme Court, in the *Morrissey* case, *supra,* went to great length to point out that the question involved "business trusts", stating, in the course of its opinion:

At page 349:

> "The Government insists that the distinction between associations and the trusts taxed under Section 219 (Revenue Acts of 1924 and 1926) is between *'business trusts* on the one side' *and other trusts 'which are engaged merely in collecting the income and conserving the property* against the day when it is to be distributed to the beneficiaries;' that Congress intended that all 'business trusts' should be taxed as associations." (Italics supplied.)

And at page 356:

> " 'Association' implies associates. It implies the entering into a joint enterprise and, as the applicable

regulation imports, *an enterprise for the transaction of business. This is not the characteristic of an ordinary trust—whether created by will, deed or declaration—by which particular property is conveyed* to a trustee or is to be held by the settler, on specified trusts, for the benefit of named or described persons. * * * *In what are called 'business trusts'* the object is not to hold and conserve particular property, with incidental powers, as in the traditional type of trust, *but to provide a medium for the conduct of a business and sharing its gains."* (Italics supplied.)

The Court, after pointing out the salient features of a trust when created and maintained as a medium for the carrying on of a business enterprise which made it analogous to a corporate organization, stated as follows:

At page 359:

"It is no answer to say that these advances flow from the very nature of trusts, for the question has arisen because of the use and adaptation of the trust mechanism. The suggestion ignores the postulate that *we are considering* those trusts which have the distinctive feature of being *created to enable the participants to carry on a business* and divide the gains which accrue from their common undertaking." (Italics supplied.)

The Morrissey trust was created for the development of a tract of land, and the Court held that the contemplated development of the tract of land held at the outset by the trust, even if other properties were not acquired, involved what was essentially a business enterprise.

In the *Swanson* case, 296 U. S. 362, the trust property
consisted of an apartment house. Under the trust agreement the trustees were given complete management and
control of the property. The Court, in applying the governing principles set forth in the opinion in the *Morrissey*
case, 296 U. S. 344, held that the trust constituted an
association.

In *Helvering v. Gilbert Associates,* 296 U. S. 369, co-
owners of real property, consisting of about twenty apartment houses, had the property conveyed to themselves as
trustees. The trust owned and operated the apartment
houses, collecting annual gross rents, which amounted to
about $420,000.00. There were approximately 1500 ten-
ants. The Court, in the course of its opinion states:

At pages 373-374:

> "Not only were they actually engaged, as the
> Board of Tax Appeals determined, in carrying on
> an extensive business for profit, but the terms of
> the trust instrument authorized a wide range of
> activities in the purchase, improvement and sale of
> properties in the cities and towns of the state. The
> parties are not at liberty to say that their purpose
> was other or narrower than that which they formerly
> set forth in the instrument under which their activ-
> ities were conducted."

In the *Helvering v. Combs et al.* case, 296 U. S. 365,
the trust was created to finance and drill a well for production and sale of oil. The Court in this case held:

At page 368:

> "The parties joined in a common enterprise for the
> transaction of business and the beneficiaries who con-

tributed money for that purpose became associated in the enterprise according to the terms of the arrangement."

In all of the foregoing cases the trusts were "doing business".

It is submitted that the petitioner was formed for the purpose of holding title to one piece of real estate subject to a long-term lease containing an option to purchase and to collect the rents provided for and to distribute the proceeds of any monies received for the sale of the trust property and that such purpose and activities do not constitute engaging in business.

In the *Morrissey* case, 296 U. S. 344, the Supreme Court did not reverse or qualify its decision in the case of *Crocker v. Malley,* 249 U. S. 223, 63 L. Ed. 573, in which the Court held the taxpayer taxable as a trust and in which the Court stated that the declaration of trust relating to mill property was, on its face, an ordinary real estate trust, in which the function of the trustees was not to manage the mills but simply to collect the rents and income of such property as may be in their hands. The Court in the *Morrissey* case, in reviewing its decisions relating to trusts, reviews *Hecht v. Malley,* 265 U. S. 144, 68 L. Ed. 949, and in the course of its opinion states:

At page 352:

"In the Hecht case the trustees of the Hecht and Haymarket trusts relied strongly upon the decision in Crocker v. Malley as conclusively determining that those trusts could not be held to be associations, unless the trust agreements vested 'the shareholders with such control over the trustees as to constitute them more than strict trusts within the Massachusetts rule.' Reviewing the reasoning of that decision, we pointed out that it was not authority for the broad proposition advanced. *We concluded that, when the nature of the trusts was considered, as the petitioners were 'not merely trustees for collecting funds and paying them over,'* but were 'associated together in much the same manner as the directors in a corporation for the purpose of carrying on business enterprises,' the trusts were to be deemed associations within the meaning of the Act of 1918." (Italics supplied.)

In the case of *Commissioner v. Vandegrift Realty and Investment Company,* 82 Fed. (2d) 387, this Court stated:

"There can hardly be a serious question as to the fact that the trust was carried on under a corporate form, but the Supreme Court indicates very clearly in Morrissey v. Commissioner, *supra,* that little consideration should be given to the form of organization under which the trust is operated, but rather that *the true rule is that purpose and actual operation of the trust should be controlling in determining whether or not the trust shall be classified as an association for tax purposes."* (Italics supplied.)

In the case of *Pelton et al. v. Commissioner,* decided March 20, 1936, 82 Fed. (2d) 473, the Seventh Circuit Court of Appeals cited *Morrissey v. Commissioner,* 296 U. S. 344, 56 S. Ct. 289; *Helvering v. Coleman Gilbert Associates,* 296 U. S. 369, 56 S. Ct. 285; *Swanson et al v. Commissioner,* 296 U. S. 362, 56 S. Ct. 283, and *Helvering v. Combs,* 296 U. S. 365, 56 S. Ct. 287, and stated:

At page 476:

"Those decisions hold that a trust is an association when (1) *it is carrying on a business enterprise for profit,* and (2) *it has substantial resemblance to a corporation."*

In the case of *Julius Blum,* 25 B. T. A. 119, the Board states:

At page 124:

" 'Organization' and the 'doing of business' must unite before the entity may be taxed as a corporation. Philadelphia & Reading Relief Ass'n, 4 B. T. A. 713; Albert M. Briggs, 7 B. T. A. 409, and Realty Associates, 17 B. T. A. 1173."

PURPOSE:

Under the rule stated by this Court in the *Vandegrift* case, *supra,* petitioner is certainly a trust and not an association. Its purpose, as set forth in the agreement and declaration of trust, is briefly summarized as follows:

Article 1 provides that the trustee shall hold all the title, right and interest in and to the real property acquired. [R. 15.]

Articles 2 and 3 provide for form of certificate to be issued to beneficiaries and for a register of the holders of certificates to be kept by the trustee. [R. 15-30.]

Article 4 provides that no assessments shall ever be made on the certificate holders. [R. 30.]

Article 5 provides "among the express purposes of this trust" is to execute a long-term lease providing for annual income and containing option to purchase the properties. [R. 30-31.]

Article 6 deals with moneys paid, if any, prior to execution of trust. [R. 32-33.]

Article 7 provides, in event of default of original lessee or any successor lessee, giving and granting to the trustee full authority to take such steps and do such things as it may deem advisable and proper to terminate the lease. In the event of termination the trustee is given full authority to do any and all things as in its opinion may be necessary or proper for the best interests of the beneficiaries, including the operation, sale or other disposition of the property. [R. 33-34.]

Articles 8 and 9 deal with the manner in which the trustee is to make semi-annual distributions of moneys received. [R. 34-40.]

Article 10 recites, as among the express purposes of the trust, the power to sell and convey the trust estate and the manner of distributing proceeds. [R. 40-44.]

Article 11 provides for the distribution of any moneys received in connection with proceedings in condemnation, expropriation or eminent domain. [R. 44-45.]

Articles 12 and 13 deals with consideration to be paid to the trustee and its duties. [R. 45-52.]

Article 14 provides after the termination of the original long-term lease to Sun Realty Co., the trustee may, in its discretion, change the dates of making semi-annual payments—seek in its own absolute discretion the advice of the holders of certificates and to pursue such course of action as may in its opinion be necessary and advisable for the best interest of the certificate holders. [R. 52-54.]

Article 15 [R. 57] declared that among the express purposes of the trust that the trustee was authorized to mortgage or otherwise bind or charge the real property of the trust *for the purpose of providing funds to meet any emergency* arising in connection therewith and for the benefit of the beneficiaries. (Italics supplied.)

Article 16 deals with the resignation of the trustee and appointment of a new trustee. [R. 59.]

Article 17 deals with the termination of the trust. [R. 61-65.]

Article 18 defines the term "trustee". [R. 66.]

Article 19 deals with the legality of the agreement and declaration of trust. [R. 66-67.]

Article 20 provides for a deposit of all funds received by the trustee. [R. 67.]

Article 21 deals with the liability of the trust for inheritance, income or other taxes and authorizes the trustee to withhold and pay such taxes out of any money in its possession. [R. 68.]

Article 22 provides that any beneficiary accepting any certificate shall be deemed a party to the agreement and declaration of trust. [R. 68-69.]

Article 23 authorizes the trustee to record the agreement and declaration of trust. [R. 69-70.]

The purposes set forth in the agreement and declaration of trust clearly show that the trust was not formed for the purpose of actively engaging in any business, but was formed for the purpose of holding title to one piece of property, improved with a twelve-story building containing storerooms on the lower floor and offices above, and to execute a long-term lease that was previously negotiated by the trustor, said lease to contain an option granting the lessee the right to purchase the trust estate throughout the term of the lease, to-wit, 98 years and 6 months. This lease was executed and is still in force and effect. [R. 156-157.] It was not the purpose, as shown by the agreement and declaration of trust, for the trustee to operate the building by leasing the separate storerooms and offices contained in the twelve-story building. These operations were to be conducted by the lessee. The trustee was not empowered to invest and reinvest any funds received, but was required to make distribution of all funds semi-annually after deducting expenses.

In the case of a default in the long-term lease by the lessee or any successor lessee or in the event the said lease shall be terminated for any reason or shall expire by limitation, the trustee had full authority to terminate the lease or to take such steps as the trustee in its opinion deems necessary and proper for the best interests of the certificate holders with respect to leasing, operating, selling, conveying, or otherwise disposing of the trust property. [R. 33.] Petitioner submits that this is an incidental power that the trustee would be required to use, even though not contained in the trust instrument, as it would have a duty to do whatever would be proper for the best interest of the certificate holders. The trustee has full power to compromise or settle claims, either in contract or tort, made by it or against it or the trust estate and to charge the expense against the income of the trust. [R. 56.] This is also an incidental power. The agreement and declaration of trust gave the trustee the right to mortgage and otherwise bind or charge the trust estate *for the purpose of providing funds to meet any exigency* arising in connection therewith and for the benefit of the certificate holders. [R. 57.] This is another incidental power. In the case of any emergency the trustee would have a duty to do that which would be for the benefit and best interests of the beneficiaries.

The case of petitioner is certainly distinguishable from the group of cases decided by the Supreme Court on December 16, 1935, hereinbefore cited, in that in all of those cases *the original purpose was to actively engage in business to produce income,* while in the petitioner's case the income is provided for in the lease that had been negotiated by the trustor prior to the execution of the agreement and declaration of trust and that was executed by the trustee. [R. 55.] The trust did not engage in business activities except those incidental activities that any trustee would be required to do to preserve the trust property. In the case of *Ittleson v. Anderson,* 67 Fed. (2d) 323, at page 326, the Second Circuit Court of Appeals states:

> "*A distinction is to be drawn between the activities of trustees under a strict trust as distinguished from the activities under a business trust.* Even in the strict trust the activities of the trustees, in preserving the trust estate, may partake of the nature of business transactions. It is a matter of degree. When, on the one hand, the trustees promote and conduct a particular business enterprise with the trust estate, it is considered an association. The usual type is a trust for the development of real estate (trust No. 5833, Security-First Nat. Bank v. Welch, *supra*) or for the active management of developed real estate (U. S. v. Neal, *supra.*) *When, on the other hand, a trustee is merely engaged in the amount of business activity necessary to preserve the corpus and otherwise discharge the functions traditionally attributable to a strict trust, it is not treated as an association.*

Lansdowne v. Com'r, *supra;* Gardiner v. Com'r, *supra;* Allen v. Com'r, *supra.* Between these extremes is the field where trustees in the management of trust property engaged in considerable business activity, and the question then presented is whether they function as a business organization or merely as trustees under the modern conception of what a strict trustee has a duty and right to do." (Italics supplied.)

In the case of *Zonne v. Minneapolis Syndicate,* 31 S. Ct. 361, the corporation had leased its property for 130 years; its activities were limited to collecting and distributing rents received under the terms of the lease or the proceeds of any sale of the land if it should be sold. The Court held the company was not doing business within the meaning of the Act of August 5, 1909 (Stat. at L. 1st Sess. 61st Cong. pp. 11-112-117, chap. 6, U. S. Comp. Stat. Supp. 1909, pp. 659-844-849). Section 38, imposing an excise upon the doing or the carrying on of business in a corporate or quasi corporate capacity.

In *Llewellyn, Collector, v. Pittsburgh, B. & L. E. R. Co.* (C. C. A.), 222 Fed. 177, 185, a case relating to the excise tax imposed by Act of August 5, 1909, Section 38 (36 Stat. 112), it is said (at page 185):

"'Carrying on business' does not mean the performance of a single disconnected business act. It means conducting, prosecuting, and continuing business by performing progressively all the acts normally incident thereto, and likewise the expression 'doing business' when employed as descriptive of an occupation, conveys the idea of business being done, not from time to time, but all the time." See, also, *Mente v. Eisner* (C. C. A.), 266 Fed. 161, 11 A. L. R. 496.

In the case of the *United Mercury Mines Co. v. John R. Viley,* decided by the United States District Court in and for the District of Idaho, Southern Division, on September 7, 1937, paragraph 1560, 1937 Prentice-Hall, the Court held the corporation was not "carrying on or doing business" for capital stock tax purposes where the only function of the corporation was to collect and distribute the purchase price of properties received from a lease and option to purchase theretofore granted upon all of its assets.

In further support of the fact that petitioner is not doing business and that the case of *Morrissey, et al. v. Commissioner,* 296 U. S. 344, and related cases decided by the Supreme Court December 16, 1935, and relied upon by the Board of Tax Appeals in its opinion are not authorities for determining what constitutes "engaged in trade or business" or "carrying on or doing business," attention is invited to General Counsel's Memorandum 18835, XVI-33-8875, issued in 1937 and printed in full in appendix at pages 30-37.

The General Counsel was dealing with the question of whether the ownership and operation of a building in the United States by a nonresident alien individual or foreign corporation constituted "engaging in trade or business" within the United States. The opinion states:

"The test of liability for income tax, excess-profits tax, and capital stock tax, in so far as such taxes were based upon, or measured by, engaging in or doing business within the United States, should be identical. * * * The mere ownership of property itself is not sufficient to constitute engaging in trade or business. It has been held that a company whose activities consisted of managing real estate and rent-

ing offices was doing business or engaging in business.
(Flint v. Stone Tracy Co., 220 U. S. 107.) *On the
other hand, it has been held that a railroad company
which leased its entire railroad for a term of years
at an annual rental was not engaging in business.*
(McCoach v. Minehill, etc., 228 U. S. 295.) * * *

"In McCoach v. Minehill, etc., *supra,* which also
arose under the Act of August 5, 1909, the Court
stated that the mere receipt of income from property
did not constitute engaging in business and commented
as follows:

"* * * The distinction is between (a) the
receipt of income from outside property or investments by a company that is otherwise engaged in.
business; in which event the investment income may
be added to the business income in order to arrive at
the measure of the tax; and (b) *the receipt of income*
from property or investments by a company that is
not engaged in business except the business of owning
the property, maintaining the investments, collecting
the income and dividing it among its stockholders.
In the former case the tax is payable; in the latter not.

"The above quoted extracts from the opinions rendered by the Supreme Court may be accepted as a
guide in determining what acts in connection with the
ownership of income-producing real property constitute engaging in business. Generally, any activities
beyond 'the mere receipt of income from property, and
the payment of organization and administration expenses incidental to the receipt and distribution thereof' (McCoach v. Minehill, etc.) constitute 'carrying
on or doing business' within the meaning of section
105 (b) of the Revenue Act of 1935, as amended,
relating to capital stock tax, and 'engaging in trade
or business' within the meaning of sections 211 (b)
and 231 (b) of the Revenue Act of 1936, relating to
income tax." (Italics supplied.)

It will be noted from the foregoing opinion that the General Counsel to the Bureau of Internal Revenue does not consider the case of *Morrissey, et al. v. Commissioner,* 296 U. S. 344, and relating cases decided by the Supreme Court on December 16, 1935, as controlling in determining the question of what constitutes "engaged in trade or business" or "carrying on or doing business." In determining this question, the older cases dealing with the excise tax on corporations engaged in business were considered controlling. Petitioner submits that General Counsel's Memorandum and the cases cited therein are controlling in this particular case.

Petitioner submits that it is clearly within the first part of the rule stated to be controlling by this Court in the *Vandegrift* case in that it was not formed for the purpose of doing business and was not doing business.

ACTUAL OPERATION:

As to actual operations, the Board found that the activities of the trustee during a year consisted of receiving twelve monthly checks and depositing the same, making two distributions a year to the beneficiaries and the performance of ordinary duties such as ascertaining whether proper insurance was carried by the lessee and the like. [R. 156-157.]

Clearly, such limited activities that obviously required such a small portion of the trustee's time do not *constitute actively engaging in business.*

In view of the foregoing, it is respectfully submitted that the Board of Tax Appeals erred in determining that the petitioner was taxable as an association.

II.

The Board's Conclusion Is Not Supported by Its Findings of Fact.

The following are the assignments of error to which this point is directed.

(4) The Board of Tax Appeals erred in failing to find that petitioner was *not* "doing business."

(5) The Board of Tax Appeals erred in failing to find as a fact that petitioner was *not* doing business in an organized capacity.

(6) The Board of Tax Appeals erred in that the opinion and decision of the Board based upon its findings of fact are contrary to law.

(7) The Board of Tax Appeals erred in that there are no findings of fact to sustain the Board's conclusion of law as set out in its opinion and decision.

(8) The Board of Tax Appeals erred in that the conclusions of law set forth in its opinion are contrary to and not in harmony with the Board's findings of fact.

In order to determine that the petitioner was taxable as an association at corporate rates, it was necessary for the Board of Tax Appeals to find that the petitioner was formed for the purpose of doing business and was an association. That was the ultimate question of fact which the Board was required to find and failed to do.

In *St. Paul Abstract Co. v. Commissioner,* 32 Fed. (2d) 225, the Eighth Circuit Court of Appeals reviewed a decision of the Board of Tax Appeals which had sustained the Commissioner's assessment against the petitioner by finding that the petitioner was a personal service corporation within the meaning of Section 200 of the Revenue Act of 1918. There the Court held that the Board's finding that the petitioner was a personal service corporation was a finding of ultimate fact which the Court said the Board was required by the statute to make. The issue is the same in this case.

In *Helvering v. Rankin,* 295 U. S. 123, 79 L. Ed. 1343, the Supreme Court in defining principles to govern review of the Board's decisions said that where the Board has failed to make an essential finding and the record is insufficient to provide the basis for a final determination, the proper procedure is to remand the case for further proceedings before the Board. It said that the same procedure would be "appropriate" even when the findings omitted by the Board might be supplied from examination of the record.

In the *Rankin* case, *supra,* the Supreme Court stated:

> "If the Board has failed to make an essential finding and the record on review is insufficient to provide the basis for a final determination, the proper procedure is to remand the case for further proceedings before the Board. * * *."

This language indicates that if the record is sufficient, as is claimed in this case, it is unnecessary for the Court to remand the case.

As stated by the Board, there is no substantial disagreement between the petitioner and the respondent as to the facts. [R. 158.] However, petitioner submits that the agreement and declaration of trust and the findings of the Board clearly show that petitioner was not formed for the purpose of doing business and that its actual operations do not constitute doing business. The Board could not, based upon the undisputed facts, find that petitioner *was* "doing business" but should have found as a fact that the petitioner was *not* "doing business."

In view of the foregoing, it is respectfully submitted that the Board's opinion and decision based upon its findings of fact are contrary to law.

In conclusion, it is respectfully submitted that petitioner is not an association taxable at the corporate rates and therefore the decision of the Board of Tax Appeals should be reversed.

Respectfully submitted,

JOHN T. RILEY,

MARSHALL D. HALL,

Attorneys for Petitioner.

APPENDIX.

Statutes.

Revenue Act of 1932, c. 209, 47 Stat. 289.

"Sec. 13, Tax on Corporations.

"(a) RATE OF TAX—There shall be levied, collected and paid for each taxable year upon the net income of every corporation, a tax of 13¾ per centum of the amount of the net income in excess of the credit against net income provided in Sec. 26. * * *

"Sec. 1111. (a) When used in this Act—

"Sec. 1111. (a) (1) The term 'person' means an individual, a trust or estate, a partnership, or a corporation.

"Sec. 1111. (a) (2) The term 'corporation' includes associations, joint-stock companies, and insurance companies.

"Sec. 161, Imposition of Tax.

"(a) APPLICATION OF TAX.—The taxes imposed by this title upon individuals shall apply to the income of estates or of any kind of property held in trust, including—

"(1) Income accumulated in trust for the benefit of unborn or unascertained persons or persons with contingent interests, and income accumulated or held for future distribution under the terms of the will or trust;

"(2) Income which is to be distributed currently by the fiduciary to the beneficiaries, and income collected by a guardian of an infant which is to be held or distributed as the court may direct;

"(3) Income received by estates of deceased persons during the period of administration or settlement of the estate: and

"(4) Income which, in the discretion of the fiduciary, may be either distributed to the beneficiaries or accumulated.

"(b) COMPUTATION AND PAYMENT.—The tax shall be computed upon the net income of the estate or trust, and shall be paid by the fiduciary, except as provided in section 166 (relating to revocable trusts) and section 167 (relating to income for benefit of the grantor). For return made by beneficiary, see Section 142."

General Counsel's Memorandum, 18835

XVI-33-8875.

REVENUE ACT OF 1936.

Withholding of income tax at the source on the gross rentals derived from real estate in the United States owned by nonresident aliens or foreign corporations.

An opinion is requested whether income tax should be withheld at the source on the gross rentals derived from real estate in the United States owned by nonresident aliens or foreign corporations.

Under the provisions of section 143 of the Revenue Act of 1936, all persons, in whatever capacity acting, including lessees or mortgagors of real or personal property, having the control, receipt, custody, disposal, or payment of rent of any nonresident alien individual are required to deduct and withhold from such income a tax equal to 10 per cent thereof. Section 211(a) imposes a tax of 10 per cent upon the amount received by every nonresident alien individual not engaged in trade or business within the United States and not having an office or place of business therein in lieu of the tax imposed by section 11 and 12 of the Revenue Act of 1936, and section 211(b) provides for the taxation of nonresident aliens in the same manner as citizens of the United States with respect to income derived from sources within the United States if they are engaged in trade or business in the United States or have an office or place of business therein. For the purpose of withholding, however, it is immaterial whether a nonresident alien individual comes within the provisions of section 211(a) or section 211(b) of the Act, and the tax must be withheld at the source from the amount of rent paid to a nonresident alien individual with respect to real property located in the United States, regardless of whether such individual is engaged in trade or business within the United States.

With respect to the rental income paid to a foreign corporation, however, section 144 of the Revenue Act of 1936 provides for the deduction of income tax at the source with respect to certain items of income, including rent, only if paid to a foreign corporation not engaged in trade or business within the United States and not having an office or place of business therein. Where income tax is required to be withheld at the source under sections 143 and 144 of the Revenue Act of 1936, the tax must be withheld from the gross amount of the income rather than the net amount. (See article 143-1, Regulations 94.) It follows that in the case of rent paid to a nonresident alien individual income tax must be withheld at the source at the rate of 10 per cent of the gross amount of rent without the allowance for any expenses incurred in connection with the income. If the nonresident alien individual is engaged in trade or business within the United States or has an office or place of business therein, he is taxable under section 211(b) of the Revenue Act of 1936. In other words, in the case of a nonresident alien individual who at any time during the taxable year was engaged in trade or business in the United States or had an office or place of business therein, the deductions allowed by section 23 for business expenses, interest, taxes, losses in trade, bad debts, depreciation, and depletion are allowed to the extent that they are connected with income from sources within the United States. (Article 213-1 of Regulations 94.) A nonresident alien individual who is taxable under section 211(b), that is, one who is engaged in trade or business within the United States or has an office or place of business therein, may receive the benefit of the deductions allowed under the statute only by filing or causing to be filed a true and accurate return of his total income received from all sources within the United States. (Section 215 of the Revenue Act of 1936.)

A foreign corporation engaged in trade or business within the United States or having an office or place of business therein is not subject to the deduction of income tax at the source with respect to rents, but is taxable at the rate of 22 per cent upon net income from sources within the United States. The benefits of deductions and credits are not allowed, however, unless a true and accurate return of total income received from all sources within the

United States is filed. (Section 233 of the Revenue Act of 1936 and article 233-1 of Regulations 94.)

In connection with the foregoing, the question has arisen whether the ownership and operation of a building in the United States by a nonresident alien individual or foreign corporation constitute "engaging in trade or business" within the United States. *The income tax regulations do not specifically state what constitute engaging in trade or business within the United States.* The question was given consideration by this office in G. C. M. 17014 (C. B. XV-2, 317 (1936)) with the idea of harmonizing the meaning of the phraseology contained in the law relating to capital stock tax with that relating to income tax. The liability of the foreign corporation for capital stock purposes under section 105(b) of the Revenue Act of 1935, as amended, is based on "carrying on or doing business" in the United States, whereas section 231 of the Revenue Act of 1936 relating to income tax uses the phrase "engaged in trade or business" within the United States. In G. C. M. 17014, *supra,* it was held that the expressions are used synonymously, citing *Lewellyn v. Pittsburgh, B. & L. E. R. Co.* (222 Fed., 177); *McCoach v. Minehill & Schuylkill Haven Railroad Co.* (228 U. S. 295); *Von Baumbach v. Sargent Land Co.* (242 U. S. 503); and *Edwards v. Chile Copper Co.* (270 U. S. 452). *It was stated that "the test of liability for income tax excess-profits tax, and capital stock tax, in so far as such taxes were based upon, or measured by, engaging in or doing business within the United States, should be identical."* It was concluded that if the foreign corporation was engaged in trade or business for income tax purposes it was doing business for capital stock tax purposes.

In the absence of income tax regulations covering the specific question, resort may be had to the capital stock tax regulations. It is stated in those regulations that the term business is very comprehensive and embraces whatever occupies the time, attention, or labor of men for profit. (Article 42 of Regulations 64.) It is also stated in the capital stock tax regulations that in general doing business includes any activities of corporations such as "(3) leasing or managing properties, collecting rents or royalties." (Article 43, Regulations 64.) The determination whether a foreign corporation is carrying on or doing business in the United States within the meaning of the Act depends upon the particular facts of each case. (Article 62, Regulations 64.) *The mere ownership of property itself is not sufficient to constitute engaging in trade or business.* It has been held that a company whose activities consisted of managing real estate and renting offices was doing business or engaging in business. (*Flint v. Stone Tracy Co.,* 220 U. S. 107.) *On the other hand, it has been held that a railroad company which leased its entire railroad for a term of years at an anuual rental was not engaging in business. (McCoach v. Minehill, etc., supra.)* It has also been held that where a corporation's activities were confined to the single purpose of purchasing and owning an apartment house for the benefit of its stockholders so that they might own their apartments, the corporation was not doing business. (*Stafford Owners, Inc., v. United States,* 39 Fed. (2d) 743.) But a corporation organized to purchase, hold, lease, and sell real estate was doing business where it acquired coal land in exchange for stock and bonds and leased the land to another corporation. (*Morrisdale Land Co. v. United States,* 66 Ct. Cls. 701.)

In *Flint v. Stone Tracy Co., supra,* which arose under the Act of August 5, 1909 (36 Stat. 11), imposing a corporation excise tax upon carrying on or doing business, it was stated in part as follows:

"* * * It remains to consider whether these corporations are engaged in business. 'Business' is a very comprehensive term and embraces everything about which a person can be employed. (Black's Law Dictionary, 158, citing *People v. Commissioners of Taxes,* 23 N. Y. 242, 244.) 'That which occupies the time, attention, and labor of men for the purpose of a livelihood or profit.' (1 Bouvier's Law Dictionary, volume 1, page 273.)

"We think it is clear that corporations organized for the purpose of doing business, and actually engaged in such activities as leasing property, collecting rents, managing office buildings, making investments of profits, or leasing ore lands and collecting royalties, managing wharves, dividing profits, and in some cases investing the surplus, are engaged in business within the meaning of this statute, and in the capacity necessary to make such organizations subject to the law."

In *McCoach v. Minehill, etc., supra,* which also arose under the Act of August 5, 1909, the Court stated that the mere receipt of income from property did not constitute engaging in business and commented as follows:

"* * * The distinction is between (*a*) the receipt of income from outside property or investments by a company that is otherwise engaged in business; in which event the investment income may be added to the business income in order to arrive at the measure of the tax; and (*b*) *the receipt of income from property or investments by a company that is not engaged in business except the business of owning the property, maintaining the investments, collecting the income and dividing it among its stockholders. In the former case the tax is payable; in the latter not.*"

The above quoted extracts from the opinions rendered by the Supreme Court may be accepted as a guide in determining what acts in connection with the ownership of income-producing real property constitute engaging in business. Generally, any activities beyond "the mere receipt of income from property, and the payment of organization and administration expenses incidental to the receipt and distribution thereof" (*McCoach v. Minehill, etc.*) constitute "carrying on or doing business" within the meaning of section 105(b) of the Revenue Act of 1935, as amended, relating to capital stock tax, and "engaging in trade or business" within the meaning of section 211(b) and 231 (b) of the Revenue Act of 1936, relating to income tax.

Where a foreign corporation or a nonresident alien individual operates business real property in the United States for the purpose of profit, whether through an agent or otherwise, such activities constitute engaging in trade or business within the United States. In the case of a foreign corporation so engaged in trade or business within the United States, the income is not subject to withholding, and the corporation is taxable at the rate of 22 per cent on its net income, provided a return is filed as required by the Act; otherwise the tax is based on gross income. A nonresident alien individual who owns or operates an apartment house or office building for the purpose of gain or profit is engaged in trade or business within the United States but the rental income is subject to withholding. Such individual may receive the benefit of the deductions to which he is entitled in connection with the operation of the building provided he files a true and accurate return of his income from all sources within the United States. As indicated above, however, the mere ownership of real property in the United States by a nonresident alien individual or foreign corporation does not in itself constitute engaging in trade or business within this country.

MORRISON SHAFROTH,
Chief Counsel, Bureau of Internal Revenue.
No. 8886.

INDEX

In the United States Circuit Court of Appeals for the Ninth Circuit

No. 8886

Taft Building Land Trust, Trust No. B–7620, Title Insurance and Trust Company, Trustee, Petitioner

v.

Commissioner of Internal Revenue, respondent

UPON PETITION TO REVIEW A DECISION OF THE UNITED STATES BOARD OF TAX APPEALS

BRIEF FOR THE RESPONDENT

OPINION BELOW

The only previous opinion is the memorandum opinion of the United States Board of Tax Appeals (R. 149–162), which is not reported.

JURISDICTION

This petition for review involves a deficiency[1] in taxpayer's income tax in the amount of $2,726.36

---

[1] The Commissioner in the deficiency notice also asserted a 25 per cent penalty in the sum of $681.59 (R. 9–12, 149) because of the taxpayer's failure to make and file its return within the time prescribed by the statute (Section 291 of

(1)

for the calendar year 1933 (R. 9–12, 149), and is taken from a decision of the Board of Tax Appeals entered March 31, 1938 (R. 163). The case is brought to this Court by petition for review filed June 4, 1938 (R. 164–169), pursuant to the provisions of Sections 1001–1003 of the Revenue Act of 1926, c. 27, 44 Stat. 9, as amended by Section 1101 of the Revenue Act of 1932, c. 209, 47 Stat. 169, and by Section 519 of the Revenue Act of 1934, c. 277, 48 Stat. 680.

QUESTION PRESENTED

Whether taxpayer is an association within the meaning of Section 1111 (a) (2) of the Revenue Act of 1932, *infra,* and is therefore taxable as a corporation, as determined by the Commissioner, or is taxable merely as a pure trust, as contended by the taxpayer.

STATUTE AND REGULATIONS INVOLVED

These will be found in the Appendix, *infra,* pp. 25–27.

STATEMENT

The facts, as found by the Board of Tax Appeals (R. 150–157), are as follows:

The taxpayer was created by an agreement and declaration of trust (a true and correct copy of

the Revenue Act of 1932). The Board found, however, that the failure to have filed the return within the statutory time was due to reasonable cause and not to willful neglect (R. 157), and therefore declined to approve the imposition of the penalty (R. 162). No petition for review was filed by the Commissioner from this portion of the decision.

which is attached to the petition) executed July
15, 1927 (but for convenience dated June 15, 1927)
between Mitchum, Tully & Company, a California
corporation, as trustor or grantor, Title Insurance
and Trust Company, a California corporation, as
trustee, and Harry L. Dunn and Albert Parker
and "such persons, partnerships, associations
and/or corporations as may become parties hereto
by the acceptance of certificates issued hereunder"
as beneficiaries (R. 150).

The declaration of trust provides, among other
things, that the trustee shall hold in trust for the
benefit of Dunn and Parker, and their respective
successors and assigns, as owners of the undivided
beneficial rights or interest represented by certificates, all the title, right and interest in and to
certain described real property located at the
southeast corner of Hollywood Boulevard and Vine
Street in Los Angeles, California; that the beneficial interest in the trust shall consist of 665 equal,
fractional, undivided parts and shall be represented by certificates to be issued by the trustee,
the certificates being transferable by the execution
of the assignment on the reverse side thereof and
transfer on the books of the trustee; that the
trustee shall issue a certificate or certificates for
the entire 665 beneficial interests to Dunn and
Parker; shall keep a register of the names of the
holders of certificates, proper transfer books in
respect of such certificates, and books of account
showing the receipts and disbursements of the

trust estate; shall have the power to rent and lease
the trust estate, or any part thereof, to Sun Realty
Company, a California corporation, under a lease
dated July 15, 1927, for a period of 98½ years for
a yearly rental of $42,000 in addition to the pay-
ment of taxes, insurance premiums, etc., with the
option to purchase the property for $725,000 prior
to June 15, 1952, and for $750,000 within the time
specified in the lease, which may contain such further terms, provisions and conditions as the trustee
may approve; that in the event the Sun Realty
Company, or any other lessee under the above-
mentioned long-term lease or any successor lessee,
shall default, or in the event such lease shall be terminated for any reason or shall expire by limitation, the trustee shall have full authority to terminate the lease or to take such steps as in its opinion
may be necessary and proper for the best interests of certificate holders with respect to leasing,
operating, selling, conveying, or otherwise disposing of the trust property; to enforce any lease
or leases made by it, to execute and deliver any
agreement in writing, modifying or supplementing
any lease or leases if and when in its discretion it
shall appear advisable, providing no such modification shall decrease the amount of the rentals and
payment or option price specified in the original
lease to Sun Realty Company; that, in the event
the Sun Realty Company shall exercise its option
to purchase, the trustee shall, upon receipt of the

purchase price, have full authority to execute the
necessary conveyance without securing the consent
from certificate holders; that the trustee may, subject to the option of Sun Realty Company, sell and
convey all of the trust property at its discretion
without the consent of the certificate holders provided the sale will make available for distribution
among the beneficiaries at least $1,250,000; that
upon the receipt of written consents of two-thirds
of the 665 interests, including two-thirds of the unredeemed certificates outstanding, the trustee may
at any time, but shall not be obligated to, sell and
convey the trust property upon such terms as may
be provided in such consents; that the trustee shall
have full power to compromise and settle claims
either in contract or tort made by it or against it
or the trust estate and to charge the expense
against the income of the trust; that it, in its discretion, may mortgage and otherwise bind or
charge the trust estate for the purpose of providing
funds to meet any exigency arising in connection
therewith and for the benefit of certificate holders:
borrow money upon any usual terms, giving notes
or other security therefor, and apply moneys, as
available from time to time, for the payment of
principal or interest in respect to any borrowings
or mortgages or other hypothecation, in preference
and with priority to any claims of beneficiaries to
periodical or other payments in respect to their
fractional interests; distribute semiannually rent-

6

als and income, less its fee as determined in the
trust agreement and expenses, pro rata to the holders of certificates whose names are registered as
such on the books of the trustee, not exceeding,
however, $30 for each fractional beneficial inter-
est, which semiannual distribution shall be cumulative without interest, the remaining rentals and
income to be applied to the redemption of certificates; that, except as otherwise provided, the
trustee shall have the exclusive right to manage
and control the trust estate and shall not be subject to any obligation to the certificate holders except as expressly assumed; that the trustee, in its
own absolute discretion, may seek the advice of the
certificate holders, and if notified in writing, by a
majority of the 665 beneficial interests, including
a majority of the interests upon which no redemption payments have been made, of their agreement
upon a course which they desire to be taken, not
inconsistent with any of the express provisions of
the trust agreement, may endeavor to effectuate
the same but shall not be obligated to do so; that
as and when moneys in excess of the semiannual
distributions and expenses become available the
trustee may redeem the certificates by inviting offers of certificate holders for such purposes and
applying such moneys for such redemption payments, which shall not be more than $1,050 on or
before June 15, 1937, nor more than $1,030 there-
after and on or before June 15, 1947, nor more than
$1,010 thereafter and on or before June 15, 1957,

and thereafter not more than $1,000, together with
accrued semiannual distribution to date of redemption; that the certificates so redeemed by payment
shall have an endorsement thereon "Redemption
Payment Made," and the certificate holders thereafter shall receive no further payments nor any
interest whatsoever until after redemption payments have been made upon all of the 665 interests,
after which time the owner of each $\frac{1}{665}$th interest,
as represented by outstanding certificates, shall
share pro rata in all further funds, less expenses,
fees, and disbursements of the trustee, as and when
available for distribution; that, when all certificates have been redeemed, the trustee may, in its
discretion, propose the modification or elimination
of terms, conditions, trusts or provisions of the
trust agreement, or any additions thereto, and, if
consented to by three-fourths of the certificate
holders, the trustee may, in its discretion, but shall
not be obligated to, make effective such changes,
provided such change shall not have the effect of
giving to any certificate holder any preference or
advantage over any other certificate holder; that
the trustee shall not be liable personally in acting
as trustee except for its personal and willful default; that no holder of any certificate shall have,
as such, any estate or interest in the trust property
but may enforce the performance of the trust and
trust agreement; that no transfer by operation of
law of the interest of any certificate holder shall
operate to terminate the trust nor entitle the suc-

cessors of such holder to an accounting or to take any action in the courts or otherwise against the trust estate or trustee; that in the event of death of any certificate holder the person or persons entitled by law shall succeed to the rights of such holder; that no assessment shall ever be made upon the holder of any certificate; that neither the trustee nor the certificate holder shall in any event be liable personally upon any contract or obligation made or entered into by the trustee in connection with the trust estate; that the trustee may resign upon giving four weeks' written notice to the certificate holders who may select its successor, and, in the event of their failure or neglect so to do, the trustee may request the Federal Judge of the District Court in and for the district in which the property is located to designate a successor trustee; and that unless sooner terminated as provided in the agreement, the trust shall terminate upon the death of the last to die of numerous persons named in the trust agreement (R. 150–155).

Mitchum, Tully & Company, grantor in the trust agreement, was, during the time herein involved and prior thereto, engaged in business as investment bankers and underwriters. It had purchased the trust property and negotiated and arranged for the lease with Sun Realty Company prior to the execution of the trust agreement. The improvements on the property consisted of a 12-story building, having stores on the ground floor and offices above. The trustee executed the Sun Realty Company lease on July 15, 1927, at or about the same time that it executed the trust agreement (R. 155).

The lease (a true and correct copy of which is attached to the petition) provides in part for a term of 98½ years commencing July 15, 1927, at a net monthly rental of $3,500 and requires the lessee to pay all taxes, general or special, which may be levied against the property or the leasehold, to keep the property insured against damage by fire and earthquake and to repair and maintain the premises leased (R. 156).

After the execution of the trust agreement the trustee issued eight certificates representing the 665 beneficial units to Dunn and Parker, who assigned them to Mitchum, Tully & Company, who in turn assigned or sold them to others. During 1933 all of the 665 beneficial units were outstanding and unredeemed certificates were held by 222 persons. Of the 665 units outstanding 17 had been redeemed as provided in the trust agreement by the end of 1933. However, the interest of the holders of beneficial units was not extinguished by redemption. Such holders merely relinquished their right to receive any further distributions until all units had been similarly redeemed (R. 156).

During the course of a year the activities of the trustee consisted of collecting the monthly rental and depositing the same, making two distributions a year, paying Federal and state (effective in 1937) income taxes and its own fees, the entry thereof in its books of account, and the performance of ordinary duties of any real estate trust, such as ascertaining whether proper insurance was carried by the lessee and the like (R. 156–157).

No meetings were ever held which were attended by the trustee or beneficiaries of the trust in connection with the management of the affairs of the trust. The rent provided for under the Sun Realty Company lease was always paid although the rent was delinquent at the time the lessee's interest in the trust property was foreclosed under a bond issue. However, the receiver appointed at that time paid the delinquent rent within the 30-day period specified in the lease. At that time the trustee had some discussions as to the status of the lease with a trust company which took over the management of the property (R. 157).

On the basis of the foregoing findings the Board affirmed (R. 158–162) the Commissioner's determination that taxpayer is an association as defined by the statute and is therefore taxable as a corporation. The Board thereupon entered its decision accordingly (R. 163), from which the taxpayer petitioned this Court for review (R. 164).

SUMMARY OF ARGUMENT

The taxpayer is a statutory association, and not merely a strict trust, within the meaning of the statute and pertinent regulations. Under the authorities cited hereafter, it was "doing business" at a profit. It is therefore taxable as a corpora- tion. The facts, as found, show that the trust contains the essential elements of a corporation and that the trustee not only had full powers to do business but actually carried on the trust as a profitable enterprise. The evidence supports these findings.

The trustee was not restricted to the mere col- lection of funds and the payment thereof to the beneficiaries of the trust, but had powers similar to or greater than those of corporate directors for the purpose of carrying on the trust enterprise. Contrary to the taxpayer's contentions, these pow- ers were not merely incidental but clearly manifest a purpose to give the trustee ample authority to operate the trust as a business for profit. There- fore, the trust is not a strict trust, but is more like an association carrying on business activities which required the trustee's constant attention.

The case is concluded by the controlling decisions cited hereafter. The many cases cited and relied on by the taxpayer are distinguishable or were de- cided prior to the controlling decisions relied on by the respondent.

ARGUMENT

The taxpayer is a statutory association within the mean- ing of the statute and is therefore taxable as a corpora- tion

We submit that the Board was correct in affirm- ing the Commissioner's determination (R. 9–12) and holding that, under the authorities, the taxpayer is not a strict trust but is a statutory association as defined by Section 1111 (a) (2) of the Revenue Act of 1932, *infra,* and is therefore taxable as a corporation (R. 158, 161–162).

The taxpayer contends that it is not an association within the meaning of Section 1111 (a) (2) and therefore taxable at corporate rates, but that since it was not "doing business" during the taxable year, it is a true trust taxable under Section 161 of the Revenue Act of 1932, *infra* (Br. 10); that the authorities relied on by the Board are distinguishable since the trusts involved in all of those cases were doing business and the original purpose was actively to engage in business to produce income (Br. 11–14, 20–24); that the instant trust was not engaged in business since it was formed merely for the purpose of holding title to one piece of real estate, collecting the rents therefrom, and distributing the proceeds received upon the sale of the trust property; that, accordingly, under the rule laid down by this Court in *Commissioner* v. *Vandegrift R. & Inv. Co.,* 82 F. (2d) 387, the taxpayer is a trust, and not an association doing business, according to its purposes as set forth in the agreement and the declaration of trust and the incidental powers of the trustee, exercised for the benefit of the certificate holders (Br. 14–20, 24); and that the Board's conclusion is not supported by a specific finding that the taxpayer is an association formed for the purpose of doing business (Br. 25–27).

The statutory definition of a corporation includes associations. Section 1111 (a) (2), Revenue Act of 1932, *infra.* The regulations interpret the statute to include associations, trusts, and organizations by whatever name known, which act or do business in an organized capacity, whether created under state laws, agreements, declarations of trust, or otherwise, the net income of which is distributable among the shareholders on the basis of the proportionate shares or capital which each has or has invested in the business or property of the organization. Regulations 77, Article 1312, *infra.* Further, they define an association as an organization in which the membership interests are transferable and the business is conducted by trustees, directors, or officers without the active participation of all the members as such. *Id.,* Article 1313, *infra.* Finally, they provide that a trust is an association, within the meaning of the Act, where the trustees are not restricted to the mere collection of funds and the distribution thereof to the beneficiaries, but have powers similar to or greater than those of corporate directors for the purpose of carrying on some business enterprise. *Id.,* Article 1314, *infra.*

If the instant trust, therefore, contains substantially the essential elements of a corporation, as provided by the foregoing statute and regulatory definitions, and was operating and doing business as a going enterprise, it is clearly a statutory association, taxable at corporate rates. We submit that, under the facts herein, it contains substantially every such essential element, was "doing business" under the authorities relied on, and was therefore an association taxable as a corporation, and not merely a pure trust, taxable as an individual.

There is no substantial disagreement between the parties as to the facts (R. 158; Br. 26). The facts, as found, show that the trust was formed for the purpose of holding title to one piece of property, improved with a 12-story building containing store rooms and offices (R. 150; Br. 18); that the beneficial interests were represented by transerable certificates (R. 150–151); that the trustee had power to and did rent and lease the trust property (R. 155), collect the rents, keep the necessary records, see that the lessee complied with all the terms of the lease, distribute the net income in accordance with the terms of the trust instrument (R. 156); and it also had full power and authority to lease, operate, mortgage, sell or otherwise dispose of the trust property, subject only to the existing lease and option given therein to the lessee to purchase property (R. 150–157). These findings (R. 161) are clearly tantamount to a finding substantially that the taxpayer was doing business. Cf. *Commissioner* v. *Vandegrift R. & Inv.*

Co., 82 F. (2d) 387, 390 (C. C. A. 9th). Since they are supported by the evidence (R. 12–74, Ex. B; R. 74–147, Ex. C), they should be sustained on review. *Phillips* v. *Commissioner,* 283 U. S. 589.

We submit that, under the facts herein, the case is governed by the rules laid down by the Supreme Court in *Morrissey* v. *Commissioner,* 296 U. S. 344; *Helvering* v. *Coleman-Gilbert,* 296 U. S. 369; *Swanson* v. *Commissioner,* 296 U. S. 362; and *Helvering* v. *Combs,* 296 U. S. 365.[2] The controlling force of those decisions was recognized in *United States* v. *Rayburn,* 91 F. (2d) 162, 167–168 (C. C. A. 8th). Those cases arose under the provisions of the Revenue Acts of 1924, 1926, and 1928 relating to the taxability of certain classes of trusts as associations or corporations instead of as strict trusts, and the provisions of those statutes are substantially the same as those of the Revenue Act of 1932, here involved.

In each of those cases, the trustees had absolute control and management of the trusts, as in this case. The trust property comprised a golf course with an adjoining real estate subdivision in the *Morrissey* case; about 20 apartment houses in the *Coleman-Gilbert* case; *a single apartment house* in the *Swanson* case; and an oil lease in the *Combs*

---

[2] Contrary to taxpayer's statement (Br. 14), these cases explain and modify *Crocker* v. *Malley,* 249 U. S. 223. See *Solomon* v. *Commissioner,* 89 F. (2d) 569, 571 (C. C. A. 5th), certiorari denied, 302 U. S. 692.

case. The trustees' powers there were similar to those of the trustee herein. Moreover, just as herein, the beneficiaries' interests in each of those trusts (except in the *Coleman-Gilbert* case) were personal property, evidenced by transferable certificates; and the trustees could not bind the beneficiaries personally, nor were they individually liable. In the *Coleman-Gilbert* case, there were no shares of beneficial interest, no meetings, and no corporate records. In the *Swanson* case, *where the trust property comprised a single apartment house,* the trustees never held formal meetings, kept no minute books, had no by-laws, elected no officers, and the operations of the business did not extend beyond the property first acquired. In the *Combs* case, the trust had no office or place of business, no seal, by-laws, or official name, and the trustees' operations were confined to the one lease acquired.

So there is a clear analogy between the determinative elements in those cases and those in the present case. Here, as in those cases, there were continuity, centralized control, transferability of certificates, continuity was unaffected by the death of the certificate holders, and the essential characteristics of an association are present in each case.

Contrary to the taxpayer's contentions (Br. 18), the instant trust was clearly formed for the purpose of engaging in business for profit—to lease, operate, mortgage, sell, or otherwise dispose of the trust property; collect the rents; keep the necessary records; see that the lessee complied with all the terms of the lease; and to distribute the net proceeds in accordance with the terms of the trust instrument—as found by the Board (R. 161). "All these things indicate the doing of and engaging in business," and "If that is not engaging in business, I do not know what is." *Von Baumbach* v. *Sargent Land Co.*, 242 U. S. 503, 516–517 (wherein the Supreme Court held (p. 517) that the corporation "handling a large property, selling lots, and seeing that the lessees lived up to their contracts" was "doing business" within the meaning of the revenue act which "requires no particular amount of business in order to bring a company within its terms."). Thus, we submit that the instant trust was engaged in business at a profit in substantially the same manner as the corporation in *Von Baumbach* v. *Sargent Land Co., supra.*

The trustee herein was not restricted to the mere collection of funds and the payment thereof to the beneficiaries of the trust. It had powers similar to or greater than those of corporate directors in carrying on business for profit. Associations, taxable as corporations, include such trusts and organizations, by whatever name called, which act or do business in an organized capacity whether created under state law, by agreements, declarations of trust, or otherwise, the net income of which, if any, is distributed or distributable among the shareholders on the basis of the proportionate share or capital which each has or has invested in the business or property of the organization.

Article 1312, Regulations 77, *infra*. The instant trust, therefore, was an association taxable as a corporation within the meaning of the statute and regulations (Section 1111 (a) (2), Revenue Act of 1932, *infra;* Articles 1312 and 1314, Regulations 77, *infra*).

Apropos of the trust's purposes herein, the Supreme Court, in *Helvering* v. *Coleman-Gilbert,* 296 U. S. 369, stated (p. 374):

> The parties are not at liberty to say that their purpose was other or narrower than that which they formally set forth in the instrument under which their activities were conducted. Undoubtedly they wished to avoid partition of the property of which they had been co-owners, *but their purpose as declared in their agreement was much broader than that.* They formed a combination to conduct the business of holding, improving, and selling real estate, with provision for management through representatives, with continuity which was not to be disturbed by death or changes in ownership of beneficial interests, and with limited liability. *They had been co-owners but they preferred to become "associates," and also not to become partners.* [Italics supplied.]

In *Morrissey* v. *Commissioner,* 296 U. S. 344, the Supreme Court said of the trust therein (p. 361):

> Its character was determined by the terms of the trust instrument. It was not a liquidating trust; it was still an organization

for profit, and the profits were still coming in. The powers conferred on the trustees continued and could be exercised for such activities as the instrument authorized.

The trustees herein had full power and authority, in the event of default in the long-term lease by the lessee or succeeding lessees, as the taxpayer admits (Br. 19), to terminate the lease or to take any other action in respect to leasing, operating, selling, conveying or otherwise disposing of the property, deemed necessary and proper in its discretion for the best interests of the certificate holders (R. 33); to compromise or settle claims made by or against it or the trust estate, and to charge the expenses thereof against the income of the trust (R. 56); and to mortgage, and otherwise bind and charge the trust estate to meet any exigencies arising in connection therewith for the benefit of the certificate holders (R. 57). It cannot properly be said, therefore, that these powers are in any wise merely incidental, as the taxpayer contends (Br. 19–20). On the contrary, they manifest a clear purpose to give the trustee full powers to operate the trust as a business for profit. *Von Baumbach* v. *Sargent Land Co., supra; United States* v. *Rayburn, supra.*

From the foregoing, therefore, we submit that the taxpayer's activities constituted the "doing of and engaging in business" (*Von Baumbach* v. *Sargent Land Co., supra*), and the facts found (R.

150–157, 161) indicate that a profitable business is conducted which requires the constant attention of the trustee herein (*Solomon* v. *Commissioner,* 89 F. (2d) 569, 571 (C. C. A. 5th), certiorari denied, 302 U. S. 692). The court also observed in the *Solomon* case (p. 571), significantly, we think, that the renting of a single apartment house was held by the Supreme Court to be a business in this connection in *Swanson* v. *Commissioner, supra,* as did the court in *United States* v. *Rayburn, supra* (pp. 167–168).

The instant case is analogous to *United States* v. *Rayburn, supra,* wherein the trust was organized to hold a tract of land to await future opportunities and to liquidate. The court there held that the trust was not purely a holding company or purely a liquidating trust, and that since there were present enough of the elements of a corporation to be classified as an association, it was taxable as a corporation. The facts there showed that the corporation, after having leased its lands and discovering that there was doubt as to its capacity legally to hold title satisfactory to oil lessees, conveyed its lands to a trust formed by the stockholders. In holding that the trust was engaged in a business enterprise for profit, as distinguished from the activities of a purely holding or liquidating trust, the court pointed out that it was created in immediate connection with the leasing of the lands for a long term of years and that obviously the creators of

the trust intended to carry on the same business
as they had been doing under the former company.
The court, reversing the District Court, stated
(pp. 166, 167–168):

> The only business carried on by the trus-
> tee was the making of these leases; the col-
> lection of bonuses and rentals (oil and
> grass); and distribution of the net proceeds
> to the beneficiaries. * * *
> During the trust, no additional land has
> been acquired; there has been no develop-
> ment of the land by the trustees. * * *
> The trial court found that during these
> tax years the trustees were not "engaged in
> carrying on a business enterprise for profit
> as the main purpose of the organization;"
> and that "such business as they may have
> done has been incidental to the ultimate
> liquidation of the property as provided in
> the trust deed."
>
> *   *   *   *   *
>
> We think no such situation is here present.
> If we consider the trust instrument alone
> and apart from all other evidence, there is
> no basis therein to conclude that this was
> purely a liquidating trust. That instru-
> ment, considered alone, reveals twenty-four
> tenants in common of a large tract of land
> conveying it to seven of their number as
> trustees to be disposed of by the trustees at
> any time within twenty years after the
> death of the survivor of such trustees; the
> trustees given the full powers as of owner-

ship to manage and control the land and all parts thereof until final disposition; provisions for succession as to trustees; provisions for unlimited modification of the trust by the trustees and two-thirds in interest of the beneficiaries. The only feature which might suggest a purely liquidation trust or a holding trust is that the corpus is a definite tract of land and the main purpose is to dispose of that land. In the leading case of *Morrissey* v. *Commissioner,* 296 U. S. 344, 360, and the companion case of *Swanson* v. *Commissioner,* 296 U. S. 362, 365, a single tract of land was involved. It is true that each of those cases dealt with trusts which contemplated improvement of the land before sale. However, it is obvious that the sale of land without prior improvement is as much a business enterprise for profit as any other business undertaking.

* * * * *

We must conclude that it was taxable as an association within the meaning of Secs. 13 (a) and 701 (a) (2) of the Revenue Act of 1928 for the two years involved here.

Likewise, in the instant case, the business activities carried on by the trustee, plus the additional powers and authority it could have exercised (R. 161; Br. 18–20), were not merely incidental to the holding of the trust property but were for substantial profit which was realized and distributed. Cf. *Solomon* v. *Commissioner, supra.*

In *Commissioner* v. *Vandegrift R. & Inv. Co.*, 82 F. (2d) 387 (C. C. A. 9th), the trust during 1924–1926 owned a substantial interest in a shoe business which was liquidated in 1927. During the period 1927–1930, however, the trust merely received and distributed rentals from a long-term lease and accumulated a reserve fund which was invested in building and loan certificates. The Board of Tax Appeals had there held that the trust was taxable as an association for the earlier but not for the later period. This Court held, however, that under the rules laid down by the Supreme Court in the *Morrissey, Swanson, Coleman-Gilbert* and *Combs* cases, *supra,* the trust there was taxable as an association for *all* of the years involved notwithstanding the fact that the trust had completed the liquidation of the shoe business which it had formerly managed.

That case, involving the element of liquidation, was a much stronger one for the taxpayer than is the present case, but this Court nevertheless properly held that, the purpose and actual operation considered, which are controlling, the trust was a taxable association. Moreover, there is no basis whatever, under the facts herein, for the taxpayer's contention (Br. 16) that, under the rule laid down by this Court in that case, the instant trust is a strict one and not an association.

The several other cases cited and relied upon by the taxpayer are distinguishable or were decided prior to the controlling decisions cited herein, as the Board held (R. 161). No useful purpose therefore could be served by a review of them herein.

In view of the foregoing, we submit that, under the controlling authorities cited herein, the instant trust was formed for the purpose of and was doing business at a profit, and that therefore the taxpayer is not merely a strict trust but is a statutory association, as defined in Section 1111 (a) (2) of the Revenue Act of 1932, *infra,* and is therefore taxable as a corporation.

CONCLUSION

The decision of the Board is correct and in accordance with law. It should therefore be affirmed.

Respectfully submitted.

JAMES W. MORRIS,

Assistant Attorney General.

SEWALL KEY,

NORMAN D. KELLER,

S. DEE HANSON,

Special Assistants to the Attorney General.

SEPTEMBER 1938.

APPENDIX

Revenue Act of 1932, c. 209, 47 Stat. 169:

SEC. 161. IMPOSITION OF TAX.

(a) *Application of tax.*—The taxes imposed by this title upon individuals shall apply to the income of estates or of any kind of property held in trust, including—

(1) Income accumulated in trust for the benefit of unborn or unascertained persons or persons with contingent interests, and income accumulated or held for future distribution under the terms of the will or trust;

(2) Income which is to be distributed currently by the fiduciary to the beneficiaries, and income collected by a guardian of an infant which is to be held or distributed as the court may direct;

(3) Income received by estates of deceased persons during the period of administration or settlement of the estate; and

(4) Income which, in the discretion of the fiduciary, may be either distributed to the beneficiaries or accumulated.

* * * *

SEC. 1111. DEFINITIONS.

(a) When used in this Act—

(1) The term "person" means an individual, a trust or estate, a partnership, or a corporation.

(2) The term "corporation" includes associations, joint-stock companies, and insurance companies. (U. S. C., Title 26, Section 1696.)

* *

Treasury Regulations 77:

ART. 1312. *Association.*—Associations and joint-stock companies include associations, common law trusts, and organizations by whatever name known, which act or do business in an organized capacity, whether created under and pursuant to State laws, agreements, declarations of trust, or otherwise, the net income of which, if any, is distributed or distributable among the shareholders on the basis of the capital stock which each holds, or, where there is no capital stock, on the basis of the proportionate share or capital which each has or has invested in the business or property of the organization. A corporation which has ceased to exist in contemplation of law but continues its business in quasi-corporate form is an association or corporation within the meaning of section 1111.

ART. 1313. *Association distinguished from partnership.*—An organization, the membership interests in which are transferable and the business of which is conducted by trustees or directors and officers without the active participation of all the members as such, is an association * * *.

ART. 1314. *Association distinguished from trust.*—Where trustees merely hold property for the collection of the income and its distribution among the beneficiaries of the trust, and are not engaged, either by themselves or in connection with the beneficiaries, in the carrying on of any business, no association exists, and the trust and the beneficiaries thereof will be subject to tax as provided by sections 161–170 and by articles 861–891. Where the trustees are not restricted to the mere collection of funds and their payment to the beneficiaries, but have similar or greater powers than the directors in a corporation for the purpose of carrying on some business enterprise, the trust is an association within the meaning of the Act.

Lightning Source UK Ltd.
Milton Keynes UK
UKHW051454020119
334537UK00024B/101/P